# THE UNITED METHODIST
# BOOK OF WORSHIP

THE UNITED METHODIST PUBLISHING HOUSE
NASHVILLE, TENNESSEE

# THE UNITED METHODIST BOOK OF WORSHIP

*Copyright © 1992 The United Methodist Publishing House*

*Twenty-sixth Printing: February 2018*

## Editions

Hard Cover (black):   978-0-687-035724
Bonded Leather (black):   978-0-687-035731
Accompaniment PDF Download:   978-1-501-800689

# PREFACE

From John Wesley's *Sunday Service of the Methodists of North America* in 1784, through the hymnals, rituals, and books of worship of our antecedent denominations, our official worship resources have defined our Church. They celebrated our heritage in worship and formed new disciples of Jesus Christ. Out of this tradition now arises *The United Methodist Book of Worship.*

This is the first worship book to carry the name United Methodist. This book and *The United Methodist Hymnal* (1989) now become the cornerstones of United Methodist worship. This book acknowledges our Anglican liturgical heritage and celebrates worship out of our cultural and ethnic diversity. It witnesses to our Evangelical United Brethren and Methodist heritage. Women, men, youth, and children have all contributed to the rich variety of ways of speaking with God in corporate worship. Underlying this diversity and variety, however, is the one God who calls us to be disciples of Christ Jesus.

The United Methodist Book of Worship Committee for four years has listened to people, explored myriad resources, and wrestled with difficult issues. Without hesitation we believe this book to be the most comprehensive worship resource ever presented to our Church. We now offer it to all who worship with joy and excitement. We believe that *The United Methodist Book of Worship* will strengthen our worship and empower our ministry and mission. May God's grace be with all who use this book in worship.

### The United Methodist Book of Worship Committee

| | |
|---|---|
| Susan M. Morrison, *Chair* | Hoyt L. Hickman, *Worship Services Editor* |
| J. Lavon Wilson, *Vice-Chair* | Diana Sanchez, *Music Editor* |
| Thomas Anderson Langford III, *General Editor* | |

Ted G. Colescott, *Chair, Service Music Subcommittee*
Lois Glory Neal, *Chair, Other Worship Resources Subcommittee*
Ann B. Sherer, *Chair, Worship Services Subcommittee*

| | | |
|---|---|---|
| William R. Auvenshine | Jerome King Del Pino | Mark Trotter |
| C. Rex Bevins | Mallonee Hubbard | Woodie W. White |
| Donald J. Bueg | Ezra Earl Jones | Sally A. Wisner |
| Sara Collins | Grace Perez-Martinez | Dal Joon Won |
| Gloster B. Current | Michael J. O'Donnell | H. Claude Young, Jr. |

### STAFF

| | |
|---|---|
| United Methodist Publishing House | General Board of Discipleship |
| Neil M. Alexander, *Book Editor, UMC* | David Schnasa Jacobsen, *Ed. Assistant* |
| Paul Franklyn, *Editor* | Joane Pettus, *Admin. Assistant* |
| Sylvia Marlow, *Typesetter* | |
| Nancy Bozeman, *Art Director* | |
| Leonardo M. Ferguson, *Designer* | |
| John Boegel, *Illustrator* | |

# CONTENTS

TERMS, ABBREVIATIONS, AND SYMBOLS_____ 12

## I. GENERAL SERVICES

### THE BASIC PATTERN OF WORSHIP
Introduction_____ 1?
The Basic Pattern of Worship_____ 1.
An Order of Sunday Worship Using the Basic Pattern_____ 1•

### SERVICES OF WORD AND TABLE
A Service of Word and Table I_____ 3•
Introduction to A Service of Word and Table II_____ 4•
Introduction to A Service of Word and Table III_____ 4•
Introduction to The Great Thanksgiving: Musical Settings_____ 4•
A Service of Word and Table IV (Traditional Methodist and E.U.B.)_____ 4•
A Service of Word and Table V with Persons Who Are Sick
    or Homebound_____ 5•
The Great Thanksgiving for Advent_____ 5•
The Great Thanksgiving for Christmas Eve, Day, or Season_____ 5•
The Great Thanksgiving for New Year, Epiphany, Baptism of the Lord,
    or Covenant Reaffirmation_____ 5•
The Great Thanksgiving for Early in Lent_____ 6•
The Great Thanksgiving for Later in Lent_____ 6•
The Great Thanksgiving for Holy Thursday Evening_____ 6•
The Great Thanksgiving for Easter Day or Season_____ 6•
The Great Thanksgiving for the Day of Pentecost_____
The Great Thanksgiving for the Season After Pentecost_____
The Great Thanksgiving for World Communion Sunday_____
The Great Thanksgiving for All Saints and Memorial Occasions_____
The Great Thanksgiving for Thanksgiving Day or for the Gift of Food_____
An Alternative Great Thanksgiving for General Use_____
A Brief Great Thanksgiving for General Use_____

### SERVICES OF THE BAPTISMAL COVENANT
Introduction_____
The Baptismal Covenant I
    (Holy Baptism, Confirmation, Reaffirmation of Faith,
    Reception of Members)_____
The Baptismal Covenant II (Baptism for Children)_____
The Baptismal Covenant II-A (Brief Order of Baptism for Children)_____

The Baptismal Covenant II-B
  (Traditional Methodist and E.U.B. for Children)_____103
The Baptismal Covenant III
  (Traditional Methodist and E.U.B. for Adults)_____106
The Baptismal Covenant IV (Congregational Reaffirmation)_____111

SERVICES OF CHRISTIAN MARRIAGE

A Service of Christian Marriage I_____115
A Service of Christian Marriage II (Traditional Methodist and E.U.B.)_____128
A Service for the Recognition or the Blessing of a Civil Marriage_____133
An Order for the Reaffirmation of the Marriage Covenant_____135
Marriage Anniversary Prayers_____138

SERVICES OF DEATH AND RESURRECTION

A Service of Death and Resurrection_____139
  An Order for Holy Communion_____152
  A Service of Committal_____155
Additional Resources for Services of Death and Resurrection_____158
  For General Use_____158
  At the Service for a Child_____161
  For an Untimely or Tragic Death_____163
  At the Service for a Person Who Did Not Profess the Christian Faith_____165
Ministry with the Dying_____166
Ministry Immediately Following Death_____167
A Family Hour or Wake_____168
A Service of Death and Resurrection for a Stillborn Child_____170

. MUSIC AS ACTS OF WORSHIP

BAPTISMAL RESPONSES_____ 173

RESPONSES FOR GENERAL ACTS OF WORSHIP_____ 176

RESPONSES FOR THE CHRISTIAN YEAR_____ 206

RESPONSES FOR DAILY PRAISE AND PRAYER_____ 220

ORDINATION HYMN (O Holy Spirit)_____ 223

. THE CHRISTIAN YEAR

THE CALENDAR_____ 224

CALENDAR FOR DATING EASTER AND RELATED HOLY DAYS    225

COLORS FOR THE CHRISTIAN YEAR    226

REVISED COMMON LECTIONARY    227

ADVENT    238
     Acts of Worship for Advent    239
     Hanging of the Greens    258
     Blessing of the Chrismon Tree    260
     Blessing of the Advent Wreath    261
     Lighting of the Advent Candles    262
     An Advent Service of Lessons and Carols    263
     Las Posadas (Service of Shelter for the Holy Family)    266

CHRISTMAS SEASON    269
     Acts of Worship for the Christmas Season    270
     Blessing of a Nativity Scene    280
     A Christmas Eve Service of Las Posadas    281
     A Festival of Nine Lessons and Carols    284
     Covenant Renewal Service    288
     Acts of Worship for New Year's Eve/Day    294
     Acts of Worship for the Epiphany of the Lord    29.

SEASON AFTER THE EPIPHANY    29.
     Acts of Worship for Baptism of the Lord    29
     Acts of Worship for the Sundays After the Epiphany    30
     Acts of Worship for Transfiguration Sunday    31

LENT    32
     A Service of Worship for Ash Wednesday    32
     Acts of Worship for Lent    32
     A Service of Worship for Passion/Palm Sunday    3:
     Acts of Worship for Holy Week    34
     A Service of Worship for Holy Thursday Evening    35
     A Service of Tenebrae    35
     A Service for Good Friday    36
     Acts of Worship for Good Friday and Holy Saturday    36

EASTER SEASON    3
     Easter Vigil, or the First Service of Easter    3
     Acts of Worship for the Easter Season    3
     Acts of Worship for Ascension Day or Sunday    4
     Acts of Worship for the Day of Pentecost    4

SEASON AFTER PENTECOST
(ORDINARY TIME, or KINGDOMTIDE)_____ 409
    Acts of Worship for Trinity Sunday_____ 410
    Acts of Worship for All Saints Day or Sunday_____ 413
    Acts of Worship for Thanksgiving Eve, Day, or Sunday____ 416
    Acts of Worship for Reign of Christ/Christ the King Sunday____ 419

# IV. SPECIAL SUNDAYS AND OTHER SPECIAL DAYS

SPECIAL SUNDAYS OF THE UNITED METHODIST CHURCH_____ 422
    Human Relations Day_____ 423
    One Great Hour of Sharing_____ 424
    Native American Awareness Sunday_____ 425
    Heritage Sunday_____ 426
    Golden Cross Sunday_____ 427
    Peace with Justice Sunday_____ 428
    Christian Education Sunday_____ 429
    Rural Life Sunday_____ 430
    World Communion Sunday_____ 431
    Laity Sunday_____ 432
    United Methodist Student Day_____ 433

OTHER SPECIAL DAYS_____ 434
    Martin Luther King, Jr. Day_____ 435
    Boy Scout Sunday/Girl Scout Sunday_____ 436
    Festival of the Christian Home_____ 437
    Mother's Day_____ 438
    Aldersgate Day or Sunday_____ 439
    Memorial Day_____ 440
    Father's Day_____ 441
    Independence Day_____ 442
    Labor Day_____ 443
    Reformation Day or Sunday_____ 444

# GENERAL ACTS OF WORSHIP

WAYS OF PRAYING_____ 445
    Tongsung Kido (Pray Aloud)_____ 446
    The Collect_____ 447

GREETINGS AND OPENING PRAYERS_____ 448
    Greetings_____ 448
    Opening Prayers_____ 459
    Acts of Congregational Centering_____ 470

CONFESSION, ASSURANCE, AND PARDON _____ 474
   Psalms of Confession _____ 474
   Confession and Pardon _____ 475
   Prayers of Confession _____ 479

A LITANY FOR THE CHURCH AND FOR THE WORLD _____ 495

THE TEN COMMANDMENTS _____ 496

PRAYERS FOR VARIOUS OCCASIONS _____ 497
   Prayers in *UMH* _____ 497
   Psalms of Petition _____ 498
   Musical Petitions _____ 499
   For Blessing, Mercy, and Courage _____ 500
   For the Church _____ 501
   For Creation _____ 502
   In Time of Natural Disaster _____ 509
   For Discernment _____ 510
   For God's Reign _____ 51
   For Guidance _____ 51
   For Justice _____ 51
   For the Mind of Christ _____ 51
   For the Nation _____ 51
   For Others _____ 51
   For Peace _____ 52
   For Purity _____ 52
   For Safety _____ 52
   For Strength _____ 52
   For Wisdom _____ 52
   For the World and Its Peoples _____ 5
   A Prayer of Susanna Wesley _____ 5
   A Prayer of Saint Patrick _____ 5
   A Prayer of Saint Thomas Aquinas _____ 5

BLESSINGS FOR PERSONS _____ 5
   Blessings in *UMH* _____ 5
   In All Occasions of Life _____ 5
   For Persons Celebrating Birthdays _____ 5
   For a Quinceañera (Girl Celebrating Fifteenth Birthday) _____ 5
   At the Beginning of a New School Year _____ 5
   For Graduates _____ 5
   For an Engaged Couple _____ 5

At the Beginning of a New Job ___ 538
For Disciples in the Marketplace ___ 539
For Those Who Work ___ 540
For Those Who Are Unemployed ___ 541
For Those in Military Service ___ 542
At the Beginning of Retirement ___ 543
For Leaders ___ 544
For Those Who Suffer ___ 545
For a Victim or Survivor of Crime or Oppression ___ 547
On the Anniversary of a Death ___ 548

PRAYERS OF THANKSGIVING ___ 549
Hymns and Psalms of Thanksgiving ___ 549
Prayers of Thanksgiving After the Offering ___ 550
General Prayers of Thanksgiving ___ 556

DISMISSAL, BLESSINGS, AND CLOSING PRAYER ___ 559
Dismissal ___ 559
Blessings ___ 560
Closing Prayer ___ 567

VI. DAILY PRAISE AND PRAYER

Introduction ___ 568
An Order for Morning Praise and Prayer ___ 569
An Order for Midday Praise and Prayer ___ 572
An Order for Evening Praise and Prayer ___ 574
An Order for Night Praise and Prayer ___ 577
A Midweek Service of Prayer and Testimony ___ 579

VII. OCCASIONAL SERVICES

The Love Feast ___ 581
Resources for Use in a Homecoming Service ___ 584
An Order of Thanksgiving for the Birth or Adoption of a Child ___ 585
An Order for the Presentation of Bibles to Children ___ 587
A Celebration of New Beginnings in Faith ___ 588
An Order of Farewell to Church Members ___ 590
An Order for Commitment to Christian Service ___ 591
An Order for Commissioning to Short-term Christian Service ___ 592
An Order for the Recognition of a Candidate ___ 593
An Order Recognizing One Who Has Been Ordained,
  Consecrated, or Certified ___ 594
An Order for the Celebration of an Appointment ___ 595
An Order of Farewell to a Pastor ___ 598

An Order for the Installation or Recognition of Leaders in the Church_____ 599
An Order for the Installation or Recognition of Church School Workers____ 601
An Order for the Commissioning of Class Leaders_____ 602
An Order for the Installation or Recognition of Persons
    in Music Ministries_____ 604
An Order for the Dedication or Consecration of an Organ
    or Other Musical Instruments_____ 606
An Order for the Dedication of Church Furnishings and Memorials_____ 607
A Service for the Blessing of Animals_____ 608
A Service for the Blessing of a Home_____ 610

## VIII. HEALING SERVICES AND PRAYERS

Introduction_____ 613
A Service of Healing I_____ 615
A Service of Healing II_____ 622
A Service of Hope After Loss of Pregnancy_____ 623
Ministry with Persons Going through Divorce_____ 626
Ministry with Persons Suffering from Addiction or Substance Abuse_____ 627
Ministry with Persons with AIDS_____ 627
Ministry with Persons with Life-threatening Illness_____ 628
Ministry with Persons in Coma or Unable to Communicate_____ 629

## IX. SERVICES RELATING TO CONGREGATIONS AND BUILDINGS

A Service for Organizing a New Congregation_____ 634
A Service for the Breaking of Ground for a Church Building_____ 63
A Service for the Laying of a Foundation Stone of a Church Building_____ 63
A Service for the Consecration or Reconsecration of a Church Building_____ 63
A Service for the Dedication of a Church Building Free of Debt_____ 64
A Service for the Consecration of an Educational Building_____ 64
An Order for the Leave-taking of a Church Building_____ 64
An Order for Disbanding a Congregation_____ 65

## X. CONSECRATIONS AND ORDINATIONS

The Order for the Consecration of Diaconal Ministers_____ 65
The Order for the Ordination of Deacons_____ 66
The Order for the Ordination of Elders_____ 6
The Order for the Consecration of Diaconal Ministers
    and the Ordination of Deacons and Elders_____ 6
The Order for the Consecration of Bishops_____ 6
Suggested Scripture Lessons_____ 7
Suggested Hymns_____ 7

# XI. OTHER ANNUAL CONFERENCE AND DISTRICT SERVICES

An Order of Commitment for Lay Speakers_____ 714

An Order for Presenting Licenses to Local Pastors_____ 717

An Order for Admission of Clergy Candidates
to Membership in an Annual Conference_____ 718

A Service Celebrating the Appointment
of a District Superintendent_____ 722

A Service Celebrating the Assignment of a Bishop to an Area_____ 724

A Service of Farewell to a Bishop or District Superintendent_____ 730

A Retirement Recognition Service_____ 734

An Annual Conference Memorial Service_____ 737

# XII. GENERAL CHURCH SERVICES

The Order for Commissioning as Missionaries I_____ 740

The Order for Commissioning to the Office of Deaconess
or as Missionaries II_____ 741

# XIII. ACKNOWLEDGMENTS

_____ 744

# TERMS, ABBREVIATIONS, AND SYMBOLS USED THROUGHOUT THIS BOOK

*UMH* is the abbreviation for *The United Methodist Hymnal.*

Numbers preceded by *UMH* refer to *The United Methodist Hymnal.*

Other crossreferences refer to *The United Methodist Book of Worship.* If the number is preceded by ♪, it indicates the page on which a musical setting for this response is found.

Scripture references are listed in lectionary order: 1) Old Testament lessons, 2) Psalms, 3) New Testament lessons other than the Gospels, and 4) Gospel lessons.

An asterisk (*) indicates an act of worship for which the congregation may be invited to stand. Printed or oral invitations to stand should show sensitivity to the fact that some persons cannot stand. Rather than use words that sound like a command to stand or that assume everyone will stand, it is better to print in the bulletin something like, "The congregation is invited to stand at points marked asterisk (*)"; or to say, "You may stand"; or gesture with upturned palms.

Brackets [    ] indicate an act of worship that is ordinarily included but may be omitted in some situations.

*Leader* means a worship leader, who may be either lay or clergy.

**R** indicates that the congregation repeats their response.


## REPRODUCTION OF MATERIALS IN THIS BOOK

United Methodist congregations may reproduce for worship and educationa purposes any item from *The United Methodist Book of Worship* for one-time use, a in a bulletin, special program, or lesson resource, provided that the copyrigh notice and acknowledgement line are included on the reproduction. Permissio requests for more than one-time use of an item should be addressed to th copyright holder noted in the Acknowledgments (744). This permission does n extend to events where admission is charged or registration fees are collectec

# I. GENERAL SERVICES

## THE BASIC PATTERN OF WORSHIP

## INTRODUCTION

The Basic Pattern of Worship is rooted in Scripture and in our United Methodist heritage and experience. It expresses the biblical, historical, and theological integrity of Christian worship and is the basis of all the General Services of the Church. This Basic Pattern serves to guide those who plan worship and to help congregations understand the basic structure and content of our worship. Though it is not an order of worship, a variety of orders of worship may be based upon it. It reveals that behind the diversity of United Methodist worship there is a basic unity.

Our worship in both its diversity and its unity is an encounter with the living God through the risen Christ in the power of the Holy Spirit. When the people of God gather, the Spirit is free to move them to worship in diverse ways, according to their needs. We rejoice that congregations of large and small membership, in different regions, in different communities, of different racial and ethnic composition, and with distinctive local traditions can each worship in a style that enables the people to feel at home.

The Spirit is also the source of unity and truth. The teachings of Scripture give our worship a basic pattern that has proved itself over the centuries, that gives The United Methodist Church its sense of identity and links us to the universal Church. This pattern goes back to worship as Jesus and his earliest disciples knew it—services in the synagogue and Jewish family worship around the meal table. It has been fleshed out by the experience and traditions of Christian congregations for two thousand years.

The Entrance and the Proclamation and Response—often called the Service of the Word or the Preaching Service—are a Christian adaptation of the ancient synagogue service.

The Thanksgiving and Communion, commonly called the Lord's Supper or Holy Communion, is a Christian adaptation of Jewish worship at family meal tables—as Jesus and his disciples ate together during his preaching and teaching ministry, as Jesus transformed it when he instituted the Lord's Supper on the night before his death, and as his disciples experienced it in the breaking of bread with their risen Lord (Luke 24:30-35; John 21:13).

After the Day of Pentecost, when the earliest Christians went out preaching and teaching, they continued to take part in synagogue worship wherever they went (Acts 9:2ff., 20; 13:5, 13ff., 44ff.; 14:1; 17:1ff., 10ff., 17ff.; 18:4, 19, 26; 19:8; 22:19; 24:12; 26:11) and to break bread as a holy meal in their own gatherings (Acts 2:42, 46).

As their preaching and teaching about Jesus led to a break between church and synagogue, the Christians held an adapted synagogue service and broke bread when they gathered on the first day of the week. Such a combined service of Word and Table is described in Acts 20:7ff. This was apparently an accepted pattern by the time Luke wrote the Emmaus account in Luke 24:13-35, which pictures the joining together of a transformed synagogue service and a transformed holy meal and indicates to readers that they can know the risen Christ in the experience of Word and Table.

The Emmaus account can be used today in preaching and teaching the Basic Pattern of Worship. As on the first day of the week the two disciples were joined by the risen Christ, so in the power of the Holy Spirit the risen and ascended Christ joins us when we gather. As the disciples poured out to him their sorrow and in so doing opened their hearts to what Jesus would say to them, so we pour out to him whatever is on our hearts and thereby open ourselves to the Word. As Jesus "opened the Scriptures" to them and caused their hearts to burn, so we hear the Scriptures opened to us and out of the burning of our hearts praise God. As they were faced with a decision and responded by inviting Jesus to stay with them, we can do likewise. As they joined the risen Christ around the table, so can we. As Jesus took, blessed, broke, and gave the bread just as the disciples had seen him do three days previously, so in the name of the risen Christ we do these four actions with the bread and cup. As he was "made known to them in the breaking of the bread," so the risen and ascended Christ can be known to us in Holy Communion. As he disappeared and sent the disciples into the world with faith and joy, so he sends us forth into the world. And as those disciples found Christ when they arrived at Jerusalem later that evening, so we can find Christ with us wherever we go.

Since New Testament times, this Basic Pattern has had a long history development. At times this pattern has been obscured and corrupted, and times it has been recovered and renewed. The Wesleyan revival continued this emphasis on Word and Table, taking the gospel into the world by preaching and singing and by celebrating of the holy meal. Today The United Methodist Church is reclaiming our biblical and historic heritage, we seek in this Basic Pattern to worship God "in spirit and in truth."

# THE BASIC PATTERN OF WORSHIP

## ENTRANCE

The people come together in the Lord's name. There may be greetings, music and song, prayer and praise.

## PROCLAMATION AND RESPONSE

The Scriptures are opened to the people through the reading of lessons, preaching, witnessing, music, or other arts and media. Interspersed may be psalms, anthems, and hymns. Responses to God's Word include acts of commitment and faith with offerings of concerns, prayers, gifts, and service for the world and for one another.

## THANKSGIVING AND COMMUNION

In services with Communion, the actions of Jesus in the Upper Room are reenacted:
   taking the bread and cup,
   giving thanks over the bread and cup,
   breaking the bread, and
   giving the bread and cup.
In services without Communion, thanks are given for God's mighty acts in Jesus Christ.

## SENDING FORTH

The people are sent into ministry with the Lord's blessing.

# AN ORDER OF SUNDAY WORSHIP
# USING THE BASIC PATTERN

While the freedom and diversity of United Methodist worship are greater than can be represented by any single order of worship, United Methodists also affirm a heritage of order and the importance of the specific guidance and modeling that an order of worship provides.

This order expands upon An Order of Sunday Worship Using the Basic Pattern on pages 3-5 of *The United Methodist Hymnal* in showing some of the variety that is possible within the Basic Pattern of Worship. It assumes that worship leaders and congregation are to be in constant prayer. Worship is a sacred time when the people are led by the Holy Spirit to pray (Romans 8:22-26) and to worship God (1 Corinthians 14:25). Like the Basic Pattern, it is a guide to help those who plan worship see the structure and flow of our services. It is not intended that the congregation follow pages 3-5 in the hymnal while at worship. The congregation may be guided through the service by a bulletin or by announcement, whether or not Holy Communion is celebrated. This order is also the basis of the Services of Word and Table and other services in this book. It rests on the same biblical foundations as the Basic Pattern and incorporates the experience and traditions of Christians through the centuries, with particular care to include what is distinctive in our United Methodist heritage. Acts of worship that reflect racial, ethnic, regional, and local customs and heritages may be used appropriately throughout this order.

As Jesus invited children to come to him, so United Methodist worship should welcome children and youth as an integral part of the community as participants in, and leaders of, worship. Congregational worship services should include stories, songs and other music, and actions that are appropriate to children and youth of various ages and abilities.

## ENTRANCE

### GATHERING

The people come together in the Lord's name.

A church bell or bells or amplified music may call persons to worship

The worship service begins when the people begin to gather for worship What takes place during the Gathering includes both what the people do as they are entering the place of worship and what happens after they are seated. This should express their coming together in the name of the God revealed to us in Jesus Christ. This time is both an outward and visible gathering of the people and an inward and spiritual gathering—a focusing of awareness that they are a people gathered in the presence of the God known to us through Jesus Christ in the power of the Holy Spirit. Even when a worship service immediately follows another activity such a

Sunday school in the same room, and some who have been at the earlier activity simply remain seated for the worship that follows, the Gathering is a crucial part of the worship service.

While they are gathering, one or more of the following may take place:

1) Informal greetings, conversation, and fellowship should have some appropriate place during the Gathering. This renewing of community is a part of our entrance into congregational worship and should not be discouraged.

2) Announcements and welcoming of visitors may come either during the Gathering or at some other time early in the service, such as at the end of the Entrance. Welcoming may include a ritual of friendship using attendance registration pads or cards and inviting persons to introduce themselves to those sitting around them.

3) Rehearsal of unfamiliar hymns and other congregational music and acts of worship may be included.

4) Informal prayer, singing, and testimony may take place as the people are gathering, or with a group such as the worship leaders and choir gathered in a separate room.

5) Quiet meditation and private prayer may be encouraged while organ or other instrumental or vocal music is being offered or in a separate prayer room or chapel.

6) Organ or other instrumental or vocal music is part of the worship service, an offering by the musician(s) to God on behalf of the entire congregation, and not a mere prelude to the worship service.

The six acts suggested above for the Gathering may be combined in various ways: (1) may be encouraged before (5) and (6) begin, or before persons have entered the place of worship; (2), (3), or (4) may also precede (5) and (6); (4) may take place during (5) and (6) but in another room. None of these combinations in itself is more valid than another, but one may be far more appropriate than another, depending on the particular congregation and circumstances.

Other acts may also be appropriate during the Gathering. If candles are used, they may be lighted by acolytes. If there is to be no processional hymn, the worship leaders and choir(s) may enter and take their places.

## GREETING AND HYMN

Facing the people, the leader greets them in the Lord's name. The Greeting should be explicitly Christian, declaring that the Lord is present and empowers our worship. A collection of such greetings is found on 448-58 and in The Christian Year, 239-421.

The Greeting may be a scripture sentence, such as:

This is the day which the Lord has made;
let us rejoice and be glad in it.                                   (PSALM 118:24)

Or it may be a responsive act between leader and people, such as:

*Leader:* The grace of the Lord Jesus Christ be with you.
*People:* **And also with you.**
*Leader:* The risen Christ is with us.
*People:* **Praise the Lord!**

The choir may also sing a Christian greeting to the congregation, sometimes called the Introit, but this should not be a substitute for the greeting by the leader. See the listing of Service Music for Greeting/Call to Worship in *UMH* 951 and also ♪ 174-222.

The hymn may precede or follow the Greeting. The people, having been greeted in the Lord's name, may return the greeting to God with a hymn of praise. On the other hand, where the architecture of the worship space or the nature of the occasion calls for a ceremonial entrance of choir and worship leaders, a processional hymn or entrance song should come before the Greeting, allowing the Greeting to be spoken with the leader facing the people. The rhythm of a processional hymn should be appropriate for walking and long enough for the completion of the procession. See the listing of Processionals in *UMH* 949-50.

This hymn is most appropriately corporate praise to God, centering on attributes and deeds of God that call forth gratitude and praise. In addition it may express the people's greetings to one another in the Lord's name and exhortations to praise. It should normally be familiar, upbeat, and affirming. See the listings under Opening Hymns in *UMH* 948.

This and other hymns and songs in the service may be related to the joy of the Lord's Day, or to the day or season in the Christian year. See the listings under Christian Year in *UMH* 937-38.

A doxology, stanza, chorus, acclamation, or canticle may also be sung at this point, possibly repeated every Sunday, at least for a season, so that the people know it by heart. Some congregations have their own theme song, which may be sung every Sunday here or later in the service. A hymn that is a call to praise may be sung. Any of these may immediately precede an opening hymn of praise.

*Doxologies (Stanzas of Praise to the Trinity) in UMH*

| | |
|---|---|
| 62 All Creatures of Our God and King (last stanza) | 91 Canticle of Praise to God (last stan- |
| 682 All Praise to Thee, My God, This Night (last stanza, sung as canon) | za) 651 Come, Holy Ghost, Our Souls Inspire (last stanza sung by choir, conclud- ing doxology by congregation) |

61 Come, Thou Almighty King (last stanza)

680 Father, We Praise Thee (last stanza)

79 Holy God, We Praise Thy Name (last stanza)

102 Now Thank We All Our God (last stanza)

727 O What Their Joy and Glory Must Be (last stanza sung by choir)

184 Of the Father's Love Begotten (last stanza)

94 Praise God, from Whom All Blessings Flow

95 Praise God, from Whom All Blessings Flow

160 Rejoice, Ye Pure in Heart (last stanza)

161 Rejoice, Ye Pure in Heart (last stanza; "Hosanna" sung by choir)

65 ¡Santo! ¡Santo! ¡Santo! (last stanza)

296 Sing, My Tongue, the Glorious Battle (last stanza)

See also:

Amen, Praise the Father ( ♪ 178)

Doxology ( ♪ 182)

Praise God from Whom All Blessings Flow ( ♪ 180 and ♪ 185)

## Opening Stanzas and Choruses in UMH

596 Blessed Jesus, at Thy Word (stanza 1)

625 Come, Let Us Eat (stanza 3)

617 I Come with Joy (stanza 1)

659 Jesus Our Friend and Brother

661 Jesus, We Want to Meet (stanza 1)

234 O Come, All Ye Faithful (refrain)

317 O Sons and Daughters, Let Us Sing (stanza 1)

184 Of the Father's Love Begotten (stanza 2)

207 Prepare the Way of the Lord

328 Surely the Presence of the Lord

657 This Is the Day

658 This Is the Day the Lord Hath Made

See also:

May the Warm Winds of Heaven ( ♪ 198 and ♪ 200)

## Acclamations in UMH

630 "Alleluia!" refrain from Become to Us the Living Bread

158 "Alleluia! Amen!" from Come, Christians, Join to Sing

711 "Alleluia!" refrain from For All the Saints

79 Holy God, We Praise Thy Name (stanza 1)

90 "Alleluia!" refrain from Ye Watchers and Ye Holy Ones

91 Canticle of Praise to God

See also:

Heleluyan ( ♪ 176)

## Hymns in UMH Suggested as Calls to Praise

91 Canticle of Praise to God

699 Come, and Let Us Sweetly Join

732 Come, We That Love the Lord

632 Draw Us in the Spirit's Tether (may be sung by choir)

662 Stand Up and Bless the Lord

See also:

Come! Come! Everybody Worship ( ♪ 199)

Introit: Sing to the Lord a New Song ( ♪ 181)

It is appropriate to stand during the singing of this hymn and rema:
standing for the Greeting if that follows the hymn.

## OPENING PRAYERS AND PRAISE

Opening prayers, together with opening hymns, establish that o'
worship is communion with God as well as with one another. The
include recognition of who we are before God by centering on the natu
and gifts of God.

Here and elsewhere in the service, the posture for prayer may va
according to local custom and circumstance. The biblical tradition
standing to pray is always appropriate, especially when the people sta:
for praise immediately before or after the prayer. Kneeling for prayer
also appropriate, especially in confession. Praying seated and bowed
acceptable, especially if the alternative is for persons to be kept standing
kneeling for an uncomfortable length of time.

Here or elsewhere in the service, when an individual leads in prayer t
**Amen** should be spoken or sung by the whole congregation. Sung **Ame**
are found in *UMH* 897-904.

The Opening Prayer(s) may take any of several forms:

1) A prayer of the day may be a printed prayer such as one of the clas
collects, or it may be an extemporaneous prayer. It may be prayed
unison or led by one person. It may be preceded or followed by silen
It may be a prayer suited to any occasion or any Lord's Day; or it n
address God in the light of the theme of the day or season of
Christian year. See the collection of prayers on 459-73. A number
such prayers—some for general use and some for particular da
seasons, or occasions—are also scattered among the hymns in *UM*
See also the hymns listed under Opening Prayer in *UMH* 951.

2) A prayer of confession and act of pardon may include the follow
sequence:
a) A formal or informal call to confession by the leader
b) A prayer of confession prayed in unison by the people
c) Silence
d) Words of assurance or declaration of pardon by the leader
e) A response by the people

A prayer of confession and declaration of pardon belong toget
neither should be used without the other. The leader may be a
liturgist. See the collection of prayers of confession and acts of par
on 474-94. See also the examples printed in *UMH* 7-8, 12, 26-27,
890-93 and the listing of hymns that can be sung as prayer:
confession (*UMH* 939-40). After the Prayer of Confession there ma
a sung response such as Jesus, Remember Me (*UMH* 488) or the refr

of Pass Me Not, O Gentle Savior (*UMH* 351) or Just As I Am (*UMH* 357). After the Words of Assurance or Declaration of Pardon there may be a sung response such as the refrain of Grace Greater Than Our Sin (*UMH* 365). See also the Hymns of Repentance and Hymns of Pardon (*UMH* 351-67).

Confession and pardon may take place either at this point in the service or later, as a Response to the Proclamation of the Word. In an opening prayer of confession the people confess the sin of which they are already aware and then come to the Proclamation of the Word in the assurance of God's pardoning grace. The acknowledgment that we are sinners saved by grace is also appropriate in opening prayers of the day or litanies. Confession as a Response to the Word includes the added awareness of personal and corporate sin to which persons are led by the Proclamation of the Word.

) If it is a litany, or responsive prayer between leader and people, the people should have a single repeated response, spoken or sung, that is simple and easily memorized, such as: **Lord, have mercy.** See the litany on 495. Suitable sung litany responses in *UMH* include:

| | |
|---|---|
| 490 Hear Us, O God | 484 Kyrie Eleison |
| 488 Jesus, Remember Me | 485 Let Us Pray to the Lord |
| 483 Kyrie Eleison | 487 This Is Our Prayer |

*See also:*
O Lord, Deliver Us ( ♪ 195)
May This Mind Be in Us ( ♪ 189 and ♪ 191)
Señor, Apiadate de Nosotros ( ♪ 188)
O Lamb of God ( ♪ 201)

fter the Opening Prayer(s), if an act of praise is desired, one or more of the llowing may be spoken or sung, actively involving the whole congregation possible:

Canticle of God's Glory (*UMH* 72, 82, or 83)

A psalm or other scripture song (canticle), especially the canticles indexed in *UMH* 935-36

The Gloria Patri (*UMH* 70 or 71) or the Glory to God on High (*UMH* 188, refrain only)

The Lord, Have Mercy (Kyrie Eleison) in threefold form (*UMH* 482)

An anthem

ioirs may sing at various points in the service, such as here, between sons, or at the Offering. Wherever an anthem is sung, it should be propriate to its place in the service. Anthems that give the whole ngregation a familiar or easily learned part to sing are increasingly common and especially recommended. The people can become active involved in any anthem by saying **Amen** at its conclusion.

Other possibilities for an act of praise at this point include a hymn, hymn stanza, chorus, doxology, or a spoken litany of praise.

If announcements and welcoming are not placed in the Gathering, they may follow the Opening Prayers and Praise.

## PROCLAMATION AND RESPONSE

### PRAYER FOR ILLUMINATION

The blessing of the Holy Spirit is invoked upon the reading, preaching, hearing, and doing of the Word. An example of such a prayer is found in Service of Word and Table I (34). The following adaptation of Psalm 19 may also be used:

Let the words of our mouths, and the meditations of our hearts
  be acceptable in your sight,
  O Lord, our Rock and our Redeemer. Amen.

*UMH* 594, 597, and 602 may also be used for this purpose. This prayer may be prayed by the congregation in unison, by someone other than the preacher, or by the preacher. Another alternative is to sing a hymn refrain such as one of the following in *UMH* (or others listed in *UMH* 9) as the Prayer for Illumination:

| | |
|---|---|
| 596 Blessed Jesus, at Thy Word | 454 Open My Eyes That I May See (ref) |
| (esp. stanza 3) | 393 Spirit of the Living God |
| 599 Break Thou the Bread of Life | 601 Thy Word Is a Lamp (refrain) |
| 473 Lead Me, Lord | 600 Wonderful Words of Life |
| 544 Like the Murmur of the Dove's Song | |
| (esp. stanza 3) | |

*See also:*
Prayer for Wisdom ( ♪ 193)
Shine on Me ( ♪ 205)

If the Opening Prayers are not followed by an Act of Praise, the Prayer Illumination may be included with the Opening Prayers, or a single prayer may serve both purposes. Many traditional collects can serve this double purpose and enable the service to move directly from the Opening Prayers to the reading of the Scriptures.

### SCRIPTURE

Two or three scripture readings should be used. The sequence of reading may be ordered so that the sermon is immediately preceded by primary text to be preached. The ancient and ecumenical order of the readings, however, embodied in the Revised Common Lectionary readings on 227-37, is as follows:

First Reading (usually from the Old Testament)
Psalm
Second Reading (from the New Testament, but not from the Gospels)
Hymn, Song, or Alleluia
Gospel (a reading from Matthew, Mark, Luke, or John)

If there are not Old Testament, Epistle, and Gospel readings at each service, care should be taken that over a period of time the people hear representative readings from each.

When laypersons, including older children and youth, are chosen to read the Scriptures in the service, they should be allowed time and opportunity to prepare.

Each reading may be introduced as follows: "A reading from (*or* Hear the Word of God in) the book of _____, the ___ chapter, beginning with the ___ verse." Following the reading, the reader may say, "The Word of the Lord (*God*)," and the people may respond, **Thanks be to God.** Or the reader may say, "Amen," and the people respond, **Amen.** If desired, the congregation may then sing a scripture acclamation such as one of those listed in *UMH* 951.

After the first reading, a psalm or psalm portions may be sung or spoken as an Act of Praise, the people standing. See *UMH* 735-862 and the lectionary for suggested psalms on 227-37. An anthem based on the psalm is also appropriate.

Before the final reading, a hymn or song related to the scriptures of the day, or an alleluia, may be sung.

Because in the reading of the four Gospels we are addressed by the words of Christ and experience this as an encounter with the living Christ, many Christians prefer to stand and greet Christ with an **Alleluia!** except during Lent (see *UMH* 78, 186, 486, and the other alleluias suggested under "Acclamations" on 19) and remain standing for the reading of the Gospel as an act of respect for the Christ who is addressing us.

## ERMON

One or more of the scripture readings is interpreted and proclaimed.

Children, youth, and adults should hear and respond to the Proclamation of the Word. The sermon should communicate effectively with as wide a range of ages and stages of faith development as possible. If necessary, sharing the Word with children may be placed earlier in the service as a response to the reading of one of the scripture lessons. This sharing should focus on the Word of the day and be in styles appropriate to the developmental levels of the children present. Specific and concrete stories and narratives are especially encouraged.

## RESPONSE TO THE WORD

This should include an Invitation to Christian Discipleship, followed by a hymn of invitation (*UMH* 337-50); or by a baptismal, confirmation, o reaffirmation hymn (*UMH* 604-11); or by one of the hymns listed unde Commitment in *UMH* 939; or by another hymn that is an appropriate response to the sermon. Responses may also include:

1) A first commitment to Christ, which may be followed if appropriate b enrollment in a preparatory group for baptism or confirmation

2) Reaffirmation of Faith (see 86-94, 106-10, or 588-89)

3) Appropriate portions of the Baptismal Covenant:
   a) Holy Baptism (see 86-110)
   b) Confirmation (see 86-94 or 106-10)
   c) Congregational reaffirmation of the Baptismal Covenant (se 111-14)
   d) Reception into The United Methodist Church of those not alread United Methodists (see 93-94 or 109-10)
   e) Reception into the Local Congregation (see 93-94 or 109-10)

4) Installation and recognition services for church officers, workers, c groups (see 593-605)

5) Other acts of worship such as services of healing that are appropriat responses to the Proclamation of the Word (see 585-90, 613-29)

6) Consecration or dedication services relating to the church building c its furnishings (see 606-07, 610-12, 630-51)

7) Congregational or individual commitment to specific actions such a missions (see 591-92) or reconciliation

8) A time of silent reflection or spoken expressions from the congregatic

9) The Apostles' Creed or another creed (see *UMH* 880-89), except whe already used in the Baptismal Covenant

   We Believe in One True God (*UMH* 85) may be sung as a creed, or or of the following in the *UMH* may be sung as a response to the cree

| | |
|---|---|
| 177 He Is Lord | 98 To God Be the Glory |
| 99 My Tribute | |

## CONCERNS AND PRAYERS

Joys and concerns to be included in the prayers may be expressed. Pray may take one or more of these forms:

1) Brief intercessions, petitions, and thanksgivings may be prayed by t leader or by members of the congregation. Each of these prayers m be followed by a common response, such as **Lord, hear our pray** spoken or sung by all, or one of the following from *UMH*:

| | |
|---|---|
| 490 Hear Us, O God | 485 Let Us Pray to the Lord |
| 488 Jesus, Remember Me | 487 This Is Our Prayer |

2) A litany of intercession and petition (see 495).

3) A bidding prayer or prayer of petition (see 497-530). This may also include blessings for persons (see 531-48) and prayers for special Sundays or days on the secular and denominational calendar (see 422-44).

4) Pastoral prayer, in which the pastor composes and offers a prayer gathering up the concerns of the church and of the world. The congregation's participation in the prayer is expressed by the unison sung or spoken **Amen** at the end of the prayer. So that the people may know when to sing or speak their **Amen,** the pastor may regularly end the prayer with words such as, "through (*in the name of*) Jesus Christ our Lord."

Prior to the prayers, prayer concerns or requests may be gathered from the congregation orally or in writing.

The choir or congregation may sing an invitation to prayer such as one of those listed in *UMH* 951-52. See also: Call to Prayer ( ♪ 196); Jesus, We Are Praying ( ♪ 192); Where Two or Three Are Gathered ( ♪ 202)

The congregation may sing **Amen** (see *UMH* 897-904), or a prayer response such as one of those listed in *UMH* 952, Heleluyan (*UMH* 78), or Remember Me (*UMH* 491).

During this time persons may be invited to kneel at the communion rail.

Congregations that do not wish to place the Concerns and Prayers and the Offering after the Proclamation of the Word may place them at the Opening Prayers and Praise in the service. The Opening Prayers may be expanded to include the Concerns and Prayers, with the Offering following, accompanied by an act of praise or by an organ or other instrumental voluntary.

## CONFESSION, PARDON, AND PEACE

See the discussion of confession and pardon on 20-21 for an explanation of this act of worship, with musical suggestions. The following is a sample of the kind of confession-pardon sequence used here or during the Entrance:

Let us confess our sin against God and our neighbors.

**Most merciful God, we confess that we have sinned against you**
**in thought, word, and deed,**
**by what we have done, and by what we have left undone.**
**We have not loved you with our whole heart;**
**we have not loved our neighbors as ourselves.**
**We are truly sorry and we humbly repent.**
**For the sake of your Son Jesus Christ, have mercy on us and forgive us;**
**that we may delight in your will, and walk in your ways,**
**to the glory of your name. Amen.**

*All offer prayers of confession in silence.*

Almighty God have mercy on you,
forgive all your sins through our Lord Jesus Christ,
strengthen you in all goodness,
and by the power of the Holy Spirit keep you in eternal life. **Amen.**

The people may offer one another signs of reconciliation and love particularly when Holy Communion is celebrated. The Peace is an act of reconciliation and blessing, based on New Testament Christian practice (Romans 16:16; 1 Corinthians 16:20; 2 Corinthians 13:12; 1 Thessalonians 5:26; 1 Peter 5:14). Its placement immediately before the Offering recalls Matthew 5:23-24. It is not simply our peace but the peace of Christ that we offer. The gestures and words used may vary widely, depending on the temperament and customs of the people and the nature of the occasion. For example, one may clasp another's hand and say, "The peace of Christ be with you," and the other respond, "And also with you." The Peace is not to be confused with the ritual of friendship or welcoming of visitors (see 17 and 22). If the Confession and Pardon are placed earlier in the service, the Peace may still be observed at this time in the service.

The choir may lead one of the following from *UMH* during the Peace or at its conclusion:

620 One Bread, One Body                    667 Shalom Chaverim
666 Shalom to You

## OFFERING

An offering may include

1) Monetary gifts or products of labor

2) Other appropriate gifts, such as memorial gifts or other items to be dedicated

3) The bread and cup, brought by representatives of the people to the Lord's table with the other gifts, or uncovered if already in place, Holy Communion is to follow

As the gifts are received and presented, there may also be offered:

1) A hymn—if Holy Communion is to follow, a hymn of invitation may be sung, such as one of these in *UMH*:

621 Be Present at Our Table, Lord
319 Christ Jesus Lay in Death's Strong
    Bands (stanza 4, sung by choir)
699 Come, and Let Us Sweetly Join
625 Come, Let Us Eat (stanzas 1, 2)
164 Come, My Way, My Truth, My
    Life (stanza 2)

616 Come, Sinners, to the Gospel Feast
    (stanza 1)
510 Come, Ye Disconsolate
618 Let Us Break Bread Together
383 This Is a Day of New Beginnings
    (stanza 5)

2) A psalm

3) An anthem

4) Instrumental music

5) A doxology or other musical response (see listings under Doxology and Offering in *UMH* 951-52 and on 18-19), especially the following in *UMH*:

588 All Things Come of Thee            640 Take Our Bread (refrain, communion)
621 Be Present at Our Table, Lord       87 What Gift Can We Bring
    (communion)
587 Bless Thou the Gifts

*See also:*
Offertory Hymn: For the Gift of Creation ( ♪ 179)

## THANKSGIVING (WITHOUT HOLY COMMUNION)

### PRAYER OF THANKSGIVING

The following or other Prayer of Thanksgiving (see 550-55) is prayed after the presentation of the gifts:

All things come from you, O God,
   and with praise and thanksgiving we return to you what is yours.
You created all that is, and with love formed us in your image.
When our love failed, your love remained steadfast.
You gave your only Son Jesus Christ to be our Savior,
   that we might have abundant and eternal life.
All that we are, and all that we have, is a trust from you.
And so, in gratitude for all that you have done,
   we offer you ourselves, and all that we have,
   in union with Christ's offering for us.
By your Holy Spirit make us one with Christ, one with each other,
   and one in ministry to all the world;
   through Jesus Christ our Lord. **Amen.**

### THE LORD'S PRAYER

All pray the Lord's Prayer, using one of the forms in *UMH* 270-71, 894-96.

A time of silence may follow the Lord's Prayer.

If Holy Communion is not celebrated, the service concludes with the Sending Forth. See 31-32.

## THANKSGIVING (WITH HOLY COMMUNION)

### TAKING THE BREAD AND CUP

This is the first of the four actions of Holy Communion, based on the actions of Jesus in the upper room.

The pastor, standing behind the Lord's table, takes the bread and cup which have been placed on the Lord's table, and prepares them for the meal. If an altar table is fixed against the wall, the pastor may stand beside it, or a freestanding Lord's table may be placed in front of it. It is traditional that there be a white linen cloth covering the top of the Lord's table under the bread and cup; but this should not be confused with the parament that hang down from the top of the Lord's table and show the color of the day or season. See the suggestions for colors on 226. It is also traditional that the bread and cup have been covered by a white linen napkin, or by a white linen-covered card over the cup, or by metal tray lids.

The bread may be either leavened or unleavened. The use of a large uncut loaf of bread, which later in the service is broken and distributed to the people, follows the practice reported by Paul in 1 Corinthians 10:16-17 and symbolizes the fact that the Church is one body in Christ. This loaf may be baked by a member of the congregation. Pita bread is especially suited for use when the people commune by intinction (dipping the bread into the chalice). If the loaf is still wrapped or covered, the pastor should unwrap or uncover it before proceeding with the Great Thanksgiving but should not cut or break the bread. If wafers or bread cubes are used, the pastor should remove the lid(s) or covering.

A large cup, commonly called the chalice, is also a symbol of unity in Christ. If the cup has not already been filled, the pastor should fill it at this time. If individual cups are used, the pastor should remove the lid(s) or covering at this time. Although the historic and ecumenical Christian practice has been to use wine, the use of unfermented grape juice by The United Methodist Church and its predecessors since the late nineteenth century expresses pastoral concern for recovering alcoholics, enables the participation of children and youth, and supports the church's witness of abstinence.

## THE GREAT THANKSGIVING

As Jesus gave thanks over (blessed) the bread and cup, so do the pastor and people. This prayer is led by the pastor appointed to that congregation and authorized by the bishop to administer the Sacraments there, or by some other ordained elder. If neither the pastor nor any other ordained person present, a Love Feast (see 581-83) rather than Holy Communion should be celebrated. The pastor stands behind the Lord's table, the people also standing. After an introductory dialogue between pastor and people, the pastor gives thanks appropriate to the occasion, remembering God's acts salvation and the institution of the Lord's Supper, and invokes the present work of the Holy Spirit, concluding with praise to the Trinity. The people responses of adoration and acclamation are interspersed, and the prayer concludes with the people's **Amen.** See the Great Thanksgivings in Service of Word and Table I-IV and on 54-80. The people's responses may be sung, using the musical settings in *UMH* 17-25.

# E LORD'S PRAYER

\ll pray the Lord's Prayer, using one of the forms in *UMH* 270-71, 894-96. 'his forms a bridge between the first pair of actions in Holy Communion Thanksgiving) and the second pair (Communion). It is both the sublime limax of our thanksgiving to God and the verbal entrance into a ommunion with God that is holy beyond words.

'he people may be called to pray the Lord's Prayer with this invitation: 'And now, with the confidence of children of God, let us pray: . . . ."

# EAKING THE BREAD

'he third of the four actions of Holy Communion, like the first, is brief and oreliminary to the act that immediately follows. It is a sequence of gestures nviting the people to come to the meal. The pastor, still standing behind he Lord's table, lifts the unbroken and uncut loaf of bread in full view of he people and breaks it by hand, in silence or with appropriate words. If ndividual wafers or cubes of bread are used, one of the wafers (preferably ι larger wafer) or a large piece of the bread from which the cubes have been ut should be broken. The pastor then raises the cup, or one of the cups, in iilence or with appropriate words. See 39 for appropriate words to ιccompany these actions.

'ollowing Breaking the Bread, the pastor may now announce that the able is ready and that people may come to be served, using a sentence iuch as, "Come, the table is ready."

# VING THE BREAD AND CUP

:n the fourth and last action of Holy Communion, the bread and cup are given to the people as Jesus gave them to the disciples. Laypersons as well as other clergy may assist the pastor in giving the bread and cup. All who ntend to lead a Christian life, together with their children, are invited to :eceive the bread and cup. We have no tradition of refusing any who oresent themselves desiring to receive. Any or all of the people may receive them while standing, kneeling, or seated. It is our custom to serve 2ach person individually, while exchanging these or other words:

[*Name,*] the body of Christ, given for you. **Amen.**
[*Name,*] the blood of Christ, given for you. **Amen.**

*or*

The body of Christ, the bread of heaven. **Amen.**
The blood of Christ, the cup of salvation. **Amen.**

*or*

Jesus Christ, the bread of heaven. **Amen.**
Jesus Christ, the cup of salvation. **Amen.**

Every effort should be made to make each person, and especially children, welcome at the table. It is particularly effective to look directly at the person being addressed, touch each person's hand while giving the bread and cup, and if possible call each person by name.

Serving one another acts out our faith that Christ is the giver of this holy meal and that we are receivers of Christ's grace. It is traditional that the pastor receive the bread and cup first and then serve those who are assisting in the giving of the bread and cup; but, if desired, the pastor and those assisting may receive last. One of those assisting may serve the pastor.

The congregation may sing hymns while the bread and cup are given. In addition to hymns UMH 612-41 and others listed under UMH 641 and in the index under Holy Communion (UMH 943), many other hymns in UMH are suitable in effectively expressing the people's loving communion with God and with one another. The day or season of the Christian year and the people's knowledge and love of particular hymns are important considerations in the selection of appropriate hymns. It is particularly effective if the people can sing from memory. Sometimes it is effective to sing and repeat a chorus such as Jesus, Remember Me (UMH 488), Remember Me (UMH 491), the refrain One Bread, One Body (UMH 620), or the alternate refrain For the Beauty of the Earth (UMH 92).

After the people have been served, the Lord's table is set in order.

What is done with the remaining bread and wine should express our stewardship of God's gifts and our respect for the holy purpose they have served.

1) They may be set aside for distribution to the sick and others wishing to commune but unable to attend. See A Service of Word and Table V on 51-53.

2) They may be reverently consumed by the pastor and others while the table is being set in order or following the service.

3) They may be returned to the earth; that is, the bread may be buried or scattered on the ground, and the wine may be reverently poured out upon the ground—a biblical gesture of worship (2 Samuel 23:16) and an ecological symbol today.

A brief prayer of thanksgiving, prayed by the pastor or in unison, may conclude the giving of the bread and cup after the people have been served (see 39, 53). Sometimes the closing hymn can serve this purpose. The earlier stanzas of some hymns may be sung while the people are being served, the final stanza(s) being sung after the people have been served (as indicated below). The following hymns and stanzas in UMH are suggested:

625 Come, Let Us Eat (last stanza)
632 Draw Us in the Spirit's Tether
　　(last stanza)
563 Father, We Thank You (may be
　　sung by choir with handbells)
565 Father, We Thank You
614 For the Bread Which You Have
　　Broken

615 For the Bread Which You Have Broken
623 Here, O My Lord (stanzas 4, 5)
617 I Come with Joy (stanzas 3-5)
634 Now Let Us from This Table Rise
102 Now Thank We All Our God
　84 Thank You, Lord
629 You Satisfy the Hungry Heart
　　(last stanza)

# SENDING FORTH

## YMN OR SONG AND DISMISSAL WITH BLESSING

Whether or not Holy Communion has been celebrated, the service concludes with a series of acts in which the congregation stands and is sent forth to active ministry in the world.

The final hymn or song of sending forth may be an entire hymn or simply one or more stanzas. It may be:

1) A hymn of thanksgiving and praise or a doxology

2) Consecration to service in the world

3) A recessional

4) A hymn of thanksgiving following Holy Communion (see list above)

5) A favorite hymn or theme song, sung every week

See the listings under Closing Hymns (*UMH* 939), Discipleship and Service (*UMH* 940), and Doxology (*UMH* 951) and the listing of doxologies on 18-19 above. If a particular hymn of sending forth is desired to be sung every week, the following in *UMH* are suggested:

376 Dona Nobis Pacem
665 Go Now in Peace
672 God Be with You till We Meet Again
673 God Be with You till We Meet Again
668 Let Us Now Depart in Thy Peace

671 Lord, Dismiss Us with Thy Blessing
664 Sent Forth by God's Blessing
666 Shalom to You
667 Shalom
　84 Thank You, Lord

*See also:*
An Indian Blessing ( ♪ 186)
Benediction ( ♪ 190)
Shawnee Traveling Song ( ♪ 197)

The Dismissal with Blessing, often called the Benediction, is given by the pastor, facing the people. It is addressed to the people, not to God, and the pastor and people appropriately look at each other as it is given. For this reason, it should be given from the front, not the back, of the sanctuary. See 39, 151, 157, 559-66.

If the closing hymn or song is a recessional in which the pastor joins,
should follow the Dismissal with Blessing; otherwise it should precede the
Dismissal with Blessing.

## GOING FORTH

Like the Gathering, the Going Forth is an act of corporate worship as long
as people are still with other people in the place of worship. One or more
of the following may be included:

1) Organ or other instrumental voluntary, during which the people are
   free to go forth, remain standing quietly in place listening, or sit down
   to listen

2) Silence before the congregation disperses

3) Extinguishing of candles and carrying out of the light (to symbolize the
   light of Christ leading us out into the world), if this was not done
   during the recessional

4) Informal greetings, conversation, and fellowship

# SERVICES OF WORD AND TABLE

# A SERVICE OF WORD AND TABLE I

*(The pure, unfermented juice of the grape **or an equivalent** shall be used during the serv-*
*ice of Holy Communion)*

*This service is found in* UMH 6-11. *A congregation may use this text for the entire service.*
*It is desirable that during the course of the year the prayers in services of Word and Table be*
*varied; see A Service of Word and Table II and III, the Great Thanksgivings (54-80), and*
*resources for the Christian year (224-421). For further directions and options see 13-32.*

## ENTRANCE

GATHERING *See 16-17.*

GREETING *See 17-20.*

The grace of the Lord Jesus Christ be with you.
**And also with you.**

The risen Christ is with us.
**Praise the Lord!**

HYMN OF PRAISE* *See 17-20.*

OPENING PRAYER* *See 20-21.*

*The following or a prayer of the day is offered:*

**Almighty God,**
**to you all hearts are open, all desires known,**
    **and from you no secrets are hidden.**
**Cleanse the thoughts of our hearts**
    **by the inspiration of your Holy Spirit,**
**that we may perfectly love you,**
    **and worthily magnify your holy name,**
**through Christ our Lord. Amen.**

[ACT OF PRAISE] *See 21-22.*

## PROCLAMATION AND RESPONSE

PRAYER FOR ILLUMINATION * *See 22.*

Lord, open our hearts and minds
  by the power of your Holy Spirit,
that, as the Scriptures are read
  and your Word proclaimed,
we may hear with joy what you say to us today. Amen.

SCRIPTURE LESSON *See 22-23 and lectionary on 227-37.*

[PSALM] * *See 22-23 and lectionary on 227-37.*

[SCRIPTURE LESSON] *See 22-23 and lectionary on 227-37.*

HYMN OR SONG * *See 23.*

GOSPEL LESSON * *See 22-23 and lectionary on 227-37.*

SERMON *See 23.*

RESPONSE TO THE WORD *See 24.*

I believe in God, the Father Almighty,
  creator of heaven and earth.
I believe in Jesus Christ, his only Son, our Lord,
  who was conceived by the Holy Spirit,
  born of the Virgin Mary,
  suffered under Pontius Pilate,
  was crucified, died, and was buried;
  he descended to the dead.
  On the third day he rose again;
  he ascended into heaven,
  is seated at the right hand of the Father,
  and will come again to judge the living and the dead.
I believe in the Holy Spirit,
  the holy catholic* church,                                    *univer
  the communion of saints,
  the forgiveness of sins,
  the resurrection of the body,
  and the life everlasting. Amen.

CONCERNS AND PRAYERS * *See 24-25.*

*Brief intercessions, petitions, and thanksgivings may be prayed by the leader*
*spontaneously by members of the congregation. To each of these, all may mak*

*common response, such as:* **Lord, hear our prayer** *or* UMH *485, 487, 488, or 490.*

*Or a litany of intercession and petition may be prayed. See 495.*

*Or a pastoral prayer may be prayed. See 25.*

## INVITATION

*Pastor stands behind the Lord's table.*

Christ our Lord invites to his table all who love him,
  who earnestly repent of their sin
  and seek to live in peace with one another.
Therefore, let us confess our sin before God and one another.

## CONFESSION AND PARDON *See 20-21, 25-26.*

**Merciful God,**
  **we confess that we have not loved you with our whole heart.**
**We have failed to be an obedient church.**
**We have not done your will,**
  **we have broken your law,**
  **we have rebelled against your love,**
  **we have not loved our neighbors,**
  **and we have not heard the cry of the needy.**
**Forgive us, we pray.**
**Free us for joyful obedience,**
**through Jesus Christ our Lord. Amen.**

*All pray in silence.*

*Leader to people:*

Hear the good news:
  Christ died for us while we were yet sinners;
  that proves God's love toward us.
In the name of Jesus Christ, you are forgiven!

*People to leader:*

**In the name of Jesus Christ, you are forgiven!**

*Leader and people:*

**Glory to God. Amen.**

## THE PEACE * *See 26.*

Let us offer one another signs of reconciliation and love.

*All, including the pastor, exchange signs and words of God's peace.*

OFFERING *See 26-27.*

As forgiven and reconciled people,
  let us offer ourselves and our gifts to God.

*A hymn, psalm, or anthem may be sung as the offering is received.*

*The bread and wine are brought by representatives of the people to the Lord's tab.*
*with the other gifts, or uncovered if already in place.*

*A hymn, doxology, or other response may be sung as the gifts are presented*

*If a Great Thanksgiving other than that which follows here is to be used, the servi*
*proceeds with A Service of Word and Table III (40). Otherwise, the servi*
*continues as follows:*

# THANKSGIVING AND COMMUNION

## TAKING THE BREAD AND CUP *See 27-28.*

*The pastor, standing if possible behind the Lord's table, facing the people from th*
*time through Breaking the Bread, takes the bread and cup; and the bread and wi*
*are prepared for the meal.*

## THE GREAT THANKSGIVING * *See 28.*

*One of the musical settings in UMH 17-25 may be used, the pastor using t*
*following text:*

The Lord be with you.
**And also with you.**
Lift up your hearts. *The pastor may lift hands and keep them raised.*
**We lift them up to the Lord.**
Let us give thanks to the Lord our God.
**It is right to give our thanks and praise.**

It is right, and a good and joyful thing,
  always and everywhere to give thanks to you,
  Father Almighty, creator of heaven and earth.
You formed us in your image
  and breathed into us the breath of life.
When we turned away, and our love failed,
  your love remained steadfast.
You delivered us from captivity,
  made covenant to be our sovereign God,
  and spoke to us through the prophets.
And so,
  with your people on earth
  and all the company of heaven
  we praise your name and join their unending hymn:

*The pastor may lower hands.*

**Holy, holy, holy Lord, God of power and might,**
**heaven and earth are full of your glory.**
  **Hosanna in the highest.**
**Blessed is he who comes in the name of the Lord.**
  **Hosanna in the highest.**

*The pastor may raise hands.*

Holy are you, and blessed is your Son Jesus Christ.
Your Spirit anointed him
  to preach good news to the poor,
  to proclaim release to the captives
    and recovering of sight to the blind,
  to set at liberty those who are oppressed,
  and to announce that the time had come
    when you would save your people.
He healed the sick, fed the hungry, and ate with sinners.
By the baptism of his suffering, death, and resurrection
  you gave birth to your Church,
  delivered us from slavery to sin and death,
  and made with us a new covenant
    by water and the Spirit.
When the Lord Jesus ascended,
  he promised to be with us always,
    in the power of your Word and Holy Spirit.

*The pastor may hold hands, palms down, over the bread, or touch the bread, or lift the bread.*

On the night in which he gave himself up for us,
  he took bread, gave thanks to you, broke the bread,
  gave it to his disciples, and said:
"Take, eat; this is my body which is given for you.
Do this in remembrance of me."

*The pastor may hold hands, palms down, over the cup, or touch the cup, or lift the cup.*

When the supper was over, he took the cup,
  gave thanks to you, gave it to his disciples, and said:
"Drink from this, all of you;
  this is my blood of the new covenant,
  poured out for you and for many
    for the forgiveness of sins.
Do this, as often as you drink it,
  in remembrance of me."

*The pastor may raise hands.*

And so,
in remembrance of these your mighty acts in Jesus Christ,
we offer ourselves in praise and thanksgiving
  as a holy and living sacrifice,
  in union with Christ's offering for us,
as we proclaim the mystery of faith.

**Christ has died; Christ is risen; Christ will come again.**

*The pastor may hold hands, palms down, over the bread and cup.*

Pour out your Holy Spirit on us gathered here,
  and on these gifts of bread and wine.
Make them be for us the body and blood of Christ,
that we may be for the world the body of Christ,
  redeemed by his blood.

*The pastor may raise hands.*

By your Spirit make us one with Christ,
  one with each other,
  and one in ministry to all the world,
until Christ comes in final victory
  and we feast at his heavenly banquet.

Through your Son Jesus Christ,
with the Holy Spirit in your holy Church,
all honor and glory is yours, almighty Father,
now and for ever. **Amen.**

THE LORD'S PRAYER * *See 29.*

*The pastor's hands may be extended in open invitation.*

And now, with the confidence of children of God, let us pray:

*The pastor may raise hands.*

**Our Father in heaven,**
  **hallowed be your name,**
  **your kingdom come,**
  **your will be done,**
    **on earth as in heaven.**
**Give us today our daily bread.**
**Forgive us our sins**
  **as we forgive those who sin against us.**
**Save us from the time of trial,**
  **and deliver us from evil.**
**For the kingdom, the power, and the glory are yours**
  **now and for ever. Amen.**

BREAKING THE BREAD *See 29.*

*The pastor, still standing behind the Lord's table facing the people, breaks the bread in silence, or while saying:*

Because there is one loaf,
we, who are many, are one body, for we all partake of the one loaf.
The bread which we break is a sharing in the body of Christ.

*The pastor lifts the cup in silence, or while saying:*

The cup over which we give thanks is a sharing in the blood of Christ.

GIVING THE BREAD AND CUP *See 29-31.*

*The bread and wine are given to the people, with these or other words being exchanged:*

The body of Christ, given for you. **Amen.**
The blood of Christ, given for you. **Amen.**

*The congregation may sing hymns while the bread and cup are given. Many hymns, songs, and choruses in* UMH *in addition to 612-41 and others listed under Holy Communion (943) are effective in expressing the people's loving communion with God and with one another. The day or season of the Christian year and the people's knowledge and love of particular hymns are important considerations in the selection of appropriate hymns. It is particularly effective if the people can sing from memory.*

*When all have received, the Lord's table is put in order. See 30.*

*The following prayer is then offered by the pastor or by all:*

**Eternal God, we give you thanks for this holy mystery**
 **in which you have given yourself to us.**
**Grant that we may go into the world**
 **in the strength of your Spirit,**
  **to give ourselves for others,**
**in the name of Jesus Christ our Lord. Amen.**

## SENDING FORTH

HYMN OR SONG * *See 30-31.*

DISMISSAL WITH BLESSING * *See 31-32.*

Go forth in peace.
The grace of the Lord Jesus Christ,
and the love of God,
and the communion of the Holy Spirit
be with you all. **Amen.**

GOING FORTH * *See 32.*

# INTRODUCTION TO
# A SERVICE OF WORD AND TABLE II

*(The pure, unfermented juice of the grape **or an equivalent** shall be used during the se~ ice of Holy Communion)*

This service is found in *UMH* 12-15 and is designed for those wishing a brief t~ beginning with the Invitation to the Lord's table. The parts of the service prec~ ing the text in *UMH* are guided by a bulletin or by announcement. The text beg~ ning with the Invitation is read by pastor and people from the hymnal.

Words appropriate to the day, season, or occasion may be added to the Gr~ Thanksgiving at points marked *. These may be words of the pastor's own co~ position or selection; or the pastor may use one of the seasonal Gr~ Thanksgivings on 54-79, all of which are designed to be used while the people f low A Service of Word and Table II or one of the musical settings in *UMH* 17-~

# INTRODUCTION TO
# A SERVICE OF WORD AND TABLE III

*(The pure, unfermented juice of the grape **or an equivalent** shall be used during the se ice of Holy Communion)*

This service is found in *UMH* 15-16 and provides only spoken congregatio~ responses for Holy Communion. It is designed to give those who design and lead service a high degree of flexibility and freedom. The service through the Entrance ~ the Proclamation and Response is guided by a bulletin or by an announcement.

The people are then directed by bulletin or announcement to *UMH* 15-16 for Thanksgiving and Communion, which they follow while the pastor prays Great Thanksgiving in one of the following forms:

1) The Great Thanksgiving in A Service of Word and Table I (see 36-38) or II ~ *UMH* 13-14)

2) One of the seasonal or alternate Great Thanksgivings (see 54-79)

3) The Great Thanksgiving for A Service of Christian Marriage (see 124-26) or A Service of Death and Resurrection (see 152-53)

4) A Great Thanksgiving composed by the pastor or taken from another sour~

# INTRODUCTION TO
# THE GREAT THANKSGIVING: MUSICAL SETTINGS

Musical settings of the Great Thanksgiving are found in *UMH* 17-25. They ar~ those congregations who wish to sing the responses to the Great Thanksgiv~ They may be used with A Service of Word and Table I or II or with the rest o~ service printed in a bulletin or announced. At the Great Thanksgiving, the ~ gregation turns to the desired musical setting, while the pastor prays the G~ Thanksgiving in one of the four forms indicated above.

# A SERVICE OF WORD AND TABLE IV

*he pure, unfermented juice of the grape **or an equivalent** shall be used during the rvice of Holy Communion.)*

*is service, beginning with the Invitation on 44, is found in UMH 26-31 and may be 'lowed by the congregation. It is a traditional text from the rituals of the former ethodist and former Evangelical United Brethren churches.*

*'e complete service text may be used as printed below; or the service text beginning with : Invitation may be used, preceded by the following:*
*The people gather in the Lord's name.*
*They offer prayer and praise, which may include Canticle of God's Glory (UMH 82).*
*The Scriptures are read and preached.*
*Responses of praise, faith and prayer are offered.*

*ien this service is used for the giving of communion to the sick, to those committed to ir homes, or to others in circumstances where the full service is impractical, it should lude the Invitation, Confession, Prayer for Pardon, Words of Assurance, Great inksgiving, Prayer of Humble Access, words with Giving the Bread and Cup, and ;missal with Blessing.*

*' further directions and options see 13-32.*

## ENTRANCE

.THERING See 16-17.

EETING See 17-20.

*: or more of the following or other suitable scripture sentences:*

is said: "Listen, I am standing at the door, knocking;
ou hear my voice and open the door,
  will come in to you and eat with you, and you with me."

(REVELATION 3:20)

is said: "I am the living bread that came down from heaven.
oever eats of this bread will live forever;
  the bread that I will give for the life of the world is my flesh."

(JOHN 6:51)

ived, let us love one another, because love is from God;
yone who loves is born of God and knows God.
's love was revealed among us in this way:
  sent his only Son into the world so that we might live through him.

(1 JOHN 4:7, 9)

HYMN OF PRAISE * *See 17-20.*

OPENING PRAYER *

The Lord be with you.
**And with thy spirit.**

**Almighty God,**
**unto whom all hearts are open, all desires known,**
 **and from whom no secrets are hid:**
**Cleanse the thoughts of our hearts**
 **by the inspiration of thy Holy Spirit,**
**that we may perfectly love thee,**
 **and worthily magnify thy holy name;**
**through Christ our Lord. Amen.**

THE LORD'S PRAYER * *See 29.*

*All pray the Lord's Prayer, using one of the forms in* UMH *270-71, 894-96, either here or following the Great Thanksgiving.*

ACT OF PRAISE

*Sung from* UMH *82 or spoken:*

**Glory be to God on high, and on earth peace, good will to all.**
**We praise thee, we bless thee, we worship thee, we glorify thee,**
 **we give thanks to thee for thy great glory:**
**O Lord God, heavenly King, God the Father Almighty.**
**O Lord, the only begotten Son, Jesus Christ;**
**O Lord God, Lamb of God, Son of the Father,**
 **that takest away the sins of the world, have mercy upon us.**
**Thou that takest away the sins of the world, receive our prayer.**
**Thou that sittest at the right hand of God the Father, have mercy upon** **us.**
**For thou only art holy; thou only art the Lord;**
**thou only, O Christ, with the Holy Ghost,**
 **art most high in the glory of God the Father. Amen.**

## PROCLAMATION AND RESPONSE

SCRIPTURE LESSON *See 22-23 and lectionary on 227-37.*

[PSALM] * *See 22-23 and lectionary on 227-37.*

[SCRIPTURE LESSON] *See 22-23 and lectionary on 227-37.*

HYMN OR ANTHEM * *See 23.*

GOSPEL LESSON * *See 22-23 and lectionary on 227-37.*

SERMON *See 23.*

RESPONSE TO THE WORD *See 24.*

CONCERNS AND PRAYERS * *See 24-25.*

*A pastoral prayer, or one of the following, may be prayed:*

**Almighty and everlasting God,**
**who hast built thy Church**
**upon the foundation of the apostles and prophets,**
**Jesus Christ being the chief cornerstone,**
**endue the universal Church with the spirit of truth, unity, and concord.**
**Grant that all who confess thy holy name may abide in the truth**
**and live in unity and godly love.**
**Give grace, O heavenly Father, to all Christian pastors,**
**that they may, both by their lives and by their doctrine,**
**set forth thy true and living Word.**
**Give thy heavenly grace to all thy people,**
**and especially to this congregation here present,**
**that with meek heart and due reverence**
**they may hear and receive thy Holy Word**
**and serve thee in holiness and righteousness all the days of their lives.**
**Of thy goodness, O Lord, comfort all who are in trouble,**
**sorrow, need, sickness, or any other adversity.**
**We bless thy name for all thy servants**
**departed this life in thy faith and fear,**
**beseeching thee to give us grace so to follow their good examples,**
**that with them we may be partakers of thy heavenly kingdom;**
**through Jesus Christ our Lord. Amen.**

Let us pray for the whole state of Christ's Church.

Most merciful Father, we humbly beseech thee
to receive these our prayers for the universal Church,
that thou wilt confirm it in the truth of thy holy faith,
inspire it with unity and concord,
and extend and prosper it throughout the world.
We beseech thee also,
so to guide and strengthen the witness of the Church
to those in authority in all nations,
that they may maintain the justice and welfare of all peoples.

**Hear us, we beseech thee, O Lord.**

Give grace, O heavenly Father, to all pastors of thy Church,
that both in their lives and in their doctrine

they may set forth thy true and lively Word,
and faithfully administer thy Holy Sacraments.
And to all thy people give thy heavenly grace,
that with willing heart and due reverence,
they may hear and receive thy Holy Word,
truly serving thee in holiness and righteousness
all the days of their lives.

**Hear us, we beseech thee, O Lord.**

And we most humbly beseech thee, of thy goodness, O Lord,
to support and strengthen all those who, in this transitory life,
are in trouble, sorrow, need, sickness, or any other adversity.

**Hear us, we beseech thee, O Lord.**

We remember with thanksgiving
those who have loved and served thee in thy Church on earth,
who now rest from their labors
[especially those most dear to us,
whom we name in our hearts before thee].

*Silence may be kept for the remembrance of names.*

Keep us in fellowship with all thy saints,
and bring us at length to the joy of thy heavenly kingdom.

**Grant this, O Father, for the sake of Jesus Christ,
our only mediator and advocate. Amen.**

## INVITATION

*Pastor stands behind the Lord's table.*

Ye that do truly and earnestly repent of your sins,
and are in love and charity with your neighbors,
and intend to lead a new life, following the commandments of Go
and walking from henceforth in his holy ways:
Draw near with faith, and take this Holy Sacrament to your comfor
and make your humble confession to almighty God.

## CONFESSION *See 20-21, 25-26.*

**Almighty God, Father of our Lord Jesus Christ,
maker of all things, judge of all people:
We acknowledge and bewail our manifold sins and wickedness,
which we from time to time most grievously have committed,
by thought, word, and deed, against thy divine majesty.
We do earnestly repent,**

and are heartily sorry for these our misdoings;
the remembrance of them is grievous unto us.
Have mercy upon us, have mercy upon us, most merciful Father.
For thy Son our Lord Jesus Christ's sake,
   forgive us all that is past;
and grant that we may ever hereafter
   serve and please thee in newness of life,
   to the honor and glory of thy name;
through Jesus Christ our Lord. Amen.

## RAYER FOR PARDON

Almighty God, our heavenly Father,
   who of thy great mercy hast promised forgiveness of sins
   to all them that with hearty repentance and true faith turn to thee:
Have mercy upon us;
   pardon and deliver us from all our sins;
   confirm and strengthen us in all goodness;
   and bring us to everlasting life;
   through Jesus Christ our Lord. **Amen.**

## ORDS OF ASSURANCE

Hear what comfortable words the Scriptures say
   to all that truly turn to the Lord:

*The leader says one or more of the following sentences:*

Come to me, all you that are weary and are carrying heavy burdens,
   and I will give you rest.           (MATTHEW 11:28)

God so loved the world that he gave his only Son,
   that everyone who believes in him
   may not perish but may have eternal life.      (JOHN 3:16)

The saying is sure and worthy of full acceptance,
   that Christ Jesus came into the world to save sinners.   (1 TIMOTHY 1:15)

If we confess our sins,
   God who is faithful and just will forgive us our sins
   and cleanse us from all unrighteousness.     (1 JOHN 1:9, alt.)

f any one sins,
   we have an advocate with the Father,
   Jesus Christ the righteous;
and he is the atoning sacrifice for our sins,
   and not for ours only but also for the sins of the whole world.
                (1 JOHN 2:1-2, alt.)

[THE PEACE] * *See 26.*

*Signs and words of God's peace may be exchanged at this point.*

OFFERING *See 26-27.*

*If an offering was not received earlier, it may be received at this time.*

*A hymn, psalm, or anthem may be sung as the offering is received.*

*The bread and wine are brought by representatives of the people to the Lord's table, or uncovered if already in place.*

*A hymn, doxology, or other response may be sung as the gifts are brought to the Lord's table.*


## THANKSGIVING AND COMMUNION


### TAKING THE BREAD AND CUP *See 27-28.*

*The pastor, standing if possible behind the Lord's table facing the people from this time, through Breaking the Bread, takes the bread and cup; and the bread and wine are prepared for the meal.*


### THE GREAT THANKSGIVING * *See 28.*

The Lord be with you.
**And with thy spirit.**
Lift up your hearts. *The pastor may lift hands and keep them raised.*
**We lift them up unto the Lord.**
Let us give thanks unto the Lord.
**It is meet and right so to do.**

It is very meet, right, and our bounden duty
   that we should at all times and in all places
   give thanks unto thee, O Lord,
   Holy Father, almighty, everlasting God.

*One of the following prefaces may be added in the day or season indicated:*

#### Advent

Because thou didst send thy beloved Son
to redeem us from sin and death,
   and to make us heirs in him of everlasting life;
that when he shall come again in power and great triumph
   to judge the world,
we may without shame or fear rejoice to behold his appearing.

### Christmas

Because thou didst give Jesus Christ, thine only Son,
  to be born as at this time for us;
who, by the operation of the Holy Spirit, was made human,
  and that without spot of sin, to make us clean from all sin.

### Epiphany or Sundays After the Epiphany

Through Jesus Christ our Lord,
who, in the substance of our mortal flesh, manifested forth his glory,
that he might bring us out of darkness into his own glorious light.

### Lent

Through Jesus Christ our Lord,
who was in every way tempted as we are, yet did not sin;
by whose grace we are able to triumph over every evil,
  and to live no longer unto ourselves,
  but unto him who died for us and rose again.

### Easter

But chiefly are we bound to praise thee
  for the glorious resurrection of thy Son Jesus Christ our Lord,
who by his death hath destroyed death,
  and by his rising to life again hath restored to us everlasting life.

### The Day of Pentecost

Through Jesus Christ our Lord,
  according to whose most true promise,
the Holy Spirit came down as at this time from heaven,
  lighting upon the disciples,
  to teach them, and to lead them into all truth,
whereby we have been brought out of darkness
  into the clear light and true knowledge of thee,
  of thy Son Jesus Christ.

*The pastor continues:*

Therefore with angels and archangels,
  and with all the company of heaven,
  we laud and magnify thy glorious name,
  evermore praising thee and saying (*singing*):

*The pastor may lower hands. The people sing (UMH 28) or say:*

**Holy, holy, holy, Lord God of hosts:**
**Heaven and earth are full of thy glory!**

**Glory be to thee, O Lord most high!**
**Blessed is he that cometh in the name of the Lord!**
**Hosanna in the highest!**

*The pastor may raise hands.*

Almighty God, our heavenly Father,
who of thy tender mercy
    didst give thine only Son Jesus Christ
    to suffer death upon the cross for our redemption;
who made there, by the one offering of himself,
    a full, perfect, and sufficient sacrifice
    for the sins of the whole world;
and didst institute,
    and in his holy Gospel command us to continue,
    a perpetual memory of his precious death until his coming again:

*The pastor may hold hands, palms down, over the bread and cup.*

Hear us, O merciful Father,
    we most humbly beseech thee;
and bless and sanctify with thy Word and Holy Spirit
    these thy gifts of bread and wine,
that we, receiving them
    according to thy Son our Savior Jesus Christ's holy institution,
    in remembrance of his passion, death, and resurrection,
    may be partakers of the divine nature through him:

*The pastor may hold hands, palms down, over the bread, or touch the bread, or l*
*the bread.*

Who, in the same night that he was betrayed, took bread;
    and when he had given thanks,
    he broke it, and gave it to his disciples, saying,
"Take, eat; this is my body which is given for you;
do this in remembrance of me."

*The pastor may hold hands, palms down, over the cup, or touch the cup, or*
*the cup.*

Likewise after supper he took the cup;
    and when he had given thanks,
    he gave it to them, saying,
"Drink ye all of this;
    for this is my blood of the New Covenant,
    which is shed for you and for many, for the forgiveness of sins;
do this as oft as ye shall drink it, in remembrance of me."

*The pastor may raise hands, as the people join in praying:*

O Lord, our heavenly Father,
  we, thy humble servants,
  desire thy fatherly goodness mercifully to accept
  this our sacrifice of praise and thanksgiving;
most humbly beseeching thee to grant that,
  by the merits and death of thy Son Jesus Christ,
  and through faith in his blood,
we and thy whole Church may obtain forgiveness of our sins,
  and all other benefits of his passion.

And here we offer and present unto thee, O Lord,
  ourselves, our souls and bodies,
  to be a reasonable, holy, and lively sacrifice unto thee;
humbly beseeching thee
  that all we who are partakers of this Holy Communion
    may be filled with thy grace and heavenly benediction.
And although we be unworthy, through our manifold sins,
  to offer unto thee any sacrifice,
yet we beseech thee to accept this our bounden duty and service,
  not weighing our merits, but pardoning our offenses;

Through Jesus Christ our Lord,
  by whom, and with whom,
  in the unity of the Holy Spirit,
  all honor and glory be unto thee, O Father Almighty,
  world without end. Amen.

*If the Lord's Prayer has not been prayed earlier in the service, it is prayed at this time.*

## BREAKING THE BREAD *See 29.*

*The pastor, still standing behind the Lord's table facing the people, breaks the bread and then lifts the cup, in silence or with appropriate words (see 39).*

*The following prayer may then be prayed:*

## PRAYER OF HUMBLE ACCESS

We do not presume to come to this thy table,
  O merciful Lord,
  trusting in our own righteousness,
  but in thy manifold and great mercies.
We are not worthy
  so much as to gather up the crumbs under thy table.
But thou art the same Lord,
  whose property is always to have mercy.
Grant us, therefore, gracious Lord,
  so to partake of this Sacrament of thy Son Jesus Christ,

that we may walk in newness of life,
may grow into his likeness,
and may evermore dwell in him, and he in us. Amen.

*Here may be sung (UMH 30-31 or ♪ 201) or spoken:*

O Lamb of God, that takest away the sins of the world,
have mercy upon us.
O Lamb of God, that takest away the sins of the world,
have mercy upon us.
O Lamb of God, that takest away the sins of the world,
grant us thy peace.

## GIVING THE BREAD AND CUP *See 29-31.*

*When the bread is given, one or both of the following sentences are said:*

The body of our Lord Jesus Christ, which was given for thee,
preserve thy soul and body unto everlasting life.

Take and eat this in remembrance that Christ died for thee,
and feed on him in thy heart by faith with thanksgiving.

*When the cup is given, one or both of the following sentences are said:*

The blood of our Lord Jesus Christ, which was shed for thee,
preserve thy soul and body unto everlasting life.

Drink this in remembrance that Christ's blood was shed for thee,
and be thankful.

*The congregation sings hymns while the bread and cup are given. Many hymns, song and choruses in UMH in addition to 612-41 and others listed under Holy Communic (943) are effective in expressing the people's loving communion with God and ot another. The day or season of the Christian year and the people's knowledge and love particular hymns are important considerations in the selection of appropriate hymns. is particularly effective if the people can sing from memory.*

*When all have received, the Lord's table is put in order, and a prayer thanksgiving after communion may be spoken or sung. See the hymns Followir Communion listed in UMH 952.*

## HYMN OR SONG OF THANKSGIVING * *See 30-31.*

## DISMISSAL WITH BLESSING * *See 31-32.*

The peace of God, which passeth all understanding,
keep your hearts and minds
in the knowledge and love of God,
and of his Son Jesus Christ our Lord;
and the blessing of God Almighty,
the Father, the Son, and the Holy Spirit,
be among you, and remain with you always. **Amen.**

## GOING FORTH * *See 32.*

# A SERVICE OF WORD AND TABLE V
# WITH PERSONS WHO ARE SICK OR HOMEBOUND

*'The pure, unfermented juice of the grape **or an equivalent** shall be used during the ;ervice of Holy Communion.)*

*;ince the earliest Christian times, communion has been brought as an extension of the ongregation's worship to sick or homebound persons unable to attend congregational )orship.*

*he following service is very flexible, depending upon the circumstances of the pastoral isit. "The people" may be simply the pastor and one other person. The service may be ery informal and conversational. There should be every possible sensitivity to the partic- lar needs of the person(s) receiving communion.*

*;uidelines for abridging A Service of Word and Table IV for use with sick or homebound ersons are found on 41.*

*he pastor, or laypersons at the direction of the pastor, may distribute the consecrated ~read and cup to sick or homebound persons as soon as feasible following a service of Word 1d Table as an extension of that service. When this service is used as a distribution of the 'nsecrated bread and cup, the Great Thanksgiving is omitted, but thanks should be given 'ter the bread and cup are received.*

*here should be whatever participation is feasible by those receiving communion. )metimes this may simply be gestures and expression. Familiar acts of worship that per- 'ns may know by memory—the Lord's Prayer, the Apostles' Creed, or the Twenty-third ;alm, for instance—may be used. Sometimes it is possible to sing one or more hymns.*

*1ose distributing communion should also be sensitive to the power of acts such as call- g the person by name, touching the person, encouraging the remembrance of significant periences, and allowing sick or homebound persons to minister to the visitors.*

*1e people come together and exchange greetings in the Lord's name.*

*riptures are read and interpreted, and prayer and praise are offered.*

## JVITATION

Christ our Lord invites to his table
  all who love him and seek to grow into his likeness.
Let us draw near with faith, make our humble confession,
  and prepare to receive this Holy Sacrament.

## ɔNFESSION AND PARDON

**We do not presume to come to this your table, merciful Lord,**
  **trusting in our own goodness, but in you unfailing mercies.**
**We are not worthy that you should receive us,**
**but give your word and we shall be healed,**
**through Jesus Christ our Lord. Amen.**

Hear the good news:
  Christ died for us while we were yet sinners;
  that is proof of God's love toward us.
In the name of Jesus Christ, you are forgiven!

## THE PEACE

*Signs and words of God's peace are exchanged.*

## TAKING THE BREAD AND CUP

*The bread and wine are prepared for the meal.*

## THE GREAT THANKSGIVING *See 28, 80.*

*The pastor prays as follows if the bread and cup are to be consecrated. If they have already been consecrated, this prayer is omitted.*

*If a layperson is distributing the consecrated bread and cup, this prayer is omitted*

Lift up your heart(s) and give thanks to the Lord our God.

Father Almighty, Creator of heaven and earth,
  you made us in your image, to love and to be loved.
When we turned away, and our love failed, your love remained steadfast
By the suffering, death, and resurrection of your only Son Jesus Christ
  you delivered us from slavery to sin and death
  and made with us a new covenant by water and the Spirit.

On the night in which Jesus gave himself up for us he took bread,
  gave thanks to you, broke the bread, gave it to his disciples, and said
"Take, eat; this is my body which is given for you.
Do this in remembrance of me."

When the supper was over he took the cup,
  gave thanks to you, gave it to his disciples, and said:
"Drink from this, all of you; this is my blood of the new covenant,
  poured out for you and for many for the forgiveness of sins.
Do this, as often as you drink it, in remembrance of me."

And so, in remembrance of these your mighty acts in Jesus Christ,
we offer ourselves in praise and thanksgiving
  as a holy and living sacrifice, in union with Christ's offering for us
Pour out your Holy Spirit on us, and on these gifts of bread and wine
Make them be for us the body and blood of Christ,
  that we may be for the world the body of Christ, redeemed by his blood

By your Spirit make us one with Christ, one with each other,
  and one in ministry to all the world,
until Christ comes in final victory, and we feast at his heavenly banquet

Through your Son Jesus Christ, with the Holy Spirit in your holy Church,
all honor and glory is yours, almighty Father, now and for ever. **Amen.**

HE LORD'S PRAYER

BREAKING THE BREAD

*In silence or with appropriate words.*

GIVING THE BREAD AND CUP

*With these or other words being exchanged:*

*Name,* the body of Christ, given for you. **Amen.**
*Name,* the blood of Christ, given for you. **Amen.**

*When all have received, the Lord's table is put in order.*

*Thanks may be given after communion. A hymn, song, or chorus may be sung. If
the consecrated bread and cup have been given and there has been no Great
Thanksgiving, the following prayer is suggested after Communion:*

Most bountiful God, we give you thanks for the world you have created,
　　for the gift of life, and for giving yourself to us in Jesus Christ,
　　whose holy life, suffering and death, and glorious resurrection
　　have delivered us from slavery to sin and death.
We thank you that in the power of your Holy Spirit
　　you have fed us in this Sacrament, united us with Christ,
　　and given us a foretaste of your heavenly banquet.
We are your children, and yours is the glory, now and for ever;
through Jesus Christ our Lord. **Amen.**

BLESSING

The grace of the Lord Jesus Christ,
and the love of God,
and the communion of the Holy Spirit
be with you [all]. **Amen.**

# THE GREAT THANKSGIVING FOR ADVENT

*This text is used by the pastor while the congregation uses A Service of Word and Table II (UMH 13-15) or III (UMH 15-16) or one of the musical settings (UMH 17-25).*

*The pastor stands behind the Lord's table. See 28.*

The Lord be with you.
**And also with you.**
Lift up your hearts. *The pastor may lift hands and keep them raised.*
**We lift them up to the Lord.**
Let us give thanks to the Lord our God.
**It is right to give our thanks and praise.**

It is right, and a good and joyful thing,
    always and everywhere to give thanks to you,
    Father Almighty (*almighty God*), creator of heaven and earth.
You formed us in your image and breathed into us the breath of life.
When we turned away, and our love failed, your love remained steadfast.
You delivered us from captivity, made covenant to be our sovereign God,
    and spoke to us through your prophets, who looked for that day
        when justice shall roll down like waters
            and righteousness like an ever-flowing stream,
        when nation shall not lift up sword against nation,
            neither shall they learn war anymore.

And so, with your people on earth and all the company of heaven
    we praise your name and join their unending hymn:

*The pastor may lower hands.*

**Holy, holy, holy Lord, God of power and might,**
**heaven and earth are full of your glory. Hosanna in the highest.**
**Blessed is he who comes in the name of the Lord. Hosanna in the highest.**

*The pastor may raise hands.*

Holy are you, and blessed is your Son Jesus Christ,
    whom you sent in the fullness of time to be a light to the nations.
You scatter the proud in the imagination of their hearts
    and have mercy on those who fear you from generation to generation.
You put down the mighty from their thrones and exalt those of low degree.
You fill the hungry with good things, and the rich you send empty away.
Your own Son came among us as a servant,
    to be Emmanuel, your presence with us.

He humbled himself in obedience to your will
    and freely accepted death on a cross.
By the baptism of his suffering, death, and resurrection
    you gave birth to your Church,
    delivered us from slavery to sin and death,
    and made with us a new covenant by water and the Spirit.

*The pastor may hold hands, palms down, over the bread, or touch the bread, or lift
the bread.*

On the night in which he gave himself up for us, he took bread,
    gave thanks to you, broke the bread, gave it to his disciples, and said:
"Take, eat; this is my body which is given for you.
Do this in remembrance of me."

*The pastor may hold hands, palms down, over the cup, or touch the cup, or lift
the cup.*

When the supper was over he took the cup,
    gave thanks to you, gave it to his disciples, and said:
"Drink from this, all of you; this is my blood of the new covenant,
    poured out for you and for many for the forgiveness of sins.
Do this, as often as you drink it, in remembrance of me."

*The pastor may raise hands.*

And so, in remembrance of these your mighty acts in Jesus Christ,
we offer ourselves in praise and thanksgiving
    as a holy and living sacrifice, in union with Christ's offering for us,
as we proclaim the mystery of faith.

**Christ has died; Christ is risen; Christ will come again.**

*The pastor may hold hands, palms down, over the bread and cup.*

Pour out your Holy Spirit on us gathered here,
    and on these gifts of bread and wine.
Make them be for us the body and blood of Christ,
that we may be for the world the body of Christ, redeemed by his blood.

*The pastor may raise hands.*

By your Spirit make us one with Christ,
one with each other, and one in ministry to all the world,
until Christ comes in final victory, and we feast at his heavenly banquet.

Through your Son Jesus Christ, with the Holy Spirit in your holy Church,
all honor and glory is yours, almighty Father (*God*), now and for ever.

**Amen.**

# THE GREAT THANKSGIVING
# FOR CHRISTMAS EVE, DAY, OR SEASON

*This text is used by the pastor while the congregation uses A Service of Word an*
*Table II (UMH 13-15) or III (UMH 15-16) or one of the musical settings (UMF*
*17-25).*

*The pastor stands behind the Lord's table. See 28.*

The Lord be with you.
**And also with you.**
Lift up your hearts. *The pastor may lift hands and keep them raised.*
**We lift them up to the Lord.**
Let us give thanks to the Lord our God.
**It is right to give our thanks and praise.**

It is right, and a good and joyful thing,
   always and everywhere to give thanks to you,
   Father Almighty (*almighty God*), creator of heaven and earth.
You created light out of darkness and brought forth life on the earth.
You formed us in your image and breathed into us the breath of life.
When we turned away, and our love failed, your love remained steadfas
You delivered us from captivity, made covenant to be our sovereign Goc
   and spoke to us through your prophets.
In the fullness of time
   you gave your only Son Jesus Christ to be our Savior,
and at his birth the angels sang
   glory to you in the highest and peace to your people on earth.

And so, with your people on earth and all the company of heaven
   we praise your name and join their unending hymn:

*The pastor may lower hands.*

**Holy, holy, holy Lord, God of power and might,**
**heaven and earth are full of your glory. Hosanna in the highest.**
**Blessed is he who comes in the name of the Lord. Hosanna in the highes**

*The pastor may raise hands.*

Holy are you, and blessed is your Son Jesus Christ.
As Mary and Joseph went from Galilee to Bethlehem
   and there found no room,
   so Jesus went from Galilee to Jerusalem and was despised and rejecte
As in the poverty of a stable Jesus was born,
   so by the baptism of his suffering, death, and resurrection
     you gave birth to your Church,

delivered us from slavery to sin and death,
and made with us a new covenant by water and the Spirit.

*he pastor may hold hands, palms down, over the bread, or touch the bread, or lift
*ie bread.*

*s your Word became flesh, born of woman, on that night long ago,
*o, on the night in which he gave himself up for us, he took bread,
    gave thanks to you, broke the bread, gave it to his disciples, and said:
Take, eat; this is my body which is given for you.
)o this in remembrance of me."

*he pastor may hold hands, palms down, over the cup, or touch the cup, or lift
*ie cup.*

*vhen the supper was over he took the cup,
    gave thanks to you, gave it to his disciples, and said:
Drink from this, all of you; this is my blood of the new covenant,
    poured out for you and for many for the forgiveness of sins.
*o this, as often as you drink it, in remembrance of me."

*he pastor may raise hands.*

*nd so, in remembrance of these your mighty acts in Jesus Christ,
*e offer ourselves in praise and thanksgiving
    as a holy and living sacrifice, in union with Christ's offering for us,
*; we proclaim the mystery of faith.

**hrist has died; Christ is risen; Christ will come again.**

*ie pastor may hold hands, palms down, over the bread and cup.*

)ur out your Holy Spirit on us gathered here,
    and on these gifts of bread and wine.
*ake them be for us the body and blood of Christ,
*at we may be for the world the body of Christ, redeemed by his blood.

*e pastor may raise hands.*

*′ your Spirit make us one with Christ,
    one with each other, and one in ministry to all the world,
*itil Christ comes in final victory, and we feast at his heavenly banquet.

*irough your Son Jesus Christ, with the Holy Spirit in your holy Church,
    all honor and glory is yours, almighty Father (*God*), now and for ever.

**nen.**

# THE GREAT THANKSGIVING
# FOR NEW YEAR, EPIPHANY, BAPTISM OF THE LORD,
# OR COVENANT REAFFIRMATION

*This text is used by the pastor while the congregation uses A Service of Word an*
*Table II (UMH 13-15) or III (UMH 15-16) or one of the musical settings (UMH*
*17-25). Either or both of the bracketed [] sections may be omitted, depending on th*
*occasion.*

*The pastor stands behind the Lord's table. See 28.*

The Lord be with you.
**And also with you.**
Lift up your hearts. *The pastor may lift hands and keep them raised.*
**We lift them up to the Lord.**
Let us give thanks to the Lord our God.
**It is right to give our thanks and praise.**

It is right, and a good and joyful thing,
    always and everywhere to give thanks to you,
    Father Almighty *(almighty God)*, creator of heaven and earth.
Before the mountains were brought forth, or you had formed the earth
    from everlasting to everlasting, you alone are God.
You created light out of darkness and brought forth life on the earth.
You formed us in your image and breathed into us the breath of life.
When we turned away, and our love failed, your love remained steadfas
You delivered us from captivity, made covenant to be our sovereign Goc
    and spoke to us through your prophets.

And so, with your people on earth and all the company of heaven
    we praise your name and join their unending hymn:

*The pastor may lower hands.*

**Holy, holy, holy Lord, God of power and might,**
**heaven and earth are full of your glory. Hosanna in the highest.**
**Blessed is he who comes in the name of the Lord. Hosanna in the highes**

*The pastor may raise hands.*

Holy are you, and blessed is your Son Jesus Christ,
in whom you have revealed yourself, our light and our salvation.

[You sent a star to guide wise men to where the Christ was born;
    and in your signs and witnesses, in every age and through all the worl
    you have led your people from far places to his light.]

    *or*

[In his baptism and in table fellowship he took his place with sinners.
Your Spirit anointed him to preach good news to the poor,

to proclaim release to the captives and recovering of sight to the blind,
to set at liberty those who are oppressed,
and to announce that the time had come
    when you would save your people.]

y the baptism of his suffering, death, and resurrection
ou gave birth to your Church, delivered us from slavery to sin and death,
and made with us a new covenant by water and the Spirit.

*he pastor may hold hands, palms down, over the bread, or touch the bread, or lift
1e bread.*

n the night in which he gave himself up for us, he took bread,
    gave thanks to you, broke the bread, gave it to his disciples, and said:
Take, eat; this is my body which is given for you.
o this in remembrance of me."

*he pastor may hold hands, palms down, over the cup, or touch the cup, or lift
1e cup.*

hen the supper was over he took the cup,
    gave thanks to you, gave it to his disciples, and said:
Drink from this, all of you; this is my blood of the new covenant,
    poured out for you and for many for the forgiveness of sins.
o this, as often as you drink it, in remembrance of me."

*he pastor may raise hands.*

nd so, in remembrance of these your mighty acts in Jesus Christ,
e offer ourselves in praise and thanksgiving
as a holy and living sacrifice, in union with Christ's offering for us,
    we proclaim the mystery of faith.

**hrist has died; Christ is risen; Christ will come again.**

*1e pastor may hold hands, palms down, over the bread and cup.*

ur out your Holy Spirit on us gathered here,
and on these gifts of bread and wine.
ake them be for us the body and blood of Christ,
at we may be for the world the body of Christ, redeemed by his blood.

*1e pastor may raise hands.*

your Spirit make us one with Christ,
one with each other, and one in ministry to all the world,
til Christ comes in final victory, and we feast at his heavenly banquet.

rough your Son Jesus Christ, with the Holy Spirit in your holy Church,
all honor and glory is yours, almighty Father (*God*), now and for ever.

nen.

# THE GREAT THANKSGIVING
# FOR EARLY IN LENT

*This text is intended for use early in Lent, such as Ash Wednesday, the First Sunday in Lent, or the first Sunday in March (if it falls within Lent).*

*It is used by the pastor while the congregation uses A Service of Word and Table I (UMH 13-15) or III (UMH 15-16) or one of the musical settings (UMH 17-25).*

*The pastor stands behind the Lord's table. See 28.*

The Lord be with you.
**And also with you.**
Lift up your hearts. *The pastor may lift hands and keep them raised.*
**We lift them up to the Lord.**
Let us give thanks to the Lord our God.
**It is right to give our thanks and praise.**

It is right, and a good and joyful thing,
   always and everywhere to give thanks to you,
   Father Almighty (*almighty God*), creator of heaven and earth.
You brought all things into being and called them good.
From the dust of the earth you formed us into your image
   and breathed into us the breath of life.
When we turned away, and our love failed, your love remained steadfast.
When rain fell upon the earth for forty days and forty nights,
   you bore up the ark on the waters, saved Noah and his family,
   and made covenant with every living creature on earth.
When you led your people to Mount Sinai for forty days and forty nights,
   you gave us your commandments and made us your covenant people.
When your people forsook your covenant,
   your prophet Elijah fasted for forty days and forty nights;
   and on your holy mountain, he heard your still small voice.

And so, with your people on earth and all the company of heaven,
   we praise your name and join their unending hymn:

*The pastor may lower hands.*

**Holy, holy, holy Lord, God of power and might,**
**heaven and earth are full of your glory. Hosanna in the highest.**
**Blessed is he who comes in the name of the Lord. Hosanna in the highest.**

*The pastor may raise hands.*

Holy are you, and blessed is your Son Jesus Christ.
When you gave him to save us from our sin,
   your Spirit led him into the wilderness,
   where he fasted forty days and forty nights to prepare for his ministry.
When he suffered and died on a cross for our sin, you raised him to life,

presented him alive to the apostles during forty days,
and exalted him at your right hand.
y the baptism of his suffering, death, and resurrection
you gave birth to your Church, delivered us from slavery to sin and death,
and made with us a new covenant by water and the Spirit.
Jow, when we your people prepare for the yearly feast of Easter,
you lead us to repentance for sin and the cleansing of our hearts,
that during these forty days of Lent we may be gifted and graced
to reaffirm the covenant you made with us through Christ.

*he pastor may hold hands, palms down, over the bread, or touch the bread, or lift*
*ie bread.*

'n the night in which he gave himself up for us, he took bread,
gave thanks to you, broke the bread, gave it to his disciples, and said:
Take, eat; this is my body which is given for you.
'o this in remembrance of me."

*he pastor may hold hands, palms down, over the cup, or touch the cup, or lift*
*'e cup.*

Jhen the supper was over he took the cup,
gave thanks to you, gave it to his disciples, and said:
Drink from this, all of you; this is my blood of the new covenant,
poured out for you and for many for the forgiveness of sins.
o this, as often as you drink it, in remembrance of me."

*'e pastor may raise hands.*

nd so, in remembrance of these your mighty acts in Jesus Christ,
e offer ourselves in praise and thanksgiving,
as a holy and living sacrifice, in union with Christ's offering for us,
we proclaim the mystery of faith.

**hrist has died; Christ is risen; Christ will come again.**

*ie pastor may hold hands, palms down, over the bread and cup.*

)ur out your Holy Spirit on us gathered here,
and on these gifts of bread and wine.
ake them be for us the body and blood of Christ,
at we may be for the world the body of Christ, redeemed by his blood.

*ie pastor may raise hands.*

' your Spirit make us one with Christ,
one with each other, and one in ministry to all the world,
til Christ comes in final victory, and we feast at his heavenly banquet.

rough your Son Jesus Christ, with the Holy Spirit in your holy Church,
all honor and glory is yours, almighty Father (*God*), now and for ever.

**nen.**

# THE GREAT THANKSGIVING
# FOR LATER IN LENT

*This text is intended for use later in Lent, such as Passion/Palm Sunday, the earl*
*days of Holy Week (prior to Thursday evening), or the first Sunday in April (if it fall*
*within Lent).*

*It is used by the pastor while the congregation uses A Service of Word and Table*
*(UMH 13-15) or III (UMH 15-16) or one of the musical settings (UMH 17-25,*

*The pastor stands behind the Lord's table. See 28.*

The Lord be with you.
**And also with you.**
Lift up your hearts. *The pastor may lift hands and keep them raised.*
**We lift them up to the Lord.**
Let us give thanks to the Lord our God.
**It is right to give our thanks and praise.**

It is right, and a good and joyful thing,
    always and everywhere to give thanks to you,
    Father Almighty (*almighty God*), creator of heaven and earth.
In love you made us for yourself;
    and when we had fallen into sin and become subject to evil and death
    your love remained steadfast.
You bid your faithful people cleanse their hearts
    and prepare with joy for the Easter feast,
that, renewed by your Word and Sacraments
    and fervent in prayer and works of justice and mercy,
we may come to the fullness of grace
    that you have prepared for those who love you.

And so, with your people on earth and all the company of heaven
    we praise your name and join their unending hymn:

*The pastor may lower hands.*

**Holy, holy, holy Lord, God of power and might,**
**heaven and earth are full of your glory. Hosanna in the highest.**
**Blessed is he who comes in the name of the Lord. Hosanna in the highes**

*The pastor may raise hands.*

Holy are you, and blessed is your Son Jesus Christ,
whom you sent in the fullness of time to redeem the world.
He emptied himself, taking the form of a servant,
    being born in our likeness.
He humbled himself and became obedient unto death,
    even death on a cross.
He took upon himself our sin and death and offered himself,
    a perfect sacrifice for the sin of the whole world.

y the baptism of his suffering, death, and resurrection
you gave birth to your Church,
delivered us from slavery to sin and death,
and made with us a new covenant by water and the Spirit.

*ie pastor may hold hands, palms down, over the bread, or touch the bread, or lift
e bread.*

n the night in which he gave himself up for us, he took bread,
gave thanks to you, broke the bread, gave it to his disciples, and said:
ake, eat; this is my body which is given for you.
o this in remembrance of me."

*ie pastor may hold hands, palms down, over the cup, or touch the cup, or lift
e cup.*

hen the supper was over he took the cup,
gave thanks to you, gave it to his disciples, and said:
)rink from this, all of you; this is my blood of the new covenant,
poured out for you and for many for the forgiveness of sins.
o this, as often as you drink it, in remembrance of me."

*ie pastor may raise hands.*

id so, in remembrance of these your mighty acts in Jesus Christ,
e offer ourselves in praise and thanksgiving
is a holy and living sacrifice, in union with Christ's offering for us,
we proclaim the mystery of faith.

**rist has died; Christ is risen; Christ will come again.**

*e pastor may hold hands, palms down, over the bread and cup.*

ur out your Holy Spirit on us gathered here,
ind on these gifts of bread and wine.
ike them be for us the body and blood of Christ,
t we may be for the world the body of Christ, redeemed by his blood.

*e pastor may raise hands.*

your Spirit make us one with Christ,
ine with each other, and one in ministry to all the world,
til Christ comes in final victory, and we feast at his heavenly banquet.

rough your Son Jesus Christ, with the Holy Spirit in your holy Church,
ill honor and glory is yours, almighty Father (*God*), now and for ever.

en.

# THE GREAT THANKSGIVING
# FOR HOLY THURSDAY EVENING

*This text is used by the pastor while the congregation uses A Service of Word and Table II (UMH 13-15) or III (UMH 15-16) or one of the musical settings (UMH 17-25).*

*The pastor stands behind the Lord's table. See 28.*

The Lord be with you.
**And also with you.**
Lift up your hearts. *The pastor may lift hands and keep them raised.*
**We lift them up to the Lord.**
Let us give thanks to the Lord our God.
**It is right to give our thanks and praise.**

It is right, and a good and joyful thing,
   always and everywhere to give thanks to you,
   Father Almighty (*almighty God*), creator of heaven and earth.
From the earth you bring forth bread and create the fruit of the vine.
You formed us in your image, delivered us from captivity,
   and made covenant to be our sovereign God.
You fed us manna in the wilderness,
   and gave grapes as evidence of the promised land.

And so, with your people on earth and all the company of heaven
   we praise your name and join their unending hymn:

*The pastor may lower hands.*

**Holy, holy, holy Lord, God of power and might,**
**heaven and earth are full of your glory. Hosanna in the highest.**
**Blessed is he who comes in the name of the Lord. Hosanna in the highest.**

*The pastor may raise hands.*

Holy are you, and blessed is your Son Jesus Christ.
When we had turned aside from your way and abused your gifts,
   you gave us in him your crowning gift.
Emptying himself, that our joy might be full,
   he fed the hungry, healed the sick,
      ate with the scorned and forgotten, washed his disciples' feet,
      and gave a holy meal as a pledge of his abiding presence.
By the baptism of his suffering, death, and resurrection
   you gave birth to your Church,
   delivered us from slavery to sin and death,
   and made with us a new covenant by water and the Spirit.

*The pastor may hold hands, palms down, over the bread, or touch the bread, or the bread.*

On the night in which he gave himself up for us, he took bread,
   gave thanks to you, broke the bread, gave it to his disciples, and said:
Take, eat; this is my body which is given for you.
Do this in remembrance of me."

*The pastor may hold hands, palms down, over the cup, or touch the cup, or lift the cup.*

When the supper was over he took the cup,
   gave thanks to you, gave it to his disciples, and said:
Drink from this, all of you; this is my blood of the new covenant,
   poured out for you and for many for the forgiveness of sins.
Do this, as often as you drink it, in remembrance of me."

*The pastor may raise hands.*

And so, in remembrance of these your mighty acts in Jesus Christ,
   we offer ourselves in praise and thanksgiving
   as a holy and living sacrifice, in union with Christ's offering for us,
   as we proclaim the mystery of faith.

**Christ has died; Christ is risen; Christ will come again.**

*The pastor may hold hands, palms down, over the bread and cup.*

Pour out your Holy Spirit on us gathered here,
   and on these gifts of bread and wine.
Make them be for us the body and blood of Christ,
   that we may be for the world the body of Christ, redeemed by his blood.

*The pastor may raise hands.*

By your Spirit make us one with Christ,
   one with each other, and one in ministry to all the world,
   until Christ comes in final victory, and we feast at his heavenly banquet.

Through your Son Jesus Christ, with the Holy Spirit in your holy Church,
   all honor and glory is yours, almighty Father (*God*), now and for ever.

**Amen.**

# THE GREAT THANKSGIVING
# FOR EASTER DAY OR SEASON

*This text is used by the pastor while the congregation uses A Service of Word an*
*Table II (UMH 13-15) or III (UMH 15-16) or one of the musical settings (UMI*
*17-25).*

*The pastor stands behind the Lord's table. See 28.*

The Lord be with you.
**And also with you.**
Lift up your hearts. *The pastor may lift hands and keep them raised.*
**We lift them up to the Lord.**
Let us give thanks to the Lord our God.
**It is right to give our thanks and praise.**

It is right, and a good and joyful thing,
   always and everywhere to give thanks to you,
   Father Almighty *(almighty God)*, creator of heaven and earth.
You formed us in your image and breathed into us the breath of life.
When we turned away, and our love failed, your love remained steadfas
You delivered us from captivity, made covenant to be our sovereign Go
   brought us to a land flowing with milk and honey,
   and set before us the way of life.

And so, with your people on earth and all the company of heaven
   we praise your name and join their unending hymn:

*The pastor may lower hands.*

**Holy, holy, holy Lord, God of power and might,**
**heaven and earth are full of your glory. Hosanna in the highest.**
**Blessed is he who comes in the name of the Lord. Hosanna in the highe**

*The pastor may raise hands.*

Holy are you, and blessed is your Son Jesus Christ.
By the baptism of his suffering, death, and resurrection
   you gave birth to your Church,
   delivered us from slavery to sin and death,
   and made with us a new covenant by water and the Spirit.
By your great mercy we have been born anew
   to a living hope through the resurrection of your Son from the dea
   and to an inheritance that is imperishable, undefiled, and unfading.
Once we were no people, but now we are your people,
   declaring your wonderful deeds in Christ,
      who called us out of darkness into his marvelous light.
When the Lord Jesus ascended, he promised to be with us always,
   in the power of your Word and Holy Spirit.

*he pastor may hold hands, palms down, over the bread, or touch the bread, or lift
*e bread.*

n the night in which he gave himself up for us, he took bread,
gave thanks to you, broke the bread, gave it to his disciples, and said:
*Take, eat; this is my body which is given for you.
o this in remembrance of me."*

*he pastor may hold hands, palms down, over the cup, or touch the cup, or lift
*e cup.*

hen the supper was over he took the cup,
gave thanks to you, gave it to his disciples, and said:
*Drink from this, all of you; this is my blood of the new covenant,
poured out for you and for many for the forgiveness of sins.
o this, as often as you drink it, in remembrance of me."*

*he pastor may raise hands.*

n the day you raised him from the dead
he was recognized by his disciples in the breaking of the bread,
d in the power of your Holy Spirit your Church has continued
in the breaking of the bread and the sharing of the cup.

d so, in remembrance of these your mighty acts in Jesus Christ,
* offer ourselves in praise and thanksgiving
as a holy and living sacrifice, in union with Christ's offering for us,
we proclaim the mystery of faith.

**rist has died; Christ is risen; Christ will come again.**

*e pastor may hold hands, palms down, over the bread and cup.*

ur out your Holy Spirit on us gathered here,
nd on these gifts of bread and wine.
ke them be for us the body and blood of Christ,
t we may be for the world the body of Christ, redeemed by his blood.

*e pastor may raise hands.*

your Spirit make us one with Christ,
ne with each other, and one in ministry to all the world,
til Christ comes in final victory, and we feast at his heavenly banquet.

rough your Son Jesus Christ, with the Holy Spirit in your holy Church,
honor and glory is yours, almighty Father (*God*), now and for ever.

**en.**

# THE GREAT THANKSGIVING
# FOR THE DAY OF PENTECOST

*This text is used by the pastor while the congregation uses A Service of Word and Table (UMH 13-15) or III (UMH 15-16) or one of the musical settings (UMH 17-25)*

*The pastor stands behind the Lord's table. See 28.*

The Lord be with you.
**And also with you.**
Lift up your hearts. *The pastor may lift hands and keep them raised.*
**We lift them up to the Lord.**
Let us give thanks to the Lord our God.
**It is right to give our thanks and praise.**

It is right, and a good and joyful thing,
    always and everywhere to give thanks to you,
    Father Almighty *(almighty God)*, creator of heaven and earth.
In the beginning your Spirit moved over the face of the waters.
You formed us in your image and breathed into us the breath of life.
When we turned away, and our love failed, your love remained steadfas
Your Spirit came upon prophets and teachers,
    anointing them to speak your Word.

And so, with your people on earth and all the company of heaven
    we praise your name and join their unending hymn:

*The pastor may lower hands.*

**Holy, holy, holy Lord, God of power and might,**
**heaven and earth are full of your glory. Hosanna in the highest.**
**Blessed is he who comes in the name of the Lord. Hosanna in the highe**

*The pastor may raise hands.*

Holy are you, and blessed is your Son Jesus Christ.
At his baptism in the Jordan your Spirit descended upon him
    and declared him your beloved Son.
With your Spirit upon him he turned away the temptations of sin.
Your Spirit anointed him to preach good news to the poor,
    to proclaim release to the captives and recovering of sight to the blir
    to set at liberty those who are oppressed,
    and to announce that the time had come
    when you would save your people.
He healed the sick, fed the hungry, and ate with sinners.
By the baptism of his suffering, death, and resurrection,
    you gave birth to your Church, delivered us from slavery to sin and dea
    and made with us a new covenant by water and the Spirit.
When the Lord Jesus ascended, he promised to be with us always,
    baptizing us with the Holy Spirit and with fire, as on the Day of Pentecc

*he pastor may hold hands, palms down, over the bread, or touch the bread, or lift
the bread.*

On the night in which he gave himself up for us, he took bread,
  gave thanks to you, broke the bread, gave it to his disciples, and said:
Take, eat; this is my body which is given for you.
Do this in remembrance of me."

*The pastor may hold hands, palms down, over the cup, or touch the cup, or lift
the cup.*

When the supper was over he took the cup,
  gave thanks to you, gave it to his disciples, and said:
Drink from this, all of you; this is my blood of the new covenant,
  poured out for you and for many for the forgiveness of sins.
Do this, as often as you drink it, in remembrance of me."

*The pastor may raise hands.*

On the day you raised him from the dead
  he was recognized by his disciples in the breaking of the bread,
and in the power of your Holy Spirit your Church has continued
  in the breaking of the bread and the sharing of the cup.

And so, in remembrance of these your mighty acts in Jesus Christ,
we offer ourselves in praise and thanksgiving
  as a holy and living sacrifice, in union with Christ's offering for us,
  we proclaim the mystery of faith.

**Christ has died; Christ is risen; Christ will come again.**

*The pastor may hold hands, palms down, over the bread and cup.*

Pour out your Holy Spirit on us gathered here,
and on these gifts of bread and wine.
Make them be for us the body and blood of Christ,
that we may be for the world the body of Christ,
redeemed by his blood and empowered by the gifts of the Spirit.

*The pastor may raise hands.*

By your Spirit make us one with Christ,
one with each other, and one in ministry to all the world,
showing forth the fruit of the Spirit until Christ comes in final victory,
and we feast at his heavenly banquet.

Through your Son Jesus Christ, with the Holy Spirit in your holy Church,
all honor and glory is yours, almighty Father (*God*), now and for ever.

**Amen.**

# THE GREAT THANKSGIVING
# FOR THE SEASON AFTER PENTECOST
# (ORDINARY TIME, OR KINGDOMTIDE)

*This text is used by the pastor while the congregation uses A Service of Word ar. Table II (UMH 13-15) or III (UMH 15-16) or one of the musical settings (UMI 17-25).*

*The pastor stands behind the Lord's table. See 28.*

The Lord be with you.
**And also with you.**
Lift up your hearts. *The pastor may lift hands and keep them raised.*
**We lift them up to the Lord.**
Let us give thanks to the Lord our God.
**It is right to give our thanks and praise.**

It is right, and a good and joyful thing,
　　always and everywhere to give thanks to you,
　　Father Almighty (*almighty God*), creator of heaven and earth.
You formed us in your image and breathed into us the breath of life.
When we turned away, and our love failed, your love remained steadfas
You delivered us from captivity, made covenant to be our sovereign Go
　　and spoke to us through your prophets, who looked for that day
　　when justice shall roll down like waters
　　　　and righteousness like an ever-flowing stream,
　　when nation shall not lift up sword against nation,
　　　　neither shall they learn war anymore.

And so, with your people on earth and all the company of heaven
　　we praise your name and join their unending hymn:

*The pastor may lower hands.*

**Holy, holy, holy Lord, God of power and might,**
**heaven and earth are full of your glory. Hosanna in the highest.**
**Blessed is he who comes in the name of the Lord. Hosanna in the highe**

*The pastor may raise hands.*

Holy are you, and blessed is your Son Jesus Christ.
Your Spirit anointed him to preach good news to the poor,
　　to proclaim release to the captives and recovering of sight to the blir
　　to set at liberty those who are oppressed,
　　and to announce that the time had come
　　when you would save your people.
He healed the sick, fed the hungry, and ate with sinners.
By the baptism of his suffering, death, and resurrection
　　you gave birth to your Church,

delivered us from slavery to sin and death,
and made with us a new covenant by water and the Spirit.
At his ascension you exalted him
to sit and reign with you at your right hand.

*The pastor may hold hands, palms down, over the bread, or touch the bread, or lift the bread.*

On the night in which he gave himself up for us, he took bread,
gave thanks to you, broke the bread, gave it to his disciples, and said:
Take, eat; this is my body which is given for you.
Do this in remembrance of me."

*The pastor may hold hands, palms down, over the cup, or touch the cup, or lift the cup.*

When the supper was over he took the cup,
gave thanks to you, gave it to his disciples, and said:
Drink from this, all of you; this is my blood of the new covenant,
poured out for you and for many for the forgiveness of sins.
Do this, as often as you drink it, in remembrance of me."

*The pastor may raise hands.*

And so, in remembrance of these your mighty acts in Jesus Christ,
we offer ourselves in praise and thanksgiving
as a holy and living sacrifice, in union with Christ's offering for us,
we proclaim the mystery of faith.

**Christ has died; Christ is risen; Christ will come again.**

*The pastor may hold hands, palms down, over the bread and cup.*

Pour out your Holy Spirit on us gathered here,
and on these gifts of bread and wine.
Make them be for us the body and blood of Christ,
that we may be for the world the body of Christ, redeemed by his blood.

*The pastor may raise hands.*

By your Spirit make us one with Christ,
one with each other, and one in ministry to all the world,
until Christ comes in final victory, and we feast at his heavenly banquet.

Through your Son Jesus Christ, with the Holy Spirit in your holy Church,
all honor and glory is yours, almighty Father (*God*), now and for ever.

**Amen.**

# THE GREAT THANKSGIVING
# FOR WORLD COMMUNION SUNDAY

*This text is used by the pastor while the congregation uses A Service of Word and Table I*
*(UMH 13-15) or III (UMH 15-16) or one of the musical settings (UMH 17-25).*
*The pastor stands behind the Lord's table. See 28.*

The Lord be with you.
**And also with you.**
Lift up your hearts. *The pastor may lift hands and keep them raised.*
**We lift them up to the Lord.**
Let us give thanks to the Lord our God.
**It is right to give our thanks and praise.**

It is right, and a good and joyful thing,
    always and everywhere to give thanks to you,
    Father Almighty (*almighty God*), creator of heaven and earth.
You have made from one every nation and people
    to live on all the face of the earth.

And so, with your people on earth and all the company of heaven
    we praise your name and join their unending hymn:

*The pastor may lower hands.*

**Holy, holy, holy Lord, God of power and might,**
**heaven and earth are full of your glory. Hosanna in the highest.**
**Blessed is he who comes in the name of the Lord. Hosanna in the highes**

*The pastor may raise hands.*

Holy are you, and blessed is your Son Jesus Christ.
By the baptism of his suffering, death, and resurrection
    you gave birth to your Church,
    delivered us from slavery to sin and death,
    and made with us a new covenant by water and the Spirit.
He commissioned us to be his witnesses to the ends of the earth
    and to make disciples of all nations,
and today his family in all the world is joining at his holy table.

*The pastor may hold hands, palms down, over the bread, or touch the bread, or l*
*the bread.*

On the night in which he gave himself up for us, he took bread,
    gave thanks to you, broke the bread, gave it to his disciples, and sa
    "Take, eat; this is my body which is given for you.
Do this in remembrance of me."

*The pastor may hold hands, palms down, over the cup, or touch the cup, or l*
*the cup.*

When the supper was over he took the cup,
  gave thanks to you, gave it to his disciples, and said:
"Drink from this, all of you; this is my blood of the new covenant,
  poured out for you and for many for the forgiveness of sins.
Do this, as often as you drink it, in remembrance of me."

*The pastor may raise hands.*

And so, in remembrance of these your mighty acts in Jesus Christ,
we offer ourselves in praise and thanksgiving
  as a holy and living sacrifice, in union with Christ's offering for us,
as we proclaim the mystery of faith.

**Christ has died; Christ is risen; Christ will come again.**

*The pastor may hold hands, palms down, over the bread and cup.*

Pour out your Holy Spirit on us gathered here,
  and on these gifts of bread and wine.
Make them be for us the body and blood of Christ,
that we may be for the world the body of Christ, redeemed by his blood.

*The pastor may raise hands.*

Renew our communion with your Church throughout the world,
and strengthen it in every nation and among every people
  to witness faithfully in your name.
By your Spirit make us one with Christ,
  one with each other, and one in ministry to all the world,
until Christ comes in final victory, and we feast at his heavenly banquet.

Through your Son Jesus Christ, with the Holy Spirit in your holy Church,
  all honor and glory is yours, almighty Father (*God*), now and for ever.

**Amen.**

# THE GREAT THANKSGIVING
## FOR ALL SAINTS AND MEMORIAL OCCASIONS

*This text is used by the pastor while the congregation uses A Service of Word and Table II (UMH 13-15) or III (UMH 15-16) or one of the musical settings (UMH 17-25).*

*The pastor stands behind the Lord's table. See 28.*

The Lord be with you.
**And also with you.**
Lift up your hearts. *The pastor may lift hands and keep them raised.*
**We lift them up to the Lord.**
Let us give thanks to the Lord our God.
**It is right to give our thanks and praise.**

It is right, and a good and joyful thing,
always and everywhere to give thanks to you,
Father Almighty (*almighty God*),
Creator of heaven and earth,
God of Abraham and Sarah,
God of Miriam and Moses,
God of Joshua and Deborah,
God of Ruth and David,
God of the priests and the prophets,
God of Mary and Joseph,
God of the apostles and the martyrs,
God of our mothers and our fathers,
God of our children to all generations.

And so, with your people on earth and all the company of heaven,
we praise your name and join their unending hymn:

*The pastor may lower hands.*

**Holy, holy, holy Lord, God of power and might,**
**heaven and earth are full of your glory. Hosanna in the highest.**
**Blessed is he who comes in the name of the Lord. Hosanna in the highest.**

*The pastor may raise hands.*

Holy are you, and blessed is your Son Jesus Christ.
By the baptism of his suffering, death, and resurrection
you gave birth to your Church,
delivered us from slavery to sin and death,
and made with us a new covenant by water and the Spirit.

*The pastor may hold hands, palms down, over the bread, or touch the bread, or lift the bread.*

On the night in which he gave himself up for us, he took bread,
gave thanks to you, broke the bread, gave it to his disciples, and said:
Take, eat; this is my body which is given for you.
Do this in remembrance of me."

*The pastor may hold hands, palms down, over the cup, or touch the cup, or lift the cup.*

When the supper was over he took the cup,
gave thanks to you, gave it to his disciples, and said:
Drink from this, all of you; this is my blood of the new covenant,
poured out for you and for many for the forgiveness of sins.
Do this, as often as you drink it, in remembrance of me."

*The pastor may raise hands.*

And so, in remembrance of these your mighty acts in Jesus Christ,
we offer ourselves in praise and thanksgiving
as a holy and living sacrifice, in union with Christ's offering for us,
as we proclaim the mystery of faith.

**Christ has died; Christ is risen; Christ will come again.**

*The pastor may hold hands, palms down, over the bread and cup.*

Pour out your Holy Spirit on us gathered here,
and on these gifts of bread and wine.
Make them be for us the body and blood of Christ,
that we may be for the world the body of Christ, redeemed by his blood.

*The pastor may raise hands.*

Renew our communion with all your saints,
especially those whom we name before you—
*Name(s)*—(*in our hearts*).

*Silence may be kept for the remembrance of names.*

Since we are surrounded by so great a cloud of witnesses,
strengthen us to run with perseverance the race that is set before us,
looking to Jesus, the Pioneer and Perfecter of our faith.

By your Spirit make us one with Christ,
one with each other, and one in ministry to all the world,
until Christ comes in final victory, and we feast at his heavenly banquet.

Through your Son Jesus Christ, with the Holy Spirit in your holy Church,
all honor and glory is yours, almighty Father (*God*), now and for ever.

**Amen.**

# THE GREAT THANKSGIVING
# FOR THANKSGIVING DAY OR
# FOR THE GIFT OF FOOD

*This text is used by the pastor while the congregation uses A Service of Word and Table II (UMH 13-15) or III (UMH 15-16) or one of the musical settings (UMH 17-25).*

*The pastor stands behind the Lord's table. See 28.*

The Lord be with you.
**And also with you.**
Lift up your hearts. *The pastor may lift hands and keep them raised.*
**We lift them up to the Lord.**
Let us give thanks to the Lord our God.
**It is right to give our thanks and praise.**

It is right, and a good and joyful thing,
  always and everywhere to give thanks to you,
  Father Almighty (*almighty God*), creator of heaven and earth.
By your appointment the seasons come and go.
You bring forth bread from the earth and create the fruit of the vine.
You formed us in your image and made us stewards of your world.
Earth has yielded its treasure,
  and from your hand we have received blessing on blessing.

And so, with your people on earth and all the company of heaven
  we praise your name and join their unending hymn:

*The pastor may lower hands.*

**Holy, holy, holy Lord, God of power and might,**
**heaven and earth are full of your glory. Hosanna in the highest.**
**Blessed is he who comes in the name of the Lord. Hosanna in the highest.**

*The pastor may raise hands.*

Holy are you, and blessed is your Son Jesus Christ.
Though he was rich, yet for our sake he became poor.
When hungry and tempted, he refused to make bread for himself
  that he might be the bread of life for others.
When the multitudes were hungry, he fed them.
He broke bread with the outcast but drove the greedy from the temple.
By the baptism of his suffering, death, and resurrection
  you gave birth to your Church,
    delivered us from slavery to sin and death,
    and made with us a new covenant by water and the Spirit.

*The pastor may hold hands, palms down, over the bread, or touch the bread, or lift the bread.*

On the night in which he gave himself up for us, he took bread,
gave thanks to you, broke the bread, gave it to his disciples, and said:
Take, eat; this is my body which is given for you.
Do this in remembrance of me."

*The pastor may hold hands, palms down, over the cup, or touch the cup, or lift
the cup.*

When the supper was over he took the cup,
gave thanks to you, gave it to his disciples, and said:
Drink from this, all of you; this is my blood of the new covenant,
poured out for you and for many for the forgiveness of sins.
Do this, as often as you drink it, in remembrance of me."

*The pastor may raise hands.*

And so, in remembrance of these your mighty acts in Jesus Christ,
we offer ourselves in praise and thanksgiving
as a holy and living sacrifice, in union with Christ's offering for us,
. we proclaim the mystery of faith.

**Christ has died; Christ is risen; Christ will come again.**

*The pastor may hold hands, palms down, over the bread and cup.*

Pour out your Holy Spirit on us gathered here,
and on these gifts of bread and wine.
Make them be for us the body and blood of Christ,
that we may be for the world the body of Christ, redeemed by his blood.

*The pastor may raise hands.*

By your Spirit make us one with Christ,
one with each other, and one in ministry to all the world,
until Christ comes in final victory, and we feast at his heavenly banquet.

Through your Son Jesus Christ, with the Holy Spirit in your holy Church,
all honor and glory is yours, almighty Father (*God*), now and for ever.
Amen.

# AN ALTERNATIVE GREAT THANKSGIVING
# FOR GENERAL USE

*This text is used by the pastor while the congregation uses A Service of Word and Table III (UMH 15-16) or one of the musical settings (UMH 17-25).*

*The pastor stands behind the Lord's table. See 28.*

The Lord be with you.
**And also with you.**
Lift up your hearts. *The pastor may lift hands and keep them raised.*
**We lift them up to the Lord.**
Let us give thanks to the Lord our God.
**It is right to give our thanks and praise.**

Blessed are you, our Alpha and our Omega,
 whose strong and loving arms encompass the universe,
 for with your eternal Word and Holy Spirit you are forever one God.
Through your Word you created all things and called them good,
 and in you we live and move and have our being.
When we fell into sin, you did not desert us.
You made covenant with your people Israel
 and spoke through prophets and teachers.
In Jesus Christ your Word became flesh and dwelt among us,
 full of grace and truth.

And so, with your people on earth and all the company of heaven
 we praise your name and join their unending hymn:

*The pastor may lower hands.*

**Holy, holy, holy Lord, God of power and might,**
**heaven and earth are full of your glory. Hosanna in the highest.**
**Blessed is he who comes in the name of the Lord. Hosanna in the highest.**

*The pastor may raise hands.*

Holy are you, and blessed is Jesus Christ, who called you Abba, Father.
As a mother tenderly gathers her children,
 you embraced a people as your own
 and filled them with a longing for a peace that would last
  and for a justice that would never fail.
In Jesus' suffering and death you took upon yourself our sin and death
 and destroyed their power for ever.
You raised from the dead this same Jesus,
 who now reigns with you in glory,
and poured upon us your Holy Spirit,
 making us the people of your new covenant.

*The pastor may hold hands, palms down, over the bread, or touch the bread, or lift the bread.*

On the night before meeting with death, Jesus took bread,
  gave thanks to you, broke the bread, gave it to the disciples, and said:
"Take, eat; this is my body which is given for you.
Do this in remembrance of me."

*The pastor may hold hands, palms down, over the cup, or touch the cup, or lift the cup.*

When the supper was over Jesus took the cup,
  gave thanks to you, gave it to the disciples, and said:
"Drink from this, all of you; this is my blood of the new covenant,
  poured out for you and for many for the forgiveness of sins.
Do this, as often as you drink it, in remembrance of me."

*The pastor may raise hands.*

And so, in remembrance of these your mighty acts in Jesus Christ,
we offer ourselves in praise and thanksgiving
  as a holy and living sacrifice, in union with Christ's offering for us,
as we proclaim the mystery of faith.

**Christ has died; Christ is risen; Christ will come again.**

*The pastor may hold hands, palms down, over the bread and cup.*

Pour out your Holy Spirit on us gathered here, and on these gifts,
that in the breaking of this bread and the drinking of this wine
  we may know the presence of the living Christ
  and be renewed as the body of Christ for the world,
    redeemed by Christ's blood.

*The pastor may raise hands.*

As the grain and grapes, once dispersed in the fields,
  are now united on this table in bread and wine,
so may we and all your people be gathered from every time and place
  into the unity of your eternal household
  and feast at your table for ever.

Through Christ, with Christ, in Christ, in the unity of the Holy Spirit,
  all honor and glory is yours, almighty God, now and for ever.

**Amen.**

# A BRIEF GREAT THANKSGIVING
# FOR GENERAL USE

*This text may be used by the pastor either in a congregational service or with sick or homebound persons as an alternative to the text on 52-53.*

Lift up your hearts and give thanks to God.

Blessed are you, O God, who with your Word and Holy Spirit
 created all things and called them good.
In Jesus Christ your Word became flesh and dwelt among us.
Through Jesus' suffering and death
you took upon yourself our sin and death
 and destroyed their power for ever.
You raised from the dead this same Jesus, who now reigns with you in glory.
 and poured upon us your Holy Spirit,
 making us the people of your new covenant.

On the night before meeting with death
 Jesus took bread, gave thanks to you, broke the bread,
 gave it to the disciples, and said:
"Take, eat; this is my body which is given for you.
Do this in remembrance of me."

When the supper was over Jesus took the cup,
 gave thanks to you, gave it to the disciples, and said:
"Drink from this, all of you;
 this is my blood of the new covenant,
 poured out for you and for many for the forgiveness of sins.
Do this, as often as you drink it, in remembrance of me."

And so, in remembrance of these your mighty acts in Jesus Christ,
we offer ourselves in praise and thanksgiving
 as a holy and living sacrifice,
 in union with Christ's offering for us.

Pour out your Holy Spirit on us gathered here, and on these gifts,
that in the breaking of this bread and the drinking of this wine
 we may know the presence of the living Christ
 and be renewed as the body of Christ for the world,
  redeemed by Christ's blood,
 until Christ comes in final victory
  and we feast at your table for ever.

Through Christ, with Christ, in Christ, in the unity of the Holy Spirit,
 all honor and glory is yours, almighty God, now and for ever.

**Amen.**

# SERVICES OF
# THE BAPTISMAL COVENANT

## INTRODUCTION

The Baptismal Covenant is God's word to us, proclaiming our adoption by grace, and our word to God, promising our response of faith and love. Those within the covenant constitute the community we call the Church; therefore, the services of the Baptismal Covenant are conducted during the public worship of the congregation where the person's membership is to be held, except in very unusual circumstances. These services are best placed in the order of worship as a response following the reading of Scripture and the sermon. If persons are to be baptized or confirmed at a special service rather than at a regular Sunday service, every effort should be made to secure attendance by the congregation.

The basic service of the Baptismal Covenant is Holy Baptism, by which we are incorporated into the Church, which is the body of Christ, and made one in Christ (1 Corinthians 12:13; Galatians 3:27-28). Because baptism initiates us into Christ's whole Church and not only into a denomination, United Methodists recognize all Christian baptisms and look upon baptism as something that should unite, rather than divide, Christians.

United Methodists may baptize by any of the modes used by Christians. Candidates or their parents have the choice of sprinkling, pouring, or immersion; and pastors and congregations should be prepared to honor requests for baptism in any of these modes. Each mode brings out part of the rich and diverse symbolism given to baptism by the Bible. Each is a form of washing which symbolizes the washing away of sin (Acts 2:38; 22:16; 1 Corinthians 6:11; Hebrews 10:22; 1 Peter 3:21). Being totally buried in water and raised from it is also a powerful symbol of our burial and resurrection with Christ (Romans 6:3-5; Colossians 2:12) and of being born anew of water and the Spirit (John 3:3-5; Titus 3:5). Pouring or sprinkling water upon the candidate's head also signifies God's pouring out of the Holy Spirit (Matthew 3:16, Mark 1:9-10; Luke 3:21-22; Acts 2:38; 19:1-7).

Baptism is an act that looks back with gratitude on what God's grace has already accomplished, it is here and now an act of God's grace, and it looks forward to what God's grace will accomplish in the future. While baptism signifies the whole working of God's grace, much that it signifies, from the washing away of sin to the pouring out of the Holy Spirit, will need to happen during the course of a lifetime. If an act of personal Christiar commitment has taken place, baptism celebrates that act and the grace o God that has made it possible. If such an act has not yet taken place, baptisn anticipates that act, declares its necessity, and celebrates God's grace tha will make it possible. In either event, baptism signifies the entry of th candidate into the general ministry of all Christians.

Baptism anticipates a lifetime of further and deeper experiences of God further acts of Christian commitment, and ministries in the world Confirmation, ordinations and consecrations to particular ministries, and a other steps in ministry grow out of what God has done as declared an signified in baptism. The covenant of Christian marriage reflects th Baptismal Covenant. Finally, as declared in the Service of Death an Resurrection, baptism signifies and anticipates death and resurrection t eternal glory.

Persons of any age are suitable candidates for baptism because Christ body, the Church, is a great family that includes persons of all ages. On th day the Church was born, Peter preached: "Repent, and be baptized ever one of you in the name of Jesus Christ so that your sins may be forgiven; an you will receive the gift of the Holy Spirit. For the promise is for you and fc your children" (Acts 2:38-39). The New Testament repeatedly records th when a believer was baptized, the believer's whole household was baptize (Acts 16:15, 33; 18:8; 1 Corinthians 1:16). Nowhere does the New Testamer record, or even suggest, that any Christian family delayed the baptism ( their children until they could make their own profession of faith. Jesu words, "Let the little children come to me, do not stop them; for it is to suc as these that the kingdom of God belongs" (Mark 10:14b), tell us that ot Lord has expressly given to little children a place among the people of Go which holy privilege must not be denied them.

As these scriptures make clear, we are not to practice indiscrimina baptism. Children and others who have not reached the development stage of making decisions for themselves are presented by parents and/ sponsors (godparents) who make the same profession of faith that candidate would make and who promise to nurture the candidate(s), in th family and in the church family, so that they will come to accept God's gra for themselves, to profess their faith openly, and to lead a Christian life. there are sponsors or godparents, they should be selected carefully becau they will help nurture the person to be baptized in the Christian faith. Th role is not only an honor, it is a serious responsibility. Parents or sponsc (godparents) should be members of Christ's holy Church; and it is the du of pastors to instruct them concerning the significance of Holy Baptism, th responsibilities for the Christian training of the baptized child, and hc these obligations may be fulfilled.

Care is also essential with candidates who take the vows for themselv They also need instruction in the significance and responsibilities of Hc Baptism. The infant being presented for baptism and the adult seeki baptism have more in common, spiritually speaking, than may at first appear. God's grace has taken the initiative and is already at work in the lives of both. Both are making responses to God's grace that are appropriate to their ages. Both need to grow in Christ within Christ's family, the Church, and with the nurturing help of other Christians. There may be sponsors or godparents when candidates can speak for themselves as well as when they cannot.

Regardless of the age of the candidate, the Christian community responds in faith to God's grace by claiming and incorporating this new member of Christ's holy Church. The congregation corporately sponsors each candidate and takes vows at each baptism that are to be taken just as seriously as the vows of parents or individual sponsors. When someone is baptized, it is a crucial event in the life both of that person and of the Church. What happens to that member of the body of Christ will make a difference to every other member, and the rest of the Church can never again be the same. By the Sacrament of Baptism the Church pledges to that member: "Your joy, your pain, your gain, your loss, are ours, for you are one of us."

There are unusual circumstances in which a candidate cannot be baptized in a congregational worship service and in which it is not feasible to use a full service. In such cases the essential acts in baptism are the vows and the baptism with water in the name of the Father, and of the Son, and of the Holy Spirit. A candidate baptized outside of a congregational worship service should, if possible, be presented at a later time to the congregation but not baptized a second time.

While the baptism of a child facing imminent death may be perceived as an emergency by the persons concerned, and while baptism may be an appropriate rite of initiation into the family of Christ under such circumstances, it should be made clear that United Methodism does not teach that infants who die before they are baptized will be denied full salvation. United Methodism has always strongly affirmed the biblical teaching that Christ died for all, and that God's prevenient grace is available to all and is sufficient for such children.

Whatever further steps in faith and life the baptized may take, baptism is not administered to any person more than once, for while our baptismal vows are less than reliable, God's promise to us in the sacrament is steadfast. Once baptized, we have been initiated into Christ's body the Church and are members of Christ's family.

Those baptized before they are old enough to take the vows for themselves make their personal profession of faith in a service called confirmation. Those who are able to take the vows for themselves at their baptism are not confirmed, for they have made their public profession of faith at baptism.

After confirmation, or after baptism when candidates take the vows for themselves, Christians are encouraged to reaffirm the Baptismal Covenant at significant moments. Individuals may make such a reaffirmation when transferring into a congregation, when renewing participation in the church after a time of lapse, or when taking further steps in their personal faith journey. Congregations make such a reaffirmation as a part of every service of the Baptismal Covenant and may do so at other appropriate times as well. Such a reaffirmation is not, however, to be understood as baptism.

While baptism, confirmation, and other services of the Baptismal Covenant may be held at any congregational service, certain occasions are especially appropriate. These include Easter, which recalls our death and resurrection with Christ; some other Lord's Day in the Easter Season, especially the Day of Pentecost; the Baptism of the Lord (the Sunday after January 6); or All Saints (the first day or Sunday in November). Easter is a particularly appropriate time for a congregational reaffirmation of the Baptismal Covenant, even when there are no candidates to be baptized or confirmed.

Other rites may also be appropriate. See An Order of Thanksgiving for the Birth or Adoption of a Child (585-87) and A Celebration of New Beginning in Faith (588-90). Naming ceremonies are traditional in some Native American and other communities. Persons may be publicly enrolled, singly or in groups, as candidates preparing for baptism and confirmation. The distinction should be kept clear, however, between such services and the Sacrament of Baptism.

The following hymns in *UMH* are suggested for services of the Baptismal Covenant, in addition to those classified Baptism (*UMH* 604-11):

### General (Appropriate for All Age Levels)

| | |
|---|---|
| 551 Awake, O Sleeper | 593 Here I Am, Lord |
| 289 Ah, Holy Jesus | 377 It Is Well with My Soul |
| 294 Alas! And Did My Savior Bleed | 398 Jesus Calls Us |
| 62 All Creatures of Our God and King (stanza 7 and refrain) | 431 Let There Be Peace on Earth |
| 186 Alleluia | 471 Move Me |
| 559 Christ Is Made the Sure Foundation | 424 Must Jesus Bear the Cross Alone |
| 731 Glorious Things of Thee Are Spoken | 102 Now Thank We All Our God |
| 100 God, Whose Love Is Reigning O'er Us | 391 O Happy Day, That Fixed My Choice |
| | 454 Open My Eyes, That I May See |
| | 497 Send Me, Lord |

*See also:*
Come Be Baptized ( ♪ 173) and Baptismal Prayer ( ♪ 174)

### For Children (Baptismal Covenant II, II-A, or II-B)

| | |
|---|---|
| 141 Children of the Heavenly Father | 585 This Little Light of Mine |

*See also:*
God Claims You ( ♪ 175)

## For Youth (Baptismal Covenant I or III)

43 On Eagle's Wings
05 Seek Ye First
45 The Church's One Foundation
   (stanza 1)

546 The Church's One Foundation
   (stanza 1)
558 We Are the Church

## For Adults or Reaffirmation (Baptismal Covenant I, III, or IV)

13 A Charge to Keep I Have
56 Blest Be the Dear Uniting Love
14 Come, My Way, My Truth, My Life
71 Go, Make of All Disciples
32 Have Thine Own Way, Lord
55 Holy Spirit, Truth Divine
40 I Love Thy Kingdom, Lord
43 Jesu, Thy Boundless Love to Me

463 Lord, Speak to Me
396 O Jesus, I Have Promised
430 O Master, Let Me Walk with Thee
415 Take Up Thy Cross
192 There's a Spirit in the Air
502 Thy Holy Wings, O Savior
383 This Is the Day of New Beginnings
252 When Jesus Came to Jordan

# THE BAPTISMAL COVENANT I

## HOLY BAPTISM
## CONFIRMATION
## REAFFIRMATION OF FAITH
## RECEPTION INTO THE UNITED METHODIST CHURCH
## RECEPTION INTO A LOCAL CONGREGATION

*This service is found in UMH 33-39 and may be used for any of the above acts or any combination of these that may be called for on a given occasion. To make it easier to determine which parts of the service to use on any given occasion, it has been marked off into the following sections:*

*1) Introduction to Baptism*
*2) Introduction to Confirmation and Reaffirmation*
*3) Presentation of Candidates*
*4) Renunciation of Sin and Profession of Faith*
*5) Parents' and Sponsors' Vow to Nurture the Child*
*6) Vows by Youth or Adult Candidates*
*7) Vows by Sponsors of Youth or Adult Candidates*
*8) Congregation's Vows*
*9) The Apostles' Creed*
*10) Thanksgiving over the Water*
*11) Baptism with Laying on of Hands*
*12) Confirmation or Reaffirmation of Faith*
*13) Congregational Reaffirmation of the Baptismal Covenant*
*14) Reception into The United Methodist Church*
*15) Reception into the Local Congregation*
*16) Commendation and Welcome*

*If there are no confirmations or reaffirmations of faith or receptions by transfer, and the only persons being baptized are (1) children who cannot take their own vows or (2) youth or adults who have not reached the developmental stage of making decisions for themselves, The Baptismal Covenant II should be used.*

*If only persons who can take the vows for themselves are being baptized and received into the Church, and there are no confirmations or reaffirmations of faith, sections 5, 12, and 13 are omitted. Section 7 is used only if there are sponsors.*

*If there are only confirmations and no baptisms, sections 5 and 11 are omitted. Section 7 is used only if there are sponsors. Section 10 is used only if water is to be used. Section 13 is optional.*

*If a confirmation class includes persons to be baptized, section 5 is omitted. Section is used only if there are sponsors. Section 13 may be omitted. Each candidate receives either Baptism with Laying on of Hands (section 11) or Confirmation (section 12), but not both.*

*If persons are being received into membership in a local congregation and wish reaffirm their faith, sections 5 and 11 are omitted. If they are transferring from*

1other United Methodist congregation, section 14 is also omitted. Section 7 is used
1ly if there are sponsors. Sections 10, 12, and 13 may also be omitted.

persons are being received into membership in a local congregation and are not
affirming their faith, only sections 14-16 are used for those coming from another
nomination, and only sections 15-16 are used for those transferring from another
nited Methodist congregation.

the whole congregation is reaffirming the Baptismal Covenant, and there are no
dividuals to be baptized, confirmed, or received into membership, The Baptismal
venant IV should be used.

## NTRODUCTION TO THE SERVICE

As persons come forward, an appropriate baptismal or confirmation hymn may be
sung. See suggestions above (84-85).

The pastor makes the following statement to the congregation:

Brothers and sisters in Christ:
Through the Sacrament of Baptism
   we are initiated into Christ's holy Church.
We are incorporated into God's mighty acts of salvation
   and given new birth through water and the Spirit.
All this is God's gift, offered to us without price.

If there are confirmations or reaffirmations, the pastor continues:

Through confirmation,
and through the reaffirmation of our faith,
we renew the covenant declared at our baptism,
acknowledge what God is doing for us,
and affirm our commitment to Christ's holy Church.

## RESENTATION OF CANDIDATES

A representative of the congregation presents the candidates with the appropriate
statements:

I present Name(s) for baptism.
I present Name(s) for confirmation.
I present Name(s) to reaffirm their faith.
I present Name(s) who come(s) to this congregation from the _____
   Church.

f desired, Thanksgiving over the Water (section 10) may precede the Renunciation
f Sin and Profession of Faith.

At this or some later point in the service, persons may add to their vows a personal
witness to their Christian faith and experience.

## RENUNCIATION OF SIN AND PROFESSION OF FAITH

4 *Since the earliest times, the vows of Christian baptism have consisted first of the renunciation of all that is evil and then the profession of faith and loyalty to Christ. Parents or other sponsors reaffirm these vows for themselves while taking the responsibilities of sponsorship. Candidates for confirmation profess for themselves the solemn vows that were made at their baptism. The pastor addresses parents or other sponsors and those candidates who can answer for themselves:*

On behalf of the whole Church, I ask you:
Do you renounce the spiritual forces of wickedness,
 reject the evil powers of this world,
 and repent of your sin?

**I do.**

Do you accept the freedom and power God gives you
 to resist evil, injustice, and oppression
 in whatever forms they present themselves?

**I do.**

Do you confess Jesus Christ as your Savior,
put your whole trust in his grace,
and promise to serve him as your Lord,
in union with the Church which Christ has opened
 to people of all ages, nations, and races?

**I do.**

5 *The pastor addresses parents or other sponsors of candidates not able to answer for themselves:*

Will you nurture *these children (persons)*
in Christ's holy Church,
that by your teaching and example *they* may be guided
 to accept God's grace for *themselves*,
 to profess *their* faith openly,
 and to lead a Christian life?

**I will.**

6 *The pastor addresses candidates who can answer for themselves:*

According to the grace given to you,
will you remain *faithful members* of Christ's holy Church
and serve as Christ's *representatives* in the world?

**I will.**

7 *If those who have answered for themselves have sponsors, the pastor addresses the sponsors:*

Will you who sponsor *these candidates*
support and encourage *them* in *their* Christian life?

**I will.**

*The pastor addresses the congregation, and the congregation responds:*

Do you, as Christ's body, the Church,
reaffirm both your rejection of sin
and your commitment to Christ?

**We do.**

Will you nurture one another in the Christian faith and life
and include *these persons* now before you in your care?

**With God's help we will proclaim the good news**
**and live according to the example of Christ.**
**We will surround *these persons***
**with a community of love and forgiveness,**
**that they may grow in *their* trust of God,**
**and be found faithful in *their* service to others.**
**We will pray for *them,***
**that *they* may be *true disciples***
**who *walk* in the way that leads to life.**

*The Apostles' Creed in threefold question-and-answer form appeared at least as early as the third century as a statement of faith used in baptisms and has been widely used in baptisms ever since. The candidate(s), sponsor(s), and local congregation join with the universal Church across the ages in this historic affirmation of the Christian faith. The pastor addresses all, and the congregation joins the candidates and their parents and sponsors in responding:*

Let us join together in professing the Christian faith
as contained in the Scriptures of the Old and New Testaments.

Do you believe in God the Father?

**I believe in God, the Father Almighty,**
**creator of heaven and earth.**

Do you believe in Jesus Christ?

**I believe in Jesus Christ, his only Son, our Lord,**
**[who was conceived by the Holy Spirit,**
**born of the Virgin Mary,**
**suffered under Pontius Pilate,**
**was crucified, died, and was buried;**
**he descended to the dead.**
**On the third day he rose again;**
**he ascended into heaven,**
**is seated at the right hand of the Father,**
**and will come again to judge the living and the dead.]**

Do you believe in the Holy Spirit?

**I believe in the Holy Spirit,**
**[the holy catholic\* church,**          *\*universal*
**the communion of saints,**

the forgiveness of sins,
the resurrection of the body,
and the life everlasting.]

## THANKSGIVING OVER THE WATER

10 *If there are baptisms, or if water is to be used for reaffirmation, the water may l*
*poured ceremonially into the font at this time in such a way that the congregatio*
*can see and hear the water. This prayer recalls scriptural images and meanings •*
*Holy Baptism and is comparable to the Great Thanksgiving at Holy Communio*

The Lord be with you.
**And also with you.**
Let us pray.

Eternal Father:
When nothing existed but chaos,
  you swept across the dark waters
  and brought forth light.
In the days of Noah
  you saved those on the ark through water.
After the flood you set in the clouds a rainbow.
When you saw your people as slaves in Egypt,
  you led them to freedom through the sea.
Their children you brought through the Jordan
  to the land which you promised.

**\*\*Sing to the Lord, all the earth.**              *\*\*See UMH 53-54 for mus*
**Tell of God's mercy each day.**

In the fullness of time you sent Jesus,
  nurtured in the water of a womb.
He was baptized by John and anointed by your Spirit.
He called his disciples
  to share in the baptism of his death and resurrection
  and to make disciples of all nations.

**\*\*Declare his works to the nations,**              *\*\*See UMH 53-54 for mu*
**his glory among all the people.**

Pour out your Holy Spirit,
to bless this gift of water and *those* who *receive* it,
to wash away *their* sin
  and clothe *them* in righteousness
  throughout *their lives,*
that, dying and being raised with Christ,
  *they* may share in his final victory.

**\*\*All praise to you, Eternal Father,**      *\*\*See UMH 53-54 for music.*
**through your Son Jesus Christ,**
**who with you and the Holy Spirit**
**lives and reigns for ever. Amen.**

## BAPTISM WITH LAYING ON OF HANDS

**11** *As each candidate is baptized, the pastor uses the Christian name(s), but not the surname:*

*Christian Name(s)*, I baptize you in the name of the Father,
and of the Son,
and of the Holy Spirit. **Amen.**

*Immediately after the administration of the water, the pastor places hands on the candidate's head and invokes the work of the Holy Spirit. Other persons, including baptized members of the candidate's family, may join the pastor in this action. During the Laying on of Hands, the pastor says:*

The Holy Spirit work within you,
that being born through water and the Spirit,
you may be a faithful disciple of Jesus Christ. **Amen.**

*If desired, one or more of the following acts may be added; but these should not be so emphasized as to seem as important as, or more important than, God's sign given in the water itself.*

   *a) The pastor may trace on the forehead of each newly baptized person the sign of the cross in silence or with the words:*"Name, [child of God], you are sealed by the Holy Spirit in baptism and marked as Christ's own forever." *Olive oil may be used in this action, following the biblical custom anointing prophets (1 Kings 19:16), priests (Exodus 29:7), and kings (1 Kings 1:39). Jesus' titles* Christ *and* Messiah *both mean "Anointed One," and the New Testament repeatedly calls Christ our High Priest and King. Christians in baptism become members of the body of Christ (1 Corinthians 12:13), which is a "royal priesthood" (1 Peter 2:9). Anointing at baptism is a reminder that all Christians are anointed into this royal priesthood.*

   *b) New clothing is sometimes presented to those just baptized, particularly in the case of infants, as a symbol that we "have put on Christ" (Galatians 3:27) as one would put on new clothing. Such clothing is traditionally white, suggesting the "white robes" in Revelation 7:9-14. Words such as these may be used:*"Receive these new clothes as a token of the new life that is given in Christ Jesus."

   *c) A lighted baptismal candle may be presented to the newly baptized, with such words as:*"Let your light so shine that others, seeing your good works, may glorify your Father in heaven." *The candle may be presented to the parents or sponsors of baptized children, in which case "others" may be changed to "this child" or "these children." It is appropriate to light the baptismal candle in the home each year on the anniversary of baptism as a reminder of the grace of God offered through baptism. A baptismal candle bears*

*either a Christian symbol or no decoration at all; it should not be confused wi*
*ornate birthday candles sold commercially to mark a child's birthdays. Th*
*candle may be lighted from the paschal candle (see 368) or from one of th*
*candles on or near the Lord's table.*

*d) A certificate of baptism may be presented to the newly baptized.*

*When all candidates have been baptized, the pastor invites the congregation*
*welcome them:*

Now it is our joy to welcome
our new *sisters and brothers* in Christ.

**Through baptism**
**you are incorporated by the Holy Spirit**
**into God's new creation**
**and made to share in Christ's royal priesthood.**
**We are all one in Christ Jesus.**
**With joy and thanksgiving we welcome you**
**as *members* of the family of Christ.**

## CONFIRMATION OR REAFFIRMATION OF FAITH

**12** *Here water may be used symbolically in ways that cannot be interpreted*
*baptism, as the pastor says:*

Remember your baptism and be thankful. **Amen.**

*Such ways of using water include the following:*

*a) Persons being confirmed or reaffirming faith may be invited to touch the wa*
*and, if desired, touch their foreheads with a moistened finger.*

*b) The pastor may scoop up a handful of water and let it flow back into the font*
*that it is heard and seen.*

*c) The pastor may touch the water and mark each person on the forehead with*
*sign of the cross.*

*As the pastor, and others if desired, place hands on the head of each person ber*
*confirmed or reaffirming faith, the pastor says to each:*

*Name*, the Holy Spirit work within you,
that having been born through water and the Spirit,
you may live as a faithful disciple of Jesus Christ. **Amen.**

**13** *When there is a congregational reaffirmation of the Baptismal Covenant, wa*
*may be used symbolically in ways that cannot be interpreted as baptism, as*
*pastor says:*

Remember your baptism and be thankful. **Amen.**

*Such ways of using water include the following:*

*a) Members of the congregation may be invited to touch the water and, if desir*
*touch their foreheads with a moistened finger.*

b) *The pastor may scoop up a handful of water up and let it flow back into the font so that it is heard and seen.*

c) *A very small amount of water may be sprinkled toward the congregation, not falling directly on them as would be the case in baptism by sprinkling. This may be done by dipping the end of a small evergreen branch into the font and shaking it toward the congregation. It may be seen as representing biblical sprinkling with hyssop for purification (Exodus 12:22; Psalm 51:7) and sprinkling as a sign of renewal (Ezekiel 36:25-26).*

d) *The pastor may touch the water and mark each person on the forehead with the sign of the cross.*

## ECEPTION INTO THE UNITED METHODIST CHURCH

*If there are persons coming into membership in The United Methodist Church from other denominations who have not yet been presented, they may be presented at this time.*

*The pastor addresses all those transferring their membership into The United Methodist Church, together with those who, through baptism or confirmation, have just professed their own faith:*

As *members* of Christ's universal Church,
will you be loyal to The United Methodist Church,
and do all in your power to strengthen its ministries?
**I will.**

## ECEPTION INTO THE LOCAL CONGREGATION

*If there are persons joining this congregation from other United Methodist congregations who have not yet been presented, they may be presented at this time.*

*The pastor addresses all those transferring membership into the congregation, together with those who, through baptism or confirmation, have just professed their own faith:*

As *members* of this congregation,
will you faithfully participate in its ministries
 by your prayers, your presence,
 your gifts, your service, and your witness?
**I will.**

## OMMENDATION AND WELCOME

*The pastor addresses the congregation:*

Members of the household of God,
I commend *these persons* to your love and care.
Do all in your power to increase *their* faith,
 confirm *their* hope, and perfect *them* in love.

*The congregation responds:*

**We give thanks for all that God has already given you**
**and we welcome you in Christian love.**
**As members together with you**
**in the body of Christ**
**and in this congregation**
**of The United Methodist Church,**
**we renew our covenant**
**faithfully to participate**
**in the ministries of the Church**
**by our prayers, our presence,**
**our gifts, our service, and our witness,**
**that in everything God may be glorified**
**through Jesus Christ.**

*The pastor addresses those baptized, confirmed, or received:*
The God of all grace,
    who has called us to eternal glory in Christ,
establish you and strengthen you
    by the power of the Holy Spirit,
that you may live in grace and peace.

*One or more laypersons, including children, may join the pastor in acts*
*welcome and peace. Baptized children may be welcomed by a kiss of peace or oth*
*acts or words immediately following Baptism with Laying on of Hands.*

*An appropriate hymn, stanza, or response may be sung. See suggestions abo*
*(84-85). Hymns listed in UMH 939 under Commitment may be used (*
*occasions other than baptism.*

*Appropriate thanksgivings and intercessions for those who have participated*
*these acts should be included in the Concerns and Prayers that follow.*

*It is most fitting that the service continue with Holy Communion, in which t*
*union of the new members with the body of Christ is most fully expressed. The ne*
*members, including children, may receive first.*

# THE BAPTISMAL COVENANT II

## HOLY BAPTISM
### FOR CHILDREN AND OTHERS UNABLE TO
### ANSWER FOR THEMSELVES

*is service is found in UMH 39-43 and is designed for use when the only persons ng baptized are (1) children who cannot take their own vows or (2) youths or adults o have not reached the developmental stage of making decisions for themselves. It is t designed for the baptism of persons who take their own vows, or for confirmation reaffirmation of faith.*

*hen it is necessary to shorten the service, use The Baptismal Covenant II-A.*

## TRODUCTION TO THE SERVICE

*As persons come forward, an appropriate baptismal hymn may be sung. See suggestions above (84).*

*The pastor makes the following statement to the congregation:*

Brothers and sisters in Christ:
Through the Sacrament of Baptism
  we are initiated into Christ's holy Church.
We are incorporated into God's mighty acts of salvation
  and given new birth through water and the Spirit.
All this is God's gift, offered to us without price.

## ESENTATION OF CANDIDATES

*A representative of the congregation presents the candidates:*

present *Name(s)* for baptism.

*If desired, Thanksgiving over the Water (section 10) may precede the Renunciation of Sin and Profession of Faith.*

## NUNCIATION OF SIN AND PROFESSION OF FAITH

*Since the earliest times, the vows of Christian baptism have consisted first of the renunciation of all that is evil and then the profession of faith and loyalty to Christ.*

*Parents or other sponsors reaffirm these vows for themselves while taking the responsibilities of sponsorship.*

*The pastor addresses parents or other sponsors:*

On behalf of the whole Church, I ask you:
Do you renounce the spiritual forces of wickedness,
  reject the evil powers of this world,
  and repent of your sin?

**do.**

Do you accept the freedom and power God gives you
to resist evil, injustice, and oppression
in whatever forms they present themselves?

**I do.**

Do you confess Jesus Christ as your Savior,
put your whole trust in his grace,
and promise to serve him as your Lord,
in union with the Church which Christ has opened
to people of all ages, nations, and races?

**I do.**

Will you nurture *these children (persons)*
in Christ's holy Church,
that by your teaching and example *they* may be guided
to accept God's grace for *themselves,*
to profess *their* faith openly,
and to lead a Christian life?

**I will.**

*The pastor addresses the congregation, and the congregation responds:*

Do you, as Christ's body, the Church,
reaffirm both your rejection of sin
and your commitment to Christ?

**We do.**

Will you nurture one another in the Christian faith and life
and include *these persons* now before you in your care?

**With God's help we will proclaim the good news
and live according to the example of Christ.
We will surround *these persons*
with a community of love and forgiveness,
that *they* may grow in *their* service to others.
We will pray for *them,*
that *they* may be *true disciples*
who *walk* in the way that leads to life.**

*See note regarding the Apostles' Creed on 89. The pastor addresses all, and
congregation joins the parents and sponsors in responding:*

Let us join together in professing the Christian faith
as contained in the Scriptures of the Old and New Testaments.

Do you believe in God the Father?

**I believe in God, the Father Almighty,
creator of heaven and earth.**

Do you believe in Jesus Christ?

I believe in Jesus Christ, his only Son, our Lord,
[who was conceived by the Holy Spirit,
born of the Virgin Mary,
suffered under Pontius Pilate,
was crucified, died, and was buried;
he descended to the dead.
On the third day he rose again;
he ascended into heaven,
is seated at the right hand of the Father,
and will come again to judge the living and the dead.]

Do you believe in the Holy Spirit?

I believe in the Holy Spirit,
[the holy catholic* church,                          *universal
the communion of saints,
the forgiveness of sins,
the resurrection of the body,
and the life everlasting.]

## ᴴANKSGIVING OVER THE WATER

*The water may be poured ceremonially into the font at this time in such a way that the congregation can see and hear the water. This prayer recalls scriptural images and meanings of Holy Baptism and is comparable to the Great Thanksgiving at Holy Communion.*

The Lord be with you.
**And also with you.**
Let us pray.

Eternal Father:
When nothing existed but chaos,
you swept across the dark waters
and brought forth light.
In the days of Noah
you saved those on the ark through water.
After the flood you set in the clouds a rainbow.
When you saw your people as slaves in Egypt,
you led them to freedom through the sea.
Their children you brought through the Jordan
to the land which you promised.

**Sing to the Lord, all the earth.**          **See UMH 53-54 for music.
Tell of God's mercy each day.**

In the fullness of time you sent Jesus,
nurtured in the water of a womb.
He was baptized by John and anointed by your Spirit.

He called his disciples
   to share in the baptism of his death and resurrection
   and to make disciples of all nations.

**\*\*Declare his works to the nations,**       \*\*See UMH 53-54 for musi*
**his glory among all the people.**

Pour out your Holy Spirit,
   to bless this gift of water and *those* who *receive* it,
   to wash away *their* sin
      and clothe *them* in righteousness
      throughout *their lives,*
   that, dying and being raised with Christ,
   *they* may share in his final victory.

**\*\*All praise to you, Eternal Father,**       \*\*See UMH 53-54 for mus*
**through your Son Jesus Christ,**
**who with you and the Holy Spirit**
**lives and reigns for ever.**
**Amen.**

## BAPTISM WITH LAYING ON OF HANDS

*As each candidate is baptized, the pastor uses the Christian name(s), but not th*
*surname:*

*Christian Name(s),* I baptize you in the name of the Father,
   and of the Son,
   and of the Holy Spirit. **Amen.**

*Immediately after the administration of the water, the pastor places hands on th*
*candidate's head and invokes the work of the Holy Spirit. Other persons, includir*
*baptized members of the candidate's family, may join the pastor in this actio*
*During the Laying on of Hands, the pastor says:*

The Holy Spirit work within you,
   that being born through water and the Spirit,
   you may be a faithful disciple of Jesus Christ. **Amen.**

*If desired, one or more of the following acts may be added: anointing, presentati*
*of new clothing, presentation of a baptismal candle, or presentation of a certifica*
*of baptism. See explanation on 91-92. These should not be so emphasized as to see*
*as important as, or more important than, God's sign given in the water itse*
*When all candidates have been baptized, the pastor invites the congregation*
*welcome them:*

Now it is our joy to welcome
   our new *sisters and brothers* in Christ.

**Through baptism**
**you are incorporated by the Holy Spirit**
   **into God's new creation**

and made to share in Christ's royal priesthood.
We are all one in Christ Jesus.
With joy and thanksgiving we welcome you
  as *members* of the family of Christ.

## COMMENDATION AND WELCOME

*Those who have been baptized into Christ's holy Church are now welcomed into this congregation of The United Methodist Church.*

*The pastor addresses the congregation:*

Members of the household of God,
I commend *these persons* to your love and care.
Do all in your power to increase *their* faith,
  confirm *their* hope, and perfect *them* in love.

*The congregation responds:*

We give thanks for all that God has already given you
  and we welcome you in Christian love.
As members together with you
  in the body of Christ
  and in this congregation
  of The United Methodist Church,
we renew our covenant
  faithfully to participate
  in the ministries of the Church
  by our prayers, our presence,
  our gifts, our service, and our witness,
that in everything God may be glorified
  through Jesus Christ.

*The pastor addresses those baptized and their parents and sponsors:*

The God of all grace,
  who has called us to eternal glory in Christ,
establish you and strengthen you
  by the power of the Holy Spirit,
that you may live in grace and peace.

*One or more laypersons, including children, may join the pastor in acts of welcome and peace. Baptized children may be welcomed by a kiss of peace or other acts or words immediately following Baptism with Laying on of Hands. Then an appropriate hymn, stanza, or response may be sung. See suggestions above (84).*

*Appropriate thanksgivings and intercessions for those who have participated in these acts should be included in the Concerns and Prayers that follow. It is most fitting that the service continue with Holy Communion, in which the union of the newly baptized children with the body of Christ is most fully expressed.*

# THE BAPTISMAL COVENANT II-A

## A BRIEF ORDER OF HOLY BAPTISM
## FOR CHILDREN AND OTHERS UNABLE TO
## ANSWER FOR THEMSELVES

*This service is designed for situations where time does not permit use of the full text
The Baptismal Covenant II and when the persons baptized are (1) children who can*
*take their own vows or (2) youths or adults who have not reached the developmen*
*stage of making decisions for themselves. It is not designed for the baptism of perso*
*who take their own vows, or for confirmation or reaffirmation of faith.*

### INTRODUCTION OF THE SERVICE
### AND PRESENTATION OF CANDIDATE(S)

*The pastor may introduce the service and present the candidate(s) eit*
*extemporaneously or using the text on 95.*

### RENUNCIATION OF SIN AND PROFESSION OF FAITH *See 95.*

*The pastor addresses parents or other sponsors:*

On behalf of the whole Church, I ask you:
Do you reject all that is evil, repent of your sin,
and accept the freedom and power God gives you
  to resist evil, injustice, and oppression
  in whatever forms they present themselves?

**I do.**

Do you confess Jesus Christ as your Savior,
put your whole trust in his grace,
and promise to serve him as your Lord,
in union with the Church which Christ has opened
  to people of all ages, nations, and races?

**I do.**

Will you nurture *these children (persons)* in Christ's holy Church,
that by your teaching and example *they* may be guided
  to accept God's grace for *themselves,*
  to profess *their* faith openly,
  and to lead a Christian life?

**I will.**

*The pastor addresses the congregation, and the congregation responds:*

Do you, as Christ's body, the Church,
reaffirm both your rejection of sin and your commitment to Christ

**We do.**

Will you nurture one another in the Christian faith and life,
include *these persons* now before you in your care,
and surround *them* with a community of love and forgiveness?
**We will.**

THANKSGIVING OVER THE WATER *See 97.*

Eternal Father, your mighty acts of salvation
    have been made known through water—
from the moving of your Spirit upon the waters of creation,
to the deliverance of your people
    through the flood and through the Red Sea.
In the fullness of time you sent Jesus,
    nurtured in the water of a womb,
    baptized by John, and anointed by your Spirit.
He called his disciples
    to share in the baptism of his death and resurrection
    and to make disciples of all nations.
Pour out your Holy Spirit,
    to bless this gift of water and *those* who *receive* it,
    to wash away *their* sin and clothe *them* in righteousness
        throughout *their lives*
that, dying and being raised with Christ,
    *they* may share in his final victory;
through the same Jesus Christ our Lord. **Amen.**

BAPTISM WITH LAYING ON OF HANDS *See 98.*

*As each candidate is baptized, the pastor uses the Christian name(s), but not the surname:*

Christian Name(s), I baptize you in the name of the Father,
    and of the Son,
    and of the Holy Spirit. **Amen.**

*Immediately after the administration of the water, the pastor places hands on the candidate's head and invokes the work of the Holy Spirit. Other persons, including baptized members of the candidate's family, may join the pastor in this action. During the laying on of hands, the pastor says:*

The Holy Spirit work within you,
that being born through water and the Spirit,
you may be a faithful disciple of Jesus Christ. **Amen.**

COMMENDATION AND WELCOME *See 99.*

*The pastor may invite the congregation to participate by turning to item 16 on UMH 38.*

*Those who have been baptized into Christ's holy Church are now welcomed into the congregation of The United Methodist Church.*

*The pastor addresses the congregation:*

Members of the household of God,
I commend *these persons* to your love and care.
Do all in your power to increase *their* faith,
  confirm *their* hope, and perfect *them* in love.

*The congregation responds:*

**We give thanks for all that God has already given you
  and we welcome you in Christian love.
As members together with you
  in the body of Christ
  and in this congregation
  of The United Methodist Church,
we renew our covenant
  faithfully to participate
  in the ministries of the Church
  by our prayers, our presence,
  our gifts, our service, and our witness,
that in everything God may be glorified
  through Jesus Christ.**

*The pastor addresses those baptized and their parents and sponsors:*

The God of all grace,
  who has called us to eternal glory in Christ,
establish you and strengthen you
  by the power of the Holy Spirit,
that you may live in grace and peace.

*One or more laypersons, including children, may join the pastor in acts of welcome and peace. Baptized children may be welcomed by a kiss of peace or other acts or words immediately following Baptism with Laying on of Hands. Then an appropriate hymn, stanza, or response may be sung. See suggestions above (84).*

*Appropriate thanksgivings and intercessions for those who have participated in the acts should be included in the Concerns and Prayers that follow. It is most fitting that the service continue with Holy Communion, in which the union of the newly baptized children with the body of Christ is most fully expressed.*

# THE BAPTISMAL COVENANT II-B

## HOLY BAPTISM
## FOR CHILDREN AND OTHERS UNABLE TO
## ANSWER FOR THEMSELVES

*..is text from the rituals of the former Methodist and former Evangelical United
..ethren churches is used by the pastor while the congregation uses The
..ongregational Pledge 1 or 2 (UMH 44).*

*..is designed for use when the only persons being baptized are (1) children who cannot
..ke their own vows or (2) youths or adults who have not reached the developmental
..ge of making decisions for themselves. It is not designed for the baptism of persons
..ho take their own vows, or for confirmation or reaffirmation of faith.*

## ..TRODUCTION TO THE SERVICE

*As persons come forward, an appropriate baptismal hymn may be sung. See
suggestions above (84).*

*The pastor addresses the congregation:*

Dearly beloved,
baptism is an outward and visible sign
  of the grace of the Lord Jesus Christ,
through which grace
  we become partakers of his righteousness
  and heirs of life eternal.
Those receiving the Sacrament
  are thereby marked as Christian disciples,
  and initiated into the fellowship of Christ's holy Church.
Our Lord has expressly given to little children
  a place among the people of God,
  which holy privilege must not be denied them.
Remember the words of the Lord Jesus Christ, how he said,
  "Let the children come to me, do not hinder them;
  for to such belongs the kingdom of God."

## ..OFESSION OF FAITH

*..he pastor addresses parents or other sponsors:*

Beloved,
..o you in presenting *these children (persons)* for Holy Baptism
  confess your faith in our Lord and Savior Jesus Christ?

  **do.**

..o you therefore accept as your bounden duty and privilege

to live before *these children (persons)*
a life that becomes the Gospel;
to exercise all godly care
that *they* be brought up in the Christian faith,
that *they* be taught the Holy Scriptures,
and that *they* learn to give reverent attendance
upon the private and public worship of God?

**I do.**

Will you endeavor to keep *these children (persons)*
under the ministry and guidance of the Church
until *they* by the power of God
shall accept for *themselves* the gift of salvation,
and be confirmed
as *full and responsible members* of Christ's holy Church?

**I will.**

## BAPTISM

*The pastor asks the parent(s) or sponsor(s) of each candidate:*

What name is given this *child (person)*?

*Then, repeating the name(s), though not including the surname, the past*
*baptizes each candidate, saying:*

*Christian Name(s)*, I baptize you in the name of the Father,
and of the Son,
and of the Holy Spirit. **Amen.**

## CONGREGATIONAL PLEDGE

*The pastor addresses the congregation, and the congregation responds with T*
*Congregational Pledge 1 or 2 (UMH 44), as follows:*

### The Congregational Pledge 1

Do you as a congregation accept the responsibility
of assisting *these parents (and sponsors)*
in fulfillment of the baptismal vows,
and do you undertake to provide facilities and opportunities
for Christian nurture and fellowship?

**We will, by the grace of God.**

### The Congregational Pledge 2

Members of the household of faith,
I commend to your love and care *these children (persons)*,
whom we this day recognize as *members* of the family of God.
Will you endeavor so to live

that *these children (persons)* may grow
   in the knowledge and love of God,
through our Savior Jesus Christ?

**With God's help
we will so order our lives after the example of Christ,
that *these children (persons)*, surrounded by steadfast love,
may be established in the faith,
and confirmed and strengthened
in the way that leads to life eternal.**

RAYER

Let us pray.

O God, our heavenly Father,
grant that *these children (persons)*, as *they grow* in years,
   may also grow in grace
   and in the knowledge of the Lord Jesus Christ,
and that
   by the restraining and renewing influence of the Holy Spirit
     *they* may ever be *true children* of thine,
   serving thee faithfully all *their* days.
So guide and uphold
   the *parents/sponsors* of *these children (persons)*
that, by loving care, wise counsel, and holy example,
   they may lead *them* into that life of faith
     whose strength is righteousness
   and whose fruit is everlasting joy and peace;
through Jesus Christ our Lord. **Amen.**

ESSING

God the Father, God the Son, and God the Holy Spirit
bless, preserve, and keep you, now and for evermore. **Amen.**

*One or more laypersons, including children, may join the pastor in acts of welcome
and peace. Baptized children may be welcomed by a kiss of peace or other acts or
words immediately following Baptism.*

*Then an appropriate hymn, stanza, or response may be sung. See suggestions
above (84).*

*Appropriate thanksgivings and intercessions for those who have participated in
these acts should be included in the Concerns and Prayers that follow.*

*It is most fitting that the service continue with Holy Communion, in which the
union of the newly baptized children with the body of Christ is most fully expressed.*

# THE BAPTISMAL COVENANT III

## HOLY BAPTISM
## FOR THOSE WHO CAN ANSWER FOR THEMSELVES
## CONFIRMATION
## REAFFIRMATION OF FAITH
## RECEPTION INTO THE UNITED METHODIST CHURCH
## RECEPTION INTO A LOCAL CONGREGATION

*This service is found in* UMH *45-49 and is a traditional text from the rituals of th*
*former Methodist and former Evangelical United Brethren churches for use wit*
*youth and adults.*

## INTRODUCTION TO THE SERVICE

*As persons come forward, an appropriate baptismal or confirmation hymn may* ●
*sung. See suggestions above (84-85). The pastor makes the following statement* ●
*the congregation:*

The Church is of God,
and will be preserved to the end of time,
for the conduct of worship
    and the due administration of God's Word and Sacraments,
the maintenance of Christian fellowship and discipline,
the edification of believers,
and the conversion of the world.
All, of every age and station,
    stand in need of the means of grace which it alone supplies.

## PRAYER FOR THOSE TO BE BAPTIZED

*This prayer is an adaptation of what was originally a thanksgiving over the wat*●

*If there are no baptisms, the service continues with the Renunciation of Sin a*
*Profession of Faith.*

*If there are candidates to be baptized, the pastor continues:*

Forasmuch as all have sinned and fallen short of the glory of God,
our Savior Christ said,
    "Unless one is born of water and the Spirit,
    one cannot enter the kingdom of God."

Let us pray.

Almighty and everlasting God,
we call upon thee for *these* thy *servants*,
that *they*, coming to thy Holy Baptism
    may receive remission of *their* sins
    and be filled with the Holy Spirit.
Receive *them*, O Lord,
    as thou hast promised by thy well-beloved Son,

and grant that *they* may be faithful to thee
   all the days of *their lives,*
and finally come to the eternal kingdom
   which thou hast promised;
through Jesus Christ our Lord. **Amen.**

## ENUNCIATION OF SIN AND PROFESSION OF FAITH

*At this or some other appropriate point in the service, persons may add a personal
witness to their Christian faith and experience.*

*Since the earliest times, the vows of Christian baptism have consisted first of the
renunciation of all that is evil and then the profession of faith and loyalty to Christ.*

*The pastor addresses those candidates for confirmation who have been previously
baptized:*

Do you in the presence of God and this congregation
renew the solemn vow and promise
made at your baptism?

**I do.**

*The pastor addresses all candidates:*

Do you truly and earnestly repent of your sins?

**I do.**

*The pastor addresses all, and the congregation joins the candidates in responding:*

Do you believe in God the Father?

**I believe in God, the Father Almighty,
   creator of heaven and earth.**

Do you believe in Jesus Christ?

**I believe in Jesus Christ, his only Son, our Lord,
   [who was conceived by the Holy Spirit,
   born of the Virgin Mary,
   suffered under Pontius Pilate,
   was crucified, died, and was buried;
   he descended to the dead.
   On the third day he rose again;
   he ascended into heaven,
   is seated at the right hand of the Father,
   and will come again to judge the living and the dead.]**

Do you believe in the Holy Spirit?

**believe in the Holy Spirit,
   [the holy catholic\* church,**          *\*universal*

the communion of saints,
the forgiveness of sins,
the resurrection of the body,
and the life everlasting.]

*The pastor addresses all candidates:*

Do you receive and profess the Christian faith
as contained in the Scriptures of the Old and New Testaments?

**I do.**

Do you promise, according to the grace given you,
to keep God's holy will and commandments
and walk in the same all the days of your life
as *faithful members* of Christ's holy Church?

**I do.**

## BAPTISM

*If there are no baptisms, the service continues with the Laying on of Hands.*

*Of the candidates for baptism, the pastor inquires:*

Do you desire to be baptized in this faith?

**I do.**

*As each candidate is baptized, the pastor uses the Christian name(s), but not th*
*surname:*

*Christian Name(s)*, I baptize you in the name of the Father,
and of the Son
and of the Holy Spirit. **Amen.**

## LAYING ON OF HANDS, CONFIRMATION, OR REAFFIRMATION OF FAITH

*As the pastor, and others if desired, place hands on the head of each person who h*
*been baptized, or is being confirmed, or is reaffirming faith, the pastor says to eac*

*Name*, the Lord defend you with his heavenly grace
and by his Spirit confirm you
in the faith and fellowship
of all true disciples of Jesus Christ. **Amen.**

*If desired, one or more of the following acts may be added: anointing, presentati*
*of new clothing, or presentation of a baptismal candle. See explanation on 91-9*
*An appropriate certificate may also be presented. These acts should not be*
*emphasized as to seem as important as, or more important than, God's sign giv*
*in the water itself.*

# RECEPTION INTO THE UNITED METHODIST CHURCH

*The pastor, addressing the people, may say:*

Let those persons who are members of other communions
in Christ's holy Church,
and who now desire to enter
into the fellowship of this congregation,
present themselves
to be received into the membership
of The United Methodist Church.

*The pastor addresses all those transferring their membership into The United
Methodist Church, together with those who, through baptism or confirmation,
have just professed their faith:*

Will you be loyal to The United Methodist Church,
and uphold it by your prayers, your presence,
your gifts, your service, and your witness?

**I will.**

# ꓤCEPTION INTO THE LOCAL CONGREGATION

*Then the pastor may say:*

Let those who are members of other congregations
of The United Methodist Church,
and who now desire to enter
into the fellowship of this congregation,
present themselves to be welcomed.

# ꓳMMENDATION AND WELCOME

*Here a lay member, selected by the Administrative Board or Council, may join with
the pastor in offering the hand of fellowship to all those received.*

*Then the pastor may have those received face the congregation and, causing the
people to stand, address them, saying:*

Brothers and sisters,
commend to your love and care
*these persons* whom we this day receive
into the membership of this congregation.
Do all in your power to increase *their* faith,
confirm *their* hope, and perfect *them* in love.

*The congregation responds:*

**We rejoice to recognize you
as *members* of Christ's holy Church,
and bid you welcome to this congregation**

of The United Methodist Church.
With you we renew our vows to uphold it
by our prayers, our presence,
our gifts, our service, and our witness,
With God's help we will so order our lives
after the example of Christ
that, surrounded by steadfast love,
you may be established in the faith,
and confirmed and strengthened in the way
that leads to life eternal.

*The pastor may give this or another blessing:*

God the Father, God the Son, and God the Holy Spirit
bless, preserve, and keep you,
now and evermore. **Amen.**

*An appropriate hymn, stanza, or response may be sung. See suggestions abo*
*(84-85). Hymns listed in* UMH *939 under Commitment may be used on occasio*
*other than baptism.*

*Appropriate thanksgivings and intercessions for those who have participated*
*these acts should be included in the Concerns and Prayers that follow.*

*It is most fitting that the service continue with Holy Communion, in which t*
*union of the new members with the body of Christ is most fully expressed. The n*
*members may receive first.*

# THE BAPTISMAL COVENANT IV

## CONGREGATIONAL REAFFIRMATION OF THE BAPTISMAL COVENANT

*This service is found in UMH 50-53 and is for use by a congregation when there are no candidates to be baptized, confirmed, or received into membership, especially on Easter, Pentecost, All Saints Day, and Baptism of the Lord.*

### INTRODUCTION TO THE SERVICE

Brothers and sisters in Christ:
Through the Sacrament of Baptism
    we are initiated into Christ's holy Church.
We are incorporated into God's mighty acts of salvation
    and given new birth through water and the Spirit.
All this is God's gift, offered to us without price.

Through the reaffirmation of our faith
we renew the covenant declared at our baptism,
    acknowledge what God is doing for us,
    and affirm our commitment to Christ's holy Church.

*If desired, the Thanksgiving over the Water may precede the Renunciation of Sin and Profession of Faith.*

### RENUNCIATION OF SIN AND PROFESSION OF FAITH

*Since the earliest times, the vows of the Baptismal Covenant have consisted first of the renunciation of all that is evil and then the profession of faith and loyalty to Christ.*

On behalf of the whole Church, I ask you:
Do you renounce the spiritual forces of wickedness,
    reject the evil powers of this world,
    and repent of your sin?

**I do.**

Do you accept the freedom and power God gives you
    to resist evil, injustice, and oppression
    in whatever forms they present themselves?

**I do.**

Do you confess Jesus Christ as your Savior,
put your whole trust in his grace,
and promise to serve him as your Lord,

in union with the Church which Christ has opened
to people of all ages, nations, and races?

**I do.**

According to the grace given to you,
will you remain *faithful members* of Christ's holy Church
and serve as Christ's *representatives* in the world?

**I will.**

Let us join together in professing the Christian faith
as contained in the Scriptures of the Old and New Testaments.

Do you believe in God the Father?

**I believe in God, the Father Almighty,
creator of heaven and earth.**

Do you believe in Jesus Christ?

**I believe in Jesus Christ, his only Son, our Lord,
[who was conceived by the Holy Spirit,
born of the Virgin Mary,
suffered under Pontius Pilate,
was crucified, died, and was buried;
he descended to the dead.
On the third day he rose again;
he ascended into heaven,
is seated at the right hand of the Father,
and will come again to judge the living and the dead.]**

Do you believe in the Holy Spirit?

**I believe in the Holy Spirit,
[the holy catholic\* church,**      *\*univers*
**the communion of saints,
the forgiveness of sins,
the resurrection of the body,
and the life everlasting.]**

## THANKSGIVING OVER THE WATER

*If water is to be used for reaffirmation, it water may be poured ceremonially into th
font at this time in such a way that the congregation can see and hear the water; an
the following prayer is offered:*

The Lord be with you.
**And also with you.**
Let us pray.

Eternal Father:
When nothing existed but chaos,
you swept across the dark waters
and brought forth light.

In the days of Noah
  you saved those on the ark through water.
After the flood you set in the clouds a rainbow.
When you saw your people as slaves in Egypt,
  you led them to freedom through the sea.
Their children you brought through the Jordan
  to the land which you promised.

**\*\*Sing to the Lord, all the earth.**          *\*\*See UMH 53-54 for music.*
**Tell of God's mercy each day.**

In the fullness of time you sent Jesus,
  nurtured in the water of a womb.
He was baptized by John and anointed by your Spirit.
He called his disciples
  to share in the baptism of his death and resurrection
  and to make disciples of all nations.

**\*\*Declare his works to the nations,**          *\*\*See UMH 53-54 for music.*
**his glory among all people.**

Pour out your Holy Spirit,
and by this gift of water call to our remembrance
  the grace declared to us in our baptism.
For you have washed away our sins,
  and you clothe us with righteousness throughout our lives,
  that dying and rising with Christ
  we may share in his final victory.

**\*\*All praise to you, eternal Father,**          *\*\*See UMH 53-54 for music.*
**through your Son Jesus Christ,**
**who with you and the Holy Spirit**
**lives and reigns for ever.**
**Amen.**

## ‡AFFIRMATION OF FAITH

*Here water may be used symbolically in ways that cannot be interpreted as baptism,
as the pastor says:*

**Remember your baptism and be thankful. Amen.**

*Such ways of using water include the following:*

*1) Members of the congregation may be invited to touch the water and, if desired,
touch their foreheads with a moistened finger.*

*2) The pastor may scoop up a handful of water and let it flow back into the font so
that it is heard and seen.*

*3) A very small amount of water may be sprinkled toward the congregation, no falling directly on them as would be the case in baptism by sprinkling. This ma be done by dipping the end of a small evergreen branch into the font and shakin it toward the congregation. It may be seen as representing biblical sprinklin with hyssop for purification (Exodus 12:22; Psalm 51:7) and sprinkling as sign of renewal (Ezekiel 36:25-26).*

*4) The pastor may touch the water and mark each person on the forehead with th sign of the cross.*

*The pastor then addresses those reaffirming the Baptismal Covenant:*

The Holy Spirit work within you,
that having been born through water and the Spirit,
you may live as faithful disciples of Jesus Christ.

**Amen.**

## THANKSGIVING

Let us rejoice in the faithfulness of our covenant God.

**We give thanks for all that God has already given us.**
**As members of the body of Christ**
    **and in this congregation of The United Methodist Church,**
**we will faithfully participate in the ministries of the Church**
    **by our prayers, our presence, our gifts, our service, and our witnes**
    **that in everything God may be glorified through Jesus Christ.**

*The pastor addresses those reaffirming the Baptismal Covenant:*

The God of all grace,
    who has called us to eternal glory in Christ,
establish and strengthen you
    by the power of the Holy Spirit,
that you may live in grace and peace.

*Signs of peace may be exchanged.*

*An appropriate hymn, stanza, or response may be sung. See suggestions abc (84-85). Other hymns of Christian commitment are also appropriate.*

*It is most fitting that the service continue with Holy Communion.*

# SERVICES OF CHRISTIAN MARRIAGE

## A SERVICE OF CHRISTIAN MARRIAGE I

*This service of Christian marriage is found in UMH 864-69. It is provided for couples who wish to solemnize their marriage in a service of Christian worship, parallel in its structure to the Sunday service, which includes the proclamation of the Word with prayer and praise. Christian marriage is proclaimed as a sacred covenant reflecting the Baptismal Covenant. Everything about the service is designed to witness that this is a Christian marriage.*

*Both words and actions consistently reflect the belief that husband and wife are equal partners in Christian marriage and that they are entering into the marriage of their own volition.*

*Those present are understood to be an active congregation rather than simply passive witnesses. They give their blessing to the couple and to the marriage, and they join in prayer and praise. It is highly appropriate that the congregation sing hymns and other acts of worship. See the wedding hymns in UMH 642-47, those listed under Weddings in UMH 953-54, and others listed in the service below.*

*Holy Communion may or may not be celebrated. If it is, it is most important that its significance be made clear. Specifically: (1) The marriage rite is included in a Service of Word and Table. (2) Not only the husband and wife but the whole congregation are to be invited to receive communion. It is our tradition to invite all Christians to the Lord's table. (3) There should be no pressure that would embarrass those who for whatever reason do not choose to receive communion.*

*The decision to perform the ceremony is the right and responsibility of the pastor, in accordance with the laws of the state and The United Methodist Church. All plans should be approved by the pastor. The pastor's "due counsel with the parties involved" prior to marriage, mandated by The Book of Discipline, should include, in addition to premarital counseling, discussing and planning the service with them and informing them of policies or guidelines established by the congregation on such matters as decorations, photography, and audio or video recording. Any leadership roles taken by other clergy should be at the invitation of the pastor of the church where the service is held. The organist or person in charge of the music should be consulted and work with the couple in all decisions on music selection.*

*Ethnic and cultural traditions are encouraged and may be incorporated into the service at the discretion of the pastor.*

*Any children of the man or the woman, other family, and friends may take a variety of roles in the service, depending on their ages and abilities. They may, for example, be members of the wedding party, participate in the Response of the Families and People, read scripture lessons, sing or play instrumental music, or make a witness in their own words.*

*In the case of couples who are not church members or are not prepared to make the Christian commitment expressed in our services, adaptations may be made at the discretion of the pastor.*

## ENTRANCE

*The congregation may participate by using A Service of Christian Marriage in UMH 864.*

## GATHERING

*While the people gather, instrumental or vocal music may be offered.*

*Here and throughout the service, the use of music appropriate for Christian worship is strongly encouraged.*

*During the entrance of the wedding party, there may be instrumental music or a hymn, a psalm, a canticle, or an anthem. The congregation may be invited to stand. The following processional hymns in UMH are suggested:*

| | |
|---|---|
| 166 All Praise to Thee, for Thou, O King Divine | 89 Joyful, Joyful We Adore Thee |
| | 93 Let All the World in Every Corner Sing |
| 559 Christ Is Made the Sure Foundation | 117 O God, Our Help in Ages Past |
| 475 Come Down, O Love Divine | 66 Praise, My Soul, the King of Heaven |
| 61 Come, Thou Almighty King | 96 Praise the Lord Who Reigns Above |
| 732 Come, We That Love the Lord | 139 Praise to the Lord, the Almighty |
| 111 How Can We Name a Love | 126 Sing Praise to God Who Reigns Above |
| 644 Jesus, Joy of Our Desiring | 90 Ye Watchers and Ye Holy Ones |

*The woman and the man, entering separately or together, now come forward with members of the wedding party. The woman and the man may be escorted by representatives of their families until they have reached the front of the church, or through the Response of the Families, at which time their escorts are seated.*

## GREETING

*Pastor to people:*

Friends, we are gathered together in the sight of God
to witness and bless the joining together of *Name* and *Name*
   in Christian marriage.
The covenant of marriage was established by God,
   who created us male and female for each other.

With his presence and power
Jesus graced a wedding at Cana of Galilee,
and in his sacrificial love
gave us the example for the love of husband and wife.
*Name* and *Name* come to give themselves to one another
in this holy covenant.

## DECLARATION OF INTENTION

**DECLARATION BY THE MAN AND THE WOMAN**

*Pastor to the persons who are to marry:*

I ask you now, in the presence of God and these people,
to declare your intention
to enter into union with each other
through the grace of Jesus Christ,
who calls you into union with himself
as acknowledged in your baptism.

*Pastor to the woman:*

*Name*, will you have *Name* to be your husband,
to live together in holy marriage?
Will you love him, comfort him, honor and keep him,
in sickness and in health,
and forsaking all others, be faithful to him
as long as you both shall live?

*Woman:* **I will.**

*Pastor to the man:*

*Name*, will you have *Name* to be your wife,
to live together in holy marriage?
Will you love her, comfort her, honor and keep her,
in sickness and in health,
and forsaking all others, be faithful to her
as long as you both shall live?

*Man:* **I will.**

**RESPONSE OF THE FAMILIES AND PEOPLE**

*Pastor to people:*

The marriage of *Name* and *Name* unites their families
and creates a new one.
They ask for your blessing.

*Parents and other representatives of the families may respond in one of th*
*following ways:*

**We rejoice in your union,**
**and pray God's blessing upon you.**

*or, in reply to the pastor's question:*

Do you who represent their families
rejoice in their union
and pray God's blessing upon them?

**We do.**

*or, children of the couple may repeat these or similar words, prompted line by line*
*by the pastor:*

**We love both of you.**
**We bless your marriage.**
**Together we will be a family.**

*If the woman and the man have been escorted by representatives of their families*
*their escorts, having blessed the marriage in the name of their families, may l*
*seated.*

*Pastor to people:*

Will all of you, by God's grace,
do everything in your power
to uphold and care for these two persons in their marriage?

*People:* **We will.**

PRAYER *

The Lord be with you.
**And also with you.**
Let us pray.

God of all peoples,
you are the true light illumining everyone.
You show us the way, the truth, and the life.
You love us even when we are disobedient.
You sustain us with your Holy Spirit.
We rejoice in your life in the midst of our lives.
We praise you for your presence with us,
    and especially in this act of solemn covenant;
through Jesus Christ our Lord. **Amen.**

# PROCLAMATION AND RESPONSE

*A hymn, psalm, canticle, anthem, or other music may be offered before or after*
*readings. The congregation may be invited to stand.*

## Suggested Scripture Lessons

| | |
|---|---|
| Genesis 1:26-28,31a | The creation of man and woman |
| Song of Solomon 2:10-14, 16a; 8:6-7 | Love is strong as death. |
| Isaiah 43:1-7 | You are precious in God's eyes. |
| Isaiah 55:10-13 | You shall go out in joy. |
| Isaiah 61:10–62:3 | Rejoice in the Lord. |
| Isaiah 63:7-9 | The steadfast love of the Lord |
| Romans 12:1-2, 9-18 | The life of a Christian |
| 1 Corinthians 13 | The greatest of these is love. |
| 2 Corinthians 5:14-17 | In Christ we are a new creation. |
| Ephesians 2:4-10 | God's love for us |
| Ephesians 4:1-6 | Called to the one hope |
| Ephesians 4:25–5:2 | Members one of another |
| Philippians 2:1-2 | The Christlike spirit |
| Philippians 4:4-9 | Rejoice in the Lord. |
| Colossians 3:12-17 | Live in love and thanksgiving. |
| 1 John 3:18-24 | Love one another. |
| 1 John 4:7-16 | God is love. |
| Revelation 19:1, 5-9a | The wedding feast of the Lamb |
| Matthew 5:1-10 | The Beatitudes |
| Matthew 7:21, 24-27 | A house built upon a rock |
| Matthew 22:35-40 | Love, the greatest commandment |
| Mark 2:18-22 | Joy in Christ as at a wedding |
| Mark 10:42-45 | True greatness |
| John 2:1-11 | The marriage feast of Cana |
| John 15:9-17 | Remain in Christ's love. |

## Suggested Hymns from UMH

| | |
|---|---|
| 542 As Man and Woman We Were Made | 645 O Perfect Love |
| 451 Be Thou My Vision | 408 The Gift of Love |
| 158 Come, Christians, Join to Sing | 138 The King of Love My Shepherd Is |
| 164 Come, My Way, My Truth, My Life | 643 When Love Is Found |
| 695 O Lord, May Church and Home | 549 Where Charity and Love Prevail |
|     Combine | 647 Your Love, O God, Has Called |
| |     Us Here |

## Suggested Psalms and Canticle

| | |
|---|---|
| 23 (*UMH* 128, 136-38, 518, 754) | The Lord is my shepherd. |
| 33 (*UMH* 767) | Rejoice in the Lord. |
| 34 (*UMH* 769) | I will bless the Lord. |
| 37 (*UMH* 772) | Trust in the Lord and do good. |
| 67 (*UMH* 791) | May God be gracious to us. |
| 100 (*UMH* 74, 75, 821) | Make a joyful noise to the Lord. |
| 103 (*UMH* 139, 824) | Bless the Lord, O my soul. |
| 112 (*UMH* 833) | Happy are those who fear the Lord. |
| 145 (*UMH* 857) | The Lord is gracious. |
| 148 (*UMH* 861) | Praise the Lord from the heavens. |
| 150 (*UMH* 96, 139, 862) | Praise the Lord. |
| Canticle of Love (*UMH* 646) | Two shall become one in love. |

SERMON OR OTHER WITNESS TO CHRISTIAN MARRIAGE

INTERCESSORY PRAYER *

*An extemporaneous prayer may be offered, or the following may be prayed by th*
*pastor or by all:*

Eternal God, Creator and Preserver of all life,
  Author of salvation, Giver of all grace:
Bless and sanctify with your Holy Spirit
  *Name* and *Name*, who come now to join in marriage.
Grant that they may give their vows to each other
  in the strength of your steadfast love.
Enable them to grow in love and peace
  with you and with one another all their days,
  that they may reach out
  in concern and service to the world;
  through Jesus Christ our Lord. **Amen.**

# THE MARRIAGE

EXCHANGE OF VOWS

*The woman and man face each other, joining hands. The pastor may prompt the*
*line by line.*

*Man to woman:*

In the name of God,
I, *Name*, take you, *Name*, to be my wife,
  to have and to hold
  from this day forward,
  for better, for worse,
  for richer, for poorer,
  in sickness and in health,
  to love and to cherish,
  until we are parted by death.
This is my solemn vow.

*Woman to man:*

In the name of God,
I, *Name*, take you, *Name*, to be my husband,
  to have and to hold
  from this day forward,
  for better, for worse,
  for richer, for poorer,
  in sickness and in health,
  to love and to cherish,
  until we are parted by death.
This is my solemn vow.

*In place of the vows given above, one of the following may be used:*

I take you, *Name*, to be my wife (*husband*),
and I promise before God and all who are present here
to be your loving and faithful husband (*wife*)
as long as we both shall live.
I will serve you with tenderness and respect,
and encourage you to develop God's gifts in you.

*Name*, in the name of God,
I take you to be my husband (*wife*) from this time onward,
to join with you and to share all that is to come,
to give and to receive,
to speak and to listen,
to inspire and to respond,
and in all our life together
to be loyal to you with my whole being,
as long as we both shall live.

## ̄LESSING AND EXCHANGE OF RINGS

*The exchange of rings is optional. Other tangible symbols may be given in addition
to, or instead of, rings.*

*The pastor, taking the rings, may say one of the following:*

These rings (*symbols*)
are the outward and visible sign
of an inward and spiritual grace,
signifying to us the union
between Jesus Christ and his Church.

These rings (*symbols*)
are the outward and visible sign
of an inward and spiritual grace,
signifying to all the uniting of *Name* and *Name* in holy marriage.

*The pastor may bless the giving of rings or other symbols of the marriage:*

Bless, O Lord, the giving of these rings (*symbols*),
that they who wear them may live in your peace
and continue in your favor
all the days of their life;
through Jesus Christ our Lord. **Amen.**

*While placing the ring on the third finger of the recipient's left hand, the giver may
say (prompted, line by line, by the pastor):*

*Name*, I give you this *ring*
as a sign of my vow,
and with all that I am,

and all that I have,
I honor you;
in the name of the Father,
and of the Son,
and of the Holy Spirit.

*If a unity candle is used, the two side candles representing the husband and wife ar*
*lighted first, and the center candle representing the marriage is lighted at this c*
*some later point in the service. The side candles are not extinguished because bot*
*husband and wife retain their personal identities.*

## DECLARATION OF MARRIAGE

*The wife and husband join hands. The pastor may place a hand on their joine*
*hands.*

*Pastor to husband and wife:*

You have declared your consent and vows
  before God and this congregation.
May God confirm your covenant
  and fill you both with grace.

*The couple may turn and face the congregation.*

*Pastor to people:*

Now that *Name* and *Name*
  have given themselves to each other by solemn vows,
  with the joining of hands,
  [and the giving and receiving of *rings*,]

I announce to you that they are husband and wife;
  in the name of the Father,
  and of the Son,
  and of the Holy Spirit.
Those whom God has joined together,
  let no one put asunder. **Amen.**

*The congregation may be invited to stand, and a doxology or other hymn may*
*sung. The following hymns from* UMH *are suggested:*

139 Praise to the Lord, the Almighty          643 When Love Is Found
408 The Gift of Love

*Intercessions may be offered for the Church and for the world.*

## BLESSING OF THE MARRIAGE *

*The husband and wife may kneel, as the pastor prays:*

O God,
you have so consecrated

the covenant of Christian marriage
that in it is represented
the covenant between Christ and his Church.
Send therefore your blessing upon *Name* and *Name,*
that they may surely keep their marriage covenant,
and so grow in love and godliness together
that their home may be a haven of blessing and peace;
through Jesus Christ our Lord. **Amen.**

*If Holy Communion is to be celebrated, the congregation turns to A Service of Word
and Table III in UMH 15, or one of the musical settings (UMH 17-25), and the
service continues with the Thanksgiving and Communion (124-27). If Holy
Communion is not to be celebrated, the service continues with the following Prayer
of Thanksgiving:*

Most gracious God,
we give you thanks for your tender love
in making us a covenant people
through our Savior Jesus Christ
and for consecrating in his name
the marriage covenant of *Name* and *Name.*
Grant that their love for each other
may reflect the love of Christ for us
and grow from strength to strength
as they faithfully serve you in the world.
Defend them from every enemy.
Lead them into all peace.
Let their love for each other
be a seal upon their hearts,
a mantle about their shoulders,
and a crown upon their heads.
Bless them
in their work and in their companionship;
in their sleeping and in their waking;
in their joys and in their sorrows;
in their lives and in their deaths.
Finally, by your grace,
bring them and all of us to that table
where your saints feast for ever
in your heavenly home;
through Jesus Christ our Lord,
who with you and the Holy Spirit
lives and reigns,
one God, for ever and ever. **Amen.**

*The Lord's Prayer, prayed by all, using one of the forms in UMH 270-71, 894-96.
The wife and husband may continue to kneel.*

*The Dismissal with Blessing. See 127.*

## THANKSGIVING AND COMMUNION

### TAKING THE BREAD AND CUP *See 27-28.*

*Pastor to people:*

Let us offer ourselves and our gifts to God.

*Here the husband and wife, or children from previous marriages, or representatives the congregation may bring bread and wine to the Lord's table.*

*The pastor, standing if possible behind the Lord's table, facing the people from t time through Breaking the Bread, takes the bread and cup; and the bread and wine prepared for the meal.*

### THE GREAT THANKSGIVING * *See 28.*

The Lord be with you.
**And also with you.**
Lift up your hearts. *The pastor may lift hands and keep them raised.*
**We lift them up to the Lord.**
Let us give thanks to the Lord our God.
**It is right to give our thanks and praise.**

It is right, and a good and joyful thing,
    always and everywhere to give thanks to you,
    Father Almighty *(almighty God)*, Creator of heaven and earth.
You formed us in your image, male and female you created us.
You gave us the gift of marriage, that we might fulfill each other.

And so,
    with your people on earth and all the company of heaven
    we praise your name and join their unending hymn:

*The pastor may lower hands.*

**Holy, holy, holy Lord, God of power and might,**
**heaven and earth are full of your glory.**
    **Hosanna in the highest.**
**Blessed is he who comes in the name of the Lord.**
    **Hosanna in the highest.**

*The pastor may raise hands.*

Holy are you, and blessed is your Son Jesus Christ.
By the baptism of his suffering, death, and resurrection
    you gave birth to your Church,
    delivered us from slavery to sin and death,
    and made with us a new covenant
    by water and the Spirit,
        from which flows the covenant love of husband and wife.

*The pastor may hold hands, palms down, over the bread, or touch the bread, or lift the bread.*

On the night in which he gave himself up for us,
  he took bread, gave thanks to you, broke the bread,
  gave it to his disciples, and said:
"Take, eat; this is my body which is given for you.
Do this in remembrance of me."

*The pastor may hold hands, palms down, over the cup, or touch the cup, or lift the cup.*

When the supper was over he took the cup,
  gave thanks to you, gave it to his disciples, and said:
"Drink from this, all of you;
  this is my blood of the new covenant,
  poured out for you and for many
    for the forgiveness of sins.
Do this, as often as you drink it,
  in remembrance of me."

*The pastor may raise hands.*

And so,
in remembrance of these your mighty acts in Jesus Christ,
we offer ourselves in praise and thanksgiving
  as a holy and living sacrifice,
  in union with Christ's offering for us,
as we proclaim the mystery of faith:

**Christ has died; Christ is risen; Christ will come again.**

*The pastor may hold hands, palms down, over the bread and cup.*

Pour out your Holy Spirit on us gathered here,
  and on these gifts of bread and wine.
Make them be for us the body and blood of Christ,
that we may be for the world the body of Christ,
  redeemed by his blood.

*The pastor may extend hands over the husband and wife.*

By the same Spirit bless *Name* and *Name*,
that their love for each other
  may reflect the love of Christ for us
  and grow from strength to strength
  as they faithfully serve you in the world.
Defend them from every enemy.
Lead them into all peace.
Let their love for each other
  be a seal upon their hearts,

a mantle about their shoulders,
and a crown upon their heads.
Bless them
in their work and in their companionship;
in their sleeping and in their waking;
in their joys and in their sorrows;
in their lives and in their deaths.
Finally, by your grace,
bring them and all of us to that table
where your saints feast for ever in your heavenly home.

*The pastor may raise hands.*

Through your Son Jesus Christ,
with the Holy Spirit in your holy Church,
all honor and glory is yours, almighty Father *(God)*,
now and for ever.

**Amen.**

## THE LORD'S PRAYER * *See 29.*

*The pastor's hands may be extended in open invitation.*

And now, with the confidence of children of God, let us pray:

*The pastor may raise hands.*
*All pray the Lord's Prayer, using one of the forms in UMH 270-71, 894-9*

## BREAKING THE BREAD *See 29.*

*The pastor, still standing behind the Lord's table facing the people, breaks the bre*
*and then lifts the cup, in silence or with appropriate words (see 39).*

## GIVING THE BREAD AND CUP *See 29-31.*

*The bread and wine are given to the people, with these or other words bei*
*exchanged. The husband and wife may assist in the distribution.*

The body of Christ, given for you. **Amen.**
The blood of Christ, given for you. **Amen.**

*While the bread and cup are given, the congregation may sing hymns, or there m*
*be vocal or instrumental music. See suggestions above (116, 119, 122) and una*
*Weddings or Holy Communion in UMH 953-54, 943.*

*When all have received, the Lord's table is put in order. See 30.*

*The pastor may then offer the following prayer:*

Eternal God, we give you thanks
that you have brought *Name* and *Name* [and their families and frienc
together at the table of your family.

Help them them grow in love and unity,
that they may rejoice together all the days of their lives
  and in the wedding feast of heaven.
Grant this through Jesus Christ our Lord. **Amen.**


## SENDING FORTH

*Here may be sung a hymn or psalm. See suggestions above (116, 119, 122).*

## SMISSAL WITH BLESSING *

*Pastor to wife and husband:*

God the Eternal keep you in love with each other,
  so that the peace of Christ may abide in your home.
Go to serve God and your neighbor in all that you do.

*Pastor to people:*

Bear witness to the love of God in this world,
  so that those to whom love is a stranger
    will find in you generous friends.
The grace of the Lord Jesus Christ,
  and the love of God,
  and the communion of the Holy Spirit
  be with you all. **Amen.**

## IE PEACE *

The peace of the Lord be with you always.
**And also with you.**

*The couple may greet each other with a kiss and be greeted by the pastor, after which greetings may be exchanged through the congregation.*

## DING FORTH *

*A hymn may be sung or instrumental music played as the couple, the wedding party, and the people leave. The following recessional hymns in UMH are suggested:*

66 All Praise to Thee, for Thou, O King
  Divine
33 Come We That Love the Lord
00 God, Whose Love Is Reigning o'er Us

89 Joyful, Joyful, We Adore Thee
384 Love Divine, All Loves Excelling
102 Now Thank We All Our God
90 Ye Watchers and Ye Holy Ones

# A SERVICE OF CHRISTIAN MARRIAGE II

*This service is a traditional text from the rituals of the former Methodist and form. Evangelical United Brethren churches.*

*The decision to perform the ceremony is the right and responsibility of the pastor, accordance with the laws of the state and The United Methodist Church. All pla should be approved by the pastor. The pastor's "due counsel with the part involved" prior to marriage, mandated by* The Book of Discipline, *should inclu in addition to premarital counseling, discussing and planning the service with th and informing them of policies or guidelines established by the congregation on su matters as decorations, photography, and audio or video recording. Any leadersh roles taken by other clergy should be at the invitation of the pastor of the church wh the service is held. The organist or person in charge of the music should be consul and work with the couple in all decisions on music selection. See the wedding hym in UMH 642-47 and others suggested in A Service of Christian Marriage I.*

*Ethnic and cultural traditions are encouraged and may be incorporated into service at the discretion of the pastor.*

*Any children of the man or the woman, other family, and friends may take a variety roles in the service, depending on their ages and abilities. They may be members of wedding party, sing or play instrumental music, or make a witness in their o words. See suggestions for including children in A Service of Christian Marriag*

*In the case of couples who are not church members or are not prepared to make Christian commitment expressed in our services, adaptations may be made at discretion of the pastor.*

## ENTRANCE

### GATHERING

*While the people gather, instrumental or vocal music may be offered.*

*Throughout the service, use of specifically Christian music is strongly encourag*

*During the entrance of the wedding party, there may be instrumental music, c hymn, a psalm, a canticle, or an anthem. The congregation may be invited to sta See the listing of suggested processional hymns (116).*

*The woman and the man may be escorted by representatives of their families ur they have reached the front of the church or until they present the woman and man, at which time their escorts are seated.*

### GREETING

*Pastor to people:*

Dearly beloved,
we are gathered together here in the sight of God,
 and in the presence of these witnesses,

to join together this man and this woman *(Name* and *Name)*
  in holy matrimony,
which is an honorable estate, instituted of God,
  and signifying unto us
    the mystical union that exists between Christ and his Church;
which holy estate Christ adorned and beautified
  with his presence in Cana of Galilee.
It is therefore not to be entered into unadvisedly,
  but reverently, discreetly, and in the fear of God.
Into this holy estate these two persons come now to be joined.

## DECLARATION OF INTENTION

### DECLARATION BY THE MAN AND THE WOMAN

*The pastor gives one of the following charges to the persons who are to marry:*

I require and charge you both, as you stand in the presence of God,
  before whom the secrets of all hearts are disclosed,
    that, having duly considered the holy covenant you are about to make,
    you do now declare before this company your pledge of faith,
      each to the other.
Be well assured that if these solemn vows are kept inviolate,
  as God's Word demands,
    and if steadfastly you endeavor to do the will of your heavenly Father,
God will bless your marriage,
  will grant you fulfillment in it,
  and will establish your home in peace.          (THE BOOK OF WORSHIP, 1965)

I charge you both, as you stand in the presence of God,
  to remember that love and loyalty alone will avail
    as the foundation of a happy home.
If the solemn vows you are about to make are kept faithfully,
  and if steadfastly you endeavor to do the will of your heavenly Father,
your life will be full of joy,
  and the home you are establishing will abide in peace.
No other ties are more tender, no other vows more sacred
  than those you now assume.          (EVANGELICAL UNITED BRETHREN, 1959)

*Pastor to the man:*

Name, will you have this woman to be your wedded wife,
  to live together in the holy estate of matrimony?
Will you love her, comfort her, honor and keep her,
  in sickness and in health;
and forsaking all others keep only to her
  so long as you both shall live?

*Man:* **I will.**

*Pastor to the woman:*

*Name*, will you have this man to be your wedded husband,
   to live together in the holy estate of matrimony?
Will you love him, comfort him, honor and keep him,
   in sickness and in health;
and forsaking all others keep only to him
   so long as you both shall live?

*Woman:* **I will.**

## PRESENTATION

*If the woman is presented in marriage, the pastor asks the presenter(s):*

Who presents this woman to be married to this man?

*Presenter(s):* **I (We) do.**

*If the man is presented in marriage, the pastor asks the presenter(s):*

Who presents this man to be married to this woman?

*Presenter(s):* **I (We) do.**

*The presenter(s) may then be seated.*

## THE MARRIAGE

## EXCHANGE OF VOWS

*The woman and man face each other, joining hands. The pastor may prompt them line by line.*

*Man to woman:*

I, *Name*, take you, *Name*,
   to be my wedded wife,
   to have and to hold,
   from this day forward,
   for better, for worse,
   for richer, for poorer,
   in sickness and in health,
   to love and to cherish,
   till death us do part,
   according to God's holy ordinance;
   and thereto I pledge you my faith.

*Woman to man:*

I, *Name*, take you, *Name*,
   to be my wedded husband,

to have and to hold,
from this day forward,
for better, for worse,
for richer, for poorer,
in sickness and in health,
to love and to cherish,
till death us do part,
according to God's holy ordinance;
and thereto I pledge you my faith.

## .ESSING AND EXCHANGE OF RINGS

*The exchange of rings is optional. Other tangible symbols may be given in addition
o, or instead of, rings.*

*The pastor, taking the rings, may say:*

The wedding ring is the outward and visible sign
of an inward and spiritual grace,
signifying to all the uniting of this man and woman in holy matrimony,
through the Church of Jesus Christ our Lord.

*The pastor may bless the giving of rings or other symbols of the marriage:*

Bless, O Lord, the giving of these rings,
hat they who wear them may abide in thy peace,
and continue in thy favor;
hrough Jesus Christ our Lord. **Amen.**

*The common custom is for the husband to give the wife her ring before the wife gives
he husband his ring. While placing the ring on the third finger of the recipient's left
and, the giver may say (prompted, line by line, by the pastor):*

n token and pledge
of our constant faith and abiding love,
vith this ring I thee wed,
n the name of the Father,
and of the Son,
and of the Holy Spirit. Amen.

## CLARATION OF MARRIAGE

*he wife and husband join hands. The pastor may place a hand on or wrap a stole
round their joined hands.*

*he couple may turn and face the congregation.*

*astor to people:*

orasmuch as *Name* and *Name* have consented together in holy wedlock,
and have witnessed the same before God and this company,

and thereto have pledged their faith each to the other,
and have declared the same
   by joining hands and by giving and receiving rings;
I pronounce that they are husband and wife together,
   in the name of the Father,
   and of the Son,
   and of the Holy Spirit.
Those whom God hath joined together, let no one put asunder. **Ame**

*If a unity candle is used, the two side candles representing the husband and wife*
*lighted first, and the center candle representing the marriage is lighted at this*
*some later point in the service. The side candles are not extinguished because b*
*husband and wife retain their personal identities.*

*The congregation may be invited to stand, and a doxology or other hymn may*
*sung. See hymn suggestions above (122).*

## BLESSING OF THE MARRIAGE

*The husband and wife may kneel, as the pastor prays:*

O eternal God,
   creator and preserver of us all,
   giver of all spiritual grace,
   the author of everlasting life:
Send thy blessing upon *Name* and *Name*,
   whom we bless in thy name;
that they may surely perform and keep
   the vow and covenant between them made,
and may ever remain in perfect love and peace together
   and live according to thy laws.
Look graciously upon them,
   that they may love, honor, and cherish each other,
   and so live together in faithfulness and patience,
      in wisdom and true godliness,
   that their home may be a haven of blessing
      and a place of peace;
through Jesus Christ our Lord. **Amen.**

*If Holy Communion is not to be celebrated, the service continues as indicated bel*

*If Holy Communion is to be celebrated, the congregation turns to A Service of W*
*and Table III in* UMH 15 *or one of the musical settings (*UMH 17-25*), and*
*pastor follows the text on 124-26 above, beginning with Taking the Bread and (*
*and concluding with the Dismissal with Blessing on 127 or the one below*

## THE LORD'S PRAYER *

*The husband and wife may continue to kneel, as all pray the Lord's Praye*

# SENDING FORTH

## ◆ISMISSAL WITH BLESSING *

God the Father, the Son, and the Holy Spirit
  bless, preserve, and keep you;
the Lord graciously with his favor look upon you,
  and so fill you with all spiritual benediction and love
    that you may so live together in this life
    that in the world to come you may have life everlasting. **Amen.**

*The couple may greet each other with a kiss and be greeted by the pastor, after which greetings may be exchanged through the congregation.*

## ◆OING FORTH *

*A hymn may be sung or instrumental music played as the couple, the wedding party, and the people leave. See the listing of suggested recessional hymns (127).*

# A SERVICE FOR THE RECOGNITION
# OR THE BLESSING OF A CIVIL MARRIAGE

*this is a separate service of worship at a time other than the regular services of the ▪ngregation, the full service below is used.*

*this is a Response to the Word in the Sunday service, the usual order may be 'lowed through the sermon. The pastor may then give the Greeting below, or ▪temporaneous introductory words, followed by the Intercessory Prayer and the ▪mainder of the service.*

## ▪ATHERING *See 116.*

## ▪REETING

*Pastor to people:*

▪Name and Name have been married by the law of the state,
  and they have made a solemn contract with each other.
◆Now, in faith, they come before the witness of the Church
  to declare their marriage covenant
  and to acknowledge God's good news for their lives.

## ▪RIPTURE LESSON(S)

*A hymn, psalm, canticle, anthem, or other music may be offered before or after the ▪readings. See the hymn and psalm suggestions in A Service of Christian Marriage I ▪(119).*

## SERMON OR OTHER WITNESS TO CHRISTIAN MARRIAGE

## INTERCESSORY PRAYER *

*An extemporaneous prayer may be offered, or the following may be prayed by th pastor or by all:*

Let us pray.

Eternal God, creator and preserver of all life,
  author of salvation, giver of all grace:
Bless and sanctify with your Holy Spirit *Name* and *Name,*
  who come now asking for your blessing upon their marriage.
Grant that they may reaffirm their vows to each other
  in the strength of your steadfast love.
Enable them to grow in love and peace
  with you and each other all their days,
  that they may reach out
  in concern and service to the world;
through Jesus Christ our Lord. **Amen.**

## DECLARATION BY THE HUSBAND AND WIFE

*Pastor to the husband and wife:*

*Name* and *Name,* you have come here today
  to seek the blessing of God and of the Church upon your marriag

*To the wife:*

*Name,* you have taken *Name* to be your lawful husband.
Now you wish to declare, before God and this congregation,
  your desire that your married life should be according to God's w

I ask you, therefore,
will you love him, comfort him, honor and keep him,
  in sickness and in health,
and forsaking all others, be faithful to him
  as long as you both shall live?

*Wife:* **I will.**

*To the husband:*

*Name,* you have taken *Name* to be your lawful wife.
Now you wish to declare, before God and this congregation,
  your desire that your married life should be according to God's w

I ask you, therefore,
will you love her, comfort her, honor and keep her,
  in sickness and in health,
and forsaking all others, be faithful to her
  as long as you both shall live?

*Husband:* **I will.**

## LESSING OF RINGS

*The husband and wife may extend their left hands, and the pastor may place a hand upon the rings and say:*

These rings are the outward and visible sign
  of an inward and spiritual grace,
signifying to us the union
  between Jesus Christ and his Church.

*The pastor may bless the wearing of rings:*

Bless, O Lord, the wearing of these rings
that they who wear them may live in your peace
  and continue in your favor
  all the days of their lives;
through Jesus Christ our Lord. **Amen.**

## ECLARATION OF MARRIAGE

*The wife and husband join hands. The pastor may place a hand on or wrap a stole around their joined hands. The pastor says to the wife and husband:*

*Name* and *Name*, you are husband and wife
  according to the witness of Christ's universal Church,
  in the name of the Father,
  and of the Son,
  and of the Holy Spirit.
Those whom God has joined together,
  let no one put asunder. **Amen.**

*The service continues with the Blessing of the Marriage and all that follows, with or without Holy Communion, in A Service of Christian Marriage I. See 122-27.*

# AN ORDER FOR THE REAFFIRMATION OF THE MARRIAGE COVENANT

*is order may be a Response to the Word during regular congregational worship, in ich case the usual order of Sunday worship may be followed through the sermon. lowing the sermon, the pastor invites the couple(s) to come forward, or to stand ere they are; and the order below is then followed. Alternatively, a special Service the Reaffirmation of the Marriage Covenant may be held. It may begin with thering and Processional Hymn (see suggestions on 116). Between the Greeting l the Reaffirmation of the Marriage Covenant there may be scripture lessons and ise (see suggestions on 119) and a sermon or other witness to Christian marriage. ? participating couple(s) should be invited to develop the order and text of the vice with the pastor and music director. A printed bulletin enables maximum ticipation.*

*If children of the couple(s) are present, they may participate by blessing the marriage reading scripture lessons, singing or playing music, or making a witness in their own words.*

## GREETING

Friends, we are gathered together in the sight of God
to witness and bless
  the reaffirmation of the marriage covenant,
  which was established by God,
  who created us male and female for each other.
With his presence and power
  Jesus graced a wedding at Cana of Galilee,
and in his sacrificial love
  gave us the example for the love of husband and wife.

## REAFFIRMATION OF THE MARRIAGE COVENANT

*The couple(s) face each other, join hands, and speak directly to each other, repeating the vows, phrase by phrase, after the pastor.*

*Husband to wife (husbands to wives):*

In the name of God, and with a thankful heart,
I once again declare that
I, *Name*, take you, *Name*, to be my wife,
  to have and to hold
  from this day forward,
  for better, for worse,
  for richer, for poorer,
  in sickness and in health,
  to love and to cherish,
  until we are parted by death.
This is my solemn vow.

*Wife to husband (wives to husbands):*

In the name of God, and with a thankful heart,
I once again declare that
I, *Name*, take you, *Name*, to be my husband,
  to have and to hold
  from this day forward,
  for better, for worse,
  for richer, for poorer,
  in sickness and in health,
  to love and to cherish,
  until we are parted by death.
This is my solemn vow.

ONGREGATIONAL RESPONSE *

Let us pray.

Eternal God, Creator and preserver of all life,
author of salvation, giver of all grace:
Bless and sanctify with your Holy Spirit
*Wife's Name* and *Husband's Name, (those)*
who have reaffirmed their marriage covenant.
Enable them to grow in love and peace
with you and with each other all their days,
that they may reach out
in concern and service to the world;
through Jesus Christ our Lord. Amen.

LESSING OF THE MARRIAGE(S) *

*Instead of, or in addition to, the following, the pastor may offer the Prayer of Thanksgiving (123). On the occasion of a marriage anniversary, the pastor and/or the couple may offer one or both of the marriage anniversary prayers on 138.*

O God, you have so consecrated
the covenant of Christian marriage
that in it is represented
the covenant between Christ and his Church.
Send therefore your blessing upon *Name* and *Name (these couples)*,
that they may surely keep their marriage covenant,
and so grow in love and godliness together
that their *homes(s)* may be (*a*) *haven(s)* of blessing and peace;
through Jesus Christ our Lord. **Amen.**

*If this order takes place during regular congregational worship, the couple(s) may be dismissed with the following blessing and the usual order of worship followed for the remainder of the service.*

God the Eternal keep you in love with each other,
so that the peace of Christ may abide in your home.
Go to serve God and your neighbor in all that you do.

*If this order is part of a special service and Holy Communion is not to be celebrated, the service continues with the Lord's Prayer.*

*If Holy Communion is to be celebrated, the congregation turns to A Service of Word and Table III in UMH 15 or one of the musical settings (UMH 17-25), and the pastor follows the text on 124-26, beginning with Taking the Bread and Cup. On a marriage anniversary, this prayer may follow communion:*

Lord, as we have gathered at the table of your Son,
bless *Name* and *Name* on their wedding anniversary.
Watch over them in the coming years,
and bring them to the feast of eternal life.
Grant this through Christ our Lord. **Amen.**

*Whether or not Holy Communion is celebrated, the service may conclude with a hymn (see suggestions in A Service of Christian Marriage I) and the Dismissal with Blessing and the Peace (see 127).*

# MARRIAGE ANNIVERSARY PRAYERS

*Marriage anniversaries present a prime opportunity for both Church and family to proclaim the joys and blessings of Christian marriage. This can happen in various ways.*

*A pastor may be invited to attend the family celebration and offer prayer, and the couple themselves may offer a prayer of thanksgiving.*

*A couple may choose the occasion of their anniversary to reaffirm their marriage covenant (see 135-38), during which the pastor may offer this or another suitable prayer as a Blessing of the Marriage.*

Lord our God,
Bless *Name* and *Name*.
We thank you for their marriage,
  [for the children they have nurtured,]
  and for all the good they have done.
As you blessed the love of their youth,
  continue to bless their life together with gifts of peace and joy.
We ask this through our Lord Jesus Christ, your Son,
  who lives and reigns with you and the Holy Spirit,
  one God, for ever and ever. **Amen.**

*The couple may offer this or another suitable prayer following, or instead of, the Blessing of the Marriage:*

O God, our heavenly Father,
  on this anniversary of our wedding
    we give you thanks for your past blessings,
  and for your continual mercies now.
We thank you that with the passing days
  you have increased and deepened our love for each other.
We praise you for all the joys of our home and family life.
Renew your blessings upon us now,
  as we renew our vows of love and loyalty;
and may your Holy Spirit strengthen us
  that we may ever remain steadfast in our faith and in your service;
through Jesus Christ our Lord. **Amen.**

# SERVICES OF DEATH AND RESURRECTION

## A SERVICE OF DEATH AND RESURRECTION

*his service is found in* UMH 870-75. *It is a service of Christian worship suitable for ʌnerals and memorial services. It should be held in the church if at all possible and at a time when members of the congregation can be present. If the service is to be held in a ʌurch and led by anyone other than the pastor of that congregation, it should be done ᵗ the invitation of that pastor. This service is intended for use with the body of the ⸰ceased present, but it can be adapted for use at memorial services or other occasions.*

*ʾse of the term* Service of Death and Resurrection *is not intended to discourage ᵹe of the more familiar terms—*funeral, burial of the dead, *or* memorial service. ʌneral *is appropriate for a service with the body of the deceased present.* Burial of ʌe Dead *is appropriate for a service where the remains of the deceased are buried.* ʌemorial Service *is appropriate when the body of the deceased is not present.* ᵊrvice of Death and Resurrection *was selected as being appropriate to any of the ʌide variety of situations in which this service might be used. It expresses clearly the ʌofold nature of what is done: the facts of death and bereavement are honestly faced, ʌd the gospel of resurrection is celebrated in the context of God's Baptismal Covenant ʌth us in Christ.*

*ʾhen circumstances make the service as it stands inappropriate, the pastor may make ʾaptations, using the alternative acts of worship on* 158-66 *and other available ᵴources. Ethnic and cultural traditions are encouraged and may be incorporated ʌo the service at the discretion of the pastor. The organist or person in charge of the ʌsic should be consulted and work with the family in all decisions on music ʾection.*

*ʌaditionally, pastors have not accepted an honorarium for this service when the ᵶeased was a member of the parish.*

*ᵉ coffin may be covered with a pall (a large cloth with a cross and other Christian ʌnbolism), an act whose meaning is declared by the words:* "As in baptism *Name* ʌt on Christ, so in Christ may *Name* be clothed with glory." *The same pall is ᵶd in a congregation for all funerals and is a witness that everyone is equal before the ʌle of the Lord. For each service the pall should be clean and free of wrinkles, and ᵶvers should never be placed on top of it. Alternatively, the coffin may be covered ʌth a flag, or flowers may be placed on it.*

*The service itself should be seen as a part of the larger ministry of the Church at death. At several times during this ministry acts of worship are especially appropriate.*

1) *In ministry with the dying, prayers and other acts of worship are crucial. See 166-67.*

2) *The pastor should be notified immediately upon the death of a member or constituent of the congregation. Prayer and other acts of worship are crucia with the bereaved at the time of death (see 167-68). The pastor may have ar important role in notifying others of the death.*

3) *Plans for the service and all other ministries following a death should be mad in consultation with the family and subject to the approval of the pastor. If th family requests that there be military, fraternal, or other rites in addition to th Service of Death and Resurrection, the pastor should plan carefully th sequence and interrelationship of these services so that the service is no interrupted with other rites, and so that its integrity is supported and no compromised.*

4) *Facing the body of the deceased and closing the coffin bring home to th mourners the reality of death and are times when the support of pastor an Christian community is important. A variety of supportive ministries b church, family, friends, and other organizations may take place between th time of death and the time of the service; see A Family Hour or Wake (168-69, Children should be invited to be present at all these services.*

5) *The Service of Death and Resurrection itself, commonly called the funeral c memorial service, brings into focus the whole ministry of the Church at deatl It presupposes that the encounter with the body of the deceased and the closin of the coffin have already taken place, and for this reason the coffin remair closed throughout the service and thereafter.*

6) *The committal service is not found in* UMH *because the congregation cann be expected to carry hymnals to the graveside, but it is found here following tr Service of Death and Resurrection. The committal may take place immediate following the funeral, or it may be a separate service at another time and plac*

7) *Reentry into the community by the chief mourners following the service tak time and can be facilitated by the supportive ministry of the Church. If t service itself does not include Holy Communion, it is sometimes helpful for t pastor to take communion to the family, perhaps at the first visit following t service.*

8 *Continuing support of representatives of the community, including ministri of prayer and worship as appropriate, is essential in the long-term process which those who mourn find healing.*

9) *Recurring memorial acts and services are occasions both of healing and celebration. Mourners are especially open to supportive ministries on su occasions as Christmas, holidays, birthdays, and anniversaries of marriage*

*of death. Celebration of All Saints (see 413-15) and other annual memorial services can also be particularly helpful (see 440 and 548, 737-39).*

10) *It is essential that ongoing congregational life in its totality be centered in the Christian gospel, which is a message of death and resurrection. The way in which persons deal with all death—past, present, and future—will depend upon how central this gospel has become in their lives.*

# ENTRANCE

*e congregation may participate by using A Service of Death and Resurrection in VIH 870.*

## ATHERING

*The pastor may greet the family.*

*Music for worship may be offered while the people gather.*

*Hymns and songs of faith may be sung during the gathering. See suggestions below '160-61) and under Eternal Life and Funerals and Memorial Services in* UMH *)40-42.*

*The coffin or urn may be carried into the place of worship in procession, in which ase the pall may be placed on it outside the place of worship with these words:*

Dying, Christ destroyed our death.
Rising, Christ restored our life.
Christ will come again in glory.
As in baptism *Name* put on Christ,
  so in Christ may *Name* be clothed with glory.
Here and now, dear friends, we are God's children.
What we shall be has not yet been revealed;
but we know that when he appears, we shall be like him,
  for we shall see him as he is.
Those who have this hope purify themselves
  as Christ is pure.

## IE WORD OF GRACE

*the coffin or urn is carried into the place of worship in procession, the pastor may o before it speaking these words, the congregation standing. Or if the coffin or urn already in place, the pastor speaks these or other words (see 158, 161, 163, 165) om in front of the congregation.*

'esus said, I am the resurrection and I am life.
Those who believe in me, even though they die, yet shall they live,
  and whoever lives and believes in me shall never die.
am Alpha and Omega, the beginning and the end, the first and the last.

I died, and behold I am alive for evermore,
and I hold the keys of hell and death.
Because I live, you shall live also.

## GREETING

Friends, we have gathered here to praise God
and to witness to our faith as we celebrate the life of *Name*.
We come together in grief, acknowledging our human loss.
May God grant us grace, that in pain we may find comfort,
in sorrow hope, in death resurrection.

*If there has been no procession, the pall may be placed at this time.*

*Whether or not the pall is placed at this time, the sentences printed above und*
*Gathering may be used here if they were not used earlier.*

## HYMN OR SONG *

*See suggestions below (160-61) and under Eternal Life and Funerals and Memor*
*Services in* UMH 940-42.

## PRAYER *

*One or more of the following or other prayers (see 158-66) may be offered, in unis*
*if desired. Petition for God's help, thanksgiving for the communion of sain*
*confession of sin, and assurance of pardon are appropriate here.*

The Lord be with you.
**And also with you.**
Let us pray.

**O God, who gave us birth,**
**you are ever more ready to hear**
**than we are to pray.**
**You know our needs before we ask,**
**and our ignorance in asking.**
**Give to us now your grace,**
**that as we shrink before the mystery of death,**
**we may see the light of eternity.**
**Speak to us once more**
**your solemn message of life and of death.**
**Help us to live as those who are prepared to die.**
**And when our days here are accomplished,**
**enable us to die as those who go forth to live,**
**so that living or dying, our life may be in you,**

and that nothing in life or in death will be able to separate us
from your great love in Christ Jesus our Lord. Amen.

Eternal God,
we praise you for the great company of all those
who have finished their course in faith
and now rest from their labor.
We praise you for those dear to us
whom we name in our hearts before you.
Especially we praise you for *Name*,
whom you have graciously received into your presence.
To all of these, grant your peace.
Let perpetual light shine upon them;
and help us so to believe where we have not seen,
that your presence may lead us through our years,
and bring us at last with them
into the joy of your home
not made with hands but eternal in the heavens;
through Jesus Christ our Lord. Amen.

*The following prayer of confession and pardon may also be used:*

Holy God, before you our hearts are open,
and from you no secrets are hidden.
We bring to you now
our shame and sorrow for our sins.
We have forgotten
that our life is from you and unto you.
We have neither sought nor done your will.
We have not been truthful in our hearts,
in our speech, in our lives.
We have not loved as we ought to love.
Help us and heal us,
raising us from our sins into a better life,
that we may end our days in peace,
trusting in your kindness unto the end;
through Jesus Christ our Lord,
who lives and reigns with you
in the unity of the Holy Spirit,
one God, now and for ever. Amen.

Who is in a position to condemn?
Only Christ, Christ who died for us, who rose for us,
who reigns at God's right hand and prays for us.
Thanks be to God who gives us the victory
through our Lord Jesus Christ.

## PSALM 130 *

*This or another version of Psalm 130 (UMH 515, 516, or 848) may be sung o* *spoken:*

**Out of the depths I cry unto thee, O Lord!**
**Lord, hear my cry.**
**Let thine ears be attentive**
**to the voice of my supplication.**
**If thou, Lord, should mark iniquities,**
**Lord, who could stand?**
**But there is forgiveness with thee,**
**that thou may be feared.**
**I wait for the Lord, my soul waits,**
**and in his word do I hope.**
**My soul waits for the Lord**
**more than those who watch for the morning.**
**O Israel, hope in the Lord!**
**For with the Lord is great mercy.**
**With him is plenteous redemption,**
**and he will redeem Israel from all their sins.**                    (RSV, AL

## PROCLAMATION AND RESPONSE

### OLD TESTAMENT LESSON

*One or both of the following or another lesson may be read:*

Comfort, O comfort my people, says your God.
Speak tenderly to Jerusalem, and cry to her
   that she has served her term, that her penalty is paid,
that she has received from the Lord's hand double for all her sins.
A voice cries out: "In the wilderness prepare the way of the Lord,
   make straight in the desert a highway for our God.
Every valley shall be lifted up,
   and every mountain and hill be made low;
the uneven ground shall become level, and the rough places a plair
Then the glory of the Lord shall be revealed,
   and all the people shall see it together,
   for the mouth of the Lord has spoken."
A voice says, "Cry out!"
   And I said, "What shall I cry?"
All people are grass, their constancy is like the flower of the field.
The grass withers, the flower fades,
   when the breath of the Lord blows upon it;
surely the people are grass.
The grass withers, the flower fades;
   but the word of our God will stand forever.                    (ISAIAH 40:

Have you not known? Have you not heard?
The Lord is an everlasting God, the Creator of the ends of the earth.
He does not faint or grow weary, his understanding is unsearchable.
He gives power to the faint, and strengthens the powerless.
Even youths will faint and be weary, and the young will fall exhausted;
but those who wait for the Lord shall renew their strength,
    they shall mount up with wings like eagles,
    they shall run and not be weary,
    they shall walk and not faint. (ISAIAH 40:28-31)

### Other Suggested Scripture Readings

| | |
|---|---|
| Exodus 14:5-14, 19-31 | Israel's deliverance |
| Isaiah 43:1-3a, 5-7, 13, | |
| 15, 18-19, 25; 44:6, 8a | God will deliver. |
| Isaiah 55:1-3, 6-13 | Hymn of joy |

See Canticle of Covenant Faithfulness (UMH 125).

For additional suggestions, see 159.

## ₃ALM 23 *

This or another version of Psalm 23 (UMH 136, 137, 138, or 754) may be sung or spoken:

The Lord is my shepherd; I shall not want.
He maketh me to lie down in green pastures:
    he leadeth me beside the still waters.
He restoreth my soul:
    he leadeth me in the paths of righteousness
        for his name's sake.
Yea, though I walk
    through the valley of the shadow of death,
    I will fear no evil:
for thou art with me;
    thy rod and thy staff they comfort me.
Thou preparest a table before me
    in the presence of mine enemies:
thou anointest my head with oil;
    my cup runneth over.
Surely goodness and mercy shall follow me
    all the days of my life:
    and I will dwell in the house of the Lord for ever. (KJV)

## ₃W TESTAMENT LESSON

One of the following or another lesson may be read:

Now I would remind you, brothers and sisters,
of the good news that I proclaimed to you,

which you in turn received, in which also you stand,
through which also you are being saved.
Now if Christ is proclaimed as raised from the dead,
how can some of you say there is no resurrection of the dead?
For if the dead are not raised, then Christ has not been raised.
If Christ has not been raised,
your faith is futile and you are still in your sins.
Then those also who have died in Christ have perished.
But in fact Christ has been raised from the dead,
the first fruits of those who have died.
But someone will ask, "How are the dead raised?
With what kind of body do they come?"
Fool! What you sow does not come to life unless it dies.
And as for what you sow, you do not sow the body that is to be,
but a bare seed, perhaps of wheat or of some other grain.
But God gives it a body as he has chosen.
What is sown is perishable, what is raised is imperishable.
It is sown in dishonor, it is raised in glory.
It is sown in weakness, it is raised in power.
It is sown a physical body, it is raised a spiritual body.
If there is a physical body, there is also a spiritual body.
When this perishable body puts on imperishability,
and this mortal body puts on immortality,
then the saying that is written will be fulfilled:
"Death has been swallowed up in victory."
"Where, O death, is your victory? Where, O death, is your sting?"
But thanks be to God,
who gives us the victory through our Lord Jesus Christ.

(1 CORINTHIANS 15:1-2a, 12, 16-18, 20, 35-38a, 42b-44, 54-55, 5

Then I saw a new heaven and a new earth;
for the first heaven and the first earth had passed away,
and the sea was no more.
And I saw the holy city, the new Jerusalem,
coming down out of heaven from God,
prepared as a bride adorned for her husband.
And I heard a loud voice from the throne saying,
"See, the home of God is among mortals.
He will dwell with them as their God;
they will be his peoples, and God himself will be with them;
he will wipe away every tear from their eyes.
Death will be no more;
mourning and crying and pain will be no more,
for the first things have passed away."
And the one who was seated on the throne said,
"See, I am making all things new."
Also he said, "Write this, for these words are trustworthy and true.

Then he said to me,
"It is done! I am the Alpha and the Omega, the beginning and the end.
To the thirsty I will give water
as a gift from the spring of the water of life.
Those who conquer will inherit these things,
and I will be their God and they will be my children."
(REVELATION 21:1-7)

There is therefore now no condemnation for those who are in Christ Jesus.
For the law of the Spirit of life in Christ Jesus
has set you free from the law of sin and of death.
If the Spirit of him who raised Jesus from the dead dwells in you,
he who raised Christ from the dead
will give life to your mortal bodies also
through his Spirit that dwells in you.
For all who are led by the Spirit of God are children of God,
and if children, then heirs,
heirs of God and joint heirs with Christ—
if, in fact, we suffer with him
so that we may also be glorified with him.
I consider that the sufferings of this present time
are not worth comparing with the glory about to be revealed to us.
We know that all things work together for good for those who love God,
who are called according to his purpose.
What then are we to say about these things?
If God is for us, who is against us?
He who did not withhold his own Son, but gave him up for all of us,
will he not with him also give us everything else?
Who will separate us from the love of Christ?
Will hardship, or distress, or persecution,
or famine, or nakedness, or peril, or sword?
As it is written, "For your sake we are being killed all day long;
we are accounted as sheep to be slaughtered."
No, in all these things we are more than conquerors
through him who loved us.
For I am convinced that neither death, nor life,
nor angels, nor rulers, nor things present, nor things to come,
nor powers, nor height, nor depth, nor anything else in all creation,
will be able to separate us from the love of God
in Christ Jesus our Lord. (ROMANS 8:1-2, 11, 14, 17-18, 28, 31-32, 35-39)

*Other Suggested Scripture Readings*

| | |
|---|---|
| 2 Corinthians 4:5-18 | Glory in God |
| Ephesians 1:15-23; 2:1-10 | Alive in Christ |
| 1 Peter 1:3-9, 13, 21-25 | Blessed by God |
| Revelation 7:2-3, 9-17 | The multitude of the redeemed |

## PSALM, CANTICLE, OR HYMN *

*Recommended, either here or after the Old Testament Lesson:*

| | |
|---|---|
| Psalm 42 (*UMH* 777) | As a deer longs for flowing streams |
| Psalm 43 (*UMH* 778) | You are the God in whom I take refuge |
| Psalm 46 (*UMH* 780) | God is our refuge and strength. |
| Psalm 90 (*UMH* 809) | From everlasting to everlasting |
| Psalm 91 (*UMH* 810) | My God in whom I trust |
| Psalm 103 (*UMH* 824) | Bless the Lord, O my soul. |
| Psalm 116 (*UMH* 837) | I will lift up the cup of salvation. |
| Psalm 121 (*UMH* 844) | I lift up my eyes to the hills. |
| Psalm 139 (*UMH* 854) | O Lord, you have searched me. |
| Psalm 145 (*UMH* 857) | The Lord is gracious and merciful. |
| Psalm 146 (*UMH* 858) | Praise the Lord, O my soul. |
| Canticle of Hope (*UMH* 734) | God shall wipe away all our tears. |
| Canticle of Remembrance (*UMH* 652) | The souls of the righteous |

*See hymns suggested below (160-61) and under Eternal Life and Funerals an Memorial Services in* UMH *940-42.*

## GOSPEL LESSON *

*The following or another lesson may be read:*

[Jesus said,] "Do not let your hearts be troubled.
Believe in God, believe also in me.
In my Father's house there are many dwelling places.
If it were not so,
would I have told you that I go to prepare a place for you?
And if I go and prepare a place for you,
I will come again and will take you to myself,
so that where I am, there you may be also.
And you know the way to the place where I am going.
I will not leave you orphaned; I am coming to you.
In a little while the world will no longer see me,
but you will see me;
because I live, you also will live.
I have said these things to you while I am still with you.
But the Advocate, the Holy Spirit, whom the Father will send in my nam
will teach you everything,
and remind you of all that I have said to you.
Peace I leave with you; my peace I give to you.
I do not give to you as the world gives.
Do not let your hearts be troubled, and do not let them be afraid."

(JOHN 14:1-4, 18-19, 25-

### Other Suggested Scripture Readings

| | |
|---|---|
| Luke 24:13-35 | Jesus at Emmaus |
| John 11:1-4, 20-27, 32-35, 38-44 | The raising of Lazarus |

# ERMON

*A sermon may be preached, proclaiming the gospel in the face of death. It may lead into, or include, the following acts of naming and witness.*

# AMING

*The life and death of the deceased may be gathered up in the reading of a memorial or appropriate statement, or in other ways, by the pastor or others.*

# ITNESS

*Pastor, family, friends, and members of the congregation may briefly voice their thankfulness to God for the grace they have received in the life of the deceased and their Christian faith and joy.*

*A poem or other reading such as If Death My Friend and Me Divide (UMH 656) may be read as a witness.*

*Signs of faith, hope, and love may be exchanged.*

# YMN OR SONG *

*See suggestions below (160-61) and under Eternal Life and Funerals and Memorial Services in* UMH 940-42.

# REED OR AFFIRMATION OF FAITH *

*See* UMH 880-89. *A hymn or musical response may either follow or precede the Creed or Affirmation of Faith.*

# COMMENDATION

*If the Committal (155-57) is to conclude this service, it may be shortened and substituted for the Commendation.*

# RAYERS *

*One or more of the following prayers may be offered, or other prayers may be used. They may take the form of a pastoral prayer, a series of shorter prayers, or a litany. Intercession, commendation of life, and thanksgiving are appropriate here.*

God of us all, your love never ends.
When all else fails, you still are God.
We pray to you for one another in our need,
    and for all, anywhere, who mourn with us this day.
To those who doubt, give light;
    to those who are weak, strength;
    to all who have sinned, mercy;
    to all who sorrow, your peace.

Keep true in us
  the love with which we hold one another.
In all our ways we trust you.
And to you,
  with your Church on earth and in heaven,
  we offer honor and glory, now and for ever. **Amen.**

O God, all that you have given us is yours.
As first you gave *Name* to us,
  now we give *Name* back to you.

*Here the pastor, with others, standing near the coffin or urn, may lay hands on i*
*continuing:*

Receive *Name* into the arms of your mercy.
Raise *Name* up with all your people.
Receive us also, and raise us into a new life.
Help us so to love and serve you in this world
  that we may enter into your joy in the world to come. **Amen.**

Into your hands, O merciful Savior,
  we commend your servant *Name.*
Acknowledge, we humbly beseech you,
  a sheep of your own fold,
  a lamb of your own flock,
  a sinner of your own redeeming.
Receive *Name* into the arms of your mercy,
  into the blessed rest of everlasting peace,
  and into the glorious company of the saints of light. **Amen.**

*The pastor may administer Holy Communion to all present who wish to share at t*
*Lord's table, the people using A Service of Word and Table III (UMH 15) or one*
*the musical settings (UMH 17-25) and the pastor using An Order for Ho*
*Communion in 152-54 below. Otherwise, the service continues as follows:*

## PRAYER OF THANKSGIVING *

God of love, we thank you
  for all with which you have blessed us
    even to this day:
for the gift of joy in days of health and strength
  and for the gifts of your abiding presence and promise
    in days of pain and grief.
We praise you for home and friends,
  and for our baptism and place in your Church
  with all who have faithfully lived and died.
Above all else we thank you for Jesus,
  who knew our griefs,
  who died our death and rose for our sake,

and who lives and prays for us.
And as he taught us, so now we pray.

HE LORD'S PRAYER *

*All pray the Lord's Prayer, using one of the forms in UMH 270-71, 894-96.*

YMN *

*This may be a recessional hymn. See suggestions below (160-61) and under Eternal Life and Funerals and Memorial Services in UMH 940-42.*

ISMISSAL WITH BLESSING *

*The pastor, facing the people, may give one or more of the following, or other, Dismissal with Blessing:*

Now may the God of peace
who brought back from the dead our Lord Jesus,
   the great Shepherd of the sheep,
   by the blood of the eternal covenant,
make you complete in everything good
   so that you may do his will,
working among us that which is pleasing in his sight,
   through Jesus Christ;
to whom be the glory for ever and ever. **Amen.** (HEBREWS 13:20-21)

The peace of God which passes all understanding
   keep your hearts and minds in the knowledge and love of God,
      and of his Son Jesus Christ our Lord.
And the blessing of God Almighty,
   the Father, Son, and Holy Spirit,
   be among you and remain with you always. **Amen.**

Now may the Father
   from whom every family in heaven and on earth is named,
   according to the riches of God's glory,
grant you to be strengthened with might
   through God's Spirit in your inner being,
   that Christ may dwell in your hearts through faith;
that you, being rooted and grounded in love,
   may be able to comprehend with all the saints
      what is the breadth and length and height and depth,
   and to know the love of Christ which surpasses knowledge,
      that you may be filled with all the fullness of God. **Amen.**
(EPHESIANS 3:14-19, PARAPHRASE)

*A Service of Committal follows at the final resting place. See 155-57.*

# AN ORDER FOR HOLY COMMUNION

*This order may be included in the Service of Death and Resurrection at the poin*
*indicated on 150, or before a common meal following the service, or with the family a*
*some time following the service. The people use A Service of Word and Table I.*
*(UMH 15) or one of the musical settings (UMH 17-25). It is our tradition to invite a*
*Christians to the Lord's table, and the invitation should be extended to everyon*
*present; but there should be no pressure that would embarrass those who for whateve*
*reason do not choose to receive Holy Communion.*

## TAKING THE BREAD AND CUP *See 27-28.*

*The pastor, standing if possible behind the Lord's table, facing the people from th*
*time through Breaking the Bread, takes the bread and cup; and the bread and wir*
*are prepared for the meal.*

## THE GREAT THANKSGIVING * *See 28.*

The Lord be with you.
**And also with you.**
Lift up your hearts. *The pastor may lift hands and keep them raised.*
**We lift them up to the Lord.**
Let us give thanks to the Lord our God.
**It is right to give our thanks and praise.**

It is right,
    that we should always and everywhere give thanks to you,
    Father Almighty *(almighty God)*, Creator of heaven and earth;
through Jesus Christ our Lord,
    who rose victorious from the dead
    and comforts us with the blessed hope of everlasting life.

And so, with your people on earth and all the company of heaven
    we praise your name and join their unending hymn:
*The pastor may lower hands.*

**Holy, holy, holy Lord, God of power and might,**
**heaven and earth are full of your glory. Hosanna in the highest!**
**Blessed is he who comes in the name of the Lord.**
**Hosanna in the highest!**
*The pastor may raise hands.*

Holy are you, and blessed is your Son Jesus Christ.
By the baptism of his suffering, death, and resurrection
    you gave birth to your Church,
    delivered us from slavery to sin and death,
    and made with us a new covenant by water and the Spirit.
When the Lord Jesus ascended, he promised to be with us always
    in the power of your Word and Holy Spirit.

*The pastor may hold hands, palms down, over the bread, or touch the bread, or lift the bread.*

On the night in which he gave himself up for us, he took bread,
  gave thanks to you, broke the bread, gave it to his disciples, and said:
"Take, eat; this is my body which is given for you.
Do this in remembrance of me."

*The pastor may hold hands, palms down, over the cup, or touch the cup, or lift the cup.*

When the supper was over he took the cup,
  gave thanks to you, gave it to his disciples, and said:
"Drink from this, all of you; this is my blood of the new covenant,
  poured out for you and for many for the forgiveness of sins.
Do this, as often as you drink it, in remembrance of me."

*The pastor may raise hands.*

And so, in remembrance of these your mighty acts in Jesus Christ,
we offer ourselves in praise and thanksgiving
  as a holy and living sacrifice, in union with Christ's offering for us,
as we proclaim the mystery of faith:

**Christ has died; Christ is risen; Christ will come again.**

*The pastor may hold hands, palms down, over the bread and cup.*

Pour out your Holy Spirit on us, gathered here,
  and on these gifts of bread and wine.
Make them be for us the body and blood of Christ,
that we may be for the world the body of Christ, redeemed by his blood.

*The pastor may raise hands.*

By your Spirit make us one with Christ,
  one with each other, and one in communion with all your saints,
  especially *Name* and all those most dear to us,
  whom we now remember in the silence of our hearts.

*A time of silence for remembrance.*

Finally, by your grace, bring them and all of us to that table
  where your saints feast for ever in your heavenly home.

Through your Son Jesus Christ, with the Holy Spirit in your holy Church,
all honor and glory is yours, almighty Father (*God*), now and for ever.
**Amen.**

## THE LORD'S PRAYER * *See 29.*

*The pastor's hands may be extended in open invitation.*

And now, with the confidence of children of God, let us pray:

*The pastor may raise hands.*

*All pray the Lord's Prayer, using one of the forms in UMH 270-71, 894-96*

## BREAKING THE BREAD *See 29.*

*The pastor, still standing behind the Lord's table facing the people, breaks the brea*
*and then lifts the cup, in silence or with appropriate words (see 39).*

## GIVING THE BREAD AND CUP *See 29-31.*

*The bread and wine are given to the people, with these or other words bein*
*exchanged:*

The body of Christ, given for you. **Amen.**
The blood of Christ, given for you. **Amen.**

*While the bread and cup are given, the congregation may sing hymns, or there ma*
*be vocal or instrumental music. In addition to the suggestions below (160-61) an*
*under Eternal Life, Funerals and Memorial Services, and Holy Communion i*
*UMH 940-43, many other hymns in UMH are effective in expressing the people*
*loving communion with God and with one another. It is particularly effective if tl*
*people can sing from memory during communion.*

*When all have received, the Lord's table is put in order. See 30.*

## DISMISSAL WITH BLESSING * *See 31-32.*

*The pastor, facing the people, may give one or more of the Dismissals with Blessir*
*in 151, or another Dismissal with Blessing.*

*A Service of Committal follows at the final resting place. See 155-57.*

# A SERVICE OF COMMITTAL

*is order is intended primarily for burial in the ground. However, it can be adapted*
*r cremation or the interment of ashes, for burial above ground or at sea, or for*
*nation of the body for medical purposes.*

*the family requests that there be military, fraternal, or other rites in addition to the*
*rvice of Committal, the pastor should approve such rites and plan carefully the*
*quence and interrelationship of these services so that the service is not interrupted.*
*e pastor will preside.*

*ayers and lessons appropriate for a service for a child or youth, or for other*
*stinctive occasions, may be used instead of the following. See 158-66.*

*hen the people have gathered, one or more of the following are said:*

the midst of life, we are in death;
from whom can we seek help?                          (NINTH CENTURY)

ur help is in the name of the Lord
who made heaven and earth.                          (PSALM 124:8, *UMH* 846)

od who raised Christ from the dead
will give life to your mortal bodies also
through the Spirit that dwells in you.              (ROMANS 8:11, ALT.)

sten, I will tell you a mystery!
e will not all die, but we will all be changed.
r this perishable body must put on imperishability,
and this mortal body must put on immortality.
en the saying that is written will be fulfilled:
"Death has been swallowed up in victory."
"Where, O death, is your victory? Where, O death, is your sting?"
t thanks be to God,
who gives us the victory through our Lord Jesus Christ.
                                    (1 CORINTHIANS 15:51, 53, 54*b*-55, 57)

erefore my heart is glad, and my soul rejoices;
my body also dwells secure.
u, [Lord,] show me the path of life;
in your presence there is fullness of joy,
in your right hand are pleasures forevermore.      (PSALM 16:9, 11, *UMH* 748)

*e following prayer is offered:*

t us pray.
God, you have ordered this wonderful world
and know all things in earth and in heaven.
ve us such faith that by day and by night,
at all times and in all places,
we may without fear commit ourselves
    and those dear to us
    to your never-failing love,
    in this life and in the life to come. **Amen.**

*One of the following or other scriptures may be read:*

Blessed be the God and Father of our Lord Jesus Christ!
By his great mercy we have been born anew to a living hope
  through the resurrection of Jesus Christ from the dead,
and to an inheritance which is imperishable, undefiled and unfading,
  kept in heaven for you.
In this you rejoice, though now for a little while you suffer trials
  so that the genuineness of your faith may prove itself worthy
    at the revelation of Jesus Christ.
Without having seen him, yet you love him;
though you do not now see him,
  you believe in him and rejoice with unutterable and exalted joy.
As the harvest of your faith you reap the salvation of your souls.

(ADAPTED FROM 1 PETER 1:3

Jesus said: "Very truly, I tell you,
  unless a grain of wheat falls into the earth and dies,
  it remains just a single grain;
  but if it dies, it bears much fruit.
Those who love their life lose it,
  and those who hate their life in this world
    will keep it for eternal life.
Whoever serves me must follow me,
  and where I am, there will my servant be also.
Whoever serves me, the Father will honor."

(JOHN 12:24-

*Standing at the head of the coffin and facing it (preferably casting earth upon it as it
lowered into the grave) the pastor says:*

Almighty God,
  into your hands we commend your *son/daughter Name,*
  in sure and certain hope of resurrection to eternal life
  through Jesus Christ our Lord. **Amen.**

This body we commit to the ground
(*to the elements, to its resting place*),
  earth to earth, ashes to ashes, dust to dust.

(TRADITION

Blessed are the dead who die in the Lord.
Yes, says the Spirit, they will rest from their labors
  for their deeds follow them.

(REVELATION 14:13, A

*One or more of the following or other prayers is offered:*

Gracious God,
  we thank you for those we love but see no more.
Receive into your arms your servant *Name,*
  and grant that increasing in knowledge and love of you,
  *he/she* may go from strength to strength
    in service to your heavenly kingdom;
through Jesus Christ our Lord. **Amen.**

Almighty God,
look with pity upon the sorrow of your servants, for whom we pray.
In midst things they cannot understand, help them to trust in your care.
Bless them and keep them.
Make your face to shine upon them, and give them peace. **Amen.**

O Lord, support us all the day long of our troubled life,
until the shadows lengthen and the evening comes,
    and the busy world is hushed,
    and the fever of life is over and our work is done.
Then in your mercy grant us a safe lodging,
    and a holy rest, and peace at the last;
through Jesus Christ our Lord. **Amen.**

Eternal God, you have shared with us the life of *Name.*
Before *he/she* was ours, *he/she* is yours.
For all that *Name* has given us to make us what we are,
    for that of *him/her* which lives and grows in each of us,
    and for *his/her* life that in your love will never end,
    we give you thanks.
As now we offer *Name* back into your arms,
    comfort us in our loneliness,
    strengthen us in our weakness,
    and give us courage to face the future unafraid.
Draw those of us who remain in this life closer to one another,
    make us faithful to serve one another,
    and give us to know that peace and joy which is eternal life;
through Jesus Christ our Lord. **Amen.**

*The Lord's Prayer may follow.*

*A hymn or song may be sung.*

*The pastor dismisses the people with the following or another blessing:*

Now to the One who is able to keep you from falling,
    and to make you stand without blemish
        in the presence of God's glory with rejoicing,
        the only God our Savior, through Jesus Christ our Lord,
    be glory, majesty, power, and authority,
        before all time and now and forever. **Amen.**     (JUDE 24-25, ALT.)

# ADDITIONAL RESOURCES FOR SERVICES OF DEATH AND RESURRECTION

## FOR GENERAL USE

*Words of Grace and Sentences*

The Lord is my light and my salvation;
  whom shall I fear?
The Lord is the stronghold of my life;
  of whom shall I be afraid?                (PSALM 27:1, *UMH* 75)

Blessed be the Lord,
  who has heard the voice of my supplications!
The Lord is my strength and shield,
  in whom my heart trusts.                  (PSALM 28:6-7a, *UMH* 76)

The Lord is merciful and gracious,
  slow to anger and abounding in steadfast love.
As a father shows compassion to his children,
  so the Lord shows compassion to the faithful.
For the Lord knows our frame, and remembers that we are dust.
The steadfast love of the Lord is from everlasting to everlasting
  upon the faithful,
and the righteousness of the Lord to children's children.
                        (PSALM 103:8, 13-14, 17, *UMH* 8:)

*Prayers*

O Jesus Christ our risen Lord, you have gone before us in death.
Grant us the assurance of your presence,
  that we who are anxious and fearful in the face of death
    may confidently face the future,
  in the knowledge that you have prepared a place for all who love yo
  **Amen.**

O God, giver of life and conqueror of death,
  our help in every time of trouble,
we trust that you do not willingly grieve or afflict us.
Comfort us who mourn;
  and give us grace, in the presence of death, to worship you,
that we may have sure hope of eternal life
  and be enabled to put our whole trust in your goodness and mercy
through Jesus Christ our Lord. **Amen.**

mighty God, our Father, from whom we come,
and to whom our spirits return:
ɔu have been our dwelling place in all generations.
ɔu are our refuge and strength, a very present help in trouble.
ʾant us your blessing in this hour,
and enable us so to put our trust in you
that our spirits may grow calm and our hearts be comforted.
ʾt our eyes beyond the shadows of earth,
and help us to see the light of eternity.
  may we find grace and strength for this and every time of need;
ʿough Jesus Christ our Lord. **Amen.**

## Scripture Readings

| | |
|---|---|
| Genesis 15:15 | Abraham's death |
| Genesis 49:1, 29-33; 50:1-2, 12-14 | Jacob's death and Joseph's response |
| Exodus 15 (*UMH 135*) | Canticle of Moses and Miriam |
| Joshua 3:14–4:7 | Crossing over Jordan |
| Job 1:21 | Job's faith |
| Job 14:1-12*a* | We are of few days. |
| Job 19:25-27 | My Redeemer lives. |
| Proverbs 31:10-13, 19-20, 30-31 | A good woman |
| Isaiah 25:1, 6-9 | God will swallow up death. |
| Isaiah 26:1-4, 19 | Your dead shall live. |
| Isaiah 35:1-6, 10 | Zion restored |
| Isaiah 41:8-10, 13 | Do not fear. |
| Isaiah 57:14-19 | Poem of consolation |
| Isaiah 61:1-4, 10-11 | The Spirit of the Lord is upon me. |
| Isaiah 66:10-13 | As a mother comforts, so does God. |
| Ezekiel 34:11-16 | Shepherd of Israel |
| Ezekiel 37:1-14, 21-28 | These bones can live. |
| Micah 6:6-8 | What does the Lord require? |
| Zephaniah 3:16-20 | Restoration of Israel |
| Psalm 27 (*UMH 758*) | Devotion and deliverance |
| Psalm 34 (*UMH 769*) | Thanksgiving for deliverance |
| Psalm 40 (*UMH 774*) | Thanksgiving for deliverance |
| Psalm 71 (*UMH 794*) | Deliverance from evil |
| Psalm 77 (*UMH 798*) | Deliverance from trouble |
| Psalm 84 (*UMH 804*) | How lovely is your dwelling place. |
| Psalm 118 (*UMH 839*) | Thanksgiving for deliverance |
| Psalm 126 (*UMH 847*) | Prayer for deliverance |
| Psalm 143 (*UMH 856*) | Prayer for deliverance |
| Acts 10:34-43 | Peter's sermon on Jesus' resurrection |
| Romans 5:1-11, 17-21 | Peace with God through faith |
| Romans 6:3-11 | Dying and rising with Christ |
| Romans 14:7-9 | Christ, Lord of the dead and the living |
| Corinthians 5:1-11*a*, 14-20 | Away from the body, at home in the Lord |
| Ephesians 3:14-21 | Bow before God; know the love of Christ. |
| Philippians 3:7-21 | The power of Christ's resurrection |

| | |
|---|---|
| Colossians 3:1-17 | Raised with Christ |
| 1 Thessalonians 4:13–5:11 | Concerning those who sleep |
| 2 Timothy 4:6-8, 17-18 | I have fought the good fight. |
| Hebrews 11–12 | The saints of God |
| 1 John 3:1-3 | We shall be like God. |
| Revelation 14:1-3, 6-7, 12-13 | Blessed are the dead in the Lord. |
| Matthew 5:1-12 | The Beatitudes |
| Matthew 6:19-21 | Do not lay up treasures on earth. |
| Matthew 11:25-30 | Come to me all who labor. |
| Matthew 25:31-46 | As you did it to one of the least |
| Matthew 28:1-10, 16-20 | Jesus' resurrection: Go make disciples. |
| Mark 16:1-8 | The open tomb: Jesus goes before you. |
| Luke 1:67-75 (UMH 208) | Canticle of Zechariah |
| Luke 12:22-40 | Do not be anxious; be ready. |
| Luke 24:1-12 | The empty tomb |
| John 3:13-17 | God's gift of eternal life |
| John 5:19-29 | Whoever hears and believes has life. |
| John 6:30-40, 47-51 | Jesus the bread of life |
| John 10:1-18, 27-30 | Jesus the Good Shepherd |
| John 12:20-36 | Unless a grain of wheat dies |
| John 15:1-17 | The vine and the branches |
| John 16:12-22, 33 | Sorrow becomes joy. |
| John 20 | Jesus' resurrection |

## Suggested Hymns from UMH

*See hymns 700-707 Death and Eternal Life and 708-712 Communion of the Sair Also see suggestions under Eternal Life and Funerals and Memorial Services UMH 940-42 and the following:*

163 Ask Ye What Great Thing I Know
557 Blest Be the Tie That Binds
141 Children of the Heavenly Father
318 Christ Is Alive
407 Close to Thee
709 Come, Let Us Join Our
    Friends Above
510 Come, Ye Disconsolate
315 Come, Ye Faithful, Raise the Strain
710 Faith of Our Fathers
129 Give to the Winds Thy Fears
654 How Blest Are They (for an
    older adult)
77 How Great Thou Art
103 Immortal, Invisible, God Only Wise
314 In the Garden
488 Jesus, Remember Me
133 Leaning on the Everlasting Arms
59 Mil Voces Para Celebrar
520 Nobody Knows the Trouble I See
57 O For a Thousand Tongues to Sing

143 On Eagle's Wings
733 Marching to Zion
368 My Hope Is Built
356 Pues Si Vivimos (When We Are Livi
66 Praise, My Soul, the King of Heav
    (stanzas 3, 4)
491 Remember Me
523 Saranam, Saranam (Refuge)
666 Shalom to You
512 Stand By Me
704 Steal Away to Jesus
496 Sweet Hour of Prayer
703 Swing Low, Sweet Chariot
395 Take Time to Be Holy
545 The Church's One Foundation
    (stanzas 1, 5)
546 The Church's One Foundation
    (stanzas 1, 5)
303 The Day of Resurrection
116 The God of Abraham Praise
504 The Old Rugged Cross

480 O Love That Wilt Not Let Me Go
247 O Morning Star, How Fair and
    Bright (stanza 3)
518 O Thou, in Whose Presence
184 Of the Father's Love Begotten

308 Thine Be the Glory
383 This Is a Day of New Beginnings
153 Thou Hidden Source of Calm Repose
322 Up from the Grave He Arose
526 What a Friend We Have in Jesus

*See also:*
Beloved, Now We Are the Saints of God ( ♪ 219).

# AT THE SERVICE FOR A CHILD

## *Words of Grace and Sentences*

Jesus said: "Truly I tell you, unless you change and become like children,
you will never enter the kingdom of heaven.
Whoever becomes humble like this child
is the greatest in the kingdom of heaven.
Take care that you do not despise one of these little ones;
for, I tell you, in heaven
their angels continually see the face of my Father in heaven.
it is not the will of your Father in heaven
that one of these little ones should be lost." (MATTHEW 18:3-4, 10, 14)

Jesus said: "Let the little children come to me,
and do not stop them;
for it is to such as these
that the kingdom of heaven belongs." (MATTHEW 19:14)

And he took them up in his arms,
laid his hands on them, and blessed them. (MARK 10:16)

The Lamb at the center of the throne will be their shepherd,
and he will guide them to springs of the water of life,
and God will wipe away every tear from their eyes. (REVELATION 7:17)

Friends, we have gathered to worship God and to witness to our faith
even as we mourn the death of this infant, the child of *Name* and *Name*.
We come together in grief, acknowledging our human loss.
May God search our hearts, that in pain we may find comfort,
in sorrow hope, in death resurrection.

*See also Psalm 103:8, 13-14, 17 (623-24).*

## *Prayers*

O God, whose dear Son took little children into his arms and blessed them:
give us grace, we pray,
to entrust this child to your never-failing love and care;
and bring us all to your eternal life;
through the same Jesus Christ our Lord. **Amen.**

O God, we pray that you will keep in your tender love
the life of this child whom we hold in blessed memory.
Help us who continue here to serve you with constancy,
trusting in your promise of eternal life, that hereafter
we may be united with your blessed children in glory everlasting;
through Jesus Christ our Lord. **Amen.**

God our Father, your love gave us life, and your care never fails.
Yours is the beauty of childhood,
and yours the light that shines in the face of age.
For all whom you have given to be dear to our hearts, we thank you,
and especially for this child you have taken to yourself.
Into the arms of your love we give *his/her* soul, remembering Jesus' word
"Let the children come unto me, for of such is the kingdom of heaven
To your love also we commend the sorrowing parents and family.
Show compassion to them as a father to his children;
comfort them as a mother her little ones.
As their love follows their hearts' treasure,
help them to trust that love they once have known is never lost,
that the child taken from their sight lives for ever in your presence.
Into your hands we also give ourselves,
our regret for whatever more we might have been or done,
our need to trust you more and to pray, all our struggle for a better li
Comfort us all. Keep tender and true the love in which we hold one anoth
Let not our longing for you ever cease.
May things unseen and eternal grow more real for us, more full of meanir
that in our living and dying you may be our peace. **Amen.**

O Lord, you keep little children in this present world,
and hold them close to yourself in the life to come.
Receive in peace the soul of your child *Name,*
for you have said, "Of such is my kingdom of heaven." **Amen.**

### Scripture Readings

| | |
|---|---|
| 2 Samuel 12:16-23 | David and the death of his child |
| Isaiah 65:17-25 | An infant who lives but a few days |
| Lamentations 3:19-26, 31-33 | Remember my affliction. God is good. |
| Joel 2:1, 12-13, 23-25a, 26-29 | Your sons and daughters will see visions. |
| Psalm 103:6-18 *(UMH 824)* | As a father pities his children |
| Matthew 11:25-30 | God revealed to infants |
| Matthew 18:1-5, 10-14 | Children are greatest in God's kingdom. |
| Matthew 19:13-15 | Let the children come to me. |
| (Also Mark 10:13-16; Luke 18:15-17) | |
| Mark 5:35-43 | Jesus' raising of the ruler's daughter |
| (Also Matthew 9:18-19, 23-26) | |

## Suggested Hymns from UMH

141 Children of the Heavenly Father        191 Jesus Loves Me
707 Hymn of Promise

# FOR AN UNTIMELY OR TRAGIC DEATH

## Words of Grace and Sentences

essed be the God who consoles us in all our affliction,
that we may be able to console those who are in any affliction
with the consolation
with which we ourselves are consoled by God.        (2 Corinthians 1:3a, 4)

ist your burden on the Lord, and God will sustain you.    (Psalm 55:22a, alt.)

## Prayers

sus our Friend, you wept at the grave of Lazarus,
you know all our sorrows.
hold our tears, and bind up the wounds of our hearts.
rough the mystery of pain,
bring us into closer communion with you and with one another.
ise us from death into life.
d grant, in your mercy, that with Name, who has passed within the veil,
we may come to live, with you and with all whom we love,
in our Father's home. **Amen.**

d of us all, we thank you for Christ's grace,
through which we pray to you in this dark hour.
life we love has been torn from us.
pectations the years once held have vanished.
e mystery of death has stricken us.
God, you know the lives we live and the deaths we die—
woven so strangely of purpose and of chance,
    of reason and of the irrational,
f strength and of frailty, of happiness and of pain.
o your hands we commend the soul of Name.
mortal life you have made is without eternal meaning.
earthly fate is beyond your redeeming.
rough your grace that can do far more than we can think or imagine,
ulfill in Name your purpose that reaches beyond time and death.
ad Name from strength to strength,
nd fit Name for love and service in your kingdom.
o your hands also we commit our lives.
u alone, God, make us to dwell in safety.

Whom, finally, have we on earth or in heaven but you?
Help us to know the measure of our days, and how frail we are.
Hold us in your keeping. Forgive us our sins.
Save our minds from despair and our hearts from fear.
And guard and guide us with your peace. **Amen.**

Everliving God, in Christ's resurrection
  you turned the disciples' despair into triumph, their sorrow into joy
Give us faith to believe that every good that seems to be overcome by evil
  and every love that seems to be buried in death,
  shall rise again to life eternal;
through Jesus Christ, who lives and reigns with you for ever more. **Amen.**

Almighty God, in your keeping there is shelter from the storm,
  and in your mercy there is comfort for the sorrows of life.
Hear now our prayer for those who mourn and are heavy laden.
Give to them strength to bear and do your will.
Lighten their darkness with your love.
Enable them to see beyond the things of this mortal world
  the promise of the eternal.
Help them to know that your care enfolds all your people,
  that you are our refuge and strength,
  and that underneath are your everlasting arms. **Amen.**

### Scripture Readings

| | |
|---|---|
| Lamentations 3:19-26, 31-33 | Remember my affliction. God is good. |
| Psalm 103 (UMH 824) | Bless the Lord, who redeems from death. |
| Revelation 21:1-6; 22:1-5 | God will wipe away every tear. |
| See Canticle of Hope (UMH 734) | |
| Mark 4:35-41 | Jesus' calming of the storm |
| Luke 15:11-32 | The prodigal son |
| John 6:35-40 | God's will that nothing be lost |

### Suggested Hymns from UMH

534 Be Still, My Soul
557 Blest Be the Tie That Binds
141 Children of the Heavenly Father
510 Come, Ye Disconsolate
129 Give to the Winds Thy Fears
128 He Leadeth Me: O Blessed Thought
707 Hymn of Promise (esp. for a youth)
452 My Faith Looks Up to Thee

528 Nearer, My God, to Thee
117 O God, Our Help in Ages Past
480 O Love That Wilt Not Let Me Go
474 Precious Lord, Take My Hand
356 Pues Si Vivimos (When We Are Living
  esp. for a young adult)
308 Thine Be the Glory (especially for
  middle adult)
525 We'll Understand It Better By and By

# AT THE SERVICE FOR A PERSON
# WHO DID NOT PROFESS THE CHRISTIAN FAITH

*he faith of the deceased or of the mourners is such that the pastor considers parts of*
*Service of Death and Resurrection inappropriate, adaptations may be made with*
*propriate consultation so that no one's integrity is violated. The acts of worship*
*ow may not be appropriate for persons who were adherents of other religions.*

### Words of Grace and Sentences

.e eternal God is our dwelling place,
and underneath are the everlasting arms.    (DEUTERONOMY 33:27 RSV, ALT.)

.e Lord is near to the brokenhearted,
and saves the crushed in spirit.    (PSALM 34:18, *UMH* 770)

e Lord heals the brokenhearted, and binds up their wounds.
eat is our Lord, and abundant in power,
whose understanding is beyond measure.    (PSALM 147:3, 5, *UMH* 859)

### Prayers

God our Father, Creator of us all, giver and preserver of all life:
confess to you our slowness to accept death as part of your plan for life.
confess our reluctance to commit to you those whom we love.
store our faith that we may come to trust in your care and providence;
'ough Jesus Christ our Lord. **Amen.**

Lord, from everlasting to everlasting you are God.
ok down upon our sorrowing hearts today, we humbly pray,
nd be gracious to us.
lp all who mourn to cast every care upon you, and find comfort;
ough Jesus Christ our Lord. **Amen.**

nighty God, the fountain of all life,
ur refuge and strength and our help in trouble:
able us, we pray, to put our trust in you,
hat we may obtain comfort,
nd find grace to help in this and every time of need;
ough Jesus Christ our Lord. **Amen.**

rnal God, you know all things in earth and heaven.
fill our hearts with trust in you
hat, by night and by day, at all times and in all seasons,
ve may without fear commit those who are dear to us
o your never-failing love, for this life and the life to come. **Amen.**

nighty and everlasting God,
ou are always more ready to hear than we are to pray,
o give more than we desire or deserve.
ir out upon us your great mercy,

forgiving those things of which our conscience is afraid,
and giving us those good things we are not worthy to ask,
but through Jesus Christ our Lord. **Amen.**

*Scripture Readings*

| | |
|---|---|
| Ecclesiastes 3:1-15 | For everything there is a season. |
| Lamentations 3:1-9, 19-26 | God's steadfast love |
| Psalm 39 *(UMH 773)* | Make me to know the measure of my days |
| Romans 14:7-13 | Why do you pass judgment? |
| Matthew 5:1-12 | The Beatitudes |
| Matthew 25:31-46 | As you did it to one of the least |
| Luke 20:27-39 | God of the living, to whom all live |
| (Also Matthew 22:23-33; Mark 12:18-27) | |

*Suggested Hymn from* UMH

707 Hymn of Promise

# MINISTRY WITH THE DYING

*When death is near, the pastor should be notified so that the ministry of the Chu*
*may be extended.*

*Holy Communion may be administered, using A Service of Word and Table V (51-*
*or adapting A Service of Word and Table IV (see 41-50).*

*The Baptismal Covenant may be reaffirmed, using portions of The Baptis*
*Covenant I (86-94) as may be appropriate.*

*The pastor, joined by others as they are able, may pray the Lord's Prayer or Psalm .*

*See also resources for Ministry with Persons with Life-threatening Illness (628-2*

*The pastor may pray one or more of the following prayers:*

Lord Jesus Christ, deliver your child *Name* from all evil
and set *him/her* free from every bond;
that *he/she* may rest with all your saints
in the joy of your eternal home, for ever and ever. **Amen.**

Gracious God, you are nearer than hands or feet, closer than breathi
Sustain with your presence our *brother/sister Name.*
Help *him/her* now to trust in your goodness
and claim your promise of life everlasting.
Cleanse *him/her* of all sin and remove all burdens.
Grant *him/her* the sure joy of your salvation,
through Jesus Christ our Lord. **Amen.**

*When a life-support system is withdrawn:*

God, you are the Alpha and Omega, the beginning and the end.
ɔu breathed into us the breath of life,
and watched over us all our days.
ɔw, in time of death, we return *Name* to you,
trusting in your steadfast love,
rough Jesus Christ our Savior. **Amen.**

*commendation at the time of death, the pastor laying his/her hand on the head of the
ing person:*

ɛpart in peace, *brother/sister Name;*
in the name of God the Father who created you;
in the name of Christ who redeemed you;
in the name of the Holy Spirit who sanctifies you.
ɪy you rest in peace, and dwell for ever with the Lord.

# MINISTRY IMMEDIATELY FOLLOWING DEATH

*ministering to the bereaved immediately following a death, the pastor may pray
emporaneously, or pray one or more of the prayers of commendation on 149-50, or
following:*

nighty God, our Creator and Redeemer,
ɪ have given us our *brother/sister Name,*
ɔ know and to love in our pilgrimage on earth.
hold us now
ɪs we entrust *him/her* to your boundless love and eternal care.
sure us that not even death can separate us from your infinite mercy.
al graciously with us who mourn,
hat we may truly know your sure consolation
ɪnd learn to live in confident hope of the resurrection;
ough your Son, Jesus Christ our Lord. **Amen.**

t of the depths we cry to you, O Lord. Hear our voice.
᾽ wait for you, O God. Our souls wait for you.
ʾe us now your word of hope.
᾽ know your love is steadfast, always there when we need it.
us feel your presence now in our time of sorrow.
lp us to look to tomorrow to see hope beyond grief,
ough Jesus Christ our Lord. **Amen.**

*er the death of a child:*

ʾing God, as your son Jesus took children into his arms
nd blessed them,
ɛ us grace to entrust *Name* into your steadfast love,
ɔugh Jesus Christ our Savior. **Amen.**

*After the birth of a stillborn child or the death of a newly born child:*

Merciful God, you strengthen us by your power and wisdom.
Be gracious to Name *(and Name)* in *their (her)* grief
  and surround *them (her)* with your unfailing love;
that *they (she)* may not be overwhelmed by *their (her)* loss
  but have confidence in your goodness,
  and courage to meet the days to come;
through Jesus Christ our Lord. **Amen.**

*See A Service of Death and Resurrection for a Stillborn Child (170-71) and prayers*
*A Service of Hope After Loss of Pregnancy (623-26).*

# A FAMILY HOUR OR WAKE

*It is appropriate for family and friends to gather for sharing and prayers in the churc*
*funeral home, or family home on the day or night before the Service of Death a*
*Resurrection.*

*This order out of an African American worship tradition may be used for su*
*occasions, or the service may be as informal as is desired. It may be led by either cler*
*or laypersons. Acts of worship suggested for the Service of Death and Resurrecti*
*may be included or substituted for those below. The coffin may be open or clos*
*depending on the wishes of the family.*

*If the deceased is a member of a fraternal or other organization that customarily ho*
*services for its deceased members, the one appointed by that organization may wish*
*conduct a special service according to its customs. Plans for such services should*
*made in consultation with the family and subject to the approval of the pasto*

## GATHERING

*Greetings and condolences may be exchanged with family and friends.*

## GREETINGS OR INTRODUCTORY REMARKS

*The leader may open with a brief greeting or introductory statement on behalf of*
*church, family, and friends, such as:*

Friends, we are gathered here
  to honor the memory of our departed friend and *brother/sister, Na*

## HYMN

*If desired, one or more stanzas of a well-known hymn or song, such as the follow*
*from UMH or those recommended above (160-61), may be sung or recited:*

700 Abide with Me                          452 My Faith Looks Up to Thee
128 He Leadeth Me: O Blessed Thought       526 What a Friend We Have in Jesus
357 Just As I Am, Without One Plea

# PRAYER

*The leader or some other designated person may pray an extemporaneous prayer, or the following or another prayer:*

Gracious God,
as your Son wept with Mary and Martha at the tomb of Lazarus,
look with compassion on those who grieve [especially *Names*].

*Silence may be kept.*

Grant them the assurance of your presence now
and faith in your eternal goodness,
that in them may be fulfilled the promise
that those who mourn shall be comforted;
through Jesus Christ our Lord. **Amen.**

# SCRIPTURE

*One of the following, or another scripture (see 144-48 and 159-60), may be read:*

| | |
|---|---|
| Psalm 23 (*UMH* 754) | The Lord is my shepherd. |
| Psalm 27 (*UMH* 758) | The Lord is my light. |
| Psalm 90:1-6, 12, 16-17 (*UMH* 809) | From everlasting to everlasting |
| Psalm 121 (*UMH* 844) | I lift up my eyes to the hills. |
| John 14:1-10a, 15-21, 25-27 | Do not let your hearts be troubled. |

# WITNESS

*Family, friends, and members of the congregation may briefly voice their thankfulness to God for the grace they have received in the life of the deceased and their Christian faith and joy. Signs of faith, hope, and love may be exchanged.*

# CLOSING PRAYER OR BLESSING

*The following or another prayer or blessing may be spoken or sung:*

The Lord bless us and keep us.
The Lord make his face to shine upon us and be gracious to us.
The Lord lift up his countenance upon us and give us peace. **Amen.**

(NUMBERS 6:24-26, ALT.)

# A SERVICE OF DEATH AND RESURRECTION FOR A STILLBORN CHILD

*In addition to, or instead of, the following acts of worship, other acts of worship fro*
*161-63 or from A Service of Hope After Loss of Pregnancy (623-26) may be include*

THE WORD OF GRACE *See 161 or 623-24.*

GREETING

Friends, we have gathered here in our grief
to praise God and witness to our faith.
We come together in grief,
acknowledging our human loss of one so young.
[*He/She* has been given the name _____ by *his/her* parents,
with the Church's blessing.]
May God grant us grace, that in pain we may find comfort,
in sorrow hope, in death resurrection.

PRAYER *

*One or both of the following is suggested:*

Almighty God, loving Parent of all your children,
we come in sorrow that *Name* has been taken from us so soon.
Sometimes the burdens of life almost overwhelm us.
Yet we put our full trust in you,
knowing that through your Son Jesus Christ you are with us alway
We take comfort that your loving arms
surround us in our time of grief.
Be with *Name's* mother, who has carried *him/her* with love for so lor
We know you feel her disappointment and pain.
May her faith be renewed in the days ahead
as she regains her strength.
Be with *Name's father and/or other family members.*
You know the heaviness of *his* (*their*) heart(s).
Pour out upon *them* (*her*) your gracious healing,
in the name of Jesus Christ, the great Physician, we pray. **Amen.**

Blessed Jesus, lover of children,
in lowliness of heart we cry to you for help.
Expecting the life of a child, we have witnessed *his/her* death.
Our despair is profound, and we know you weep with us in our lo
Help us to hear your consoling voice,
and give healing to our grief, merciful Savior. **Amen.**

*In some circumstances a prayer of confession and pardon (see 143) may*
*appropriate. If the pastor feels this is the case, the issue should also be addressee*
*the sermon and in counseling.*

## CRIPTURE

*One or more of the following is suggested:*

| | |
|---|---|
| Psalm 23 (*UMH* 754) | The Lord is my shepherd. |
| Psalm 130 (*UMH* 848) | Out of the depths I cry to you. |
| 2 Corinthians 1:3-7 | God consoles us in all our affliction. |
| Matthew 11:28-30 | Come to me, all who carry heavy burdens. |

*See also the readings listed on 159-60.*

## ERMON

## RAYER OF COMMENDATION *

All-loving and caring God, Parent of us all,
   you know our grief in our loss,
   for you too suffered the death of your child.
Give us strength to go forward from this day,
   trusting, where we do not understand, that your love never ends.
When all else fails, you still are God.
We thank you for the life and hope
   that you give
   through the resurrection of your Son Jesus Christ.
We pray to you for one another in our need,
   and for all, anywhere, who mourn with us this day.
To those who doubt, give light; to those who are weak, strength;
   to all who have sinned, mercy; to all who sorrow, your peace.
Keep true in us the love with which we hold one another.
And to you, with your Church on earth and in heaven,
   we offer honor and praise, now and for ever. **Amen.**

*Here the pastor, with others, standing near the coffin or urn, may lay hands on it,
continuing:*

Receive *Name* into the arms of your mercy.
Receive us also, and raise us into a new life.
Help us so to love and serve you in this world
   that we may enter into your joy in the world to come. **Amen.**

*The pastor may administer Holy Communion. See 152-54.*

## RAYER OF THANKSGIVING *See 150-51.*

*If the Committal is part of the service, it occurs at this point.*

## E LORD'S PRAYER * *See UMH 270-71, 894-96.*

## SMISSAL WITH BLESSING * *See 151.*

*A Service of Committal may follow at the final resting place. The service on 155-57
may be adapted in accord with the specific needs.*

# II. MUSIC AS ACTS OF WORSHIP

## INTRODUCTION

"Sing all. See that you join with the congregation as frequently as you ca
Let not a slight degree of weakness or weariness hinder you. If it is a cross
you, take it up, and you will find it a blessing" *From John Wesley's Directio*
*for Singing.*

From the beginning of the early Church, worship has involved t
community singing. The following pages maintain this tradition of variety
music for worship.

This music provides focus to the congregation's acts of singing. Most
these pieces are for use throughout the Christian year, and some piec
relate to specific litanies, prayers, and orders of worship. Also note th
many pieces are particularly appropriate for children and youth.

Much of the music presented here is new. Rehearsal for the worship leade
and the congregation is highly recommended. The Gathering time
especially appropriate to rehearse the congregation. A songleader in t
pulpit, lectern, or other designated place may also enhance the learning a
singing of these pieces.

Limited permission is given for reprinting and using these acts of worship
congregational worship. See page 744 for more information.

For harmonizations, see the *Accompaniment Edition to The United Methodist Book of Worship.*
available as a supplement to the seven-ring binder that contains the Keyboard Edition of *The Un*
*Methodist Hymnal,* 1989.

## BAPTISMAL RESPONSES

# Come, Be Baptized

173

Come, be bap-tized in the name of the Fa-ther,

come, be bap-tized in the name of the Son,

come, be bap-tized in the name of the Spir-it,

come, be bap-tized in love.

)RDS and MUSIC: Gary Alan Smith
)82 Hope Publishing Company

**174**

# Baptismal Prayer

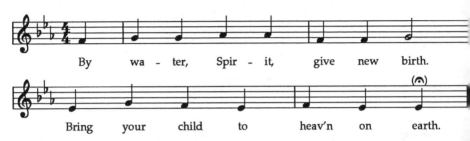

By wa - ter, Spir - it, give new birth.

Bring your child to heav'n on earth.

WORDS and MUSIC: Steve Garnaas-Holmes
© 1992 Abingdon Press

**175**

# God Claims You

*Sing Refrain twice at beginning and end, and once between stanzas.*

*"Dan - iel, Dan - iel," God claims you, God
or Child of prom - ise,

helps you, pro - tects you, and loves you, too.

1. We this day do all a - gree a
** 2. We your fam - ily love you so, we
3. We are here to say this day that
4. And if you should tire or cry then

child of God you'll al - ways be.
vow to help your faith to grow.
we will help you on your way.
we will sing this lul - la - by.

* *may insert child's name*
** *may insert parents' names "Jeff and Kathy love you so, we vow ..."*

WORDS and MUSIC: Stanley M. Farr
© 1981 Stanley M. Farr

# RESPONSES FOR GENERAL ACTS OF WORSHIP

## Heleluyan (Hallelujah) 176

**Paraphrase (for information only):**

*Refrain*

I will sing hallelujah,
I will sing hallelujah.

Christian people are there (in heaven)
and I will sing hallelujah with them
when I get there.

Erkenakvlke (Elth-kee-nah-kah-kee) ...
(The ministers ...)

Purahvlket (Po-thla-hah-ket) ...
(The elders ...)

Pucusvlket (Po-cho-sah-ket) ...
(The younger ones ...)

5   Puwantaket (Po-wahn-ta-ket) ...
(Our sisters ...)

6.   Hopuetaket (Ho-po-ee-ta-ket) ...
(Our children ...)

7.   Vkvsamvlket (Ah-kah-sah-mah-ket) ...
(Believers ...)

8.   Emestvlket (E-mess-tah-ket) ...
(God's people ...)

9.   Pumetvlwvlket (Po-me-tah-wah-ket) ...
(Our communities ...)

)RDS: Traditional Muscogee (Creek); phonetic transliteration by Marilyn M. Hofstra, Choctaw,
Chickasaw; English paraphrase by Leona Sullivan, Creek

'SIC: Traditional Muscogee (Creek); transcription by Marilyn M. Hofstra, Choctaw, Chickasaw
netic transliteration and transcription © 1992 Marilyn M. Hofstra. All rights reserved.
lish paraphrase © 1992 Leona Sullivan

## 177 Amen Siakudumisa (Great Amen)

Ma - si - thi: A - men, si - ya - ku - du - mi - sa, Ma - si - thi:
Sing a - men: A - men, we praise your name, O Lord, Sing a - men:

A - men, si - ya - ku - du - mi - sa, Ma - si - thi: A - men. Ba - wo,
A - men, we praise your name, O Lord, Sing a - men: A - men, a - men,

A - men, Ba - wo, A - men, si - ya - ku - du - mi - sa.
a - men, a - men, A - men, we praise your name, O Lord.

WORDS: Traditional South African originally from the Xhosa language
MUSIC: Attributed to S. C. Molefe as taught by George Mxadana
Words and Music © The Lumko Institute

## 178 Amen, Praise the Father

1. A - men, Praise the Fa - ther; A - men, Praise our Mak - er
2. A - men, Praise the Son; ___ A - men, Praise our Sav - ior
3. A - men, Praise the Spir - it; A - men, Praise our Teach - er

3rd time only

A - men, ___ A - men. ___ A - men.

WORDS and MUSIC: Leng Loh, Asian American
© 1983 Leng Loh

# Offertory Hymn: For the Gift of Creation  179

For the gift of cre - a - tion, the gift of your love,

and the gift of the Spir - it by which we live,

we thank you and give you the fruit of our hands.

May your grace be pro - claimed by the gifts _____ that we give.

ORDS and MUSIC: Steve Garnaas-Holmes
.992 Abingdon Press

# Praise God, from Whom All Blessings Flow  180

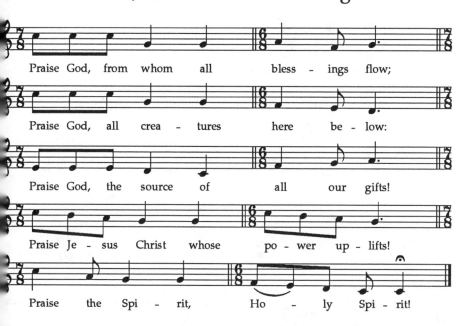

Praise God, from whom all bless - ings flow;

Praise God, all crea - tures here be - low:

Praise God, the source of all our gifts!

Praise Je - sus Christ whose po - wer up - lifts!

Praise the Spi - rit, Ho - ly Spi - rit!

ORDS: Thomas Ken, 1674; adapted by Gilbert H. Vieira, 1978
USIC: Constance Biau-Oan Fang, Asian American
ptation © 1989 The United Methodist Publishing House; music © 1992 Abingdon Press

## 181 Introit: Sing to the Lord a New Song

Sing to the Lord a new song,_____

for God has done_____ mar - ve - lous things.

*Congregation repeats this Refrain after Choir sings Verse*

WORDS: Psalm 98
MUSIC: Skinner Chávez-Melo, Mexican
© 1992 Abingdon Press

## 182 Doxology

Dadd9 ... Gadd9

1. Glad - ly we praise you and bless you, Cre -
2. Christ, we a - dore you and thank you, com -

Aadd9 ... Gadd9 ... Aadd9 ... Dadd9

a - tor, O God of Life._____
pas - sion of God, our Light._____

Bb ... C

3. Great Ho - ly Spir - it, by you we are

C ... D ... G ... A ... G ... D

born from a - bove!_____ Al - le - lu - ia!

Em ... A ... D ... D7 ... G

Praise the God of bless - ing! Al -

A ... D ... Em ... A7 ... D

le - lu - ia! Bless the God of Love!_____

WORDS and MUSIC: Steve Garnaas-Holmes
© 1992 Abingdon Press

## God Hears Our Every Need 183

God hears our ev - ery need.

WORDS and MUSIC: James Kriewald
1992 Abingdon Press

## Kiowa Hymn: A Call to Worship 184

♩ = 40

1. Dau - kgeah-ee, Ai dau - chai____ ahn,
2. Dau - kgeah-ee, Ai dau - chai____ ahn,

Dau - kgeah-ee, Ai dau - chai ahn,
Dau - kgeah-ee, Ai dau - chai ahn,

Ahm thdoe ____ gah dau, doi ahn,
Aim key - dah day, doi ahn,

Ai chain_____ doe ghat thi ahm.
Ai chain_____ doe ghat thi ahm.

*Kiowa*

Daukgeahee, Ai dauchai ahn,
Daugeahee, Ai dauchai ahn,
Ahm thdoe gah dau, doi ahn,
Ai chain doe ghat thi ahm.

Daukgeahee, Ai dauchai ahn,
Daukgeahee, Ai dauchai ahn,
Aim keydah day, doi ahn,
Ai chain doe ghat thi ahm.

*Paraphrase (for information only)*

Son of God, we have come to pray,
We have come to your house to pray.
Because we have come, help us.

Son of God, we have come to pray,
We have come to pray because it is your
day.
Because we have come, help us.

WORDS: Traditional Kiowa; phonetic transliteration by Marilyn M. Hofstra, Choctaw, Chickasaw;
English paraphrase by Dorothy Gray, Kiowa

MUSIC: Traditional Kiowa; transcription by Marilyn M. Hofstra, Choctaw, Chickasaw

## 185   Praise God, from Whom All Blessings Flow

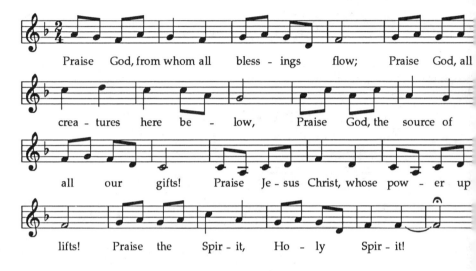

Praise God, from whom all bless - ings flow; Praise God, all
crea - tures here be - low, Praise God, the source of
all our gifts! Praise Je - sus Christ, whose pow - er up
lifts! Praise the Spir - it, Ho - ly Spir - it!

WORDS: Thomas Ken, 1674; adapted by Gilbert H. Vieira, 1978
MUSIC: Constance Biau-Oan Fang, Asian American
Adaptation © 1989 The United Methodist Publishing House; music © 1992 Abingdon Press

## 186   An Indian Blessing

Ye - shu   su - pri - ya,
Je - sus,   lov - ing   Lord;

Ye - shu   a - shra - ye,
Je - sus,   strength and   stay,

Ye - shu   pri - ya   ta - ra - ka,   sa -
in   your   mer - cy   bless   us   all   and

ha - ya   ho - ma - la.
keep   us   night and   day.

WORDS and MUSIC: Traditional Hindi

## Jesus, We Are Here 187

Je - sus, we are here, Je - sus, we are here,

Je - sus. we are here, we are here for you.

ORDS and MUSIC: Patrick Matsikenyiri, African

usic © 1990 Patrick Matsikenyiri; Eng. trans. © 1990 Iona Community. G.I.A. Publications, Inc. North American Agents

## Señor, Apiádate de Nosotros 188
## (O Lord, Have Mercy Upon Us)

Se - ñor, a - piá - da - te de no - so - tros.
O Lord, have mer-cy up-on your peo - ple.

Cris - to, a - piá - da - te de no - so - tros.
O Christ, have mer - cy up - on your peo - ple.

O Cris - to, da - nos la vi - da e - ter - na.
O Mas - ter, give us your life for - ev - er.

Se - ñor, a - piá - da - te de no - so - tros.
O Lord, have mer-cy up-on your peo - ple.

Cris - to, a - piá - da - te de no - so - tros.
O Christ, have mer-cy up-on your peo - ple.

ORDS and MUSIC: Traditional Colombia; arranged by Alvin Schutmaat; trans. by Gertrude Suppe

189
# May This Mind Be in Us

MUSIC: James Ritchie

Music © 1992 Abingdon Press; text used by permission of Oxford University Press

(See 514 for full litany)

# Benediction

*Narrative:*
> The Lord bless you and keep you,

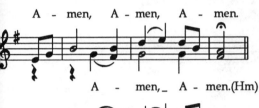

*Narrative:*
> The Lord make his face to shine upon you and be gracious unto you,

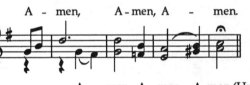

*Narrative:*
> The Lord lift up his countenance upon you and give you peace.

*e hum should begin immediately as each "amen" is sung.*

WORDS: Numbers 6:24-26
MUSIC: William Farley Smith, African American
1975 William Farley Smith

191 **May This Mind Be in Us**

May this mind be in us which was in Je-sus Christ.

WORDS: Philippians 2:5 (alt.)
MUSIC: Philip E. Baker
Music © 1992 Abingdon Press

*(See 514 for full litany.)*

192 **Jesus, We Are Praying**

*Choir (or Leader)* *All*

Je-sus, we are pray-ing. Je-sus, are you lis-tening?

*Choir*

Oh, yes, I'm lis-ten-ing to you.

*All*

Je-sus, we are pray-ing, Je-sus, are you lis-tening

*Choir*

Oh, lis-ten, I am pray-ing, too. I'm pray-ing for you.

WORDS and MUSIC: Steve Garnaas-Holmes
© 1992 Abingdon Press

# Prayer for Wisdom 193

Wis - dom, you are my sis - ter, _____ let us
walk to - geth - er hand in hand.
Teach me the ways of your heart; _____
help me to un - der - stand. _____

WORDS: Proverbs 7:4 and 3:13-18; Psalm 25:4
MUSIC: Steve Garnaas-Holmes
1992 Abingdon Press

# Teach Me to Hear in Silence 194

♩ = 54

Teach me to hear in si - lence, _____
_____ to lis - ten and un - der - stand,
in qui - et com - mun - ion with you.

WORDS: Susan Gregg-Schroeder
MUSIC: Daniel Burton
1992 Abingdon Press

195

# O Lord, Deliver Us

*last time only*

O Lord, de - liv - er us! A - men.

MUSIC: Sally Ahner
© 1992 Abingdon Press

*(See 520 for full litany.)*

196

# Call to Prayer

While I'm down here pray-ing, Lord, search my heart.

While I'm down here moan-ing, Lord, search my heart;

While I'm down here cry-ing, Lord, search my heart! You

know Lord, all a - bout me! Do, Lord, search my heart.

WORDS: African American spiritual (Psalm 139)
MUSIC: African American spiritual; adapted by William Farley Smith, African American
Adaptation © 1992 Abingdon Press

# Shawnee Traveling Song 197

*The grandfathers teach us that sometimes the best way to think deep thoughts is to ccupy a part of the mind with the trivial. Thus the traveling song is made up of repeated llables with no meaning, but we are taught to sing another song in our hearts. That dwelling song is as follows.*

I am walking upon the earth;
 the earth is my mother.
Wherever I walk,
 I will be home.

I am walking with the people who
 love me
 their love surrounds me.
Wherever I walk,
 I will be loved.

I am walking on the circle of Creator;
 Creator above, Creator below.
Wherever I walk,
 I am with Creator.

I am walking upon the earth
 with people who love me
 on the circle of Creator.
I will always be home.
I will always be loved.
I will be with Creator.

Hey a lo - ma, Hey a lo - ma. Hey o - pa - lo - ma.

Hey o - pa - lo - ma, Hey o - pa - lay,

Hey o - pa - lo - ma, Hey o - pa - lay.

Hey o - pa - lo - ma, Hey o - pa - lay.

Hey o - pa - lo - ma, Hey o - pa - lay

a Hey o - pa - lay a Hey o - pa - lay. a Hey!

ORDS: Fred A. Shaw / Neeake
USIC: Traditional Shawnee as used by the Shawnee Nation United Remnant Band
987 Fred Shaw / Neeake, Shawnee Nation United Remnant Band

*is may be sung as a song of sending forth or congregational benediction. All may sing "Hey a loma"
choir alone) as the leader or congregation reads the indwelling song.*

## 198     May the Warm Winds of Heaven

May the warm winds of hea - ven blow soft - ly on your house.

May the Great Spir - it bless all who en - ter here.

WORDS: Traditional Cherokee Nation prayer
MUSIC: John Thornburg
Music © 1992 Abingdon Press

## 199     Come! Come! Everybody Worship!

*Refrain*

Come!     Come!     Eve - ry - bod - y wor - ship
¡Ven - gan     to - dos a - do - re - mos

with a prayer or song of praise! Come! Come!
con can - tos y o - ra - ción! ¡Ven - gan *Fi*

Eve - ry - bod - y wor - ship! Wor - ship God al - ways!
to - dos a - do - re - mos a nues - tro Se - ñor!

1. Wor - ship and re - mem - ber to keep the Sab - bath day.
2. Wor - ship and re - mem - ber the Lord's un - end - ing care,
3. Wor - ship and re - mem - ber your bless - ings great and small.
4. Wor - ship and re - mem - ber how Je - sus long a - go
5. Wor - ship and re - mem - ber that God is like a light,

Take a rest and think of God; put your work a - way!
reach - ing out to love and help peo - ple ev - 'ry - where!
Give to God an of - fer - ing; show your thanks for all!
taught us how to talk to God; some thing we should know!
show - ing you the way to go; ev - er burn - ing bright!

WORDS and MUSIC: Natalie Sleeth; Spanish trans. by Mary Lou Santillán-Baert
© 1991 by Cokesbury. Used by permission.

## May the Warm Winds of Heaven   200

May the warm winds of hea-ven blow soft - ly on your house. May the

May the warm winds blow soft - ly on your house. May the

Great Spir - it bless all who en - ter here. _____

WORDS: Traditional Cherokee Nation prayer
MUSIC: Sally Ahner
Music © 1992 Abingdon Press

## O Lamb of God   201

**Leader**

O Lamb of God that tak - est a - way the sins of ___ the

1. *All*   2. *All*

world, ___ have mer - cy___ up - on us. have mer - cy___ up -

**Leader**

on us. O Lamb of God that tak - est a - way the

*All*

sins _____ of the world, grant us___ thy peace.

(♪·)

MUSIC: Raquel Mora Martínez, Mexican American
© 1992 Abingdon Press

## 202   Where Two or Three Are Gathered

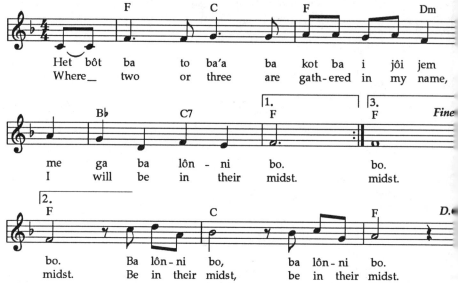

Het bôt ba to ba'a ba kot ba i jôi jem
Where_ two or three are gath-ered in my name,

me ga ba lôn - ni bo.   bo.
I will be in their midst.   midst.

bo.   Ba lôn - ni bo,   ba lôn - ni bo.
midst.   Be in their midst,   be in their midst.

WORDS: Matthew 18:20
MUSIC: Alfred Bayiga, Cameroon
© Alfred Bayiga

## 203   Tino tenda Jesu (Thank You Jesus)

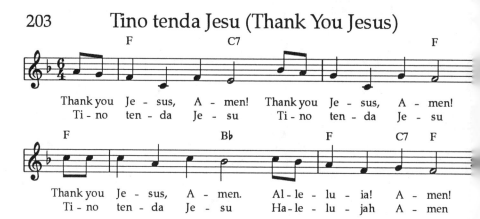

Thank you Je - sus, A - men! Thank you Je - sus, A - men!
Ti - no ten - da Je - su Ti - no ten - da Je - su

Thank you Je - sus, A - men. Al - le - lu - ia! A - men!
Ti - no ten - da Je - su Ha - le - lu - jah A - men

WORDS: Original Shona language, trans. by Patrick Matsikenyiri, African
MUSIC: African folk song, transcription by Patrick Matsikenyiri, African
Eng. trans. and music transcription © Church Music Service, The United Methodist Church of Zimbabwe

## Praised Be Our Lord

Praised_____ be our Lord.

IC: Daniel Burton
2 Abingdon Press

*507 for full litany.)*

## Shine on Me

**205**

Shine on me,_____ shine on me, let the

light from the light-house _____ shine on me.

Shine on me,_____ shine on me. Let the

light from the light-house_____ shine on me.

RDS: African American spiritual (Matthew 11:28; Luke 11:36)
SIC: African American spiritual; adapted by William Farley Smith, African American
otation © 1992 Abingdon Press

## RESPONSES FOR THE CHRISTIAN YEAR

206      ## Entrance Song for Advent

Came he not in fire, _____ on - ward came the

Lord. _____ Not in wind or rain, _____

on - ward came the Lord. _____ Hail nor sleet or

snow, _____ on - ward came the Lord. _____

In a still small voice came He, ____ on - ward came the Lord!

WORDS and MUSIC: William Farley Smith (1 Kings 19:12), African American

# Come, Lord Jesus 207

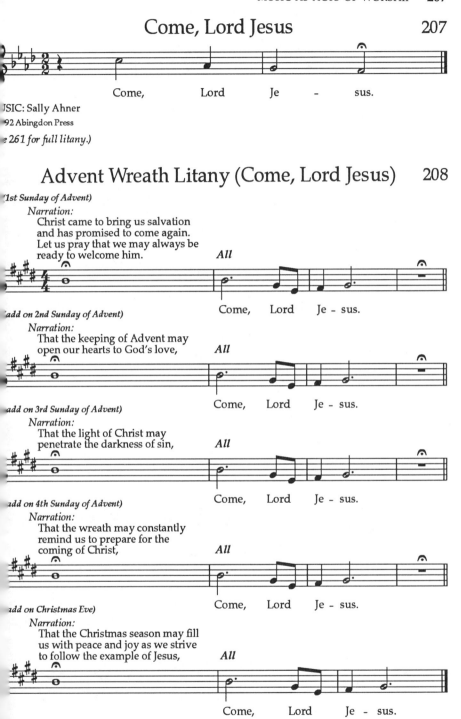

Come, Lord Je - sus.

JSIC: Sally Ahner
92 Abingdon Press
*e 261 for full litany.)*

# Advent Wreath Litany (Come, Lord Jesus) 208

*(1st Sunday of Advent)*

*Narration:*
Christ came to bring us salvation
and has promised to come again.
Let us pray that we may always be
ready to welcome him.  *All*

Come, Lord Je - sus.

*(add on 2nd Sunday of Advent)*

*Narration:*
That the keeping of Advent may
open our hearts to God's love,  *All*

Come, Lord Je - sus.

*(add on 3rd Sunday of Advent)*

*Narration:*
That the light of Christ may
penetrate the darkness of sin,  *All*

Come, Lord Je - sus.

*(add on 4th Sunday of Advent)*

*Narration:*
That the wreath may constantly
remind us to prepare for the
coming of Christ,  *All*

Come, Lord Je - sus.

*(add on Christmas Eve)*

*Narration:*
That the Christmas season may fill
us with peace and joy as we strive
to follow the example of Jesus,  *All*

Come, Lord Je - sus.

SIC: Gary Alan Smith

*c* © 1992 Gamut Music Productions; words © 1988 by the United States Catholic Conference, Washington, D.C.

*261 for full litany.)*

209   # Advent Candle Song

1. Light one can - dle:   Christ is com - ing,
2. Light two can - dles:   Christ is com - ing,
3. Light three can - dles:   Christ is com - ing,
4. Light four can - dles:   Christ is com - ing,
5. Light the white one   Christ is born, _____

Christ, the Hope of the world.   Light one can - dle:
Christ, the Way for the world.   Light two can - dles:
Christ, the Joy of the world.   Light three can - dles:
Christ, the Peace of the world.   Light four can - dles:
Christ, the Light of the world.   Light the white one:

Christ is com - ing,   Christ is com - ing   soon!
Christ is com - ing,   Christ is com - ing   soon!
Christ is com - ing,   Christ is com - ing   soon!
Christ is com - ing,   Christ is com - ing   soon!
Christ is born, ____   Christ is born to - day!
                                              (to - night!)

WORDS and MUSIC: Sally Ahner
© 1992 Abingdon Press

210   # I Am the Lamp

I am the lamp _____ and

Je - sus is the light; _____   I am the

can - dle _____ and Je - sus is the flame. _____

*May be sung unaccompanied as a two-part round*

WORDS and MUSIC: James Ritchie
© 1984, 1990 James Ritchie

# Prepare the Way

Pre - pare the way of the Lord. Make straight in the de - sert a high - way for our God. (Pre - pare ye the way.)

Opt. 2nd part

ORDS: Isaiah 40:3
USIC: Gary Alan Smith
sic © 1992 Gamut Music Productions

# Christ Is Born

212

Christ is born; give him glo - ry! Christ is born; give him glo - ry!

Christ has come down from heav - en; re - ceive him, re - ceive him!

Christ is now on the earth; ex - alt him, ex - alt him!

Sing, O earth, to the Lord! Na - tions, praise him in joy, for

he has been glo - ri - fied, for he has been glo - ri - fied!

table for instruments such as congo drums, maracas, claves.
y be sung antiphonally by leader/all or choir/congregation.

RDS: Traditional Byzantine Christmas prayer
SIC: Raquel Mora Martínez, Mexican American
ic © 1992 Abingdon Press

## 213 Christ Is Born

Christ is born; give him glo - ry!

Christ has come down from heav - en; re - ceive him!

Christ is now on earth; \_\_\_\_\_ ex - alt him!

O you earth, sing to the Lord!

O you na - tions, praise him in joy, _____

for he has been glo - ri - fied! _____

WORDS: Traditional Byzantine Christmas prayer
MUSIC: Daniel Burton

## 214 Spirit of God

Al - le - lu - ia, come, Spir - it,

come. _____ come. _____

*May be sung several times.*

WORDS and MUSIC: Steve Garnaas-Holmes

## Holy God

Ho - ly God.  Ho - ly and Might - y.

Ho - ly and Im - mor - tal One, have mer - cy up-on us.

MUSIC: James Kriewald
1992 Abingdon Press
(See 363 for *The Reproaches*.)

## Arise, Shine

**216**

*Leader*

A - rise, shine;  for your light _ has come,

*All*

A - rise, shine;  for your

and the glo - ry of the Lord _____

light ___ has come,  and the

has ris - en _____ up -

glo - ry of the Lord

on you.

has ris - en _____ up - on you.

WORDS: Isaiah 60:1
MUSIC: Gary Alan Smith
Music © 1992 Gamut Music Productions

## 217 Remember that You Are Dust

Re - mem - ber that you are dust, and to dust you shall re - turn.

MUSIC: Skinner Chávez-Melo, Mexican
Music © 1992 Abingdon Press

*(See 323 for Ash Wednesday service.)*

## 218 Benediction for Pentecost

My good Lord done been here; done blessed my soul and gone a - way.__ My good Lord done been here; his spir - it now re - ceive. Sing it o - ver chil-dren, ceive!

1. | D.C. | 2. Fine

WORDS and MUSIC: African American spiritual (Luke 24:51; John 20:22b); adapted by William
  Farley Smith, African American
Music adaptation © 1992 Abingdon Press

# Beloved, Now We Are the Saints of God   219

Be - loved, be - loved, now we are the saints of God,

and it does not yet ap - pear what we shall _____ be.

But we know_____ when he shall ap - pear, _____ but we know___

__ when he shall ap - pear _____ we shall be like him, _____

we shall be like him, _____ we shall see him, as he is.

ᴡ ᴼRDS: 1 John 3:2

ᴹ ᴜSIC: James Edward Hoy, African American

ᴹ ᴜsic © 1992 Abingdon Press

## RESPONSES FOR DAILY PRAISE AND PRAYER

220 # O Lord, Open Our Lips
### (Morning Praise and Prayer)

O___ Lord, o - pen our lips.

And___ we shall de - clare ___ your praise.

MUSIC: David Goodrich
Music © 1983 by David Goodrich

*(See 569 for Order of Morning Praise and Prayer.)*

221 # Light and Peace
### (Evening Praise and Prayer)

Light and peace in Je - sus Christ. Thanks __ be to God.

MUSIC: David Goodrich
Music © 1983 by David Goodrich

*(See 574 for Order of Evening Praise and Prayer.)*

222 # O Lord, Come to Our Assistance
### (Night Praise and Prayer)

O Lord, come to our as - sist - ance. O Lord, hast-en to help us.

MUSIC: Skinner Chávez-Melo, Mexican
Music © 1992 Abingdon Press

*(See 577 for Order of Night Praise and Prayer)*

## ORDINATION HYMN
# O Holy Spirit

1. O Ho-ly Spi-rit, by whose breath
2. You are the seek-er's sure re-source,
3. In you God's en-er-gy is shown,
4. Flood our dull sen-ses with your light;
5. From in-ner strife grant us re-lief;
6. Praise to the Fa-ther, Christ, his Word,

life ris-es vi-brant out of death;
of burn-ing love the liv-ing source,
to us your var-ied gifts make known.
in mu-tual love our hearts u-nite.
turn na-tions to the ways of peace.
and to the Spir-it: God the Lord,

come to cre-ate, re-new, in-spire;
pro-tec-tor in the midst of strife,
Teach us to speak, teach us to hear;
Your power the whole cre-a-tion fills;
To ful-ler life your peo-ple bring
to whom all hon-or, glo-ry be

come, kin-dle in our hearts your fire.
the giv-er and the Lord of life.
yours is the tongue and yours the ear.
con-firm our weak, un-cer-tain wills.
that as one bo-dy we may sing:
both now and for e-ter-ni-ty.

WORDS: Att. Rabanus Maurus; tr. John Webster Grant, alt.; para. of *Veni Creator Spiritus*    HAMBURG
MUSIC: Lowell Mason    LM
Words © 1971 John Webster Grant

# III. THE CHRISTIAN YEAR
## THE CALENDAR

ADVENT (purple or blue)
 First Sunday of Advent to the Fourth Sunday of Advent

CHRISTMAS SEASON (white or gold)
 Nativity of the Lord (Christmas Eve, Christmas Day)
 First Sunday After Christmas Day
 New Year's Eve or New Year's Day
 Epiphany of the Lord

SEASON AFTER THE EPIPHANY (ORDINARY TIME; green)
 First Sunday After the Epiphany (Baptism of the Lord; white)
 Second Sunday After the Epiphany
  to the Eighth Sunday After the Epiphany
 Last Sunday After the Epiphany (Transfiguration Sunday; white)

LENT (purple; red as an alternative for Holy Week)
 Ash Wednesday
 First Sunday in Lent to the Fifth Sunday in Lent
 Sixth Sunday in Lent (Passion/Palm Sunday)
 Monday of Holy Week
 Tuesday of Holy Week
 Wednesday of Holy Week
 Holy Thursday+
 Good Friday+ (no color)
 Holy Saturday+ (no color)

EASTER SEASON (white or gold)
 Resurrection of the Lord (Easter Eve, Easter Day, Easter Evening) +
 Second Sunday of Easter to the Sixth Sunday of Easter
 Ascension of the Lord
 Seventh Sunday of Easter
 Day of Pentecost (red)

SEASON AFTER PENTECOST (ORDINARY TIME; green)
 First Sunday After Pentecost (Trinity Sunday; white)
 Second Sunday After Pentecost to the Twenty-sixth Sunday After Pentecos
 All Saints (white)
 Thanksgiving (red or white)
 Last Sunday After Pentecost (Christ the King/Reign of Christ Sunday; wh

+*The Great Three Days from sunset Holy Thursday to sunset Easter Day are a unity—the clim*
*of the Christian year.*

# CALENDAR FOR DATING EASTER AND RELATED HOLY DAYS

| Year | Ash Wednesday | Easter Day | Day of Pentecost | First Sunday of Advent |
|---|---|---|---|---|
| 2015 | February 18 | April 5 | May 24 | November 29 |
| 2016 | February 10 | March 27 | May 15 | November 27 |
| 2017 | March 1 | April 16 | June 4 | December 3 |
| 2018 | February 14 | April 1 | May 20 | December 2 |
| 2019 | March 6 | April 21 | June 9 | December 1 |
| 2020 | February 26 | April 12 | May 31 | November 29 |
| 2021 | February 17 | April 4 | May 23 | November 28 |
| 2022 | March 2 | April 17 | June 5 | November 27 |
| 2023 | February 22 | April 9 | May 28 | December 3 |
| 2024 | February 14 | March 31 | May 19 | December 1 |
| 2025 | March 5 | April 20 | June 8 | November 30 |
| 2026 | February 18 | April 5 | May 24 | November 29 |
| 2027 | February 10 | March 28 | May 16 | November 28 |
| 2028 | March 1 | April 16 | June 4 | December 3 |
| 2029 | February 14 | April 1 | May 20 | December 2 |
| 2030 | March 6 | April 21 | June 9 | December 1 |
| 2031 | February 26 | April 13 | June 1 | November 30 |
| 2032 | February 11 | March 28 | May 16 | November 28 |
| 2033 | March 2 | April 17 | June 5 | November 27 |
| 2034 | February 22 | April 9 | May 28 | December 3 |
| 2035 | February 7 | March 25 | May 13 | December 2 |

# COLORS FOR THE CHRISTIAN YEAR

The Christian year contains two cycles: the Christmas Cycle (Advent Christmas-Epiphany) and the Easter Cycle (Lent-Easter-Pentecost). Withi each cycle are a preparatory season symbolized by the color purple and festival season symbolized by the color white. After each cycle there is a ordinary time of growth symbolized by the color green. Thus there is sequence of seasons using purple, white, and green in that order twice eac year.

Purple is a color of both penitence and royalty used during the preparator seasons of Advent and Lent. Blue, a color of hope, may also be used durin Advent.

White and gold are joyous and festive colors used during the Christmas an Easter Seasons (except on the Day of Pentecost) and in other seasons o festive days such as Baptism of the Lord, Transfiguration, Trinity, All Saint and Christ the King. White may also be used at weddings and at service where the Sacrament of Baptism is central. White is recommended services of death and resurrection because it symbolizes both death ar resurrection. At services of Holy Communion white linens on top of tl Lord's table are customary, but the paraments hanging over the front sides of the table and the other visuals should reflect the day or season of tl year.

Green, is a color of growth, used in the Seasons After the Epiphany ar After Pentecost, except when special days call for white or red.

Red is a color of fire, symbolizing the Holy Spirit. It is used on the Day Pentecost and at other times when the work of the Holy Spirit emphasized. Red is also the color of blood—the blood of Christ and tl blood of martyrs. Because of its intensity, red is most effective when use occasionally rather than continuously for a whole season. It is appropria for evangelistic services, for ordinations and consecrations, for chur anniversaries and homecomings, and for civil observances such as Mart Luther King, Jr. Day or Memorial Day. It may be used beside white and go through the Easter Season. It may be used during Holy Week, beginni with Passion/Palm Sunday, to symbolize the blood of Christ.

Although use of these colors is based on broad ecumenical tradition, oth colors have been and are being used in Christian churches. Creativity wi colors and other signs for days and seasons is encouraged.

# REVISED COMMON LECTIONARY

The Revised Common Lectionary *(1992) is a calendar and table of suggested scripture readings for a three-year cycle. The readings for each Sunday and holy day—typically one each from the Old Testament, Epistles, and Gospels—are meant for the weekly service of worship on the Lord's Day. It provides a systematic approach to the use of Scripture in worship.*

*The lectionary follows the outline of the Christian year. In it the Church celebrates the central mystery of our faith: the life, death, and resurrection of Christ Jesus. The foundation is the Lord's Day, the first day of the week, on which we recall Christ's triumph over sin and death. Each year there are two Christ-centered cycles: Advent-Christmas-Epiphany and Lent-Easter-Pentecost. In each cycle, days of preparation (Advent and Lent) are followed by days of celebration (Christmas-Epiphany and Easter-Pentecost).*

*The lectionary is a tool for voluntary use in planning and leading worship. Its widespread use by United Methodists as well as other Christians testifies to its value in helping congregations hear the whole message of Scripture.*

*The following lectionary is based on the* Revised Common Lectionary, *with selections made on the basis of United Methodist needs and traditions. Other denominations may use other options. The* Revised Common Lectionary *is the best possible table of lessons at this time of publication. Through the life of this book of worship, this lectionary may be amended. Future program resources of The United Methodist Church will describe these changes when appropriate.*

*Versification is based on the* New Revised Standard Version *of the Bible.*

| *YEAR A* | *YEAR B* | *YEAR C* |
|---|---|---|
| Advent 1992, 1995, 1998, 2001, 2004, 2007, 2010, 2013, 2016, 2019 | Advent 1993, 1996, 1999, 2002, 2005, 2008, 2011, 2014, 2017, 2020 | Advent 1994, 1997, 2000, 2003, 2006, 2009, 2012, 2015, 2018 |

**First Sunday of Advent**

| | | |
|---|---|---|
| Isa 2:1-5 | Isa 64:1-9 | Jer 33:14-16 |
| Ps 122 | Ps 80:1-7, 17-19 | Ps 25:1-10 |
| (*UMH* 845) | (*UMH* 801) | (*UMH* 756) |
| Rom 13:11-14 | 1 Cor 1:3-9 | 1 Thess 3:9-13 |
| Mt 24:36-44 | Mk 13:24-37 | Lk 21:25-36 |

**Second Sunday of Advent**

| | | |
|---|---|---|
| Isa 11:1-10 | Isa 40:1-11 | Mal 3:1-4 |
| Ps 72:1-7, 18-19 | Ps 85:1-2, 8-13 | Lk 1:68-79) |
| (*UMH* 795) | (*UMH* 806) | (*UMH* 208) |
| Rom 15:4-13 | 2 Pet 3:8-15*a* | Phil 1:3-11 |
| Mt 3:1-12 | Mk 1:1-8 | Lk 3:1-6 |

### Third Sunday of Advent

| | | |
|---|---|---|
| Isa 35:1-10 | Isa 61:1-4, 8-11 | Zeph 3:14-20 |
| Lk 1:47-55 (*UMH* 199) | Ps 126 (*UMH* 847) | Isa 12:2-6 |
| Jas 5:7-10 | 1 Thess 5:16-24 | Phil 4:4-7 |
| Mt 11:2-11 | Jn 1:6-8, 19-28 | Lk 3:7-18 |

### Fourth Sunday of Advent

| | | |
|---|---|---|
| Isa 7:10-16 | 2 Sam 7:1-11, 16 | Mic 5:2-5*a* |
| Ps 80:1-7, 17-19 | Lk 1:47-55 | Lk 1:47-55 |
| (*UMH* 801) | (*UMH* 199) | (*UMH* 199) |
| Rom 1:1-7 | Rom 16:25-27 | Heb 10:5-10 |
| Mt 1:18-25 | Lk 1:26-38 | Lk 1:39-45 |

### Christmas Eve (A, B, and C)

Isa 9:2-7
Ps 96 (*UMH* 815)
Titus 2:11-14
Lk 2:1-20

### Christmas Day (A, B, and C)

Isa 52:7-10
Ps 98 (*UMH* 818)
Heb 1:1–4 (5–12)
Jn 1:1-14

### First Sunday After Christmas Day

| | | |
|---|---|---|
| Isa 63:7-9 | Isa 61:10–62:3 | 1 Sam 2:18-20, 26 |
| Ps 148 (*UMH* 861) | Ps 148 (*UMH* 861) | Ps 148 (*UMH* 861) |
| Heb 2:10-18 | Gal 4:4-7 | Col 3:12-17 |
| Mt 2:13-23 | Lk 2:22-40 | Lk 2:41-52 |

### January 1—New Year (A, B, and C)

Eccl 3:1-13
Ps 8 (*UMH* 743)
Rev 21:1-6*a*
Mt 25:31-46

### Epiphany of the Lord (January 6 or first Sunday of January; A, B, and C)

Isa 60:1-6
Ps 72:1-7, 10-14 (*UMH* 795)
Eph 3:1-12
Mt 2:1-12

### Baptism of the Lord (First Sunday After the Epiphany; Sunday between January 7 and inclusive)

| | | |
|---|---|---|
| Isa 42:1-9 | Gen 1:1-5 | Isa 43:1-7 |
| Ps 29 (*UMH* 761) | Ps 29 (*UMH* 761) | Ps 29 (*UMH* 761) |
| Acts 10:34-43 | Acts 19:1-7 | Acts 8:14-17 |
| Mt 3:13-17 | Mk 1:4-11 | Lk 3:15-17, 21-22 |

**Second Sunday After the Epiphany** (Sunday between January 14 and 20 inclusive)

| | | |
|---|---|---|
| Isa 49:1-7 | 1 Sam 3:1-10 (11-20) | Isa 62:1-5 |
| Ps 40:1-11 | Ps 139:1-6, 13-18 | Ps 36:5-10 |
| (*UMH* 774) | (*UMH* 854) | (*UMH* 771) |
| 1 Cor 1:1-9 | 1 Cor 6:12-20 | 1 Cor 12:1-11 |
| Jn 1:29-42 | Jn 1:43-51 | Jn 2:1-11 |

**Third Sunday After the Epiphany** (Sunday between January 21 and 27 inclusive)

| | | |
|---|---|---|
| Isa 9:1-4 | Jonah 3:1-5, 10 | Neh 8:1-3, 5-6, 8-10 |
| Ps 27:1, 4-9 (*UMH* 758) | Ps 62:5-12 (*UMH* 787) | Ps 19 (*UMH* 750) |
| 1 Cor 1:10-18 | 1 Cor 7:29-31 | 1 Cor 12:12-31a |
| Mt 4:12-23 | Mk 1:14-20 | Lk 4:14-21 |

**Fourth Sunday After the Epiphany** (Sunday between January 28 and February 3 inclusive; if it is the Last Sunday After the Epiphany, see Transfiguration.)

| | | |
|---|---|---|
| Mic 6:1-8 | Deut 18:15-20 | Jer 1:4-10 |
| Ps 15 (*UMH* 747) | Ps 111 (*UMH* 832) | Ps 71:1-6 (*UMH* 794) |
| 1 Cor 1:18-31 | 1 Cor 8:1-13 | 1 Cor 13:1-13 |
| Mt 5:1-12 | Mk 1:21-28 | Lk 4:21-30 |

**Fifth Sunday After the Epiphany** (Sunday between February 4 and 10 inclusive; if it is the Last Sunday After the Epiphany, see Transfiguration.)

| | | |
|---|---|---|
| Isa 58:1-9a (9b-12) | Isa 40:21-31 | Isa 6:1-8 (9-13) |
| Ps 112:1-10 | Ps 147:1-11, 20c | Ps 138 |
| (*UMH* 833) | (*UMH* 859) | (*UMH* 853) |
| 1 Cor 2:1-12 (13-16) | 1 Cor 9:16-23 | 1 Cor 15:1-11 |
| Mt 5:13-20 | Mk 1:29-39 | Lk 5:1-11 |

**Sixth Sunday After the Epiphany** (Sunday between February 11 and 17 inclusive; if it is the Last Sunday After the Epiphany, see Transfiguration.)

| | | |
|---|---|---|
| Deut 30:15-20 | 2 Kings 5:1-14 | Jer 17:5-10 |
| Ps 119:1-8 (*UMH* 840) | Ps 30 (*UMH* 762) | Ps 1 (*UMH* 738) |
| 1 Cor 3:1-9 | 1 Cor 9:24-27 | 1 Cor 15:12-20 |
| Mt 5:21-37 | Mk 1:40-45 | Lk 6:17-26 |

**Seventh Sunday After the Epiphany** (Sunday between February 18 and 24 inclusive; if it is the Last Sunday After the Epiphany, see Transfiguration.)

| | | |
|---|---|---|
| Lev 19:1-2, 9-18 | Isa 43:18-25 | Gen 45:3-11, 15 |
| Ps 119:33-40 | Ps 41 | Ps 37:1-11, 39-40 |
| (*UMH* 840) | (*UMH* 776) | (*UMH* 772) |
| 1 Cor 3:10-11, 16-23 | 2 Cor 1:18-22 | 1 Cor 15:35-38, 42-50 |
| Mt 5:38-48 | Mk 2:1-12 | Lk 6:27-38 |

**Eighth Sunday After the Epiphany** (Sunday between February 25 and 29 inclusive; if it is the Last Sunday After the Epiphany, see Transfiguration.)

| | | |
|---|---|---|
| Isa 49:8-16a | Hos 2:14-20 | Isa 55:10-13 |
| Ps 131 or Ps 62:5-12 | Ps 103:1-13, 22 | Ps 92:1-4, 12-15 |
| (*UMH* 787) | (*UMH* 824) | (*UMH* 811) |
| 1 Cor 4:1-5 | 2 Cor 3:1-6 | 1 Cor 15:51-58 |
| Mt 6:24-34 | Mk 2:13-22 | Lk 6:39-49 |

**Transfiguration Sunday** (Last Sunday After the Epiphany)
Readings for Transfiguration are used on the Sunday prior to Ash Wednesd

| | | |
|---|---|---|
| Ex 24:12-18 | 2 Kings 2:1-12 | Ex 34:29-35 |
| Ps 99 (*UMH* 819) | Ps 50:1-6 (*UMH* 783) | Ps 99 (*UMH* 819) |
| 2 Pet 1:16-21 | 2 Cor 4:3-6 | 2 Cor 3:12–4:2 |
| Mt 17:1-9 | Mk 9:2-9 | Lk 9:28-36 (37-43) |

**Ash Wednesday** (A, B, and C)

Joel 2:1-2, 12-17
Ps 51:1-17 (*UMH* 785)
2 Cor 5:20b–6:10
Mt 6:1-6, 16-21

**First Sunday in Lent**

| | | |
|---|---|---|
| Gen 2:15-17; 3:1-7 | Gen 9:8-17 | Deut 26:1-11 |
| Ps 32 (*UMH* 766) | Ps 25:1-10 (*UMH* 756) | Ps 91:1-2, 9-16 (*UMH* |
| Rom 5:12-19 | 1 Pet 3:18-22 | Rom 10:8b-13 |
| Mt 4:1-11 | Mk 1:9-15 | Lk 4:1-13 |

**Second Sunday in Lent**

| | | |
|---|---|---|
| Gen 12:1-4a | Gen 17:1–7, 15-16 | Gen 15:1-12, 17-18 |
| Ps 121 (*UMH* 844) | Ps 22:23-31 (*UMH* 752) | Ps 27 (*UMH* 758) |
| Rom 4:1-5, 13-17 | Rom 4:13-25 | Phil 3:17–4:1 |
| Jn 3:1-17 | Mk 8:31-38 | Lk 13:31-35 |

**Third Sunday in Lent**

| | | |
|---|---|---|
| Ex 17:1-7 | Ex 20:1-17 | Isa 55:1-9 |
| Ps 95 (*UMH* 814) | Ps 19 (*UMH* 750) | Ps 63:1-8 (*UMH* 788) |
| Rom 5:1-11 | 1 Cor 1:18-25 | 1 Cor 10:1-13 |
| Jn 4:5-42 | Jn 2:13-22 | Lk 13:1-9 |

**Fourth Sunday in Lent**

| | | |
|---|---|---|
| 1 Sam 16:1-13 | Num 21:4-9 | Josh 5:9-12 |
| Ps 23 | Ps 107:1-3, 17-22 | Ps 32 |
| (*UMH* 754 or 137) | (*UMH* 830) | (*UMH* 766) |
| Eph 5:8-14 | Eph 2:1-10 | 2 Cor 5:16-21 |
| Jn 9:1-41 | Jn 3:14-21 | Lk 15:1-3, 11b-32 |

**Fifth Sunday in Lent**

| | | |
|---|---|---|
| Ezek 37:1-14 | Jer 31:31-34 | Isa 43:16-21 |
| Ps 130 (*UMH* 848) | Ps 51:1-12 (*UMH* 785) | Ps 126 (*UMH* 847) |
| Rom 8:6-11 | Heb 5:5-10 | Phil 3:4b–14 |
| Jn 11:1-45 | Jn 12:20-33 | Jn 12:1-8 |

**Passion/Palm Sunday** (Sixth Sunday in Lent)

Liturgy of the Palms

| | | |
|---|---|---|
| Mt 21:1-11 | Mk 11:1-11 | Lk 19:28-40 |
| Ps 118:1-2, 19-29 | Ps 118:1-2, 19-29 | Ps 118:1-2, 19-29 |
| (*UMH* 839) | (*UMH* 839) | (*UMH* 839) |

Liturgy of the Passion

| | | |
|---|---|---|
| Isa 50:4-9*a* | Isa 50:4-9*a* | Isa 50:4-9*a* |
| Ps 31:9-16 (*UMH* 764) | Ps 31:9-16 (*UMH* 764) | Ps 31:9-16 (*UMH* 764) |
| Phil 2:5-11 | Phil 2:5-11 | Phil 2:5-11 |
| Mt 26:14–27:66 | Mk 14:1–15:47 | Lk 22:14–23:56 |
| or Mt 27:11-54 | or Mk 15:1-39 (40-47) | or Lk 23:1-49 |

**Monday of Holy Week** (A, B, and C)

Isa 42:1-9
Ps 36:5–11 (*UMH* 771)
Heb 9:11-15
Jn 12:1-11

**Tuesday of Holy Week** (A, B, and C)

Isa 49:1-7
Ps 71:1-14 (*UMH* 794)
1 Cor 1:18-31
Jn 12:20-36

**Wednesday of Holy Week** (A, B, and C)

Isa 50:4-9*a*
Ps 70 (*UMH* 793)
Heb 12:1-3
Jn 13:21-32

**Holy Thursday** (A, B, and C)

Ex 12:1-4 (5-10) 11-14
Ps 116:1-4, 12-19 (*UMH* 837)
1 Cor 11:23-26
Jn 13:1-17, 31*b*-35

**Good Friday** (A, B, and C)

Isa 52:13–53:12
Ps 22 (*UMH* 752)
Heb 10:16-25
Jn 18:1–19:42

**Easter Vigil**
The number of readings may vary, but Exodus 14 and at least two other readings from the Old Testament should be used in addition to the New Testament readings.

Old Testament Readings and Psalms (A, B, and C)

| | |
|---|---|
| Gen 1:1–2:4*a* | Isa 55:1-11 |
| Ps 136:1-9, 23-26 or Ps 33 (*UMH* 767) | Isa 12:2-6 |
| Gen 7:1-5, 11-18; 8:6-18; 9:8-13 | Ezek 36:24-28 |
| Ps 46 (*UMH* 780) | Ps 42 (*UMH* 777) |
| Gen 22:1-18 | Ezek 37:1-14 |
| Ps 16 (*UMH* 748) | Ps 143 (*UMH* 856) |
| Ex 14:10-31; 15:20-21 | |
| Ex 15:1*b*-13, 17-18 (*UMH* 135) | |

Second Reading and Psalm (A, B, and C)

Rom 6:3-11
Ps 114 (*UMH* 835)

Gospel Reading

Mt 28:1-10                    Mk 16:1-8                    Lk 24:1-12

**Easter Day**

| | | |
|---|---|---|
| Acts 10:34-43 | Acts 10:34-43 | Acts 10:34-43 |
| Ps 118:1-2, 14-24 | Ps 118:1-2, 14-24 | Ps 118:1-2, 14-24 |
| (*UMH* 839) | (*UMH* 839) | (*UMH* 839) |
| Col 3:1-4 | 1 Cor 15:1-11 | 1 Cor 15:19-26 |
| Jn 20:1-18 | Jn 20:1-18 | Jn 20:1-18 |
| or Mt 28:1-10 | or Mk 16:1-8 | or Lk 24:1-12 |

**Second Sunday of Easter**

| | | |
|---|---|---|
| Acts 2:14*a*, 22-32 | Acts 4:32-35 | Acts 5:27-32 |
| Ps 16 (*UMH* 748) | Ps 133 (*UMH* 850) | Ps 150 (*UMH* 862) |
| 1 Pet 1:3-9 | 1 Jn 1:1–2:2 | Rev 1:4-8 |
| Jn 20:19-31 | Jn 20:19-31 | Jn 20:19-31 |

**Third Sunday of Easter**

| | | |
|---|---|---|
| Acts 2:14*a*, 36-41 | Acts 3:12-19 | Acts 9:1-6 (7-20) |
| Ps 116:1-4, 12-19 | Ps 4 | Ps 30 |
| (*UMH* 837) | (*UMH* 741) | (*UMH* 762) |
| 1 Pet 1:17-23 | 1 Jn 3:1-7 | Rev 5:11-14 |
| Lk 24:13-35 | Lk 24:36*b*-48 | Jn 21:1-19 |

**Fourth Sunday of Easter**

| | | |
|---|---|---|
| Acts 2:42-47 | Acts 4:5-12 | Acts 9:36-43 |
| Ps 23 | Ps 23 | Ps 23 |
| (*UMH* 754 or 137) | (*UMH* 754 or 137) | (*UMH* 754 or 137) |
| 1 Pet 2:19-25 | 1 Jn 3:16-24 | Rev 7:9-17 |
| Jn 10:1-10 | Jn 10:11-18 | Jn 10:22-30 |

**Fifth Sunday of Easter**

| | | |
|---|---|---|
| Acts 7:55-60 | Acts 8:26-40 | Acts 11:1-18 |
| Ps 31:1-5, 15-16 | Ps 22:25-31 | Ps 148 |
| (*UMH* 764) | (*UMH* 752) | (*UMH* 861) |
| 1 Pet 2:2-10 | 1 Jn 4:7-21 | Rev 21:1-6 |
| Jn 14:1-14 | Jn 15:1-8 | Jn 13:31-35 |

**Sixth Sunday of Easter**

| | | |
|---|---|---|
| Acts 17:22-31 | Acts 10:44-48 | Acts 16:9-15 |
| Ps 66:8-20 (*UMH* 790) | Ps 98 (*UMH* 818) | Ps 67 (*UMH* 791) |
| 1 Pet 3:13-22 | 1 Jn 5:1-6 | Rev 21:10, 22–22:5 |
| Jn 14:15-21 | Jn 15:9-17 | Jn 14:23-29 |

scension of the Lord (A, B, and C)
These readings may also be used on the Seventh Sunday of Easter.

Acts 1:1-11
Ps 47 (*UMH* 781)
Eph 1:15-23
Lk 24:44-53

**·venth Sunday of Easter**

| | | |
|---|---|---|
| Acts 1:6-14 | Acts 1:15-17, 21-26 | Acts 16:16-34 |
| Ps 68:1-10, 32-35 | Ps 1 | Ps 97 |
| (*UMH* 792) | (*UMH* 738) | (*UMH* 816) |
| 1 Pet 4:12-14; 5:6-11 | 1 Jn 5:9-13 | Rev 22:12-14, 16-17, 20-21 |
| Jn 17:1-11 | Jn 17:6-19 | Jn 17:20-26 |

**·ay of Pentecost**

| | | |
|---|---|---|
| Acts 2:1-21 | Acts 2:1-21 | Acts 2:1-21 |
| Ps 104:24-34, 35*b* | Ps 104:24-34, 35*b* | Ps 104:24-34, 35*b* |
| (*UMH* 826) | (*UMH* 826) | (*UMH* 826) |
| 1 Cor 12:3*b*-13 | Rom 8:22-27 | Rom 8:14-17 |
| Jn 7:37-39 | Jn 15:26-27; 16:4*b*-15 | Jn 14:8-17 (25–27) |

**inity Sunday** (First Sunday After Pentecost)

| | | |
|---|---|---|
| Gen 1:1–2:4*a* | Isa 6:1-8 | Prov 8:1-4, 22-31 |
| Ps 8 (*UMH* 743) | Ps 29 (*UMH* 761) | Ps 8 (*UMH* 743) |
| 2 Cor 13:11-13 | Rom 8:12-17 | Rom 5:1-5 |
| Mt 28:16-20 | Jn 3:1-17 | Jn 16:12-15 |

**·nday between May 29 and June 4 inclusive** (if after Trinity Sunday)

| | | |
|---|---|---|
| Gen 6:11-22; 7:24; 8:14-19 | 1 Sam 3:1-20 | 1 Kings 18:20-39 |
| Ps 46 | Ps 139:1-6, 13-18 | Ps 96 |
| (*UMH* 780) | (*UMH* 854) | (*UMH* 815) |
| Rom 1:16-17; 3:22*b*–28 (29-31) | 2 Cor 4:5-12 | Gal 1:1-12 |
| Mt 7:21-29 | Mk 2:23–3:6 | Lk 7:1-10 |

**·nday between June 5 and 11 inclusive** (if after Trinity Sunday)

| | | |
|---|---|---|
| Gen 12:1-9 | 1 Sam 8:4-20 (11:14-15) | 1 Kings 17:8-24 |
| Ps 33:1-12 (*UMH* 767) | Ps 138 (*UMH* 853) | Ps 146 (*UMH* 858) |
| Rom 4:13-25 | 2 Cor 4:13–5:1 | Gal 1:11-24 |
| Mt 9:9-13, 18-26 | Mk 3:20-35 | Lk 7:11-17 |

**·nday between June 12 and 18 inclusive** (if after Trinity Sunday)

| | | |
|---|---|---|
| Gen 18:1-15 | 1 Sam 15:34–16:13 | 1 Kings 21:1-21*a* |
| Ps 116:1-2, 12-19 | Ps 20 or Ps 72 | Ps 5:1–8 |
| (*UMH* 837) | (*UMH* 795) | (*UMH* 742) |
| Rom 5:1-8 | 2 Cor 5:6-10 (11-13), 14-17 | Gal 2:15-21 |
| Mt 9:35–10:8 (9-23) | Mk 4:26-34 | Lk 7:36–8:3 |

**Sunday between June 19 and 25 inclusive** (if after Trinity Sunday)

| | | |
|---|---|---|
| Gen 21:8-21 | 1 Sam 17:(1*a*, 4-11, 19-23) 32-49 | 1 Kings 19:1-15*a* |
| Ps 86:1-10, 16-17 or Ps 17 | Ps 9:9-20 | Ps 42 |
| (*UMH* 749) | (*UMH* 744) | (*UMH* 777) |
| Rom 6:1*b*-11 | 2 Cor 6:1-13 | Gal 3:23-29 |
| Mt 10:24-39 | Mk 4:35-41 | Lk 8:26-39 |

**Sunday between June 26 and July 2 inclusive**

| | | |
|---|---|---|
| Gen 22:1-14 | 2 Sam 1:1, 17-27 | 2 Kings 2:1-2, 6-14 |
| Ps 13 | Ps 130 | Ps 77:1-2, 11-20 |
| (*UMH* 746) | (*UMH* 848) | (*UMH* 798) |
| Rom 6:12-23 | 2 Cor 8:7-15 | Gal 5:1, 13-25 |
| Mt 10:40-42 | Mk 5:21-43 | Lk 9:51-62 |

**Sunday between July 3 and 9 inclusive**

| | | |
|---|---|---|
| Gen 24:34-38, 42-49, 58-67 | 2 Sam 5:1-5, 9-10 | 2 Kings 5:1-14 |
| Ps 45:10-17 or Ps 72 | Ps 48 | Ps 30 |
| (*UMH* 795) | (*UMH* 782) | (*UMH* 762) |
| Rom 7:15-25*a* | 2 Cor 12:2-10 | Gal 6:(1-6) 7-16 |
| Mt 11:16-19, 25-30 | Mk 6:1-13 | Lk 10:1-11, 16-20 |

**Sunday between July 10 and 16 inclusive**

| | | |
|---|---|---|
| Gen 25:19-34 | 2 Sam 6:1-5, 12*b*-19 | Amos 7:7-17 |
| Ps 119:105-112 or Ps 25 | Ps 24 | Ps 82 |
| (*UMH* 756) | (*UMH* 755) | (*UMH* 804) |
| Rom 8:1-11 | Eph 1:3-14 | Col 1:1-14 |
| Mt 13:1-9, 18-23 | Mk 6:14-29 | Lk 10:25-37 |

**Sunday between July 17 and 23 inclusive**

| | | |
|---|---|---|
| Gen 28:10-19*a* | 2 Sam 7:1-14a | Amos 8:1-12 |
| Ps 139:1-12, 23-24 | Ps 89:20-37 | Ps 52 or Ps 82 |
| (*UMH* 854) | (*UMH* 807) | (*UMH* 804) |
| Rom 8:12-25 | Eph 2:11-22 | Col 1:15-28 |
| Mt 13:24-30, 36-43 | Mk 6:30-34, 53-56 | Lk 10:38-42 |

**Sunday between July 24 and 30 inclusive**

| | | |
|---|---|---|
| Gen 29:15-28 | 2 Sam 11:1-15 | Hos 1:2-10 |
| Ps 105:1-11, 45*b* | Ps 14 | Ps 85 |
| (*UMH* 828) | (*UMH* 746) | (*UMH* 806) |
| Rom 8:26-39 | Eph 3:14-21 | Col 2:6-15 (16-19) |
| Mt 13:31-33, 44-52 | Jn 6:1-21 | Lk 11:1-13 |

**Sunday between July 31 and August 6 inclusive**

| | | |
|---|---|---|
| Gen 32:22-31 | 2 Sam 11:26–12:13*a* | Hos 11:1-11 |
| Ps 17:1-7, 15 | Ps 51:1-12 | Ps 107:1-9, 43 |
| (*UMH* 749) | (*UMH* 785) | (*UMH* 830) |
| Rom 9:1-5 | Eph 4:1-16 | Col 3:1-11 |
| Mt 14:13-21 | Jn 6:24-35 | Lk 12:13-21 |

**Sunday between August 7 and 13 inclusive**

| | | |
|---|---|---|
| Gen 37:1-4, 12-28 | 2 Sam 18:5-9, 15, 31-33 | Isa 1:1, 10-20 |
| Ps 105:1-6, 16-22, 45b | Ps 130 | Ps 50:1-8, 22-23 |
| (UMH 828) | (UMH 848) | (UMH 783) |
| Rom 10:5-15 | Eph 4:25–5:2 | Heb 11:1-3, 8-16 |
| Mt 14:22-33 | Jn 6:35, 41-51 | Lk 12:32-40 |

**Sunday between August 14 and 20 inclusive**

| | | |
|---|---|---|
| Gen 45:1-15 | 1 Kings 2:10-12; 3:3-14 | Isa 5:1-7 |
| Ps 133 (UMH 850) | Ps 111 (UMH 832) | Ps 80:1-2, 8-19 (UMH 801) |
| Rom 11:1-2a, 29-32 | Eph 5:15-20 | Heb 11:29–12:2 |
| Mt 15:(10-20) 21-28 | Jn 6:51-58 | Lk 12:49-56 |

**Sunday between August 21 and 27 inclusive**

| | | |
|---|---|---|
| Ex 1:8–2:10 | 1 Kings 8:(1, 6, 10-11) 22-30, 41-43 | Jer 1:4-10 |
| Ps 124 (UMH 846) | Ps 84 (UMH 804) | Ps 71:1-6 (UMH 794) |
| Rom 12:1-8 | Eph 6:10-20 | Heb 12:18-29 |
| Mt 16:13-20 | Jn 6:56-69 | Lk 13:10-17 |

**Sunday between August 28 and September 3 inclusive**

| | | |
|---|---|---|
| Ex 3:1-15 | Song 2:8-13 | Jer 2:4-13 |
| Ps 105:1-6, 23-26, 45c | Ps 45:1-2, 6-9 or Ps 72 | Ps 81:1, 10-16 |
| (UMH 828) | (UMH 795) | (UMH 803) |
| Rom 12:9-21 | Jas 1:17-27 | Heb 13:1-8, 15-16 |
| Mt 16:21-28 | Mk 7:1-8, 14-15, 21-23 | Lk 14:1, 7-14 |

**Sunday between September 4 and 10 inclusive**

| | | |
|---|---|---|
| Ex 12:1-14 | Prov 22:1-2, 8-9, 22-23 | Jer 18:1-11 |
| Ps 149 or Ps 148 | Ps 125 or Ps 124 | Ps 139:1-6, 13-18 |
| (UMH 861) | (UMH 846) | (UMH 854) |
| Rom 13:8-14 | Jas 2:1-10 (11-13), 14-17 | Philem 1-21 |
| Mt 18:15-20 | Mk 7:24-37 | Lk 14:25-33 |

**Sunday between September 11 and 17 inclusive**

| | | |
|---|---|---|
| Ex 14:19-31 | Prov 1:20-33 | Jer 4:11-12, 22-28 |
| Ex 15:1b-11, 20-21 | Ps 19 | Ps 14 |
| (UMH 135) | (UMH 750) | (UMH 746) |
| Rom 14:1-12 | Jas 3:1-12 | 1 Tim 1:12-17 |
| Mt 18:21-35 | Mk 8:27-38 | Lk 15:1-10 |

**Sunday between September 18 and 24 inclusive**

| | | |
|---|---|---|
| Ex 16:2-15 | Prov 31:10-31 | Jer 8:18–9:1 |
| Ps 105:1-6, 37-45 or Ps 78 | Ps 1 | Ps 79:1-9 or Ps 4 |
| (UMH 799) | (UMH 738) | (UMH 741) |
| Phil 1:21-30 | Jas 3:13–4:3, 7-8a | 1 Tim 2:1-7 |
| Mt 20:1-16 | Mk 9:30-37 | Lk 16:1-13 |

**Sunday between September 25 and October 1 inclusive**

| | | |
|---|---|---|
| Ex 17:1-7 | Esth 7:1-6, 9-10; 9:20-22 | Jer 32:1-3a, 6-15 |
| Ps 78:1-4, 12-16 | Ps 124 | Ps 91:1-6, 14-16 |
| (*UMH* 799) | (*UMH* 846) | (*UMH* 810) |
| Phil 2:1-13 | Jas 5:13-20 | 1 Tim 6:6-19 |
| Mt 21:23-32 | Mk 9:38-50 | Lk 16:19-31 |

**Sunday between October 2 and 8 inclusive**

| | | |
|---|---|---|
| Ex 20:1-4, 7-9, 12-20 | Job 1:1; 2:1-10 | Lam 1:1-6 |
| Ps 19 | Ps 26 or Ps 25 | Ps 137 |
| (*UMH* 750) | (*UMH* 756) | (*UMH* 852) |
| Phil 3:4b-14 | Heb 1:1-4; 2:5-12 | 2 Tim 1:1-14 |
| Mt 21:33-46 | Mk 10:2-16 | Lk 17:5-10 |

**Sunday between October 9 and 15 inclusive**

| | | |
|---|---|---|
| Ex 32:1-14 | Job 23:1-9, 16-17 | Jer 29:1, 4-7 |
| Ps 106:1-6, 19-23 | Ps 22:1-15 | Ps 66:1-12 |
| (*UMH* 829) | (*UMH* 752) | (*UMH* 790) |
| Phil 4:1-9 | Heb 4:12-16 | 2 Tim 2:8-15 |
| Mt 22:1-14 | Mk 10:17-31 | Lk 17:11-19 |

**Sunday between October 16 and 22 inclusive**

| | | |
|---|---|---|
| Ex 33:12-23 | Job 38:1-7 (34-41) | Jer 31:27-34 |
| Ps 99 | Ps 104:1-9, 24, 35c | Ps 119:97-104 or Ps 19 |
| (*UMH* 819) | (*UMH* 826) | (*UMH* 750) |
| 1 Thess 1:1-10 | Heb 5:1-10 | 2 Tim 3:14–4:5 |
| Mt 22:15-22 | Mk 10:35-45 | Lk 18:1-8 |

**Sunday between October 23 and 29 inclusive**

| | | |
|---|---|---|
| Deut 34:1-12 | Job 42:1-6, 10-17 | Joel 2:23-32 |
| Ps 90:1-6, 13-17 | Ps 34:1-8 (19-22) | Ps 65 |
| (*UMH* 789) | (*UMH* 769) | (*UMH* 789) |
| 1 Thess 2:1-8 | Heb 7:23-28 | 2 Tim 4:6-8, 16-18 |
| Mt 22:34-46 | Mk 10:46-52 | Lk 18:9-14 |

**Sunday between October 30 and November 5 inclusive**

| | | |
|---|---|---|
| Josh 3:7-17 | Ruth 1:1-18 | Hab 1:1-4; 2:1-4 |
| Ps 107:1-7, 33-37 | Ps 146 | Ps 119:137-144 |
| (*UMH* 830) | (*UMH* 858) | (*UMH* 840) |
| 1 Thess 2:9-13 | Heb 9:11-14 | 2 Thess 1:1-4, 11-12 |
| Mt 23:1-12 | Mk 12:28-34 | Lk 19:1-10 |

**All Saints** (November 1 or may be used on first Sunday in November)

| | | |
|---|---|---|
| Rev 7:9-17 | Isa 25:6-9 | Dan 7:1-3, 15-18 |
| Ps 34:1-10, 22 | Ps 24 | Ps 149 or Ps 150 |
| (*UMH* 769) | (*UMH* 755) | (*UMH* 862) |
| 1 Jn 3:1-3 | Rev 21:1-6a | Eph 1:11-23 |
| Mt 5:1-12 | Jn 11:32-44 | Lk 6:20-31 |

**Sunday between November 6 and 12 inclusive**

| | | |
|---|---|---|
| Josh 24:1-3a, 14-25 | Ruth 3:1-5; 4:13-17 | Hag 1:15b–2:9 |
| Ps 78:1-7 | Ps 127 or Ps 42 | Ps 145:1-5, 17-21 |
| (*UMH* 799) | (*UMH* 777) | (*UMH* 857) |
| 1 Thess 4:13-18 | Heb 9:24-28 | 2 Thess 2:1-5, 13-17 |
| Mt 25:1-13 | Mk 12:38-44 | Lk 20:27-38 |

**Sunday between November 13 and 19 inclusive**

| | | |
|---|---|---|
| Judg 4:1-7 | 1 Sam 1:4-20 | Isa 65:17-25 |
| Ps 123 or Ps 76 | 1 Sam 2:1-10 or Ps 113 | Isa 12 or Ps 118 |
| (*UMH* 797) | (*UMH* 834) | (*UMH* 839) |
| 1 Thess 5:1-11 | Heb 10:11-14 (15–18) 19-25 | 2 Thess 3:6-13 |
| Mt 25:14-30 | Mk 13:1-8 | Lk 21:5-19 |

**Christ the King/Reign of Christ** (Sunday between November 20 and 26 inclusive)

| | | |
|---|---|---|
| Ezek 34:11-16, 20-24 | 2 Sam 23:1-7 | Jer 23:1-6 |
| Ps 100 (*UMH* 821) | Ps 132:1-12 (*UMH* 849) | Lk 1:68-79 (*UMH* 208) |
| Eph 1:15-23 | Rev 1:4b-8 | Col 1:11-20 |
| Mt 25:31-46 | Jn 18:33-37 | Lk 23:33-43 |

**Thanksgiving Day**

| | | |
|---|---|---|
| Deut 8:7-18 | Joel 2:21-27 | Deut 26:1-11 |
| Ps 65 (*UMH* 789) | Ps 126 (*UMH* 847) | Ps 100 (*UMH* 821) |
| 2 Cor 9:6-15 | 1 Tim 2:1-7 | Phil 4:4-9 |
| Lk 17:11-19 | Mt 6:25-33 | Jn 6:25-35 |

# ADVENT

Advent is a season of four weeks including four Sundays. *Advent* derive from the Latin *adventus*, which means "coming." The season proclaims th comings of the Christ—whose birth we prepare to celebrate once again, wh comes continually in Word and Spirit, and whose return in final victory w anticipate. Each year Advent calls the community of faith to prepare fc these comings; historically, the season was marked by fasts for preparatior Each Sunday of Advent has its distinctive theme: Christ's coming in fin. victory (First Sunday), John the Baptist (Second and Third Sundays), and th events immediately preceding the birth of Jesus Christ (Fourth Sunday). I addition to the acts and services of worship on the following pages, see Th Great Thanksgiving for Advent (54-55) and the scripture readings fc Advent in the lectionary (227-28).

Use purple or blue for paraments, stoles, and banners. Visuals of the seasc may include an Advent wreath (an evergreen wreath with four purp candles and a central white Christ candle added on Christmas Eve/Day evergreen wreaths and branches, a Chrismon tree (an evergreen tr covered with white monograms of Christ), and a Jesse tree (a tree with sigr of the ancestors of Christ). Other symbols include trumpets for Isaia messianic rose, star of Jacob, and fleur-de-lis.

## 239   ACTS OF WORSHIP FOR ADVENT

*Hymns and Canticles from* UMH

195-216 Christ's Gracious Life:
  Promised Coming
722 I Want to Be Ready
626 Let All Mortal Flesh
  Keep Silence
718 Lo, He Comes with
  Clouds Descending
719 My Lord, What a Morning

730 O Day of God, Draw Nigh
729 O Day of Peace That Dimly Shines
184 Of the Father's Love Begotten
724 On Jordan's Stormy Banks I Stand
706 Soon and Very Soon
717 The Battle Hymn of the Republic
  (stanzas 1, 3, 5)
720 Wake, Awake, for Night Is Flying

*Musical Responses from* UMH

211 O Come, O Come, Emmanuel (stanza 1, refrain)
207 Prepare the Way of the Lord

e also:

rise, Shine ( ♪ 216)
ntrance Song for Advent ( ♪ 206)
repare the Way ( ♪ 211)

## Greetings

**240**

ft up your heads, O gates!
**and be lifted up, O ancient doors!**
**that the King of glory may come in.**    (Psalm 24:7)

**241**

voice cries out:
n the wilderness prepare the way of the Lord,
**make straight in the desert a highway for our God."**    (Isaiah 40:3)

**242**

ng and rejoice, O daughter Zion!
**or lo, I will come and dwell in your midst, says the Lord.**
any nations shall join themselves to the Lord in that day,
**and shall be my people; and I will dwell in your midst.**
(Zechariah 2:10-11b)

**243**

ou know what time it is,
**how it is now the moment for you to wake from sleep.**
or salvation is nearer to us now than when we became believers;
**the night is far gone, the day is near.**
t us then lay aside the works of darkness
**and put on the armor of light.**    (Romans 13:11-12)

also:

| | |
|---|---|
| alm 131:3 | Hope in the Lord. |
| niah 35:3-4 | Be strong; do not fear. |
| niah 40:1-2 | Comfort my people. |
| niah 40:9 | Here is your God. |
| ekiel 30:1-3 | The day of the Lord is near. |
| el 2:1 | The day of the Lord is coming. |
| phaniah 2:1-3 | Seek the Lord. |
| atthew 25:31-34 | When the Son of man comes |
| ark 1:15 | The time is fulfilled. |
| ke 3:4-6 | One crying out in the wilderness |
| ke 12:35-38 | Watchful slaves |
| Corinthians 6:2 | Now is the acceptable time. |
| ilippians 4:4-5 | Rejoice in the Lord. |

**244**

e! The ruler of earth shall come,
**the Lord who will take from us the heavy burden of our exile.**
(Traditional Monastic Liturgy)

## 245

Praise be to God!
**Blessed be the Lord God of Israel,**
**who has visited and redeemed the people.**

Blessed is he who comes in the name of the Lord.
**Blessed be the name of the Lord.** (THE BOOK OF WORSHIP 1965, AL*

## 246

Tell the timid to take heart.
**The Lord our God will come!** (TRADITIONAL MONASTIC LITURG

## 247

We wait for the word of the Lord as we wait for the rains
**and our God shall come down upon us like gentle dew.**
(TRADITIONAL MONASTIC LITURG

## 248

The hills and the mountains will be singing praise to God.
**Every tree in the forest will be clapping its hands.**
**The Lord will come and rule for ever. Alleluia.**
(TRADITIONAL MONASTIC LITURC

*Opening Prayers*

*See Advent (UMH 201) and the O Antiphons (UMH 211). The antiphons (sho*
*phrases based on scripture) may be used over several Sundays, with each one bei*
*read before its corresponding hymn stanza is sung.*

## 249

Eternal God, in your providence you made all ages
a preparation for the kingdom of your Son.
Make ready our hearts for the brightness of your glory
and the fullness of your blessing in Jesus Christ our Lord. Amen.
(THE BOOK OF WORSHIP 1944, AL

## 250

Merciful God, you sent your messengers the prophets
to preach repentance and prepare the way for our salvation.
Give us grace to heed their warnings and forsake our sins,
that we may greet with joy the coming of Jesus Christ, our Redeemer;
who lives and reigns with you and the Holy Spirit,
one God, now and for ever. Amen.
(THE BOOK OF COMMON PRAYER, U.S.A., 20TH CENT., AL

## 251

O God, you so loved the world as to give your only begotten Son,
that whosoever believes in him should not perish,
but have everlasting life.

rant to us the precious gift of faith,
that we may know that the Son of God is come,
ıd may have power to overcome the world
and gain a blessed immortality;
ırough Jesus Christ our Lord. Amen. (THE BOOK OF WORSHIP 1965, ALT.)

**252**

God, whose will is justice for the poor and peace for the afflicted,
let your herald's urgent voice pierce our hardened hearts
    and announce the dawn of your kingdom.
ɔfore the advent of the One who baptizes with the fire of the Holy Spirit,
let our complacency give way to conversion, oppression to justice,
and conflict to acceptance of one another in Christ.
'e ask this through the One whose coming is certain,
whose day draws near:
your Son, our Lord Jesus Christ,
who lives and reigns with you and the Holy Spirit,
one God, for ever and ever. Amen. (SACRAMENTARY, U.S.A., 20TH CENT.)

**253**

the advent seasons, when the past has fled, unasked, away
and there is nothing left to do but wait,
od, shelter us.
ɂ our surrounding darkness;
be the fertile soil out of which hope springs in due time.
uncertain times, help us to greet the dawn and labor on, love on,
in faith awaiting your purpose hid in you
    waiting to be born in due time. Amen. (RUTH DUCK, U.S.A., 20TH CENT.)

**254**

ʿer present God,
you taught us that the night is far spent and the day is at hand.
ɾant that we may ever be found watching for the coming of your Son.
ɪve us from undue love of the world,
that we may wait with patient hope for the day of the Lord,
and so abide in him,
that when he shall appear, we may not be ashamed;
rough Jesus Christ our Lord. Amen. (CHURCH OF SCOTLAND, 20TH CENT., ALT.)

*Prayer of Thanksgiving and Intercession* **255**

ɪlent prayer may follow each intercession.

ɔd of the ages, we praise you,
for in the dawn of time you created the world,
sending light by your Word to dispel darkness.
Jesus Christ you began a new creation,
sending him to be the Light of the world,

to drive away fear and despair,
and to rule in peace and justice, holiness and love.

Especially we thank you
for the order and beauty of your creation . . .
for coming in Jesus Christ to share our human life . . .
for the place you give us in your continuing creation . . .
for the promise of peace among nations, and justice for all peoples . .
for the Church as the sign of your coming kingdom . . .

Mighty God, prepare the world for your rule,
for we long for the day when there shall be no more crying or tears
and death will be destroyed.
Help us to share the ministry of Christ and be agents of his compassior

Especially we pray
for the nations of the earth and peace in the world . . .
for victims and survivors of violence . . .
for those who are sick and suffering . . .
for our families and friends . . .
for the Church and those who serve in Christ's name . . .

All this we pray in the name of Jesus Christ our Lord. Amen.

(Presbyterian Daily Prayer, U.S.A., 20th cent., al

## 256            *The Annunciation to Mary*

*Suggested Scripture Readings*

| | |
|---|---|
| Isaiah 7:10-14 | The young woman shall bear a son. |
| Psalm 40:1-11 (*UMH* 774) | I delight to do your will, O my God. |
| Hebrews 10:5a-10 | I have come to do your will, O God. |
| Luke 1:26-38 | The annunciation to Mary |

*Suggested Hymns from* UMH

199 Canticle of Mary
198 My Soul Gives Glory to My God
200 Tell Out, My Soul
215 To a Maid Engaged to Joseph
197 Ye Who Claim the Faith of Jesus

*Prayer*

Holy God,
the mystery of your eternal Word took flesh among us in Jesus Chris
At the message of an angel,
the virgin Mary placed her life at the service of your will.
Filled with the light of your Spirit,
she became the temple of your Word.
Strengthen us by the example of her humility,
that we may always be ready to do your will,
and welcome into our lives Jesus Christ our Lord. Amen.

(Liturgy of the Hours, U.S.A., 20th cen

The Visitation of Mary to Elizabeth                    257

ggested Scripture Readings

| | |
|---|---|
| ;amuel 2:1-10 | Hannah's prayer of thanksgiving |
| alm 113 (*UMH* 834) | God gives children to a barren woman. |
| mans 12:9-16*b* | Share joys and sorrows. |
| ke 1:39-57 | The visitation of Mary to Elizabeth |

*ayer*

mighty God, you inspired the virgin Mary, mother of your Son,
to visit Elizabeth and assist her in her need.
:ep us open to the working of your Spirit,
and with Mary may we praise you for ever.
e ask this through Jesus Christ our Lord,
10 lives and reigns with you and the Holy Spirit,
.e God, now and for ever. Amen.          (SACRAMENTARY, U.S.A., 20TH CENT., ALT.)

# HANGING OF THE GREENS          258

*is service may take place at any time during Advent. It may be used on a Sunday*
*rning during the Entrance or as a Response to the Word, or it may be used as an*
*ning service. During the singing of Come, Thou Long-Expected Jesus (UMH*
*6), greens may be brought in and the Advent candle(s) lighted.*

*ch lesson should, if possible, be read by a different reader. Each reader should*
*nounce the lesson by the descriptive title preceding it. At the end of the lesson, the*
*der or another person reads the narrative.*

TRODUCTION *

How shall we prepare this house for the coming of the King?
**With branches of cedar, the tree of royalty.**

How shall we prepare this house for the coming of the eternal Christ?
**With garlands of pine and fir, whose leaves are ever living, ever green.**

How shall we prepare this house for the coming of our Savior?
**With wreaths of holly and ivy,**
    **telling of his passion, death, and resurrection.**

How shall we prepare our hearts for the coming of the Son of God?
**By hearing again the words of the prophets,**
    **who foretold the saving work of God.**

For God did not send the Son into the world to condemn the world,
    but that the world through him might be saved.
**Glory to God in the highest!**

## GOD WILL SEND A RIGHTEOUS KING Jeremiah 23:5-6

In ancient times the cedar was revered as the tree of royalty.
It also signified immortality and was used for purification.
We place this cedar branch as a sign of Christ,
   who reigns as King for ever,
   and whose coming, in justice and righteousness, will purify our hear

HYMN *Suggested from* UMH:

196 Come, Thou Long-Expected Jesus      202 People, Look East (stanza 1)
                                        207 Prepare the Way of the Lord

## THE PROPHET DECLARES A CHILD WILL BE BORN Isaiah 9:2, 6-

Because the needles of pine and fir trees appear not to die each seaso
   the ancients saw them as signs of things that last for ever.
Isaiah tells us that there will be no end to the reign of the Messiah.
Therefore, we hang this wreath of evergreens shaped in a circle,
   which itself has no end,
   to signify the eternal reign of Jesus, the Christ.

HYMN *Suggested from* UMH:

211 O Come, O Come, Emmanuel (stanzas 5, 6, 7)
210 Toda la Tierra (All Earth Is Waiting; stanzas 1, 2)

## THE FOURTH SERVANT SONG Isaiah 53:1-6

For Christians, this passage from Isaiah reflects the sufferings of Jesu
   who saved us from our sins by his death on the cross,
   and by his resurrection from the dead.
In ancient times,
   holly and ivy were considered signs of Christ's passion.
Their prickly leaves suggested the crown of thorns,
   the red berries the blood of the Savior,
   and the bitter bark the drink offered to Jesus on the cross.
As we hang the holly and ivy,
   let us rejoice in the coming of Jesus, our Savior.

HYMN *Suggested from* UMH:

203 Hail to the Lord's Anointed      190 Who Is He in Yonder Stall?
626 Let All Mortal Flesh Keep
   Silence (stanzas 1, 2)

## THE MYSTERY OF THE INCARNATION * John 1:1-5, 9-14

As we prepare for the coming of Jesus, the Light of the World,
   we light the *Christmas (Chrismon)* tree.

During this Advent, wherever you see a lighted Christmas tree,
    let it call to mind the One who brings light to our darkness,
    healing to our brokenness, and peace to all who receive him.

*The tree is now lighted, and the Blessing of the Chrismon Tree (260) may be prayed.*

ΥMN * *Suggested from* UMH:

205 Canticle of Light and                206 I Want to Walk as a Child of
    Darkness (response 1 or 2)               the Light (stanzas 1, 2, 3)
                                         585 This Little Light of Mine

# BLESSING OF THE CHRISMON TREE    260

*e Chrismon tree, a sign begun in the Lutheran Church of the Ascension in
nville, Virginia, has now spread to many other congregations. This evergreen tree
overed with signs of Christ, such as stars. Many congregations save the Chrismon
e trunk to make a cross for Lent. Titus 3:4-7 may be read before the blessing. This
ssing may also be used when a Christmas tree is set up at home.*

)ly Lord, we come with joy to celebrate the birth of your Son,
who rescued us from the darkness of sin
    by making the cross a tree of life and light.
ιy this tree, arrayed in splendor,
remind us of the life-giving cross of Christ,
that we may always rejoice in the new life that shines in our hearts.
e ask this through Jesus Christ our Lord. Amen.

(BOOK OF BLESSINGS, U.S.A., 20TH CENT.)

# BLESSING OF THE ADVENT WREATH    261

*e Advent wreath is a simple circle of evergreen branches, a sign of life without end;
four Advent candles encircle a central white Christ candle. Some traditions use the
ɔr rose on the Third Sunday of Advent and for this reason use three purple candles
l one rose candle. United Methodists, however, encourage purple for the whole
son of Advent and therefore use four purple candles. The following blessing, with a
ding from Isaiah 9:2, 6-7, may precede the lighting of the first Advent candle. This
ssing may also be used for blessing an Advent wreath in a home.*

' *a complete musical setting of this litany see* ♪ 208.

ᵣrist came to bring us salvation and has promised to come again.
t us pray that we may always be ready to welcome him.
me, **Lord Jesus.** *See* ♪ 207.

at the keeping of Advent may open our hearts to God's love, **R**
at the light of Christ may penetrate the darkness of sin, **R**

That this wreath may constantly remind us
to prepare for the coming of Christ, **R**

That the Christmas season may fill us with peace and joy
as we strive to follow the example of Jesus, **R**

**Loving God, your Church joyfully awaits the coming of its Savior,
who enlightens our hearts
and dispels the darkness of ignorance and sin.
Pour forth your blessings upon us as we light the candles of this wreat
May their light reflect the splendor of Christ,
who is Lord, for ever and ever. Amen.**

(BOOK OF BLESSINGS, U.S.A., 20TH CEN

# 262  LIGHTING OF THE ADVENT CANDLES

*Each Sunday of Advent may include the lighting of the Advent candles by
appointed family or person, usually during the Entrance. Each Sunday one addition
candle is lighted until all four are lighted. Finally, on Christmas Eve and Day,
middle white candle is lighted. A nativity scene replaces the Advent wreath af
Christmas Day; for the Blessing of a Nativity Scene for the Christmas Season,
280. The person lighting the candles or another person may say the words provided
each Sunday. The candles may be lighted during or after the reading of the script
lessons or while a hymn is sung or appropriate words are spoken.*

### Suggested Hymns from UMH

206 I Want to Walk as a Child of the Light    585 This Little Light of Mine
211 O Come, O Come, Emmanuel          205 Canticle of Light and Darkness
   (stanzas 1, 2, 6, 7)                (response 1 or 2)

*See also* Advent Candle Song ( ♪ 209)

### Suggested Readings

FIRST SUNDAY Isaiah 60:2-3

We light this candle as a symbol of Christ our Hope.
May the light sent from God shine in the darkness
to show us the way of salvation.
O come, O come, Emmanuel.

SECOND SUNDAY Mark 1:4

We light this candle as a symbol of Christ the Way.
May the Word sent from God through the prophets
lead us to the way of salvation.
O come, O come, Emmanuel.

HIRD SUNDAY Isaiah 35:10

We light this candle as a symbol of Christ our Joy.
May the joyful promise of your presence, O God,
    make us rejoice in our hope of salvation.
O come, O come, Emmanuel.

OURTH SUNDAY Isaiah 9:6-7

We light this candle as a symbol of the Prince of Peace.
May the visitation of your Holy Spirit, O God,
    make us ready for the coming of Jesus, our hope and joy.
O come, O come, Emmanuel.

(FROM HOPE TO JOY, U.S.A., 20TH CENT., ALT.)

# AN ADVENT SERVICE 263
# OF LESSONS AND CAROLS

*iis service for Advent, with a focus on the prophets, is an adaptation of the*
*iristmas Festival of Nine Lessons and Carols (284-88).*

ATHERING

ROCESSIONAL HYMN * *Suggested from* UMH:

196 Come, Thou Long-Expected Jesus     197 Ye Who Claim the Faith of Jesus
202 People, Look East

HE BIDDING PRAYER *

Beloved in Christ, as we await the great festival of Christmas,
    let us prepare ourselves so that we may be shown its true meaning.
Let us hear, in lessons from Holy Scripture,
    how the prophets of Israel foretold
        that God would visit and redeem the waiting people.
Let us rejoice, in our carols and hymns,
    that the good purpose of God is being mightily fulfilled.
Let us celebrate the promise that our Lord and Savior, Jesus Christ,
    will bring all peoples and all things
        into the glory of God's eternal kingdom.
The blind receive their sight, and the lame walk,
    the lepers are cleansed, and the deaf hear,
    the dead are raised up, and the poor have the gospel preached to them.

But first, let us pray for the world that God so loves,
    for those who have not heard the good news of God,
    or who do not believe it;

for those who walk in darkness and the shadow of death;
and for the Church in this place and everywhere,
   that it may be freed from all evil and fear,
   and may in pure joy lift up the light of the love of God.

These prayers and praises let us humbly offer to God,
   in the words that Christ himself taught us.

THE LORD'S PRAYER * *See 29.*

CAROL * O Come, O Come, Emmanuel (*UMH* 211, stanzas 1-4)

*Each lesson should, if possible, be read by a different reader. Each reader shou announce the lesson by the descriptive sentence printed. At the end of the lesson t reader may pause and say,* **The Word of the Lord,** *and all may respond,* **Than be to God,** *or the reader may say,* Thanks be to God.

FIRST LESSON Isaiah 40:1-8

To God's people in exile in a faraway land,
   the prophet Isaiah announces good news:
God is coming back, and bringing the exiles home!

CAROL *Suggested from* UMH:

| | |
|---|---|
| 211 O Come, O Come, Emmanuel (stanzas 1-3) | 210 Toda la Tierra (All Earth Is Waiting)<br>207 Prepare the Way of the Lord |

SECOND LESSON Jeremiah 23:5-6

The prophet Jeremiah offers hope for a righteous branch,
   a just king who is yet to come.

CAROL *Suggested from* UMH:

| | |
|---|---|
| 204 Emmanuel, Emmanuel<br>203 Hail to the Lord's Anointed | 211 O Come, O Come, Emmnauel (stanzas 4-6) |

THIRD LESSON Zechariah 9:9-10

To a nation grown weary of war and weapons,
   God promises a king who will establish a reign of peace.

CAROL *Suggested from* UMH:

209 Blessed Be the God of Israel
196 Come, Thou Long-Expected Jesus

FOURTH LESSON Haggai 2:6-9

The prophet Haggai promises to God's people
   a temple even more glorious than the temple of old.

CAROL Lift Up Your Heads, Ye Mighty Gates (*UMH* 213)

FIFTH LESSON Isaiah 35:1-6

The prophet Isaiah announces the renewal
  both of the land and of God's people
  on the coming day of redemption.

CAROL *Suggested from* UMH:

209 Blessed Be the God of Israel     211 O Come, O Come, Emmanuel (stanza 7)
216 Lo, How a Rose E'er
     Blooming

SIXTH LESSON Luke 1:26-35, 38

The angel Gabriel announces to the virgin Mary
  that she will give birth to a ruler whose reign shall never end.

CAROL *Suggested from* UMH:

198 My Soul Gives Glory to     215 To a Maid Engaged to Joseph
     My God                   197 Ye Who Claim the Faith of Jesus
200 Tell Out, My Soul

SEVENTH LESSON * Mark 1:1-15

Jesus proclaims the coming of the kingdom of God.

CAROL * *Suggested from* UMH:

209 Blessed Be the God of Israel
252 When Jesus Came to Jordan

COLLECT * *See Advent (UMH 201) or another Advent prayer (249-55).*

DISMISSAL WITH BLESSING *

Go forth into the world in peace; be of good courage;
  hold fast that which is good; render to no one evil for evil;
  strengthen the fainthearted; support the weak;
  help the afflicted; honor everyone;
  love and serve the Lord, rejoicing in the power of the Holy Spirit.
And the blessing of God Almighty,
  the Father, the Son, and the Holy Spirit,
  be upon you, and remain with you always. **Amen.**

GOING FORTH *

# LAS POSADAS
## (SERVICE OF SHELTER FOR THE HOLY FAMILY)

*In the Hispanic tradition of Latin American countries, especially in Mexico, one of the oldest celebrations is* Las Posadas. *It was created by the Augustinian Father Dieg de Soria about 1587 to introduce Christianity to the New World, and now it is revis by United Methodists Carlos Avendano, Raquel M. Martinez, and Robe Escamilla. This celebration takes place during Advent, from December 16 throu December 23, with a special service on December 24 (see 281-84 for A Christmas E Service of Las Posadas). It is a preparation for, and anticipation of, the birth of Savior, commemorating the nine months when Mary carried the infant Jesus in womb and emphasizing his coming again and the need of all persons for repenta and God's mercy.* Las Posadas *is a Christian, biblical, and evangelistic service ou the Hispanic culture.*

*Well ahead of time, eight homes of church members are chosen in different areas for eight nights prior to Christmas Eve. These homes should be willing to have a ho party, including a piñata to be broken by a child. The piñata represents the devil, w cannot be recognized, and therefore the child is blindfolded. The child is fight against evil with the rod of virtue, symbolized in the stick provided to break the piñc When the child perseveres to the end, the glory of God will come down on everyone shown by the candy hidden within the piñata. The homes may also offer cups of chocolate, coffee, apple cider, or punch; buñuelos (thin, fried pastry); tamales; doughnuts; sweet rolls; all kinds of avocado and other dips; or other refreshmer Each family should also visit neighbors and invite them to* Las Posadas.

*On the appointed day, people meet at the corner near the home to be visited. In sr communities this procession of pilgrims would walk from one home to another, bu large communities it could be a car caravan. Traditionally, persons carry ligh candles and sing as they walk. In the lead may be Mary, seated on a donkey, u Joseph. Children, possibly dressed as shepherds and the magi, accompany procession. Then, in procession, the people approach the darkened house and proc with the following service:*

*Knocking on the door, a person begins:*

Listen! I am standing at the door, knocking;
if you hear my voice and open the door,
I will come in to you and eat with you, and you with me.

(REVELATION 3

*People outside the home say:*

Who will give lodging to these pilgrims
who are weary of traveling the roads?
We have come exhausted from Nazareth.
I'm a carpenter, by the name of Joseph.
In the name of the heavens, I beg you for lodging,
my beloved wife can no longer travel.

*eople inside the home answer:*

lthough you tell us that you are weary,
we do not give lodging to strangers.
'e don't care what your name is; let us sleep.
'e are telling you that we will not let you enter.

*eople outside say:*

e was in the world, and the world came into being through him;
yet the world did not know him.
e came to what was his own, and his own people did not accept him.
it to all who received him, who believed in his name,
he gave power to become children of God. (JOHN 1:10, 12)

*eople inside say:*

ho are the children of God?

*eople outside say:*

l who are led by the Spirit of God are children of God. (ROMANS 8:14)

*eople inside say:*

) what does the Spirit of God guide us?

*eople outside say:*

)u shall love the Lord your God with all your heart,
and with all your soul, and with all your mind.
)u shall love your neighbor as yourself. (MATTHEW 22:37, 39)

ie fruit of the Spirit is love, joy, peace, patience, kindness,
generosity, faithfulness, gentleness, and self-control. (GALATIANS 5:22-23a)

*eople inside say:*

)w do we know we love the Lord and have faith?

*eople outside say:*

hat good is it, my brothers and sisters,
if you say you have faith but do not have works?
n faith save you?
a brother or sister is naked and lacks daily food,
and one of you says to them,
"Go in peace; keep warm and eat your fill,"
d yet you do not supply their bodily needs, what is the good of that?
faith by itself, if it has no works, is dead. (JAMES 2:14-17)

*ople inside switch on all the lights and say:*

dging we will give you with much happiness;
ter, good Joseph; enter with Mary.

*The doors of the home open, and all enter.*

*People inside say:*

Enter, holy pilgrims. Receive this corner
not of this humble home, but of our hearts.

*Host family offers the following prayer:*

God all-powerful,
grant that we may rid ourselves of the works of darkness,
and that we may invest ourselves with the weapons of light
in this life to which your Son, Jesus Christ,
with great humility came to visit us;
so that in the final day,
when he returns in majestic glory to judge the living and the dead,
we shall rise to eternal life through Jesus Christ,
who lives and reigns with you and the Holy Spirit,
now and for ever. **Amen.**

*The people may sing one or more of the following hymns in* UMH:

| 217 Away in a Manger | 222 Niño Lindo (Child So Lovely) |
| 243 De Tierra Lejana Venimos (From a Distant Home) | 219 What Child Is This |

*A member of the host family or another person reads Psalm 80 (UMH 801) and one the following:*

| December 16 | Malachi 3:1-6*a* | Mark 1:1-8 |
| December 17 | Malachi 4:1-6 | Luke 1:5-17 |
| December 18 | Isaiah 62:1-12 | Luke 1:26-38 |
| December 19 | Isaiah 11:1-10 | Luke 1:39-56 |
| December 20 | Isaiah 35:1-10 | Luke 1:57-66 |
| December 21 | Isaiah 42:1-9 | Matthew 3:1-12 |
| December 22 | Isaiah 9:2-7 | Matthew 1:12-17 |
| December 23 | Zephaniah 3:14-20 | Luke 1:67-80 |

*The host family now serves refreshments, and the piñata may be broken.*

# CHRISTMAS SEASON

hristmas is a season of praise and thanksgiving for the incarnation of God
Jesus Christ, which begins with Christmas Eve or Day and continues
rough the Day of Epiphany. The name *Christmas* comes from the season's
rst service, the *Christ Mass. Epiphany* comes from the Greek word *epiphania,*
hich means "manifestation." New Year's Eve or Day is often celebrated in
e United Methodist tradition with a Covenant Renewal Service (see 288).
addition to acts and services of worship for the Christmas Season on the
llowing pages, see The Great Thanksgivings on 56-59 and the scripture
adings for the Christmas Season in the lectionary (228).

se the colors of white and gold and materials of the finest texture for
raments, stoles, and banners. Signs of the season include a Chrismon
ee, a nativity scene (include the magi on the Day of Epiphany), a Christmas
ar, angels, poinsettias, and roses. Gold, frankincense, myrrh, and three
owns are appropriate on the Day of Epiphany.

## ACTS OF WORSHIP                                              270
## FOR THE CHRISTMAS SEASON

*Suggested Hymns and Canticles from* UMH

217-55 Christ's Gracious Life:          188 Christ Is the World's Light
    Birth and Baptism              173 Christ, Whose Glory
 82 Canticle of God's Glory               Fills the Skies
    (Gloria in Excelsis)           206 I Want to Walk as a Child of the Light
 83 Canticle of God's Glory           179 O Sing a Song of Bethlehem
    (Gloria in Excelsis)           679 O Splendor of God's Glory Bright
205 Canticle of Light                   214 Savior of the Nations, Come
    and Darkness                   190 Who Is He in Yonder Stall

*Suggested Musical Responses from* UMH

 90 Alleluia! refrain from Ye          158 Alleluia! Amen! from Come,
    Watchers and Ye Holy Ones          Christians, Join to Sing
630 Alleluia! refrain from Become        72 Gloria, Gloria
    to Us the Living Bread         190 Who Is He in Yonder Stall (stanza 1)
711 Alleluia! refrain from              188, 234, 237, 238 Refrains
    For All the Saints             240, 244, 245, 248 Refrains

*See also:*
Christ Is Born ( ♪ 212)
Christ Is Born ( ♪ 213)
Heleluyan ( ♪ 176)

*Greetings*

## 271

Do not be afraid;
for see—I am bringing you good news of a great joy for all the people
**to you is born this day in the city of David a Savior,**
**who is the Messiah, the Lord.** (LUKE 2:1

## 272

In the beginning was the Word,
and the Word was with God, and the Word was God.
**And the Word became flesh and lived among us,**
**and we have seen his glory.** (JOHN 1:1, 1

## 273

The grace of God has appeared bringing salvation to all. (TITUS 2:1

*See also:*

| | |
|---|---|
| Isaiah 9:6 | A child has been born. |
| Micah 5:2-4 | Bethlehem of Ephrathah |
| Luke 2:10-14 | Good news of great joy |
| 2 Corinthians 9:15 | Thanks be to God |
| 1 John 1:5-7 | God is light. |
| Revelation 21:23-24 | The city of God |

## 274

Let us dance with delight in the Lord
and let our hearts be filled with rejoicing,
**for eternal salvation has appeared on the earth. Alleluia!**
(LITURGY OF THE HOURS, U.S.A., 20TH CEN

## 275

Christ is born; give him glory!
**Christ has come down from heaven; receive him!**
**Christ is now on earth; exalt him!**

O you earth, sing to the Lord!
**O you nations, praise him in joy, for he has been glorified!**
(TRADITIONAL BYZANTINE CHRISTMAS PRAYER, A

*See also* ♪ 213 and ♪ 214.

*Opening Prayers*

## 276

O God our Father, you have brought us again to the glad season
when we celebrate the birth of your Son, Jesus Christ our Lord.
Grant that his Spirit may be born anew in our hearts this day
and that we may joyfully welcome him to reign over us.
Open our ears that we may hear again the angelic chorus of old.
Open our lips that we, too, may sing with uplifted hearts.
Glory to God in the highest,
and on earth, peace, goodwill toward all;
through Jesus Christ our Lord. Amen. (THE BOOK OF WORSHIP 1944, A

**277**

) almighty God, by the birth of your holy child Jesus
  you gave us a great light to dawn on our darkness.
;rant that in his light we may see light.
estow upon us that most excellent Christmas gift of love to all people,
  so that the likeness of your Son may be formed in us,
  and that we may have the ever brightening hope of everlasting life;
irough Jesus Christ our Savior. Amen.    (THE BOOK OF WORSHIP 1965, ALT.)

**278**

end, O God, into the darkness of this troubled world,
  the light of your Son.
et the star of your hope touch the minds of all people
  with the bright beams of mercy and truth;
id so direct our steps that we may ever walk in the way revealed to us,
  as the shepherds of Bethlehem walked with joy
    to the manger where he dwelled,
  who now and ever reigns in our hearts, Jesus Christ our Lord. Amen.
                                        (JOHN SUTER, U.S.A., 20TH CENT., ALT.)

*e also Christmas (UMH 231) and Epiphany (UMH 255).*

*Prayer of Thanksgiving and Intercession*   **279**

*lent prayer may follow each petition.*

oly God, heaven and earth are met this day
  in the newborn Child, Savior of the world.
e celebrate his birth;
r in him you come to be close to us, that we might be close to you.

pecially, we give thanks
  for the birth, life, death, and resurrection of our Lord Jesus Christ
    and all he means to us . . .
  for prospects of peace in the world . . .
  for confidence in your almighty love . . .
  for those who generously give . . .
  for those who graciously receive . . .
  for the Church's nurturing us in the faith . . .

)d of all mercy,
as you have come in Jesus Christ to be our guest,
inspire our hearts to a hospitality
    that welcomes all your children in his name.

pecially we pray
for those who have not heard your good news . . .
for the sick and suffering . . .
for those who know no laughter, only tears . . .

for those who govern and rule . . .
for those enslaved by tyranny . . .
for prisoners of addiction or abuse . . .
for the Church as a refuge for the needy . . .
All this we pray in the name of Jesus Christ our Lord. Amen.

(PRESBYTERIAN DAILY PRAYER, U.S.A., 20TH CENT., AL˥

# 280   BLESSING OF A NATIVITY SCENE

*A nativity scene, including the holy family, animal, shepherds, and angels, may ▪*
*placed before the congregation. An empty manger may be used during Advent. C*
*Christmas Eve or Day, the infant is added to the scene. The magi may be added on t▪*
*Day of Epiphany. The Friendly Beasts (UMH 227) may be sung during or after t▪*
*placing of the animals. Luke 2:1-7 may be read before the blessing.*

God of every nation and people,
   from the very beginning of creation you have made manifest your lov
When our need for a Savior was great
   you sent your Son to be born of the virgin Mary.
To our lives he brings joy and peace, justice, mercy, and love.
Lord, bless all who look upon this manger.
May it remind us of the humble birth of Jesus,
   and raise up our thoughts to him,
   who is God-with-us and Savior of all,
   and who lives and reigns for ever and ever. Amen.

(BOOK OF BLESSINGS, U.S.A., 20TH CENT., AL

# 281 A CHRISTMAS EVE SERVICE OF LAS POSADAS

*See the Advent service of Las Posadas (266-68) for an introduction to the service. C*
*Christmas Eve the service is held at the church, using the following order of worsh▪*

## ENTRANCE

*Joseph and Mary stand outside the sanctuary, accompanied by youths a*
*children. One member of the group outside knocks on the sanctuary door and sa▪*

Listen! I am standing at the door, knocking;
if you hear my voice and open the door,
   I will come in to you and eat with you, and you with me.

(REVELATION 3:

*he following sections are sung to the tune* ST. KEVIN *(UMH 315).*

*eople outside the sanctuary sing:*

1 the name of God, we beg: will you let us enter?
Je are tired and we are cold. May we please have shelter?

*eople inside the sanctuary sing:*

ou look dirty and you smell. Will you please keep moving.
or your kind there is no place, for our inn is decent.

*eople outside sing:*

is not by our own choice that today we travel.
Jt the emperor has said that all must be counted.

*eople inside sing:*

or your reasons we care not, every room is taken.
an't you see the place is full? You are bad for business.

*:ople outside say:*

e was in the world, and the world came into being through him;
  yet the world did not know him.
e came to what was his own, and his own people did not accept him.
Jt to all who received him, who believed in his name,
  he gave power to become children of God. (JOHN 1:10, 12)

*'ople inside say:*

ho are the children of God?

*'ople outside say:*

1 who are led by the Spirit of God are children of God. (ROMANS 8:14)

*ople inside say:*

what does the Spirit of God guide us?

*ople outside say:*

ou shall love the Lord your God with all your heart,
  and with all your soul, and with all your mind.
ou shall love your neighbor as yourself. (MATTHEW 22:37, 39)

e fruit of the Spirit is love, joy, peace, patience, kindness,
  generosity, faithfulness, gentleness, and self-control.
(GALATIANS 5:22-23*a*)

*ople inside say:*

ow do we know we love the Lord and have faith?

*People outside say:*

What good is it, my brothers and sisters,
  if you say you have faith but do not have works?
Can faith save you?
If a brother or sister is naked and lacks daily food,
  and one of you says to them, "Go in peace; keep warm and eat your f
and yet you do not supply their bodily needs, what is the good of t
So faith by itself, if it has no works, is dead.                    (JAMES 2:1

*People outside sing:*

Will the child be born tonight out on a street corner?
Can't you find a place for him? Do you have no pity?

*As the outsiders come into the sanctuary at this time, the people inside may s
and sing:*

Oh, my goodness, do come in. You can use the manger.
For the rooms that we do have are for a rich trav'ler.

*All sing:*

**Gentle Mary laid her child lowly in a manger;**
**There he lay, the undefiled, to the world a stranger.**
**Such a babe in such a place, can he be the Savior?**
**Ask the saved of all the race who have found his favor.**

*All pray:*

**God all-powerful,**
  **grant that we may rid ourselves of the works of darkness,**
**and that we may invest ourselves with the weapons of light**
  **in this life**
    **to which your Son, Jesus Christ,**
    **with great humility came to visit us;**
  **so that in the final day,**
    **when he returns in majestic glory to judge the living and the d**
  **we shall rise to eternal life through Jesus Christ,**
    **who lives and reigns with you and the Holy Spirit,**
    **now and for ever. Amen.**

THE CANTICLE OF MARY Luke 1:47-55 (*UMH* 197, 198, 199, 200

THE PRINCE OF PEACE IS BORN Isaiah 9:2-7

HYMN * Niño Lindo (Child So Lovely; *UMH* 222)

PSALM 98 (*UMH* 818)

HYMN * De Tierra Lejana Venimos (From a Distant Home; *UMH* 2

ERMON

*Following the sermon, Holy Communion may be celebrated. The congregation turns to A Service of Word and Table III (UMH 15) or one of the musical settings in UMH 17-25, the pastor praying The Great Thanksgiving (56-57). Whether or not Holy Communion is celebrated, the service concludes as follows:*

RAYER *

*A child prays:*

Visit your family, O God.
Give us love, joy, and your peace.
Purify our thoughts, words, and deeds, so that when Jesus Christ comes,
    he will find a place prepared for his coming.

*A youth prays:*

O heavenly Father,
    as we prepare ourselves for the coming of your Son,
    fill our hearts and lives with praise.
Grant that we may be just and merciful,
    ready to help in the needs of our neighbor
        and conscious of your great love for all the world.
Fill the Christian family with your spiritual gifts
    of forgiveness, patience, mutual love, and unending joy.
All this we ask in the name of Jesus Christ our Lord. **Amen.**

SMISSAL WITH BLESSING *

God bless you, brothers and sisters.
May Christ keep us in the faith
    until the day we shall appear before his presence.

CESSIONAL HYMN * Good Christian Friends, Rejoice (*UMH* 224)

*The people sing as they leave the sanctuary and go to an area for breaking the piñata and having refreshments.*

# A FESTIVAL OF NINE LESSONS AND CAROLS 284

*1880 E. W. Benson, then Anglican Bishop of Truro, England, composed a Festival Nine Lessons and Carols, based on ancient sources, for Christmas Eve. In 1918 it s adapted for the chapel of King's College, Cambridge, by its Dean, Eric Iner-White, who also wrote The Bidding Prayer. The Blessing after The Lord's yer, added by Milner-White, was first included in its present form in 1930. The e Lessons given here have been customarily used in recent years at King's College. e service has been edited for United Methodist congregations.*

GATHERING

PROCESSIONAL HYMN * Once in Royal David's City (*UMH* 250)

THE BIDDING PRAYER *

Beloved in Christ,
this Christmas *Eve* (*Day, Season*) it is our duty and delight
  to prepare ourselves to hear again the message of the angels,
  and to go in heart and mind to Bethlehem,
  and see this thing which is come to pass,
  and the Babe lying in a manger.

Therefore let us hear again from Holy Scripture
  the tale of the loving purposes of God from the first days of our si
    until the glorious redemption brought us by this holy Child;
  and let us make this house of prayer glad with our carols of praise.

But first, because this of all things would rejoice Jesus' heart,
  let us pray to him for the needs of the whole world, and all his peopl
    for peace upon the earth he came to save;
    for love and unity within the one Church he did build;
    for goodwill among all peoples.

And particularly at this time let us remember
  the poor, the cold, the hungry, the oppressed;
  the sick and them that mourn; the lonely and the unloved;
  the aged and the little children;
  and all who know not the Lord Jesus, or who love him not,
    or who by sin have grieved his heart of love.

Lastly let us remember all those who rejoice with us,
  but upon another shore and in a greater light,
  that multitude which no one can number,
  whose hope was in the Word made flesh,
  and with whom, in this Lord Jesus, we for evermore are one.

These prayers and praises let us humbly offer up to the throne of heave
  in the words that Christ himself has taught us.

THE LORD'S PRAYER * *See 29.*

BLESSING *

The almighty God bless us with divine grace,
  Christ give us the joys of everlasting life,
  and unto the fellowship of the citizens above
  may the King of Angels bring us all. **Amen.**

CAROL * Of the Father's Love Begotten (*UMH* 184)

*Each lesson should, if possible, be read by a different reader. Each reader should announce the lesson by the descriptive sentence printed. At the end of the lesson, the reader may pause and say,* **The Word of the Lord,** *and all may respond,* **Thanks be to God,** *or the reader may say,* Thanks be to God.

FIRST LESSON Genesis 3:8-15, 17-19

God announces in the Garden of Eden
    Adam and Eve's punishment for their rebellion
    and that the seed of woman shall bruise the serpent's head.

CAROL Come, Thou Long-Expected Jesus (*UMH* 196)

SECOND LESSON Genesis 22:15-18

God promises to Abraham that by his descendants
    all the nations of the earth shall obtain blessing.

CAROL *Suggested from* UMH:

211 O Come, O Come, Emmanuel (stanzas 1, 2, 4, 7)
116 The God of Abraham Praise (stanzas 1-3)

THIRD LESSON Isaiah 9:2, 6-7

The prophet announces the birth of a king to a people in darkness.

CAROL *Suggested from* UMH:

205 Canticle of Light          210 Toda la Tierra (All Earth Is Waiting;
    and Darkness                   stanzas 1, 4)
216 Lo, How a Rose E'er
    Blooming (stanzas 1, 2)

FOURTH LESSON Isaiah 11:1-4a, 6-9 *or* Micah 5:2-5a

The king is coming and will usher in a reign of justice for the poor
    and peace for all of God's creation.

CAROL *Suggested from* UMH:

216 Lo, How a Rose E'er          230 O Little Town of Bethlehem
    Blooming                    210 Toda la Tierra (All Earth Is Waiting)

FIFTH LESSON Luke 1:26-35, 38

The angel Gabriel announces to the virgin Mary
    that she will give birth to God's promised Son
    whose kingdom shall never end.

CAROL *Suggested from* UMH:

| | |
|---|---|
| 199 Canticle of Mary | 200 Tell Out, My Soul |
| 198 My Soul Gives Glory to My God | 215 To a Maid Engaged to Joseph |
| | 197 Ye Who Claim the Faith of Jesus |

## SIXTH LESSON Luke 2:1-7

Against a backdrop of emperors and taxes,
Jesus is born.

CAROL *Suggested from* UMH:

| | |
|---|---|
| 228 He Is Born | 241 That Boy-Child of Mary |
| 235 Rock-a-Bye, My Dear Little Boy | 245 The First Noel (stanza 1) |

## SEVENTH LESSON Luke 2:8-16

The shepherds go to see the Savior of the world, lying in a manger.

CAROL *Suggested from* UMH:

| | |
|---|---|
| 72 Gloria, Gloria | 221 In the Bleak Midwinter (stanzas 1, 2) |
| 229 Infant Holy, Infant Lowly | 245 The First Noel (stanzas 1, 2) |

## EIGHTH LESSON Matthew 2:1-11

The wise men follow a star to find the child Jesus, the King of the Jews

CAROL *Suggested from* UMH:

| | |
|---|---|
| 243 De Tierra Lejana Venimos (From a Distant Home) | 254 We Three Kings |
| 248 On This Day Earth Shall Ring | 221 In the Bleak Midwinter |

## NINTH LESSON * John 1:1-14

John unfolds the great mystery of the Incarnation.

CAROL * *Suggested from* UMH:

234 O Come, All Ye Faithful
239 Silent Night, Holy Night

COLLECT * *See Christmas (UMH 231) or one of the prayers on 276-79.*

*Instead of a collect, Break Forth, O Beauteous Heavenly Light (UMH 223) may sung.*

## DISMISSAL WITH BLESSING *

May the Christ who by his Incarnation
gathered into One things earthly and heavenly,

fill you with the sweetness of inward peace and goodwill;
and the blessing of God Almighty,
the Father, the Son, and the Holy Spirit,
be upon you and remain with you always.
**Amen.**

Go forth in peace and joy.
**Thanks be to God. Alleluia!**

## ᴏING FORTH *

*Congregations at this point, or immediately prior to the Dismissal with Blessing, may choose to have a candle lighting service. Candles should be distributed prior to the service. The pastor or other worship leader may light a candle from the Christ candle and then light the candles of others, dipping only the unlighted candle. The congregation may then exit the sanctuary with the candles. Children enjoy participating but need the supervision of adults.*

## COVENANT RENEWAL SERVICE       288

*1663 Richard Alleine, a Puritan, published* Vindiciae Pietatis: or, A ndication of Godliness in the Greater Strictness and Spirituality of It. *In 53, it was again published in John Wesley's* A Christian Library. *Wesley used one apter, "The Application of the Whole," on Monday, August 11, 1755, in what obably was the first real celebration of the Covenant Service in the Methodist ovement.*

*esley found the service rich and meaningful, as expressed in his* Journal: *"Many ourned before God, and many were comforted" (April 1756); "It was, as usual, a ne of remarkable blessing" (October 1765); "It was an occasion for a variety of ritual experiences . . . I do not know that ever we had a greater blessing. terwards many desired to return thanks, either for a sense of pardon, for full vation, or for a fresh manifestation of His graces, healing all their backslidings" nuary 1, 1775). In London these services were usually held on New Year's Day. ound the country the Covenant Service was conducted whenever John Wesley ited the Methodist Societies.*

*er the time of Wesley several versions of the Covenant Service were developed, dually giving Wesley's material less place in the total service. The present service lows our Basic Pattern of worship, enables the congregation to participate more ly, and updates language. Most significant, the liturgy beginning with the vitation is taken directly from Wesley's service of 1780.*

*e heart of the service, focused in the Covenant Prayer, requires persons to commit mselves to God. This covenant is serious and assumes adequate preparation for and atinual response to the covenant. Leaders of worship must take seriously the need to pare the congregation for this service, possibly through study sessions and prayer.*

*The leaders must also assume responsibility to assist persons to be faithful to t*
*covenant, possibly through meetings for spiritual discipline.*

*The Covenant Service is most commonly held on New Year's Eve or Day and therefo*
*is sometimes called a Watch Night Service. Historically, a Watch Night Servi*
*would be three hours or longer, including readings from Scripture and hymn singin*
*This Covenant Service would also be appropriate on one of the Sundays After t*
*Epiphany, during Lent, on a church anniversary, or during a revival or preachir*
*mission. Ideally, the service should be used only once a year on the same Sunday. R*
*is an appropriate color for paraments and vestments.*

*Individual copies of the Covenant Service are recommended for all worshipers so th*
*they may sign and keep them as reminders.*

# ENTRANCE

## GATHERING  *See 16-17.*

## GREETING *  *See 17-20.*

## HYMN *  Come, Let Us Use the Grace Divine (*UMH* 606)

*Charles Wesley wrote this hymn specifically for this service.*

## OPENING PRAYER *  *See 20-21.*

**O God, Searcher of all our hearts,**
**you have formed us as a people and claimed us for your own.**
**As we come to acknowledge your sovereignty and grace,**
    **and to enter anew into covenant with you,**
    **reveal any reluctance or falsehood within us.**
**Let your Spirit impress your truth on our inmost being,**
    **and receive us in mercy, for the sake of our Mediator, Jesus Chri**
    **who lives and reigns with you in the unity of the Holy Spirit,**
    **one God, for ever and ever. Amen.**

(DAVID TRIPP, ENGLAND, 20TH CE

## LITANY OF THANKSGIVING

*The following or another litany of thanksgiving may be used:*

Let us give thanks for all of God's mercies.

O God, our Covenant Friend,
you have been gracious to us through all the years of our lives.
We thank you for your loving care,
    which has filled our days and brought us to this time and place.
**We praise your holy name, O God.**

You have given us life and reason,
  and set us in a world filled with your glory.
You have comforted us with family and friends,
  and ministered to us through the hands of our sisters and brothers. R

You have filled our hearts with a hunger after you,
  and have given us your peace.
You have redeemed us, and called us to a high calling in Christ Jesus.
You have given us a place in the fellowship of your Spirit
  and the witness of your Church. R

You have been our light in darkness
  and a rock of strength in adversity and temptation.
You have been the very Spirit of joy in our joys
  and the all-sufficient reward in all our labors. R

You remembered us when we forgot you.
You followed us even when we tried to flee from you.
You met us with forgiveness when we returned to you.
For all your patience and overflowing grace. R


# PROCLAMATION

RAYER FOR ILLUMINATION * *See 22.*

CRIPTURE LESSON(S)

*These lessons may be interspersed with hymns (see 294) and psalms:*

| | |
|---|---|
| Deuteronomy 31:9-13 | A covenant renewal |
| 2 Kings 23:1-3 | Renewal of covenant |
| 2 Chronicles 34:29-33 | Renewal of covenant |
| Jeremiah 31:31-34 | A new covenant |
| Psalm 50 (UMH 783) | Gathering of the faithful |
| 1 Peter 1 | Call of holy living |
| Matthew 25:14-30 | Parable of talents |
| Matthew 25:31-46 | Judgment of the nations |
| John 15:1-8 | Jesus is the true vine. |


ROCLAMATION

Brothers and sisters in Christ,
  the Christian life is redeemed from sin and consecrated to God.
Through baptism, we have entered this life
  and have been admitted into the new covenant
    of which Jesus Christ is the Mediator.
He sealed it with his own blood, that it might last for ever.

On the one side, God promises to give us new life in Christ,
the Source and Perfecter of our faith.
On the other side, we are pledged
to live no more for ourselves but only for Jesus Christ,
who loved us and gave himself for us.

From time to time we renew our covenant with God,
especially when we reaffirm the Baptismal Covenant
and gather at the Lord's table.

Today, however, we meet, as the generations before us have met,
to renew the covenant that binds us to God.
Let us make this covenant of God our own.

# WESLEY'S COVENANT SERVICE

## INVITATION

Commit yourselves to Christ as his servants.
Give yourselves to him, that you may belong to him.
Christ has many services to be done.
Some are more easy and honorable,
others are more difficult and disgraceful.
Some are suitable to our inclinations and interests,
others are contrary to both.
In some we may please Christ and please ourselves.
But then there are other works where we cannot please Christ
except by denying ourselves.
It is necessary, therefore,
that we consider what it means to be a servant of Christ.

Let us, therefore, go to Christ, and pray:

**Let me be your servant, under your command.**
**I will no longer be my own.**
**I will give up myself to your will in all things.**

Be satisfied that Christ shall give you your place and work.

**Lord, make me what you will.**
**I put myself fully into your hands:**
**put me to doing, put me to suffering,**
**let me be employed for you, or laid aside for you,**
**let me be full, let me be empty,**
**let me have all things, let me have nothing.**
**I freely and with a willing heart**
**give it all to your pleasure and disposal.**

Christ will be the Savior of none but his servants.
He is the source of all salvation to those who obey.
Christ will have no servants except by consent;
Christ will not accept anything except full consent
  to all that he requires.
Christ will be all in all, or he will be nothing.

Confirm this by a holy covenant.

To make this covenant a reality in your life, listen to these admonitions:

First, set apart some time, more than once,
  to be spent alone before the Lord;
in seeking earnestly God's special assistance
  and gracious acceptance of you;
in carefully thinking through all the conditions of the covenant;
in searching your hearts
  whether you have already freely given your life to Christ.
Consider what your sins are.
Consider the laws of Christ, how holy, strict, and spiritual they are,
  and whether you, after having carefully considered them,
  are willing to choose them all.
Be sure you are clear in these matters, see that you do not lie to God.

Second, be serious and in a spirit of holy awe and reverence.

Third, claim God's covenant,
rely upon God's promise of giving grace and strength,
  so you can keep your promise.
Trust not your own strength and power.

Fourth, resolve to be faithful.
You have given to the Lord your hearts,
  you have opened your mouths to the Lord,
  and you have dedicated yourself to God.
With God's power, never go back.

And last, be then prepared to renew your covenant with the Lord.
Fall down on your knees, lift your hands toward heaven,
  open your hearts to the Lord, as we pray:

## COVENANT PRAYER

*The people kneel or bow.*

O righteous God, for the sake of your Son Jesus Christ,
  see me as I fall down before you.
Forgive my unfaithfulness in not having done your will,
  for you have promised mercy to me
    if I turn to you with my whole heart.

God requires that you shall put away all your idols.

**I here from the bottom of my heart renounce them all,**
  **covenanting with you that no known sin shall be allowed in my life**
**Against your will, I have turned my love toward the world.**
**In your power**
  **I will watch all temptations that will lead me away from you.**
**For my own righteousness is riddled with sin,**
  **unable to stand before you.**

Through Christ, God has offered to be your God again
  if you would let him.

**Before all heaven and earth,**
  **I here acknowledge you as my Lord and God.**
**I take you, Father, Son, and Holy Spirit, for my portion,**
  **and vow to give up myself, body and soul, as your servant,**
  **to serve you in holiness and righteousness all the days of my life**

God has given the Lord Jesus Christ
  as the only way and means of coming to God.

**Jesus, I do here on bended knees accept Christ**
  **as the only new and living Way,**
  **and sincerely join myself in a covenant with him.**
**O blessed Jesus, I come to you,**
  **hungry, sinful, miserable, blind, and naked,**
  **unworthy even to wash the feet of your servants.**
**I do here, with all my power, accept you as my Lord and Head.**
**I renounce my own worthiness,**
  **and vow that you are the Lord, my righteousness.**
**I renounce my own wisdom, and take you for my only guide.**
**I renounce my own will, and take your will as my law.**

Christ has told you that you must suffer with him.

**I do here covenant with you, O Christ,**
  **to take my lot with you as it may fall.**
**Through your grace I promise**
  **that neither life nor death shall part me from you.**

God has given holy laws as the rule of your life.

**I do here willingly put my neck under your yoke, to carry your burden**
**All your laws are holy, just, and good.**
**I therefore take them as the rule for my words, thoughts, and actions**
  **promising that I will strive**
    **to order my whole life according to your direction,**
  **and not allow myself to neglect anything I know to be my duty.**

The almighty God searches and knows your heart.

O God, you know that I make this covenant with you today
   without guile or reservation.
If any falsehood should be in it, guide me and help me to set it aright.
And now, glory be to you, O God the Father,
   whom I from this day forward shall look upon as my God and Father.
Glory be to you, O God the Son,
   who have loved me and washed me from my sins in your own blood,
   and now is my Savior and Redeemer.
Glory be to you, O God the Holy Spirit,
   who by your almighty power have turned my heart from sin to God.

O mighty God, the Lord Omnipotent, Father, Son, and Holy Spirit,
   you have now become my Covenant Friend.
And I, through your infinite grace, have become your covenant servant.
So be it.
And let the covenant I have made on earth be ratified in heaven.
Amen.

*You are advised to make this covenant not only in your heart, but in word; not only
in word, but in writing. Therefore, with all reverence, lay the service before the
Lord as your act and deed. And when you have done this, sign it. Then keep it as a
reminder of the holy agreement between God and you that you may remember it
during doubts and temptations.*

*See also A Covenant Prayer in the Wesleyan Tradition (UMH 607).*

*The pastor may now celebrate Holy Communion, the people using A Service of
Word and Table III (UMH 15) or one of the musical settings (UMH 17-25) and the
pastor using The Great Thanksgiving on 58-59. Otherwise, the service continues
as follows:*

YMN * *Suggested from UMH:*

563/4 Father, We Thank you       117 O God, Our Help in Ages Past
698 God of The Ages              501 O Thou Who Camest from Above
561 Jesus, United by Thy Grace

SMISSAL WITH BLESSING * *See 31-32.*

# ACTS OF WORSHIP                                   294
# FOR NEW YEAR'S EVE OR DAY

*Suggested Hymns from UMH*

* Hymns listed under New Year

*Greeting*

rd, you have been our dwelling place in all generations.
>m everlasting to everlasting, you are God.          (PSALM 90:1, 2c)

*Prayer*

Creative God, you make all things new in heaven and on earth.
We come to you in a new year with new desires and old fears,
  new decisions and old controversies,
  new dreams and old weaknesses.
Because you are a God of hope,
  we know that you create all the possibilities of the future.
Because you are a God of love,
  we know that you accept all the mistakes of the past.
Because you are the God of our faith,
  we enter your gates with thanksgiving and praise,
  we come into your presence with gladness and a joyful noise,
  and we serve and bless you. Amen.    (Maren C. Tirabassi, U.S.A., 20th cent., Al

*See A Covenant Prayer in the Wesleyan Tradition (UMH 607).*

*If Holy Communion is to be celebrated, see The Great Thanksgiving on 58-59.*
*Covenant Renewal service (see 288-94) or A Congregational Reaffirmation of t*
*Baptismal Covenant (see 111-14) may also be celebrated.*

# 295    ACTS OF WORSHIP
# FOR THE EPIPHANY OF THE LORD

*The Epiphany (Manifestation) of the Lord (January 6), an even more ancie*
*celebration among Christians than Christmas, originally focused on the nativi*
*incarnation, and baptism of Christ. Today we celebrate the coming of the three w*
*men (magi), who brought gifts to the Christ child. For this reason, in Puerto Rico a*
*in most Latin American countries this day is observed as* Three Kings Day *or* Dia
*Los Reyes. It marks the end of the Christmas Cycle, which began the First Sunday*
*Advent.*

*The Latino culture has preserved and developed this ancient celebration in a way th*
*is a great gift to the whole Church. Within the church service, this day is celebra*
*with plays and special songs emphasizing the coming of the kings and their gifts*
*the Christ child. In the home the children are told to place boxes filled with hay un*
*their beds so that the camels will eat the hay and the kings leave presents for*
*children.*

ongregations that do not worship on January 6 unless it is a Sunday may celebrate
piphany on the first Sunday in January.

## Suggested Hymns from UMH

7 Hymns listed under Epiphany
7-54 Christ's Gracious Life: Birth and Baptism

### Greeting     **296**

o we have the prophetic message more fully confirmed.
ou will do well to be attentive to this,
as to a lamp shining in a dark place,
ntil the day dawns and the morning star rises in your hearts.

(2 PETER 1:19)

### Prayer     **297**

verlasting God, the radiance of faithful souls,
you brought the nations to your light
    and kings to the brightness of your rising.
ll the world with your glory, and show yourself to all the nations;
rough him who is the true light and the bright and morning star,
en Jesus Christ your Son our Lord. Amen.

(LATIN SACRAMENTARY, 5TH-7TH CENT., ALT.)

e Epiphany (UMH 255).

Holy Communion is to be celebrated, see The Great Thanksgiving on 58-59.

# SEASON AFTER THE EPIPHANY (ORDINARY TIME)

The Season After the Epiphany is a season of Ordinary Time, which includ• four to nine Sundays, depending on the date of Easter. It is ordinary in that stands between the two great christological cycles of Advent-Christma• Epiphany and Lent-Easter-Pentecost and has no central theme. The Fir• Sunday focuses on the Baptism of Christ and the Last Sunday on t• Transfiguration. The Gospel readings in the lectionary center on stories fro• the early ministry of Christ. In addition to the acts of worship for Sunda• After the Epiphany on the following pages, see The Great Thanksgivings • 36-38, 58-59, and 70-71 and the scripture readings for the Sundays After t• Epiphany in the lectionary (228-30).

Use white paraments, stoles, and banners on the First Sunday (Baptism the Lord) and the Last Sunday (Transfiguration Sunday); add green on t• other Sundays. Contrasting colors will accentuate these more neutral colo• Visuals may include a baptismal font, water jars for the miracle at Cana, a• bright candles for the Transfiguration.

## 299 ACTS OF WORSHIP FOR BAPTISM OF THE LORD

*This Sunday, which falls between January 7 and 13 inclusive, celebrates Chris• baptism by John and reminds all Christians of our one baptism. It is an especia• appropriate time for baptisms and for A Congregational Reaffirmation of • Baptismal Covenant (111-14 and UMH 50).*

### Suggested Hymns from UMH

193 Jesus! the Name High over All  
252 When Jesus Came to Jordan

604-11 Baptism, Confirmation, Reaffirmatio•

## 300  *Greeting*

Ascribe to the Lord, O heavenly beings,
**ascribe to the Lord glory and strength.**

Ascribe to the Lord the glory of God's name,
**worship the Lord in holy array.**

The voice of the Lord is upon the water.
**The God of glory thunders, the Lord upon many waters.**

ιe voice of the Lord is powerful.
**he voice of God is full of majesty.**
**ːt us praise the name of the Lord!**          (PSALM 29, ALT.)

*Prayer*          **301**

ving God,
hen the Spirit descended on Jesus at his baptism in Jordan's water
you revealed him as your own beloved Son.
ɔu anointed him with the Holy Spirit.
ιant that all who are baptized into his name
may keep the covenant they have made,
and boldly confess Jesus Christ as Lord and Savior
     now and for ever. Amen. (THE BOOK OF COMMON PRAYER, U.S.A., 20TH CENT., ALT.)

*e Baptism of the Lord (UMH 253).*

*Holy Communion is to be celebrated, see The Great Thanksgiving on 58-59.*

# ACTS OF WORSHIP          302
# FOR THE SUNDAYS AFTER THE EPIPHANY

*though the following hymns and other acts of worship are most suitable for this*
*ιson, the General Acts of Worship (445-567) are also suitable.*

### Suggested Hymns from UMH

7-54 Christ's Gracious Life:          193 Jesus! the Name High over All
   Birth and Baptism          679 O Splendor of God's Glory Bright
5 Canticle of Light and Darkness          258 O Wondrous Sight! O Vision Fair
8 Christ Is the World's Light          187 Rise, Shine, You People
0 Christ upon the Mountain Peak          418 We Are Climbing Jacob's Ladder
3 Christ, Whose Glory Fills the Skies

### Suggested Musical Responses

ise, Shine ( ♪ 216)
ιm the Lamp ( ♪ 210)

### Greetings

**303**

ιe Lord has declared victory,
ιd has revealed his vindication in the sight of the nations.
          (PSALM 98:2 UMH)

**304**

ːise, shine; for your light has come,
ιand the glory of the Lord has risen upon you.          (ISAIAH 60:1)

*e ♪ 216 for musical setting.*

**305**

And the Word became flesh and lived among us,
  **and we have seen his glory,**
  **the glory as of a father's only son, full of grace and truth.**   (JOHN 1:)

**306**

For it is the God who said, "Let light shine out of darkness,"
  who has shone in our hearts
    **to give the light of the knowledge of the glory of God**
    **in the face of Jesus Christ.**   (2 CORINTHIANS 4)

**307**

So he came and proclaimed peace to you who were far off
  and peace to those who were near;
**for through him all of us have access in one Spirit to the Father.**
                                    (EPHESIANS 2:17 18, AI)

*Prayers*

**308**

Almighty God,
  your Son, our Savior Jesus Christ, is the light of the world.
Grant that your people, illumined by your Word and Sacraments,
  may shine with the radiance of Christ's glory,
that he may be known, worshiped, and obeyed
  to the ends of the earth, now and for ever. Amen.
                    (THE BOOK OF COMMON PRAYER, U.S.A., 20TH CENT., AI)

**309**

O Christ, who commanded the apostles to go into all the world,
  and to preach the gospel to every creature,
let your name be great among the nations
  from the rising up of the sun to its going down,
  now and for ever. Amen.   (LANCELOT ANDREWES, ENGLAND, 16TH CENT., A)

**310**

Eternal Light, shine into our hearts.
Eternal Goodness, deliver us from evil.
Eternal Power, be our support.
Eternal Wisdom, scatter the darkness of our ignorance.
Eternal Pity, have mercy upon us.
That with all our heart and mind and soul and strength
  we may seek your face
  and be brought by your infinite mercy to your holy presence;
through Jesus Christ our Lord. Amen.   (ALCUIN OF YORK, ENGLAND, 8TH CEN)

**311**

living Christ, you changed Cana's water into festal wine.
ransform our common worship into celebration,
that we may taste your glory here and now
ıd anticipate that heavenly banquet
where we shall behold your face for ever. Amen.

(DAVID SCHNASA JACOBSEN, U.S.A., 20TH CENT.)

**312**

ʳerlasting God, you gave us the faith of Christ
for a light to our feet amid the darkness of this world.
ave pity on all who, by doubting or denying it,
are gone astray from the path of safety.
ʳing home the truth to their hearts, and grant them to receive it;
ᵗrough the same Jesus Christ our Lord. Amen.

(WILLIAM BRIGHT, ENGLAND, 19TH CENT., ALT.)

**313**

Lord God, your chosen dwelling is the heart of the lowly.
ʾe give you thanks that you revealed yourself in the holy child Jesus,
thereby sanctifying all childhood in him.
ake us humble in faith and love, that we may know the joy of the gospel
hidden from the wise and prudent and revealed unto babes.
ᵘis we ask in the name of the One, who, wearing our mortal flesh,
grew in wisdom and in favor with God and all people,
Jesus Christ our Lord. Amen.

(CONGREGATIONAL WORSHIP, ENGLAND AND WALES, 20TH CENT., ALT.)

**314**

God of all the nations,
you manifested your love by sending your only Son into the world
    that all might live through him.
ᵘur your Spirit on your Church,
that it may fulfill his command to preach the gospel everywhere;
nd forth laborers into your harvest;
ᵉfend them in all dangers and temptations;
ʳve them grace to bear faithful witness to you;
ᵻdue them with zeal and love, that they may turn many to righteousness;
ᵗrough the same your Son, Jesus Christ our Lord. Amen.

(THE BOOK OF WORSHIP 1965, ALT.)

**315**

God,
ᵘu made of one blood
    all nations that dwell on the face of the whole earth,
ᵻd sent your blessed Son to preach peace
    to them that are afar off and to them that are near.
ʳant that all people everywhere may seek after you and find you.

Bring the nations into your fold, pour out your Spirit on all flesh,
   and hasten your kingdom;
through the same Jesus Christ our Lord. Amen.

(THE BOOK OF COMMON PRAYER, U.S.A., 20TH CENT., AL

## 316          *Presentation of Jesus in the Temple*

*This day, traditionally February 2, remembers that Mary and Joseph took Jesus
Simeon in the Temple for purification on the fortieth day after his birth.*

### Suggested Scripture Readings

| | |
|---|---|
| Malachi 3:1-4 | The Lord will come to his temple. |
| Psalm 24:7-10 (*UMH* 755) or | The Lord enters the gates of his temple. |
|   Psalm 84 (*UMH* 804) | The joy of being in God's temple |
| Hebrews 2:14-18 | Christ was a Jew in every respect. |
| Luke 2:22-40 | Presentation of Jesus in the Temple |

### Suggested Hymns from UMH

225 Canticle of Simeon
226 My Master, See, the Time Has Come

### Prayer

God of compassion, on this day your Holy Spirit revealed
   the salvation you had prepared for all peoples
      to the devout Simeon and Anna,
   who had waited until late in life.
Grant that we, too, may adore your Son, Jesus Christ,
   a light to the Gentiles and the glory of Israel,
so we may proclaim him to all your world;
through Jesus Christ our Lord. Amen.    (DON E. SALIERS, U.S.A., 20TH CENT., AI

# ACTS OF WORSHIP 317
# FOR TRANSFIGURATION SUNDAY

s last Sunday before Lent recalls Christ's transfiguration on the mountain with
ah and Moses.

### Suggested Hymns from UMH

Hymns listed under Transfiguration

### Greeting 318

e Lord is Sovereign; let the people tremble in awe.
**·d is enthroned upon the cherubim; let the earth shake.**
e Lord is great in Zion, and is high above all peoples.
**·claim the greatness of the Lord our God,**
**ɪnd worship Yahweh upon the holy mountain.**

(FROM HOPE TO JOY, U.S.A., 20TH CENT., ALT.)

### Prayer 319

d of glory and mercy,
ɔefore his death in shame your Son went to the mountain top,
ɪnd you revealed his life in glory.
ɪere prophets witnessed to him, you proclaimed him your Son,
ɔut he returned to die among us.
lp us face evil with courage,
:nowing that all things, even death,
ɪre subject to your transforming power.
: ask this through Christ our Lord. Amen.

(JAMES F. WHITE, U.S.A., 20TH CENT.)

*Transfiguration (UMH 259).*

# LENT

Lent is a season of forty days, not counting Sundays, which begins on A
Wednesday and ends on Holy Saturday. *Lent* comes from the Anglo-Sax
word *lencten*, which means "spring." The season is a preparation
celebrating Easter. Historically, Lent began as a period of fasting a
preparation for baptism by converts and then became a time for penance
all Christians. The First Sunday describes Jesus' temptation by Satan; a
the Sixth Sunday (Passion/Palm Sunday), Christ's triumphal entry i
Jerusalem and his subsequent passion and death. Because Sundays
always little Easters, the penitential spirit of Lent should be tempered w
joyful expectation of the Resurrection.

The Great Three Days—sometimes called the Triduum or Pasch—fr
sunset Holy Thursday through sunset Easter Day are the climax of Lent (a
of the whole Christian year) and a bridge into the Easter Season. These da
proclaim the paschal mystery of Jesus Christ's passion, death, a
resurrection. During these days, the community journeys with Jesus fr
the upper room, to the cross, to the tomb, and to the garden. They should
seen as a great unified service beginning with a service of Holy Commun
on Holy Thursday and concluding with the services of Easter Day. Th
services may be connected with a prayer vigil lasting from Holy Thurs(
evening (or Good Friday) until the first service of Easter and may
accompanied by fasting.

In addition to the acts and services of worship on the following pages,
the two Great Thanksgivings for Lent (60-63) and the scripture readings
Lent in the lectionary (230-231).

Somber colors such as purple or ash gray and rough-textured cloth are m
appropriate for paraments, stoles, and banners. Unbleached muslin cl(
with red stitching is also appropriate. Remove all shiny objects from
worship area. Some may wish to omit flowers. Other visuals may includ
large rough cross (possibly made from the trunk of the Chrismon tree) c
veil over the sanctuary cross.

Other visuals for Holy Week may include red paraments, stoles, a
banners, and symbols such as perfume, coins, a whip, a crown of thorn:
torn garment, nails, a spear, a sponge, or a broken reed. On Good Friday a
Holy Saturday the church may be stripped bare of visuals.

# A SERVICE OF WORSHIP FOR ASH WEDNESDAY

*sh Wednesday emphasizes a dual encounter: we confront our own mortality and ·nfess our sin before God within the community of faith. The form and content of the ·rvice focus on the dual themes of sin and death in the light of God's redeeming love in sus Christ.*

*·epending upon circumstances, this service may be held (1) early in the morning, ·fore the work and school day begin; (2) at noontime, perhaps observing a fast with ·e deletion of the regular noon meal; or (3) early in the evening, perhaps following a ·ared sacrificial meal of bread and water.*

*·he visual environment should be solemn and stark. Purple is the most traditional ·lor throughout Lent; but on Ash Wednesday gray, with its suggestion of ashes, is ·pecially appropriate. Dark earth colors or any somber hues are also appropriate. ·ough, coarse textures such as burlap—sackcloth and ashes—suggest the character of ·e day and season.*

*·he use of ashes as a sign of mortality and repentance has a long history in Jewish and ·hristian worship, and the Imposition of Ashes can be a powerful nonverbal and ·periential way of participating in the call to repentance and reconciliation. This ·actice is the historic focus of Ash Wednesday observance and gave the day its name. · is traditional to save the palm branches from the previous Passion/Palm Sunday ·rvice and burn them ahead of time to produce the ashes for this service. ·lternatively, ushers may distribute small cards or pieces of paper on which each ·rson may be invited to write a particular sin or hurtful or unjust characteristic. ·ey may then be brought forward by the ushers following the sermon and placed ·on a grate to be burned with palm branches for the ashes. The ashes may be mixed ·th a small amount of water for Imposition of Ashes. A towel for cleansing the ·stor's hands should be provided.*

*·stead of Imposition of Ashes or in addition to it, Holy Communion may be ·lebrated. Immediately before Confession and Pardon, the congregation may be ·vited to turn for the rest of the service to A Service of Word and Table IV (UMH 26). · the service may continue as given below through the Offering, during which the ·ead and wine are brought by representatives of the people to the Lord's table with the ·her gifts or uncovered if already in place. After the offering, the congregation may be ·vited to turn to A Service of Word and Table III (UMH 15) or one of the musical ·ttings in UMH 17-25, the pastor praying The Great Thanksgiving on 60-61. If both ·position of Ashes and Holy Communion are included in the service, they should ·ways be separated, with the people coming forward for each action.*

**·ATHERING** *See 16-17.*

*If a brief explanation of the service is necessary, it may be done quietly during this time, allowing for a return to silence before the Greeting.*

*If a choir is to process, it should do so in silence immediately before the Greeting.*

GREETING * *See 17-20.*

The grace of the Lord Jesus Christ be with you.
**And also with you.**

Bless the Lord who forgives all our sins.
**God's mercy endures for ever.**

OPENING PRAYER * *See Ash Wednesday (UMH 353).*

HYMN * Lord, Who Throughout These Forty Days (*UMH* 269)

SCRIPTURE LESSON Joel 2:1-2, 12-17

[PSALM] *

*If Psalm 51:1-17 (UMH 785) is not used as the Prayer of Confession later, it may* *used here.*

SCRIPTURE LESSON 2 Corinthians 5:20b–6:10

HYMN * *See suggestions under Imposition of Ashes below.*

GOSPEL LESSON * Matthew 6:1-6, 16-21

SERMON

INVITATION TO THE OBSERVANCE OF LENTEN DISCIPLINE

*The following or similar words may be spoken:*

Dear brothers and sisters in Christ:
the early Christians observed with great devotion
    the days of our Lord's passion and resurrection,
and it became the custom of the Church that before the Easter celebrati
    there should be a forty-day season of spiritual preparation.
During this season converts to the faith were prepared for Holy Baptis
It was also a time when persons who had committed serious sins
    and had separated themselves from the community of faith
        were reconciled by penitence and forgiveness,
    and restored to participation in the life of the Church.
In this way the whole congregation was reminded
    of the mercy and forgiveness proclaimed in the gospel of Jesus Chr
    and the need we all have to renew our faith.
I invite you, therefore, in the name of the Church,
    to observe a holy Lent:
    by self-examination and repentance;
    by prayer, fasting, and self-denial;
    and by reading and meditating on God's Holy Word.

To make a right beginning of repentance,
 and as a mark of our mortal nature,
 let us now kneel *(bow)* before our Creator and Redeemer.

*A brief silence is kept, the congregation kneeling or bowed.*

*If there is to be no Imposition of Ashes, the service continues with Confession and Pardon.*

## ᴴANKSGIVING OVER THE ASHES

Almighty God, you have created us out of the dust of the earth.
Grant that these ashes may be to us a sign of our mortality and penitence,
 so that we may remember that only by your gracious gift
  are we given everlasting life;
through Jesus Christ our Savior. **Amen.**

## ᴵPOSITION OF ASHES *

*The pastor, and any others assisting, take their places in front of the congregation*
*ₐnd with word or gesture invite the congregation to come forward. The leaders dip a*
*ᵗhumb in the ashes and make a cross on the forehead of each person.*

*They sing ( ♪ 217) or say:*

◀Remember that you are dust, and to dust you shall return.

*Ɔr they say:*

◀Repent, and believe the gospel.

*The Imposition may be done in silence, or one or more of the following hymns in*
*ᴜMH may be sung:*

| | |
|---|---|
| ₄58 Dear Lord and Father | 357 Just as I Am, Without One Plea |
|   of Mankind | 402 Lord, I Want to Be a Christian |
| ₄55 Depth of Mercy | 351 Pass Me Not, O Gentle Savior |
| ₄82 Have Thine Own Way, Lord | 491 Remember Me |
| ₃54 I Surrender All | 346 Sinners, Turn: Why Will You Die? |
| ₃52 It's Me, It's Me, O Lord | 356 When We Are Living |
| ₄88 Jesus, Remember Me | |

## ƆNFESSION AND PARDON *See 20-21, 25-26.*

*The congregation prays Psalm 51:1-17 (UMH 785).*

*Ɑll offer prayers of confession in silence.*

*The pastor then says:*

◀May the almighty and merciful God,
 who desires not the death of a sinner
  but that we turn from wickedness and live,
◀accept your repentance, forgive your sins,
 and restore you by the Holy Spirit to newness of life. Amen.

*Or one of the confession-pardon sequences in UMH 890-93 or on 474-94 may used.*

THE PEACE * *See 26.*

Let us offer one another signs of reconciliation and love.

*All exchange signs and words of God's peace.*

OFFERING *See 26-27.*

PRAYER OF THANKSGIVING * *See 27.*

THE LORD'S PRAYER * *See 29.*

HYMN * *See suggestions above.*

DISMISSAL WITH BLESSING * *See 31-32.*

GOING FORTH * *See 32.*

*If the choir is to recess, it should be in silence following Dismissal with Blessi*
*The people may depart in silence.*

# 324     ACTS OF WORSHIP FOR LENT

*Suggested Hymns and Canticles from* UMH

278-301 Christ's Gracious Life:
    Passion and Death
166 All Praise to Thee, for Thou,
    O King Divine
163 Ask Ye What Great Thing I Know
168 At the Name of Jesus
167 Canticle of Christ's Obedience
125 Canticle of Covenant Faithfulness
527 Do, Lord, Remember Me
142 If Thou But Suffer God
    to Guide Thee

213 Lift Up Your Heads,
    Ye Mighty Gates
194 Morning Glory, Starlit Sky
267 O Love, How Deep
137 Psalm 23 (King James Version)
161 Rejoice, Ye Pure in Heart
124 Seek the Lord
415 Take Up Thy Cross
277 Tell Me the Stories of Jesus
622 There Is a Fountain Filled with Blood
549 Where Charity and Love Prevail

*Suggested Musical Responses from* UMH

488 Jesus, Remember Me        491 Remember Me

*See also:*
Holy God ( ♪ 215)
O Lamb of God ( ♪ 201)
Señor Apiádate de Nosotros ( ♪ 188)

*Greetings*

**325**

Come now, let us reason together, says the Lord:
though your sins are like scarlet, they shall be like snow;
**though they are red like crimson, they shall become like wool.**

(ISAIAH 1:18, ALT.)

**326**

Come, let us walk in the light of the Lord,
**that he may teach us his ways and that we may walk in his paths.**

(ISAIAH 2:5, 3c)

**327**

In returning and rest you shall be saved;
**in quietness and in trust shall be your strength.** (ISAIAH 30:15b-c)

**328**

Rend your hearts and not your clothing.
Return to the Lord, your God,
**for he is gracious and merciful,**
  **slow to anger, and abounding in steadfast love,**
  **and relents from punishing.** (JOEL 2:13)

**329**

Since, then, we have a great high priest
  who has passed through the heavens,
  Jesus, the Son of God,
**let us hold fast to our confession.**

For we do not have a high priest
  who is unable to sympathize with our weaknesses,
**but we have one who in every respect has been tested as we are,**
  **yet without sin.**

Let us therefore approach the throne of grace with boldness,
**so that we may receive mercy and find grace to help in time of need.**

(HEBREWS 4:14-16)

*also:*

| | |
|---|---|
| Psalm 139:23-24 | Search me, O God, and know my heart. |
| Isaiah 53:6 | All we like sheep have gone astray. |
| 1 Corinthians 10:13 | God is faithful. |
| James 4:10 | Humble yourselves before the Lord. |
| 1 John 1:8-9 | We deceive ourselves. |

**330**

Savior of the world,
who by your cross and precious blood has redeemed us,
save us and help us. (SARUM LITURGY, ENGLAND, 13TH CENT., ALT.)

# 331

The Lord is merciful and gracious,
  slow to anger and abounding in steadfast love.
**He does not deal with us according to our sins,**
  **nor requite us according to our iniquities.**

What shall I render to the Lord for all his bounty to me?
**I will lift up the cup of salvation**
  **and call on the name of the Lord.** (THE BOOK OF WORSHIP 19⦿

# 332

Let us test and examine our ways, and return to the Lord!
**God has blessed us; let all the ends of the earth fear him!**

Seek the Lord while he may be found,
  call upon him while he is near;
let the wicked forsake their way,
  and the unrighteous their thoughts;
let them return to the Lord.
**The sacrifice acceptable to God is a broken spirit;**
**a broken and contrite heart, O God, you will not despise.**

(THE BOOK OF WORSHIP 1965, A⦿

*Prayers*

# 333

Almighty God, your blessed Son was led by the Spirit
  to be tempted by Satan.
Come quickly to help us who are assaulted by many temptations.
And, as you know the weakness of each of us,
  let each one find you mighty to save;
through Jesus Christ your Son, our Lord. Amen.

(THE BOOK OF COMMON PRAYER, U.S.A., 20TH CENT., A

# 334

O God, your glory is always to have mercy.
Be gracious to all who have gone astray from your ways,
  and bring them again with penitent hearts and steadfast faith
    to embrace and hold fast the unchangeable truth of your Word,
Jesus Christ your Son,
who with you and the Holy Spirit lives and reigns,
one God, for ever and ever. Amen.

(THE BOOK OF COMMON PRAYER, U.S.A., 20TH CENT., A⦿

# 335

Everlasting God,
  because of your tender mercy toward all people,
  you sent your Son, our Savior Jesus Christ,
  to take upon himself our flesh,

and to suffer death upon the cross,
that all should follow the example of his great humility.
Mercifully grant that we may follow the example of his patience
and also be made partakers of his resurrection;
through the same Jesus Christ our Lord. Amen.

(THE BOOK OF COMMON PRAYER, U.S.A., 20TH CENT., ALT.)

**336**

O merciful Father, in compassion for your sinful children
you sent your Son Jesus Christ to be the Savior of the world.
Grant us grace to feel and to lament our share of the evil
that made it necessary for him to suffer and to die for our salvation.
Help us by self-denial, prayer, and meditation
to prepare our hearts for deeper penitence and a better life.
And give us a true longing to be free from sin,
through the deliverance won by Jesus Christ our Redeemer. Amen.

(JOSEPH NEWTON, U.S.A., 20TH CENT., ALT.)

**337**

Lord our God, teach us temperance and self-control,
that we may live in the Spirit
and be mindful of all that Jesus endured and sacrificed for our sakes,
and how he was made perfect through sufferings.
Help us so to keep the fast that you have chosen,
that we may loose the bonds of wickedness,
undo the heavy burdens, and let the oppressed go free;
through the grace of Christ Jesus our crucified and risen Savior. Amen.

(HENRY VAN DYKE, U.S.A., 20TH CENT., ALT.)

*See Lent (UMH 268).*

# A SERVICE OF WORSHIP  338
# FOR PASSION/PALM SUNDAY

*This service embodies the sharp contrasts of Holy Week. In the Entrance with the Palms we experience the joyous demonstration of loyalty to Jesus as he enters Jerusalem, including festive Palm Sunday music. In the Proclamation and Response we confront and respond to the story of Jesus' passion, including somber Passion Sunday music.*

*It is important not to let the celebration of Palm Sunday crowd out the observance of Passion Sunday. The passion narratives in Scripture are highly unified and dramatic,*

*and we need to experience the story in its wholeness before we reflect at greater leng*
*on its various parts during the following weekdays. We need also to remember th*
*many persons who attend on Passion/Palm Sunday will not be in church again un*
*Easter Day. Going directly from the lesser joy of the entry into Jerusalem to the joy*
*Easter, without being addressed by the passion and the cross of our Lor*
*misrepresents the gospel. There is no triumph without suffering, no crown without*
*cross.*

*Because so much of significance is in this service, and because this day and all of Ho*
*Week are preliminary to the supreme joy of Easter, this day is unsuitable f*
*celebrating baptism, confirmation, or the reception of new members. Baptisms ar*
*confirmations at this time of year are most appropriately held during the East*
*Season—the Great Fifty Days from the Easter Vigil through the Day of Pentecos*

## ENTRANCE WITH THE PALMS

### GATHERING *See 16-17.*

*When circumstances permit, the congregation may gather at a designated pla*
*outside the church building or in a room other than the place of worship. T*
*branches of palm, olive, or other trees or shrubs to be carried in the procession m*
*be distributed to the people, and a brief introduction to the whole service may*
*given. Palm leaves may be saved until the following year and burned to provi*
*ashes for Ash Wednesday.*

### PROCLAMATION OF THE ENTRANCE INTO JERUSALEM *

Hear from the Gospel according to ____
how our Lord Jesus entered Jerusalem.

*One of the following is read:*

| | |
|---|---|
| Matthew 21:1-11 | (Year A) |
| Mark 11:1-11 | (Year B) |
| Luke 19:28-40 | (Year C) |

### THE PEOPLE'S RESPONSE *

*Psalm 118:1-2, 19-29 (UMH 839) may be sung or spoken by the leader and t*
*congregation, or by the leader and the choir if the congregation does not have acc*
*to hymnals; or the following acclamation may be used:*

Hosanna to the Son of David!
**Hosanna in the highest!**

Blessed is the One who comes in the name of the Lord.
**Hosanna in the highest!**

### PROCESSIONAL HYMN *

*The congregation, choir(s), and leaders then process into the place of worship. T*
*participation of children is especially effective and encouraged even if the wh*
*congregation does not process. Suggested from UMH:*

280 All Glory, Laud, and Honor
278 Hosanna, Loud Hosanna

213 List Up Your Heads, Ye Mighty Gates
279 Mantos y Palmas (Filled with Excitement)
161 Rejoice, Ye Pure in Heart

OPENING PRAYER] * See 20-21.

Almighty God,
on this day your Son Jesus Christ entered the holy city of Jerusalem
and was proclaimed King
by those who spread their garments and palm branches along his way.
Let those branches be for us signs of his victory,
and grant that we who bear them in his name
may ever hail him as our Lord,
and follow him in the way that leads to eternal life.
In his name we pray. Amen.

## PROCLAMATION AND RESPONSE

PRAYER FOR ILLUMINATION * See Passion/Palm Sunday (UMH 281).

SCRIPTURE LESSON Isaiah 50:4-9a

PSALM 31:1-16 (UMH 764)

SCRIPTURE LESSON Philippians 2:5-11

This scripture may be sung as a canticle (UMH 167) or as a hymn, All Praise to Thee, for Thou, O King Divine (UMH 166), omitting the alleluia refrain. If it is sung, both the preceding psalm and the following hymn may be omitted.

HYMN * The people may sing one of the following in UMH:

168 At the Name of Jesus
692 Creator of the Stars of Night
177 He Is Lord

193 Jesus! the Name High over All
536 Precious Name

## PROCLAMATION OF THE PASSION STORY

Matthew 26:14–27:66 or Matthew 27:11-54 (Year A)
Mark 14:1–15:47 or Mark 15:1-39 [40-47] (Year B)
Luke 22:14–23:56 or Luke 23:1-49 (Year C)

Several possibilities will allow the congregation to experience the whole passion story in this service:

1) One of the above versions of the passion story may be read dramatically, with members of the congregation taking the various roles: the narrator, Jesus, Pilate, the apostles, other characters, and the crowd. As few as three persons can do this if all the voices except the narrator and Jesus are spoken by one person. If

*members of the congregation are provided a text or proper cues, they may take the role of the crowd, or the choir may take this role. The passion narratives are printed in a format suited for dramatic reading in various publications.*

2) *The passion narrative may also be sung by the choir. Although settings such as Bach's would be far too long, many shorter choral settings are available Selections from the larger works may be woven together with dramatize readings as well. Advance planning, rehearsal, and wise choice in the level of difficulty of the music are essential. Something simple, done well, is better than something beyond the capacity of the choir.*

3) *A lessons-and-hymns pattern similar to the lessons-and-carols pattern for a Advent or a Christmas service may be used. Segments of Scripture are read, most effectively by several readers, interspersed with passion hymns and possibly accompanied by mime. This pattern begins with the scripture lessons from Isaiah and Philippians above and continues with the passion narrative, divided into shorter readings as indicated below and interspersed with hymns. Readings from the Gospel of John (355-61), which are suitable any year, provide an alternative to the passion narrative suggested by the lectionary for the current year.*

## A Service of Lessons and Hymns

### Matthew 26:14-29; Mark 14:1-25; or Luke 22:14-23

*Suggested hymns from* UMH:

628 Eat This Bread
614-15 For the Bread Which You
    Have Broken (stanzas 1, 2)

584 Lord, You Give the Great Commissio
    (stanza 3)
84 Thank You, Lord

Tino Tenda Jesu (Thank You, Jesus) ( ♪ 203)

### Matthew 26:30-56; Mark 14:26-50; Luke 22:31-53; or Readings 1-2 (355-5

*Suggested hymns from* UMH:

290 Go to Dark Gethsemane
    (stanza 1)

371 I Stand Amazed in the Presence
    (stanzas 1, 2; add stanza 3 with Luk

### Matthew 26:57-75; Mark 14:53-72; Luke 22:54-62; or Readings 3-4 (35€

*Suggested hymns from* UMH:

289 Ah, Holy Jesus (stanzas 1, 2)

292 What Wondrous Love Is This
    (stanzas 1, 2)

### Matthew 27:1-23, 26-30; Mark 15:1-19; Luke 22:63–23:25; or Readings 5-8 (357-58)

*Suggested hymns from* UMH:

290 Go to Dark Gethsemane
    (stanza 2)
286 O Scared Head, Now
    Wounded (except with Luke)

285 To Mock Your Reign, O Dearest Lord
    (except with Luke)
292 What Wondrous Love Is This
    (stanzas 1, 2)

Matthew 27:31-50; Mark 15:20-37; Luke 23:26-46; or Readings 9-11 (358-59)

*Suggested hymns from UMH:*

294 Alas! and Did My Savior
    Bleed" (stanzas 1, 3)
530 Are Ye Able (with Luke)
527 Do, Lord, Remember Me
    (with Luke)
291 He never Said a Mubalin'
    Word (stanzas 1, 2, 5)
488 Jesus, Remember Me (with
    (with Luke)

584 Lord, You Give the Great
    Commission (stanza 4 with Luke)
424 Must Jesus Bear the Cross Alone
    (stanzas 1, 3)
425 O Crucified Redeemer
287 O Love Divine, What Hast Thou Done
491 Remember Me (with Luke)
282 'Tis Finished! The Messiah Dies
288 Were You There (stanzas 1, 4)

Matthew 27:51-66; Mark 15:38-47; Luke 23:47-56; or Readings 12-16 (359-61)

*Suggested hymns from UMH:*

359 Alas! and Did My Savior
    Bleed (stanzas 1, 2)
297 Beneath the Cross of Jesus
301 Jesus, Keep Me Near the
    Cross
504 The Old Rugged Cross

282 'Tis Finished! The Messiah Dies
    (stanzas 2, 4)
288 Were You There (stanza 5)
292 What Wondrous Love Is This
298-99 When I Survey the
    Wondrous Cross

ERMON]

*The Proclamation of the Passion Story may take the place of a sermon, but situations may arise that call for preaching a sermon and shortening the reading of the passion story to the selected portion on which the sermon is based. If this is done, it is strongly urged that the other portions of the story be read at some later time(s) in Holy Week.*

SPONSE TO THE PROCLAMATION *See 24.*

ONCERNS AND PRAYERS *See 24-25.*

ONFESSION AND PARDON] *See 20-21, 25-26.*

*If expression of confession and pardon has not been adequately included in the hymns previously sung, it may be included here.*

IE PEACE * *See 26.*

FERING *See 26-27.*

# THANKSGIVING AND COMMUNION

*If Holy Communion is not celebrated, the service continues with a Prayer of Thanksgiving (see 27) and the Lord's Prayer (see 29).*

*If Holy Communion is to be celebrated, the congregation may be invite immediately after the Concerns and Prayers to turn for the rest of the service to Service of Word and Table IV (UMH 26). Or the service may continue as give above through the Offering, during which the bread and wine are brought b representatives of the people to the Lord's table with the other gifts or uncovered already in place. After the offering, the congregation may be invited to turn to Service of Word and Table III (UMH 15) or one of the musical settings in UMI 17-25, the pastor praying The Great Thanksgiving on 62-63.*

*In any event, the service concludes as follows:*

## SENDING FORTH

HYMN * *See suggestions above.*

DISMISSAL WITH BLESSING * *See 31-32.*

GOING FORTH * *See 32.*

# ACTS OF WORSHIP FOR HOLY WEEK

*Greetings*

## 343
If any want to become my followers,
  let them deny themselves and take up their cross and follow me.
**For those who want to save their life will lose it,**
  **and those who lose their life**
  **for my sake and for the sake of the gospel, will save it.** (MARK 8:34b-;

## 344
It is that very Spirit bearing witness with our spirit
  that we are children of God, and if children, then heirs,
  heirs of God and joint heirs with Christ—
**if, in fact, we suffer with him**
  **so that we may also be glorified with him.** (ROMANS 8:16-

## 345
Let us run with perseverance the race that is set before us,
looking to Jesus the pioneer and perfecter of our faith,
**who for the sake of the joy that was set before him**
  **endured the cross, disregarding its shame,**
  **and has taken his seat at the right hand of the throne of God.**
(HEBREWS 12:1

*Prayers*

*Monday of Holy Week*                                                    **346**

God of strength and mercy, by the suffering and death of your Son,
  free us from slavery to sin and death and protect us in all our weakness;
  through Jesus Christ our Lord. Amen.          (DON E. SALIERS, U.S.A., 20TH CENT.)

*Tuesday of Holy Week*                                                   **347**

Holy and compassionate God, your dear Son went not up to joy
  before he suffered pain,
  and entered not into glory before he was crucified.
Mercifully grant that we, walking in the way of the cross,
  may find it the way of life and peace;
through Jesus Christ your Son, our Savior. Amen.
                              (THE BOOK OF COMMON PRAYER, U.S.A., 20TH CENT., ALT.)

*Wednesday of Holy Week*                                                 **348**

Most merciful God,
  our blessed Son, our Savior, was betrayed, whipped,
  and his face spat upon.
Grant us grace to endure the sufferings of the present time,
  to overcome all that seeks to overwhelm us,
  confident of the glory that shall yet be revealed;
through Jesus Christ our Redeemer. Amen.
                              (THE BOOK OF COMMON PRAYER, U.S.A., 20TH CENT., ALT.)

*Holy Thursday*                                                          **349**

God, by the example of your Son, our Savior Jesus Christ,
  you taught us the greatness of true humility,
  and call us to watch with him in his passion.
Give us grace to serve one another in all lowliness,
  and to enter into the fellowship of his suffering;
  his name and for his sake. Amen.
                              (W. E. ORCHARD, ENGLAND, 20TH CENT., ALT.)

*The Seder*                                                              **350**

*The Seder, or Passover meal, on the night of the fifteenth day of Nisan in the Jewish
calendar is the most important of all Jewish household ceremonies. It is an enduring
witness to God's promise of freedom for the Jewish people. Jews share this meal of
celebration, remembering the Exodus from Egypt and rejoicing that the Lord passed
over (pesaḥ) and spared the children of Israel in Egypt (Exodus 12:27). The Feast of
Unleavened Bread, which became an alternative name for Passover in the Bible (Luke
22:1), recalls how Israel left Egypt in such haste that the dough for the bread was
unleavened (Exodus 13). The meal celebrated in each Jewish home includes foods that
remind the family members of the Exodus and features a recitation of the sacred
story of the Jewish people.*

*United Methodists are encouraged to celebrate the Seder as invited guests in a Jewish home or in consultation with representatives of the Jewish community, thu respecting the integrity of what is a Jewish tradition and continuing the worth practice of Jews and Christians sharing at table together. Celebrating the modern me without a Jewish family as host is an affront to Jewish tradition and sometimes creat misunderstanding about the meaning of the Lord's Supper.*

**351**

# A SERVICE OF WORSHIP
# FOR HOLY THURSDAY EVENING

*On this night Christians commemorate the supper Jesus shared with his discipl before his crucifixion, when Jesus washed the disciples' feet (John 13:1-17) ar instituted the Sacrament of the Lord's Supper (Matthew 26:26-29; Mark 14:22-2 Luke 22:13-20; 1 Corinthians 11:23-25).*

*Six actions traditional on this night are included in the following service. They a (1) confession and pardon, (2) proclamation of the Word, (3) footwashing, (4) t Lord's Supper, (5) stripping of the church, and (6) Tenebrae. Of these, (1), (2), a (4) are essential; (3), (5), and (6) are optional and are thus marked with brackets. Th require careful preparation when introduced to a congregation.*

*Footwashing is a powerful symbolic response to the Word, dramatizing servanthood of Jesus, both on the night before his death and in his continuing preser in our midst. The alternative title for this day, Maundy Thursday, recalls the n commandment (mandatum novum in Latin) in John 13:34. The service m appropriately be called Maundy Thursday when footwashing occurs in imitation Jesus' actions and as a response to his new commandment to love one another. Care advance planning and advance notice to the people are essential. It may be sugges that participants come without socks or hose and that persons are welcome to obse rather than participate. Representatives of the people or those volunteering participate may come forward to the place(s) where chairs, a basin and pitcher water, and towels have been placed. Mutual footwashing among pastor(s) c laypersons should be clearly visible, yet not overly dramatic. Love and care for c another may be expressed in the gestures. During the footwashing the congregatior choir may sing, or the footwashing may be done in silence.*

*The ancient practice of stripping the Lord's table and sanctuary following commun is a vivid and dramatic way of showing the desolation and abandonment of the l night in Gethsemane and what followed. Designated persons pick up the cloths on Lord's table and the pulpit and other hangings, banners, candlesticks, decorations and quietly carry them from the sanctuary. This may be done in silence Psalm 22 (UMH 752) may be used. The church then remains bare until the Ea Vigil, when the process is reversed.*

*A Service of Tenebrae, or Service of the Shadows, is found on 354-61.*

# ENTRANCE

GATHERING *See 16-17.*

GREETING * *See 17-20.*

The grace of the Lord Jesus Christ be with you.
**And also with you.**

Taste and see the goodness of the Lord.
**Christ has prepared a feast of love.**

HYMN * *Suggested from* UMH:

| | |
|---|---|
| 285-301 Christ's Gracious Life:<br>       Passion and Death<br>635 Because Thou Hast Said | 626 Let All Mortal Flesh<br>      Keep Silence<br>425 O Crucified Redeemer<br>633 The Bread of Life for All Is Broken |

CONFESSION AND PARDON

My sisters and brothers,
   Christ shows us his love by becoming a humble servant.
Let us draw near to God and confess our sin in the truth of God's Spirit.

*All may sing O Lamb of God ( ♪ 201) or Señor, Apiádate de Nosotros ( ♪ 188).*

*A brief silence for individual confession.*

**Most merciful God,**
**we your Church confess**
   **that often our spirit has not been that of Christ.**
**Where we have failed to love one another as he loves us,**
**where we have pledged loyalty to him with our lips**
   **and then betrayed, deserted, or denied him,**
**forgive us, we pray;**
**and by your Spirit make us faithful in every time of trial;**
**through Jesus Christ our Lord. Amen.**

Who is in a position to condemn? Only Christ.
But Christ suffered and died for us,
   was raised from the dead and ascended on high for us,
   and continues to intercede for us.
Believe the good news:
In the name of Jesus Christ, you are forgiven!

**In the name of Jesus Christ, you are forgiven!**
**Glory to God. Amen.**

## PROCLAMATION AND RESPONSE

PRAYER FOR ILLUMINATION *

SCRIPTURE LESSON Exodus 12:1-14

PSALM 116:1-2, 12-19 (*UMH* 837)

SCRIPTURE LESSON 1 Corinthians 11:23-26

HYMN * *See suggestions above.*

GOSPEL LESSON John 13:1-17, 31*b*-35

SERMON

RESPONSES TO THE WORD *See 24.*

[FOOTWASHING] *See introduction.*

*During the footwashing the following in* UMH *may be sung:*
432 Jesu, Jesu, Fill Us With Your Love
549 Where Charity and Love Prevail

CONCERNS AND PRAYERS * *See 24-25 and Holy Thursday (UMH 283)*

THE PEACE * *See 26.*

OFFERING *See 26-27.*

## THANKSGIVING AND COMMUNION

TAKING THE BREAD AND CUP *See 27-28.*

THE GREAT THANKSGIVING *

*The congregation turns to A Service of Word and Table III (UMH 15) or to one the musical settings in* UMH *17-25, the pastor praying The Great Thanksgiving on 29.*

THE LORD'S PRAYER * *See 29.*

BREAKING THE BREAD *See 29.*

*The pastor breaks the bread and then lifts the cup, in silence or with appropria words.*

IVING THE BREAD AND CUP * *See 29-31.*

*The bread and wine are given to the people, with appropriate words being exchanged.*

*The congregation sings Lenten hymns while the bread and cup are given.*

*When all have received, the Lord's table is put in order.*

*The pastor or congregation may give thanks after communion.*

## SENDING FORTH

YMN * *See suggestions above.*

TRIPPING OF THE CHURCH] *See introduction.*

ENEBRAE] *See text on 354-61.*

ISMISSAL WITH BLESSING * *See 31-32. May also be omitted.*

Go in peace.
May Jesus Christ,
   who for our sake became obedient unto death, even death on a cross,
   keep you and strengthen you this night and for ever. Amen.

OING FORTH * *See 32.*

# A SERVICE OF TENEBRAE          354

*Service of Tenebrae, or "Darkness," is based on a twelfth-century late night/early*
*rning service and is an extended meditation on the passion of Christ. It may be used*
*(1) a concluding service following Holy Communion on Holy Thursday, or (2) the*
*ning service on Good Friday, particularly as the beginning of a prayer vigil lasting*
*ough Saturday.*

*e readings given below are by James H. Charlesworth. He accurately translates*
*n 18:1–19:42, with special sensitivity to Jews, Judaism, Jesus' Jewishness, and the*
*ish origins of Christianity.*

ATHERING] *Omitted if part of Holy Thursday service.*

REETING *

God is light, in whom there is no darkness at all.
**Jesus Christ is the light of the world.**

And this is the judgment, that the light has come into the world,
**and we loved darkness rather than light.**

[HYMN *] *Suggested from UMH:*

| | |
|---|---|
| 285-301 Christ's Gracious Life: Passion and Death | 626 Let All Mortal Flesh Keep Silence |
| 635 Because Thou Hast Said | 425 O Crucified Redeemer |
| | 633 The Bread of Life for All Is Broken |

[PRAYER] *

*If the service is on Good Friday, pray in unison Good Friday (UMH 284).*

## THE PASSION OF JESUS CHRIST

*Fourteen candles, along with a central Christ candle, are lighted at this point or befo*
*the service begins; then one is extinguished at the conclusion of each section. Hym*
*or hymn stanzas may be interspersed, provided there is enough light to read, or t*
*hymns may be sung from memory. See also Lessons and Hymns 341-42.*

### 1

Jesus . . . went forth with his disciples across the Kidron valley,
    where there was a garden, which he and his disciples entered.
Now Judas, who betrayed him, also knew the place;
    for Jesus often met there with his disciples.
So Judas, procuring a band of soldiers
    and some officers from the chief priests and the Pharisees,
    went there with lanterns and torches and weapons.
Then Jesus, knowing all that was to befall him,
    came forward and said to them, "Whom do you seek?"
They answered him, "Jesus of Nazareth."
Jesus said to them, "I am he."
Judas, who betrayed him, was standing with them.
When he said to them, "I am he," they drew back and fell to the groun
Again he asked them, "Whom do you seek?"
And they said, "Jesus of Nazareth."
Jesus answered, "I told you that I am he;
    so, if you seek me, let these men go."
This was to fulfill the word which he had spoken,
    "I did not lose a single one of those whom you gave me."
Then Simon Peter, having a sword,
    drew it and struck the high priest's slave and cut off his right ear
The slave's name was Malchus.
Jesus said to Peter, "Put your sword into its sheath;
    shall I not drink the cup which the Father has given me?"

*A reader extinguishes the first candle.*

## 2

So the band of soldiers and their captain
and the officers of the Judean authorities seized Jesus and bound him.
First they led him to Annas;
for he was the father-in-law of Caiaphas, who was high priest that year.
It was Caiaphas who had given counsel to the religious authorities
that it was expedient that one man should die for the people.

*The second candle is extinguished.*

## 3

Simon Peter followed Jesus, and so did another disciple.
As this disciple was known to the high priest,
he entered the court of the high priest along with Jesus,
while Peter stood outside at the door.
So the other disciple, who was known to the high priest,
went out and spoke to the woman who guarded the gate,
and brought Peter in.
The woman who guarded the gate said to Peter,
"Are not you also one of this man's disciples?"
He said, "I am not."
Now the servants and officers had made a charcoal fire,
because it was cold,
and they were standing and warming themselves;
Peter also was with them, standing and warming himself.

*The third candle is extinguished.*

## 4

The high priest then questioned Jesus about his disciples and his teaching.
Jesus answered him, "I have spoken openly to the world;
I have always taught in synagogues and in the temple,
where all Jewish people come together;
I have said nothing secretly. Why do you ask me?
Ask those who have heard me, what I said to them;
they know what I said."
When he had said this,
one of the officers standing by struck Jesus with his hand, saying,
"Is that how you answer the high priest?"
Jesus answered him,
"If I have spoken wrongly, bear witness to the wrong;
but if I have spoken rightly, why do you strike me?"
Annas then sent him bound to Caiaphas the high priest.

*The fourth candle is extinguished.*

## 5

Now Simon Peter was standing and warming himself.
They said to him, "Are not you also one of his disciples?"
He denied it and said, "I am not."
One of the servants of the high priest,
 a kinsman of the man whose ear Peter had cut off, asked,
"Did I not see you in the garden with him?"
Peter again denied it; and at once the cock crowed.

*The fifth candle is extinguished.*

## 6

Then they led Jesus from the house of Caiaphas to Pilate's headquarters
It was early.
They themselves did not enter the headquarters,
 so that they might not be defiled, but might eat the Passover.
So Pilate went out to them and said,
"What accusation do you bring against this man?"
They answered him,
"If this man were not an evildoer,
 we would not have handed him over."
Pilate said to them,
"Take him yourselves and judge him by your own law."
The religious authorities said to him,
"It is not lawful for us to put any man to death."
This was to fulfill the word which Jesus had spoken
 to show by what death he was to die.

*The sixth candle is extinguished.*

## 7

Pilate entered the headquarters again and called Jesus, and said to him
"Are you the King of the Jews?"
Jesus answered, "Do you say this of your own accord,
 or did others say it to you about me?"
Pilate answered, "Am I a Jew?
 Your own nation and the chief priests have handed you over to me
 what have you done?"
Jesus answered, "My kingship is not of this world;
 if my kingship were of this world, my servants would fight,
 that I might not be handed over to the religious authorities;
 but my kingship is not from the world."
Pilate said to him, "So you are a king?"
Jesus answered, "You say that I am a king.
For this I was born, and for this I have come into the world,
 to bear witness to the truth.

Every one who is of the truth hears my voice."
Pilate said to him, "What is truth?"

*The seventh candle is extinguished.*

### 8

After Pilate had said this,
 he went to the religious authorities again, and told them,
 "I find no crime in him.
But you have a custom
 that I should release one man for you at the Passover;
will you have me release for you the King of the Jews?"
They cried out again, "Not this man, but Barabbas!"
Now Barabbas was a robber.

*The eighth candle is extinguished.*

### 9

Then Pilate took Jesus and scourged him.
And the soldiers plaited a crown of thorns, and put it on his head,
 and arrayed him in a purple robe;
they came up to him, saying, "Hail, King of the Jews!"
 and struck him with their hands.
Pilate went out again, and said to them,
 "See, I am bringing him out to you,
 that you may know that I find no crime in him."
So Jesus came out, wearing the crown of thorns and the purple robe.
Pilate said to them, "Behold the man!"
When the chief priests and the officers saw him,
 they cried out, "Crucify him, crucify him!"
Pilate said to them,
 "Take him yourselves and crucify him, for I find no crime in him."
The religious authorities answered him,
 "We have a law, and by that law he ought to die,
 because he has made himself the Son of God."
When Pilate heard these words, he was the more afraid;
he entered the headquarters again and said to Jesus,
 "Where are you from?"
But Jesus gave no answer.
Pilate therefore said to him, "You will not speak to me?
 Do you not know that I have power to release you,
 and power to crucify you?"
Jesus answered him,
 "You would have no power over me
  unless it had been given you from above;
 therefore he who delivered me to you has the greater sin."

*The ninth candle is extinguished.*

## 10

Upon this Pilate sought to release him,
  but the religious authorities cried out,
"If you release this man, you are not Caesar's friend;
  every one who makes himself a king sets himself against Caesar."
When Pilate heard these words, he brought Jesus out
  and sat down on the judgment seat
    at a place called The Pavement, and in Hebrew, *Gab'·ba·tha.*
Now it was the day of Preparation of the Passover;
  it was about the sixth hour.
He said to the religious authorities, "Behold your King!"
They cried out, "Away with him, away with him, crucify him!"
Pilate said to them, "Shall I crucify your King?"
The chief priests answered, "We have no king but Caesar."
They handed him over to them to be crucified.

*The tenth candle is extinguished.*

## 11

So they took Jesus, and he went out, bearing his own cross,
  to the place called the place of a skull,
  which is called in Hebrew, *Gol'·go·tha.*
There they crucified him,
  and with him two others, one on either side, and Jesus between them
Pilate also wrote a title and put it on the cross;
  it read, "Jesus of Nazareth, the King of the Jews."
Many of the Judeans read this title,
  for the place where Jesus was crucified was near the city;
  and it was written in Hebrew, in Latin, and in Greek.
The Jewish chief priests then said to Pilate,
  "Do not write, 'The King of the Jews,'
  but, 'This man said, I am King of the Jews.'"
Pilate answered, "What I have written I have written."

*The eleventh candle is extinguished.*

## 12

When the soldiers had crucified Jesus
  they took his garments and made four parts, one for each soldier;
  also his tunic.
But the tunic was without seam, woven from top to bottom;
  so they said to one another,
  "Let us not tear it, but cast lots for it to see whose it shall be."
This was to fulfill the scripture,

"They parted my garments among them,
and for my clothing they cast lots."

*The twelfth candle is extinguished.*

## 13

So the soldiers did this.
But standing by the cross of Jesus were his mother,
and his mother's sister, Mary the wife of Clopas, and Mary Magdalene.
When Jesus saw his mother,
and the disciple whom he loved standing near,
he said to his mother, "Woman, behold, your son!"
Then he said to the disciple, "Behold, your mother!"
And from that hour the disciple took her to his own home.

*The thirteenth candle is extinguished.*

## 14

After this Jesus, knowing that all was now finished,
said (to fulfill the scripture), "I thirst."
A bowl full of vinegar stood there;
so they put a sponge full of the vinegar on hyssop
and held it to his mouth.
When Jesus had received the vinegar, he said, "It is finished";
and he bowed his head and gave up his spirit.

*The fourteenth candle is extinguished.*

## 15

Since it was the day of Preparation,
in order to prevent the bodies from remaining on the cross
on the sabbath (for that sabbath was a high day),
the religious authorities asked Pilate that their legs might be broken,
and that they might be taken away.
So the soldiers came and broke the legs of the first,
and of the other who had been crucified with him;
but when they came to Jesus and saw that he was already dead,
they did not break his legs.
But one of the soldiers pierced his side with a spear,
and at once there came out blood and water.
He who saw it has borne witness—his testimony is true,
and he knows that he tells the truth—that you also may believe.
For these things took place that the scripture might be fulfilled,
"Not a bone of him shall be broken."
And again another scripture says,
"They shall look on him whom they have pierced."

*The Christ candle is taken away or extinguished. A loud noise is made by a cymb or other means. The last section is read in darkness.*

## 16

After this Joseph of Arimathea, who was a disciple of Jesus,
   but secretly, for fear of the religious authorities,
asked Pilate that he might take away the body of Jesus,
   and Pilate gave him leave.
So he came and took away his body.
Nicodemus also, who had at first come to him by night,
came bringing a mixture of myrrh and aloes,
   about a hundred pounds' weight.
They took the body of Jesus, and bound it in linen cloths with the spice
   as is the burial custom of the Jews.
Now in the place where he was crucified there was a garden,
   and in the garden a new tomb where no one had ever been laid.
So because of the Jewish day of Preparation,
   as the tomb was close at hand,
   they laid Jesus there.                                    (JOHN 18:1–19:

*Silence. The room remains darkened with only illumination necessary for safet
The room now remains barren until the Easter Vigil. The final hymn and Dismiss
may be omitted to be a sign of waiting for the coming resurrection and to show t
essential unity between the services of the Great Three Days.*

[HYMN *] *See suggestions above.*

[DISMISSAL *]

Go in peace.
May Jesus Christ,
   who for our sake became obedient unto death, even death on a cros
   keep you and strengthen you this night and for ever. Amen.

## GOING FORTH *

*All depart in silence, except those beginning a prayer vigil.*

# A SERVICE FOR GOOD FRIDAY

*'iis service may be used either at noon or in the evening of Good Friday. It is ·eferable that there are no paraments, banners, flowers, or decorations on Good ·iday except, perhaps, representations of the way of the cross (see 366). The Lord's ble, pulpit, and other furnishings should be bare of cloth, candles, or anything else )t actually used in the service. The cross remains visible, but it and any permanently ced images may be veiled. By partly concealing the cross, the veil also calls attention it. The color scarlet is suggested for a veil over the cross.*

## ENTRANCE

ATHERING

*Appropriate music may be offered while the people gather, but silence is preferable. The pastor, choir, and other leaders of worship enter in silence.*

REETING *

Christ himself bore our sins in his body on the tree.
**That we might die to sin and live to righteousness.**

Let us pray.

*The following or Good Friday (UMH 284) is said:*

Almighty God,
  your Son Jesus Christ was lifted high upon the cross
    so that he might draw the whole world to himself.
Grant that we, who glory in this death for our salvation,
  may also glory in his call to take up our cross and follow him;
through Jesus Christ our Lord. Amen.

IYMN *] *Suggested from UMH:*

285-301 Christ's Gracious Life:       626 Let All Mortal Flesh Keep Silence
          Passion and Death            425 O Crucified Redeemer
635 Because Thou Hast Said            633 The Bread Life for All Is Broken
167 Canticle of Christ's Obedience

## PROCLAMATION AND RESPONSE

CRIPTURE LESSON Isaiah 52:13–53:12

5ALM 22 (*UMH* 752)

CRIPTURE LESSON] Hebrews 10:16-25

IYMN or ANTHEM*]

## PROCLAMATION OF THE PASSION STORY John 18:1–19:42

*The Good Friday narrative may be proclaimed in one of several ways:*

*1) The longer or shorter version of the passion story may be read dramatically as suggested for Passion/Palm Sunday (341-42), or a single reader may be preferred. John's passion narrative is printed on 355-61.*

*2) A choral setting of the passion narrative may be sung by the choir. See 341*

*3) Hymns may be interspersed at appropriate intervals within the reading of John passion narrative, as on Passion/Palm Sunday (341-42) or in the Service of Tenebrae (355-61).*

## [SERMON]

*Ordinarily the Proclamation of the Passion Story takes the place of a sermon, but situations may arise that call for preaching a sermon.*

## CONCERNS AND PRAYERS

## [OFFERING]

## MEDITATION AT THE CROSS

HYMN *See suggestions above.*

*If desired, a plain wooden cross may now be brought into the church and placed in the sight of the people.*

## SILENT MEDITATION

*During Silent Meditation and The Reproaches, persons may be invited to come forward informally to kneel briefly before the cross or touch it.*

## THE REPROACHES: CHRIST'S LAMENT AGAINST HIS FAITHLESS CHURCH

*Any or all of the following reproaches may be spoken, with the congregation responding as indicated below or singing after each stanza, Jesus, Remember Me (UMH 488) or Remember Me (UMH 491). A time of silence may be kept after each stanza.*

1) O my people, O my Church,
 what have I done to you, or in what have I offended you?
 I led you forth from the land of Egypt
 and delivered you by the waters of baptism,
 but you have prepared a cross for your Savior.

**Holy God, holy and mighty, holy and immortal One,
 have mercy upon us.** *See* ♪ *215.*

2) I led you through the desert forty years and fed you with manna;
   I brought you through times of persecution and of renewal
       and gave you my body, the bread of heaven;
   but you have prepared a cross for your Savior. R

3) I made you branches of my vineyard
       and gave you the water of salvation,
   but when I was thirsty you gave me vinegar and gall
       and pierced with a spear the side of your Savior. R

4) I went before you in a pillar of cloud,
       but you have led me to the judgment hall of Pilate.
   I brought you to a land of freedom and prosperity,
       but you have scourged, mocked, and beaten me. R

5) I gave you a royal scepter, and bestowed the keys to the kingdom,
       but you have given me a crown of thorns.
   I raised you on high with great power,
       but you have hanged me on the cross. R

6) My peace I gave, which the world cannot give,
       and washed your feet as a servant,
   but you draw the sword to strike in my name
       and seek high places in my kingdom. R

7) I accepted the cup of suffering and death for your sakes,
       but you scatter and deny and abandon me.
   I sent the Spirit of truth to lead you,
       but you close your hearts to guidance. R

8) I called you to go and bring forth fruit,
       but you cast lots for my clothing.
   I prayed that you all may be one,
       but you continue to quarrel and divide. R

9) I grafted you into the tree of my chosen people Israel,
       but you turned on them with persecution and mass murder.
   I made you joint heirs with them of my covenants,
       but you made them scapegoats for your own guilt. R

10) I came to you as the least of your brothers and sisters.
   I was hungry but you gave me no food,
       thirsty but you gave me no drink.
   I was a stranger but you did not welcome me,
       naked but you did not clothe me,
       sick and in prison but you did not visit me. R

*A brief silence follows.*

## THE LORD'S PRAYER * *See 29.*

*The final hymn and Dismissal may be omitted to signify that we are waiting for t* *coming resurrection and to show the essential unity among the services of the Gre* *Three Days.*

[HYMN *] *See suggestions above.*

[DISMISSAL *]

May Jesus Christ,
who for our sake became obedient unto death, even death on a cros
keep you and strengthen you, now and for ever. Amen.

## GOING FORTH *

*All depart in silence, except those beginning a prayer vigil.*

# ACTS OF WORSHIP
# FOR GOOD FRIDAY AND HOLY SATURDAY

**365**                        *The Seven Last Words*

*Services based on the seven last words (phrases) of Jesus from the cross a* *traditionally developed from harmonies of the Gospel passion narratives. Also know* *as the Devotion of the Three Hours (from noon on Friday to 3:00 P.M., to rememb* *Christ's hours on the cross), it was first conducted by a Jesuit priest in Peru in t* *eighteenth century as a service of scripture readings with prayers and hym* *interspersed. Over the years it has become popular in Protestant circles in Engla* *and North America. The common order of the readings is presented here. Visua* *music, drama, or liturgical dance may be employed imaginatively.*

| | |
|---|---|
| 1) Luke 23:34 | Father, forgive them. |
| 2) Luke 23:43 | Today you will be with me in paradis |
| 3) John 19:26-27 | Woman, here is your son. |
| 4) Mark 15:34 (Matthew 27:46) | My God, why have you forsaken me? |
| 5) John 19:28 | I am thirsty. |
| 6) John 19:30a | It is finished. |
| 7) Luke 23:46 | Into your hands I commend my spirit |

## The Way of the Cross   366

he Way (or Stations) of the Cross has been a common way of participating in the
*ssion (suffering) of Christ as a part of Good Friday services. The service may be
*nducted in the church or outdoors with stops (stations) at various locations.
*opping at each station reminds the participant of different moments of Christ's
*ssion journey and encourages reflection and contemplation. Visuals, music,
*ama, or liturgical dance may be employed imaginatively. A prayer, with kneeling,
*d hymn may follow each reading. Its inspiration came from the desire to imitate the
*urneys of early Christian pilgrims to the Holy Land, especially to the places of
*hrist's redemptive suffering. The version offered here differs from traditional ones in
*at it includes only stations with a biblical basis.

| *ation of the Cross | Scripture | Summary |
|---|---|---|
| ) Jesus prays alone. | Luke 22:39-44 | Take this cup from me. |
| ) Jesus is arrested. | Matthew 26:47-56 | Have you come with swords? |
| ) Sanhedrin tries Jesus. | Mark 14:61-64 | Are you the Christ? |
| ) Pilate tries Jesus. | John 18:33-37 | Are you King of the Jews? |
| ) Pilate sentences Jesus. | Mark 15:6-15 | Crucify him. |
| ) Jesus wears crown. | John 19:5 | Here is the man. |
| ) Jesus carries his cross. | John 10:17-18 | I lay it down of my own. |
| ) Simon carries cross. | Luke 23:26 | Simon the Cyrene |
| ) Jesus speaks to the women. | Luke 23:27-31 | Weep for yourselves. |
| ) Jesus is crucified. | Luke 23:33-34 | Jesus on the cross |
| ) Criminals speak to Jesus. | Luke 23:39-43 | Today you will be with me. |
| ) Jesus speaks to Mary, John. | John 19:25*b*-27 | Woman, this is your son. |
| ) Jesus dies on the cross. | John 19:28-34 | It is accomplished. |
| ) Jesus is laid in tomb. | John 19:38-42 | There they laid Jesus. |

## Holy Saturday   367

*erciful and everliving God, Creator of heaven and earth,
   the crucified body of your Son was laid in the tomb
      and rested on this holy day.
*rant that we may await with him the dawning of the third day
   and rise in newness of life, through Jesus Christ our Redeemer. Amen.

(THE BOOK OF COMMON PRAYER, U.S.A., 20TH CENT., ALT.)

# EASTER SEASON

The Easter Season, also known as the Great Fifty Days, begins at suns
Easter Eve and continues through the Day of Pentecost. It is the most joyo
and celebrative season of the Christian year. It focuses on Chris
resurrection and ascension and on the givings of the Holy Spirit on the fir
Easter (John 20:22-23) and the Day of Pentecost (Acts 2). Lessons from th
Acts of the Apostles replace readings from the Old Testament because th
early church, empowered by the Holy Spirit, is the best witness to th
Resurrection. The ancient Christian name for this festival is *Pasch*, deriv
from the Hebrew *pesaḥ* ("deliverance" or "passover"), thus connecting th
Resurrection to the Exodus. The origin of the English word *Easter* is disput
but may come from the Anglo-Saxon spring goddess Eastre and her festiv
*Pentecost* comes from the Greek *pentekoste*, which means "fiftieth." It refers
the Jewish Feast of Weeks, which Greek-speaking Jews called the Day
Pentecost (Acts 2:1). Early Christians also used the term Pentecost to refer
the Great Fifty Days as a season. In addition to the acts and services
worship on the following pages, see The Great Thanksgivings on 66-69 ar
the scripture readings for the Easter Season in the lectionary on 231-3

Baptisms, confirmations, and congregational reaffirmation of the Baptism
Covenant are highly appropriate throughout this season, most especially
the First Service of Easter and on the Day of Pentecost.

Use the colors of white and gold and materials of the finest texture f
paraments, stoles, and banners. On the Day of Pentecost use bright re
Bright red symbols may also be used on a white background earlier in th
season. A focus on the baptismal font is appropriate throughout the seaso
A large freestanding white candle called a paschal candle may be used
every service during this season and at baptisms and funerals during the re
of the year. Standing for prayer is most traditional. Flowers of all colors a
appropriate. Visuals for the Day of Pentecost may include red flowe
doves, flames of fire, a ship, or a rainbow.

## 369  EASTER VIGIL OR THE FIRST SERVICE OF EASTER

*During the Great Three Days, from sunset Holy Thursday to sunset Easter Day,*
*celebrate the saving events of Jesus Christ's suffering, death, and resurrection. In t*
*development of Christian worship, each event came to be remembered on a separa*

. In the earliest centuries, however, these events were celebrated as a unity in an
raordinary single liturgy that began Saturday night and continued until the dawn
Easter Day. It was known as the great Paschal (Easter) Vigil. Preceded by a fast
, it was the most holy and joyful night of the entire Christian year, for it
claimed and celebrated the whole of salvation history and Christ's saving work. It
he most appropriate time for baptisms; persons baptized symbolically die and rise
h Christ (Romans 6:3-11). It has also come to be seen as a most appropriate time for
gregational reaffirmation of the Baptismal Covenant.

Easter (Paschal) Vigil has both historic and symbolic roots in the Jewish Passover.
t is why so many images are from the Old Testament and why so many analogies
experienced in Christ. In this service we experience the passage from slavery to
dom, from sin to salvation, from death to life.

Easter Vigil is the First Service of Easter. The following service is an adaptation of
ancient Paschal Vigil service and consists of four parts: (1) The Service of Light,
The Service of the Word, (3) The Service of the Baptismal Covenant, and (4) The
vice of the Table. The length of the service may suggest that the sermon be brief.
us we celebrate God's saving work in Christ through the symbols of light, word,
ter, and the heavenly banquet.

s service may be celebrated in one of several ways:
It may be an Easter Eve service, comparable to a Christmas Eve service, reaching
its climax after midnight. This comes closest to the ancient pattern and is
appropriately called the Easter Vigil.
It may be a predawn Easter service, like a modern Easter sunrise service but
beginning while it is still dark so as to experience the transition from darkness to
light. In this case it may be called the First Service of Easter and may be followed by
a festive breakfast.
Because the service is very long, it may be divided into two services: a
predawn/sunrise Service of Light and Service of the Word, followed by a festive
breakfast, followed by a Service of the Baptismal Covenant and Service of the
Table. With the Easter Day service, a sequence of three different services would
make a unity. Persons could attend any or all of them.

# THE SERVICE OF LIGHT

ATHERING

The service begins in darkness. If possible, the people should gather outside the
building or in a room or hall other than the sanctuary that can accommodate the
whole congregation. A fire, built on the ground or in a large brazier and
symbolizing the Resurrection, is kindled while the people gather. The central sign is
the paschal candle, a large freestanding white candle signifying the triumph of the
Resurrection over the darkness of death. Each person may also be given a candle.
Silence is kept until all have assembled.

## GREETING AND INTRODUCTION *

*The leader addresses the people with these or similar words:*

Grace and peace to you from Jesus Christ our Lord.

My brothers and sisters in Christ:
On this most holy night (*morning*)
  in which Jesus Christ passed over from death to life,
we gather as the Church to watch and pray.
This is the Passover of Christ,
  in which we share in Christ's victory over death.

## OPENING PRAYER *

God of life,
  through Jesus Christ
    you have bestowed upon the world the light of life.
Sanctify this new fire,
and grant that our hearts and minds may also be kindled
  with holy desire to shine forth with the brightness of Christ's risir
  that we may attain to the feast of everlasting light;
through Jesus Christ our Lord. Amen.

## LIGHTING OF THE PASCHAL CANDLE *

*The leader lights the paschal candle from the fire, saying:*

The light of Christ rises in glory,
  overcoming the darkness of sin and death.

*The paschal candle is lifted so that all may see it, and the leader says:*

Christ is our light!

*A procession then forms.*

## PROCESSION INTO THE CHURCH *

*If candles have been given to members of the congregation, they may be lighted fr
others that have been lighted from the paschal candle. As the room fills, station
candles in the sanctuary may be lighted.*

*As the congregation processes into the darkened sanctuary, the following
another appropriate hymn from UMH may be sung:*

173 Christ, Whose Glory Fills the Skies

## EASTER PROCLAMATION

*When the paschal candle is placed on a stand visible to the people, the ancient Eas
Proclamation (the* Exsultet) *follows. The stanzas may be divided among differ
readers.*

Rejoice, heavenly powers! Sing, choirs of angels!
Exult, all creation around God's throne!
Jesus Christ, our King, is risen!
Sound the trumpet of salvation!

**Rejoice, heavenly powers!**
**Sing, choirs of angels!**
**Jesus Christ, our King, is risen!**

Rejoice, O earth, in shining splendor,
    radiant in the brightness of our King!
Christ has conquered! Glory fills you!
Darkness vanishes for ever! **R**

Rejoice, O holy Church! Exult in glory!
The risen Savior shines upon you!
Let this place resound with joy,
    echoing the mighty song of all God's people! **R**

It is truly right that we should praise you,
    invisible, almighty, and eternal God, and your Son, Jesus Christ.
For Christ has ransomed us with his blood,
    and paid the debt of Adam's sin to deliver your faithful people. **R**

This is our Passover feast, when Christ, the true Lamb, is slain.
This is the night when first you saved our forebears,
    you freed the people of Israel from their slavery
        and led them with dry feet through the sea. **R**

This is the night when the pillar of fire destroyed the darkness of sin!
This is the night when Christians everywhere,
    washed clean of sin and freed from all defilement,
    are restored to grace and grow together in holiness. **R**

This is the night when Jesus Christ broke the chains of death
    and rose triumphant from the grave.
Night truly blessed, when heaven is wedded to earth,
    and we are reconciled to you! **R**

Accept this Easter candle, a flame divided but undimmed,
    a pillar of fire that glows to your honor.
Let it mingle with the lights of heaven,
    and continue bravely burning to dispel the darkness of the night! **R**

May the Morning Star, which never sets, find this flame still burning.
Christ, that Morning Star, who came back from the dead,
    and shed his peaceful light on all creation,
        your Son who lives and reigns for ever and ever. **R Amen.**

*The members of the congregation extinguish their candles. The lights in the church*
*are turned on. The paschal candle remains burning, and it is lighted at all services*
*from Easter Day through the Day of Pentecost.*

# THE SERVICE OF THE WORD

## INTRODUCTION

Let us hear the record of God's saving deeds in history,
and pray that each of us may receive the fullness of this grace.

*The number of readings may vary, but Exodus 14 and at least two other readings*
*from the Old Testament should be used in addition to the New Testament reading.*

*Each reading may be introduced with the words given and followed by silence,*
*psalm or a hymn, and then a prayer.*

## THE CREATION

With a word God creates order out of the primeval, watery chaos.
God's good creation reaches its pinnacle in humankind,
the bearer of God's image.

Genesis 1:1–2:4*a*

*Silence, then one of the following from UMH:*

767 Psalm 33                     145 Morning Has Broken

Almighty God, you wonderfully created, yet more wonderfully restored
the dignity of human nature.
Grant that we may share the divine life
of the One who shared our humanity,
Jesus Christ our Savior. Amen.

## THE COVENANT BETWEEN GOD AND THE EARTH

God causes the earth, overcome by sin, to be drowned in a watery deluge.
Yet in Noah and his family, God saves a remnant
and binds all together in a covenant with the sign of a rainbow.

Genesis 7:1-5, 11-18; 8:6-18; 9:8-13

*Silence, then one of the following from UMH:*

780 Psalm 46                     110 A Mighty Fortress Is Our God

Almighty God of heaven and earth, you set in the clouds a rainbow
to be a sign of your covenant with every living creature.
Grant that we may be faithful stewards
of the dominion you have entrusted to us on earth,
according to your grace given to us through Jesus Christ our Lord.
Amen.

## ABRAHAM'S TRUST IN GOD

Abraham is tested when God commands him to sacrifice his own son,
the embodiment of God's promise to him.
Through God's own provision on the mountain, the promise holds.

Genesis 22:1-18

*Silence, then one of the following from* UMH:

748 Psalm 16                                    467 Trust and Obey
116 The God of Abraham Praise

Gracious God of all believers, through Abraham's trust in your promise
  you made known your faithful love to countless numbers.
By the grace of Christ's sacrifice
  fulfill in your Church and in all creation
  the joy of your promise and new covenant. Amen.

## RAEL'S DELIVERANCE AT THE RED SEA

The ruler who kept God's people in slavery
  pursues them to the Red Sea as they try to escape.
Despite a hopeless situation, God rescues God's people,
  leading them on dry land through the parted sea
  and closing the waters on their former masters.
Miriam then sings a song about God's marvelous deliverance.

Exodus 14:10-31 (and 15:20-21 if canticle does not follow)

*Silence, then one of the following from* UMH:

135 Canticle of Moses and Miriam
315 Come, Ye Faithful, Raise the Strain
134 O Mary, Don't You Weep, Don't You Mourn

God our Savior, as once you delivered by the power of your mighty arm
  your chosen Israel through the waters of the sea,
so now deliver your Church and all the peoples of the earth
  from bondage and oppression, to rejoice and serve you in freedom,
through Jesus Christ our Deliverer. Amen.

## LVATION OFFERED FREELY TO ALL

The prophet Isaiah issues an invitation of abundant life
  to the hungry and thirsty.

Isaiah 55:1-11 (or 1-5 if canticle follows)

*Silence, then one of the following from* UMH:

125 Canticle of Covenant Faithfulness       641 Fill My Cup, Lord

Creator of all things,
  you freely offer water to the thirsty and food to the hungry.
Refresh us by the water of baptism
  and feed us with the bread and wine of your table,
  that your Word may bear fruit in our lives,
  and bring us all to your heavenly banquet;
through Jesus Christ our Lord. Amen.

## A NEW HEART AND A NEW SPIRIT

The prophet promises that God will renew God's people.
God will replace their heart of stone with a new heart.

Ezekiel 36:24-28

*Silence, then one of the following from* UMH:

777 Psalm 42                 393 Spirit of the Living God

*Prayer for a New Heart (UMH 392) or the following is said:*

God of holiness and light, in the mystery of dying and rising with Chr
    you have established a new covenant of reconciliation.
Cleanse our hearts and give a new spirit to all your people,
    that your saving grace may be made known to the whole world;
    through Jesus Christ our Lord. Amen.

## NEW LIFE FOR GOD'S PEOPLE

The prophet Ezekiel sees a vision:
God will take the dry bones of God's people,
    reconnect them, breathe into them, and restore them to life.

Ezekiel 37:1-14

*Silence, then one of the following from* UMH:

856 Psalm 143                 420 Breathe on Me, Breath of God

Eternal God, you raised from the dead our Lord Jesus
    and by your Holy Spirit brought to life your Church.
Breathe upon us again with your spirit and give new life to your peop
    through the same Jesus Christ our Redeemer. Amen.

## BURIED AND RAISED WITH CHRIST IN BAPTISM

The apostle Paul reminds us that in Christ we have already died,
    drowned in baptism.
Yet we who have died are raised to newness of life.

Romans 6:3-11

*Psalm 114 (UMH 835) and/or an alleluia (UMH 78, 162, 186, 486) may be us*

## GOSPEL LESSON *

Matthew 28:1-10 (Year A)          Jesus is raised while the guards shak
Mark 16:1-8 (Year B)              Who will roll away the stone for us?
Luke 24:1-12 (Year C)             Why look for the living among the de

## SERMON

# THE SERVICE OF THE BAPTISMAL COVENANT

persons are to be baptized, confirmed, or received into membership in the local
ngregation, or to make a personal reaffirmation of faith, The Baptismal Covenant I
6-94, UMH 33), II (95-99, UMH 39), or III (106-10, UMH 45) is used.

there are no candidates for any of these acts, the congregation may use The
aptismal Covenant IV (111-14, UMH 50).

## THE SERVICE OF THE TABLE

**FFERING** See 26-27.

**AKING THE BREAD AND CUP** See 27-28.

**HE GREAT THANKSGIVING** *

*The congregation turns to A Service of Word and Table III (UMH 15) or one of the
musical settings in UMH 17-25, and the pastor prays The Great Thanksgiving on 66.*

**HE LORD'S PRAYER** * See 29.

**REAKING THE BREAD** See 29.

*The pastor breaks the bread and then lifts the cup, in silence or with appropriate
words.*

**IVING THE BREAD AND CUP** * See 29-31.

*The bread and wine are given to the people, with appropriate words being
exchanged.*

*The congregation sings joyous Easter hymns while the bread and cup are given.*

*When all have received, the Lord's table is put in order.*

*The pastor or congregation may give thanks after communion.*

## SENDING FORTH

**YMN** * See suggestions for Easter.

**ISMISSAL WITH BLESSING** * See 31-32.

We are sent forth in the power of Christ's resurrection. Alleluia!
The grace of the Lord Jesus Christ,
and the love of God,
and the communion of the Holy Spirit
be with you all. Amen.

**OING FORTH** * See 32.

377
# ACTS OF WORSHIP
# FOR THE EASTER SEASON

### Suggested Hymns and Canticles from UMH

302-27 Christ's Gracious Life:          937 Hymns listed under Easter Vigil,
      Resurrection and Exaltation              Easter, Ascension, and Pentecost
328-36 In Praise of the Holy Spirit     166 All Praise to Thee, for Thou, O King Divi
537-44 The Nature of the Church:        384 Love Divine, All Loves Excelling
      Born of the Spirit                388 O Come and Dwell in Me

### Suggested Musical Responses from UMH

318 Christ Is Alive (stanza 1)           306 Alleluia from The Strife Is O'er
305 Refrain from Camina, Pueblo de Dios  308 Refrain from Thine Be the Glory
   (Walk On, O People of God)

### Greetings
378
Praise the Lord!
Praise the Lord from the heavens, praise the Lord in the heights!
**Let them praise the name of the Lord, whose name alone is exalted,**
  **whose glory is above earth and heaven.** (PSALM 148:1, 13, UM

379
Sing for joy, O heavens, and exult, O earth;
  break forth, O mountains, into singing!
**For the Lord has comforted his people,**
  **and will have compassion on his suffering ones.** (ISAIAH 49:

380
Break forth together into singing, you ruins of Jerusalem;
**for the Lord has comforted his people.** (ISAIAH 52:9

381
Jesus said, "I am the resurrection and the life.
**Those who believe in me, even though they die, will live,**
  **and everyone who lives and believes in me will never die."**
(JOHN 11:

382
In fact Christ has been raised from the dead,
  the first fruits of those who have died. (1 CORINTHIANS 15:

383

or this perishable body must put on imperishability,
and this mortal body must put on immortality.
**When this perishable body puts on imperishability,**
**and this mortal body puts on immortality,**
**hen the saying that is written will be fulfilled:**
**"Death has been swallowed up in victory."**
'Where, O death, is your victory?
**Where, O death, is your sting?"**              (1 CORINTHIANS 15:53-55)

384

ince then we have a great high priest
who has passed through the heavens, Jesus, the Son of God,
**et us therefore approach the throne of grace with boldness,**
**so that we may receive mercy and find grace to help in time of need.**
                                                (HEBREWS 4:14a, 16)

385

scribe to the Lord glory and strength.
**o the one seated on the throne and to the Lamb**
**be blessing and honor and glory and might forever and ever.**
                                        (PSALM 96:7b; REVELATION 5:13b)

*ee also:*

| | |
|---|---|
| aiah 12:2 | God is my salvation. |
| aiah 43:1-3a | I have redeemed you. |
| aiah 60:19 | The Lord will be your everlasting light. |
| uke 12:49-50 | I have a baptism. |
| Corinthians 15:20-22 | All will be made alive in Christ. |
| olossians 3:1-4 | New life in Christ |
| Peter 1:3-4 | New birth into a living hope |

386

hrist is risen!
**hrist is risen indeed! Alleluia!**

387

oar we now where Christ has led, following our exalted Head;
**ade like him, like him we rise;**
**urs the cross, the grave, the skies!**      (CHARLES WESLEY, ENGLAND, 18TH CENT.)

388

or Judah's Lion bursts his chains,
**rushing the serpent's head;**
**nd cries aloud through death's domains**
**o wake the imprisoned dead.**               (LATIN HYMN, 11TH CENT.)

389

y your cross you destroyed the curse of the tree.
**y your burial you slayed the dominion of death.**

By your rising, you enlightened the human race.
**O benefactor, Christ our God, glory to you.**

(TRADITIONAL ORTHODOX LITURG)

## 390

Come, Holy Spirit, fill the hearts of your faithful.
**And kindle in them the fire of your love.**

Send forth your Spirit and they shall be created.
**And you will renew the face of the earth.**

(BOOK OF PRAYERS, U.S.A., 20TH CEN)

## 391

Glory to the Father, who has woven garments of glory for the resurrectio)
Worship to the Son, who was clothed in them at his rising.
Thanksgiving to the Spirit, who keeps them for all the saints.

(SYRIAN ORTHODOX CHURC)

*Opening Prayers*

## 392

O Lord, your wondrous birth means nothing unless we are born agair
   your death and sacrifice mean nothing unless we die to sin,
   your resurrection means nothing if you be risen alone.
Raise and exalt us, O Savior,
   both now to the estate of grace and hereafter to the state of glory;
   where with the Father and the Holy Spirit
   you live and reign, God for ever and ever. Amen.

(ERIC MILNER-WHITE, ENGLAND, 20TH CENT., AL)

## 393

Almighty God, through your only Son you overcame death
   and opened to us the gate of everlasting life.
Grant that we who celebrate our Lord's resurrection,
   by the renewing of your Spirit,
   arise from the death of sin to the life of righteousness;
through the same Jesus Christ our Lord. Amen.

(GELASIAN SACRAMENTARY, 5TH CENT., AI)

## 394

Lord of Life, submitting to death, you conquered the grave.
By being lifted on a cross you draw all peoples to you.
By being raised from the dead
   you restored to humanity all that we had lost through sin.
Throughout these fifty days of Easter
   we proclaim the marvelous mystery of death and resurrection.
For all praise is yours, now and throughout eternity. Amen.

(JAMES F. WHITE, U.S.A., 20TH CENT., A)

*he following prayers from* UMH:

20 Easter Vigil or Day                 542 Day of Pentecost
21 Sundays of Easter                   329 Prayer to the Holy Spirit
23 Ascension                           335 An Invitation to the Holy Spirit

### Prayers of Thanksgiving and Intercession

**395**

God of power and majesty:
With the rising of the sun you have raised Jesus Christ
   and delivered him and us from death's destruction.
We praise you on this bright day for all your gifts of new life.
Especially we thank you
   for all victories over sin and evil in our lives . . .
   for loyalty and love of friends and family . . .
   for the newborn, the newly baptized,
      and those now in your eternal home . . .
   for the renewal of nature . . .
   for the continuing witness of the church of Christ . . .
God of eternity:
You are present with us because of Christ's rising from the dead,
   and you persist in lifting us to new life in him.
We bring to you our prayers for this world in need of resurrection.
Especially we pray
   for nations and peoples in strife . . .
   for the poor and impoverished, at home and abroad . . .
   for those we know in particular circumstances of distress . . .
   for the diseased and the dying . . .
   for all who follow the risen Christ . . . ;
through the same Jesus Christ our Lord. Amen.

(PRESBYTERIAN DAILY PRAYER, U.S.A., 20TH CENT., ALT.)

**396**

On the first day of the week, at early dawn,
   the women went to the tomb, taking the spices they had prepared.
And they found the stone rolled away from the tomb.
**Allelujah!**

And the women departed quickly from the tomb with fear and great joy.
And behold, Jesus met them and said, "Hail!" **R**

And Mary stood weeping outside the tomb.
And she said, "They have taken away my Lord,
   and I do not know where they have laid him."
Saying this, she turned around and saw Jesus standing,
   but she did not know that it was Jesus.
And Jesus said to her, "Mary."
And she turned and said to him, "Master." **R**

That very day, two of the disciples were going to a village named Emmaus
While they were talking and discussing together,
    Jesus himself drew near and went with them.
And they recognized him in the breaking of the bread. R

On the evening of that day, the doors being shut where the disciples were
    Jesus came and stood among them, and said to them,
    "Peace be with you."
When he had said this, he showed them his hands and his side. R

Simon Peter said unto the disciples, "I am going fishing."
They said to him, "We will go with you."
And that night they caught nothing.
But just as the day was breaking, Jesus stood on the beach.
And the disciple whom Jesus loved said to Peter, "It is the Lord." R

Now may the God of peace,
    who brought again from the dead our Lord Jesus,
    that great shepherd of the sheep, by the blood of the eternal covenan
equip you with everything good that you may do God's will,
    working in you that which is pleasing in God's sight,
through Jesus Christ: to whom be glory for ever and ever. **Amen.**

(W. E. ORCHARD, ENGLAND, 20TH CENT., AL

## 397

*Each petition may be followed by silent prayer.*

In the peace of the risen Christ, let us pray to the Lord:
that our risen Savior may grant us victory over all our enemies,
    seen and unseen . . . ;
that he may crush beneath our feet the prince of darkness
    and all evil powers . . . ;
that he may raise us up and set us with him in heaven . . . ;
that he may fill us with the joy of his holy and life-giving resurrection . .
that he may provide through us
    for those who lack food, work, and shelter . . . ;
that by his love, wars and famine may cease through all the earth . . .
that isolated and persecuted churches find fresh strength
    in the gospel . . . ;
that all those who have gone before us in the faith of Christ
    may find refreshment, light, and peace;
through Jesus Christ our Lord. Amen.

(U.S.A., 20TH CENT., AL

## 398

And you, Jesus, good Lord, are you not also Mother?
Would a mother not be one who, like a hen,
    gathers her young beneath her wings?
In truth, Lord, you are my Mother! Amen.

(ANSELM OF CANTERBURY, ENGLAND, 11TH CEN

*Intercessions for the Weeks of the Easter Season*

Week 1 **399**

) God, our light, our beauty, our rest:
ι the resurrection of your Son you have brought us into your new creation.
orm us into your people, and order our lives in you;
ιrough Christ our Lord. Amen. Alleluia. (Ps 27:1; Ps 27:4; Mt 11:29)

## Week 2

) God, our bread, our milk, and our honey:
ι the resurrection of your Son you have brought us to your table.
ɛed us with your plenty, and enlarge our table for all the hungry;
ιrough Christ our Lord. Amen. Alleluia. (Jn 6:35; 1 Pet 2:2; Ezek 3:3)

## Week 3

٠ God, our rainbow, our dove, our promised land:
ι the resurrection of your Son you have brought us into your ark.
rotect us from storms, and ferry us to your welcoming shore;
ιrough Christ our Lord. Amen. Alleluia. (Rev 4:3; Mk 1:10; Ps 119:57)

## Week 4

٠ God, our shepherd, our gate, our lamb:
ι the resurrection of your Son you have brought us into your pasture.
uide us to your clear streams, and tame the wolf at our gate;
ιrough Christ our Lord. Amen. Alleluia. (Jn 10:11; Jn 10:9; Jn 1:36)

## Week 5

God, our grove, our lover, our well:
. the resurrection of your Son you have brought us into your garden.
'arry us for now and for ever, and give us to eat from the tree of life;
rough Christ our Lord. Amen. Alleluia. (Ezek 47:12; Isa 5:1; Jn 4:14)

## Week 6

God, our sovereign, our banquet, our crown:
the resurrection of your Son you have brought us into your palace.
'ain us to be heirs to your throne, that we may shield the needy;
rough Christ our Lord. Amen. Alleluia. (Ps 8:1; Ps 99:1; Isa 25:6; Isa 28:5)

## Week 7

God, Holy One, our altar, our cloud:
the resurrection of your Son you have brought us into your temple.
:cept the sacrifices we offer, and draw us into the fire of your Spirit;
rough Christ our Lord. Amen. Alleluia. (Ps 71:22; Ps 43:4; Ex 16:10)

*The Day of Pentecost*

O God, when all things come to their end,
    you bring us into the city of resurrection of your Son.
Shelter every nation and tongue with your Spirit,
    and feed us all with joy unending;
through Christ our Lord. Amen. Alleluia.    (GAIL RAMSHAW, U.S.A., 20TH CENT

**400**    *Signs of the Resurrection*

*These Signs of the Resurrection focus on the appearances of the resurrected Jesu
during the forty days from Easter Day to the Ascension. Each sign reminds th
participant of different events in Christ's resurrection and encourages reflection ar
contemplation. A hymn or stanza may be sung after each sign. Visuals, musi
drama, or liturgical dance may be employed imaginatively. The service may be use
any time during the first forty days of Easter.*

| Sign | Scripture | Summary |
| --- | --- | --- |
| 1) The empty tomb | John 20:1-18 | Appearance to Mary |
| 2) In the garden | Matthew 28:1-10 | Jesus with Mary and Mary |
| 3) Walk to Emmaus | Luke 24:13-35 | Appearance to travelers |
| 4) The upper room | John 20:19-23 | Appearance with disciples |
| 5) The upper room | John 20:24-29 | Jesus and Thomas |
| 6) The Sea of Tiberias | John 21:1-19 | Peter called |
| 7) Mount in Galilee | Matthew 28:16-20 | Great Commission |
| 8) Jerusalem | Luke 24:36-49 | Wait for power. |
| 9) The Ascension | Acts 1:4-11 | Jesus ascends. |

**401**    **ACTS OF WORSHIP
FOR ASCENSION DAY OR SUNDAY**

*Ascension Day is the fortieth day after Easter (Sixth Thursday of Easter), whe
Christ ascended into heaven (Acts 1:1-11). It may be celebrated the following Sunda*

*Suggested Hymns from UMH*

937 Hymns listed under Ascension    312 Hail the Day That Sees Him Rise
168 At the Name of Jesus

**402**    *Greeting*

Risen with Christ, let us seek the realities of the Spirit.
**Our life is hidden with Christ in God.**

He who descended is also ascended far above the heavens,
that he might fill all things.
**When Christ, our Life, appears,
we shall appear with him in glory! Alleluia!**

(DON E. SALIERS, U.S.A., 20TH CEN

Prayer                                              403

lmighty God,
your blessed Son, our Savior Jesus Christ,
ascended far above all heavens,
that he might fill all things.
lercifully give us faith to perceive that, according to his promise,
he abides with his Church on earth, even to the end of the world;
irough the same your Son, Jesus Christ our Lord. Amen.

(SCOTTISH BOOK OF COMMON PRAYER, SCOTLAND, 20TH CENT., ALT.)

*e The Ascension (UMH 323).*

A Prayer for the Sunday After the Ascension        404

• God, the King of glory,
you have exalted your only Son Jesus Christ
   with great triumph to your kingdom in heaven.
•o not leave us comfortless,
but send us your Holy Spirit to strengthen us,
and exalt us to that place where our Savior Christ has gone before;
ho lives and reigns with you and the Holy Spirit,
ie God, in glory everlasting. Amen.

(THE BOOK OF COMMON PRAYER, U.S.A., 20TH CENT.)

# ACTS OF WORSHIP                405
# FOR THE DAY OF PENTECOST

*e Day of Pentecost is the fiftieth and last day of the Easter Season, when the Church eived the gift of the Holy Spirit (Acts 2). It is a most appropriate day for baptisms, ıfirmations, and congregational reaffirmation of the Baptismal Covenant. For ıual suggestions see 368.*

### Suggested Hymns from UMH

3-36 In Praise of the Holy Spirit     140 Great Is Thy Faithfulness
7-44 The Nature of the Church:        114 Many Gifts, One Spirit
     Born of the Spirit               388 O Come and Dwell in Me
7 Hymns listed under Pentecost        143 On Eagle's Wings
$ Hymns listed under Holy Spirit      347 Spirit Song
) Help Us Accept Each Other

   *also:*
ıediction for Pentecost ( ♪ 218)
ırit of God ( ♪ 214)

**406**                                    *Greeting*

And in the last days it shall come to pass, God declares,
   that I will pour out my Spirit on all flesh,
**And your sons and daughters shall prophesy,**
   **your old shall dream dreams, and your young shall see visions.**

When the Day of Pentecost had come,
   they were all gathered together in one place.
**And suddenly a sound came from heaven like the rush of a mighty wind**
   **and it filled all the house where they were sitting.**

And there appeared to them tongues as of fire,
   distributed and resting on each of them.
**And they were all filled with the Holy Spirit.** (THE BOOK OF WORSHIP 1965, AL

*Prayers*

**407**

O God, you sent the Holy Spirit to enkindle the zeal of Christ's followe:
   waiting in Jerusalem for his promised gift.
Pour the same inspiration on your people here assembled,
   and on the Church of Christ throughout the world.
Revive the power of the gospel in our hearts,
   that it may be to us a sacred trust for the blessing of all creation.
Enable your Church to spread the good news of salvation,
   so that all nations may hear it in their own tongues,
   and welcome it into their own lives.
Protect, encourage, and bless all ministers of the cross,
   and prosper their words and works,
so that Jesus, being lifted up, may draw all people unto him,
and the kingdoms of the world
   may become the kingdom of our Lord and of Jesus Christ. Amen.
                                    (HENRY VAN DYKE, U.S.A., 20TH CENT., AI

**408**

God of wind, word, and fire, we bless your name this day
   for sending the light and strength of your Holy Spirit.
We give you thanks for all the gifts, great and small,
   that you have poured out upon your children.
Accept us with our gifts
   to be living praise and witness to your love throughout all the earth
through Jesus Christ, who lives with you in the unity of the Holy Spir
   one God, for ever. Amen.          (DON E. SALIERS, U.S.A., 20TH CEN

*See Day of Pentecost (UMH 542).*

*If Holy Communion is to be celebrated, see The Great Thanksgiving on 68-69*

# SEASON AFTER PENTECOST
## (ORDINARY TIME OR KINGDOMTIDE)

he Season After Pentecost, also called Ordinary Time, begins the day after Pentecost and ends the day before the First Sunday of Advent. It may nclude twenty-three to twenty-eight Sundays, depending on the date of Easter, but the first Sunday is always Trinity Sunday, and the last Sunday is always the Sunday of the Reign of Christ or Christ the King. The season also ncludes All Saints and Thanksgiving.

Jnited Methodists have the option of calling this season Kingdomtide, a erm first used in 1937 in a book sponsored by the former Federal Council of Churches as a name for the half of the year between the Day of Pentecost and Advent, during which churches were urged to emphasize Jesus' teachings oncerning the kingdom of God. In 1940 the season was shortened to three nonths, beginning the last Sunday in August. The former Methodist Church adopted it in its shortened three-month form in the 1945 and 1965 ditions of *The Book of Worship*. Today, no other denomination uses the term Kingdomtide.

Although the scripture lessons in the lectionary for this half of the year go in semicontinuous cycle through books of the Bible rather than follow a heme, the gospel lessons cover Jesus' teaching ministry and tend to center n the theme of the kingdom and reign of God. Thus this half of the year can illy serve the purposes intended for Kingdomtide in its original six-month orm.

araments, stoles, and banners may show a variety of color, texture, and ymbols. Regardless of the name given to this season, its basic color is green, ymbolizing growth in Christ. White is the customary color for Trinity unday, All Saints, and Reign of Christ/Christ the King Sunday. Red is ppropriate for homecomings, anniversaries, evangelistic services, conse- ations, and civil holidays. The scripture readings or theme for a particular unday may suggest colors, textures, or symbols for the visuals used that ay. A lesson on children, for example, might suggest using art by children.

cts of worship are chosen more because they relate to the scripture eadings or theme of the particular day than because they fit the season as a hole. In addition to the acts and services of worship on the following ages, see General Acts of Worship (445-567), The Great Thanksgivings on )-77, and the scripture readings in the lectionary on 233-37.

# 410   ACTS OF WORSHIP FOR TRINITY SUNDAY

*The Sunday After Pentecost is a celebration of the Trinity: one God in three persons*
*In addition to the acts of worship suggested below, the Nicene Creed (UMH 880) i₁*
*especially appropriate on this day because of its classic statement of the doctrine of the*
*Trinity.*

### Suggested Hymns from UMH

938 Hymns listed under
   Trinity Sunday

95 Praise God, from Whom
   All Blessings Flow
113 Source and Sovereign, Rock and Cloud

## 411   *Greeting*

No one has ever seen God;
**if we love one another,**
   **God lives in us, and his love is perfected in us.**   (1 JOHN 4:1₂

## 412   *Prayer*

Everlasting God:
You have revealed yourself as Father, Son, and Holy Spirit,
   and ever live and reign in the perfect unity of love.
Grant that we may always hold firmly and joyfully to this faith,
   and, living in praise of your divine majesty,
   may finally be one in you;
who are three persons in one God, for ever and ever. Amen.
        (CHURCH OF SOUTH INDIA, 20TH CENT., ALT

*See Trinity Sunday (UMH 76).*

*If Holy Communion is to be celebrated, see The Great Thanksgiving on 70-71.*

## 413   ACTS OF WORSHIP
## FOR ALL SAINTS DAY OR SUNDAY

*All Saints (November 1 or the first Sunday in November) is a day of remembran₁*
*for the saints, with the New Testament meaning of all Christian people of every tim*
*and place. We celebrate the communion of saints as we remember the dead, both of th*
*Church universal and of our local congregations. For this reason, the names*
*persons in the congregation who have died during the past year may be solemnly rec*
*as a Response to the Word.*

### Suggested Hymns from UMH

938 Hymns listed under
   All Saints Day

708-12 Communion of the Saints
652-56 Funeral and Memorial Service

*See also:*
Beloved, Now We Are the Saints of God ( ♪ 219)

*Greeting* **414**

race to you and peace from God
who is, and was, and is to come. **Amen.**
nd from Jesus Christ the faithful witness,
the firstborn of the dead, and ruler of kings on earth. **Amen.**
he grace of the Lord Jesus be with all the saints. **Amen.**

(U.S.A., 20TH CENT., ALT.)

*Prayer* **415**

'e bless your holy name, O God,
for all your servants who, having finished their course,
now rest from their labors.
ive us grace to follow the example
of their steadfastness and faithfulness,
to your honor and glory;
rough Christ Jesus our Lord. Amen. (ENGLAND, 20TH CENT., ALT.)

e *All Saints (UMH 713). See also On the Anniversary of a Death (548).*

*Holy Communion is to be celebrated, see The Great Thanksgiving on 74-75.*

# ACTS OF WORSHIP  416
# FOR THANKSGIVING EVE, DAY, OR SUNDAY

*anksgiving Day in the U.S.A. is celebrated on the fourth Thursday in November or
 Sunday before or after Thanksgiving Day. It is a harvest festival, giving thanks for
 God's blessings, often characterized by prayer and feasts. It was first celebrated in
rth America in 1619 in Charles City, Virginia.*

*anksgiving may also be a time to remember when the Native American tribal
oples made survival possible for the early immigrants to the U.S.A. Native
nericans have a variety of ceremonies for thanksgiving which are related to the
sons of nature, for families to feast and pray, and to offer thanks to the Creator.
ited Methodists are encouraged to celebrate Thanksgiving in consultation with
resentatives of the Native Americans in their region. Such a service should respect
 traditions of the native peoples, and it may be a service of repentance and
onciliation between indigenous and immigrant peoples. See Native American
areness Sunday 425 for additional suggestions.*

### Suggested Hymns from UMH

 Hymns listed under Thanksgiving Day

## 417 *Greeting*

Let the nations be glad and sing for joy,
 for you judge the peoples with equity
 and guide all the nations upon the earth.
**Let all the peoples praise you, O God;**
**let all the peoples praise you.**

The earth has brought forth its increase;
may God, our own God, bless us.
**Let all the peoples praise you, O God;**
**let all the peoples praise you.**  (U.S.A., 20TH CENT., AL'

## 418 *Prayer*

Most gracious God, you crown the year with your goodness.
We praise you that you have ever fulfilled your promise
 that, while earth remains, seedtime and harvest shall not cease.
We bless you for the order and constancy of nature,
 for the beauty of earth and sky and sea,
 and for the providence that year by year supplies our need.
We thank you for your blessing
 on the work of those who plowed the soil and sowed the seed,
 and have now gathered in the fruits of the earth.
And with our thanksgiving for these blessings,
 accept our praise, O God,
 for the eternal riches of your grace in Christ our Lord;
to whom, with you, O Father, and the Holy Spirit,
 be all glory and honor and worship, for ever and ever. Amen.
(J. M. TODD, ENGLAND, 20TH CENT., AI

*See also Prayers of Thanksgiving on 549-58.*

*If Holy Communion is to be celebrated, see The Great Thanksgiving on 76-77*

## 419 ACTS OF WORSHIP
## FOR REIGN OF CHRIST/CHRIST THE KING SUNDAY

*The Last Sunday After Pentecost, which is also the last Sunday of the Christian ye*
*is a celebration of the coming reign of Jesus Christ and the completion of creatic*

### Suggested Hymns from UMH

938 Hymns listed under  722-34 The Completion of Creation
  Christ the King  706 Soon and Very Soon
714-21 Return and Reign of the Lord

*Greeting* 420

I am the Alpha and the Omega," says the Lord God,
"who is, and who was, and who is to come, the Almighty."
**lessing and honor and glory and might be unto the Lamb!**
Worthy is Christ who has ransomed us by his blood
from every tribe and tongue and nation,
and made his people a kingdom, and priests to our God.
**Holy, holy, holy, is the Lord God Almighty,**
**who was and is and is to come! Amen.** (U.S.A., 20TH CENT.)

*Prayer* 421

Almighty God, who gave your Son Jesus Christ a realm
where all peoples, nations, and languages should serve him;
make us loyal followers of our living Lord,
that we may always hear his word,
follow his teachings, and live in his Spirit;
and hasten the day when every knee shall bow
and every tongue confess that he is Lord;
to your eternal glory. Amen. (A. CAMPBELL FRAZIER, ENGLAND, 20TH CENT., ALT.)

*See Christ the King (UMH 721).*

# IV. SPECIAL SUNDAYS
# AND OTHER SPECIAL DAYS

## SPECIAL SUNDAYS OF
## THE UNITED METHODIST CHURCH

Human Relations Day      Sunday before the observance of
     Martin Luther King, Jr.'s birthday
One Great Hour of Sharing      Fourth Sunday in Lent
Native American Awareness      Third Sunday of Easter
     Sunday
Heritage Sunday      April 23 or the following Sunday
Golden Cross Sunday      First Sunday in May
Peace with Justice Sunday      First Sunday After Pentecost
Christian Education Sunday      Date set by each Annual Conference
Rural Life Sunday      Date set by each Annual Conference
World Communion Sunday      First Sunday in October
Laity Sunday      Third Sunday in October
United Methodist Student Day      Last Sunday in November

*The Special Sundays of The United Methodist Church, celebrated annually, illustrate the nature and calling of the Church. These special Sundays approved by General Conference are the only Sundays of churchwide emphasis. Such special Sundays should never take precedence over the particular day in the Christian year. The special Sundays are placed on the calendar in the context of the Christian year, which is designed to make clear the calling of the Church as the people of God. Several give persons the opportunity of contributing offerings to special programs. The "Special Sundays with Churchwide Offerings" are set by each General Conference, to do deeds expressive of our commitment, and remain constant for a quadrennium. Other "Special Sundays Without Offerings" and "Special Sundays" with Annual Conference offerings are also set by General Conference. Annual Conferences may also determine other Special Sundays with or without offerings. Throughout the life of this book, such days are likely to change, and persons need to plan with yearly program calendars from the denomination.*

# HUMAN RELATIONS DAY              423

*bserved on the Sunday before the observance of Martin Luther King, Jr.'s birthday,*
*is day calls the Church to recognize the right of all God's children to realize their*
*tential as human beings in relationship with one another. See also resources for*
*artin Luther King, Jr. Day on 435.*

## *Suggested Hymns and Prayers from* UMH

7-93 Called to God's Mission
9-36 Strength in Tribulation
0 Hymns listed under
   Reconciliation
0-93 Prayers of Confession,
   Assurance and Pardon

401 For Holiness of Heart
101 From All That Dwell Below the Skies
548 In Christ There Is No East or West
733 Marching to Zion
131 We Gather Together

## *Litany*

irit of the living God, fall afresh on us.
s we gather in this place, allow your Spirit to fill our very being.
**s we worship today,**
**we remember our brothers and sisters**
  **who are worshiping elsewhere throughout the world.**
**spire each of us to work more faithfully**
  **for justice and dignity of life everywhere.**

ise our vision above the barriers
  of color, culture, and creed that separate us.
ve us wisdom as we deal with one another.
elp us to recognize and to respect different ways, rather than to judge.
**the Spirit of Jesus who came not to be served, but to serve,**
**we now must walk in the world.**
e must reach out our hands with help and open our hearts in love.
**wake in us the desire to seek your way of serving you in the world.**
**men.**
              (NANCY R. MCMASTER, U.S.A., 20TH CENT., ALT.)

# ONE GREAT HOUR OF SHARING        424

*bserved on the Fourth Sunday in Lent, this day calls the Church to share the*
*odness of life with those who hurt.*

*Suggested Hymns and Prayers from* UMH

567-93 Called to God's Mission
434 Cuando El Pobre
    (When the Poor Ones)
456 For Courage to Do Justice

548 In Christ There Is No East or West
726 O Holy City Seen of John
446 Serving the Poor

*Greeting*

Jesus said:
"I was hungry and you gave me food,
  I was thirsty and you gave me something to drink."
**Let us act justly.**

"I was a stranger and you welcomed me,
  I was naked and you gave me clothing."
**Let us love tenderly.**

"I was sick and you took care of me,
  I was in prison and you visited me."
**Let us walk humbly with our God.**

May we see Christ in one another,
  **that we may be healers and peacemakers in Christ's name.**

(MATTHEW 25:31-46; MICAH 6:8, AL

# 425 NATIVE AMERICAN AWARENESS SUNDAY

*Observed on the Third Sunday of Easter, this Sunday reminds the Church of the gif
and contributions made by Native Americans to our Church and society. It was fir
celebrated in 1989. United Methodists are encouraged to celebrate Native Americ
Awareness Sunday in consultation with representatives of the Native Americ
community in their region. Such a service should respect the traditions of the nati
peoples, and may be a service of repentance and reconciliation between indigenous ar
immigrant peoples.*

*Suggested Hymns from* UMH

378 Amazing Grace (note stanzas in
    Native American languages)
330 Daw-Kee, Aim Daw-Tsi-Taw
    (Great Spirit, Now I Pray)

78 Heleluyan
191 Jesus Loves Me (stanza in Cherokee)
148 Many and Great, O God
244 'Twas in the Moon of Wintertime

*See also:*
Shawnee Traveling Song ( ♪ 197)

Kiowa Hymn: A Call to Worship ( ♪ 184)

*Greeting*

Every part of this earth is sacred.
**Every shining pine needle, every sandy shore,
  every mist in the dark woods,
  every clearing and humming insect is holy.**

e rocky crest, the meadow, the beasts and all the people,
all belong to the same family.
each your children that the earth is our mother.
**'hatever befalls the earth befalls the children of the earth.**
**'e are part of the earth, and the earth is a part of us.**

e rivers are our brothers, they quench our thirst.
**he perfumed flowers are our sisters, the air is precious,**
**for all of us share the same breath.**

e wind that gave our grandparents breath also receives their last sigh.
**he wind gave our children the spirit of life.**

is we know, the earth does not belong to us.
**e belong to the earth.**

is we know, all things are connected.
**ke the blood which unites one family, all things are connected.**

ur God is the same God, whose compassion is equal for all.
**r we did not weave the web of life.**
**'e are merely a strand in it.**

'hatever we do to the web we do to ourselves.
**t us give thanks for the web and the circle that connects us.**
**anks be to God, the God of all.**

(INSPIRED BY CHIEF SEATTLE, NATIVE AMERICAN, U.S.A., 19TH CENT.)

### Prayers

e Prayer to the Holy Spirit (UMH 329).
e also 455, 458, 468, 470, 487, 521, 558, 562.

# HERITAGE SUNDAY 426

*bserved on April 23 or the following Sunday, this day calls The United Methodist*
*iurch to honor its heritage by committing itself to the continuing call of God,*
*membering that on April 23, 1968, The United Methodist Church was created by*
*e union of The Evangelical United Brethren Church and The Methodist Church.*

### Suggested Hymns from UMH

8 Hymns listed under           363 And Can It Be That I Should Gain
  Church Anniversaries         342 Where Shall My Wondering Soul Begin*

*Read as poetry or sing to the tune ST. PETERSBURG (UMH 153).*

### Litany

lmighty God, you have raised up servants
to proclaim the gift of redemption and a life of holiness.

For our spiritual forebears,
  Susanna, John, and Charles Wesley;
  Barbara Heck, Jacob Albright,
  Philip William Otterbein, and Martin Boehm,
  inspired by your Spirit, we give thanks.
In their ministry, through their difficulties,
  and in spite of their weaknesses,
  you were their hope and their salvation.
**You led them and their followers to create the heritage that is ours.**
We praise you for the women and men, young and old,
  who followed them,
  who gave themselves unselfishly for the welfare of the Church,
  whose commitment and vision encouraged
    and supported the Church.
Their talents, enthusiasm, idealism, and dedication
  infused the Church with energy.
**Their outstanding gifts and witness shaped our thought and life.**
**We praise you for these countless members of your Church,**
  **whose names we now remember . . .**

*Silence is kept to remember the names of saints.*

And we give you thanks for the place of our rich tradition
  among the churches which comprise the Body of Christ.
**With all your people throughout creation,**
  **give us a new vision, new love, new wisdom,**
    **and fresh understanding,**
  **that we may serve you more fully;**
**through Jesus Christ our Lord. Amen.** (CHARLES YRIGOYEN, U.S.A., 20TH CENT., AL⸀

# 427 GOLDEN CROSS SUNDAY

*Observed on a date determined by the Annual Conference, this day supports Annua*
*Conference health and welfare ministries. This day was created by the North Texa*
*Conference to finance charity work in Dallas and was adopted in 1922 as an offici*
*program of the Methodist Episcopal Church, South. See also the resources in Healir*
*Services and Prayers (613-29) and hymns under Healing in UMH 943.*

### Prayer

O God, you sent your Son to be a physician,
  healing broken bodies and diseased minds.
Bless those who are afflicted with sickness, pain, and disability.

urround with your love
those who lack the full use of their limbs or their minds.
less those who stand and watch while dear ones suffer.
less those who care for these persons—
the pastors, counselors, doctors, nurses, and others—
who minister to those unable to care fully for themselves.
nd bless us as we provide hospitals, homes, and services
for all those who need our help.
lake us all instruments of your healing power;
Jesus' name we pray. Amen.                    (U.S.A., 20TH CENT., ALT.)

*e also Litany for the Church and for the World (495).*

## PEACE WITH JUSTICE SUNDAY          428

*bserved on the First Sunday After Pentecost, this day witnesses to God's demand for faithful, just, disarmed, and secure world.*

### Suggested Hymns and Prayers from UMH

5-50 Social Holiness                107 La Palabara Del Senor Es Recta
9 Hymns listed under Peace          (Righteous and Just Is the Word of the Lord)
6 For Courage to Do Justice

*Prayer*

om self-righteousness that will not compromise,
and from selfishness that gains by the oppression of others,
**Lord, deliver us.** *See also* ♪ *195.*

om the lust for money or power that drives to kill, **R**
om trusting in the weapons of war,
and mistrusting the councils of peace, **R**
om hearing, believing, and speaking lies about other nations, **R**
om suspicions and fears that stand in the way of reconciliation, **R**
om words and deeds that encourage discord, prejudice, and hatred;
om everything that prevents us from fulfilling your promise of peace, **R**
**men.**                                       (U.S.A., 20TH CENT., ALT.)

*e also 495, 511, 513, 515-21, 526-27.*

## CHRISTIAN EDUCATION SUNDAY          429

*n a date set by each Annual Conference, this Sunday calls the Church as the people of d to be open to growth and learning as disciples of Jesus Christ. See An Order for e Installation or Recognition of Church School Workers on 601, An Order for the esentation of Bibles to Children on 587, and hymns listed under Education in MH 938 for resources.*

# 430        RURAL LIFE SUNDAY

*On a date set by each Annual Conference, this Sunday calls the Church to celebrate t. rural heritage of The United Methodist Church, to affirm worldwide the people ar communities who work with and on the land by raising food and fiber, and recognize the ongoing crisis occuring in the rural areas of the nation and world toda Emphases may include honoring persons who have been leaders in the rural chur. and community, observing Rogation Sunday (a service asking for God's blessir upon the earth and its crops, traditionally held on the three days prior to the Day Ascension in the spring), and celebrating and showing a concern for God's creat. order. Also see A Service for the Blessing of Animals (608-10), and 425, 507.*

## Suggested Scripture Readings

| | |
|---|---|
| Deuteronomy 26:1-11 (at harvest) | Give God the first fruits of the harvest. |
| Joel 2:21-27 (at planting) | Promise of abundant harvest |
| Psalm 90 | Prosper the work of our hands. |
| 2 Corinthians 9:6, 10 | Sow bountifully. |
| Mark 4:26-29 | The earth produces and the harvest come |

*Suggested Hymns from* UMH*:* 144-52 Creation

### Prayer

O Lord, you have given us the gift of land.
**May we ever protect and preserve it.**

O Lord, you have given us the gift of water.
**May we keep it pure and safe.**

O Lord, you have given us the gift of air.
**May we keep it pure and fresh.**

O Lord, you have given us the gift of plants and trees.
**May we ever use and protect them justly.**

O Lord, you have given us the gift of birds and animals.
**May we preserve and enjoy them.**

O Lord, you have given us care of the earth.
**O Lord, we accept the care of these gifts as our sacred stewardshi**
**Amen.**              (MELVIN E. WEST, U.S.A., 20TH CEN

# 431        WORLD COMMUNION SUNDAY

*Observed on the first Sunday in October, this day calls the Church to be the univers. inclusive Church. The day was first observed by Presbyterians in 1936, adopted by t Federal Council of Churches in 1940, and shortly thereafter observed in Method. and Evangelical United Brethren churches.*

### Suggested Hymns and Prayers from UMH

| | |
|---|---|
| 2-41 Holy Communion | 191 Jesus Loves Me |
| 8 For the Healing of the Nations | 556 Litany for Christian Unity |
| 4 For the Unity of Christ's Body | 547 O Church of God, United |
| 8 In Christ There Is No East or West | 702 Sing with All the Saints in Glory |

### Prayers

lmighty God: from the ends of the earth
you have gathered us around Christ's holy table.
**e come to feast together.**
ave mercy on your church, troubled and divided.
**enew us and make us one. Amen.**    (ANDY LANGFORD, U.S.A., 20TH CENT.)

God, we join with our sisters and brothers around the world
in remembering Christ's sacrifice for us.
or the opportunity to eat and drink together
and for the life we have received,
we give you thanks and praise.
the abundance of your many gifts,
grant us grace to fill one another's lives with love.
edeem, restore and remold us until we are made new.
ansform our daily bread into the bread of life,
and the cup that we drink into the cup of salvation.
e pray in Jesus' name. Amen.    (BARBARA DUNLAP-BERG, U.S.A., 20TH CENT., ALT.)

*e the prayers for the Church on 495, 501-06.*
*e The Great Thanksgiving on 72-73.*

# LAITY SUNDAY                     432

*bserved on the third Sunday in October, this day calls the Church to celebrate the
nistry of Christians of all ages in the home, workplace, congregation, community,
d world.*

### Suggested Hymns from UMH

| | |
|---|---|
| 7-93 Called to God's Mission | 558 We Are the Church |

### Litany

om the beginning, God entered into covenant with the human family:
with Adam and Eve, Noah, Abraham and Sarah,
Moses, Deborah, Ruth, and Jeremiah.
**rough baptism, Jesus Christ calls us into the covenant
and makes us ministers of Christ's righteousness.**

All Christian ministry is Christ's work of outreaching love.
It demonstrates a common life of gratitude and devotion,
  witness and service, celebration and discipleship.
**All Christians are called to Christ's servanthood in the world,**
  **to the glory of God and for human fulfillment.**

The Church, as the community of the new covenant,
  participates in Christ's ministry of grace.
**It stretches out to human needs**
  **wherever service may convey God's love and ours.**

In our ministry of servanthood is this ultimate concern:
**that all may be renewed in the image of their Creator,**
**and that all Christians are called to minister**
  **in deeds and words that heal and free. Amen.**

(ADAPTED FROM THE BOOK OF DISCIPLINE 1992, ¶¶101-•

# 433    UNITED METHODIST STUDENT DAY

*Observed on the last Sunday in November, this day calls the Church to suppc*
*students in uniting faith with knowledge.*

*Suggested Hymns in* UMH: 567-93 Called to God's Mission

### *Litany*

Gracious God, eternal God, you have led us to curiosity
  about our creation, ourselves, and all things unknown.
**Let us never lose our sense of wonder about the world you have given u**

God of Abraham and Sarah,
  you lead us to new understandings when we least expect them.
**Let us never see ourselves as too young, too old, or too wise**
  **to learn new lessons from you.**

God of the prophets,
  you call us to speak truth with love to a reluctant world.
**Give us courage to judge ourselves,**
  **and wisdom to learn from those you send to teach us.**

God of the rich young ruler,
  you love us though we shrink from the challenge of discipleship.
**Teach us to surrender our own wills,**
  **that we might seek yours and draw closer to your grace.**

Everlasting, everloving God, teacher, creator,
  giver of knowledge and freedom, fear and courage, doubt and faith,
**grant that we might always use your gifts to build a world**
  **where peace, justice, love, and hope reign in wisdom and in trut**
**Amen.** (KATHIE NEAL, U.S.A., 20TH CENT., AI

# OTHER SPECIAL DAYS 434

| | |
|---|---|
| Martin Luther King, Jr. Day | Third Monday in January |
| Boy Scout Sunday | Second Sunday in February |
| Girl Scout Sunday | Second Sunday in March |
| Festival of the Christian Home | Second Sunday in May |
| Mother's Day | Second Sunday in May |
| Aldersgate Day or Sunday | May 24 |
| Memorial Day | Last Monday in May |
| Father's Day | Third Sunday in June |
| Independence Day | July 4 |
| Labor Day | First Monday in September |
| Reformation Day or Sunday | October 31 |

*These special days are commonly observed in many United Methodist congregations and are recognized in the* Book of Discipline *but not given churchwide emphasis. Although set in the context of the Christian year, such special days should never take precedence over the particular day in the Christian year.*

## MARTIN LUTHER KING, JR. DAY 435

*This day is observed on the third Monday in January to remember the life and ministry of Martin Luther King, Jr.*

*Suggested Hymns and Prayers from* UMH

| | |
|---|---|
| 529-36 Strength in Tribulation | 401 For Holiness of Heart |
| 89 For God's Gifts | 106 God Is Able |

*Prayer*

*The left and right sides of the congregation may pray alternate paragraphs of the following prayer. Silent prayers may follow each paragraph.*

We remember the conviction of Martin Luther King, Jr., that
  "freedom is never voluntarily given by the oppressor;
  it must be demanded by the oppressed."
Therefore, let us pray
  for courage and determination by those who are oppressed. . . .

We remember Martin's warning that
  "a negative peace which is the absence of tension"
  is less than "a positive peace which is the presence of justice."
Therefore, let us pray
  that those who work for peace in our world
    may cry out first for justice. . . .

We remember Martin's insight that
"injustice anywhere is a threat to justice everywhere.
We are caught in an inescapable network of mutuality
tied in a single garment of destiny.
Whatever affects one directly affects all indirectly."
Therefore, let us pray that we may see nothing in isolation,
but may know ourselves bound to one another
and to all people under heaven. . . .

We remember Martin's lament that
"the contemporary church is often a weak, ineffectual voice
with an uncertain sound.
It is so often the arch-supporter of the status quo.
Far from being disturbed by the presence of the Church,
the power structure of the average community is consoled
by the Church's silent and often vocal sanction of things as they are
Therefore, let us pray
that neither this congregation nor any congregation of Christ's peopl
may be silent in the face of wrong,
but that we may be disturbers of the status quo
when that is God's call to us. . . .

We remember Martin's
"hope that dark clouds of racial prejudice will soon pass away
and the deep fog of misunderstanding will be lifted
from our fear-drenched communities
and in some not too distant tomorrow
the radiant stars of love and brotherhood
will shine over our great nation with all their scintillating beauty."
Therefore, in faith, let us commend ourselves and our work for justice
to the goodness of almighty God.

> (QUOTATIONS FROM LETTER FROM THE BIRMINGHAM CITY JAIL BY MARTIN LUTHER KING, J
> LITANY BY W. B. McCLAIN AND L. H. STOOKEY, U.S.A., 20TH CEN

## 436   BOY SCOUT SUNDAY/GIRL SCOUT SUNDAY

*Boy Scout Sunday is observed on the second Sunday in February; Girl Scout Sunde
is observed on the second Sunday in March. When it is not practical to honor Be
Scouts and Girl Scouts separately, it is acceptable to have a joint recognition in c
inclusive service between the second Sunday in February and the second Sunday
March. Scout Sunday offers an excellent opportunity for the local congregation
recognize the Scouting program, the Scouts, and their leaders as an integral ar
intentional part of the Church's ministry. Use Scout members as ushers, acolyte
worship leaders, and musicians.*

### Suggested Hymns from UMH

A Charge to Keep I Have          150 God, Who Stretched the Spangled Heavens
Thy Word Is a Lamp

### Prayer

God, your will is that all your children should grow into fullness of life.
e lift to you the ministry of scouting.
e offer you thanks for camping,
to teach us that the world is our great home;
for study and work, to build character;
for service, to see our responsibility to those in need;
for encouragement in genuine patriotism and vital faith.
ess the work of scouting, in this place and around the world,
that, through its efforts, the young may, like our Lord,
increase in wisdom and in stature, and in favor with you and all people.
nen.                                            (MARK TROTTER, U.S.A., 20TH CENT.)

## FESTIVAL OF THE CHRISTIAN HOME          437

*served the second Sunday in May, this day celebrates the gift of Christian homes*
*d affirms the Christian family in its wholeness.*

### Suggested Hymns from UMH

Hymns listed under Home          445 Happy the Home When God Is There
    and Family                    695 O Lord, May Church and Home Combine
Blest Be the Tie that Binds       447 Our Parent, By Whose Name

### Prayer

you, O God, every family on earth receives its name.
umine the homes of this earth with the light of your love,
granting courage to those who are hurt or lonely,
endurance to those who care for sick family members,
and wisdom to those in fearful times of change.
e thank you for gifts of love we have received
from mother, father, spouse, child, or companion.
we have been loved by you and by others, so may we love.
ant us your peace, through Jesus the Christ. Amen.
                                            (RUTH DUCK, U.S.A., 20TH CENT., ALT.)

## MOTHER'S DAY          438

*served the second Sunday in May, this day honors all mothers. It began in its*
*sent form with a special service in May 1907 at the Methodist Episcopal Church in*

*Grafton, West Virginia. The service was organized by a Methodist laywoman, An*
*Jarvis, to honor her mother, who had died on May 9, 1905. By 1908 Anna Jarvis t*
*advocating that all mothers be honored on the second Sunday in May, and in 1912*
*Methodist Episcopal Church recognized the day and raised it to the national agen*
*It has some parallels with the old English Mothering Sunday in mid-Lent, wh*
*focused on returning home and paying homage to one's mother, and with Mothe*
*Day for Peace, introduced in 1872 by Julia Ward Howe in Boston as a day dedicated*
*peace.*

### *Suggested Hymns from* UMH

*See* Festival of the Christian Home (437).

### *Prayer*

*Silent prayer may follow each petition.*

For our mothers, who have given us life and love,
    that we may show them reverence and love,
we pray to the Lord. . .

For mothers who have lost a child through death,
    that their faith may give them hope,
    and their family and friends support and console them,
we pray to the Lord. . .

For women, though without children of their own,
    who like mothers have nurtured and cared for us,
we pray to the Lord. . .

For mothers, who have been unable to be a source of strength,
    who have not responded to their children
        and have not sustained their families,
we pray to the Lord. . .

Loving God, as a mother gives life and nourishment to her children,
    so you watch over your Church.
Bless these women, that they may be strengthened as Christian mothe
Let the example of their faith and love shine forth.
Grant that we, their sons and daughters,
    may honor them always with a spirit of profound respect.
Grant this through Christ our Lord. Amen.

(BOOK OF BLESSINGS, U.S.A., 20TH CENT., A

## 439　ALDERSGATE DAY OR SUNDAY

*On Wednesday, May 24, 1738, John Wesley experienced his "heart strang*
*warmed." This Aldersgate experience was crucial for his own life and becam*
*touchstone for the Wesleyan movement.*

## Suggested Scripture Readings

| | |
|---|---|
| ,alm 130 (*UMH* 515, 516, 848) * | Out of the depths I cry to you, O Lord. |
| :ts 2:1-21 | The giving of the Holy Spirit |
| )mans 5:1-11 | By faith we have peace with God. |
| Peter 1:4* | Great and precious promises |
| atthew 9:27-30*a* | According to your faith, let it be done. |
| ark 12:28-34*a** | You are not far from the kingdom of God. |

*hese scriptures were read or heard by John Wesley on May 24, 1738.*

Soul Begin *

7 O for a Thousand Tongues to Sing

*ead as poetry or sing to the tune* St. Petersburg *(UMH 153).*

## Prayer

⁀mighty God, in a time of great need
you raised up your servants John and Charles Wesley,
▮d by your Spirit inspired them to kindle a flame of sacred love
which leaped and ran, an inextinguishable blaze.
⁀ant that all those whose hearts have been warmed at these altar fires,
being continually refreshed by your grace, may be so devoted
     to the increase of scriptural holiness throughout the land
at in this our time of great need,
your will may fully and effectively be done on earth as it is in heaven;
⁀rough Jesus Christ our Lord. Amen. (Fred D. Gealy, U.S.A., 20th cent., alt.)

# MEMORIAL DAY 440

*ɔserved the last Monday in May or the previous Sunday, this day honors the war*
*d of the United States. It was first celebrated in 1866 in Waterloo, New York.*
*any observe the day by decorating graves, especially of persons who died in war.*

## Suggested Resources from UMH

| | |
|---|---|
| 2 Canticle of Remembrance | 656 If Death My Friend and Me Divide |
| 3 Christ the Victorious | 717 The Battle Hymn of the Republic |
| 4 How Blest Are They Who Trust in Christ | 437 This Is My Song |

## Prayer

*ent prayer may follow each petition.*

.mighty God, before whom stand the living and the dead,
we your children, whose mortal life is but a hand's breadth,
give thanks to you:

For all those through whom you have blessed our pilgrimage,
  whose lives that have empowered us,
  whose influence is a healing grace,
**We lift up thankful hearts.**

For the dear friends and family members
  whose faces we see no more, but whose love is with us for ever . . .

For the teachers and companions of our childhood and youth,
  and for the members of our household of faith
    who worship you now in heaven . . . R

For those who sacrificed themselves,
  our brothers and sisters who have given their lives
    for the sake of others . . . R

That we may hold them all in continual remembrance,
  and ever think of them as with you
in that city whose gates are not shut by day
  and where there is no night . . . R

That we may now be dedicated to working for a world
  where labor is rewarded, fear dispelled, and the nations made one,
**O Lord, save your people and bless your heritage.**
**Day by day we magnify you,**
  **and worship your name, for ever and ever. Amen.**

(JOHN HUNTER, SCOTLAND, 20TH CENT., AL

## 441                      FATHER'S DAY

*Observed the third Sunday in June, this day honors all fathers. It was first celebrate*
*in Spokane, Washington, in 1910.*

*Suggested Hymns from* UMH

*See* Festival of the Christian Home (437).

*Prayer*

*Silent prayers may follow each petition.*

For our fathers, who have given us life and love,
  that we may show them respect and love,
we pray to the Lord. . .

For fathers who have lost a child through death,
  that their faith may give them hope,
    and their family and friends support and console them,
we pray to the Lord. . .

>r men, though without children of their own,
who like fathers have nurtured and cared for us,
e pray to the Lord. . .

>r fathers, who have been unable to be a source of strength,
who have not responded to their children
    and have not sustained their families,
e pray to the Lord. . .

>d our Father, in your wisdom and love you made all things.
ess these men, that they may be strengthened as Christian fathers.
:t the example of their faith and love shine forth.
rant that we, their sons and daughters,
    may honor them always with a spirit of profound respect.
'ant this through Christ our Lord. Amen.

(BOOK OF BLESSINGS, U.S.A., 20TH CENT., ALT.)

## INDEPENDENCE DAY 442

*'y 4 celebrates the Declaration of Independence of the United States of America, but
: resources may be used for the Independence Day of any nation.*

### Suggested Scripture Readings

uteronomy 10:12-13, 17-21          What does God require of a nation?
alm 72                             A prayer for justice and righteousness
latians 5:13-26                    The proper use of freedom
n 8:31-36                          True freedom

### Suggested Hymns and Prayers from UMH

; America the Beautiful              698 God of the Ages
' America (My Country, 'Tis of Thee) 519 Lift Every Voice and Sing
) For Our Country                    437 This Is My Song

### Prayer

mighty God, you rule all the peoples of the earth.
spire the minds of all women and men to whom you have committed
the responsibility of government and leadership
in the nations of the world.
ve to them the vision of truth and justice,
that by their counsel all nations and peoples may work together.
ve to the people of our country
zeal for justice and strength of forbearance,
that we may use our liberty in accordance with your gracious will.
rgive our shortcomings as a nation;
purify our hearts to see and love the truth.
e pray all these things through Jesus Christ. Amen.

(ANDY LANGFORD, U.S.A., 20TH CENT.)

# 443                       LABOR DAY

*Observed the first Monday in September, this day of rest and relaxation honoring ⬦ who work originated in 1882 in New York City with a parade organized by machinist and a carpenter. Churches sometimes observe the previous day as Lab Day Sunday.*

### Suggested Scripture Readings

| | |
|---|---|
| Amos 5:11-15 | Establish justice. |
| Psalm 2 (*UMH* 739) | Warning to rulers of the earth |
| Psalm 71:1-12 (*UMH* 794) | Rescue me from injustice and cruelty. |
| 2 Thessalonians 3:6-13 | Exhortation to labor |
| John 6:5-14, 26-27 | Work for the food that endures. |

### Suggested Hymns from UMH

954 Hymns listed under Work        501 O Thou Who Camest from Above
411 Dear Lord, Lead Me Day by Day

### Prayer

O God, you have bound us together in this life.
Give us grace to understand how our lives depend
   on the courage, the industry, the honesty,
   and the integrity of all who labor.
May we be mindful of their needs, grateful for their faithfulness,
   and faithful in our responsibilities to them;
through Jesus Christ our Lord. Amen. (REINHOLD NIEBUHR, U.S.A., 20TH CENT., AI

# 444          REFORMATION DAY OR SUNDAY

*This day is observed on October 31 or the last Sunday in October to remind us that October 31, 1517, Martin Luther issued his Ninety-five Theses in Wittenberg a began the Protestant Reformation.*

### Prayers

*See prayers "For the Church" on 501-06.*

### Suggested Hymns from UMH

110 A Mighty Fortress Is Our God       598 O Word of God Incarnate
577 God of Grace and God of Glory      589 The Church of Christ, in Every A⬦

# V. GENERAL ACTS OF WORSHIP

## 5    WAYS OF PRAYING

rough prayer the Holy Spirit testifies with our spirit that we are God's
ldren. The Holy Spirit enables our prayers. "Likewise the Spirit helps us
th our weakness; for we do not know how to pray as we ought, but that
y Spirit intercedes with sighs too deep for words" (Romans 8:26).

yer is vital to faithful worship. Public prayer enables the community at
rship to speak and listen collectively to God. Persons may kneel, stand, or
for prayer, with their eyes either open or closed. Prayers may be led by a
person—a child, a youth, or an older adult—or a pastor. Corporate
yer, however, should avoid lengthy discourses. Silent prayers, bidding
yers, and prayers of petition are excellent alternatives to a traditional
toral prayer.

ny ways of praying are found in our United Methodist heritage. From the
e of John Wesley we have encouraged both formal, written prayers and
e, spontaneous prayers. The prayers and acts of worship in this section
ness to the great variety of effective prayer, and they are intended to
ourage worship leaders and congregations to find their own styles of
aking and listening to God. Two of these styles are described below.

## 6    TONGSUNG KIDO (PRAY ALOUD)

*orean congregations, among others, Tongsung Kido is popular and an important*
*t of prayer life. Usually the congregation is given a specific time period, with a*
*mon theme of petition or supplication. Then all pray aloud at the same time. The*
*es of others will not bother them when they concentrate on their own earnest*
*yers, longing for the empowerment of the Holy Spirit.*

# THE COLLECT

*The collect, an ancient pattern of prayer, is short and to the point, yet has a ri content. Not only are many collects included in this and other collections of prayer but persons who learn to pray in this form can quickly and easily compose appropria prayers for all kinds of occasions. These are the elements of a collect, as illustrated the traditional Collect for Purity and a contemporary version of it:*

| | | |
|---|---|---|
| 1) *Address to God* | Almighty God, | Almighty God, |
| 2) *God's attribute or acts on which this prayer is based* | unto whom all hearts are open, all desires known, and from whom no secrets are hid: | to you all hearts are open, all desires known, and from you no secrets are hidden. |
| 3) *The petition itself* | Cleanse the thoughts of our hearts by the inspiration of thy Holy Spirit, | Cleanse the thoughts of our hearts by the inspiration of your Holy Spirit, |
| 4) *Intended result of the petition* | that we may perfectly love thee, and worthily magnify thy holy name; | that we may perfectly love you, and worthily magnify your holy name, |
| 5) *Final doxology* | through Christ our Lord. Amen. | through Christ our Lor Amen. |

# GREETINGS AND OPENING PRAYERS

*or a description of Greetings and Opening Prayers, see 17-22, which includes*
*usical suggestions for these acts of worship.*

## GREETINGS 448

| | |
|---|---|
| shua 24:24 | We will serve God. |
| salm 15 (*UMH* 747) | Who shall abide in God's tent? |
| salm 24:1 | The earth is the Lord's. |
| salm 84 (*UMH* 804) | The joy of worship |
| salm 95 (*UMH* 814) | Call to worship and obedience |
| salm 96:1, 13 | Sing to the Lord. |
| salm 100 (*UMH* 821) | Make a joyful noise to the Lord. |
| salm 117 (*UMH* 838) | Call to worship |
| salm 118:24 | This is the day that the Lord has made. |
| salm 139:7-10 | Where shall I go from God? |
| salm 145 (*UMH* 857) | The Lord is gracious and merciful. |
| salm 145:10-11 | All works give thanks. |
| salm 146 (*UMH* 858) | Praise the Lord. |
| salm 147 (*UMH* 859) | Praise the Lord. |
| salm 148 (*UMH* 861) | Praise for God's universal glory |
| salm 150 (*UMH* 862) | Praise for God's greatness |
| el 2:28 | God will pour out the Spirit. |
| aniel 12:3 | The wise shall shine. |
| mos 5:24 | Let justice roll down. |
| atthew 9:37-38 | The harvest is plentiful. |
| hn 3:6-8 | What is born of the Spirit is spirit. |
| hn 4:23-24 | Worship in spirit and truth. |
| hn 14:15-17 | Love me and keep my commandments. |
| ts 1:8 | Receive power from the Holy Spirit. |
| mans 5:5b | The Holy Spirit has been given to us. |
| ohn 4:13 | He has given us his Spirit. |

449

ust in the Lord and do good.
**ay the Lord give strength to the people!**
taste and see that the Lord is good!
**od is our refuge and strength.** (THE BOOK OF WORSHIP 1965, ALT.)

450

iis is the day that the Lord has made; let us rejoice and be glad in it.
**iis is none other than the house of God, and this is the gate of heaven.**

ie hour is coming, and now is,
when true worshipers will worship the Father in spirit and truth,
for such the Father seeks to worship him.
**iter his gates with thanksgiving, and his courts with praise!**
**ive thanks to him, bless his name!** (THE BOOK OF WORSHIP 1965, ALT.)

## 451

In the midst of the congregation I will praise you.
**Rejoice in the Lord, O you righteous,**
  **and give thanks to God's holy name!**

I will extol you, my God and King,
  and bless your name for ever and ever.
**Great is the Lord, and greatly to be praised,**
  **and God's greatness is unsearchable.**  (THE BOOK OF WORSHIP 1965, AL)

## 452

May those who love your salvation say continually, "Great is the Lord!
**Yea, our heart is glad in God, because we trust in God's holy name.**

Let us make a joyful noise to God with songs of praise!
**We praise you, O God;**
**we acknowledge you to be the Lord.**  (THE BOOK OF WORSHIP 1965, AL)

## 453

Sing praises to God, O you saints,
  and give thanks to God's holy name!
**We exalt you, O God, for you have restored us to life!**

We may cry through the night, but your joy comes with the morning.
**You hear us, O God, and you are gracious in our distress.**

You turn our mourning into dancing!
**Our souls cannot be silent!**
**O God, our Savior, we give thanks to you for ever!**

(JANN C. WEAVER, U.S.A., 20TH CEN)

## 454

As a shepherd seeks a lost sheep,
**so God seeks and saves the lost.**

Like a woman who searches for a lost coin until it is found,
**so God rejoices over one soul restored to wholeness.**

As a father receives a returning wayward son,
**so God welcomes us, and lets the past be the past.**

Therefore let us praise God in thanksgiving that we are received.
**Let us receive and welcome and rejoice over one another**
  **in the name of Jesus Christ.**  (RUTH DUCK, U.S.A., 20TH CENT., AL)

## 455

You have come from afar and waited long and are wearied.
Let us sit side by side,

sharing the same bread drawn from the same source
   to quiet the same hunger that makes us weak.
hen standing together let us share the same spirit, the same thoughts
   that once again draw us together in friendship and unity and peace.

(PRIERES D'OZAWAMICK, CANADIAN INDIAN, 20TH CENT.)

**456**

ome to Christ, that living stone,
   rejected by the world, but in God's sight chosen and precious.
**Je have responded to Christ's call,**
   **and seek to be built into a spiritual house,**
   **a living reminder of God's presence on earth.**

nce we were no people, but now we are God's people,
   called out of the darkness into God's marvelous light.
herefore we sing with the Church in all ages:
**lessed be your name, O God, our Redeemer.**
**y your mercy we have been born anew to a living hope**
   **through the resurrection of Jesus Christ from the dead.**

(RUTH DUCK, U.S.A., 20TH CENT.)

**457**

ith all our heart, we take refuge in God most high,
   who created all things,
   the merciful Father, Source of all goodness.
ith all our heart, we take refuge in Christ,
   the Redeemer from sin,
   who restores our true nature,
   the perfect and mysterious Word.
ith all our heart, we take refuge in the One who embraces the universe,
   who at all times and in all places responds to our needs,
   the pure and tranquil Holy Spirit.

(KARL LUDVIG REICHELT, CHRISTIAN MISSION TO BUDDHISTS, HONG KONG, 20TH CENT., ALT.)

**458**

ay the warm winds of heaven blow softly on our house.
**ay the Great Spirit bless all who enter here.**

(TRADITIONAL CHEROKEE NATION PRAYER)

e also ♪ 198 and ♪ 200.

# OPENING PRAYERS

*pening Prayers are frequently collects. See 447.*

**459**

mighty and everlasting God,
   in whom we live and move and have our being,

you created us for yourself,
so that our hearts are restless until they find rest in you.
Grant to us such piety of heart and strength of purpose
that no selfish passion may hinder us from knowing your will,
and no weakness from doing it.
In your light may we see life clearly
and in your service find perfect freedom;
through Jesus Christ our Lord. Amen. (THE BOOK OF WORSHIP 1965, ALT)

## 460

O God, our Guide and Guardian,
you have led us apart from the busy world into the quiet of your house
Grant us grace to worship you in Spirit and in truth,
to the comfort of our souls
and the upbuilding of every good purpose and holy desire.
Enable us to do more perfectly the work to which you have called us,
that we may not fear the coming of night,
when we shall resign into your hands
the tasks which you have committed to us.
So may we worship you not with our lips at this hour,
but in word and deed all the days of our lives;
through Jesus Christ our Savior. Amen. (THE BOOK OF WORSHIP 1965, ALT)

## 461

We believe, O Lord,
that you have not abandoned us to the dim light of our own reason
to conduct us to happiness,
but that you have revealed in Holy Scriptures
whatever is necessary for us to believe and practice.
How noble and excellent are the precepts,
how sublime and enlightening the truth,
how persuasive and strong the motives,
how powerful the assistance of your holy religion.
Our delight shall be in your statutes,
and we will not forget your Word. Amen.

(RICHARD ALLEN, AFRICAN METHODIST EPISCOPAL BISHOP, U.S.A., 19TH CENT., AL

## 462

Our heavenly Father,
we your humble children invoke your blessing on us.
We adore you, whose name is love,
whose nature is compassion, whose presence is joy,
whose Word is truth, whose Spirit is goodness,
whose holiness is beauty, whose will is peace,
whose service is perfect freedom,
and in knowledge of whom stands our eternal life.

nto you be all honor and all glory;
rough Jesus Christ our Lord. Amen.　　(THE BOOK OF WORSHIP 1944, ALT.)

**463**

God, the Parent of our Lord Jesus Christ, and our Parent,
  you are to us both Father and Mother.
/e who are your children draw around your lotus feet to worship you.
our compassion is as the fragrance of the lotus.
hough you are enthroned in the heavens, we may draw nigh to you,
  for your feet stand upon the earth where we humans dwell.
/e see your compassion in Jesus.
each us that we belong to you and that you alone belong to us.
nd you are enough. Amen.
　　(D. T. NILES, METHODIST CHURCH OF SRI LANKA BISHOP, 20TH CENT., ALT.)

**464**

God, in mystery and silence you are present in our lives,
  bringing new life out of destruction,
  hope out of despair, growth out of difficulty.
'e thank you that you do not leave us alone but labor to make us whole.
elp us to perceive your unseen hand in the unfolding of our lives,
  and to attend to the gentle guidance of your Spirit,
  that we may know the joy you give your people. Amen.
　　(RUTH DUCK, U.S.A., 20TH CENT.)

**465**

ive us, Señor, a little sun, a little happiness, and some work.
ive us a heart to comfort those in pain.
ive us the ability to be good, strong, wise, and free,
  so that we may be as generous with others as we are with ourselves.
nally, Señor, let us all live as your own one family. Amen.
　　(FROM A CHURCH WALL IN MEXICO, 20TH CENT.)

**466**

od our Mother and Father, we come to you as children.
 with us as we learn to see one another with new eyes,
  hear one another with new hearts,
  and treat one another in a new way. Amen.
　　(CORRYMEELA COMMUNITY, IRELAND, 20TH CENT.)

**467**

Lord our God,
u are always more ready to bestow your good gifts on us
  than we are to seek them,
  and are willing to give more than we desire or deserve.
elp us so to seek that we may truly find,

so to ask that we may joyfully receive,
so to knock that the door of your mercy may be opened to us;
through Jesus Christ our Savior. Amen.

(THE BOOK OF COMMON PRAYER OF THE CHURCH OF ENGLAND, 20TH CENT., ALT

## 468
Grandfather, Great Spirit,
    you have always been, and before you nothing has been.
There is no one to pray to but you.
The star nations all over the heaven are yours,
    and yours are the grasses of the earth.
You are older than all need, older than all pain and prayer.
Grandfather, Great Spirit, fill us with light.
Give us strength to understand and eyes to see.
Teach us to walk the soft earth as relatives to all that live.
Help us, for without you we are nothing. Amen.

(TRADITIONAL DAKOTA TRIBE PRAYE

## 469
God, like a bakerwoman,
    you bring the leaven which causes our hopes to rise.
With your strong and gentle hands, shape our lives.
Warm us with your love.
Take our common lives and touch them with your grace,
    that we may nourish hope among humanity.
We pray trusting in your name, through Jesus our Christ. Amen.

(RUTH DUCK, U.S.A., 20TH CENT., AL

# ACTS OF CONGREGATIONAL CENTERING

## 470
*Also see The Circle of Love Is Broken (488) for a related Prayer of Confession. Befo
the prayer, determine the four points of the compass: North, East, South, and Wes
Then all persons present form a circle, facing the center. After a period of silence, t
prayer begins:*

Paul reminds us that Christ is the center of creation,
    of our lives, and of the world.
We seek the wisdom of directions.
From each direction we return to the center
    reminded that Christ brings healing and salvation
        and by God's Spirit renews the face of the earth.
Let us be silent as we face our center point.

Let us face East. *All persons face East.*
From the East, the direction of the rising sun,
    we glean wisdom and knowledge

through desert silences and humble service.
**nable us, O God, to be wise in our actions**
**and in our use of the resources of the earth,**
**sharing them in justice, partaking of them in gratitude.**

*ll persons return facing center.*

et us face South. *All persons face South.*
rom the South come guidance and the beginning and end of life.
**ay we walk good paths, O God,**
**living on the earth as sisters and brothers should,**
**rejoicing in one another's blessing,**
**sympathizing in one another's sorrows,**
**and together look to you, seeking the new heaven and earth.**

*ll persons return facing center.*

et us face West. *All persons face West.*
om the West come purifying waters.
**'e pray that water might be pure and available to all,**
**and that we, too, may be purified**
**that life may be sustained and nurtured**
**over the entire face of the earth.**

*l persons return facing center.*

et us face North. *All persons face North.*
om the North come strong winds and gentle breezes.
**ay the air we breathe be purified**
**d may our lives feel that breath of the Spirit,**
**strengthening and encouraging us.**

*l persons return facing center.*

we walked a path in each direction, the sacred paths would form a cross.
**turning to the center, we discover Christ,**
**who calls us and challenges us.**         (TRADITIONAL LAKOTA TRIBE PRAYER, ALT.)

**471**

hold: the ripples of fire buried deep in the dark, rich ground.
**e are here; we bring our memories and legacy.**
**e bring our bamboo and rice, our taro and palm.**
**e bring our earth and ocean.**

hold: the rice shoots
**that burst out from the ground and reach toward the sun.**
**e are here; we bring our struggles and hopes.**
**e bring our shovels, picks, and irons.**
**e bring our broken hands and weeping hearts.**

Behold: the golden flower that blooms
   with all the beauty and power and fragrance of almighty God.
**We are not yet here; but we are coming.**
**Help us, O God,**
   **to open our minds; to open our hearts; to open our spirits**
      **to the bright potential you have given us in each moment of life.**
(NATIONAL CONVOCATION OF ASIAN AMERICAN CHURCHES, U.S.A., 20TH CENT., AL

## 472

*Silent prayer may follow each petition.*

As we come together, let us settle into stillness. . .
Slowly, ever so slowly, we center our minds and our hearts. . .
Let your cares and your weariness fall away. . .
Enter deeply into silence. . .
We are one with the universe. . .
We are one with the sun and the stars. . .
We are one with the One who is Mystery,
   who created the heavens and the earth. . .
O marvelous Mystery!
I am one with the One who is Mystery,
   the One who created me, and loves me,
   and whose Spirit lives in me. Amen.      (MIRIAM THERESE WINTER, U.S.A., 20TH CEN

## 473

Like the sun that is far away and yet close at hand to warm us,
   so God's Spirit is ever present and around us.
Come Creator into our lives.
We live and move and have our very being in you.
Open now the windows of our souls. Amen.
(UNITED METHODIST CLERGYWOMEN'S CONSULTATION, U.S.A., 20TH CENT., AL

# CONFESSION, ASSURANCE, AND PARDON

or a description of Prayers of Confession and Acts of Pardon, see 20-21, which
ncludes musical suggestions for these acts of worship.

ee Prayers of Confession, Assurance, and Pardon in UMH 890-893.

## PSALMS OF CONFESSION                474

| | |
|---|---|
| salm 25 (*UMH* 756) | Prayer for guidance |
| salm 51:1-17 (*UMH* 785) | Have mercy on me, O God. |
| salm 90 (*UMH* 809) | God's eternity and human frailty |
| salm 130 (*UMH* 848) | If you mark our iniquities |
| salm 139 (*UMH* 854) | The inescapable God |

## CONFESSION AND PARDON

475

lave mercy upon us, O God, according to your lovingkindness.
.ccording to the multitude of your tender mercies,
  blot out our transgressions.
Jash us thoroughly from our iniquities, and cleanse us from our sins.
or we acknowledge our transgressions, and our sin is ever before us.
reate in us clean hearts, O God, and renew a right spirit within us;
irough Jesus Christ our Lord.          (W. E. ORCHARD, ENGLAND, 20TH CENT., ALT.)

*ll offer prayers of confession in silence.*

he Lord is gracious and merciful,
  slow to anger and abounding in steadfast love.          (PSALM 145:8)

lay the almighty and merciful Lord grant us remission of all our sins,
  true repentance, amendment of life,
  and the grace and consolation of the Holy Spirit. Amen.
                                        (THE BOOK OF COMMON PRAYER, U.S.A.)

476

holy and merciful God,
  we confess that we have not always taken upon ourselves
    the yoke of obedience,
  nor been willing to seek and to do your perfect will.
'e have not loved you
  with all our heart and mind and soul and strength,
either have we loved our neighbors as ourselves.
ou have called to us in the need of our sisters and brothers,
  and we have passed unheeding on our way.

In the pride of our hearts, and our unwillingness to repent,
  we have turned away from the cross of Christ,
  and have grieved your Holy Spirit.

(WESLEYAN METHODIST CONFERENCE, ENGLAND, 20TH CENT., ALT.

*All offer prayers of confession in silence.*

This is the message we have heard from God and proclaim to you,
  that God is light and in God there is no darkness at all.
If we walk in the light, as God is in the light,
  we have fellowship with one another,
  and the blood of Jesus the Son cleanses us from all sin.

(1 JOHN 1:5, 7, ALT

May almighty God, who caused light to shine out of darkness,
  shine in our hearts, cleansing us from all our sins,
  and restoring us to the light of the knowledge of God's glory,
  in the face of Jesus Christ, our Savior. Amen.

(THE BOOK OF WORSHIP 1944, ALT)

## 477

Almighty and most merciful God, you know the thoughts of our hearts
We confess that we have sinned against you and done evil in your sight
We have transgressed your holy laws.
We have disregarded your Word and Sacraments.
Forgive us, O Lord.
Give us grace and power to put away all hurtful things,
  that, being delivered from the bondage of sin,
  we may bring forth fruit worthy of repentance,
  and from henceforth may ever walk in your holy ways;
through Jesus Christ our Lord.

(WESLEYAN METHODIST CONFERENCE, ENGLAND, 20TH CENT., ALT)

*All offer prayers of confession in silence.*

If we confess our sins,
God who is faithful and just will forgive us our sins
  and cleanse us from all unrighteousness.          (1 JOHN 1:9, ALT)

May the almighty and merciful Lord grant us remission of all our sins,
  true repentance, amendment of life,
and the grace and consolation of the Holy Spirit. Amen.

(THE BOOK OF COMMON PRAYER U.S.A., 20TH CENT., ALT)

## 478

Holy and awesome God, we stand in your presence
  filled with regret for our many sins and failings.
Though there is greatness in us, and a deep longing for goodness,
  we have often denied our better selves
  and refused to hear your voice

calling us to rise to the full height of our humanity.
or there is weakness in us, as well as strength.
t times we choose to walk in darkness, our vision obscured.
Je do not care to look within,
  and we are unwilling to look beyond at those who need our help.
• God, we are too weak to walk unaided.
e with us as a strong and wise friend,
  and teach us to walk by the light of your truth.
*ll offer prayers of confession in silence.*

he Lord God is merciful and gracious,
  endlessly patient, loving, and true,
  showing mercy to thousands,
  forgiving iniquity, transgression, and sin, and granting pardon. Amen.

(JEWISH PRAYER FOR FORGIVENESS, U.S.A., 20TH CENT.)

# PRAYERS OF CONFESSION

479

lmighty God,
  we confess that we are often swept up in the tide of our generation.
'e have failed in our calling to be your holy people,
  a people set apart for your divine purpose.
Je live more in apathy born of fatalism than in passion born of hope.
Je are moved more by private ambition than by social justice.
Je dream more of privilege and benefits than of service and sacrifice.
'e try to speak in your name without relinquishing our glories,
  without nourishing our souls, without relying wholly on your grace.
elp us to make room in our hearts and lives for you.
orgive us, revive us, and reshape us in your image. Amen.

(LYDIA S. MARTINEZ, HISPANIC, U.S.A., 20TH CENT., ALT.)

480

'e confess to you, all-knowing God, what we are.
'e are not the people we like others to think we are.
'e are afraid to admit, even to ourselves,
  what lies in the depths of our souls.
ıt we cannot hide our true selves from you.
ou know us as we are, and yet you love us.
elp us not to shrink from self-knowledge.
ach us to respect ourselves for your sake.
ive us the courage to put our trust in your guiding power.
ise us out of the paralysis of guilt
  into the freedom and energy of forgiven people.

And for those who through long habit find forgiveness hard to accept,
  we ask you to break their bondage and set them free;
through Jesus Christ our Redeemer. Amen.          (ENGLAND, 20TH CENT., ALT

## 481

Almighty and merciful God,
  we know that when we offend another, we offend you.
We are aware that we have often allowed the shadow of hate
  to cloud our souls, hiding the light from our unseeking eyes.
We have said unpleasant and hurtful things to our brothers and sisters
  when they failed to live up to our expectations.
Grant that we might find that spark of love that ever burns within us,
  the love that you have shown to us even when we failed you.
Fan the embers of that love until it roars again
  in flames of love, peace, and reconciliation.
Forgive us our sins
  and help us to forgive those who have sinned against us.
Lead us into new life through your Son Jesus Christ,
  who died for the sins of all. Amen.  (MICHAEL J. O'DONNELL, U.S.A., 20TH CEN

## 482

Lord Jesus Christ, you are the way of peace.
Come into the brokenness of our lives and our land
  with your healing love.
Help us to be willing to bow before you in true repentance,
  and to bow to one another in real forgiveness.
By the fire of your Holy Spirit, melt our hard hearts
  and consume the pride and prejudice which separate us.
Fill us, O Lord, with your perfect love, which casts out our fear,
  and bind us together in that unity
  which you share with the Father and the Holy Spirit. Amen.

                            (CECIL KERR, NORTHERN IRELAND, 20TH CEN

## 483

God of grace and glory,
  we thank you that you judge us not by the perfection of our actions,
  but by our readiness to live boldly by faith.
Help us, as individuals and as a congregation,
  to trust you and follow where you lead,
that in Christ your name may be glorified in all the earth. Amen.

                                      (RUTH DUCK, U.S.A., 20TH CEN

## 484

All-merciful, tender God, you have given birth to our world,
  conceiving and bearing all that lives and breathes.

We come to you as your daughters and sons,
  aware of our aggression and anger,
  our drive to dominate and manipulate others.
We ask you to forgive us,
  and by the gentle touch of your Spirit
  help us to find a renewed sense of compassion,
  that we may truly live as your people in service to all. Amen.

(JANET WELLER, ENGLAND, 20TH CENT., ALT.)

**485**

O God, source of all that makes life possible,
  giver of all that makes life good:
We gather to give you our thanks,
  yet we confess that we have often failed to live our thankfulness.
What we have we take for granted,
  and we grumble about what we lack.
We have squandered your bounty,
  with little thought of those who will come after us.
We are more troubled by the few who have more
  than by the many who have less.
Forgive us, O God.
In this hour of worship, accept our thanksgiving;
  and teach us to make gratitude and sharing our way of life;
through the grace of Jesus Christ. Amen. (PAUL J. FLUCKE, U.S.A., 20TH CENT., ALT.)

**486**

O Lord God,
  the watchers of Zion have called peace, peace,
  when there was no peace.
Therefore have you so long withheld from us
  the influence of your Holy Spirit?
Why have you hardened our hearts?
  is because we have honored you with our lips,
  when our hearts were far from you.
Return again to us, O Lord God,
  and pardon this iniquity of your servants.
Cause your face to shine upon us, and we shall be saved.
  visit us with your salvation.
Raise up sons and daughters from Abraham and Sarah,
  and grant that there might come
    a mighty shaking of dry bones among us,
  and a great ingathering of souls.
Be pleased to grant
  that the kingdom of our Lord Jesus Christ may be built up;
that all nations and kindreds and tongues and peoples

might be brought to the knowledge of the truth,
and we at last meet around your throne,
and join in celebrating your praises. Amen.

(MARIA STEWARD, AFRICAN AMERICAN, U.S.A., 19TH CENT., ALT

## 487

O Great Spirit *(Gitchi Manitou, Most Awesome of the Awesome)*,
  whose voice we hear in the winds,
  and whose breath gives life to all the world, hear us.
We come before you as your children.
We are small and weak; we need your strength and wisdom.
Let us walk in beauty
  and make our eyes ever behold the red and purple sunset.
May our hands respect the things you have made,
  our ears be sharp to hear your voice.
Make us wise,
  so that we may know the things you have taught your people,
  the lessons you have hidden in every leaf and rock.
We seek strength not to be superior to our brothers and sisters,
  but to live in harmony with ourselves and all of your creation.
Help us to be ever ready to come to you,
  so when life fades as a fading sunset,
  our spirits may come to you without shame. Amen.

(TRADITIONAL NATIVE AMERICAN PRAYER

## 488

We confess that the circle of love is repeatedly broken
  because of our sin of exclusion.
We create separate circles: the inner circle and the outer circle,
  the circle of power and the circle of despair,
  the circle of privilege and the circle of deprivation.
**Forgive us our sins, as we forgive all who have sinned against us.**

We confess that the circle of love is broken
  whenever there is alienation, whenever there is misunderstanding,
  whenever there is insensitivity or a hardening of the heart. **R**

We confess that the circle of love is broken
  whenever we cannot see eye to eye,
  whenever we cannot link hand to hand,
  whenever we cannot live heart to heart and affirm our differences. **R**

Through God's grace we are forgiven,
  by the mercy of our Creator,
  through the love of the Christ,
  and in the power of the Spirit.
Let us rejoice and be glad!
**Glory to God! Amen.**
(MIRIAM THERESE WINTER, U.S.A., 20TH CENT., ALT

*See 470 for a related Act of Congregational Centering.*

**489**

lmighty and all-loving God,
  through your Son Jesus Christ
    you have reconciled the world to yourself.
.elp us now to be reconciled with one another,
  that again we might dwell in the warmth of your love.
ispire us with your Holy Spirit
  to put aside the cloak of pride and put on Christ,
  that we might forgive and be forgiven;
irough Jesus Christ our Lord. Amen.      (MICHAEL J. O'DONNELL, U.S.A., 20TH CENT.)

**490**

' merciful God,
  we confess that we have not acknowledged you
    as the source of our successes, our substance, our selves.
'e have been far more ready to complain when things go wrong
  than to praise when all is well.
'e have fed our bodies a rich diet while neglecting to feed our souls.
)wer and wealth have assumed greater importance to us
  than sensitivity and service.
'e have allowed religious words and forms to substitute
  for living encounters with the persons you have called us to love.
)rgive us, compassionate Redeemer,
  and grant us the opportunity to start over again.
eep us from repeating the mistakes of the past
  or from new evils that could mislead or destroy.
i the name of Christ,
  we offer our earnest prayers for pardon and deliverance. Amen.
                              (LAVON BAYLER, U.S.A., 20TH CENT., ALT.)

**491**

'e are reluctant, O Author of Love,
  to set aside our hurt, our anger, our disappointment.
eal us with your tender touch,
  that we might be cleansed of all unclean thoughts,
  all schemes of revenge, all hope of vindictive retribution.
pen our eyes to the power of love,
  shown to us in the unselfish sacrifice
    of your Son, our Savior, Jesus Christ. Amen.
                              (MICHAEL J. O'DONNELL, U.S.A., 20TH CENT.)

**492**

od of all nations, we praise you that in Christ
  the barriers that have separated humanity are torn down.
it we confess our slowness to open our hearts and minds
  to those of other lands, tongues, and races.

Deliver us from the sins of fear and prejudice,
that we may move toward the day
when all are truly one in Jesus Christ. Amen.

(Ruth Duck, U.S.A., 20th cent

## 493

O God of Shalom,
we have built up walls to protect ourselves from our enemies,
but these walls also shut us off from receiving your love.
Break down those walls.
Help us to see that the way to your heart
is through the reconciliation of our own hearts with our enemies.
Bless them and us,
that we may come to grow in love for each other and for you;
through Jesus Christ. Amen.  (Michael J. O'Donnell, U.S.A., 20th cent

## 494

Creator God, breathing your own life into our being,
you gave us the gift of life.
You placed us on this earth with its minerals and waters,
flowers and fruits, living creatures of grace and beauty.
You gave us the care of the earth.
Today you call us: "Where are you; what have you done?"

*Silent prayer for creation.*

We hide in utter shame, for we are naked.
We violate the earth and plunder it.
We refuse to share the earth's resources.
We seek to own what is not ours, but yours.
**Forgive us, Creator God, and reconcile us to your creation.**

O God of Love, you gave us the gift of peoples—
of cultures, races, and colors—
to love, to care for, to share our lives with.
Today you ask us: "Where is your brother, your sister?"

*Silent prayer for others.*

We hide ourselves in shame and fear.
Poverty, hunger, hatred, and war rule the earth.
The refugees, the oppressed, and the voiceless cry out to you.
Forgive us, O God of Love,
and reconcile us to yourself and to one another.
**Teach us, O Creator God of Love,**
**that the earth and all its fullness is yours,**
**the world and those who dwell in it.**
**Call us yet again to safeguard the gift of life. Amen.**

(Sixth Assembly of the World Council of Churches, 20th cent., al

# A LITANY FOR THE CHURCH AND FOR THE WORLD

*r musical and other suggestions regarding litanies, see 21.*

ɔt us pray for the Church and for the world.

rant, almighty God,
that all who confess your name may be united in your truth,
live together in your love, and reveal your glory in the world.
ɔrd, in your mercy, **hear our prayer.** *Silent prayer.*

ɹuide the people of this land, and of all the nations,
in the ways of justice and peace;
ɑat we may honor one another and serve the common good.
ɔrd, in your mercy, **hear our prayer.** *Silent prayer.*

ɨve us all a reverence for the earth as your own creation,
that we may use its resources rightly
in the service of others and to your honor and glory.
ɔrd, in your mercy, **hear our prayer.** *Silent prayer.*

ɹess all whose lives are closely linked with ours,
and grant that we may serve Christ in them,
and love one another as Christ loves us.
ɔrd, in your mercy, **hear our prayer.** *Silent prayer.*

ɔmfort and heal all those who suffer in body, mind, or spirit;
ve them courage and hope in their troubles,
and bring them the joy of your salvation.
ɔrd, in your mercy, **hear our prayer.** *Silent prayer.*

ʾe commend to your mercy all who have died,
that your will for them may be fulfilled;
ɪd we pray that we may share with all your saints
in your eternal kingdom.
ɔrd, in your mercy, **hear our prayer.** *Silent prayer.*

ʾe offer these prayers through Jesus Christ our Lord. **Amen.**

(THE BOOK OF COMMON PRAYER, U.S.A., 20TH CENT., ALT.)

# THE TEN COMMANDMENTS

God spoke from the mountain and said:
"I am the Lord your God,
  who brought you out of the land of Egypt, out of the house of slavery
you shall have no other gods before me."
**Almighty God, write your law upon our hearts.**

"You shall not make for yourself an idol.
You shall not make wrongful use of the name of the Lord your God.
Remember the sabbath day, and keep it holy." **R**

"Honor your father and your mother.
You shall not murder.
You shall not commit adultery.
You shall not steal.
You shall not bear false witness.
You shall not covet . . . anything that belongs to your neighbor." **R**

(EXODUS 20:1-17, ABRIDGED; RESPONSE FROM THE BOOK OF COMMON PRAYER, U.S.A., 20TH CEN

# PRAYERS
# FOR VARIOUS OCCASIONS

## PRAYERS IN *UMH*

*e 25 for musical Invitations to Prayer in* UMH, *which may precede any of the
llowing prayers.*

*e 24-25 for musical Prayer Responses in* UMH, *which may follow any of these
·ayers.*

1 Adversity, For Overcoming
0 Alves, Prayer of Rubem
3 Augustine of Hippo, Prayer of
9 Bonhoeffer, Prayer of Dietrich
3 Chichester, Prayer of Richard of
6 Christ, An Invitation to
2 Chrysostom, Prayer of John
4 Church, For Renewal of the
6 Come, my Light
9 Country, For Our
6 Courage to Do Justice, For
7 Covenant Prayer in the Wesleyan
    Tradition, A
9 Day, At the Close of
1 Day, For Help for the Forthcoming
6 Dimitri of Rostov, Prayer of
5 Direction, For
5 Distraction, A Refuge Amid
3 Finding Rest in God
1 Francis of Assisi, The Prayer of
0 Freedom in Christ
9 Gealy, Prayer of Fred D.
9 Gifts, For God's
6 God Is Able (litany)
4 God of Many Names, Praising
6 Guidance, For
2 Hammerskjöld, Prayer of Dag
0 Harkness, Prayer of Georgia
1 Heart, For Holiness of
2 Heart, Prayer for a New
5 Holy Spirit, An Invitation to the
9 Holy Spirit, Prayer to the
0 Ignatius of Loyola, Prayer of
0 Illness, In Time of
7 Illumination, For
6 Invitation to Christ, An

677 Johnson, Prayer of James Weldon
456 Justice, For Courage to Do
429 Kagawa, Prayer of Toyohiko
106 King, Martin Luther, Jr., Litany of
403 Life, For True
535 Like an ant on a stick
677 Listen, Lord
481 Lord, make me an instrument
270-71, 894-96 Lord's Prayer, The
104 Mechthild of Magdeburg, Prayer of
335 Milner-White, Prayer of Eric
677 Morning, We come this
446 Mother Teresa of Calcutta, Prayer of
392 New Heart, Prayer for a
693 Night, For a Peaceful
691 Night, For Protection at
456 Paton, Prayer of Alan
446 Poor, Serving the
556 Pope John Paul II, Prayer of
104 Praising God of Many Names
477 Rossetti, Prayer of Christina G.
481 Saint Francis, The Prayer of
531 Savonarola, Prayer of Girolamo
602 Scriptures, Concerning the
459 Serenity Prayer, The
423 Singh, Prayer of Sundar
69 Singing, For True
412 Supplication, Common
570 Teach us, good Lord
403 Teresa of Avila, Prayer of
493 Three Things We Pray
489, 401 Thurman, Howard, Prayers of
403 True Life, For
597 Truth, For the Spirit of
556 Unity, Litany for Christian
564 Unity of Christ's Body, For the

# 498 PSALMS OF PETITION

| | |
|---|---|
| Psalm 4 (*UMH* 741) | Plea for deliverance from enemies |
| Psalm 10 (*UMH* 745) | Plea for deliverance from enemies |
| Psalm 13 (*UMH* 746) | Plea for deliverance from enemies |
| Psalm 17 (*UMH* 749) | Plea for deliverance from enemies |
| Psalm 22 (*UMH* 752) | Plea for deliverance from suffering |
| Psalm 25 (*UMH* 756) | Prayer for guidance and deliverance |
| Psalm 28 (*UMH* 760) | Prayer for help |
| Psalm 39 (*UMH* 773) | Prayer for wisdom and forgiveness |
| Psalm 42 (*UMH* 777) | Longing for God and God's assistance |
| Psalm 43 (*UMH* 778) | Prayer in time of trouble |
| Psalm 44 (*UMH* 779) | National lament and prayer for help |
| Psalm 51 (*UMH* 785) | Prayer for cleansing and pardon |
| Psalm 70 (*UMH* 793) | Prayer for deliverance from enemies |
| Psalm 71 (*UMH* 794) | Prayer for protection and help |
| Psalm 82 (*UMH* 804) | Plea for justice |
| Psalm 85 (*UMH* 806) | Prayer for restoration of God's favor |
| Psalm 130 (*UMH* 848) | Waiting for redemption |
| Psalm 143 (*UMH* 856) | Prayer for deliverance from enemies |

# 499 MUSICAL PETITIONS

596 Blessed Jesus, At Thy Word
560 Help Us Accept Each Other
521 I Want Jesus to Walk with Me
483 Kyrie Eleison

484 Kyrie Eleison
485 Let Us Pray to the Lord
482 Lord, Have Mercy
393 Spirit of the Living God

*See also*
Call to Prayer ( ♪ 196)
God Hears Our Every Need ( ♪ 183)
Jesus, We Are Here ( ♪ 187)
Jesus, We Are Praying ( ♪ 192)
O Lamb of God ( ♪ 201)
Prayer for Wisdom ( ♪ 193)
Señor, Apiadate de Nosotros ( ♪ 188)
Shine on Me ( ♪ 205)
Teach Me to Hear in Silence ( ♪ 194)

# 500 FOR BLESSING, MERCY, AND COURAGE

O God, that we may receive your blessing,
   touch our brows, touch our heads, and do not look upon us in anger
In a hard year, offer us mercy; in a year of affliction, offer us kindness
dark spirits banish from us, bright spirits bring close to us;
gray spirits put away from us, good spirits draw near to us.
When we are afraid, offer us courage;
when we are ashamed, be our true face;
be over us like a blanket, be under us like a bed of furs. Amen.

(TRADITIONAL PRAYER, MONGOLIA, AL

# FOR THE CHURCH

501

gracious God, we pray for your holy Church universal,
that you would be pleased to fill it with all truth, in all peace.
here it is corrupt, purify it;
here it is in error, direct it;
here in any thing it is amiss, reform it;
here it is right, establish it;
here it is in want, provide for it;
here it is divided, reunite it;
r the sake of him who died and rose again,
and ever lives to make intercession for us,
Jesus Christ, your Son, our Lord. Amen.

(THE BOOK OF COMMON PRAYER, U.S.A., 20TH CENT., ALT.)

502

ost merciful Father,
send your heavenly blessings upon this your Church,
that all its members may dwell together in unity and love.
:ep far from us all self-will and discord.
ndue your pastors with righteousness,
and enable them faithfully to fulfill their ministry,
to bring again the outcasts, and to seek the lost.
nd grant to us so to receive their ministrations,
and to use your means of grace,
that in all our words and deeds
    we may seek your glory and the advancement of your kingdom;
rough Jesus Christ our Lord. Amen.

(THE BOOK OF COMMON PRAYER, U.S.A., 20TH CENT., ALT.)

503

)irit of promise, Spirit of unity,
we thank you that you are also the Spirit of renewal.
:new in the whole Church
that passionate desire for the coming of your kingdom
which will unite all Christians in one mission to the world.
ay we all grow up together into him who is our head,
the Savior of the world. Amen.

(OLIVE WYON, ENGLAND, 20TH CENT., ALT.)

504

God of all times and places,
we pray for your Church,
which is set today amid the perplexities of a changing order,
and face to face with new tasks.
iptize her afresh in the life-giving spirit of Jesus.

Bestow upon her a great responsiveness to duty,
  a swifter compassion with suffering,
  and an utter loyalty to your will.
Help her to proclaim boldly the coming of your kingdom.
Put upon her lips the ancient gospel of her Lord.
Fill her with the prophets' scorn of tyranny,
  and with a Christlike tenderness for the heavyladen and downtrodde:
Bid her cease from seeking her own life, lest she lose it.
Make her valiant to give up her life to humanity,
  that, like her crucified Lord,
  she may mount by the path of the cross to a higher glory;
through the same Jesus Christ our Lord. Amen.

(WALTER RAUSCHENBUSCH, U.S.A., 20TH CENT., AL

## 505

O God, the Giver of life, we pray for the Church throughout the worl
Sanctify its life, renew its worship, empower its witness, restore its unit
Remove from your people all pride
  and every prejudice that dulls their will for unity.
Strengthen the work of all those who strive to seek
  that common obedience that will bind us together.
Heal the divisions which separate your children from one another,
  that they may keep the unity of the spirit in the bond of peace. Ame

(PRAYER USED IN THE ECUMENICAL CENTRE, GENEVA, ON THE OCCASION
THE VISIT OF POPE JOHN PAUL II, 20TH CEN

## 506

O God, you have built your Church
  upon the foundation of the apostles and prophets,
  Jesus Christ himself being the chief cornerstone.
Save the community of your people
  from cowardly surrender to the world,
  from rendering unto Caesar what belongs to you,
  and from forgetting the eternal gospel
    amid the temporal pressures of our troubled days.
For the unity of the Church we pray,
  and for fellowship across the embittered lines of race and nation;
to growth in grace, building in love, enlargement in service,
  increase in wisdom, faith, charity, and power,
  we dedicate our lives;
through Jesus Christ our Savior. Amen.

(HARRY EMERSON FOSDICK, U.S.A., 20TH CENT., AL

# FOR CREATION

### *Prayer of Saint Francis of Assisi for All Created Things*    **507**

most high, omnipotent, good Lord God,
to you belong praise, glory, honor, and all blessing.

ѵr our brother the sun, who is our day and who brings us the light,
who is fair, and radiant with a very great splendor;
**ѵaised be our Lord.** *See also* ♪ *204.*

ѵr our sister the moon, and for the stars,
which you have set clear and lovely in heaven;

ѵr our brother the wind,
and for air and clouds, calms and all weather;

ѵr our sister water,
who serves us and is humble and precious and chaste;

ѵr our brother fire, by whom you light up the night,
and who is fair and merry, and very mighty and strong;

ѵr our mother the earth, who sustains us and keeps us,
and brings forth various fruits,
and flowers of many colors, and grass;

ѵr all those who pardon one another for your love's sake,
and who bear weakness and tribulation;

essed are they who peaceably shall endure,
walking by your most holy will;
for you, O Most High, shall give them a crown.
ѵaise and bless the Lord,
**and give thanks unto God,**
**ѵd serve God with great humility. Amen.**

(SAINT FRANCIS OF ASSISI, ITALY, 12TH CENTURY, ALT.)

ѵe *also* All Creatures of Our God and King *(UMH 62).*

### *Psalm of the Woodlands*    **508**

ѵs a tree in the forest becomes tall reaching for the light
may we grow above the shadows of sin, fear, and doubt.
**ѵs it gives shelter and shade to its friends of fur and feather,**
**so may we help those brothers and sisters**
**who are smaller and weaker than ourselves.**

ѵhe tree sends down roots deep into the soil
that it may be nourished by mother earth.
**ѵay we be as firmly grounded by the love of Christ**
**and sustained by his grace.**

If a tree falls and decays, it provides nourishment for new plants
   and gives its place in the sun for others.
**Our Lord and Savior died to make a new life and a new place for us**

When a tree in the forest is cut down,
   its wood is used for shelter and fuel.
**Jesus taught that only when life is surrendered,**
   **when love is poured out,**
**can we build his kingdom and reflect the warmth of his Spirit. Amen**

(MILTON VAHEY, U.S.A., 20TH CEN

*See also Prayer of Confession on 494.*

*Following the prayer, all may sing one of these hymns from UMH:*

147 All Things Bright and Beautiful    151 God Created Heaven and Earth
150 God, Who Stretched the
     Spangled Heavens


# 509          IN TIME OF NATURAL DISASTER

O God, you divided the waters of chaos at creation.
In Christ you stilled storms, raised the dead,
   and vanquished demonic powers.
Tame the earthquake, wind, and fire,
   and all the forces that defy control or shock us by their fury.
Keep us from calling disaster your justice.
Help us, in good times and in distress,
   to trust your mercy and yield to your power, this day and for eve
Amen.                                    (ANDY LANGFORD, U.S.A., 20TH CEN


# 510          FOR DISCERNMENT

Almighty God, in a world of change you placed eternity in our hearts
   and gave us power to discern good from evil.
Grant us sincerity,
   that we may persistently seek the things that endure,
   refusing those which perish,
and that, amid things vanishing and deceptive,
   we may see the truth steadily, follow the light faithfully,
   and grow ever richer in that love which is the life of all people;
through Jesus Christ our Savior. Amen.    (HUGH CAMERON, SCOTLAND, 20TH CEN

# FOR GOD'S REIGN 511

 believe in you, O God,
or you have made the suffering of humanity your suffering.
u have come to establish a kingdom of the poor and humble.
day we sing to you,
 ecause you are alive, you have saved us, you have made us free.
 nen. (CUBA, 20TH CENT.)

# FOR GUIDANCE 512

eternal God,
 n whose appointment our life stands,
 and who committed our work to us,
 we commit our cares to you.
 thank you that we are your children, and that you have assured us
 that, while we are intent upon your will, you will heed our wants.
 us with that compassion for others' troubles
 which comes from forgetfulness of our own;
 th the charity of those who know their own unworthiness;
 d with the glad hope of the children of eternity.
 d to you,
 the Beginning and the End, Lord of the living, Refuge of the dying,
 be thanks and praise for ever. Amen.
(JAMES MARTINEAU, ENGLAND, 19TH CENT., ALT.)

# FOR JUSTICE 513

 mighty God, you created us in your own image.
 ant us grace fearlessly to contend against evil,
 and to make no peace with oppression.
 d, that we may reverently use our freedom,
 help us to employ it in the maintenance of justice
 to the glory of your holy name;
 rough Jesus Christ our Savior. Amen.
(THE BOOK OF COMMON PRAYER, U.S.A., 20TH CENT., ALT.)

## 514  FOR THE MIND OF CHRIST

Let us remember Jesus:
Who, though he was rich,
    yet for our sakes became poor and dwelt among us.
Who was content to be subject to his parents,
    the child of a poor couple's home.
Who lived for thirty years the common life,
    earning his living with his own hands and declining no humble task
Whom the people heard gladly, for he understood their ways.
**May this mind be in us which was in Christ Jesus.**
*See also* ♪ *189 and* ♪ *191.*

Let us remember Jesus:
Who was mighty in deed, healing the sick and the disordered,
    using for others the powers he would not invoke for himself.
Who refused to force people's allegiance.
Who was Master and Lord to his disciples,
    yet was among them as their companion and as one who served.
Whose desire was to do the will of God who sent him. **R**

Let us remember Jesus:
Who loved people, yet retired from them to pray,
    rose a great while before day, watched through the night,
    stayed in the wilderness, went up into a mountain, sought a garden
Who, when he would help a tempted disciple, prayed for him.
Who prayed for the forgiveness of those who rejected him,
    and for the perfecting of those who received him.
Who observed the traditions,
    but defied convention that did not serve the purposes of God.
Who hated the sins of pride and selfishness, of cruelty and impurity.

Let us remember Jesus:
Who believed in people and never despaired of them.
Who through all disappointment never lost heart.
Who disregarded his own comfort and convenience,
    and thought first of others' needs,
    and, though he suffered long, was always kind.
Who, when he was reviled, uttered no harsh word in return,

and when he suffered, did not threaten retaliation.
ho humbled himself and carried obedience to the point of death,
even death on the cross,
herefore God has highly exalted him. **R**

et us unite in prayer that Christ may dwell in our hearts.
**Christ, our only Savior,**
**so come to dwell in us that we may go forth**
**with the light of your hope in our eyes,**
**and with your faith and love in our hearts. Amen.**

(ENGLAND, 20TH CENT., ALT.)

# FOR THE NATION

**515**

each us, God of every nation,
to see every question of national policy in the light of our faith,
that we may check in ourselves and in others
every passion that makes for war, all ungenerous judgment,
all promptings of self-assurance, all presumptuous claims.
rant us insight to recognize the needs and aspirations of other nations,
and remove our suspicions and misunderstandings,
that we may honor all people in Jesus Christ our Lord. Amen.

(ENGLAND, 20TH CENT., ALT.)

**516**

ook graciously, O Lord, upon this land.
here it is in pride, subdue it.
here it is in need, supply it.
here it is in error, rectify it.
here it is in default, restore it.
nd where it holds to that which is just and compassionate, support it.
men.                    (CHURCH OF PAKISTAN, 20TH CENT.)

*A Prayer in a Time of National Crisis*          **517**

od of all the ages,
in your sight nations rise and fall, and pass through times of peril.
ow when our land is troubled, be near to judge and save.
ay leaders be led by your wisdom;
may they search your will and see it clearly.
we have turned from your way,
reverse our ways and help us to repent.
ive us your light and your truth, let them guide us;
rough Jesus Christ, who is Lord of this world, and our Savior. Amen.

(PRESBYTERIAN WORSHIPBOOK, U.S.A., 20TH CENT., ALT.)

or a related *Prayer of Confession see 482.*

# FOR OTHERS

## 518

Strong covenant God, save us from being self-centered in our prayers,
and teach us to remember to pray for others.
May we be so bound up in love with those for whom we pray
that we may feel their needs as acutely as our own,
and intercede for them with sensitiveness,
with understanding and with imagination.
This we ask in Christ's name. Amen.

(BASED ON WORDS FROM JOHN CALVIN, SWITZERLAND, 16TH CEN'

## 519

Teach us, Ruler of the universe,
to see people by the light of the faith we profess,
that we may check in ourselves
all ungenerous judgments, all presumptuous claims,
that, recognizing the needs and rightful claims of others,
we may remove old hatreds and rivalries
and hasten new understandings,
that we may bring our tributes of excellence
to the treasury of our common humanity;
through Jesus Christ our Lord. Amen.

(ENGLAND, 20TH CENT., AL

## 520  FOR PEACE

Remember, Prince of Peace,
the peoples of the world divided into many nations and tongues.
Deliver us from every evil that obstructs your saving purpose,
and fulfill your promises of old to establish your kingdom of peace.

From the curse of war and all that creates it,
**O Lord, deliver us.** See ♪ 195.

From believing and speaking lies against other nations, R

From narrow loyalties and selfish isolation, R

From fear and distrust of other nations,
from all false pride, vainglory, and self-conceit, R

From the lust of the mighty for riches,
that drives peaceful people to slaughter, R

rom putting our trust in the weapons of war,
  and from want of faith in the power of justice and good will, R

rom every thought, word, and deed that divides the human family
  and separates us from the perfect realization of your love, R **Amen.**

(ENGLAND, 20TH CENT., ALT.)

### A Vision of Hope 521

/e pray that someday an arrow will be broken,
  not in something or someone, but by each of humankind,
  to indicate peace, not violence.
ɔmeday, oneness with creation,
  rather than domination over creation,
  will be the goal to be respected.
ɔmeday fearlessness to love and make a difference
  will be experienced by all people.
hen the eagle* will carry our prayer for peace and love,
  and the people of the red, white, yellow, brown, and black communities
     can sit in the same circle together to communicate in love
  and experience the presence of the Great Mystery in their midst.
ɔmeday can be today for you and me. Amen.

(WANDA LAWRENCE, CHIPPEWA, 20TH CENT.)

\n eagle in the Native American tradition is often a carrier of prayer.

## FOR PURITY 522

Lord, this solemn prayer comes from deep desire,
  may our lives be as pure as candle fire.
ɛt our every breath dispel the world's gloom,
  let our spirit glow so brightly that darkness meets its doom.
.ay we be faithfully drawn to learning
  as the moth is drawn to the candle's burning.
.ay our lives be devoted to serving the needy
  and to loving a sorrowful, ever suffering humanity.
:ad us away from the path of temptation.
  Lord, let truth alone be our destination. Amen.

(TRADITIONAL CHILD'S PRAYER, PAKISTAN, ALT.)

: also the Collect for Purity on 447.

## FOR SAFETY 523

\mighty and merciful God,
  of your bountiful goodness keep us from all things that may hurt us,
  that we, being ready in both body and soul,

may cheerfully accomplish those things you command;
through Jesus Christ our Savior. Amen.

(THE BOOK OF COMMON PRAYER, U.S.A., 20TH CENT., AI

## 524                    FOR STRENGTH

O creator and mighty God,
  you have promised strength for the weak,
  rest for the laborers, light for the way,
  grace for the trials, help from above,
  unfailing sympathy, undying love.
O creator and mighty God,
  help us to continue in your promise. Amen.

(TRADITIONAL PRAYER, PAKISTAN, AI

## 525                    FOR WISDOM

O Wisdom on High, by you the meek are guided in judgment,
  and light rises up in darkness for the godly.
Grant us, in all doubts and uncertainties,
  the grace to ask what you would have us do,
  that we may be saved from all false choices,
  and that in your light we may see light,
    and in your straight path may not stumble;
through Jesus Christ our Savior. Amen.

(THE BOOK OF COMMON PRAYER, U.S.A., 20TH CENT., A

## FOR THE WORLD AND ITS PEOPLES

### 526

O God, you are the hope of all the ends of the earth,
  the God of the spirits of all flesh.
Hear our humble intercession for all races and families on earth,
  that you will turn all hearts to yourself.
Remove from our minds hatred, prejudice, and contempt
  for those who are not of our own race or color, class or creed,
that, departing from everything that estranges and divides,
  we may by you be brought into unity of spirit, in the bond of peac
Amen.                              (CHURCH OF SCOTLAND, 20TH CENT., A

527

'e are people who journey as vessels containing wellsprings of hope;
haring, replacing, and adding new waters
of proclamation, power, prophecy, and prayer
to the containers of our life and faith.
'e pause and reflect on the movement of the tide in this journey,
as it washes upon our shores,
cleansing and calling us back to ministry and faith.

*ue people are invited to stand where they are and share their prayers after each*
*vitation is given.*

**Creator God, let the waters of your womb heal.**
at us pray for our global community . . . R
at us pray for the bent-overness of our lives and world . . . R
at us pray for those living in the midst of violence . . . R
at us pray for those living in poverty . . . R
at us pray for the effort of peace . . . R
at us pray to trust the validity of our experience . . . R
at us pray for the call within
by the One who creates in us wellsprings of hope . . . R

**Creator God, may the waters that covered us at our birth**
**once again remind us of our creation in you.**
**emind us that we are vessels of the waters of hope**
**and that your outpourings have power to heal**
**and make whole our bruised world.**
**at the living waters of creation, womb, baptism, and Spirit**
**encircle us that we may remember we are yours and be thankful.**
(Elizabeth Lopez Spence, U.S.A., 20th cent., alt.)

# A PRAYER OF SUSANNA WESLEY 528

ou, O Lord, have called us to watch and pray.
herefore, whatever may be the sin against which we pray,
make us careful to watch against it,
and so have reason to expect that our prayers will be answered.
 order to perform this duty aright,
grant us grace to preserve a sober, equal temper,
and sincerity to pray for your assistance. Amen.
(Susanna Wesley, England, 18th cent., alt.)

529            A PRAYER OF SAINT PATRICK

Christ be with us, Christ before us, Christ behind us,
Christ in us, Christ beneath us, Christ above us,
Christ on our right, Christ on our left,
Christ where we lie, Christ where we sit, Christ where we arise,
Christ in the heart of every one who thinks of us,
Christ in every eye that sees us,
Christ in every ear that hears us.
    Salvation is of the Lord,
    Salvation is of the Christ,
May your salvation, O Lord, be ever with us.

(SAINT PATRICK, IRELAND, 5TH CENT., AL)

530    A PRAYER OF SAINT THOMAS AQUINAS

Give us, O Lord,
    steadfast hearts, which no unworthy thought can drag downward,
    unconquered hearts, which no tribulation can wear out,
    upright hearts, which no unworthy purpose may tempt aside.
Bestow upon us also, O Lord our God,
    understanding to know you, diligence to seek you, wisdom to find you
    and a faithfulness that may finally embrace you;
through Jesus Christ our Lord. Amen.

(SAINT THOMAS, ITALY, 13TH CENT., AL)

# BLESSINGS FOR PERSONS

## BLESSINGS INCLUDED IN *UMH*  531

46 At the Birth of a Child  
57 For the Sick  
460 In Time of Illness  
461 For Those Who Mourn

## IN ALL OCCASIONS OF LIFE  532

ord God, from the abundance of your mercy
  enrich your servants and safeguard them.
trengthened by your blessing,
  may they always be thankful to you and bless you with unending joy.
'e ask this through Christ our Lord. Amen.

(BOOK OF BLESSINGS, U.S.A., 20TH CENT.)

## FOR PERSONS CELEBRATING BIRTHDAYS

*ne of the following may be read before the blessing:*

ilippians 1:3-11  
Thessalonians 3:11-13  
Give thanks for you.  
May you grow in holiness.

### 533

od of all creation,
  we offer you grateful praise for the gift of life.
ear the prayers for *Name*, your servant,
  who recalls today the day of *his/her* birth
    and rejoices in your gifts of life and love, family and friends.
ess *him/her* with your presence and surround *him/her* with your love,
  that *he/she* may enjoy many happy years, all of them pleasing to you.
'e ask this through Christ our Savior. Amen.

(BOOK OF BLESSINGS, U.S.A., 20TH CENT., ALT)

## FOR A QUINCEAÑERA  534
(GIRL CELEBRATING FIFTEENTH BIRTHDAY)

Creator, God of the universe,
  we praise your holy name for the life of *Name*.
'e rejoice that she has come to that time in her life
  when she assumes new and greater responsibilities.
'e affirm her at this time of joy and celebration.
is is a time of thanksgiving for the past

and visions and challenges for the future.
We acknowledge that this is a time of commitment,
   not only to the highest ideals of life
      but also to the saving grace and sovereignty of Christ in her life.
Accept her life in true commitment and fill her heart with joy,
   and grant that your peace may come to abide in her heart for ever,
through Jesus Christ, our Sovereign and Savior. Amen.

(ROBERTO ESCAMILLA, HISPANIC AMERICAN, 20TH CENT

# 535 AT THE BEGINNING OF A NEW SCHOOL YEAR

UMH 383, *This Is a Day of New Beginnings, may be sung before the blessing*

At the beginning of a new school year, O God of wisdom,
we offer thanks and praise for the gift of new beginnings
   and for the opportunity to learn and to wonder.
We pray for teachers, students, and staff
   that this year might be rewarding for all.
Be with us as we face the challenge of new tasks,
   the fear of failure, the expectations of parents, friends, and self.
In our learning and our teaching,
   may we grow in service to others and in love for your world,
through Jesus Christ our Savior. Amen.

(U.S.A., 20TH CENT., AL'

# 536                FOR GRADUATES

UMH 383, *This Is a Day of New Beginnings, may be sung before the blessing*

God of truth and knowledge,
   by your wisdom we are taught the way and the truth.
Bless *Name(s)* as they now finish this course of study.
We thank you for those who taught and worked beside them,
   and all who supported them along the way.
Walk with *these* graduate(s) as *they* leave and move forward in life.
Take away *their* anxiety and confusion of purpose.
Strengthen *their* many talents and skills,
   instill in *them* a confidence in the future you plan,
      where energies may be gathered up and used for the good of all peopl
for the sake of Jesus Christ. Amen.

(ANDY LANGFORD, U.S.A., 20TH CEN

# FOR AN ENGAGED COUPLE

*One of the following may be read before the blessing:*

Hosea 2:19-20           Faithfulness
John 15:9-12            Remain in my love.
1 Corinthians 13:4-13   Love
Philippians 2:1-5       United in spirit

### 537

We praise you, Lord,
 for your gentle plan that draws together your children, *Name* and *Name,*
 in their love for each other.
Strengthen their hearts,
 so that they will keep faith with each other, please you in all things,
 and so come to the happiness of celebrating their marriage.
We ask this through Christ our Lord. Amen.

(BOOK OF BLESSINGS, U.S.A., 20TH CENT., ALT.)

# AT THE BEGINNING OF A NEW JOB   538

*MH 383, This Is a Day of New Beginnings, may be sung before the blessing.*

Lord Jesus Christ, carpenter of creation,
 you knew the satisfactions and responsibilities of human work
 and hallowed it for ever in a carpenter's shop in Nazareth.
As *Name* begins a new job,
 as a worthy occupation, may it be useful in the human enterprise.
May *Name* be a blessing to others
 by living and working to the honor and glory of your holy name. Amen.

(U.S.A., 20TH CENT.)

# FOR DISCIPLES IN THE MARKETPLACE   539

God, we realize you do not call us to be successful in the marketplace;
 you call us to be faithful as disciples of Jesus.
You do not call us to achievement in work, but to responsible living.
You do not call us to make a great fortune, but to labor for your reign.
Guide us into greater understanding of your priorities. Amen.

(ANTON K. JACOBS, U.S.A., 20TH CENT.)

# FOR THOSE WHO WORK   540

Living Word, by whom all things are created,
 bless all who work daily in home, field, and marketplace.
Labor with them until the creation of the new heaven and earth.
 Jesus' name we pray. Amen.         (ANDY LANGFORD, U.S.A., 20TH CENT.)

# 541 FOR THOSE WHO ARE UNEMPLOYED

O God of the vineyard,
  you call us all to productive labor,
  to employ our gifts and talents for you.
We pray for those who are unemployed.
Strengthen them in this difficult hour,
uplift their spirits,
and grant them a place among your laborers
  until all be employed for the common good,
  and we share fully in our true work
  of praising you with heart and mind and soul forever. Amen.

(DAVID SCHNASA JACOBSEN, U.S.A., 20TH CENT

# 542 FOR THOSE IN MILITARY SERVICE

Righteous God, you rule the nations.
Guard brave men and women in military service.
Give them compassion for those who confront them as enemies.
Keep our children from hate that hardens,
  or from scorekeeping with human lives.
Though for a season they must be people of war,
  let them live for peace, as eager for agreement as for victory.
Encourage them as they encourage one another,
  and never let hard duty separate them from loyalty to your Son,
  our Savior, Jesus Christ. Amen.

(PRESBYTERIAN WORSHIPBOOK, U.S.A., 20TH CENT., ALT

# 543 AT THE BEGINNING OF RETIREMENT

*UMH 383, This Is a Day of New Beginnings, may be sung before the blessin*

Eternal God,
  you hold the times and seasons,
  endings and beginnings, in your hands.
Bless *Name*, who now enters a new time of life.
We give you thanks for tasks accomplished,
  for the joys and pains woven into the fabric of *his/her* years.
Give *Name* the guidance of your Holy Spirit.
May days no longer filled with old obligations
  be free for new activities and associations.
May fears and uncertainties about the future
  be transformed into quiet confidence.
May each new day be received as a sacred trust and lived to your glory
through Jesus Christ our Savior. Amen. (U.S.A., 20TH CENT., ALT

## FOR LEADERS 544

God, as you anointed leaders and called prophets of old,
lead us to recognize our true representatives and authentic leaders:
men and women who love your people and can walk with them,
who feel their pain and share their joys,
who dream their dreams and strive to accompany them
to their common goal.
your fire, with your Spirit, embolden and commission us
to transform our political system, to serve your people,
and to bring real glory to your name. Amen. (PHILIPPINES, 20TH CENT.)


## FOR THOSE WHO SUFFER 545

Almighty God, shield of the oppressed,
hear us as we pray for the friendless and the lonely,
the tempted and the unbelieving.
merciful to those who suffer, in body or in mind,
to those who are in danger or distress, and who have suffered loss.
et your love surround the infirm and the aged.
especially near to those who are passing through the valley of death.
May they find eternal rest, and light at evening time;
through Jesus Christ our Lord. Amen.

(PRESBYTERIAN CHURCH OF SOUTH AFRICA, 20TH CENT., ALT.)


546

*lent prayers may follow each petition.*

Healer of Galilee,
you are afflicted in the sufferings of your people
and are full of compassion and tender mercy.
ear us as we pray for those who suffer:

r all who suffer trauma in body or mind. . .

r those whose livelihood is insecure,
the overworked, the hungry, the homeless, and the destitute,
for those who have been downtrodden, ruined,
and driven to despair. . .

r little children,
whose surroundings hide them from your love and beauty,
for all the fatherless and motherless. . .

For those who have to bear their burdens alone,
   and for all who have lost those whom they love. . .

For those who are in doubt and anguish of soul,
   for those who are oversensitive and afraid. . .

For those who suffer through their own wrongdoing. . .

For those whose suffering is unrelieved
   by the knowledge of your love. . .

Set free, Helper of the weak,
   the souls of your servants from all restlessness and anxiety.

Give us the peace and power that flow from you.
Keep us in all perplexities and distresses,
   in all griefs and grievances, from any fear or faithlessness;
that, being upheld by your strength
   and stayed on the rock of your faithfulness,
through storm and stress we may abide in you. Amen.

(U.S.A. 20TH CENT

*See also Healing Services and Prayers on 613-29.*

# FOR A VICTIM OR SURVIVOR
# OF CRIME OR OPPRESSION

*One of the following may be read before the blessing:*

| | |
|---|---|
| Job 3:1-26 | Lamentation of Job |
| Isaiah 59:6b-8, 15b-18 | God appalled by evil and injustice |
| Lamentations 3:1-24 | One who knows affliction |
| Lamentations 3:49-59 | You come to my aid. |
| Matthew 5:1-10 | The Beatitudes |
| Matthew 10:28-31 | Do not be afraid. |
| Luke 10:25-37 | The good Samaritan |

*One of the following hymns from UMH may be sung before the blessing:*

| | |
|---|---|
| 479 Jesus, Lover of My Soul | 512 Stand By Me |
| 488 Jesus Remember Me | 507 Through It All |
| 480 O Love That Wilt Not Let Me Go | |

## 547

Lord God of liberation,
   you saw your people as slaves in Egypt
      and delivered them from captivity,
   you see works of violence and weep.
Relieve the suffering of *Name*,
   grant *him/her* peace of mind
      and a renewed faith in your protection and care.
Protect us all from the violence of others,

keep us safe from the weapons of hate,
and restore us to tranquillity and peace.
We ask this through Christ our Lord. Amen.

(BOOK OF BLESSINGS, U.S.A., 20TH CENT., ALT.)

*See also Healing Services and Prayers on 613-29.*

## ON THE ANNIVERSARY OF A DEATH

*One of the following hymns from* UMH *may be sung before the blessing:*

708-12 Communion of the Saints          707 Hymn of Promise

**548**

Overliving God,
this day revives in us memories of loved ones who are no more.
That happiness we shared when they walked among us.
That joy, when, loving and being loved, we lived our lives together.
**Their memory is a blessing for ever.**

Months or years may have passed, and still we feel near to them.
Our hearts yearn for them.
Though the bitter grief has softened, a duller pain abides;
for the place where once they stood is empty now.
The links of life are broken, but the links of love and longing cannot break.
**Their souls are bound up in ours for ever.**

We see them now with the eye of memory,
their faults forgiven, their virtues grown larger.
So does goodness live, and weakness fade from sight.
We remember them with gratitude and bless their names.
**Their memory is a blessing for ever.**

And we remember as well the members
who but yesterday were part of our congregation and community.
To all who cared for us and labored for all people, we pay tribute.
May we prove worthy of carrying on the tradition of our faith,
for now the task is ours.
**Their souls are bound up in ours for ever.**

We give you thanks that they now live and reign with you.
As a great crowd of witnesses,
they surround us with their blessings,
and offer you hymns of praise and thanksgiving.
**They are alive for ever more. Amen.**

(BASED ON JEWISH MEMORIAL PRAYER, U.S.A., 20TH CENT.)

*See also All Saints (UMH 713) and Acts of Worship for All Saints Day or
Sunday (413-15).*

# PRAYERS OF THANKSGIVING

## 549 HYMNS AND PSALMS OF THANKSGIVING

57-101 Hymns of Praise and Thanksgiving to the Triune God
328-36 Hymns in Praise of the Holy Spirit
153-94 Hymns in Praise of Christ

| | | | | | |
|---|---|---|---|---|---|
| 743 | Psalm 18 | 803 | Psalm 81 | 832 | Psalm 111 |
| 761 | Psalm 29 | 811 | Psalm 92 | 834 | Psalm 113 |
| 767 | Psalm 33 | 815 | Psalm 96 | 838 | Psalm 117 |
| 769 | Psalm 34 | 816 | Psalm 97 | 851 | Psalm 135 |
| 780 | Psalm 46 | 818 | Psalm 98 | 853 | Psalm 138 |
| 789 | Psalm 65 | 819 | Psalm 99 | 858 | Psalm 146 |
| 790 | Psalm 66 | 821 | Psalm 103 | 859 | Psalm 147 |
| 791 | Psalm 67 | 824 | Psalm 103 | 861 | Psalm 148 |
| 792 | Psalm 68 | 830 | Psalm 107 | 862 | Psalm 150 |

# PRAYERS OF THANKSGIVING AFTER THE OFFERING

*When Holy Communion is celebrated, The Great Thanksgiving follows the offerin*
*When Holy Communion is not celebrated, a prayer such as one of the following*
*appropriate after the Offering.*

## 550

Almighty and forgiving God,
we your unworthy servants give you most humble thanks
for all your goodness and lovingkindness,
to us and to all whom you have made.
We bless you for our creation, preservation,
and all the blessings of this life;
but above all for your immeasurable love
in the redemption of the world by our Lord Jesus Christ,
for the means of grace, and for the hope of glory.
Give us such an awareness of your mercies,
that our hearts may be thankful,
and that we may show forth your praise,
not only with our lips, but in our lives,
by giving up ourselves to your service
and by walking before you in holiness and righteousness all our day
through Jesus Christ our Lord, to whom, with you and the Holy Spiri
be all honor and glory, for ever and ever. Amen.

(THE BOOK OF COMMON PRAYER, U.S.A., 20TH CENT., AL

**551**

Almighty and most merciful God,
  from you comes every good and perfect gift.
We give you praise and thanks for all your mercies.
Your goodness has created us, your bounty has sustained us,
  your discipline has chastened us, your patience has borne with us,
  your love has redeemed us.
Give us a heart to love and serve you,
and enable us to show our thankfulness for all your goodness and mercy
  by giving up ourselves to your service,
  and cheerfully submitting in all things to your blessed will;
through Jesus Christ our Savior. Amen.          (THE BOOK OF WORSHIP 1965, ALT.)

**552**

All things come from you, O God,
  and with gratitude we return to you what is yours.
You created all that is, and with love formed us in your image.
When our love failed, your love remained steadfast.
You gave your only Son Jesus Christ to be our Savior.
All that we are, and all that we have, is a trust from you.
And so, in gratitude for all your gifts,
  we offer you ourselves, and all that we have,
  in union with Christ's offering for us.
By your Holy Spirit make us one with Christ, one with each other,
  and one in ministry to all the world;
through Jesus Christ our Savior. Amen.

(HOYT L. HICKMAN, U.S.A., 20TH CENT., ALT.)

**553**

O Lord our God, the author and giver of all good things,
  we thank you for all your mercies,
  and for your loving care over all your creatures.
We bless you for the gift of life, for your protection round about us,
  for your guiding hand upon us,
  and for the tokens of your love within us.
We thank you for friendship and duty,
  for good hopes and precious memories, for the joys that cheer us,
  and the trials that teach us to trust in you.
Most of all we thank you
  for the saving knowledge of your Son our Savior,
  for the living presence of your Spirit, the Comforter,
  for your Church, the body of Christ,
  for the ministry of Word and Sacrament, and all the means of grace.
In all these things, O heavenly God,
  make us wise for a right use of your benefits,

that we may render an acceptable thanksgiving unto you
   all the days of our lives;
through Jesus Christ our Lord. Amen.

(THE BOOK OF COMMON ORDER, SCOTLAND, 20TH CENT., ALT.)

## 554

O God, most merciful and gracious,
   of whose bounty we have all received,
   accept this offering of your people.
Remember in your love those who have brought it
   and those for whom it is given,
and so follow it with your blessing
   that it may promote peace and goodwill among all peoples,
and advance the kingdom of our Lord and Savior Jesus Christ. Amen.

(PRESBYTERIAN, U.S.A, 20TH CENT.

## 555

Almighty God, giver of every good and perfect gift,
   teach us to render to you all that we have and all that we are,
   that we may praise you, not with our lips only,
      but with our whole lives,
   turning the duties, the sorrows, and the joys of all our days
      into a living sacrifice to you;
through our Savior Jesus Christ. Amen.    (THE BOOK OF WORSHIP 1965, ALT

# GENERAL PRAYERS OF THANKSGIVING

## 556

O Supreme Lord of the Universe,
   you fill and sustain everything around us.
With the touch of your hand you turned chaos into order,
   darkness into light.
Unknown energies you hid in the heart of matter.
From you burst forth the splendor of the sun
   and the mild radiance of the moon.
Stars and planets without number you set in ordered movement.
You are the source of the fire's heat and the wind's might,
   of the water's coolness and the earth's stability.
Deep and wonderful are the mysteries of your creation. Amen.

(INDIA, 20TH CENT

## 557

Lord of lords, Creator of all things,
   God of all things, God over all gods, God of sun and rain,
   you created the earth with a thought and us with your breath.

ord, we brought in the harvest.
he rain watered the earth, the sun drew cassava and corn out of the clay.
our mercy showered blessing after blessing over our country.
reeks grew into rivers, swamps became lakes.
ealthy fat cows graze on the green sea of the savanna.
he rain smoothed out the clay walls.
he mosquitoes perished in the high waters.
ord, the yam is fat like meat, the cassava melts on the tongue,
oranges burst in their peels, dazzling and bright.
ord, nature gives thanks, your creatures give thanks.
our praise rises in us like the great river.
ord of lords, Creator, Provider, we thank you in the name of Jesus Christ.
men. (FRITZ PAWELZIK, WEST AFRICA, 20TH CENT.)

## 558

hank you, Creator of the universe,
for the people gathered around us today.
'e give thanks for the things of the earth that give us the means of life.
**hank you for the plants, animals, and birds
that we use as food and medicine.**

hank you for the natural world,
in which we find the means to be clothed and housed.
**hank you, Lord, for the ability
to use these gifts of the natural world.**

elp us to see our place among these gifts,
not to squander them or think of them as means for selfish gain.
**ay we respect the life of all you have made.
ay our spirits be strengthened by using only what we need,
and may we use our strength to help those who need us. Amen.**

(SUE ELLEN HERNE, MOHAWK, 20TH CENT., ALT.)

# DISMISSAL, BLESSINGS, AND CLOSING PRAYER

*For musical and other suggestions regarding Dismissals with Blessing, see 31-3*

## 559          DISMISSAL

Serve your God with patience and passion.
Be deliberate in enacting your faith.
Be steadfast in celebrating the Spirit's power.
And may peace be your way in the world. Amen.

(GLEN E. RAINSLEY, U.S.A., 20TH CENT

## BLESSINGS

### 560
The Lord bless you and keep you;
the Lord make his face to shine upon you, and be gracious to you;
the Lord lift up his countenance upon you, and give you peace. Amen

(NUMBERS 6:24-2

### 561
May the God of hope fill you with all joy and peace in believing,
  so that you may abound in hope by the power of the Holy Spirit. Amer

(ROMANS 15:1

### 562
Before us it is blessed, behind us it is blessed,
  below us it is blessed, above us it is blessed,
  around us it is blessed as we set out with Christ.
Our speech is blessed as we set out for God.
With beauty before us, with beauty behind us,
  with beauty below us, with beauty above us,
  with beauty around us, we set out for a holy place indeed. Amen.

(TRADITIONAL NAVAHO PRAYER, AL<sup></sup>

### 563
May the presence of God the Creator give you strength;
May the presence of God the Redeemer give you peace;
May the presence of God the Sustainer give you comfort.
May the presence of God the Sanctifier give you love. Amen.

(UNITED METHODIST CLERGYWOMEN'S CONSULTATION, U.S.A., 20TH CENT., AL<sup></sup>

**564**

May the blessing of God, fountain of living water,
flow within us as a river of life.
May we drink deep of her wisdom.
May we never thirst again.
May we go through life refreshing many,
as a sign of healing for all;
through the One who is Life eternal. Amen.

(MIRIAM THERESE WINTER, U.S.A., 20TH CENT.)

**565**

May the road rise to meet you,
may the wind be always at your back,
may the sun shine warm upon your face,
may the rains fall soft upon your fields,
and until we meet again,
may God hold you in the palm of his hand. Amen.

(TRADITIONAL GAELIC PRAYER)

*Sarum Blessing*                    **566**

God be in your head, and in your understanding.
God be in your eyes, and in your looking.
God be in your mouth, and in your speaking.
God be in your heart, and in your thinking.
God be at your end, and at your departing.

(SARUM LITURGY, ENGLAND, 13TH CENT., ALT.)

# CLOSING PRAYER          567

Grant, O Lord,
that what has been said with our lips we may believe in our hearts,
and that what we believe in our hearts we may practice in our lives;
through Jesus Christ our Lord. Amen.

(JOHN HUNTER, SCOTLAND, 19TH CENT., ALT.)

# VI. DAILY PRAISE AND PRAYER

## INTRODUCTION

From the earliest days of the Church, Christian worshipers saw the rising of the sun and lighting of the evening lamps as symbolic of Christ's victory over death. Additional hours of the day were also designated as significant moments of celebrating Christ's presence in the world. The following Orders of Daily Praise and Prayer enable United Methodists to celebrate daily the life, death, and resurrection of Jesus Christ.

These services, following an ancient pattern of congregational prayer, focus upon the praise of God and prayer for God's creation rather than the proclaiming of the Word. Therefore, preaching and other devotional talks are inappropriate in these services. When scripture is used, passages should be chosen that will encourage the community in its praise and prayer.

Each order reflects a simple yet flexible pattern. The openings, hymns, songs of praise, responses to prayers, and Lord's Prayer may all be sung, with or without accompaniment; the more singing, the stronger the service. Scripture and Silence are optional, as indicated by brackets.

Each order is to be celebrated in a community of Christians at various occasions in their life together. Daily prayer may begin in the already existing gatherings of persons in the congregation. Rather than starting a prayer group for using these services, encourage persons who already gather for the work of the church to use these orders. The desire is for every gathering of every group in a congregation to pray together. Families may also choose to adapt these services for use in homes. These orders may be used on any occasion when Christians gather, but they are not adequate substitutes for the full Sunday Service of Word and Table.

As in the early church, when Christians worshiped in homes rather than in church buildings, the services are appropriate in any setting, including classroom, fellowship hall, garden, or home. The communal quality of prayer is emphasized when the people stand or sit in a circle or other arrangement facing one another.

The visible objects or signs are symbols pointing beyond themselves to

piritual reality. They are important, but secondary. A single candle,
vening lamp, or simple oil lamp may be a powerful sign of the light of Christ
umining the darkness. Leaders may use a lectern or reading desk.

aity are encouraged to lead these services. Different parts of the service
ay be led by different people.

# AN ORDER FOR MORNING PRAISE AND PRAYER

*his service is for use by groups at dawn or as they begin their day in prayer. The
rvice is most effective when morning sunlight is visible.*

*he people may participate by using An Order for Morning Praise and Prayer in
MH 876.*

*he congregation may be invited to stand for the entire service, except during the
ading of Scripture and Silence, when used.*

ALL TO PRAISE AND PRAYER * *Sung ( ♪ 220) or spoken:*

O Lord, open our lips.
**And we shall declare your praise.**                    (Psalm 51:15, alt.)

IORNING HYMN *

*A hymn appropriate to the morning may be sung. Suggested from* UMH:

674-81 Morning Hymns                  658 This Is the Day the Lord Hath Made
947 Hymns listed under Morning Prayer  185 When Morning Gilds the Skies
173 Christ, Whose Glory Fills the Skies  65 Santo! Santo! Santo!
 64 Holy, Holy, Holy!                  657 This Is the Day

RAYER OF THANKSGIVING *

*One of the following or other prayers of thanksgiving may be said by the leader or by
all together:*

New every morning is your love, great God of light,
    and all day long you are working for good in the world.
Stir up in us desire to serve you,
    to live peacefully with our neighbors,
    and to devote each day to your Son,
    our Savior, Jesus Christ the Lord. **Amen.**
                    (Presbyterian Worshipbook, U.S.A., 20th cent.)

Eternal God, hallowed be your name.
Early in the morning, before we begin our work, we praise your glory.
Renew our bodies as fresh as the morning flowers.

Open our inner eyes, as the sun casts new light upon the darkness.
Deliver us from all captivity.
Like the birds of the sky,
    give us wings of freedom to begin a new journey.
As a mighty stream running continuously,
    restore justice and freedom day by day.
We thank you for the gift of this morning,
    and a new day to work with you. **Amen.**

(MASAO TAKENAKA, JAPAN, 20TH CENT., ALT.

*See also For a New Day (UMH 676), Listen, Lord (UMH 677), and For Help fo
the Forthcoming Day (UMH 681).*

## SCRIPTURE

*The following or other readings appropriate to the morning, or to the day or seaso
of the Christian year, or to the nature of the occasion, may be used:*

Deuteronomy 6:4-7          The Shema
Isaiah 55:1-3              Invitation to abundant life
Psalm 51 (*UMH 785*)       Prayer for cleansing and pardon
Psalm 63 (*UMH 788*)       Comfort and assurance
Psalm 95 (*UMH 814*)       Call to worship and obedience
Romans 12:1-2             Be transformed by God.
John 1:1-5, 9-14          In the beginning was the Word.

### SILENCE

*Silent meditation on the scripture that has been read. This may be concluded with
short prayer, such as* Let our prayers be acceptable to you, O God, our rock
and our salvation. **Amen.**

## SONG OF PRAISE *

*The traditional morning Song of Praise is the Song of Zechariah (UMH 208, 209
The following psalms and canticles, or other scripture songs or hymns, may also b
sung:*

Psalm 100 (*UMH 821*)                    Canticle of Light and Darkness (*UMH 205*
Psalm 148 (*UMH 861*)                    Canticle of Moses and Miriam (*UMH 135*
Psalm 150 (*UMH 862*)                    Canticle of Praise to God (*UMH 91*)
Canticle of God's Glory (*UMH 82, 83*)   Canticle of Thanksgiving (*UMH 74*)
Canticle of the Holy Trinity (*UMH 80*)

## PRAYERS OF THE PEOPLE *

*The following or other of litany of intercession (see 495 for another litany) may b
prayed, during which any person may offer a brief prayer of intercession or petitior*

*After each prayer, the leader may conclude:* Lord, in your mercy, *and all may respond:* **Hear our prayer.**

*Or the leader may intone:* Let Us Pray to the Lord (UMH 485), *and all respond singing:* **Lord, have mercy.**

Together, let us pray

for the people of this congregation . . .

for those who suffer and those in trouble . . .

for the concerns of this local community . . .

for the world, its peoples, and its leaders . . .

for the Church universal—its leaders, its members, and its mission . . .

in communion with the saints . . . .

*Following these prayers, all may sing one of the following from* UMH:

490 Hear Us, O God            491 Remember Me
488 Jesus, Remember Me        487 This Is Our Prayer
485 Let Us Pray to the Lord

*See also:*
God Hears Our Every Need ( ♪ 183)      Tino tenda Jesu ( ♪ 203)
Jesus, We Are Here ( ♪ 187)            Señor Apiádate de Nosotros ( ♪ 188)
Teach Me to Hear in Silence ( ♪ 194)   O Lamb of God ( ♪ 201)

HE LORD'S PRAYER * *Sung or spoken. See* UMH 270-71, 894-96.

LESSING *

The grace of the Lord Jesus Christ,
and the love of God,
and the communion of the Holy Spirit
be with you all. **Amen.**

HE PEACE * *Signs of peace may be exchanged. See 26.*

# AN ORDER FOR MIDDAY PRAISE AND PRAYER

*This service is for use by groups in the middle of the day, possibly before a noon meal or following a morning meeting.*

*The congregation may be invited to stand for the entire service. The service is most effective when sunlight is visible.*

## CALL TO PRAISE AND PRAYER *

Even youths will faint and be weary,
  and the young will fall exhausted;
but those who wait for the Lord shall renew their strength,
  they shall mount up with wings like eagles,
they shall run and not be weary,
  they shall walk and not faint. (ISAIAH 40:30-3⟩

## HYMN *

*A hymn for the midday may be sung. Suggested from UMH:*

62 All Creatures of Our God and King
154 All Hail the Power of Jesus' Name
155 All Hail the Power of Jesus' Name
451 Be Thou My Vision
527 Do, Lord, Remember Me
404 Every Time I Feel the Spirit
465 Holy Spirit, Truth Divine
397 I Need Thee Every Hour
521 I Want Jesus to Walk with Me
494 Kum Ba Yah
402 Lord, I Want to Be a Christian

102 Now Thank We All Our God
119 O God in Heaven
480 O Love That Wilt Not Let Me Go
454 Open My Eyes, That I May See
96 Praise the Lord Who Reigns Above
492 Prayer Is the Soul's Sincere Desire
116 The God of Abraham Praise
601 Thy Word Is a Lamp
67 We, Thy People, Praise Thee
526 What a Friend We Have in Jesus

## PRAYER OF THANKSGIVING *

God of mercy, this midday moment of rest is your welcome gift.
Bless the work we have begun, make good its defects,
  and let us finish it in a way that pleases you.
Grant this through Christ our Lord. **Amen.**

(THE WESTMINSTER PRESS/JOHN KNOX PRESS, U.S.A., 20TH CEN⟩

## SONG OF PRAISE *

*A scripture song or hymn may be sung. Suggested from UMH:*

834 Psalm 113
844 Psalm 121
845 Psalm 122
846 Psalm 124

847 Psalm 126
74 Canticle of Thanksgiving
91 Canticle of Praise to God

RAYERS OF THE PEOPLE *

*The following or other of litany of intercession (see 495 for another litany) may be prayed, during which any person may offer a brief prayer of intercession or petition.*

*After each prayer, the leader may conclude:* Lord, in your mercy, *and all may respond:* **Hear our prayer.**

*Or the leader may intone:* Let Us Pray to the Lord *(UMH 485), and all respond singing:* **Lord, have mercy.**

Together, let us pray

for the people of this congregation . . .

for those who suffer and those in trouble . . .

for the concerns of this local community . . .

for the world, its peoples, and its leaders . . .

for the Church universal—its leaders, its members, and its mission . . .

in communion with the saints . . . .

*Following these prayers, all may sing a response. Suggested from* UMH:

| | |
|---|---|
| 490 Hear Us, O God | 491 Remember Me |
| 488 Jesus, Remember Me | 487 This Is Our Prayer |
| 485 Let Us Pray to the Lord | |

| | |
|---|---|
| *See also:* | Tino tenda Jesu ( ♪ 203) |
| God Hears Our Every Need ( ♪ 183) | Señor Apiádate de Nostros ( ♪ 188) |
| Jesus, We Are Here ( ♪ 187) | O Lamb of God ( ♪ 201) |
| Teach Me to Hear in Silence ( ♪ 194) | |

THE LORD'S PRAYER * *Sung or spoken. See UMH 270-71, 894-96.*

BLESSING *

The God of peace be with us.
**Amen.**

Let us bless the Lord.
**Thanks be to God.**

THE PEACE * *Signs of peace may be exchanged. See 26.*

# AN ORDER FOR EVENING PRAISE AND PRAYER

*This service is for use by groups as they end their day in prayer, especially before c
after an evening meeting.*

*The people may participate by using An Order for Evening Praise and Prayer i
UMH 878.*

*The congregation may be invited to stand for the entire service, except during th
reading of Scripture and Silence, when used.*

## PROCLAMATION OF THE LIGHT *

*A large unadorned candle may be lighted and lifted in the midst of the communit*
*The following may be sung ( ♪ 221) or spoken:*

Light and peace in Jesus Christ.
**Thanks be to God.**

## [SERVICE OF INCENSE *]

*Since the fourth century of the early church, the burning of incense has served as*
*devotional sign of prayer, based on Psalm 141. A stick of incense may be lighted, c*
*pieces of incense may be dropped onto a lighted piece of charcoal. During this time*
*the following may be read:*

I call upon you, O Lord; come quickly to me;
give ear to my voice when I call to you.
Let my prayer be counted as incense before you,
and the lifting up of my hands as an evening sacrifice.    (PSALM 141:1-

*See also Psalm 134 (UMH 850).*

## EVENING HYMN * *Suggested from UMH:*

682-93 Evening Hymns
941 Hymns listed under Evening Prayer
498 My Prayer Rises to Heaven
686 O Gladsome Light (traditional opening hymn for Evening Prayer)

## PRAYER OF THANKSGIVING *

*One of the following or other prayers of thanksgiving may be said by the leader or b*
*all together:*

We praise and thank you, O God,
for you are without beginning and without end.
Through Christ, you created the whole world;
through Christ, you preserve it.
You made the day for the works of light
and the night for the refreshment of our minds and bodies.

Keep us now in Christ; grant us a peaceful evening,
a night free from sin; and bring us at last to eternal life.
Through Christ and in the Holy Spirit,
we offer you all glory, honor, and worship,
now and for ever. **Amen.** (LITURGY OF EVENING PRAYER, SYRIA, 4TH CENT.)

In the brightness of your Son we spend each day;
in the darkness of the night you light our way;
always you protect us with the umbrella of your love.
To you, God, be all praise and glory forever and forever. **Amen.**
(1985 CHRISTIAN CONFERENCE OF ASIA YOUTH)

*See also For Protection at Night (UMH 691) and For a Peaceful Night (UMH 693).*

## CRIPTURE

*The following or other readings appropriate to the evening, or to the day or season of the Christian year, or to the nature of the occasion, may be used:*

| | |
|---|---|
| Genesis 1:1-5, 14-19 | The creation |
| Exodus 13:21-22 | Pillar of cloud and pillar of fire |
| Psalm 23 (*UMH* 137, 754) | The divine shepherd |
| Psalm 90 (*UMH* 809) | God's eternity and human frailty |
| Psalm 121 (*UMH* 844) | Song of praise and prayer |
| Romans 5:6-11 | Christ died for the ungodly. |
| 1 Thessalonians 5:2-10 | The day of the Lord |
| Revelation 22:1-5 | The city of God |
| Matthew 25:1-13 | Parable of ten bridesmaids |

## ILENCE

*Silent meditation on the scripture that has been read. This may be concluded with a short prayer.*

## ONG OF PRAISE *

*The traditional evening Song of Praise is the Song of Mary (UMH 198, 199, 200, 197 [stanza 4]). The following psalms and canticles, or other scripture songs or hymns, may also be sung:*

| | |
|---|---|
| Psalm 134 (*UMH* 850) | Canticle of Light and Darkness (*UMH* 205) |
| Canticle of Hope (*UMH* 734) | Canticle of Simeon (*UMH* 225) |
| Canticle of Covenant Faithfulness (*UMH* 125) | |

## RAYERS OF THE PEOPLE *

*The following or other litany of intercession (see 495 for another litany) may be prayed, during which any person may offer a brief prayer of intercession or petition.*

*After each prayer, the leader may conclude:* Lord, in your mercy, *and all may respond:* **Hear our prayer.**

*Or the leader may intone:* Let Us Pray to the Lord (UMH 485), *and all respond singing:* **Lord, have mercy.**

Together, let us pray

for the people of this congregation . . .

for those who suffer and those in trouble . . .

for the concerns of this local community . . .

for the world, its peoples, and its leaders . . .

for the Church universal—its leaders, its members, and its mission . .

in communion with the saints . . .

*Or prayers of confession and words of pardon may be offered. See UMH 890-93 ar 474-94.*

*Following these prayers, all may sing a response such as one of the following fro UMH:*

| | |
|---|---|
| 490 Hear Us, O God | 482 Lord, Have Mercy |
| 483 Kyrie Eleison | 491 Remember Me |
| 484 Kyrie Eleison | |

| | |
|---|---|
| *See also:* | Tino tenda Jesu ( ♪ 203) |
| God Hears Our Every Need ( ♪ 183) | Señor Apiádate de Nosotros ( ♪ 188) |
| Jesus, We Are Here ( ♪ 187) | O Lamb of God ( ♪ 201) |
| Teach Me to Hear in Silence ( ♪ 194) | |

THE LORD'S PRAYER * *Sung or spoken. See UMH 270-71, 894-96.*

BLESSING *

The grace of Jesus Christ enfold you.
Go in peace.
**Thanks be to God.**

THE PEACE *

*Signs of peace may be exchanged, or all may depart in silence. See 26.*

# AN ORDER FOR NIGHT PRAISE AND PRAYER

*his service of serenity and silence is for use by groups immediately prior to sleep or hen retiring at night as they end their day in prayer. The people may remain seated r the entire service.*

## ALL TO PRAISE AND PRAYER

*A large unadorned candle may be lighted. The following may be sung ( ♪ 222) or spoken:*

O God, come to our assistance.
**O Lord, hasten to help us.**

The Lord Almighty grant us a restful night and peace at the last.
**Amen.**

## IGHT HYMN *Sung or spoken. Suggested from UMH:*

682-93 Evening Hymns
Hymns listed under Evening Prayer 941
498 My Prayer Rises to Heaven
486 O Gladsome Light

## RAYERS OF CONFESSION

*Prayers of confession and words of pardon may be offered. See UMH 890-93 and 474-94.*

*Following these prayers, all may sing. Suggested from UMH:*

| | |
|---|---|
| 490 Hear Us, O God | 484 Kyrie Eleison |
| 482 Lord, Have Mercy | 491 Remember Me |
| 483 Kyrie Eleison | |

*See also:*
O Lamb of God ( ♪ 201)
O Lord, Deliver Us ( ♪ 195)
Señor, Apiádate de Nosotras ( ♪ 188)

## ILENCE

## ONG OF PRAISE

*The following or other scripture song or hymn from UMH may be sung:*

| | |
|---|---|
| 741 Psalm 4 | 810 Psalm 91 |
| 767 Psalm 33 | 850 Psalm 134 |
| 769 Psalm 34 | 854 Psalm 139:1-12 |

SILENCE

## PRAYER OF THANKSGIVING

*One of the following or other prayers of thanksgiving may be said by the leader or by all together:*

As you have made this day, O God,
   you also make the night.
Give light for our comfort.
Come upon us with quietness and still our souls
   that we may listen for the whisper of your Spirit
      and be attentive to your nearness in our dreams.
Empower us to rise again in new life to proclaim your praise,
   and show Christ to the world. **Amen.**

(LITURGY OF THE HOURS, U.S.A., 20TH CEN°

Grant, O eternal God,
   that we may lie down in peace,
   and raise us up, O Sovereign, to life renewed.
Spread over us the shelter of your peace;
   guide us with your good counsel;
   and for your name's sake, be our Help.
Shield us from hatred and plague;
   keep us from war and famine and anguish;
   subdue our inclination to evil.
O God our Guardian and Helper,
   our gracious and merciful Ruler,
   give us refuge in the shadow of your wings.
O guard our coming and our going,
   that now and always we have life and peace.
Blessed is the Lord, Guardian of the people Israel for ever. **Amen.**

(JEWISH PRAYER FOR PROVIDENCE, U.S.A., 20TH CEN°

*See also: At the Close of Day (UMH 689), For Protection at Night (UMH 691, and For a Peaceful Night (UMH 693).*

THE LORD'S PRAYER *Sung or spoken. See UMH 270-71, 894-96.*

## COMMENDATIONS

In peace we will lie down and sleep.
**In the Lord alone we safely rest.**

Guide us waking, O Lord, and guard us sleeping,
**that awake we may watch with Christ,**
   **and asleep we may rest in peace.**

May the divine help remain with us always.
**And with those who are absent from us.**

(ORDER OF ST. LUKE, U.S.A., 20TH CENT., ALT.)

IE SONG OF SIMEON (*UMH* 225, 226)

ESSING

May the God of hope
   fill you with all joy and peace in believing,
so that you may abound in hope
   by the power of the Holy Spirit.

(ROMANS 15:13)

IE PEACE

*Signs of peace may be exchanged, and all may depart in silence. See 26.*

# A MIDWEEK SERVICE OF PRAYER AND TESTIMONY

*is may be used for an informal midweek prayer service. It reflects a distinctively*
*esleyan and North American style of worship.*

ALL TO PRAISE AND PRAYER *

*Brief invitations to praise and prayer, such as* Our help is in the name of the
Lord, who made heaven and earth, *or other scripture sentences may be offered,*
*such as Psalm 118:24, Isaiah 40:30-31, Lamentations 3:25-26, John 4:23-24, or*
*Romans 6:4.*

YMN(S) *

*Hymns appropriate to the time of day, or to the day or season of the Christian year,*
*or to the nature of the occasion may be used. Use Index of Topics and Categories*
*(UMH 934-54) for suggestions. A wide variety of hymns and choruses may be*
*chosen, as the Spirit moves.*

RAYER OF THANKSGIVING *

*A brief prayer thanking God for the gift of one another, the occasion, and Jesus*
*Christ. Also see 556-58 for other prayers of thanksgiving.*

## SCRIPTURE

*One or more readings, appropriate to the time of day, or to the day or season of t*
*Christian year, or to the nature of the occasion, may be used.*

## TESTIMONIES

*Testimonies may include personal witness to God's grace or accounts of what G*
*is doing in the lives of others. The pastor may also give a witness to the scriptur*

## PRAISE AND PRAYERS OF THE PEOPLE

*Praise may take the form of hymns, songs, choruses, or spoken exclamations.*
*may vary from the relative formality of a hymn, to spontaneous calling o*
*requests, and singing and praying as the Spirit moves.*

*Spontaneous prayers may be offered by the people, or a litany of intercession a*
*petition may be prayed, during which any person may offer a brief prayer*
*intercession or petition. See also 497-530 for a variety of prayers.*

*After each prayer, the leader may conclude,* **Lord, in your mercy,** *and all m*
*respond:* **Hear our prayer.**

*Or prayers for the day, season, or gathering may be offered by individuals, as th*
*are moved, or by a leader.*

## THE LORD'S PRAYER *Sung or spoken. See UMH 270-71, 894-96.*

## HYMN(S) *

*See above for suggestions.*

## BLESSING *

*A brief blessing may be given, such as 1 Timothy 1:17:*

To . . . God be honor and glory forever and ever.

# VII. OCCASIONAL SERVICES

## THE LOVE FEAST

*ιe Love Feast, or Agape Meal, is a Christian fellowship meal recalling the meals
ʒus shared with disciples during his ministry and expressing the koinonia
ɔmmunity, sharing, fellowship) enjoyed by the family of Christ.*

*ıthough its origins in the early church are closely interconnected with the origins of
ε Lord's Supper, the two services became quite distinct and should not be confused
ith each other. While the Lord's Supper has been practically universal among
ʼristians throughout church history, the Love Feast has appeared only at certain
ʼnes and among certain denominations.*

*ıe modern history of the Love Feast began when Count Zinzendorf and the
ʼoravians in Germany introduced a service of sharing food, prayer, religious
ʼnversation, and hymns in 1727. John Wesley first experienced it among the
ʼoravians in Savannah, Georgia, ten years later. His diary notes: "After evening
ʼayers, we joined with the Germans in one of their love-feasts. It was begun and
ʼded with thanksgiving and prayer, and celebrated in so decent and solemn a manner
ʼ a Christian of the apostolic age would have allowed to be worthy of Christ."*

*ʼ quickly became a feature of the Evangelical Revival and a regular part of Methodist
ʼciety meetings in Great Britain and throughout the English-speaking world. As
ʼethodists immigrated to North America they made Love Feasts an important part of
ʼrly American Methodism.*

*ʼhile Love Feasts became less frequent in the years that followed, they continued to be
ʼld in some places; and in recent years the Love Feast has been revived. Love Feasts
ʼve often been held at Annual Conferences and Charge Conferences, where persons
ʼay report on what God has been doing in their lives and on the hope and trust they
ʼace in God for the future. The Love Feast is also an important part of the practice of
ʼovenant Discipleship groups. Christmas, New Year's Eve or Day, the weekdays of
ʼoly Week, and the Day of Pentecost are also fitting occasions for a Love Feast. A
ʼve Feast may also be held during a congregational supper.*

*ʼhe Love Feast has often been held on occasions when the celebration of the Lord's
ʼupper would be inappropriate—where there is no one present authorized to
ʼdminister the Sacrament, when persons of different denominations are present who*

*do not feel free to take Holy Communion together, when there is a desire for a service more informal and spontaneous than the communion ritual, or at a full meal or some other setting to which it would be difficult to adapt the Lord's Supper.*

*The Love Feast is most naturally held around a table or with persons seated in a circle but it is possible to hold it with persons seated in rows. A church sanctuary, fellowship hall, or home is an appropriate location.*

*One of the advantages of the Love Feast is that any Christian may conduct it. Congregational participation and leadership are usually extensive and important especially involving children.*

*Testimonies and praise are the focal point in most Love Feasts. Testimonies may include personal witness to God's grace or accounts of what God has been doing in the lives of others. Praise may take the form of hymns, songs, choruses, or spoken exclamations and may vary from the relative formality of an opening and closing hymn to spontaneous calling out of requests and singing as the Spirit moves. Sometimes the leader guides those present alternating spontaneous singing and sharing in free and familiar conversation for as long as the Spirit moves. Wesley counseled that all the above be done decently and in order.*

*Prayer is vital to a Love Feast. A fixed form of prayer may be used, especially something like the* Lord's Prayer *or* Be present at our table, Lord, *that is familiar to the people. Spontaneous prayer requests and prayers may come from the people.*

*Scripture is also important. There may be scripture readings, or persons may quote Scripture spontaneously as the Spirit moves. There may be a sermon, an exhortation, or an address; but it should be informal and consist of the leader's adding personal witness to what spontaneously comes from the congregation.*

*Most Love Feasts include the sharing of food. It is customary not to use communion bread, wine, or grape juice because to do so might confuse the Love Feast with the Lord's Supper. The bread may be a loaf of ordinary bread, crackers, rolls, or a sweet bread baked especially for this service. If a loaf of bread, it may be broken in two or more pieces and then passed from hand to hand as each person breaks off a piece. Crackers, rolls, or slices of bread may be passed in a basket. The beverage has usually been water, but other beverages such as lemonade, tea, or coffee have been used. Early Methodists commonly passed a loving cup with two handles from person to person, but later the water was served in individual glasses. The food is served quietly without interrupting the service.*

*The Love Feast may also be followed by a full meal, in which case persons or families may bring dishes of food for all to share. During the meal there may be informal conversation in Christian fellowship, or the leader may direct the conversation by suggesting matters of mutual concern, or there may be spontaneous witnessing and praise. If there is food left over, it may be taken as an expression of love to persons not present.*

## OPENING HYMN OR CHORUS *Suggested from* UMH:

947 Hymns listed under Love Feast

*See also* Jesus, We Are Here ( ♪ 187) and Tino tenda Jesu ( ♪ 203).

RAYERS

*One or more persons may pray aloud, the others responding with* **Amen,**
**Hallelujah, Praise the Lord,** *or other responses as the Spirit moves, or one of the*
*following or another prayer or table grace may be spoken or sung (UMH 621):*

Be present at our table, Lord;
Be here and everywhere adored;
Thy creatures bless, and grant that we
May feast in paradise with Thee. (JOHN CENICK)

*The following prayer by Charles Wesley was written especially for the Love Feast*
*and recommended for use at all Love Feasts by both John and Charles Wesley. It*
*may be sung to the tune* TERRA BEATA *(UMH 144).*

Father of earth and heaven,
    Thy hungry children feed,
Thy grace be to our spirits given,
    That true immortal bread.
Grant us and all our race
    In Jesus Christ to prove
The sweetness of thy pardoning grace,
    The manna of thy love.

SCRIPTURE *Suggested lessons:*

| | |
|---|---|
| Psalm 145:8-21 (*UMH* 857) | God's abounding love |
| Canticle of Love (*UMH* 646) | Scripture selections concerning love |
| 1 Corinthians 13 | The gift of love |
| 2 Corinthians 9:6-15 | Our generous sharing glorifies God. |
| Philippians 2:5-11 | God's self-emptying in Christ Jesus |
| 1 John 4:7-21 | God is love. |
| Matthew 22:34-40 | Love of God and neighbor |
| Luke 9:12-17 | Feeding the five thousand |
| Luke 14:16-24 | Parable of the great dinner |
| John 6:25-35 | Jesus the Bread of Life |

ADDRESS OR PERSONAL WITNESS TO THE SCRIPTURE

*One or more persons may give a personal witness to the scripture.*

PASSING OF THE BREAD

*The bread is passed from person to person. Each person may be invited in passing*
*the bread to quote a scripture verse. The leader may receive last and close with a few*
*words, a short prayer, or an invitation to new commitment to Christ and a holy life.*

[COLLECTION FOR THE POOR]

[CIRCULATION OF THE LOVING CUP]

TESTIMONIES, PRAYERS, SINGING

[CLOSING EXHORTATION]

HYMN OR CHORUS *Suggested from* UMH:

| | |
|---|---|
| 566 Blest Be the Dear Uniting Love | 572 Pass It On |
| 557 Blest Be the Tie That Binds | 558 We Are the Church |

*See also suggestions above under Opening Hymn or Chorus.*

DISMISSAL WITH BLESSING *See 31-32.*

# RESOURCES FOR USE
# IN A HOMECOMING SERVICE

*Prayer*

Eternal and loving God, today we give thanks to you for your goodne
through all the years of worship and witness in this place.

For your grace in calling us to be your people,
  for your love revealed to us in Christ your Son,
  for your gift of the Spirit and the joy of salvation:
**We give you thanks, O God.**

For those who established this congregation,
  for their faith and vision, for their gifts and abilities: **R**

For all who have been members of this congregation,
  for those who have given freely of their time and money,
  for those whose wisdom guided our congregation: **R**

For all who have preached and taught here;
  for all who have confessed here that Jesus is Lord;
  for all who today lead in worship, witness, and service: **R**

Give us the assurance that we too belong to that great company,
  and that we too may find the peace that passes understanding;
through Jesus Christ our Savior. **Amen.**

*Suggested Hymns from* UMH

| | |
|---|---|
| 708-14 Communion of the Saints | 653 Christ the Victorious |
| 938 Hymns listed under Anniversaries. | 555 Forward Through the Ages |
| 557 Blest Be the Tie That Binds | 654 How Blest Are They |
| 652 Canticle of Remembrance | 356 Pues Si Vivimos (When We Are Livir |

# AN ORDER OF THANKSGIVING
# FOR THE BIRTH OR ADOPTION OF A CHILD

*)llowing the birth or adoption of a child, the parent(s), together with other members of e family, may present the child in a service of worship to be welcomed by the congre- tion and to give thanks to God. Part or all of this order may be included in any service ' congregational worship. Either a pastor or a deacon may lead. If a pastor leads and a 'acon is present, it is most appropriate for the deacon to offer or lead the prayer.*

*'anksgiving for the birth or adoption of a child may also be offered to God in a hospital ' home, using such parts of this order as are appropriate.*

*should be made clear to participants that this act is neither an equivalent of nor a bstitute for Holy Baptism but has an entirely different history and meaning. This act appropriate (1) prior to the presentation of the child for baptism, or (2) if the child has 'en baptized elsewhere and is being presented for the first time in the congregation where s or her nurture is to take place. For a statement concerning the meaning of baptism, e 81-85.*

*'hile this order will not normally be the theme of an entire service, one or more of the llowing Scriptures may be read as a lesson or sung as an act of praise and thanksgiving:*

| | |
|---|---|
| euteronomy 6:4-9 | Diligently teach your children. |
| euteronomy 31:12-13 | Do this that children may hear and learn. |
| Samuel 1:9-11, 19b-20, 26-28 | Samuel born and lent to the Lord |
| alm 8 (UMH 743) | O Lord, how majestic is your name. |
| alatians 4:4-7 | We are God's adopted children. |
| atthew 18:1-5 | The greatest are humble like children. |
| ark 10:13-16 | Jesus blesses the children. |
| ike 1:47-55 (UMH 198-200) | The Canticle of Mary |
| ike 2:22-40 | The presentation of Jesus in the Temple |

*s a Response to the Word, the pastor invites those presenting children to come forward d then continues:*

## RESENTATION AND CALL TO THANKSGIVING

*There may be informal and spontaneous acts of presentation and thanksgiving, and/ or the following:*

Brothers and sisters in Christ:
The *birth (adoption)* of a child is a joyous and solemn occasion
  in the life of a family.
It is also an occasion for rejoicing in the church family.
I bid you, therefore, to join with *parent's Name* [and *parent's Name*]
  in giving thanks to God, whose children we all are,
  for the gift of *Child's Name* to be *their son/daughter*
[and with *sibling's Name(s)*, for a new *brother/sister*].

*See also At the Birth of a Child (UMH 146).*

## PRAYER OF THANKSGIVING AND INTERCESSION *

*One or more of the following prayers is offered.*

### For the Birth of a Child

O God, as a mother comforts her children,
  you strengthen us in our solitude, sustain and provide for us.
As a father cares for his children,
  so continually look upon us with compassion and goodness.
We come before you with gratitude for the gift of this child,
  for the joy that has come into this family,
  and the grace with which you surround them and all of us.
Pour out your Spirit.
Enable your servants to abound in love,
  and establish our homes in holiness;
through Jesus Christ our Lord. **Amen.**

### For a Safe Delivery

Gracious God, we give you humble and hearty thanks
  that you have preserved through the pain and anxiety of childbirt
    your servant *mother's Name*
  and upheld your servant(s) *Names of father and/or other family member*
*They desire (She desires)* now to offer you
  *their (her)* praises and thanksgivings.
Grant in your mercy that by your help
  *they (she)* may live faithfully according to your will in this life,
  and finally partake of everlasting glory in the life to come;
through Jesus Christ our Lord. **Amen.**

### For the Adoption of a Child

O God, you have adopted all of us as your children.
We give thanks to you for the child
  who has come to bless *Name(s) of parent(s)*
  [and *Name(s) of siblings*]
  who have welcomed this child as *their* own.
By the power of your Holy Spirit,
  fill their home with love, trust, and understanding;
through Jesus Christ our Lord. **Amen.**

### For the Family

Gracious God, from whom every family in heaven and on earth is name
Out of the treasures of your glory, strengthen us through your Spiri
Help us joyfully to nurture *child's Name* within your Church.
Bring *him/her* by your grace to *baptism (Christian maturity)*,
  that Christ may dwell in *his/her* heart through faith.

Give power to *child's Name* and to us,
that with all your people we may grasp
the breadth and length, the height and depth, of Christ's love.
Enable us to know this love,
and to be filled with your own fullness;
through Jesus Christ our Lord. **Amen.**

*A hymn or response may be sung and a blessing given. Suggested from* UMH:

| | | | |
|---|---|---|---|
| 951 | Listings under Doxology | 141 | Children of the Heavenly Father |
| 186 | Alleluia | 92 | For the Beauty of the Earth |
| 53 | All Praise to You | | (stanzas 1, 4, 6) |
| 54 | All Praise to You | 72 | Gloria, Gloria |
| 611 | Child of Blessing, Child of Promise | 78 | Heleluyan |
| | (stanzas 2, 4) | 84 | Thank You, Lord |

*See also:*
Tino tenda, Jesu (*BOW* 203).

# AN ORDER FOR THE PRESENTATION
# OF BIBLES TO CHILDREN

*This service may be used on Sunday morning as a Response to the Word. A Bible may be handed to each child by a pastor, deacon, parent, teacher, or friend. Luke 2:41-52 may be read prior to the giving of the Bibles, preferably by an older child.*

*Pastor, deacon, parents, teachers, and friends, facing the children, say:*

Receive the Word of God.
Learn its stories and study its words.
Its stories belong to us all,
and these words speak to us all.
They tell us who we are.
They tell us that we belong to one another,
for we are the people of God.

*Children respond:*

We receive these Bibles with our hands, our hearts, and our minds.
Thank you.
We will read and study the Bible together.

*The children and leaders face the congregation.*

*Congregation to children:*

**We rejoice in this step in your journey with God.**
**We pray God will guide you, your family, and us**
**as you use this Holy Bible in your home,**
**in your church school classes, and in our worship.**
**We will learn together and grow in our love for God's Word.**

*Children to congregation:*

The Word of God is a lamp to our feet,
and a light to our path.
Thanks be to God.

*A hymn may be sung. Suggested from* UMH:

602 Concerning the Scriptures
936 Hymns listed under Children

558 We Are the Church
601 Thy Word Is a Lamp Unto My Feet

*See also:*
Come! Come! Everybody Worship (*BOW* 199)

# A CELEBRATION OF NEW BEGINNINGS IN FAITH

*This service witnesses to the fact that the Holy Spirit is constantly working in the lives* ·
*God's people, awakening faith and calling them to make a new beginning in the Christia*
*pilgrimage. While many persons at this time wish to reaffirm the Baptismal Covenan*
*using The Baptismal Covenant I (UMH 33, 86-94), others may wish to use another se*
*vice such as this one. It may be used to meet particular situations such as the following*

*1) When a person has recently come to faith in Christ and desires to celebrate t*
*experience and witness to it before the congregation in a service before or after baptis*

*2) When a person has recently made a recommitment of life to Christ*

*3) When a person intends to return to active involvement in the life of the congregatio*

*This order may be used on Sunday morning or at A Midweek Service of Prayer and Te*
*timony (572). It may be placed after the sermon as a Response to the Word.*

INTRODUCTION

*The pastor or deacon and the person celebrating a new beginning in faith stand*
*together before the congregation, as the pastor or deacon begins:*

Brothers and sisters,
from time to time we experience a new beginning in our faith journe
when the Holy Spirit breaks into our lives to inspire us, to lead u
and to deepen our commitment to Christ.

Today, we praise the Lord
for what has been happening in *Name's* life.

SCRIPTURE *Suggested readings:*

Psalm 139 (*UMH* 854)
Micah 6:6-8
Romans 5:6-10
Romans 8:12-17
Galatians 2:15-20

The inescapable God
What does the Lord require of you?
Christ died for us.
We are children of God.
Christ lives in me.

Ephesians 4:22-24        Be renewed in the Spirit.
Matthew 7:7-11        Ask, and it will be given to you.

## WITNESS

*The person may give a brief witness to an experience of Christ or a new beginning in faith, or the pastor or another person may outline briefly the experiences that have brought the person to make this witness.*

## CONGREGATIONAL RESPONSE

*The pastor begins:*

Name, we rejoice in your experience
   of the grace of the Lord Jesus Christ,
     the love of God, and the communion of the Holy Spirit.

*The congregation responds:*

**In the love of Christ we encourage you,
   and pray that God will continue to bless you.
To God's name be glory and praise. Hallelujah!**

## [PRAYER WITH THE LAYING ON OF HANDS]

*Members of the congregation, family, and friends may be invited to come forward and gather around the person. The person kneels. The pastor or deacon and others lay hands on the person's head, as the pastor or deacon begins:*

Let us pray for *Name.*

*After a brief time of silence, the leader continues:*

O God, like a good shepherd searching for a lost lamb,
   like a woman looking for a lost coin,
   like a father redeeming his son,
   your love is rich beyond our deserving.
You never forsake us, no matter how far we move from you.
We thank you for all you have done for *Name.*
Strengthen *him/her* by the Holy Spirit,
   that *he/she* may grow in faith and increase in love for you.
May *his/her* service and witness bring you honor and glory;
in the name of Jesus Christ. **Amen.**

## BLESSING

*The pastor offers this blessing:*

Name, you are a child of God,
a servant of Christ, and a temple of the Holy Spirit.
May almighty God bless you and keep you in eternal life. **Amen.**

[HYMN]

*A hymn or song significant to the person may be sung. The following in UMH ar*
*also suggested:*

382-94 Rebirth and the New Creature        153 Thou Hidden Source of Calm Repos
154-5 All Hail the Power of Jesus' Name

## AN ORDER OF FAREWELL TO CHURCH MEMBERS

*This is an act of public farewell to a church member or family moving to anothe*
*community.*

*In any service of congregational worship, as a Response to the Word, or at some othe*
*suitable point in the service, the pastor calls forward the person(s) who are moving t*
*be recognized. They face the congregation. The pastor may briefly describe th*
*contributions of the person(s) to the congregation and then proceed with this orde*

*Pastor:*

The church is a family.
United by the common recognition of Jesus Christ as our Savior,
    we are all brothers and sisters.
And, for a time, *Name of congregation* is our home.

Like every human family,
our church family is formed and reformed over time:
    as members are born, as they die,
    as members are adopted into our family,
        and as they leave our congregation for a new home, in a different place

For a time, *Name(s) has/have* lived with us.
We have shared with each other good times and bad,
    we have shared each other's joys and sorrows,
    we have lightened each other's heavy loads.
Together we have laughed and cried,
    together we have worshiped and praised God,
    together we have lived.

*Congregation:*

**We feel sorrow in your leaving,**
    **yet we rejoice with you in anticipation of this new phase of your life**
**We will miss your love and support,**
    **yet we know you will add much to the lives**
        **of those who will be your new church family,**
    **as you have added much to our lives.**

*Congregation and pastor:*

**We will pray for you and for the whole family of God.**

*Pastor:*

Let us pray:
O God, you are the strength and the protector of your people.
We humbly place in your hands *Name(s)* of this congregation
  who *is/are* about to leave us.
Keep and preserve *him/her/them*, O Lord,
  in all health and safety, both of body and soul;
through Jesus Christ our Lord. **Amen.**
Go in the peace of Christ. Our prayers go with you. **Amen.**

*A hymn or response may be sung. Suggested from* UMH:

52 Hymns listed under Sending Forth          438 Forth in Thy Name, O Lord
57 Blest Be the Tie That Binds                    383 This Is a Day of New Beginnings


# AN ORDER FOR COMMITMENT
# TO CHRISTIAN SERVICE

*This order is intended to recognize and consecrate a commitment to the service of*
*Christ in the world, either in general terms or in connection with a particular*
*responsibility in the world or in the Church. It is designed to be used within a service*
*of worship. When used separately, it should follow appropriate praise and prayer,*
*scripture lessons, and sermon.*

*Individual reaffirmation of the Baptismal Covenant, using appropriate parts of the*
*service on 86-94, may be used as an alternative to this form, since baptism is the*
*Christian's basic consecration to ministry and its reaffirmation is appropriate to*
*celebrate any form of commitment to Christian service.*

*As a Response to the Word or at some other appropriate place within a public worship*
*service, the pastor invites the person(s) undertaking some special responsibility to*
*come forward and then says to the congregation:*

Dear friends, today we recognize the ministry of *Name(s)*
  and consecrate *him (her, each of them)* to a special task
    in the service of Jesus Christ.

*The pastor briefly describes the form of service to which each person is being*
*consecrated.*

*The person(s) may either remain standing or kneel for the act of consecration. The*
*pastor may lay hands on the head of each person and say to that person:*

*Name*, in the name of this congregation I commend you to this work
  and pledge to you our prayers, encouragement, and support.
May the Holy Spirit guide and strengthen you,
  that in this and in all things
    you may do God's will in the service of Jesus Christ.

*After the consecration(s) the pastor or deacon leads the congregation in extemporaneou
prayer or offers the following:*

Almighty God, look with favor upon *Name (these persons)*
who *reaffirm(s)* commitment to follow Christ and to serve in his name.
Give *him (her, each of them)* courage, patience, and vision;
and strengthen us all in our Christian vocation
of witness to the world and of service to others;
through Jesus Christ our Lord. **Amen.**

*A hymn may be sung and a blessing given. Jesus, We Are Here (BOW 187) and the
following hymns in UMH are suggested:*

| | |
|---|---|
| 425-50 Social Holiness | 548 In Christ There Is No East or West |
| 567-93 Called to God's Mission | 383 This Is a Day of New Beginnings |
| 939 Hymns listed under Commitment | 344 Tú Has Venido a la Orilla |
| 413 A Charge to Keep I Have | (Lord, You Have Come to the Lakeshore |
| 251 Go, Tell It on the Mountain | |

# AN ORDER FOR COMMISSIONING
# TO SHORT-TERM CHRISTIAN SERVICE

*This order may be used when persons are leaving for a work trip or project.*

*As a Response to the Word or at some other appropriate place within a public worship
service, the pastor invites the person(s) undertaking this service to come forward. The
pastor briefly describes the work trip or project and then says to the congregation:*

All who take upon themselves the name of Christ
are called into ministries of love and service by the example of Christ.
As these members of our community begin their work
among the people of *location,*
we pray the blessings of God and this community upon their endeavors.

*Congregation:*

**We recognize you as ambassadors of this congregation
in ministry with the people of** *location*
**and dedicate you to service in the name of Jesus Christ.
Through our prayers we will be united with you in your work.
May God richly bless your labors.**

*Pastor or deacon:*

Let us affirm our belief in the responsibilities of Christian service.

*The congregation may join those being commissioned in saying The World Methodist
Social Affirmation (UMH 886) or the following abbreviated version of The United
Methodist Social Creed:*

We believe in God, Creator of the world;
and in Jesus Christ, the Redeemer of creation.
We believe in the Holy Spirit, through whom we acknowledge God's gifts.
We commit ourselves to the rights and dignity of all persons
and to the improvement of the quality of life.
We dedicate ourselves to peace throughout the world
and to the rule of justice and law among all nations.
We believe in the present and final triumph
of God's Word in human affairs,
and gladly accept our commission
to manifest the life of the gospel in the world.

*A hymn may be sung and a blessing given. See hymn suggestions on 592.*

# AN ORDER FOR THE RECOGNITION OF A CANDIDATE

*This order may be used within a service of worship by a congregation to recognize a candidate for the ordained or licensed ministry after he or she has been certified as a candidate by the district Committee on Ordained Ministry or the conference Board of Ordained Ministry.*

*As a Response to the Word or immediately prior to taking some leadership role in the service, the candidate comes forward.*

*Pastor to congregation:*

Today we are happy to recognize *Name*
and celebrate *his/her* certification
as a candidate for the *ordained (licensed)* ministry
by the Committee on Ordained Ministry of the *Name* District
*(by the Board of Ordained Ministry of the* Name *Annual Conference)*
of The United Methodist Church.

*Pastor to candidate:*

*Name*, we rejoice with you
that you have heard God's call to the I *ordained (licensed)* ministry
and have said, with Isaiah: Here am I; send me!
The Church has certified you as a candidate for this ministry.
As you prepare for it in the months and years ahead,
we will stand with you and offer you our fullest support.

*Pastor or deacon to congregation:*

I invite you to stand and join with me in prayer for *Name*
as *he/she* prepares for *his/her* ministry.

*The pastor or deacon may pray extemporaneously, or the leader and congregation may join in the following prayer:*

Spirit of the living God,
   we pray for Name as he/she prepares to answer your call.
Guide him/her as he/she faces further decisions
   and strengthen him/her when the path is long and hard.
Keep us open to your guidance
   as we continue to offer our support
   and as we listen for your call in our own lives.
This we ask in Jesus' name. Amen.

*A hymn may be sung and a blessing given. See hymn suggestions on 713.*

# RECOGNITION OF ONE WHO HAS BEEN ORDAINED, COMMISSIONED, OR CERTIFIED

*This order may be used within a service of worship by a congregation to recogni:
someone after he or she has been ordained, commissioned, or certified by the Annu
Conference.*

*It is fitting that the person being recognized take a role in the service appropriate to th
ministry into which he or she has been ordained, commissioned, or certified.*

*The order may be led by the pastor or, if the pastor is the one being recognized, by anoth
leader such as the lay member of Annual Conference.*

*Prior to the Proclamation and Response, or as a Response to the Word, the person wh
has been ordained, commissioned, or certified stands before the people and faces the leade*

*The leader to the congregation:*

Today we are happy to recognize *Name*
   and celebrate *his/her* entry into this ministry.

*Leader to person being recognized:*

*Name*, we rejoice with you as you enter into this ministry.
As you carry on this ministry
   we will stand with you and offer you our fullest support.

*Leader to congregation:*

I invite you to stand and join with me in prayer for *Name*
   and for *his/her* ministry.

*The leader may pray extemporaneously, or the leader and congregation may join in the
following prayer:*

God of grace and power,
   pour out your Spirit on Name as he/she ministers [among us].
Guide and strengthen him/her for his/her ministry
   in all that lies ahead,

that together we may be one in ministry to all the world;
through the One in whom we all are one,
  your Son Jesus Christ our Lord. Amen.

*An appropriate gift or symbol of ministry may be presented.*

*A hymn may be sung and a blessing given. See hymn suggestions on 713.*

# AN ORDER FOR THE CELEBRATION
# OF AN APPOINTMENT

*This order is intended to be used within a service of worship by a congregation whose pastor or deacon has been newly appointed or reappointed by the bishop according to the polity of The United Methodist Church. The leader may be the chairperson of the Pastor-Parish Relations Committee or another designated leader in the congregation. The service may be adapted as needed where ministers other than the pastor are also appointed, reappointed, or assigned to ministry in a particular congregation.*

*Before the reading of the scripture lessons, the pastor, deacon, and any other staff under appointment come before the Lord's table, and the person officiating says to the congregation:*

Dear friends, today we welcome Name(s),
  who *has (have)* been (re)appointed to serve as our pastor(s).
We believe that *he/she is (they are)* well qualified
  and *has (have)* been prayerfully appointed by our bishop, *Name.*

*Leader to newly appointed staff:*

Name(s), you have been sent to live among us
  as *a bearer* of the Word of God;
  *a minister* of the Sacraments;
  and *a sustainer* of the love, order, and discipleship of the people of God.

*Leader to diaconal minister:*

Name, you are to represent the ministry of servanthood
  and to equip all Christians to be in ministry
    and in service to the community.]

*Pastor (and other staff):*

Today I (*we*) reaffirm this commitment in the presence of this congregation.

*Leader to congregation:*

Brothers and sisters in Christ,
as a people committed to participate in the ministries of the Church
  by your prayers, your presence, your gifts, your service, and your witness,
will you who celebrate this new beginning
  support and uphold Name(s) in these ministries?

*Congregation:*

**We reaffirm our commitment to support you
with our prayers, presence, gifts, service, and witness.**

*Leader:*

How beautiful upon the mountains are the feet of the messenger

*Congregation:*

**who announces peace, who brings good news, who announces salvation.**

*Praise God, from Whom All Blessings Flow (UMH 94-95), Glory Be to the Father
(UMH 70-71), or another doxology may be sung. See list of doxologies in UMH 951.
See also Doxology ( ♪ 182), Praise God, from Whom All Blessings Flow ( ♪ 180 and
♪ 185)*

*The leader continues with one of the following prayers or one of the prayers "For the
Church" on 501-06.*

Let us pray.

Eternal God, strengthen and sustain us in our ministries together,
    with *Name(s)* as our pastor(s) [and *Name* as our diaconal minister].
Give *him (her, them)* and us patience, courage, and wisdom
    so to care for one another and challenge one another
    that together we may follow Jesus Christ,
    living together in love,
    and offering our gifts and talents in your service;
through Jesus Christ our Lord. **Amen.**

Almighty God, you still call us to go into your service
    and spread the message of the salvation of your Son.
Bless richly, we pray, your servant(s) *Name(s)* entrance into our fellowship.
Fill *him (her, them)* with the power of your Holy Spirit
    and let *him (her, them)* find with us an open door for the Word.
We also pray for your Church on earth.
Equip us all with a spirit of willingness,
    that we with courage can witness about you
        by the profession of our mouths and through our way of living.
Grant us all to partake in your strength and joy,
    so that we can enter into the anxiety and suffering of the world,
        to be radiating and make alive that hope which Christ gives.
All this we dare to pray of you;
    for you are to us the Father of mercy and the God of all grace;
    you are the Son, the Savior and the Redeemer;
    you are the Holy Spirit, the Lord, the Helper and the Giver of Life.
Blessed be you. **Amen.**                    (UNITED METHODIST, SWEDEN, 20TH CENT., ALT

*esus, We Are Here (BOW 187) or another suitable hymn may be sung.*

*When a reappointment is being celebrated, the service continues with the congregational prayer below.*

*When a pastor, associate pastor, deacon, or diaconal minister is being appointed to a congregation for the first time, representatives of the congregation may make any or all of these presentations, or others as may be deemed appropriate. After each presentation, the newly appointed person responds* **Amen** *and places it on a table.*

*Presenter to pastor:*

*Name,* accept this Bible,
and be among us as one who proclaims the Word. **Amen.**

*Name,* take this water,
and baptize new Christians in this place. **Amen.**

*Name,* take this bread and cup,
and keep us in communion with Christ and his Church. **Amen.**

*Presenter to deacon or diaconal minister:*

*Name,* take this towel and basin,
and lead us to be servants of all. **Amen.**

*Presenter to pastor, deacon, or diaconal minister:*

*Name,* use this hymnal and book of worship
to guide us in our prayer and praise. **Amen.**

*Name,* receive this *Book of Discipline,*
and help us keep the covenant
that strengthens our connections as United Methodists. **Amen.**

*Name,* receive this globe,
and lead us in our mission to this community and all the world. **Amen.**

*Presenter to pastor:*

*Name,* receive this stole, signifying your ordination,
and shepherd us as our pastor. **Amen.**

*Presenter to deacon or diaconal minister:*

*Name,* receive this stole signifying your consecration,
and equip us for our ministries in the world. **Amen.**

*Then the pastor, deacon, or diaconal minister may take from the Lord's table the stole left by the previous pastor (see 598), put it on, and say:*

This yoke has been laid upon me, and I willingly take it upon myself.

*Pastor:* Let us pray.

*Congregation:*

**Lord God, bless the ministries of your Church.**
**We thank you for the variety of gifts you have bestowed upon us.**
**Draw us together in one Spirit,**
**that each of us may use our differing gifts as members of one body.**
**May your Word be proclaimed with faithfulness,**
**and may we be doers of your Word and not hearers only.**
**As we who have died and risen with Christ in baptism**
**gather at his table and then scatter into the world,**
**may we be one in service to others,**
**in the name of Jesus Christ our Lord. Amen.**

*The appointed minister may kneel, and the leader and others may lay hands on his/her head. The congregation may join hands and unite in this blessing:*

**The Lord bless you and keep you;**
**the Lord make his face to shine upon you, and be gracious to you;**
**the Lord lift up his countenance upon you, and give you peace. Amen.**

*Pastor:* The peace of the Lord be always with you.

*Congregation:* **And also with you.**

*A hymn or chorus may be sung. Tino tenda, Jesu (BOW 203); Jesus, We Are Here (BOW 187); and the following hymns from UMH are suggested:*

939  Hymns listed under Commitment      383  This Is a Day of New Beginnings
545  The Church's One Foundation        558  We Are the Church
546  The Church's One Foundation

# AN ORDER OF FAREWELL TO A PASTOR OR DEACON

*This order may be used within a service of worship on the last Sunday before a pastor or deacon moves to another congregation or retires, or it may take place at a special service. It may be adapted to be an order of farewell to a member of the church staff other than the pastor or deacon.*

*As a Response to the Word, the lay leader or another designated leader comes forward and announces that the time has come to say farewell to the pastor or deacon.*

*One or more persons may recall with thanksgiving the person's ministry.*

*A gift or symbol may be given with appropriate words of thanks. A stole may be left to put on the next pastor or deacon. See An Order for the Celebration of an Appointment (595).*

*The pastor or deacon and congregation may release one another with these or similar words:*

I thank you, the members and friends of *Name* United Methodist Church,
for the love and support you have shown me
while I have ministered among you.

am grateful for the ways my leadership has been accepted.
ask forgiveness for the mistakes I have made.
\s I leave, I carry with me all that I have learned here.

**Ve receive your thankfulness, offer forgiveness,**
 **and accept that you now leave to** *minister elsewhere (retire).*
**Ve express our gratitude for your time among us.**
**Ve ask your forgiveness for our mistakes.**
**(our influence on our faith and faithfulness**
 **will not leave us with your departure.**

accept your gratitude and forgiveness, and I forgive you,
 trusting that our time together and our parting
 are pleasing to God.
release you from turning to me and depending on me.
encourage your continuing ministry here
 and will pray for you and for your new *pastor (deacon), Name.*

*The pastor or deacon may pray extemporaneously, or lead the congregation in the
ollowing prayer:*

.et us pray.

**:ternal God, whose steadfast love for us is from everlasting to everlasting,**
 **we give you thanks for cherished memories**
 **and commend one another into your care as we move in new directions.**
**<eep us one in your love forever, through Jesus Christ our Lord. Amen.**

*A hymn may be sung. Suggested from* UMH:

| | |
|---|---|
| ;66 Blest Be the Dear Uniting Love | 670 Go Forth for God |
| 57 Blest Be the Tie That Binds | 667 Shalom Chaverim |
| 72 God Be with You | 666 Shalom to You |
| 73 God Be with You | |

*ee also:* Benediction (*BOW* 190); Shawnee Traveling Song (*BOW* 197); An Indian Blessing
*BOW* 186)

# AN ORDER FOR THE INSTALLATION OR RECOGNITION
# OF LEADERS IN THE CHURCH

*This order may be included in a service of worship when elected or appointed leaders in
he congregation are to be installed or recognized.*

*As a Response to the Word or at some other appropriate place within a public worship ser-
*ice, the pastor invites the leaders being recognized to come forward. The pastor presents
he leaders to the congregation and then says to them:*

)ear friends,
 you have been called by God and chosen by the people of God
 for leadership in the church.
'his ministry is a blessing and a serious responsibility.

It recognizes your special gifts
  and calls you to work among us and for us.
In love we thank you for accepting your obligation
  and challenge you to offer your best
    to the Lord, to this people, and to our ministry in the world.
Live a life in Christ
  and make him known in your witness and your work.

Today we *install* (*recognize*) *Names.*

*The pastor or deacon continues:*

Do you this day acknowledge yourself a faithful disciple of Jesus Christ?

**I do.**

Will you devote yourself to the service of God in the world?

**I will.**

Will you so live
  that you enable this church to be a people of love and peace?

**I will.**

Will you do all in your power
  to be responsible to the task for which you have been chosen?

**I will.**

[We also recognize those persons who have been elected to office
  by the United Methodist Men, United Methodist Women,
  and United Methodist Youth (*and other organizations as appropriate*)
  and are already installed in those organizations.]

Let us pray.

Almighty God, pour out your blessings upon these your servants
  who have been given particular ministries in your church.
Grant them grace to give themselves wholeheartedly in your service.
Keep before them the example of our Lord,
  who did not think first of himself, but gave himself for us all.
Let them share his ministry and consecration,
  that they may enter into his joy.
Guide them in their work.
Reward their faithfulness with the knowledge
  that through them your purposes are accomplished;
through Jesus Christ our Lord. **Amen.**

*The pastor addresses the congregation:*

Dear friends, rejoice that God provides laborers for the vineyards.
Will you do all you can to assist and encourage them
  in the responsibilities to which they have been called,
    giving them your cooperation, your counsel, and your prayers?

*he congregation responds:*

**Je will.**

*he pastor and deacon may greet the leaders individually.*

*hymn may be sung and a blessing given (see 598). Suggested hymns from* UMH:

| | |
|---|---|
| 39 Hymns listed under Commitment | 583 Sois la Semilla (You Are the Seed) |
| 44 Hymns listed under Installation | 415 Take Up Thy Cross |
| Services | 545 The Church's One Foundation |
| 78 God of Love and God of Power | 546 The Church's One Foundation |
| 70 Go Forth for God | 585 This Little Light of Mine |
| 31 Lord, Whose Love Through Humble | 558 We Are the Church |
| Service | 338 Where He Leads Me |
| 54 Sent Forth by God's Blessing | 582 Whom Shall I Send? |

# AN ORDER FOR THE INSTALLATION OR RECOGNITION OF CHURCH SCHOOL LEADERS

*his order may be included as a Response to the Word or at some other appropriate place*
*a service of congregational worship.*

*uring the singing of a hymn, the church school staff may gather in front of the*
*ngregation.*

*ollowing the hymn, the chairperson of education or the pastor introduces the staff. The*
*istor then says to the congregation:*

**ear friends,**
**let us recognize those who have responded to the call of God**
**to become workers in the church school.**
**teach, to administer the work of teaching,**
**and to support the work of teaching**
**are ministries of Christ among us.**
**hose called to these ministries need our loyal support and our prayers.**

*he pastor prays the following or another prayer:*

**et us pray.**

**ternal God, you have entrusted us with the message**
**of your power, grace, justice, and love.**
**rovide for us your guidance,**
**that we may be teachers and learners together.**
**elieving that you are in our midst,**
**we set apart those who would serve in our church school.**
**lay they serve you in nurturing the spiritual growth**
**of all who are entrusted in their care.**
**less each one gathered before us,**
**enabling them to be channels of your grace.**
**Je pray through Jesus Christ our Savior. Amen.**

*Pastor to church school staff:*

You have recognized God's call in your lives.
Will you endeavor to develop your gifts for teaching
  so as to continue to pass on the Christian faith?
Will you be faithful to the task,
  taking seriously the commitments of time and talent?
Will you take seriously your role as learner,
  studying diligently the Scriptures and traditions of the faith?

*Church school staff:*

We have heard God's call to teach
  and have responded to that call.
We teach, trusting in God's promises
  to support, sustain, and encourage us
  through gifts sufficient for the task.
We teach, relying on prayer and the presence of the Holy Spirit.
We teach, inviting others to recognize and respond
  to God's call in their lives.
We teach, depending on this congregation to uphold us in this task.

*Congregation:*

**We pledge ourselves to pray for you**
  **and for the educational ministry of this congregation.**
**We pledge ourselves to enable, encourage, and love you in this ministry**
**We pledge ourselves to be learners with you,**
  **diligently studying with you the Scriptures and traditions of the faith**

*The pastor may greet the church school workers individually.*

*A hymn may be sung and a blessing given. Suggested hymns from UMH:*

939 Hymns listed under Commitment
938 Hymns listed under Education
156 I Love to Tell the Story
381 Savior, Like a Shepherd Lead Us
583 Sois la Semilla (You Are the Seed)

277 Tell Me the Stories of Jesus
601 Thy Word Is a Lamp
344 Tu Has Venido a la Orilla (Lord, Yo
  Have Come to the Lakeshore)
558 We Are the Church

# AN ORDER FOR THE COMMISSIONING
# OF CLASS LEADERS

*This order is intended for the public commissioning of class leaders following the*
*appointment by a Charge or Church Conference of the congregation.*

*The order may be led by the pastor of the congregation, the district superintendent, of*
*the bishop of the area.*

*As a Response to the Word or at some other appropriate place within a service of*
*congregational worship, the pastor invites the newly appointed class leader(s) to com*
*forward.*

*astor to congregation:*

ear friends,

e office of class leader is one of the most important contributions
made by world Methodism
    to the pastoral leadership of Christ's holy Church.

the General Rules of 1743,
John Wesley described the Methodist societies
as companies of men and women who,
aving the form, and seeking the power of godliness,"
me together in order to pray,
to receive the word of exhortation,
and "to watch over one another in love
    that they may help each other work out their salvation."
this end, the societies were divided into small companies, called classes,
each with an appointed leader
"to advise, reprove, comfort, or exhort, as occasion may require."

ass leaders of today continue this tradition.
the founding *Discipline* of our church, they are described as persons
"not only of sound judgment, but truly devoted to God,"
who are willing to help others in the congregation
"to grow in the knowledge and love of God."

*astor to class leader(s):*

o you accept the office of class leader
in this congregation of The United Methodist Church?

**do.**

ill you exercise this office
helping other members of the congregation
to fulfill the general rule of discipleship:
witness to Jesus Christ in the world, and to follow his teachings
through acts of compassion, justice, worship, and devotion,
under the guidance of the Holy Spirit?

**will.**

ill you help other members of the congregation
to be accountable for their discipleship,
not by judging them, but by watching over them in love?

**will.**

ill you meet weekly in covenant with others of like mind
and purpose to be accountable for your own discipleship?

**I will.**

*Pastor to congregation:*

Will you affirm the call of *these men and women* to be *class leaders*
in this congregation of The United Methodist Church?

**We will.**

Will you acknowledge *them* as your *leaders* in discipleship,
and accept *their* guidance as *they* watch over you in love?

**We will.**

*Pastor to class leader(s):*

You are hereby commissioned as *class leaders*
in this congregation of The United Methodist Church.

Let us pray.

Most gracious God,
bless your servant(s)
whom we now entrust with the office of class leader.
Grant *them* wisdom tempered by your love,
and courage tempered by your justice,
so that Jesus Christ might be honored and served
by all in this congregation,
to the furtherance of your coming reign, on earth as in heaven;
through the same Jesus Christ our Lord. **Amen.**

UMH 438, *Forth in Thy Name, O Lord, may then be sung.*

# AN ORDER FOR THE INSTALLATION
# OR RECOGNITION
# OF PERSONS IN MUSIC MINISTRIES

*This order may be included as a Response to the Word or at some other appropria*
*place in a service of worship when choirs, their directors, song leaders, an*
*instrumentalists are to be installed or recognized.*

*The pastor addresses the congregation:*

Dear friends, let us recognize those who have responded to the call of Go
to the ministry of music in the church.
To direct, to sing, and to play instruments
are ministries of Christ among us.
Those called to these ministries need our loyal support and our prayer

*he chairperson of worship or the pastor reads the names of the persons and choirs to
recognized, and they come forward to stand before the pastor, who says to them:*

Making music to the praise of God in the congregation
is a ministry that requires devotion and discipline.
Do you accept responsibility for this ministry?

**do.**

Will you be faithful to the disciplines of music?

**will.**

May the faith expressed by your music live in your heart,
and what you believe in your heart, practice in your life.
And may God give you grace
to offer your music and your life in faithfulness and consecration,
now, and in the world to come.

*he pastor then says to the congregation:*

Dear friends, I commend to you these persons.
To them has been given the ministry of music in the church.
Will you sustain them with your encouragement and your prayers,
as together we seek to offer praise to God?

*he congregation responds:*

**We will.**

*he pastor and congregation pray together:*

**Lord, our God, bless these ministries of music
and those who offer them in your service.
Give to these persons love for you and your people,
fullness of heart as they praise you,
and diligence that their music may be a worthy offering to your glory;
through Jesus Christ our Lord. Amen.**

*he pastor may greet those engaged in music ministries, or their leaders,
individually.*

*hymn may be sung and a blessing given. Suggested hymns from UMH:*

| | |
|---|---|
| 99 Hymns listed under Commitment | 105 God of Many Names |
| 62 All Creatures of Our God and King | 100 God, Whose Love Is Reigning o'er Us |
| 62 Alleluia, Alleluia | 333 I'm Goin' a Sing When the Spirit Says |
| 81 ¡Canta, Debora, Canta! | Sing |
| (Sing, Debora, Sing!) | 89 Joyful, Joyful, We Adore Thee |
| 149 Cantemos al Senor | 93 Let All the World in Every Corner Sing |
| (Let's Sing unto the Lord) | 733 Marching to Zion |
| 568 Christ for the World We Sing | 160-161 Rejoice, Ye Pure in Heart |
| 158 Come, Christians, Join to Sing | 126 Sing Praise to God Who Reigns Above |
| 304 Easter People, Raise Your Voices | 68 When in Our Music God Is Glorified |

# AN ORDER FOR THE DEDICATION OR CONSECRATION OF AN ORGAN OR OTHER MUSICAL INSTRUMENTS

*This order is intended to be used within a service of worship. If the instrument is give in memory of a person who has died or in honor of someone living, the phrases i brackets [ ] are added.*

*If a special dedication service is held, it may begin with appropriate prayer and praisе scripture lessons, and sermon; and it may close with a hymn and Dismissal wit Blessing.*

### Scripture Lessons and Psalms

| | |
|---|---|
| 2 Samuel 6:1-5 | David praises God with instruments. |
| Psalm 33:1-3 (*UMH* 767) | Play skillfully on instruments. |
| Psalm 81:1-3 (*UMH* 803) | Sing and play instruments to God. |
| Psalm 150 (*UMH* 862) | Praise God with instruments. |
| Colossians 3:12-17 | Sing to God. |

### Suggested Hymns from UMH

587 Bless Thou the Gifts
149 Cantemos al Señor
    (Let's Sing unto the Lord)
93 Let All the World in Every Corner Sing

380 There's Within My Heart a Melody
87 What Gift Can We Bring
68 When in Our Music God Is Glorifiе

*The donor, or someone designated to present the instrument, stands before th congregation and says:*

We present this *instrument* to be consecrated
to the glory of almighty God and for service in this congregation
[in *loving memory (honor)* of *Name*].

*The pastor and people respond:*

It is good to give thanks to the Lord,
**to sing praises to your name, O Most High,**

to declare your steadfast love in the morning,
**and your faithfulness at night,**

to the music of the lute and the harp,
**to the melody of the lyre.**

For you, O Lord, have made me glad by your work;
**at the works of your hands I sing for joy.**

*All sing the Gloria Patri or other doxology. See 18-19.*

*Dedicatory music is played on the instrument(s) to be consecrated.*

et us pray.

ternal God,
whom the generations have worshiped through the gift of music,
ccept our praise to you in the sound of this instrument,
which we consecrate in your name and to your glory.
rant that its music may be a blessing to all who worship here,
and that they may be consecrated to you,
whose sound has gone out through all the earth
   and whose words to the end of the world.
et our music be so joined to your holy Word
that your glory may surround us
   and empower us for the service to which you call us in the world;
rough Jesus Christ our Lord. **Amen.**

# AN ORDER FOR THE DEDICATION
# OF CHURCH FURNISHINGS AND MEMORIALS

*his order is intended to be used within a service of worship. When used separately, it ould follow praise, prayer, scripture lessons, and sermon. It can be used for the dication not only of indoor furnishings but also of gardens, signs, bells, and parking ts. If the gift is given in memory of a person who has died or in honor of someone ring, the phrases in brackets [ ] are added.*

*he donor, or someone designated to present the gift or memorial, stands before the ngregation and says:*

Ve present this _____ to be consecrated
to the glory of almighty God and for service in this church
[in *loving memory (honor) of Name*].

*ther phrases may also be added as appropriate.*

*he person designated to accept the gift says:*

Ve accept this _____as a sacred trust and will guard and use it reverently
[in *loving memory (honor) of Name*].

*ther phrases may also be added as appropriate. Then the pastor says:*

the name of the Father, and of the Son, and of the Holy Spirit
(*in the name of the holy and triune God*),
e consecrate this _____ to the glory of God
[and in *memory (honor)* of God's servant *Name*.
The memory of the righteous is ever blessed].

*ther phrases may also be added as appropriate. The pastor continues:*

et us pray.

Most loving God, without you no words or works of ours have meaning
Accept the gifts of our hands as symbols of our devotion.
Grant us your blessing, as we have consecrated this gift to your glory,
   that it may be an enduring witness before all your people,
   and that our lives may be consecrated in your service;
through Jesus Christ our Lord. **Amen.**

*A hymn may be sung. Suggested from* UMH:

942 Hymns listed under Gratitude
938 Hymns listed under Thanksgiving Day
587 Bless Thou the Gifts

555 Forward Through the Ages
712 I Sing a Song of the Saints of God
589 The Church of Christ, in Every Age

*See also:* Tino tenda Jesu (♪ 203).

# A SERVICE FOR THE BLESSING OF ANIMALS

*A Blessing of Animals, in many congregations, witnesses to God's and the Church*
*love, care, and concern for creation. As we recognize our mutual interdependenc*
*with God's creatures, the Church's witness of stewardship of creation is strengthenec*
*It is also a service with special appeal to children.*

*The Blessing is best celebrated during daylight in the outdoors—in the churchyard c*
*in a park. It may be celebrated at any time of the year, especially in early spring, or o*
*the Feast Day of St. Francis of Assisi, October 4. Make allowances for the arrival c*
*larger animals such as horses and other livestock. The space may contain a table o*
*which the Bible or musical instruments may be placed. Music is best led b*
*instruments that work well outdoors—trumpets, accordions, drums, and guitars*
*Bulletins are awkward and should be used only to provide the texts of hymns to b*
*sung.*

## GATHERING AND GREETING

*When most animals and their friends have arrived, the leader invites all to form*
*large circle around the table. The leader begins:*

The animals of God's creation inhabit the skies, the earth, and the sea
They share in the fortunes of human existence
   and have a part in human life.
God, who confers gifts on all living things,
   has often used the service of animals
   or made them reminders of the gifts of salvation.
Animals were saved from the flood
   and afterwards made a part of the covenant with Noah. (GENESIS 9:9-1

The paschal lamb recalls the passover sacrifice
   and the deliverance from slavery in Egypt. (EXODUS 12:3-1

A giant fish saved Jonah; (JONAH 2:1-1

ravens brought bread to Elijah;                    (1 KINGS 17:6)

animals were included in the repentance of Nineveh;        (JONAH 3:7)

and animals share in Christ's redemption of all God's creation.
We, therefore, invoke God's blessing on these animals.
As we do so, let us praise the Creator
    and thank God for setting us as stewards
        over all the creatures of the earth.

**YMN** *Suggested hymns from UMH:*

| | |
|---|---|
| 62 All Creatures of Our God and King | 122 God of the Sparrow, God of the Whale |
| 147 All Things Bright and Beautiful | 152 I Sing the Almighty Power of God |
| 149 Cantemos al Señor | 148 Many and Great, O God |
| (Let's Sing unto the Lord) | 144 This Is My Father's World |
| 227 The Friendly Beasts | |

**CRIPTURE** *Suggested lessons and psalms:*

| | |
|---|---|
| Genesis 1 | The creation |
| Genesis 6:17-22 | Animals on the ark |
| Isaiah 11:6-9 | The wolf and the lamb |
| Psalm 8 (*UMH* 743) | The work of your fingers |
| Psalm 148 (*UMH* 861) | Praise the Lord for creation. |

**RAYER**

*The following, or St. Francis' Prayer for All Created Things (507), or a prayer from 507-08 may be prayed.*

God created us and placed us on the earth
    to be stewards of all living things,
        therefore let us proclaim the glory of our Creator, saying:
**O God, how wonderful are the works of your hands.**

Blessed are you, O Lord of the Universe; you create the animals
    and give us the ability to train them to help us in our work. R

Blessed are you, O Lord of the Universe;
    you give us food from animals to replenish our energies. R

Blessed are you, O Lord of the Universe; for the sake of our comfort
    you give us domestic animals as companions. R

Blessed are you, O Lord of the Universe; you care for us
    even as you care for the birds of the air. R

Blessed are you, O Lord of the Universe;
    you offered your Son to us as the passover lamb
    and in him willed that we should be called your children. R

PRAYER OF BLESSING

*The leader says the following prayer with hands outstretched or may touch an*
*bless each animal. The animals may form a procession to be blessed.*

Bless, O Lord, *this (these)* creature(s),
   and fill our hearts with thanksgiving for *its (their)* being.

HYMN *See suggestions on 609.*

DISMISSAL WITH BLESSING

May God, who created the animals of this earth,
   continue to protect and sustain us all,
   now and for ever. **Amen.**

# A SERVICE FOR THE BLESSING OF A HOME

GATHERING *Family and friends gather inside or outside the home.*

GREETING *The leader addresses the family and friends:*

Jesus said: "Listen! I am standing at the door, knocking;
   if you hear my voice and open the door, I will come in."

Dear friends,
   we have gathered together to seek God's blessing upon this home,
   which by the favor of God and human labor has been made ready
This home is not only a dwelling
   but a symbol to us of God's loving care
      and of our life together as the family of Christ.
Let us therefore bring praise and thanksgiving
   for goodness and mercy and for our communion,
offering ourselves as God's servants
   and as loving sisters and brothers to one another.

OPENING PRAYER

Let us pray.

Almighty and everlasting God,
   grant to this home the grace of your presence,
   that you may be known to inhabit this dwelling
      and defend this household;
through Jesus Christ our Lord, who with you and the Holy Spirit
   lives and reigns, one God, for ever and ever. **Amen.**

SCRIPTURE *Suggested lessons:*

| | |
|---|---|
| Joshua 24:14-15 | As for me and my household, we will serve the Lord. |
| 1 John 4:11-21 | Those who abide in love abide in God. |
| Acts 2:43-47 | Day by day . . . they broke bread at home. |
| Ephesians 3:14-21 | Every family takes its name from God. |
| Matthew 6:25-33 | Do not worry about your life. |
| Matthew 7:24-27 | A house built on rock |
| John 14:1-3 | In my Father's house are many dwellings. |

## CONSECRATION OF THE HOME

In the name of the Father, and of the Son, and of the Holy Spirit
*(in the name of the holy and triune God),*
    we consecrate this home,
    committing to God's love and care *all (the one)* who dwell(s)
therein.
**Amen.**
Let us pray.
Eternal God, bless this home.
Let your love rest upon it and your promised presence be manifested
in it.
May *the members of this household (Name)*
    grow in grace and in the knowledge of our Lord Jesus Christ.
Teach *them (him, her)* to love, as you have loved us;
and help us all to live in the peace of Jesus Christ our Lord. **Amen.**

*The service may conclude with the Lord's Prayer and Dismissal with
Blessing or as indicated below.*

## CONSECRATION OF A PARSONAGE

*This may be used in place of Consecration of the Home above.*

In the name of the Father, and of the Son, and of the Holy Spirit
    *(in the name of the holy and triune God),*
    we consecrate this home for the pastors *(diaconal ministers)*
        and their families
    of *Name* United Methodist Church. **Amen.**

Let us pray.
Eternal God, bless this home provided as a parsonage
    to assure the domestic comfort of those called of God
        and appointed by the Bishop to serve this congregation.
May those who reside here
    experience the love and support of this congregation
        as very special persons in this family of God.
Help us love each other as you have loved us
    and help us all to live in the peace of Jesus Christ our Lord.
**Amen.**

*The service may conclude with the Lord's Prayer and Dismissal with
Blessing or as indicated below.*

## SYMBOLIC ACTS

*At this point symbolic expressions may be appropriate: the presentation of a gift such as a cross, painting, or other gift, or the planting of a tree or shrub. These actions may be accompanied by suitable blessings.*

## HOLY COMMUNION

*It is appropriate to gather the people for a household celebration of Holy Communion, with the pastor presiding, using the dining table as the Lord's table and perhaps bread baked in the oven of the new home. See The Great Thanksgiving on 52-53 or 81 and hymn suggestions on UMH 943.*

## BLESSING

# VIII. HEALING SERVICES
# AND PRAYERS

## INTRODUCTION

cripture strongly affirms ministries of spiritual healing, which in recent
ears have received renewed emphasis throughout Christ's holy Church.
he root of the word *healing* in New Testament Greek, *sozo*, is the same as
at of *salvation* and *wholeness*. Spiritual healing is God's work of offering
ersons balance, harmony, and wholeness of body, mind, spirit, and
lationships through confession, forgiveness, and reconciliation. Through
ich healing, God works to bring about reconciliation between God and
imanity, among individuals and communities, within each person, and
tween humanity and the rest of creation. The New Testament records that
sus himself healed the estranged and sick and sent out his disciples on
inistries of healing. James (5:14-16a) calls us also to pray for and anoint the
ck, that they may be healed.

ll healing is of God. The Church's healing ministry in no way detracts from
e gifts God gives through medicine and psychotherapy. It is no substitute
r either medicine or the proper care of one's health. Rather, it adds to our
tal resources for wholeness.

ealing is not magic, but underlying it is the great mystery of God's love.
hose who minister spiritual healing are channels of God's love. Although
one can predict what will happen in a given instance, many marvelous
ealings have taken place.

od does not promise that we shall be spared suffering but does promise to
with us in our suffering. Trusting that promise, we are enabled to
cognize God's sustaining presence in pain, sickness, injury, and
trangement.

ikewise, God does not promise that we will be cured of all illnesses; and we
l must face the inevitability of death. A Service of Healing is not necessarily
service of curing, but it provides an atmosphere in which healing can

happen. The greatest healing of all is the reunion or reconciliation of human being with God. When this happens, physical healing sometime occurs, mental and emotional balance is often restored, spiritual health i enhanced, and relationships are healed. For the Christian the basic purpos of spiritual healing is to renew and strengthen one's relationship with th living Christ.

Patterns of healing services grow out of both Church traditions and th needs of the moment. Prayers for healing, accompanied if desired b anointing with the laying on of hands, may be incorporated into any servic of congregational worship as a Response to the Word. Also, there may be healing service at a stated time each week or month, or healing may b ministered privately to individuals. Many find not only prayer but also Hol Communion, laying on of hands, and anointing with oil to be healing.

Laying on of hands, anointing with oil, and the less formal gesture c holding someone's hand all show the power of touch, which plays a centr role in the healings recorded in the New Testament. Jesus often touche others—blessing children, washing feet, healing injuries or disease, an raising people from death. Biblical precedent combines with our natur desire to reach out to persons in need in prompting us to touch gently an lovingly those who ask for healing prayers. Such an act is a tangibl expression of the presence of the healing Christ, working in and throug those who minister in his name.

Anointing the forehead with oil is a sign act invoking the healing love c God. The oil points beyond itself and those doing the anointing to the actio of the Holy Spirit and the presence of the healing Christ, who is God' Anointed One. Olive oil is traditionally used in anointing but can becom rancid. Sweet oil, which is olive oil with a preservative, is available in an pharmacy. Fragrant oils may be used, but care must be taken because som people are allergic to perfumes.

In addition to the general services of healing provided below, resources ar included for special needs: for persons grieving after loss of pregnancy, fc persons going through divorce, for a person suffering from addiction c substance abuse, for a person with AIDS, for a person with life-threatenin illness, and for a person in a coma or unable to communicate. The suggeste scriptures, prayers, and hymns may be used in a Service of Healing or on an suitable occasion. The prayers of confession in UMH 890-93 and on 474-9 will be useful in many situations, particularly when there is a need fc reconciliation (healing of relationships) with God, with other people, an with oneself. Also, the following prayers for healing are found in UMH

466 An Invitation to Christ
458 Dear Lord, for All in Pain (may be
 spoken or sung)
457 For the Sick

461 For Those Who Mourn
460 In Time of Illness
481 Prayer of Saint Francis
459 The Serenity Prayer

is important that those ministering in services of healing be sensitive to the
fferences that exist among those who come for healing ministries. Sound
eaching, teaching, and pastoral care are essential for healing ministries to
complish their purpose.

# A SERVICE OF HEALING I

*is is a congregational service centered on healing and is for use at some time other
in that of the principal weekly congregational worship service. It may be freely
apted to meet specific needs.*

ATHERING *See 16-17.*

REETING * *One of the following may be used:*

Are any among you sick?
They should call for the elders of the church
    and have them pray over them,
    anointing them with oil in the name of the Lord.
The prayer of faith will save the sick,
    and the Lord will raise them up;
    and anyone who has committed sins will be forgiven.
Therefore confess your sins to one another,
    and pray for one another,
    so that you may be healed.         (JAMES 5:14-16a)

May grace and peace be yours in abundance
    in the knowledge of God and of Jesus our Lord.     (2 PETER 1:2)
We have come to lift up our brothers and sisters before the Lord
    that they might receive healing.
Let those who seek God's healing
    open their hearts to the Spirit of the Lord.

Bless the Lord, O my soul!
**And all that is within me, bless God's holy name!**

Bless the Lord, O my soul, and forget not all God's benefits.
**The Lord forgives all our iniquity, and heals all our diseases.**

The Lord redeems our lives from the pit,
    and crowns us with steadfast love and mercy.
**God satisfies us with good as long as we live**
    **so that our youth is renewed like the eagle's.**

YMN OF PRAISE * *See 17-20.*

*A hymn of adoration and praise (see UMH 57-152 and the listing in UMH 934) or
one of the hymns of healing listed below on 620 may be sung.*

OPENING PRAYER * *The following or another prayer may be used. See 20-2*

Almighty and everlasting God,
who can banish all affliction both of soul and of body,
show forth your power upon those in need,
that by your mercy they may be restored to serve you afresh
in holiness of living, through Jesus Christ our Lord. **Amen.**

SCRIPTURE *Suggested lessons and psalms:*

| | |
|---|---|
| Ecclesiastes 3:1-11a | For everything there is a season. |
| Isaiah 26:3-4 | Trust in the Lord forever. |
| Isaiah 35:1-10 | Restoration of all that is broken |
| Isaiah 40:28-31 | The weak shall renew their strength. |
| Isaiah 43:1-3a, 18-19, 25 | When you pass through the waters |
| Isaiah 53:3-5 | With his stripes we are healed. |
| Isaiah 61:1-3a | Good tidings to the afflicted |
| Psalm 13 (*UMH* 746) | A prayer of pain and sorrow |
| Psalm 23 | You have anointed my head with oil. |
| | *See* UMH *128, 136, 137, 138, 518, 754.* |
| Psalm 27 (*UMH* 758) | God is the strength of my life. |
| Psalm 30 (*UMH* 762) | Recovery from grave illness |
| Psalm 41 (*UMH* 776) | Assurance of God's help |
| Psalm 42 (*UMH* 777) | My soul longs for you. |
| Psalm 51:1-12, 15-17 (*UMH* 785) | Create in me a clean heart. |
| Psalm 91 (*UMH* 810) | Refuge under God's wings |
| Psalm 103 (*UMH* 824) | God forgives all your sins. |
| Psalm 130 (*UMH* 515, 516, 848) | Out of the depths |
| Psalm 138 (*UMH* 853) | Fulfill your purpose for me. |
| Psalm 139 (*UMH* 854) | The inescapable God |
| Psalm 146 (*UMH* 858) | God lifts the bowed down. |
| Acts 3:1-10 | Peter and John heal the lame man. |
| Acts 5:12-16 | Healings in Jerusalem |
| Romans 8 | Nothing can separate us from God's love. |
| Romans 14:7-12 | We live to the Lord. |
| 2 Corinthians 1:3-5 | God comforts us in affliction. |
| 2 Corinthians 4:16-18 | What can be seen is temporary. |
| Colossians 1:11-29 | May you be strengthened with all power. |
| Hebrews 12:1-2 | Jesus, the perfecter of our faith |
| James 5:13-16 | Is any among you sick? |
| 1 John 4:16b-19 | There is no fear in love. |
| 1 John 5:13-15 | The confidence we have in Christ |
| Revelation 21:1-4 | New heaven and new earth |
| Matthew 5:1-12 | Blessed are they. |
| Matthew 8:1-13 | The healing of a leper and servant |
| Matthew 10:1-8 | Jesus sends the twelve disciples to heal. |
| Matthew 11:28-30 | All who labor and are heavy laden |
| Matthew 15:21-28 | The Canaanite woman's faith |
| Matthew 26:36-39 | Not what I want, but what you want |
| Mark 1:21-28 | Jesus heals a man with an unclean spirit. |
| Mark 5:1-20 | My name is Legion, for we are many. |
| Mark 5:21-43 | Girl restored to life, a woman healed |

| | |
|---|---|
| Mark 6:7-13 | Anointing of the sick with oil |
| Mark 6:53-56 | People brought the sick to Jesus. |
| Mark 8:22-26 | A blind man at Bethsaida |
| Mark 10:46-52 | Take heart; rise, Jesus is calling you. |
| Luke 5:17-26 | Take up your pallet and walk. |
| Luke 7:11-17 | Jesus raises the widow's son at Nain. |
| Luke 8:43-48 | The woman with an issue of blood |
| Luke 17:11-19 | Thanksgiving for healing |
| John 3:16-17 | God so loved the world |
| John 5:2-18 | Do you want to be healed? |
| John 9 | Healing of the man born blind |
| John 11:1-44 | Raising of Lazarus |

SERMON, MEDITATION, OR TESTIMONY

[AFFIRMATION OF FAITH OR OTHER RESPONSE TO THE WORD]

CONFESSION AND PARDON

*If James 5:14-16a has not been read earlier in the service, it may be read as a call to confession.*

*The congregation may pray a confession such as one of those in* UMH 890-93 *or on 474-94, or an appropriate psalm (see above).*

*The confession is followed by silence and these or other words of pardon.*

*Leader to people:*

Hear the good news:
   Christ died for us while we were yet sinners;
   that proves God's love toward us.
In the name of Jesus Christ, you are forgiven!

*People to leader:*

**In the name of Jesus Christ, you are forgiven.**

*Leader and people:*

**Glory to God. Amen.**

*The congregation may then sing a response of praise and thanksgiving such as one of the following from* UMH:

| | |
|---|---|
| 162 Alleluia, Alleluia | 78 Heleluyan |
| 72 Gloria, Gloria | 84 Thank You, Lord |

*See also:*
Tino tenda Jesu ( ♪ 203)
Heleluyan ( ♪ 176)
Praised Be Our Lord ( ♪ 204)

THE PEACE *] *See 26.*

*If desired, the Peace, Offering, and Holy Communion may follow the Anointing and Laying on of Hands.*

[OFFERING] *See 26-27.*

[HOLY COMMUNION]

*The pastor may administer Holy Communion to all present who wish to share at th*
*Lord's table, the people using A Service of Word and Table III (UMH 15) or one c*
*the musical settings (UMH 17-25) and the pastor using the following.*

*The pastor, standing if possible behind the Lord's table, facing the people from thi*
*time through the Breaking of Bread, takes the bread and cup; and the bread and win*
*are prepared for the meal. The pastor then prays:*

The Lord be with you.
**And also with you.**
Lift up your hearts. *The pastor may lift hands and keep them raised.*
**We lift them up to the Lord.**
Let us give thanks to the Lord our God.
**It is right to give our thanks and praise.**

It is right, and a good and joyful thing,
    always and everywhere to give thanks to you,
    Father Almighty (*almighty God*), creator of heaven and earth.
In the beginning, when darkness covered the face of the earth
    and nothing existed but chaos,
    your Spirit swept across the waters.
You spoke but a word, and light was separated from darkness.

And so, with your people on earth and all the company of heaven
    we praise your name and join their unending hymn:

*The pastor may lower hands.*

**Holy, holy, holy Lord, God of power and might,**
**heaven and earth are full of your glory. Hosanna in the highest.**
**Blessed is he who comes in the name of the Lord. Hosanna in the highest**

*The pastor may raise hands.*

Holy are you, and blessed is your Son Jesus Christ:
    who lived among us and knew human pain and suffering;
    who called all who were burdened and heavy laden and gave them rest
    who healed the sick, fed the hungry, and ate with sinners;
    who cast out demons and showed us the way to you through faith
    who took our suffering upon himself,
        that we might be cleansed of our sins and receive eternal life.
By the baptism of his suffering, death, and resurrection,
    you gave birth to your Church,
    delivered us from slavery to sin and death,
    and made with us a new covenant by water and the Spirit.

*The pastor may hold hands, palms down, over the bread, or touch the bread, or lift the bread.*

On the night in which he gave himself up for us, he took bread,
gave thanks to you, broke the bread, gave it to his disciples, and said:
"Take, eat; this is my body which is given for you.
Do this in remembrance of me."

*The pastor may hold hands, palms down, over the cup, or touch the cup, or lift the cup.*

When the supper was over he took the cup,
gave thanks to you, gave it to his disciples, and said:
"Drink from this, all of you; this is my blood of the new covenant,
poured out for you and for many for the forgiveness of sins.
Do this, as often as you drink it, in remembrance of me."

*The pastor may raise hands.*

And so, in remembrance of these your mighty acts in Jesus Christ,
we offer ourselves in praise and thanksgiving
as a holy and living sacrifice, in union with Christ's offering for us,
as we proclaim the mystery of faith:

**Christ has died; Christ is risen; Christ will come again.**

*The pastor may hold hands, palms down, over the bread and cup.*

Pour out your Holy Spirit on us gathered here,
and on these gifts of bread and wine.
Make them be for us the body and blood of Christ,
that we may be for the world the body of Christ, redeemed by his blood.

*The pastor may raise hands.*

By the same Spirit heal us in body, mind, and spirit,
cleansing away all that would separate us from you.
By your Spirit make us one with Christ,
one with each other, and one in ministry to all the world,
until Christ comes in victory, and we feast at his heavenly banquet.

Through your Son Jesus Christ, with the Holy Spirit in your holy Church,
all honor and glory is yours, almighty Father (*God*), now and for ever.

**Amen.**

*All pray the Lord's Prayer, using one of the forms in* UMH *270-71, 894-96.*

*The pastor, still standing behind the Lord's table, facing the people, breaks the bread and then lifts the cup, in silence or with appropriate words.*

*The bread and wine are given to the people, with these or other words being exchanged:*

The body of Christ, given for you. **Amen.**
The blood of Christ, given for you. **Amen.**

*When all have received, the Lord's table is put in order (see 30).*

## [THANKSGIVING OVER THE OIL *]

*If desired, this act may precede Holy Communion.*

*If James 5:14-16a has not been read earlier in the service, it may be read here as a introduction to the anointing.*

Let us pray.

O God, the giver of health and salvation,
 we give thanks to you for the gift of oil.
As your holy apostles anointed many who were sick and healed them,
 so pour out your Holy Spirit on us and on this gift,
 that those who in faith and repentance receive this anointing
  may be made whole;
through Jesus Christ our Lord. **Amen.**

## [HYMN OF HEALING *]

*One of the hymns listed in UMH 943-44 under Healing or Hope or in UMH 94 under Courage, or one of the following hymns in UMH, or another suitable hym may be sung by the congregation or by a choir or solo voice.*

516 Canticle of Redemption
130 God Will Take Care of You
560 Help Us Accept Each Other
474 Precious Lord, Take My Hand

523 Saranam, Saranam
393 Spirit of the Living God
375 There Is a Balm in Gilead

## PRAYERS FOR HEALING AND WHOLENESS
## WITH ANOINTING AND/OR LAYING ON OF HANDS

*People may be invited to come forward individually or as a group to the communio rail or other designated prayer area and express any specific concerns they ma have. They may be ministered to by the pastor, by other designated persons, or b prayer teams of two or three persons each. All prayer team members lay on hand and share in silent and spoken prayer.*

*The congregation and choir may sing hymns. See hymns suggested above.*

*If there is anointing with oil, a leader touches a thumb to the oil and makes the sig of the cross on the person's forehead, in silence or using these or similar word*

*Name,* I anoint you with oil
in the name of the Father, and of the Son, and of the Holy Spirit
 (*in the name of the holy and triune God*)
 (*in the name of Jesus, the Christ, your Savior and Healer*)
[for *specified purpose*].

*If there is laying on of hands, a leader, who may be joined by others, lays hands upon each person's head, in silence or using these or similar words:*

Name, I (*we*) lay my (*our*) hands on you
(*These hands are laid upon you*)
in the name of the Father, and of the Son, and of the Holy Spirit
  (*in the name of the holy and triune God*)
  (*in the name of Jesus, the Christ, your Savior and Healer*)
[for *specified purpose*].

May the power of God's indwelling presence heal you of all illnesses—
  of body, mind, spirit, and relationships—
that you may serve God with a loving heart. **Amen.**

## ³RAYER AFTER ANOINTING AND/OR LAYING ON OF HANDS *

*The following, or one of the prayers for special concerns on 626-29, or another suitable prayer may be used.*

Almighty God,
  we pray that *Names* (*our brothers and sisters*)
    may be comforted in their suffering and made whole.
When they are afraid, give them courage;
when they feel weak, grant them your strength;
when they are afflicted, afford them patience;
when they are lost, offer them hope;
when they are alone, move us to their side;
[when death comes, open your arms to receive *him/her*].
In the name of Jesus Christ we pray. **Amen.**

## SHARING OF THANKSGIVINGS]

*Persons who feel so led may give thanks for healing or other blessings.*

## ⁴YMN * *One of the hymns suggested above or another suitable hymn.*

## ⁾ISMISSAL WITH BLESSING * *See 31-32.*

The Lord who heals all your iniquity bless and keep you;
the face of the Lord who heals all your afflictions
  shine upon you and be gracious to you;
the light of the countenance of the Lord who redeems your life
  be lifted upon you and give you peace. **Amen.**

## ⌐OING FORTH * *See 32.*

# A SERVICE OF HEALING II

*This service may be used in private or in corporate worship. It may take place in a church, home, or hospital, or at a meeting of a prayer group. The service may be adapted for special needs by selecting appropriate portions from it and from any of the additional resources on 626-29. Hymns suggested in A Service of Healing I may also be used.*

## GREETING AND PREPARATION

SCRIPTURE *See lessons suggested above (616-17).*

*Comments on the lesson(s) may be added as appropriate.*

## CONFESSION AND PARDON

*If it seems appropriate, the person(s) present may be invited to share any trouble or difficulty that hinders his or her relationship with God, using one of the following or another suitable invitation:*

*Name*, the Scriptures tell us to bear one another's burdens
 and so fulfill the law of Christ.
As your *sister/brother* in Christ, I ask you now,
are you at peace with God,
or is there anything in your life
 that causes you to feel separated from God
 and less than the full person God calls you to be?

*Name*, the Scriptures tell us not to be anxious about our lives
 or about tomorrow.
Are there anxieties that cause you to feel separated
 from the peace that God promises?

*There may be silence, reflection, or personal sharing.*

*A Confession and Pardon from 474-94 or A Service of Word and Table V (51-52) or UMH 890-93, or an appropriate psalm (see 616) may be used.*

## [HOLY COMMUNION]

*The pastor may administer Holy Communion, using A Service of Word and Table V on 51-53.*

## PRAYERS FOR HEALING AND WHOLENESS
## WITH ANOINTING AND/OR LAYING ON OF HANDS

*If there is anointing with oil, a leader touches a thumb to the oil and makes the sign of the cross on the person's forehead, in silence or using these or similar words*

*Name,* I anoint you with oil
in the name of the Father, and of the Son, and of the Holy Spirit
   (*in the name of the holy and triune God*)
[for *specified purpose*].

*If there is laying on of hands, a leader, who may be joined by others, lays hands upon each person's head, in silence or using these or similar words:*

*Name,* I (*we*) lay my (*our*) hands on you
in the name of the Father, and of the Son, and of the Holy Spirit
   (*in the name of the holy and triune God*)
[for *specified purpose*].

**'RAYERS OF INTERCESSION**

*One of the prayers for special concerns on 626-29, or another suitable prayer.*

**'HE LORD'S PRAYER** *See 29.*

**'LESSING** *See 31-32.*

# A SERVICE OF HOPE AFTER LOSS OF PREGNANCY

*'his service may be held in a church, hospital, or home. Any of the scriptures and 'rayers may also be used by themselves.*

*ny of the acts of worship suggested at the death of a child (161-63) or in A Service of 'eath and Resurrection for a Stillborn Child (170-71) may be included or substituted.*

**'ATHERING**

**'ORDS OF GRACE** *One or more of the following:*

Blessed be the God who consoles us in all our affliction,
   so that we may be able to console those who are in any affliction
   with the consolation with which we ourselves are consoled by God.
(2 CORINTHIANS 1:3a, 4)

Thus says the Lord:
A voice is heard in Ramah, lamentation and bitter weeping.
Rachel is weeping for her children;
she refuses to be comforted for her children, because they are no more.
(JEREMIAH 31:15)

The Lord is merciful and gracious,
   slow to anger and abounding in steadfast love.
As a father shows compassion to his children,
   so the Lord shows compassion to the faithful.

For the Lord knows our frame, and remembers that we are dust.
But the steadfast love of the Lord
  is from everlasting to everlasting upon the faithful,
and the righteousness of the Lord to children's children,
  to those who keep his covenant
    and remember to do his commandments.

(P<small>SALM</small> 103:8, 13-14, 17-18, UMH 824-2)

PRAYER *One or more of the following:*

Life-giving God,
  your love surrounded each of us in our mothers' wombs,
  and from that secret place you called us forth to life.
Pour out your compassion upon *mother's Name.*
Her heart is heavy with the loss of the promise
  that once took form in her womb.
Have compassion upon *Names of father and/or other family members.*
*Their hearts are* also heavy with the loss of promise.
*They grieve* the death of the hopes *they* (*she*) anticipated,
  the dreams *they* (*she*) envisioned, the relationship *they* (*she*) desired
Give *them* (*her*) the courage to admit *their* (*her*) pain and confusion,
  and couple that confession with the simplicity to rest in your care.
Allow *them* (*her*) to grieve, and then to accept this loss.
Warm *them* (*her*) with the embrace of your arms.
Knit together *their* (*her*) frayed emotions,
  and bind *their* (*her*) heart(s) with the fabric of your love for *them* (*her*
In the strong name of Jesus Christ we pray. **Amen.**

Lord, we do not understand why this life,
  which we had hoped to bring into this world,
  is now gone from us.
We only know that where there was sweet expectation,
  now there is bitter disappointment;
where there were hope and excitement, there is a sense of failure and loss
We have seen how fragile life is,
and nothing can replace this life, this child, whom we have loved
  before seeing, before feeling it stirring in the womb,
  even before it was conceived.
In our pain and confusion we look to you, Lord,
  in whom no life is without meaning, however small or brief.
Let not our limited understanding confine our faith.
Draw us closer to you and closer to one another.
Lay our broken hearts open in faith to you
  and in ever greater compassion to one another.
So raise us from death to life; we pray in Christ's name. **Amen.**

Ever-loving and caring God,
we come before you humbled by the mysteries of life and death.
Help us to accept what we cannot understand,
    to have faith where reason fails,
    to have courage in the midst of disappointment.
Comfort *mother's Name*, who has lost a part of herself,
    and *Names of father and/or other family members*.
Help *them* (*her*) to see the hope of life beyond grief.
Through Jesus we know that you love all your children
    and are with us always.
Let us feel that presence now as we seek to live in faith,
    through Jesus Christ our Lord. **Amen.**

CRIPTURE *Suggested lessons:*

| | |
|---|---|
| 2 Samuel 12:15b-23 | David and the death of his child |
| Isaiah 25:6-9 | God will wipe away the tears. |
| Psalm 23 (*UMH* 754, 137) | The good shepherd |
| Psalm 42 (*UMH* 777) | Longing for God's presence |
| Psalm 90 (*UMH* 809) | God's eternal presence |
| Psalm 103 (*UMH* 824) | The steadfast love of God |
| Psalm 118 (*UMH* 839) | God's love endures forever. |
| Psalm 121 (*UMH* 844) | From where will my help come? |
| Psalm 130 (*UMH* 515, 516, 848) | Out of the depths I cry. |
| Psalm 139 (*UMH* 854) | Where can I flee? |
| Romans 14:7-8 | Living or dying, we are the Lord's. |
| 1 Thessalonians 4:13-18 | Do not grieve as those who have no hope. |
| 1 John 3:1-2 | See what love the Father has given us. |
| Matthew 5:1-12 | The Beatitudes |
| Matthew 11:25-30 | God revealed to babes |
| Matthew 18:1-5, 10-14 | Children are greatest in God's kingdom. |
| Mark 10:13-16 | Let the little children come to me. |
| John 14:1-6a | Do not let your hearts be troubled. |

ITNESS

*Pastor, family, and friends may briefly voice their feelings and Christian witness.*

*Signs of faith, hope, and love may be exchanged.*

RAYER *One or both of the following may be used:*

Lord God, as your Son, Jesus,
    took children into his arms and blessed them,
    so we commit this child *Name* into your loving care.
Grant us the assurance that you have received this life, which you gave,
    and grant that when we stand before you
    we might be as innocent and trusting as little children. **Amen.**

Compassionate God,
    soothe the heart(s) of *Name(s)* and enlighten *their* (*her*) faith.

Give hope to *their hearts* and peace to *their lives*.
Grant mercy to *all members of this family* (*her*)
and comfort *them* (*her*) with the hope
that one day we shall all live with you,
through Jesus Christ our Lord. **Amen.**

*Here or elsewhere in the service a familiar and beloved hymn of comfort may b*
*sung.*

THE LORD'S PRAYER *See 29.*

BLESSING *See 31-32.*

# MINISTRY WITH PERSONS GOING THROUGH DIVORCE

*Prayer*

God of infinite love and understanding,
pour out your healing Spirit upon *Name,*
as *he/she* reflects upon the failure of *his/her* marriage
and makes a new beginning.
Where there is hurt or bitterness,
grant healing of memories
and the ability to put behind the things that are past.
Where feelings of despair or worthlessness flood in,
nurture the spirit of hope and confidence
that by your grace tomorrow can be better than yesterday.
Where *he/she* looks within and discovers faults
that have contributed to the destruction of the marriage
and have hurt other people,
grant forgiveness for what is past
and growth in all that makes for new life.
[Heal *children's names,* and help us minister your healing to *them.*]
We pray for [other] family and friends,
for the healing of their hurts and the acceptance of new realities.
All this we ask in the name of the One
who sets us free from slavery to the past and makes all things new,
even Jesus Christ our Savior. **Amen.**

*Suggested Scripture Readings*

| | |
|---|---|
| Philippians 3:12-16 | Press forward. |
| Luke 7:36-50 | Jesus forgives a woman in the city. |
| Luke 13:10-17 | Jesus heals a woman bent over. |
| Luke 18:35-43 | Jesus heals a blind beggar. |

*Suggested hymns from* UMH *are listed under Hymn of Healing (620).*

# MINISTRY WITH PERSONS SUFFERING FROM ADDICTION OR SUBSTANCE ABUSE

## Prayer

God of mercy,
  we bless you in the name of your Son, Jesus Christ,
  who ministered to all who came to him.
Give your strength to *Name*, your servant,
  [bound by the chains of addiction].
Enfold *him/her* in your love
  and restore *him/her* to the freedom of your children.
Look with compassion on all those who have lost their health and freedom.
Restore to them the assurance of your unfailing mercy.
Strengthen them in the work of recovery,
  [and help them to resist all temptation].
To those who care for them,
  grant patient understanding and a love that perseveres.
We ask this through Christ our Lord. **Amen.**

*See also The Serenity Prayer (UMH 459).*

## Suggested Scripture Readings

| | |
|---|---|
| Kings 5:1-14 | Healing of Naaman by Elisha |
| Isaiah 63:7-9 | God has mercifully favored us. |
| Psalm 121 *(UMH 844)* | My help comes from the Lord. |
| Psalm 130 *(UMH 515, 516, 848)* | Out of the depths |
| Romans 8:18-25 | Present sufferings and future glory |
| Matthew 15:21-28 | Woman, you have great faith. |
| Matthew 17:14-21 | Jesus heals an epileptic boy. |
| Luke 4:31-37 | Man with unclean spirit |

*Suggested hymns from UMH are listed under Hymn of Healing (620).*

# MINISTRY WITH PERSONS WITH AIDS

## Prayer

Most merciful God, you hold each of us dear to your heart.
Hold *Name(s)* in your loving arms
  and tenderly draw *them* into your love,
  together with all who are living with AIDS and HIV infection.
Assure them that they are not alone,
  and give them courage and faith for all that is to come.
Strengthen those who care for them and treat them,
  and guide those who do research.

Forgive those who have judged harshly,
and enlighten those who live in prejudice or fear.
Nourish those who have lost sight of you,
and heal the spirits of those who are broken.
We pray this in the name of Jesus, who suffered and died,
and then rose from the dead to lead us into new life,
now and for ever. **Amen.**

*Suggested Scripture Readings*

| | |
|---|---|
| Psalm 13 (*UMH* 746) | Trust in the midst of suffering |
| Psalm 121 (*UMH* 844) | My help comes from the Lord. |
| Psalm 130 (*UMH* 515, 516, 848) | Out of the depths |
| Romans 8:31-39 | Nothing can separate us from God's love. |
| Colossians 1:11-20 | May you be strengthened with all power. |
| 1 Peter 2:21-25 | By Christ's wounds you have been healed. |
| Matthew 5:1-16 | The Beatitudes |
| Matthew 8:1-4 | The healing of a leper |
| Mark 2:1-12 | Rise, take your mat, and go. |
| Luke 10:25-37 | The good Samaritan |
| Luke 17:11-19 | The healing of the ten lepers |

*Suggested hymns from* UMH *are listed under Hymn of Healing (620).*

# MINISTRY WITH PERSONS WITH
# LIFE-THREATENING ILLNESS

*Prayer*

Lord Jesus Christ,
we come to you sharing the suffering that you endured.
Grant us patience during this time,
that as we and *Name* live with pain, disappointment, and frustration,
we may realize that suffering is a part of life,
a part of life that you know intimately.
Touch *Name* in *his/her* time of trial,
hold *him/her* tenderly in your loving arms,
and let *him/her* know you care.
Renew us in our spirits,
even when our bodies are not being renewed,
that we might be ever prepared to dwell in your eternal home,
through our faith in you, Lord Jesus,
who died and are alive for evermore. **Amen.**

*Suggested Scripture Readings*

| | |
|---|---|
| Ecclesiastes 3:1-11*a* | For everything there is a season. |
| Isaiah 25:6-10 | God will swallow up death. |

salm 23          The Lord is my shepherd.
salm 42          My soul longs for you.
omans 8:18-25    Present sufferings and future glory
omans 14:7-9     We are the Lord's.

*amiliar beloved hymns, or hymns suggested under Hymn of Healing (620), may be ing to or with persons life-threatening illness.*

*ee also the resources in Ministry with the Dying (166-67).*

# MINISTRY WITH PERSONS
# IN COMA OR UNABLE TO COMMUNICATE

*Prayer*

ternal God, you have known us before we were here
  and will continue to know us after we are gone.
ouch *Name* with your grace and presence.
.s you give your abiding care,
  assure *him/her* of our love and presence.
.ssure *him/her* that our communion together remains secure,
  and that your love for *him/her* is unfailing.
1 Christ, who came to us, we pray. **Amen.**

*Suggested Scripture Readings*

salm 23 (*UMH* 137)    The Lord is my shepherd.
salm 42 (*UMH* 777)    My soul longs for you.
aiah 61:1-3            The Spirit of the Lord
omans 8:18-25          Present sufferings and future glory
omans 14:7-9           We are the Lord's.

*amiliar beloved hymns may be sung to persons in coma or unable to communicate.*

# IX. SERVICES RELATING TO CONGREGATIONS AND BUILDINGS

## A SERVICE FOR ORGANIZING
## A NEW CONGREGATION

*This service may also be used when creating a new congregation as a result of a merge of previous congregations.*

GATHERING *See 16-17.*

*The people and the district superintendent or pastor convening them assemble (the appointed place.*

GREETING AND DECLARATION OF PURPOSE

Dear friends, the Scriptures teach us
that the Church is the household of God,
  the body of which Christ is the head,
and that it is the design of the gospel to bring together in one
  all who are in Christ.
We have come together to form a new congregation
  of The United Methodist Church,
  which is a part of Christ's holy Church.
Let us dedicate ourselves to this purpose.

HYMN OF PRAISE * *See 17-20. Suggested from* UMH:

| | |
|---|---|
| 57-152 The Glory of the Triune God | 559 Christ Is Made the Sure Foundation |
| 948 Hymns listed under Opening Hymns | 660 God Is Here |
| | 577 God of Grace and God of Glory |
| 934 Hymns listed under Adoration and Praise | 529 How Firm a Foundation |
| | 545 The Church's One Foundation |

OPENING PRAYER * *See 20-21.*

Lord God, preserve your Church.
Let your Word be heard and your Sacraments lived out among this people
so that they may live in harmony with you and one another,

be confirmed in steadfast faith,
and be your brave witnesses and workers in the world. **Amen.**

SCRIPTURE *Suggested lessons:*

| | |
|---|---|
| Isaiah 2:1-4 | Let us go up to the mountain of the Lord. |
| Jeremiah 31:31-34 | God will make a new covenant. |
| Jeremiah 32:36-41 | They shall be my people, and I their God. |

PSALM 100 * (*UMH* 821, 74, 75)

SCRIPTURE *Suggested lessons:*

| | |
|---|---|
| 1 Corinthians 3:10-17 | You are God's temple. |
| 1 Peter 2:4-10 | You are a royal priesthood. |
| 2 Peter 1:3-10 | Be eager to confirm your call. |
| Revelation 21:9-27 | The new Jerusalem |

HYMN * *Suggested from* UMH:

| | |
|---|---|
| Hymns listed above and under | 563 Father, We Thank You |
| 938 Dedication of a Building | 558 I Am the Church |
| 590 Christ Loves the Church | 540 I Love Thy Kingdom, Lord |
| 632 Draw Us in the Spirit's Tether | |

GOSPEL * *Suggested lessons:*

| | |
|---|---|
| Matthew 16:13-18 | On this rock I will build my Church. |
| Matthew 20:20-28 | Whoever wishes to be first among you |

SERMON

ORGANIZATION OF THE CONGREGATION

*The leader gives opportunity for any to present themselves for membership by certificate of transfer or on profession of faith, receives them according to one of the services of the Baptismal Covenant (81-110), completes the organization of the congregation as prescribed in* The Book of Discipline, *and then says:*

By what name shall this church be known?

*The pastor or designated lay official answers:*

It shall be called the *Name* United Methodist Church.

*The leader then says:*

In accordance with the laws and *Discipline*
of The United Methodist Church,
I hereby declare that *Name* United Methodist Church
is duly constituted and organized for the glory of God,
the proclamation of the gospel, and the service of humanity.

PRAYER *

*Concerns and prayers, a pastoral prayer, or the following:*

Almighty God,
upon your Son Jesus Christ you built your Church.
Bless this your congregation.
Watch over its beginning,
increase its ministry and mission,
and sustain it to the end,
through Jesus Christ our foundation. **Amen.**

OFFERING *See 26-27.*

*Holy Communion may be celebrated, using A Service of Word and Table II (UMH 12-15), III (UMH 15-16), or IV (UMH 26-31). One of the musical settings (UMH 17-25) may be used for the Great Thanksgiving. See hymn suggestions on 30.*

*If Holy Communion is not celebrated, the service may conclude as follows:*

THE LORD'S PRAYER * *See 29.*

HYMN * *See suggestions on 630 and 631.*

DISMISSAL WITH BLESSING * *See 31-32.*

GOING FORTH * *See 32.*

# A SERVICE FOR THE BREAKING OF GROUND
# FOR A CHURCH BUILDING

*The people may assemble at the construction site, or they may gather in a suitable place and process to the site. If the people process to the site following a service in their present house of worship, the service at the site may begin with the Breaking of Ground.*

*A wooden cross may be erected at the place where the Lord's table will be located, if this is appropriate to the condition of the construction site.*

*The use of banners and colorful vestments can add to the joyful, festive character of the celebration.*

GATHERING *See 16-17.*

GREETING *See 17-20.*

Our help is in the name of the Lord, who made heaven and earth.
**Except the Lord build the house, they labor in vain who build it.**

HYMN OF PRAISE * See 17-20. *Suggested from* UMH:

57-152 The Glory of the Triune God
934 Hymns listed under Adoration and
    Praise
559 Christ Is Made the Sure Foundation

529 How Firm a Foundation
733 Marching to Zion
545 The Church's One Foundation

*If the hymn is a processional, it may precede the Greeting.*

OPENING PRAYER * See 20-21.

Almighty and everlasting God, ever exalted yet always near:
Be present with us, gathered together here
    to set apart this ground upon which we stand
    to the honor and glory of your great name.
Let your Spirit descend upon your church that will come together here,
    and within these walls let your glory dwell.
Fill with your love all who shall seek your face here;
    and as they depart from this place,
    go with them in the peace and power of your Holy Spirit;
through Jesus Christ our Lord. **Amen.**

ANTHEM, HYMN, OR OTHER ACT OF PRAISE

SCRIPTURE *Suggested lessons:*

Genesis 28:11-22
1 Chronicles 21:28–22:16
Ezra 3

Jacob's dream moves him to erect a pillar.
David prepares to build the Temple.
Foundation laid for the Second Temple

PSALM 122 * (*UMH* 845, response 2) or
PSALM 118 (*UMH* 839, response 2)

*Psalm 122 may be shortened to verses 1-2, 6-9. The response may be:*
**"I have chosen and sanctified this place"** *(1 Chronicles 7:16).*

SCRIPTURE *Suggested lessons:*

1 Corinthians 3:10-17
Ephesians 4:1-7, 11-13
Revelation 21:9-27

You are God's temple.
There is one body and one spirit.
The new Jerusalem

HYMN OR SONG *

*In addition to the hymns listed above, those listed under Dedication of a Building in UMH 938 are suggested.*

GOSPEL * *Suggested lessons:*

Matthew 7:24-27
Matthew 16:13-18

A house built on rock
On this rock I will build my church.

| Matthew 21:12-17 | My house shall be a house of prayer. |
| John 4:19-24 | Worship God in spirit and truth. |

## SERMON

## OFFERING *See 26-27.*

## BREAKING OF GROUND

*Pastor:*

To the glory of God, in the presence of this congregation,
I now direct that ground be broken
 for the *Name* United Methodist Church.
The responsibility and the privilege rest upon us
 to cause a building to rise here
  that shall be a house of this people of God
  and a place devoted to the worship of almighty God
  and to the glory of our Lord and Savior Jesus Christ.

*As each one of those selected turns a spadeful of earth, the pastor says one of th*
*following sentences, to which the people respond:*

That a church may meet here
 where children shall learn to love God
  and grow in grace and goodness,
  and in favor with God and all people,
**we break this ground today.**

That a church may meet here
 where youth shall be inspired to pray and serve, **R**

That a church may meet here
 where the weary and heavy laden shall find inner peace
  that the world can neither give nor take away, **R**

That a church may meet here
 where God is worshiped in prayer and praise,
 where the Word of God shall be so read and preached
  that it shall become the living Word,
 and the Sacraments so celebrated
  that all life shall become sacramental, **R**

That a church may meet here
 where multitudes shall be refreshed in spirit, relieved from pain,
  released from bondage, and redeemed from sin, **R**

That a church may meet here
 where the grace of God may make our human lives into a Christlike lov
  and our homes places of living witness
  for that realm where Christ is Lord, **R**

That a church may meet here
 from which, by the power of your Holy Spirit,

your people are sent forth into this community and all the world
as champions of justice and peace to all peoples, R

## LOSING PRAYER *

Lord God, you fill the whole world with your presence,
that your name may be hallowed everywhere.
Bless us who meet here, on this ground made holy by your worship.
Consecrate those whose vision and work provide this site.
Help us to rejoice in this work just begun
and to persevere to its completion,
so that this place may resound with your praises
and become for us a home
where we may together be nurtured
in the faith of our Lord Jesus Christ. **Amen.**

HE LORD'S PRAYER * *See 29.*

[YMN * *See suggestions on 630 and 631.*

*The following hymns in* UMH *are also suggested:*

548 In Christ There Is No East or West    733 Marching to Zion

»ISMISSAL WITH BLESSING * *See 31-32.*

;OING FORTH * *See 32.*

# A SERVICE FOR THE LAYING
# OF A FOUNDATION STONE OF A CHURCH BUILDING

*he people may assemble at the site of the new building, or they may gather in a*
*litable place and process to the site. If the people process to the site following a service*
*t their present house of worship, the service at the site may begin with the Laying of*
*ie Foundation Stone.*

;ATHERING *See 16-17.*

;REETING *See 17-20.*

Our help is in the name of the Lord, who made heaven and earth.
**Except the Lord build the house, they labor in vain who build it.**

IYMN OF PRAISE * *See 17-20. Suggested from* UMH:

57-152 The Glory of the Triune God      529 How Firm a Foundation
934 Hymns listed under Adoration and    139 Praise to the Lord
    Praise                                   545 The Church's One Foundation
559 Christ Is Made the Sure Foundation   546 The Church's One Foundation

*If the hymn is a processional, it may precede the Greeting.*

## DECLARATION OF PURPOSE

Friends,
we are assembled to lay the foundation stone of a new house of worship
Let us faithfully and devoutly seek the blessing of God on what we do

## OPENING PRAYER * *See 20-21.*

Almighty and everlasting God, exalted yet near,
we offer to you this foundation for a house of praise and prayer
  where your glory shall be manifest among us,
  and from which your people shall go forth in ministry to all the world
through Jesus Christ our Lord. **Amen.**

## ANTHEM, HYMN, OR OTHER ACT OF PRAISE

SCRIPTURE *Suggested lessons:*

| | |
|---|---|
| Isaiah 28:16-17 | I am laying in Zion a foundation stone. |
| Ezra 3 | Foundation stone laid for Second Temple |

## PSALM 24 * (*UMH* 755, 212, 213) or PSALM 118 (*UMH* 839)

SCRIPTURE *Suggested lessons:*

| | |
|---|---|
| 1 Corinthians 3:10-17 | You are God's temple. |
| Ephesians 2:13-22 | Christ Jesus himself the cornerstone |
| Revelation 21:9-27 | The new Jerusalem |

## HYMN OR SONG *

*See hymns suggested above or following Dedication of a Building* (UMH 938)

## GOSPEL * *Suggested lessons:*

| | |
|---|---|
| Matthew 7:24-27 | A house built on rock |
| Matthew 16:13-18 | On this rock I will build my Church. |
| Matthew 21:12-17 | My house shall be a house of prayer. |

## SERMON

## OFFERING *See 26-27.*

## LAYING OF THE FOUNDATION STONE

*If items are to be placed in the foundation stone, they may be brought forward at this time and displayed before the people. These items may include a Bible,* The United Methodist Hymnal, The United Methodist Book of Worship, The Book of Discipline, *church periodicals, appropriate names and pictures, and other things suitable. When these have been placed in a box and put in the foundation stone the pastor stands at the side of the stone and says:*

According to the grace of God given to me,
like a skilled master builder I laid a foundation.
For no one can lay any foundation other than the one that has been laid;
that foundation is Jesus Christ. (1 CORINTHIANS 3:10a, 11)

*Then with the aid of the builder or other persons chosen, the stone is put in place.*

Praise the Lord, because the foundation of the house of the Lord is laid!
**Praise the Lord. Hallelujah!**

*An alleluia may be sung. Suggested alleluias from* UMH:

186 Alleluia                              78 Heleluyan
162 Alleluia, Alleluia (refrain)

LOSING PRAYER *

Almighty God, on whom we build all our hopes,
with your lovingkindness bless this place
    where we lay the foundation of a house
        to the praise and honor of your holy name.
Accept the act by which we lay this foundation stone.
Bless those whose offerings enable us to build this house.
Guard and direct those who labor in building it,
    shielding them from accident and peril.
May the walls of this building rise in security and in beauty;
and may the hearts of these your people
    be joined together into a living temple,
        built upon the foundation of the apostles and prophets,
        Jesus Christ being the chief foundation stone. **Amen.**

HE LORD'S PRAYER * *See 29.*

IYMN * *See suggestions on 630 and 631.*

ISMISSAL WITH BLESSING * *See 31-32.*

OING FORTH * *See 32.*

# A SERVICE FOR THE CONSECRATION
# OR RECONSECRATION
# OF A CHURCH BUILDING

*Upon acquisition or completion of any church building, parsonage, or other church nit, a service of consecration may be held" (The Book of Discipline 1992, ¶ 2544). he following service is based on the ancient tradition that the consecration*

of a church building is the proclamation of the Word and the celebration of Hol;
Communion as the first act of worship in the new building. For the dedication of ;
parsonage, see 610-12.

This may also be the first service after the renovation or reopening of a churc;
building. If the building or renovation costs have been fully paid, the term dedicatio;
may be substituted whenever the term consecration occurs.

## GATHERING See 16-17.

It is appropriate and also an ancient tradition that the congregation and leaders c
worship gather at some place outside the building and enter in procession for th
consecration service.

Before the procession the people may read or sing Psalm 24 (UMH 755, 212, 213)

## PROCESSIONAL HYMN * See 17-20. Suggested from UMH:

| | |
|---|---|
| 57-152 The Glory of the Triune God | 731 Glorious Things of Thee Are Spoken |
| 934 Hymns listed under Adoration and | 660 God Is Here |
| Praise | 577 God of Grace and God of Glory |
| 553 And Are We Yet Alive? | 529 How Firm a Foundation |
| 559 Christ Is Made the Sure Foundation | 545 The Church's One Foundation |
| 92 For the Beauty of the Earth | 546 The Church's One Foundation |
| (especially stanzas 5, 6) | 87 What Gift Can We Bring? |

Certain items that will be used in worship may be carried in the procession, such a
a Bible, water for the baptismal font, plate for the communion bread and cup, ;
cross, paraments for the Lord's table, and other works of art. If a choir leads th
procession, it may assemble in the church and sing anthems as the people enter

## DECLARATION OF PURPOSE

Brothers and sisters in Christ, this is a day of rejoicing.
We have come together to *consecrate (reconsecrate)* this building
of *Name* United Methodist Church.
Let us open our hearts and minds to receive God's Word with faith.
May our blessed communion,
born of one baptism and nurtured at one table of the Lord,
become one temple of the Holy Spirit as we gather in love.

## PRESENTATION OF THE BUILDING

A person or persons designated come(s) forward and say(s):

I (we) present this building to be *consecrated (reconsecrated)*
for the worship of God and the service of all people.

## NAMING OF THE BUILDING

Bishop, district superintendent, or their representative, hereafter called th
officiating minister:

By what name shall this house be known?

*Pastor or designated lay official:*

It shall be called the *Name* United Methodist Church.

## ONSECRATION OF THE BUILDING *

Dear friends, rejoice that God so moved the hearts of people
　that this house has been built for praise and prayer.
Let us now *consecrate* it for service and celebrate its holy use.

*Several persons may lead sections of the following prayer of consecration, which the officiating minister should begin and conclude:*

O eternal God, mighty in power and of incomprehensible majesty,
　whom the heavens cannot contain,
　　much less the walls of temples made with hands,
you have promised your special presence
　whenever two or three are assembled in your name
　　to offer praise and prayer.

By the power of your Holy Spirit *consecrate* this house of your worship.
Bless us and sanctify what we do here,
that this place may be holy for us and a house of prayer for all people.

Guide and empower in this place by the same Spirit
　the proclamation of your Word and the celebration of your Sacraments,
　the pouring out of prayer and the singing of your praise,
　professions of faith and testimonies to your grace,
　the joining of men and women in marriage
　　and the celebration of death and resurrection.

Save us from that failure of vision
　which would confine our worship within these walls,
but send us out from here to be your servants in the world,
　sharing the blessings of Christ with the world he came to redeem.

*The officiating minister concludes:*

Now, O God, sanctify this place,
　for everything in heaven and on earth is yours.
Yours, Lord, is the dominion, and you are exalted as head above all.

## NTHEM, HYMN, OR OTHER ACT OF PRAISE

## ONSECRATION OF THE PULPIT

*Those leading in worship process to the pulpit.*
*The officiating minister lays a hand upon the pulpit and says:*

Eternal God, we thank you that Christ your living Word
  speaks to us through the words of Holy Scripture,
    written of old by the inspiration of your Holy Spirit
    and proclaimed today by the anointing of the same Spirit.
When your Word is read and preached from this pulpit,
  purify the lives and lips of those who speak here,
    that your Word alone may be proclaimed
    and your Word alone may be heard and obeyed.
May the words of our mouths and the meditations of our hearts
  be acceptable to you, our Rock and our Redeemer,
through Jesus Christ our Lord. **Amen.**

God's Word is a lantern to our feet and a light upon our path.
We consecrate this pulpit
  in the name of the Father, and of the Son, and of the Holy Spirit
  (*in the name of the holy and triune God*). **Amen.**

*A Bible is placed upon the pulpit at this time.*

SCRIPTURE *Suggested lessons:*

| | |
|---|---|
| Genesis 28:10-22 | The house of God |
| 1 Kings 8:22-30 | Solomon's prayer dedicating the Temple |
| Ezra 6:13-22 | Dedication of the Second Temple |

PSALM 122 * (*UMH* 845, response 2) or
PSALM 118 (*UMH* 839, response 2)

*Psalm 122 may be shortened to verses 1-2, 6-9. The response may be:*
**"I have chosen and consecrated this house"** (*2 Chronicles 7:16*).

SCRIPTURE *Suggested lessons:*

| | |
|---|---|
| 1 Corinthians 3:9-13, 16-17 | Jesus Christ is the foundation. |
| Hebrews 10:19-25 | Confidence to enter the sanctuary |
| 1 Peter 2:4-10 | You are a royal priesthood. |
| Revelation 21:9-27 | The new Jerusalem |

HYMN OR SONG *

*Suggested from* UMH, *in addition to those suggested under Processional Hymn f this service (638):*

| | |
|---|---|
| 938 Hymns listed under Dedication of a Building | 584 Lord, You Give the Great Commission |
| 97 For the Fruits of This Creation | 114 Many Gifts, One Spirit |
| | 139 Praise to the Lord, the Almighty |

OSPEL * *Suggested lessons:*

| | |
|---|---|
| Matthew 7:24-27 | A house built on rock |
| Matthew 16:13-18 | On this rock I will build my Church. |
| Matthew 21:12-17 | My house shall be a house of prayer. |

ERMON

YMN OF INVITATION OR RESPONSE * *See suggestions above.*

## ONSECRATION OF THE BAPTISMAL FONT

*Those leading in worship process to the baptismal font.*

*The officiating minister lays a hand upon the font and says:*

Most gracious God, we thank you that through the waters of baptism
    you have given us new life, adopted us as your children,
    and made us members of your Church.
When we pour the water of baptism,
    making and renewing our covenant vows,
    pour out your Spirit and give new birth;
    wash away sin and clothe your people in righteousness;
that, dying and being raised with Christ,
    we may walk in new and abundant life;
through the same Jesus Christ our Lord. **Amen.**

There is one Lord, one faith, one baptism, one God and Father of us all.
We consecrate this font
    in the name of the Father, and of the Son, and of the Holy Spirit
    (*in the name of the holy and triune God*). **Amen.**

*Water is poured into the font at this time. Persons may be baptized using Services of
the Baptismal Covenant. See 81-110 and* UMH *32-49.*

*A hymn or stanza may be sung. See* UMH *604-11.*

*See also:*
Baptismal Prayer ( ♪ 174)
Come, Be Baptized ( ♪ 173)

## ONSECRATION OF THE LORD'S TABLE

*Those leading in worship process to the Lord's table.*

*The officiating minister lays a hand upon the table and says:*

Lord God, we thank you that when we gather at the Lord's table
    the living Christ is known to us
        in the breaking of the bread and the sharing of the cup;
and we are renewed as his body, whose life is in his blood.
When we eat this bread and drink from this cup,
    refresh all those who partake at this holy table.

Feed the hunger of our hearts with the bread of heaven,
and quench our deepest thirst with the cup of salvation.
Strengthen us for your service in the world,
and give us a foretaste of the feast to come,
through Jesus Christ our Lord. **Amen.**
Jesus said: "Whoever comes to me shall not hunger,
and whoever believes in me shall never thirst."
We consecrate this table
in the name of the Father, and of the Son, and of the Holy Spirit
(*in the name of the holy and triune God*). **Amen.**

*A response may be sung, such as the refrain of* One Bread, One Body *(UMH 620) or* Be Present at Our Table, Lord *(UMH 621).*

**OFFERING** *See 26-27.*

*An offering may be received.*

*A hymn may be sung while the gifts are brought to the Lord's table. See hymn suggestions on 638 and 640.*

*Communion vessels, bread, and wine are placed upon the table at this time. Flower may be placed near the table, and candles may be lighted.*

**HOLY COMMUNION**

*The people may use* A Service of Word and Table II *(UMH 12-15), III (UMH 15-16), or IV (UMH 26-31). One of the musical settings (UMH 17-25) may b used for the Great Thanksgiving. See hymn suggestions on 30.*

**HYMN OR SONG** \* *See suggestions on 638 and 640.*

**DISMISSAL WITH BLESSING** \* *See 31-32.*

**GOING FORTH** \* *See 32.*

# A SERVICE FOR THE DEDICATION
# OF A CHURCH BUILDING
# FREE OF DEBT

*"Before any church building, parsonage, or other church unit is formally dedicated all indebtedness against the same shall be discharged"* (The Book of Disciplin 1992, ¶ 2545). *The following service, commonly called a mortgage-burning service may be used for the dedication of a church sanctuary, or an education or activitie building, when the building has become free of debt.*

ATHERING *See 16-17.*

REETING *See 17-20.*

This is the day which the Lord has made; let us rejoice and be glad in it.
**I was glad when they said to me, "Let us go to the house of the Lord!"**

This is none other than the house of God, and this is the gate of heaven.
**Blessed be the Lord; may God's glory fill the whole earth.**

YMN OF PRAISE * *See 17-20.*

*If the hymn is a processional, it may precede the Greeting. See the hymns suggested on 638 and 640 and Dedication of a Building (UMH 938).*

PENING PRAYER * *See 20-21.*

Eternal God, let this building, which we dedicate to your name,
    be a house of salvation and grace where Christians gathered together
        may worship you in spirit and truth,
    may learn of you, and may grow together in love.
Grant this through Christ our Lord. **Amen.**

NTHEM, HYMN, OR OTHER ACT OF PRAISE

CRIPTURE *Suggested lessons:*

| | |
|---|---|
| 1 Kings 8:22-30 | Solomon's prayer dedicating the Temple |
| Isaiah 55:6-13 | God's Word shall not return empty. |
| Jeremiah 31:31-34 | The new covenant |

SALM 24 * (*UMH* 755, 212, 213)

CRIPTURE *Suggested lessons:*

| | |
|---|---|
| 1 Corinthians 3:9-13, 16-17 | Jesus Christ is the foundation. |
| Ephesians 2:13-22 | Christ Jesus is the cornerstone. |
| Revelation 21 | The holy city |

YMN OR SONG * *See the hymns suggested on 638 and 640.*

OSPEL * *Suggested lessons:*

| | |
|---|---|
| Matthew 7:24-27 | A house built on rock |
| Matthew 16:13-18 | On this rock I will build my Church. |
| Matthew 21:12-17 | My house shall be a house of prayer. |

ERMON

URNING OF THE MORTGAGE

*A copy of the mortgage ought to be burned, not the original mortgage itself, which should be preserved. In some communities fire codes may require that the service or*

*part of it be held outdoors. The service might begin in the church building and mo*
*outdoors in a procession for the mortgage burning. Such a procession is appropria*
*in any event, either at the beginning of the service or immediately before t*
*burning ceremony, and may include the bringing forward of the document to*
*burned, a vessel such as a large bowl in which the burning will take place, and a*
*the persons who will be involved in the service.*

*In the burning ceremony itself the copy of the mortgage may be presented to t*
*pastor or district superintendent by one of the trustees. The burning may*
*accompanied by an anthem of praise or a brief witness to the congregation by sever*
*representatives of the different ministries of the church—such as worshi*
*education, evangelism, mission—concerning the meaning of this event and hop*
*for the future.*

## OFFERING *See 26-27.*

## ACT OF DEDICATION

*Any sections below that do not apply to the functions of the building being dedicat*
*may be omitted.*

Dear friends, now that we have completed building,
    and paid all indebtedness on it,
let us dedicate this building and rejoice in its holy use.

To the glory of God, who has called us by grace;
to the honor of Jesus Christ, who loved us and gave himself for us;
to the praise of the Holy Spirit, who illumines and sanctifies us;
**we dedicate this house.**

For the worship of God in prayer and praise;
for the preaching of the everlasting gospel;
for the celebration of the Holy Sacraments; **R**

For the comfort of all who mourn;
for strength to those who are tempted;
for light to those who seek the way; **R**

For the hallowing of family life;
for teaching and guiding the young;
for the perfecting of the saints; **R**

For the conversion of sinners;
for the promotion of righteousness;
for the extension of God's reign; **R**

In the unity of the faith;
in the bond of brotherhood and sisterhood;
in love and goodwill to all; **R**

In gratitude for the labors of all who love and serve this church;
in loving remembrance of those who have finished their course;
in the hope of eternal life through Jesus Christ our Lord; **R**

LOSING PRAYER *

We now, the people of this congregation,
surrounded by a great cloud of witnesses,
grateful for our heritage,
aware of the sacrifices of our mothers and fathers in the faith,
and confessing that apart from us their work cannot be made perfect,
dedicate ourselves anew to the worship and service of almighty God;
through Jesus Christ our Lord. **Amen.**

[YMN * See suggestions on 638 and 640.

ISMISSAL WITH BLESSING * See 31-32.

OING FORTH * See 32.

# A SERVICE FOR THE CONSECRATION OF AN EDUCATIONAL BUILDING

*his service of worship may be used for the opening and consecration of an educational
education-administration building of a local church or church-related school. For
1 order to be used for celebrating the payment of the indebtedness on such a building,
e 642-45.*

ATHERING See 16-17.

REETING See 17-20.

Blessed be the name of God for ever and ever,
to whom belong wisdom and might.
**God gives wisdom to the wise
and knowledge to those who have understanding.**

[YMN OF PRAISE * See 17-20. Suggested from UMH:

87 What Gift Can We Bring?
938 Hymns listed under Education

ECLARATION OF PURPOSE

Dear friends, this building,
which by the favor of God and human labor has been so far completed,
embodies the obligation of each generation
to impart its treasures of wisdom and knowledge
to the generation following.

For the fulfillment of this task we need
  not only the best that we can do
    but above all the blessing of almighty God.
Let us, therefore, bring praise for God's aid in this undertaking,
giving thanks for those who, by their gifts of their service,
  shall unite in fulfilling the purpose
    for which this building is prepared.

## ANTHEM, HYMN, OR OTHER ACT OF PRAISE

SCRIPTURE *Suggested lessons:*

| | |
|---|---|
| Proverbs 3:13-18 | Happy are those who find wisdom. |
| Jeremiah 31:31-34 | The new covenant |

## PSALM 119:1-8, 33-40* (*UMH* 840)

SCRIPTURE *Suggested lessons:*

| | |
|---|---|
| Philippians 2:1-11 | Let the mind of Christ Jesus be in you. |
| 1 Timothy 4:6-16 | These are the things you must teach. |

HYMN OR SONG* *See suggestions in* UMH *under Education (938).*

GOSPEL* *Suggested lessons:*

| | |
|---|---|
| Luke 2:41-52 | I must be in my Father's house. |
| John 14:15-17, 25-26; 16:12-13 | The Advocate will teach you. |

## SERMON

## OFFERING *See 26-27.*

## HYMN OR ANTHEM

## PRESENTATION OF THE BUILDING

*Members of the Board of Trustees or of another appropriate committee stand befo*
*the congregation, and an appointed member says:*

We present this building to be consecrated to the glory of almighty Go
  and for service in the preparation of God's people for discipleship.

*If the building is to be a memorial, the phrase is added:*
in loving memory (*honor*) of *Name.*

## ACT OF CONSECRATION

Dear friends, it is with joy that we gather to consecrate this building
But the consecration of this building is vain

without the consecration of those whose gifts it represents.
Let us give ourselves anew to the service of God:
  our minds, that they may be renewed after the image of Christ;
  our bodies,
    that they may be fit temples for the indwelling of the Holy Spirit;
  and our labors, that they may be according to God's will,
    and that their fruit may glorify God's name
    and serve God's eternal purposes.
In the name of the Father, and of the Son, and of the Holy Spirit
  (*in the name of the holy and triune God*),
  **we consecrate this building.**

To the spiritual enrichment of all who shall come here seeking knowledge,
  **we consecrate this building.**

To the loyal service of those whose training and devotion
  have prepared them to lead students toward the truth,
  **we consecrate this building.**

To that ministry of administration
  upon whose ability and faithfulness depends
    the wise conduct of our life together and our ministry in the world,
  **we consecrate this building;**
  **and we consecrate ourselves anew to that service of humanity**
    **in which we perform the true service of God.**

CLOSING PRAYER *

Almighty God,
hear us who gather here to consecrate ourselves to your service.
Grant that those who come here,
  whether as leaders, staff, teachers, or students,
  may come with inquiring minds, honest purpose,
    and steadfast endeavor to do your holy will.
We give thanks to you for all your servants,
  our parents, teachers, benefactors, and friends,
  by whose love and devotion
    we have come into our great inheritance of health, truth, and faith.
Help us guard this treasure, be blessed by it, nurture it,
  and pass it on to the coming generation, that they may serve you;
in the name of Jesus Christ our Lord. **Amen.**

THE LORD'S PRAYER * *See 29.*

HYMN * *See suggestions on 638 and 640.*

DISMISSAL WITH BLESSING * *See 31-32.*

GOING FORTH * *See 32.*

# AN ORDER FOR THE LEAVE-TAKING
# OF A CHURCH BUILDING

*This order is intended to be used within the final service of worship held in a chur*
*building or sanctuary that is about to be razed or that is hereafter to be used for oth*
*purposes. The service as a whole should follow a pattern familiar to the congregatio*
*with this order concluding the service. If the service begins in an old building*
*sanctuary and continues with a procession to a new building or sanctuary and*
*service there, this order should immediately precede the procession. If this order*
*being used by a congregation that is disbanding, the italicized words within brackets*
*and An Order for Disbanding a Congregation (650-51) may be added.*

*Included in the bulletin or in the earlier portions of the service may be:*

*1) A brief history of the congregation and of its building(s)*

*2) Reminiscences by members of the congregation*

*3) A listing of former pastors and leaders*

*4) Greetings from former pastors, some of whom may be present and participating*
   *the service*

## DECLARATION OF PURPOSE

The time has come for this congregation of Christ's holy Church,
   under God's leadership,
   to [*disband and*] take leave of this building.
It has been consecrated
   for the ministry of God's Holy Word and Sacraments.
It has provided refuge and comfort for God's people.
It has served well our holy faith.
It is fitting, therefore, that we should take our leave
   [*of one another and*] of this consecrated house,
   lifting up our hearts in thanksgiving for this common store of memorie

## LITANY OF THANKSGIVING *

Blessed be the name of God,
   whose Word has long been proclaimed within this hallowed place
   **We give you thanks, O God.**

As generations have prayed their prayers and sung your praises her
   your Spirit has blessed countless worshipers. **R**

We have celebrated the Lord's Supper here
   and been nurtured by it through our journey in faith. **R**

We have rejoiced here as believers have confessed faith in Christ. **R**

Here we have baptized our children and mourned our dead. **R**

As new families have been created through marriage,
   we, our parents, and our children have vowed at this altar
   to love, honor, and cherish always. **R**

From within these walls many have gone out to serve you in the world. **R**

As we go now from this house into a further journey of faith,
**we give you thanks, O God, through Jesus Christ our Lord. Amen.**

**IYMN** * *Suggested from* UMH:

| | |
|---|---|
| 563 Father, We Thank You | 102 Now Thank We All Our God |
| 565 Father, We Thank You | 393 Spirit of the Living God |
| 92 For the Beauty of the Earth | 558 We Are the Church |

*As this hymn is sung, the Bible, sacramental vessels, cross, and other objects may be removed from their places in the chancel and held by designated persons until they are carried out during the recessional hymn.*

*A statement may be made regarding the disposition of the pulpit, Lord's table, baptismal font, and other furnishings that cannot be carried out during the recessional hymn.*

## DECLARATION OF DECONSECRATION]

*The bishop or bishop's representative (who may be the pastor) may say:*

This building,
   having been consecrated
      and named the *Name* United Methodist Church,
together with the land on which it stands and all objects remaining in it,
   we now deconsecrate and release for any honorable use.
We declare that it is no longer
   the place of meeting of a United Methodist congregation.

*If the congregation is disbanding, a Declaration Disbanding the Congregation (see 650-51) immediately follows the Declaration of Deconsecration.*

*A response such as* Tino tenda Jesu ( ♪ *203) or* Shalom to You (UMH *666) may be sung.*

## LOSING PRAYER *

O God, as in your great goodness
   you have blessed the many ministries carried on
      by this congregation in this building,
so, now and in the days and years to come,
we pray that you may greatly bless your many ministries
   in your ongoing Church.
Bless those persons who have worshiped in this building,
   and will now be worshiping
      *in their new building (in other congregations and other buildings).*

As disciples of the risen Christ,
may we be channels at all times of your steadfast love;
through the same Jesus Christ our Lord. **Amen.**

THE LORD'S PRAYER * *See 29.*

RECESSIONAL HYMN * *See 30-31. Suggested from* UMH:

671 Lord, Dismiss Us with Thy Blessing     664 Sent Forth by God's Blessing
117 O God, Our Help in Ages Past

*See also hymns listed on 31.*

GOING FORTH * *See 32.*

*If the congregation is moving to a new building nearby, the procession begu*
*during the Recessional Hymn may continue to the new building, where there ma*
*be an opening service of worship (see 637-42).*

# AN ORDER FOR DISBANDING A CONGREGATION

*The final service of worship of a congregation that is disbanding should follow*
*pattern familiar to the congregation, concluding with An Order for the Leave-takin*
*of a Church Building (648-50). Following the Declaration of Deconsecration of th*
*Church Building (649), the congregation may form a circle and be disbanded wit*
*these or other words.*

*The bishop or bishop's representative (who may be the pastor) may make this o*
*another Declaration Disbanding the Congregation:*

This congregation, named the *Name* United Methodist Church,
was organized as a part of Christ's holy Church
   and of The United Methodist Church.
It was God's gift for a season.
We are thankful for the many ways it has served the mission
   given to it by Jesus Christ.
It has accomplished its purpose.
We declare that it is no longer a United Methodist congregation
   and is now disbanded.
But Christ's holy Church is of God,
   and will be preserved to the end of time,
   for the conduct of worship
      and the due administration of God's Word and Sacraments,
   the maintenance of Christian fellowship and discipline,
   the edification of believers,
   and the conversion of the world.
We remain part of Christ's ongoing Church,
   and as we scatter into other congregations
   we shall still be one with Christ, one with each other,

and one in ministry to all the world,
until Christ comes in final victory and we feast at his heavenly banquet.

*he congregation may continue in a circle and conclude the service as on 649-50, with*
*ing response, Closing Prayer, The Lord's Prayer, Closing Hymn, and Going Forth.*
*he Closing Hymn may be one that is especially beloved by the congregation.*

# X. CONSECRATIONS AND ORDINATIONS

## INTRODUCTION TO THE
## CONSECRATION OF DIACONAL MINISTERS

"The New Testament witness to Jesus Christ makes clear that the primar form of his ministry, in God's name, was that of service (*diakonia*) in th world. Very early in its history the Church came to understand that all of it members were commissioned, in Baptism, to ministries of love, justice, an service, within local congregations and the larger communities in whic they lived; all who follow Jesus have a share in the ministry of Jesus, wh came not to be served, but to serve. There is thus a general ministry of a baptized Christians.

"The Church also affirms that particular persons are called and set apart fc representative ministries of leadership within the body, to help the whole c the membership of the Church be engaged in and fulfill its ministry c service. The purpose of such leadership is the equipping of the genera ministry of the Church, to the end that the whole Church may be built up a the Body of Christ for the work of ministry. This set-apart ministry is not substitute for the diaconal responsibility of all members of the genera ministry. Rather, it exists to intensify and make more effective the sel understanding of the whole People of God as servants in Christ's name" (*Tf Book of Discipline 1992,* ¶ 301).

"The words *deacon, deaconess, diaconate,* and *diaconal* all spring from common Greek root—*diakonia,* or 'service.' Very early in its history th Church instituted an order of . . . ministers to personify or focus th servanthood to which all Christians are called.

"Those who are called to this representative ministry of service in th Church and world may be set apart to the office of diaconal minister. Th ministry exemplifies the servanthood every Christian is called to live in bot Church and world. Participating with the elder in the leadership of worshir working in a serving-profession in the Church, and serving the needs of th poor, the sick, or oppressed, the diaconal minister embodies the unity of th congregation's worship with its life in the world" (*The Book of Discipline 199. ¶* 302).

Consecration includes prayer in which the Holy Spirit is invoked t empower a person for the exercise of a particular ministry.

To be set apart to diaconal ministry means that a person has received a call t a particular ministry, has responded to that call, has prepared through stud

652

nd the meeting of all the standards for this form of ministry, is committed to quip others for ministry, has been affirmed by the Annual Conference, has een consecrated by a bishop of the Church, and is accountable to the faith ommunity.

The diaconal minister's relationship to the Annual Conference of The Jnited Methodist Church shall be conferred by the act of consecration. Consecration should take place in the Annual Conference where local nembership is held" (*The Book of Discipline 1992,* ¶ 307).

'he resident bishop should be responsible for the service of consecration, ollowing the approved order, and should plan it in consultation with the onference Board of Diaconal Ministry and the conference Worship Committee.

'he bishop shall preside at the consecration service during a session of the nnual Conference. Laity, diaconal ministers, and ordained clergy may articipate in leadership during the Entrance, Presentation, and Proclamation.

'he bishop shall lay hands on the head of the candidate. A district uperintendent, a sponsor, a lay member of the conference, and a diaconal ninister chosen by the bishop may also participate in the laying on of hands. pouses and other family members of candidates for consecration should ot participate in the laying on of hands. Family members and friends may e invited to stand where they are for silent prayer during the laying on of ands.

'are should be taken to enable members of the congregation to see the ying on of hands. Cameras, videocassette recorders, and other equipment hould not be allowed to intrude upon the service.

he candidates for consecration are presented to the bishop using each andidate's full name.

/hen Holy Scriptures are presented to candidates, complete texts of the Old nd New Testaments are to be used.

ollowing the presentation of the Bible to each candidate, a diaconal's stole, )wel and basin, or other appropriate sign may be presented to each andidate. It is recommended that diaconal ministers wear the stole as a sash ver the left shoulder, fastened below the right arm. The color of the stole may e the liturgical color of the day, season, or occasion. At consecration services e stoles are usually red, signifying the work and gifts of the Holy Spirit.

he service normally takes place within the service of Word and Table, with loly Communion served to the entire congregation.

ed is an appropriate color for paraments.

ecause consecrations are acts of the whole Church, the text and rubrics of he Order for the Consecration of Diaconal Ministers are to be used as pproved by the General Conference.

# THE ORDER FOR THE CONSECRATION OF DIACONAL MINISTERS

## ENTRANCE

### GATHERING

*The service begins with the gathering of the people. Festive music may be offered while the people gather. The service may then continue with a procession including the worship leaders, other participants in worship, candidates, and bishop(s).*

### PROCESSIONAL HYMN *

*If the hymn is to be a hymn of praise, it follows the Greeting. Processional hymn are listed on 713.*

### GREETING AND OPENING PRAYER *

*The bishop begins; the people respond.*

We come together as the Church
  to offer praise and thanksgiving to God,
  to hear the Holy Word,
  and to seek for ourselves and others
  the power, presence, and direction of the Holy Spirit.
Let us pray.

**Eternal God, by Jesus Christ and the Holy Spirit**
  **you gave to your apostles many excellent gifts.**
**Give your grace to all servants of your Church**
  **that we may with diligence and faithfulness**
    **fulfill our various ministries.**
**Grant that we your people may follow where you lead**
  **and live in joyful obedience to your will;**
**through Jesus Christ our Savior. Amen.**

*The people are seated.*

## RECOGNITION OF OUR COMMON MINISTRY

*The bishop begins:*

Ministry is the work of God,
  done by the people of God

and given to each Christian as vocation.
Through baptism
　all Christians are made part of the priesthood of all believers,
　the Church made visible in the world.
God in Christ through the Holy Spirit
　empowers us to live as witnesses of God's grace and love.
We are to bear witness in and through the life of the Church
　and to be faithful in our daily lives.

Therefore, in celebration of our common ministry,
　I call upon all God's people gathered here:
Remember your baptism and be thankful.
**We remember our baptism and affirm our common ministry.**

# PRESENTATION

*One layperson and one diaconal minister from the conference Board of Diaconal Ministry, chosen by the bishop, present to the bishop those who are to be consecrated.*

*Layperson:*

This day,
　these are the witnesses who have come forth from among us.
They are responding to their call by the Holy Spirit
　to diaconal ministry.

Bishop *Name,*
on behalf of the laity of the local congregations
　who have examined and approved these candidates,

*Diaconal minister:*

and on behalf of the Board of Diaconal Ministry,
　which has recommended these candidates,
and the Annual Conference, which has approved them,
　we present to you these persons
　to be consecrated diaconal ministers in Christ's holy Church:

*The full name of each candidate is read aloud by a presenter, and each candidate stands.*

*After the candidates have been presented, all candidates remain standing, and the bishop says:*

These persons are by God's grace
　to be consecrated to diaconal ministry.
Those authorized by the Church to inquire about them
　have discerned that they are persons
　　of sound learning and of Christian character.

They possess the necessary gifts and evidence of God's grace,
and have demonstrated a profound commitment to serve Jesus Christ
Therefore, we believe them to be duly called
to serve God in this representative ministry.

We ask you, people of God, to declare your assent
to the consecration of these persons.
Do you trust that they are worthy, by God's grace, to be consecrated

**We do! Thanks be to God!**

Will you uphold them in their ministry?

**With God's help, we will!**

Let us pray.

**Almighty God,**
**the giver of every good and perfect gift,**
**to whom all work must be consecrated,**
**we commend to you these persons**
**to be consecrated to diaconal ministry within your Church.**
**Grant to them a vision of service;**
**give them strength for the performance of their duties,**
**an understanding heart,**
**and a willingness to work with all others**
**in the ministry of the Church,**
**through Jesus Christ our Savior. Amen.**

*The bishop and candidates are seated.*

## PROCLAMATION

*Suggested scripture readings are found on 711-12.*

OLD TESTAMENT LESSON

PSALM *

NEW TESTAMENT LESSON

HYMN OR ANTHEM *

*Hymns are listed on 713.*

GOSPEL LESSON *

SERMON

THE APOSTLES' CREED * *See UMH 881, 882.*

HYMN *

*Hymns are listed on 713. During the hymn, the candidates come forward.*

## EXAMINATION

*All are seated, except the candidates and the bishop, who stand facing each other. The bishop examines the candidates, saying:*

All baptized Christians are called to share in Christ's ministry
of love and service in the world,
to the glory of God
and for the redemption of the human family and the whole of creation.

My *brothers and sisters,*
you are to be consecrated to diaconal ministry
in Christ's holy Church.
You are to represent to the Church
the ministry of servanthood in the world.

God has called you to a special ministry
that will exemplify Christ's servanthood.
You are to lead the people of God to be obedient servants,
to participate in the leadership of worship,
to demonstrate concern for love, justice, and freedom,
to counsel the troubled in spirit,
to teach from the riches of God's grace,
to serve the poor, the sick, and the oppressed,
to equip all Christians to be in ministry
and in service to the community,
and to embody the unity of the congregation's worship
with its life in the world.

As a diaconal minister in the Church,
you are to be a coworker with other diaconal ministers,
and with the bishops, deacons, and elders.
It is your task to proclaim by word and deed
the gospel of Jesus Christ,
and to lead your life in accordance with it.

So that we may know that you believe yourselves
to be called by God
and that you profess the Christian faith,
we ask you:
Do you believe that you have been called by God
to the life and work of a diaconal minister?

**I do so believe.**

Do you believe in the Triune God,
and confess Jesus Christ as your Lord and Savior?

**I do so believe and confess.**

Do you believe the doctrines of the Christian faith?

**I do so believe them.**

Are you persuaded
   that the scriptures of the Old and New Testaments
   contain all things necessary for salvation,
through faith in Jesus Christ, and are the unique and authoritative
   standard for the church's faith and life?

**I am so persuaded, by God's grace.**

Will you be faithful in prayer,
   in the reading and study of the Holy Scriptures,
   and with the help of the Holy Spirit
   continually rekindle the gift of God that is in you?

**I will, God being my helper.**

Will you live
   so that the power of God may be manifest in your life and ministry
   enabling others to become disciples of Jesus Christ?

**I will, by God's grace.**

Will you accept the duties that have been committed to your care,
   and will you discharge them faithfully
   in serving all persons to the glory of God?

**I will, God being my helper.**

Will you be loyal to The United Methodist Church,
   accepting its order, liturgy, doctrine, and discipline,
   committing yourself to be accountable with those serving with you
and to those who are appointed to supervise your ministry?

**I will, God being my helper.**

Remember that you are called
   to serve rather than to be served,
   to proclaim the faith of the Church and no other,
   to look after the concerns of Christ above all.

May God,
   who has given you the will to do these things,
   give you grace to perform them
   that the work begun in you may be brought to perfection. **Amen.**

# LAYING ON OF HANDS AND PRAYER

*The bishop calls the people to prayer, saying:*

As these persons are consecrated by God and the Church
    as diaconal ministers,
let us pray for them.

*The candidates kneel. The people pray for them in silence.*

*The bishop prays:*

We give thanks to you, eternal God,
    that in your great love
    you sent Jesus Christ,
    to take the form of a servant for the sake of us all,
    becoming obedient even to death on the cross.
We praise you that you have highly exalted Jesus Christ your servant
    and that you have taught us, by his word and example,
    that whoever would be great among us must be servant of all.

We thank you that Jesus Christ has poured forth your gifts,
    for equipping the saints for the work of ministry,
    for serving the poor, the sick, and the oppressed,
    for building up Christ's body the Church,
    and for fulfilling your gracious purpose in the world.

Give to these servants the grace and power
    to serve you in this ministry
    so that your people may be strengthened
    and your name glorified in all the world.

*Family members and friends may be invited to stand where they are for silent prayer
during the laying on of hands.*

*One by one, the candidates stand, go to the bishop, and kneel. Calling each
candidate by name, the bishop lays both hands on the head of each one. Other
participating persons also lay on hands. While hands are imposed, the prayer
continues:*

Eternal God, pour upon *Name* your Holy Spirit
for the office and work of a diaconal minister,
in the name of the Father, and of the Son, and of the Holy Spirit.

*After all have received the laying on of hands, the bishop, with both hands extended,
concludes the prayer:*

We thank you, God,
    for raising up among us faithful servants
    for diaconal ministry in your Church.
Clothe them with your righteousness,

and grant that we, with them,
may glorify you by giving ourselves to others;
through Jesus Christ our Savior,
who lives and reigns with you,
in the unity of the Holy Spirit,
one God, now and for ever. **Amen.**

*The following sign act of delivering a Bible may be done immediately after the laying on of hands and prayer for the Holy Spirit.*

*Then the bishop shall deliver to each one a Bible, saying:*

*Name,* take authority as a diaconal minister in the Church
to teach the Word,
to practice justice,
and to serve God's people.

*A diaconal's stole, a towel and basin, or other appropriate sign may be given to the diaconal ministers.*

*If the Lord's Supper is celebrated, the new diaconal ministers remain to assist the bishop. The service on 678-82 may be followed. If the Lord's Supper is not celebrated, they return to their seats.*

*When the Lord's Supper is not celebrated, the service concludes as follows.*

## SENDING FORTH

## HYMN *

*If the closing hymn is a recessional, it should follow Dismissal with Blessing otherwise it should precede Dismissal with Blessing.*
*Closing hymns are listed on 713.*

## DISMISSAL WITH BLESSING *

*The bishop dismisses and blesses the people, saying:*

The grace of our Savior Jesus Christ,
the love of God,
and the communion of the Holy Spirit be with you all. **Amen.**

Go forth in the power of the Holy Spirit!
Proclaim the gospel throughout the earth!
Serve God with gladness, in deeds of justice and mercy!

**We are sent in the name and with the power of Jesus Christ!
Thanks be to God!**

## GOING FORTH *

# NTRODUCTION TO THE ORDINATION OF DEACONS

Ordination is a public act of the Church which indicates acceptance by an dividual of God's call to the upbuilding of the Church through the ministry f Word, Sacrament, and Order and acknowledgment and authentication of is call by the Christian community through prayers and the laying on of ands.

It is a rite of the Church following New Testament usage as appears in the ords of Paul to Timothy: 'I remind you to rekindle the gift of God that is ithin you through the laying on of my hands' (2 Timothy 1:6).

United Methodist tradition has entrusted persons in the ordained ministry ith the responsibility for maintaining standards: for education and training nd for examination and granting credentials to those who seek ordination. y the authorization of the clergy members of the Annual Conference, andidates are elected into the Annual Conference and are ordained by the ishop, who will use the historic language of the Holy Trinity: Father, Son, nd Holy Spirit. Because ordinations are acts of the whole Church, the text nd rubrics of the orders for ordination are to be used as approved by the eneral Conference.

Ordination, thus, is that act by which the Church symbolizes a shared elationship between those ordained for sacramental and functional eadership and the Church community from which the person being rdained has come. The community is initiated by God, is given meaning nd direction by Christ, and is sustained by the Holy Spirit. This relationship a gift which comes through the grace of God in assurance of the ministry of hrist throughout the world" (*The Book of Discipline 1992*, ¶ 432).

Ordination includes prayer in which the Holy Spirit is invoked to empower a erson for the exercise of a particular ministry.

he resident bishop should be responsible for the service of ordination and hould plan it in consultation with the conference Board of Ordained linistry and the conference Worship Committee.

he bishop shall preside at the ordination service. Laity, diaconal ministers, nd ordained clergy may participate in leadership during the Entrance, resentation, and Proclamation.

he service should take place during Annual Conference. Red is the ppropriate color for paraments.

Orders from another denomination are recognized in accordance with isciplinary requirements, ordination is not repeated for any person. ersons whose Orders are recognized should participate as candidates in the ervice except in the laying on of hands.

The candidates for ordination are presented to the bishop using each candidate's full name.

Deacons "shall be ordained by a bishop, employing the Order of Service for the Ordination of Deacons" (*The Book of Discipline 1992*, ¶ 434.3).

Care should be taken to enable members of the congregation to see the laying on of hands. Cameras, videocassette recorders, and other equipment should not be allowed to intrude upon the service.

The resident bishop alone shall lay on hands. Spouses and other family members of candidates for ordination should not participate in the laying on of hands. Family members and friends may be invited to stand where they are for silent prayer during the laying on of hands.

When Holy Scriptures are presented to candidates, complete texts of the Old and New Testaments are to be used.

Following the presentation of the Bible to each candidate, a deacon's stole may be presented. It is recommended that deacons wear the stole as a sash over the left shoulder, fastened below the right arm. The color of the stole may be the liturgical color of the day, season, or occasion. At ordination services the stoles are usually red, signifying the work and gifts of the Holy Spirit.

The service of ordination normally takes place within the service of Word and Table, with Holy Communion served to the entire congregation.

Updates to this service can be found at:
www.umcdiscipleship.org/services-for-the-ordering-of-ministry-in-the-united-methodist-church

# THE ORDER FOR
# THE ORDINATION OF DEACONS

## ENTRANCE

**GATHERING**

*The service begins with the gathering of the people. Festive music may be offered while the people gather. The service may then continue with a procession including the worship leaders, other participants in worship, candidates, and bishop(s).*

**PROCESSIONAL HYMN ***

*If the hymn is to be a hymn of praise, it follows the Greeting. Processional hymns are listed on 713.*

**GREETING AND OPENING PRAYER ***

*The bishop begins; the people respond.*

The grace of our Lord Jesus Christ be with you all.

**And also with you.**

Our help is in the name of the Lord.

**The Creator of heaven and earth.**

Let us pray.

**Almighty God, by your Son Jesus Christ and the Holy Spirit
  you gave to your apostles many excellent gifts.
Give your grace to all
  who have been called to representative ministry,
  that they may with diligence and faithfulness
  fulfill their various ministries.
Grant that we your people may follow where you lead,
  perfect our ministries,
  and live in joyful obedience to your will;
through Jesus Christ our Lord. Amen.**

*The people are seated.*

# PRESENTATION

*One layperson and one elder from the conference Board of Ordained Ministry, chosen by the bishop, present to the bishop those who are to be ordained deacons. The bishop stands before the Lord's table, facing the people.*

*Layperson:*

Bishop *Name,*
   on behalf of the laity of the local congregations
   who have examined and approved these candidates,

*Elder:*

and on behalf of the elders of the Annual Conference,
   who have also examined and approved these candidates,
   we present to you these persons
   to be ordained deacons in Christ's holy Church:

*The full name of each candidate is read aloud by a presenter, and each candidate stands.*

*After the candidates have been presented, all candidates remain standing, and the bishop says:*

These persons are by God's grace
   to be ordained to the ministry of deacons.
Those authorized by the Church to inquire about them
   have found them to be of sound learning
   and of Christian character,
   to possess the necessary gifts and evidence of God's grace,
   and believe them to be duly called
   to serve God in this ministry.

We ask you, people of God,
   to declare your assent to the ordination of these persons.
Do you trust that they are worthy, by God's grace, to be ordained?

**We do! Thanks be to God!**

Will you uphold them in their ministry?

**With God's help, we will!**

*The bishop and candidates are seated.*

# PROCLAMATION

*Suggested scripture lessons are found on 711-12.*

## OLD TESTAMENT LESSON

SALM *

EW TESTAMENT LESSON

YMN OR ANTHEM *

*Hymns are listed on 713.*

OSPEL LESSON *

ERMON

HE APOSTLES' CREED * *See UMH 881, 882.*

YMN *

*Hymns are listed on 713.*

*During the hymn, the candidates come forward.*

## EXAMINATION

*All are seated, except the candidates and the bishop, who stand facing each other. The bishop examines the candidates, saying:*

My *brothers and sisters,*
    you are to be ordained to the ministry of deacons
    in the Church of God.

God has called you to represent to the Church
    the ministry of servanthood in the world,
    a ministry to which all Christians are called in baptism.
You are to preach the Word of God,
    to assist in the leadership of worship,
    and to assist the elders at Holy Baptism and Holy Communion.
You are to be a coworker with other deacons,
    and with the bishops, diaconal ministers, and elders.
In the name of Jesus Christ
    you are to serve all people,
    particularly the poor, the sick, and the oppressed.
You are to interpret to the Church
    the needs, concerns, and hopes of the world.
At all times, by your life and teaching
    you are to show Christ's people
    that in serving the helpless they are serving Christ.

So that we may know that you believe yourselves
    to be called by God

and that you profess the Christian faith,
we ask you:

Do you trust that you are called by God
to the life and work of a deacon?

**I do so trust.**

Do you believe in the Triune God,
and confess Jesus Christ as your Lord and Savior?

**I do so believe and confess.**

Do you believe the doctrines of the Christian faith?

**I do so believe them.**

Are you persuaded
that the scriptures of the Old and New Testaments
contain all things necessary for salvation
through faith in Jesus Christ,
and are the unique and authoritative standard
for the Church's faith and life?

**I am so persuaded, by God's grace.**

Will you be faithful in prayer,
in the reading and study of the Holy Scriptures,
and with the help of the Holy Spirit
continually rekindle the gift of God that is in you?

**I will, with the help of God.**

Will you do your best to pattern your life
in accordance with the teachings of Christ?

**I will, with the help of God.**

Will you, in the exercise of your ministry,
lead the people of God
to faith in Jesus Christ,
to participate in the life and work of the community,
and to seek peace, justice, and freedom for all people?

**I will, with the help of God.**

Will you be loyal to The United Methodist Church,
accepting its order, liturgy, doctrine, and discipline,
and accepting the authority of those who are appointed
to supervise your ministry?

**I will, with the help of God.**

May God,
who has given you the will to do these things,
give you grace to perform them
that the work begun in you may be brought to perfection. **Amen.**

# LAYING ON OF HANDS AND PRAYER

*The bishop calls the people to prayer, saying:*

As these persons are ordained by God and the Church
 for the ministry of deacons
 to which we believe they have been called by the Holy Spirit,
let us pray for them.

*The candidates kneel.*

*The people pray for them in silence.*

*The bishop addresses the candidates:*

My *sisters and brothers,*
 from the time of the apostles
 persons with suitable gifts and grace have been set apart
 by the laying on of hands and prayer
 for a ministry of service in the Church of Jesus Christ our Lord.
We trust that the Spirit of God
 has called you to the ministry of deacons.
As earnest prayer is made
 for the fulfillment of the Spirit's gift in you,
 the Church of God now calls you
 to receive the laying on of hands
 as the seal of your vocation by the Spirit.

*Family members and friends may be invited to stand where they are for silent prayer during the laying on of hands.*

*One by one, the candidates stand, go to the bishop, and kneel. Calling each candidate by name, the bishop lays both hands on the head of each one. While hands are imposed, the bishop prays:*

Lord, pour upon *Name* the Holy Spirit
for the office and work of a deacon,
in the name of the Father, and of the Son, and of the Holy Spirit.

*After all have received the laying on of hands, the bishop facing the candidates, with both hands extended over them, prays:*

Let us pray.

We give thanks to you, Lord God,
 that in your great love
 you sent Jesus Christ, your only begotten,
 to take the form of a servant for the sake of us all,
 becoming obedient even to death on the cross.
We praise you that you have highly exalted Jesus Christ your servant
 whom you have made to be Lord of all,
 and that you have taught us, by his word and example,

that whoever would be great among us must be servant of all.
Increase within the lives of these your servants
    the gift of the Holy Spirit,
    through Jesus Christ your Son,
    for the ministry of a deacon in your Church.
Give them grace to be faithful to their promises,
    constant in their discipleship,
    and always ready for the works of loving service.
Make them modest and humble, gentle and strong,
    that, having the assurance of faith and rejoicing in hope,
    they may be rooted and grounded in love.
Give them a share in the ministry of Jesus Christ,
    who came not to be served but to serve;
who now lives and reigns with you,
in the unity of the Holy Spirit,
one God, now and for ever. **Amen.**

*The following sign act of delivering a Bible may be done immediately after the*
*laying on of hands and prayer for the Holy Spirit.*

*Then the bishop shall deliver to each deacon a Bible, saying:*

*Name,* take authority as a deacon in the Church
    to preach the Word of God,
    and to serve all God's people.

*A deacon's stole or other gift may be given to each deacon.*


## RECOGNITION OF ORDERS

*The bishop addresses all those whose orders as deacons are recognized. If the bishop*
*prefers, this may be done immediately prior to the laying on of hands.*

After due examination
    of your call and ministry in another part of Christ's holy Church,
    we now welcome you to this communion.
You have given assurance of your faith and Christian experience.
You have renewed the vows of your ordination
    and committed yourself to uphold faithfully
    The United Methodist Church.
We rejoice that you have been called to serve among us,
    and pray that the Spirit of God may guide your ministry.

*As each candidate comes forward, the bishop uses the following greeting:*

*Name,* we now recognize you as a deacon
    in The United Methodist Church.

HYMN *

*Hymns are listed on 713.*

*If the Lord's Supper is celebrated, the deacons remain to assist the bishop. The service on 678-82 may be followed. If the Lord's Supper is not celebrated, they return to their seats.*

*When the Lord's Supper is not celebrated, the service concludes as follows.*

## SENDING FORTH

PRAYER

*The following is used only if the Lord's Supper has not been celebrated. The bishop says:*

Let us pray.

We thank you, Lord God,
   for raising up among us faithful servants
   for the ministry of deacons in your Church.
Clothe them with your righteousness,
   and grant that we, with them, may glorify you
   by giving ourselves to others;
through Jesus Christ our Lord,
who lives and reigns with you,
in the unity of the Holy Spirit,
one God, now and for ever. **Amen.**

HYMN *

*If the closing hymn is a recessional, it should follow Dismissal with Blessing; otherwise it should precede Dismissal with Blessing.*
*Closing hymns are listed on 713.*

DISMISSAL WITH BLESSING *

*The bishop dismisses and blesses the people, saying:*

Go in peace
   to serve God and your neighbor in all that you do.
**We go in the name of Christ. Thanks be to God!**

The blessing of almighty God,
   Father, Son, and Holy Spirit, be with you always. **Amen.**

GOING FORTH *

# INTRODUCTION TO THE ORDINATION OF ELDERS

"Ordination is a public act of the Church which indicates acceptance by a individual of God's call to the upbuilding of the Church through th ministry of Word, Sacrament, and Order and acknowledgment an authentication of this call by the Christian community through prayer and the laying on of hands.

"It is a rite of the Church following New Testament usage as appears in th words of Paul to Timothy: 'I remind you to rekindle the gift of God that i within you through the laying on of my hands' (2 Timothy 1:6).

"United Methodist tradition has entrusted persons in the ordained ministr with the responsibility for maintaining standards: for education and trainin and for examination and granting credentials to those who seek ordinatior By the authorization of the clergy members of the Annual Conference candidates are elected into the Annual Conference and are ordained by th bishop, who will use the historic language of the Holy Trinity: Father, Sor and Holy Spirit. Because ordinations are acts of the whole Church, the te> and rubrics of the orders for ordination are to be used as approved by th General Conference.

"Ordination, thus, is that act by which the Church symbolizes a share relationship between those ordained for sacramental and functional leade> ship and the Church community from which the person being ordaine has come. The community is initiated by God, is given meaning an direction by Christ, and is sustained by the Holy Spirit. This relationship i a gift which comes through the grace of God in assurance of the ministry c Christ throughout the world" (*The Book of Discipline 1992*, ¶ 432).

Ordination includes prayer in which the Holy Spirit is invoked to empower person for the exercise of a particular ministry.

The resident bishop should be responsible for the service of ordination an should plan it in consultation with the conference Board of Ordaine Ministry and the conference Worship Committee.

The bishop shall preside at the ordination service. Laity, diaconal ministers and ordained clergy may participate in leadership during the Entrance Presentation, and Proclamation.

The service should take place during Annual Conference. Red is th appropriate color for paraments.

If Orders from another denomination are recognized in accordance wit disciplinary requirements, ordination is not repeated for any persor Persons whose Orders are recognized should participate as candidates in th service except in the laying on of hands.

The candidates for ordination are presented to the bishop using eac candidate's full name.

lders "shall be ordained by a bishop, employing the Order of Service for the rdination of Elders. The bishops shall be assisted by other elders." The rvice "may include laity designated by the bishop representing the Church mmunity and representatives of other Christian communions, especially ember churches of the Consultation on Church Union in the laying on of ands" *(The Book of Discipline 1992, ¶ 435.3)*.

are should be taken to enable members of the congregation to see the ying on of hands by the bishop and others. Cameras, videocassette corders, and other equipment should not be allowed to intrude upon the rvice. The bishop may limit the number of persons participating in the ying on of hands to ensure that candidates are not hidden from the ngregation.

pouses and other family members of candidates for ordination should not articipate in the laying on of hands. Family members and friends may be vited to stand where they are for silent prayer during the laying on of ands.

hen Holy Scriptures are presented to candidates, complete texts of the Old nd New Testaments are to be used.

ollowing the presentation of the Bible to each candidate, an elder's stole or a alice and paten together may be presented. It is recommended that elders ear the stole around the backs of their necks, hanging down in front. The olor of the stole may be the liturgical color of the day, season, or occasion. t ordination services the stoles are usually red, signifying the work and ifts of the Holy Spirit.

he service of ordination normally takes place within the service of Word nd Table, with Holy Communion served to the entire congregation.

Updates to this service can be found at:
www.umcdiscipleship.org/services-for-the-ordering-of-ministry-in-the-united-methodist-church

# THE ORDER FOR
# THE ORDINATION OF ELDERS

## ENTRANCE

### GATHERING

*The service begins with the gathering of the people. Festive music may be offere while the people gather. The service may then continue with a procession includin the worship leaders, other participants in worship, candidates, and bishop(s)*

### PROCESSIONAL HYMN *

*If the hymn is to be a hymn of praise, it follows the Greeting. Processional hymn are listed on 713.*

### GREETING AND OPENING PRAYER *

*The bishop begins; the people respond.*

The grace of our Lord Jesus Christ be with you all.

**And also with you.**

Our help is in the name of the Lord.

**The creator of heaven and earth.**

Let us pray.

**God of light and truth,**
  **you led your holy apostles**
  **to appoint ministers in every place.**
**Guide your Church,**
  **through the wisdom of your Holy Spirit,**
  **that we may choose men and women with gifts of grace**
  **for the ministry of Word, Sacrament, and Order.**
**May we uphold them in their work,**
  **and may your reign be extended;**
**through Jesus Christ, the Shepherd of our souls,**
**who with you and the Holy Spirit,**
**is worshiped and glorified,**
**one God, for ever and ever. Amen.**

*The people are seated.*

# PRESENTATION

*One layperson and one elder from the conference Board of Ordained Ministry, chosen by the bishop, present to the bishop those who are to be ordained elders. The bishop stands before the Lord's table, facing the people.*

*Layperson:*

Bishop *Name,*
on behalf of the laity of the local congregations
who have examined and approved these candidates,

*Elder:*

and on behalf of the elders of the Annual Conference,
who have also examined and approved these candidates,
we present to you these persons
to be ordained elders in Christ's holy Church:

*The full name of each candidate is read aloud by a presenter, and each candidate stands.*

*After the candidates have been presented, all candidates remain standing, and the bishop says:*

These persons are by God's grace
to be ordained to the ministry of elders.
Those authorized by the Church to inquire about them
have found them to be of sound learning
and of Christian character,
to possess the necessary gifts and evidence of God's grace,
and believe them to be duly called
to serve God in this ministry.

We ask you, people of God,
to declare your assent to the ordination of these persons.
Do you trust that they are worthy, by God's grace, to be ordained?

**We do! Thanks be to God!**

Will you uphold them in their ministry?

**With God's help, we will!**

*The bishop and candidates are seated.*

# PROCLAMATION

*Suggested scripture lessons are found on 711-12.*

## OLD TESTAMENT LESSON

## PSALM *

## NEW TESTAMENT LESSON

## HYMN OR ANTHEM *

*Hymns are listed on 713.*

## GOSPEL LESSON *

## SERMON

## THE APOSTLES' CREED * *See* UMH *881, 882.*

## HYMN *

*Hymns are listed on 713.*

*During the singing of the hymn, the candidates come forward.*


# EXAMINATION

*All are seated, except the candidates and the bishop, who stand facing each other*
*The bishop examines the candidates, saying:*

My brothers and sisters,
    you are to be ordained to the ministry of elders
    in the Church of God.

All baptized Christians are called to share in Christ's ministry
    of love and service in the world,
    to the glory of God
    and for the redemption of the human family and the whole of creation

As an elder in the Church,
    you are called to share in the ministry of Christ
    and of the whole Church:
by preaching and teaching the Word of God
    and faithfully administering
        the Sacraments of Baptism and Holy Communion;
by leading the people of God in worship and prayer;
by leading persons to faith in Jesus Christ;

by exercising pastoral supervision of the people committed to your care,
    ordering the life of the congregation,
    counseling the troubled in spirit,
    and declaring the forgiveness of sin;
by leading the people of God
    in obedience to mission in the world,
    to seek justice, peace, and freedom for all people;
by taking a responsible place in the government of the Church
    and in service to the community;
and by being conformed to the life of Christ,
    who took the form of a servant for our sake.

As an elder in the Church,
    you are to be in covenant with the elders in this Annual Conference,
    and a coworker with the bishop, other elders,
    deacons, and diaconal ministers.
It is your task to proclaim by word and deed
    the gospel of Jesus Christ,
    and to fashion your life in accordance with its precepts.
You are to love, serve, and pray
    for all the people among whom you work,
    caring alike for young and old,
    strong and weak, rich and poor.

Remember that you are called
    to serve rather than to be served,
    to proclaim the faith of the Church and no other,
    to look after the concerns of Christ above all.

So that we may know that you believe yourselves
    to be called by God
    and that you profess the Christian faith,
we ask you:

Do you trust that you are called by God
    to the life and work of an elder?

**I do so trust.**

Do you believe in the Triune God,
    and confess Jesus Christ as your Lord and Savior?

**I do so believe and confess.**

Are you persuaded
    that the scriptures of the Old and New Testaments
    contain all things necessary for salvation
    through faith in Jesus Christ,
    and are the unique and authoritative standard
    for the Church's faith and life?

**I am so persuaded, by God's grace.**

Will you be faithful in prayer,
   in the reading and study of the Holy Scriptures,
   and with the help of the Holy Spirit
   continually rekindle the gift of God that is in you?

**I will, with the help of God.**

Will you be a steadfast disciple of Christ,
   so that your life may be fashioned by the gospel,
   and provide a faithful example for all God's people?

**I will, with the help of God.**

In covenant with other elders,
   will you be loyal to The United Methodist Church,
   accepting its order, liturgy, doctrine, and discipline,
   defending it against all doctrines contrary to God's Holy Word,
   and accepting the authority of those who are appointed
      to supervise your ministry?

**I will, with the help of God.**

May God,
   who has given you the will to do these things,
   give you grace to perform them
   that the work begun in you may be brought to perfection. **Amen.**

## LAYING ON OF HANDS AND PRAYER

*The bishop calls the people to prayer, saying:*

As these persons are ordained by God and the Church
   for the ministry of elders
   to which we believe they have been called by the Holy Spirit,
let us pray for them.

*The candidates kneel.*

*The people pray for them in silence.*

*The hymn O Holy Spirit, By Whose Breath ( ♪ 223 or UMH 651) may* ♦
*sung.*

*The bishop, standing and facing the candidates, with both hands extended ove*
*them, begins the prayer of ordination:*

We praise you, eternal God,
   because you have called us in your infinite love
   to be a priestly people,
   offering to you acceptable worship through Jesus Christ our Lord,

Apostle and High Priest, Shepherd and Bishop of our souls.
We thank you that, by dying, Christ has overcome death
    and, having ascended into heaven,
    has poured forth gifts abundantly on your people,
    making some apostles, some prophets,
        some evangelists, some pastors and teachers,
    to equip the saints for the work of ministry,
    to build up Christ's body, the Church,
    and to fulfill your gracious purpose in the world.

*Family members and friends may be invited to stand where they are for silent
prayer during the laying on of hands.*

*One by one, the candidates stand, go to the bishop, and kneel. Calling each
candidate by name, the bishop lays both hands on the head of each one. Other
participating elders also lay on their hands. Bishops and others with ordaining
responsibilities from other communions may be invited to lay on hands also. Laity
designated by the bishop to represent the Church community may be included in the
laying on of hands. While hands are imposed, the prayer continues:*

Lord, pour upon *Name* the Holy Spirit
for the office and work of an elder,
in the name of the Father, and of the Son, and of the Holy Spirit.

*After laying on of hands of all candidates, the bishop, facing the candidates, with
both hands extended over them, concludes the prayer:*

Gracious God,
    give to these your servants the grace and power they need
    to serve you in this ministry,
    so that your people may be strengthened
    and your name glorified in all the world.
Make them faithful pastors, patient teachers, and wise counselors.
Enable them to serve without reproach,
    to proclaim the gospel of salvation,
    to administer the Sacraments of the new covenant,
    to order the life of the Church,
    and to offer with all your people
        spiritual sacrifices acceptable to you;
through Jesus Christ our Lord,
who lives and reigns with you,
in the unity of the Holy Spirit,
one God, now and for ever. **Amen.**

*The following sign act of delivering a Bible may be done immediately after the
laying on of hands and prayer for the Holy Spirit.*

*Then the bishop shall deliver to each candidate a Bible, saying:*

*Name*, take authority as an elder in the Church
to preach the Word of God,
and to administer the Holy Sacraments.

*An elder's stole, or chalice and paten together, may be given to each elder.*


## RECOGNITION OF ORDERS

*The bishop addresses all those whose Orders as elders are recognized. If the bishop prefers, this may be done immediately prior to the laying on of hands.*

After due examination
of your call and ministry in another part of Christ's holy Church,
we now welcome you to this communion.
You have given assurance of your faith and Christian experience.
You have renewed the vows of your ordination
and committed yourself to uphold faithfully
The United Methodist Church.
We rejoice that you have been called to serve among us,
and pray that the Spirit of God may guide your ministry.

*As each candidate comes forward, the bishop uses the following greeting:*

*Name*, we now recognize you as an elder in The United Methodist Church

## HYMN*

*Hymns are listed on 713.*

*If the Lord's Supper is celebrated, the elders remain to assist the bishop, and the service continues as follows. If the Lord's Supper is not celebrated, they return to their seats.*

*When the Lord's Supper is not celebrated, the service concludes with Sending Forth (682).*


## THANKSGIVING AND COMMUNION

### TAKING THE BREAD AND CUP

*The bread and wine are brought by representatives of the people to the Lord's table or uncovered if already in place. Deacons prepare the table for the Lord's Supper.*

*A hymn, doxology, or other response may be sung as the gifts are presented.*

### THE GREAT THANKSGIVING *

*This text is used by the bishop, while the congregation uses A Service of Word and Table III (UMH 15-16) or one of the musical settings (UMH 17-25).*

*The bishop may use the gestures suggested in the text.*

*The presiding bishop, standing behind the Lord's table, facing the people from this time through Breaking the Bread, begins the prayer:*

The Lord be with you.
**And also with you.**
Lift up your hearts. *The bishop may lift hands and keep them raised.*
**We lift them up to the Lord.**
Let us give thanks to the Lord our God.
**It is right to give our thanks and praise.**

It is right, and a good and joyful thing,
    always and everywhere to give thanks to you,
    almighty God, Creator of heaven and earth.

You built your Church
    on the foundation of the apostles and prophets,
    and instituted a holy ministry
    so that your prophetic and apostolic Word
    might be heard in the Church and in the world until the end of time.

And so,
    with your people on earth
    and all the company of heaven
    we praise your name and join their unending hymn:

*The bishop may lower hands.*

**Holy, holy, holy Lord, God of power and might,
heaven and earth are full of your glory.
    Hosanna in the highest.
Blessed is he who comes in the name of the Lord.
    Hosanna in the highest.**

*The bishop may raise hands.*

Holy are you, and blessed is your Son Jesus Christ.
Your Spirit anointed him
    to preach good news to the poor,
    to proclaim release to the captives
    and recovering of sight to the blind,
    to set at liberty those who are oppressed,
    and to announce that the time had come
    when you would save your people.
He healed the sick, fed the hungry, and ate with sinners.
By the baptism of his suffering, death, and resurrection
    you gave birth to your Church,

delivered us from slavery to sin and death,
  and made with us a new covenant by water and the Spirit.
When the Lord Jesus,
  the great Shepherd of your flock, ascended,
  he sent forth the apostles
  to preach the gospel and make disciples of all nations.
He promised to be with them always,
  and sent the Holy Spirit to lead them.

*The bishop may hold hands, palms down, over the bread, or touch the bread, or li*
*the bread.*

On the night in which he gave himself up for us,
  he took bread, gave thanks to you, broke the bread,
  gave it to his disciples, and said:
"Take, eat; this is my body which is given for you.
Do this in remembrance of me."

*The bishop may hold hands, palms down, over the cup, or touch the cup, or lift tʰ*
*cup.*

When the supper was over, he took the cup,
  gave thanks to you, gave it to his disciples, and said:
"Drink from this, all of you;
  this is my blood of the new covenant,
  poured out for you and for many
  for the forgiveness of sins.
Do this, as often as you drink it,
  in remembrance of me."

*The bishop may raise hands.*

And so,
in remembrance of these your mighty acts in Jesus Christ,
we offer ourselves in praise and thanksgiving
  as a holy and living sacrifice,
  in union with Christ's offering for us,
as we proclaim the mystery of faith.

**Christ has died; Christ is risen; Christ will come again.**

*The bishop may hold hands, palms down, over the bread and cup.*

Pour out your Holy Spirit on us gathered here,
  and on these gifts of bread and wine.
Make them be for us the body and blood of Christ,
that we may be for the world the body of Christ,
  redeemed by his blood.

*The bishop may raise hands.*

By your Spirit make us one with Christ,
  one with each other,

and one in ministry to all the world,
until Christ comes in final victory
and we feast at his heavenly banquet.

Through your Son Jesus Christ,
with the Holy Spirit in your holy Church,
all honor and glory is yours, almighty Father,
now and for ever. **Amen.**

## THE LORD'S PRAYER *

## BREAKING THE BREAD

*The bishop, still standing behind the Lord's table, facing the people, assisted by the elders as necessary, while the deacons prepare the cups, breaks the bread in silence, or while saying:*

Because there is one loaf,
we, who are many, are one body, for we all partake of the one loaf.
The bread which we break is a sharing in the body of Christ.

*The bishop lifts the cup in silence, or while saying:*

The cup over which we give thanks is a sharing
in the blood of Christ.

## GIVING THE BREAD AND CUP

*The bread and wine are given to the people by elders, deacons, diaconal ministers, and laity, with these or other words being exchanged:*

The body of Christ, given for you. **Amen.**

The blood of Christ, given for you. **Amen.**

*The congregation sings hymns while the bread and cup are given. In addition to hymns 612-41 and others listed in the index under Holy Communion (UMH 943), many other hymns in UMH are effective in expressing the people's loving communion with God and with one another. The people's knowledge and love of particular hymns are important considerations in the selection of appropriate hymns. It is particularly effective if the people can sing from memory during communion.*

*When all have received, the Lord's table is put in order by the deacons.*

## PRAYER AFTER RECEIVING

*A bishop says:*

Let us pray.

We thank you, gracious Lord, for giving yourself to us,
    and for uniting us in the communion of your Holy Spirit.

We bless you for raising up among us your faithful servants.
Clothe them with your righteousness
   and grant that we, with them,
   may glorify you by giving ourselves to others;
through Jesus Christ our Lord,
who lives and reigns with you,
in the unity of the Holy Spirit,
one God, now and for ever. **Amen.**


## SENDING FORTH

### PRAYER

*The following prayer is used only if the Lord's Supper has not been celebrated. Th*
*bishop says:*

Let us pray.

We thank you, Lord God,
   for raising up among us faithful servants
   for the ministry of elders in your Church.
Clothe them with your righteousness,
   and grant that we, with them,
   may glorify you by giving ourselves to others;
through Jesus Christ our Lord,
who lives and reigns with you,
in the unity of the Holy Spirit,
one God, now and for ever. **Amen.**


### HYMN *

*If the closing hymn is a recessional, it should follow Dismissal with Blessin*
*otherwise it should precede Dismissal with Blessing. Closing hymns are listed o*
*713.*


### DISMISSAL WITH BLESSING *

*The bishop dismisses and blesses the people, saying:*

Go in peace
   to serve God and your neighbor in all that you do.

**We go in the name of Christ. Thanks be to God!**

The blessing of almighty God,
   Father, Son, and Holy Spirit, be with you always. **Amen.**


### GOING FORTH *

# INTRODUCTION TO THE ORDER FOR CONSECRATIONS AND ORDINATIONS

This service is a combination of The Order for the Consecration of Diaconal Ministers (652-60), The Order for the Ordination of Deacons (661-69), and The Order for the Ordination of Elders (670-82). It is designed for use when these three events take place in one service. Worship planners and leaders should review the other services and introductory comments before planning this service.

This service emphasizes various ministries of the Church. It also recognizes the unity and validity of the ministry of Jesus Christ by all Christians and the representative ministries to which individuals are called.

The resident bishop should be responsible for the service and should plan it in consultation with the conference Board of Ordained Ministry, the conference Board of Diaconal Minstry, and the conference Worship Committee.

The bishop should preside at the service. Laity, diaconal ministers, and ordained clergy may participate in leadership during the Entrance, Presentation, and Proclamation.

The service should take place during a session of Annual Conference. Red is an appropriate color for paraments.

If Orders from another denomination are recognized in accordance with disciplinary requirements, ordination is not repeated for any person. Persons whose Orders are recognized should participate as candidates in the service except in the laying on of hands.

The candidates are presented to the bishop using each candidate's full name.

Care should be taken that the sermon address the candidates for the office of diaconal ministry, the order of deacon, and the order of elder.

Diaconal ministers shall be consecrated by a bishop. A district superintendent, a sponsor, the conference lay leader, and a diaconal minister chosen by the bishop may also participate in the laying on of hands.

Deacons "shall be ordained by a bishop" (*The Book of Discipline 1992*, ¶ 434.3).

Elders "shall be ordained by a bishop," and "the bishops shall be assisted by other elders." The service "may include laity designated by the bishop representing the Church community and representatives of other Christian communions, especially member churches of the Consultation on Church Union in the laying on of hands" (*The Book of Discipline 1992*, ¶ 435.3).

Care should be taken to enable members of the congregation to see the laying on of hands by the bishop and others. Cameras, videocassette recorders, and other equipment should not be allowed to intrude upon the service. The bishop may limit the number of persons participating in the laying on of hands to ensure that candidates are not hidden from the congregation.

Spouses and other family members of candidates should not participate in the laying on of hands. Family members and friends may be invited to stand where they are for silent prayer during the laying on of hands.

When Holy Scriptures are presented to candidates, complete texts of the Old and New Testaments are to be used.

Following the presentation of the Bible to each candidate, a stole appropriate to the office (or a towel and basin for diaconal ministers, or a chalice and paten together for elders) may be presented. It is recommended that deacons and diaconal ministers wear the stole as a sash over the left shoulder fastened below the right arm. Elders wear the stole around the backs of their necks, hanging down in front. The color of the stole may be the liturgical color of the day, season, or occasion. At consecration and ordination services, the stoles are usually red, signifying the work and gifts of the Holy Spirit.

The service normally takes place within the service of Word and Table, with Holy Communion served to the entire congregation.

Because consecrations and ordinations are acts of the whole Church, the text and rubrics of the service are to be used as approved by the General Conference.

Updates to the combined service can be found at:
www.umcdiscipleship.org/services-for-the-ordering-of-ministry-in-the-united-methodist-church

# THE ORDER FOR CONSECRATIONS AND ORDINATIONS

## ENTRANCE

### GATHERING

*The service begins with the gathering of the people. Festive music may be offered while the people gather. The service may then continue with a procession including the worship leaders, other participants in worship, candidates, and bishop(s).*

### PROCESSIONAL HYMN *

*If the hymn is to be a hymn of praise, it follows the Greeting. Processional hymns are listed on 713.*

### GREETING AND PRAYER *

*The bishop begins; the people respond.*

The grace of our Lord Jesus Christ be with you all.

**And also with you.**

Our help is in the name of the Lord.

**The Creator of heaven and earth.**

We come together as the Church
　　to offer praise and thanksgiving to God,
　　to hear the Holy Word,
　　and to seek for ourselves and others
　　　　the power, presence, and direction of the Holy Spirit.
Let us pray.

**Eternal God, by Jesus Christ and the Holy Spirit**
　　**you gave to your apostles many excellent gifts.**
**Give your grace**
　　**to all who have been called to representative ministry,**
　　**that they may with diligence and faithfulness**
　　**fulfill their various ministries.**
**Grant that we your people may follow where you lead,**
　　**perfect our ministries,**

**and live in joyful obedience to your will;
through Jesus Christ our Savior. Amen.**

*The people are seated.*

## RECOGNITION OF OUR COMMON MINISTRY

*The bishop begins:*

Ministry is the work of God,
  done by the people of God
  and given to each Christian as vocation.
Through baptism
  all Christians are made part of the priesthood of all believers,
  the Church made visible in the world.
God in Christ through the Holy Spirit
  empowers us to live as witnesses of God's grace and love.
We are to bear witness in and through the life of the Church
  and to be faithful in our daily lives.

Therefore, in celebration of our common ministry,
  I call upon all God's people gathered here:
Remember your baptism and be thankful.

**We remember our baptism and affirm our common ministry.**

## PRESENTATION

*One layperson, one diaconal minister from the conference Board of Diacona*
*Ministry, and one elder from the conference Board of Ordained Ministry, chosen b*
*the bishop, present to the bishop those who are to be consecrated and ordained. Th*
*bishop stands before the Lord's table.*

*Layperson:*

This day,
  these are the witnesses who have come forth from among us.
They are responding to their call by the Holy Spirit
  to representative ministry.

Bishop *Name,*
  on behalf of the laity of the local congregations
  who have examined and approved these candidates,

*Diaconal minister:*

and on behalf of the Board of Diaconal Ministry of the Annual Conference
  which has recommended these candidates,

and the Annual Conference, which has approved them,
  we present to you these persons
  to be consecrated diaconal ministers in Christ's holy Church:

*Elder:*

and on behalf of the elders of the Annual Conference,
  who have examined and approved these candidates,
  we present to you
  these persons to be ordained as deacons,
  and these persons to be ordained as elders in Christ's holy Church:

*The full name of each candidate is read aloud by a presenter—the diaconal minister reading the names of diaconal candidates and the elder reading the names of deacon and elder candidates—and each candidate stands.*

*After the candidates have been presented, all candidates remain standing, and the bishop says:*

These persons are by God's grace
  to be consecrated or ordained to representative ministry.
Those authorized by the Church to inquire about them
  have discerned that they are persons
  of sound learning and of Christian character.
They possess the necessary gifts and evidence of God's grace,
  and have demonstrated a profound commitment to serve Jesus Christ.
Therefore, we believe them to be duly called
  to serve God in this representative ministry.

We ask you, people of God,
  to declare your assent
  to the consecration or ordination of these persons.
Do you trust that they are worthy, by God's grace,
  to be consecrated or ordained?

**We do! Thanks be to God!**

Will you uphold them in their ministry?

**With God's help, we will!**

*The bishop and candidates are seated.*

## PROCLAMATION

*Suggested scripture lessons are found on 711-12.*

OLD TESTAMENT LESSON

PSALM *

NEW TESTAMENT LESSON

## HYMN OR ANTHEM *

*Hymns are listed on 713.*

## GOSPEL LESSON *

## SERMON

## THE APOSTLES' CREED * *See* UMH *881, 882.*

## HYMN *

*Hymns are listed on 713.*

## GENERAL EXAMINATION

*The candidates remain standing, and the bishop addresses all the candidates:*

My *sisters and brothers,*
   all Christians are called through baptism
   to share in Christ's ministry of love and service.
This ministry is empowered by God's Holy Spirit
   for the redemption of the human family and the whole of creation.

You have been called,
   by the Spirit of God working in you,
   to a representative ministry within the people of God.
Christ's body, the Church,
   now confirms your calling through consecration or ordination.

You are to lead the people of God in worship and prayer,
   and to nurture, teach, and encourage them
   from the riches of God's grace.
You are to exemplify Christ's servanthood;
   to build up the people of God
      in their obedience to Christ's mission in the world,
   and to seek justice, peace, and salvation for all people.

As representative ministers in the Church,
   you are to be coworkers with the bishops,
   deacons, diaconal ministers, and elders.
It is your task to proclaim by word and deed the gospel of Jesus Christ
   to lead persons to faith in Jesus Christ,
   and to conform your life in accordance with the gospel.

Remember that you are called
   to serve rather than to be served,
   to proclaim the faith of the Church and no other,
   to look after the concerns of Christ above all.

So that we may know that you believe yourselves
  to be called by God
  and that you profess the Christian faith,
we ask you:

Do you trust that you are called by God
  to the life and work of representative ministry in the Church?

**I do so trust.**

Do you believe in the Triune God,
  and confess Jesus Christ as your Lord and Savior?

**I do so believe and confess.**

Are you persuaded
  that the scriptures of the Old and New Testaments
  contain all things necessary for salvation
  through faith in Jesus Christ,
  and are the unique and authoritative standard
  for the Church's faith and life?

**I am so persuaded, by God's grace.**

Will you be faithful in prayer,
  in the reading and study of the Holy Scriptures,
  and with the help of the Holy Spirit
  continually rekindle the gift of God that is in you?

**I will, God being my helper.**


## ADMONITION AND PRAYER

*The bishop addresses all the candidates:*

May God,
  who has given you the will to do these things,
  give you grace to perform them
  that the work begun in you may be brought to perfection. **Amen.**

*The bishop calls the people to prayer, saying:*

Let us pray for these persons
  to be consecrated or ordained by God and the Church
  for representative ministry.

*The candidates kneel.*

*The people pray for them in silence, and the bishop concludes:*

We give you thanks, eternal God,
  that in your great love

you sent Jesus Christ, your only begotten,
to take the form of a servant for the sake of us all.
You have taught us, by his word and example,
    that whoever would be great among us must be servant of all.
Give to these your servants the grace and power
    to serve you in their ministry
    so that your people may be strengthened
    and your name glorified in all the world. **Amen.**

*The hymn O Holy Spirit, By Whose Breath ( ♪ 223 or UMH 651) is sung.*

*The deacon and elder candidates are seated. The diaconal candidates come forward and face the bishop.*

## EXAMINATION OF DIACONAL MINISTERS

*The bishop addresses the candidates for diaconal ministry:*

A diaconal minister is called to exemplify Christ's servanthood,
    to participate in the leadership of worship,
    to teach the gospel,
    to counsel the troubled in spirit,
    to serve God's people with special concern
        for love, justice, and ministry to the poor, the sick, and the oppressed
    to equip the people of God for the ministry of all baptized Christians
    and to embody the unity of the congregation's worship
        with its life in the world.

These are the duties of a diaconal minister.

Do you believe that you have been called by God
    to the life and work of a diaconal minister?

**I do so believe.**

Will you be loyal to The United Methodist Church
    accepting its order, liturgy, doctrine, and discipline,
        committing yourself to be accountable with those serving with you,
    and to those who are appointed to supervise your ministry?

**I will, God being my helper.**

## LAYING ON OF HANDS
## AND PRAYER FOR DIACONAL MINISTERS

*The bishop begins:*

Let us pray.

We give thanks to you, eternal God,
    that in your great love
    you sent Jesus Christ,

to take the form of a servant for the sake of us all,
becoming obedient even to death on the cross.
We praise you that you have highly exalted Jesus Christ your servant
and that you have taught us, by his word and example,
that whoever would be great among us must be servant of all.

We thank you that Jesus Christ has poured forth your gifts,
for equipping the saints for the work of ministry,
for serving the poor, the sick, and the oppressed,
for building up Christ's body the Church,
and for fulfilling your gracious purpose in the world.

Give to these servants the grace and power
to serve you in this ministry
so that your people may be strengthened
and your name glorified in all the world.

*Family members and friends may be invited to stand where they are for silent prayer during the laying on of hands.*

*One by one, the candidates go to the bishop and kneel. Calling each candidate by name, the bishop lays both hands on the head of each one. Other participating persons also lay on hands. While hands are imposed, the prayer continues:*

Eternal God, pour upon *Name* your Holy Spirit
for the office and work of a diaconal minister in your Church,
in the name of the Father, and of the Son, and of the Holy Spirit.

*After all have received the laying on of hands, the bishop facing the candidates, with both hands extended over them, concludes the prayer:*

We thank you, God,
for raising up among us faithful servants
for diaconal ministry in your Church.
Clothe them with your righteousness,
and grant that we, with them,
may glorify you by giving ourselves to others;
through Jesus Christ our Savior,
who lives and reigns with you,
in the unity of the Holy Spirit,
one God, now and for ever. **Amen.**

*The following sign act of delivering a Bible may be done immediately after the laying on of hands and prayer for the Holy Spirit.*

*Then the bishop shall deliver to each one a Bible, saying:*

*Name*, take authority as a diaconal minister in the Church
to teach the Word,
to practice justice,
and to serve God's people.

*A diaconal's stole, towel and basin, or other appropriate sign may be given to t,*
*diaconal ministers.*

## HYMN *

*Hymns are listed on 713.*

*During the hymn, the diaconal ministers return to their seats. The deacc*
*candidates now come forward.*

## EXAMINATION OF DEACONS

*The bishop addresses the deacon candidates:*

A deacon in the Church
is called to preach the Word of God,
to assist in the leadership of worship,
and to assist the elders at Holy Baptism and Holy Communion;
to serve all people, particularly the poor, the sick, and the oppressec
to interpret to the Church
the needs, concerns, and hopes of the world;
and at all times, by your life and teaching,
to show Christ's people
that in serving the helpless they are serving Christ.

These are the duties of a deacon.

Do you believe that you have been called by God
to the life and work of a deacon?

**I do so believe.**

Will you be loyal to The United Methodist Church,
accepting its order, liturgy, doctrine, and discipline,
and accepting the authority of those who are appointed
to supervise your ministry?

**I will, with the help of God.**

## LAYING ON OF HANDS AND PRAYER FOR DEACONS

*The bishop addresses the candidates:*

My *sisters and brothers,*
from the time of the apostles
persons with suitable gifts and grace have been set apart
by the laying on of hands and prayer
for a ministry of service in the Church of Jesus Christ our Lord.
We trust that the Spirit of God
has called you to the ministry of deacons.

As earnest prayer is made
  for the fulfillment of the Spirit's gift in you,
  the Church of God now calls you
    to receive the laying on of hands
    as the seal of your vocation by the Spirit.

*Family members and friends may be invited to stand where they are for silent
prayer during the laying on of hands.*

*One by one the candidates go to the bishop and kneel. Calling each candidate by
name, the bishop lays both hands on the head of each one. While hands are imposed,
the bishop prays:*

Lord, pour upon *Name* the Holy Spirit
for the office and work of a deacon
in the name of the Father, and of the Son, and of the Holy Spirit.

*After all have received the laying on of hands, the bishop facing the candidates, with
both hands extended over them, prays:*

Let us pray.

We give thanks to you, Lord God,
  that in your great love
  you sent Jesus Christ, your only begotten,
    to take the form of a servant for the sake of us all,
    becoming obedient even to death on the cross.
We praise you that you have highly exalted Jesus Christ your servant
  whom you have made to be Lord of all,
  and that you have taught us, by his word and example,
    that whoever would be great among us must be servant of all.
Increase within the lives of these your servants
  the gift of the Holy Spirit,
  through Jesus Christ your Son,
  for the ministry of a deacon in your Church.
Give them grace to be faithful to their promises,
  constant in their discipleship,
  and always ready for the works of loving service.
Make them modest and humble, gentle and strong,
  that, having the assurance of faith and rejoicing in hope,
  they may be rooted and grounded in love.
Give them a share in the ministry of Jesus Christ,
  who came not to be served but to serve;
who now lives and reigns with you,
in the unity of the Holy Spirit,
one God, for ever and ever. **Amen.**

*The following sign act of delivering a Bible may be done immediately after the
laying on of hands and prayer for the Holy Spirit.*

*Then the bishop shall deliver to each deacon a Bible, saying:*

**Name,** take authority as a deacon in the Church
to preach the Word of God,
and to serve all God's people.

*A deacon's stole or other gift may be given to each deacon.*

## RECOGNITION OF ORDERS

*The bishop addresses all those whose Orders as deacons are recognized. If the bishop prefers, this may be done immediately prior to the laying on of hands.*

After due examination
of your call and ministry in another part of Christ's holy Church,
we now welcome you to this communion.
You have given assurance of your faith and Christian experience.
You have renewed the vows of your ordination
and committed yourself to uphold faithfully
The United Methodist Church.
We rejoice that you have been called to serve among us,
and pray that the Spirit of God may guide your ministry.

*As each candidate comes forward, the bishop uses the following greeting:*

**Name,** we now recognize you as a deacon in
The United Methodist Church.

## HYMN *

*Hymns are listed on 713.*

*During the hymn, the deacons return to their seats. The elder candidates now come forward.*

## EXAMINATION OF ELDERS

*The bishop examines the elder candidates, saying:*

An elder in the Church,
in covenant with other elders in this Annual Conference,
is called to share in the ministry of Christ
and of the whole Church:
by preaching and teaching the Word of God
and faithfully administering
the Sacraments of Baptism and Holy Communion;
by leading the people of God in worship and prayer;
by leading persons to faith in Jesus Christ;

by exercising pastoral supervision of the people committed to your care,
  ordering the life of the congregation,
  counseling the troubled in spirit,
  and declaring the forgiveness of sin;
by leading the people of God
  in obedience to mission in the world,
  to seek justice, peace, and freedom for all people;
and by taking a responsible place in the government of the Church
  and in service to the community.

These are the duties of an elder.

Do you believe that you are called by God
  to the life and work of an elder?

**I do so believe.**

In covenant with other elders,
  will you be loyal to The United Methodist Church,
  accepting its order, liturgy, doctrine, and discipline,
  defending it against all doctrines contrary to God's Holy Word,
  and accepting the authority of those who are appointed
    to supervise your ministry?

**I will, with the help of God.**

## LAYING ON OF HANDS AND PRAYER FOR ELDERS

*The bishop, standing and facing the candidates, with both hands extended toward them, begins the prayer of ordination:*

We praise you, eternal God,
  because you have called us in your infinite love
  to be a priestly people,
  offering to you acceptable worship through Jesus Christ our Lord,
  Apostle and High Priest, Shepherd and Bishop of our souls.
We thank you that, by dying, Christ has overcome death
  and, having ascended into heaven,
  has poured forth gifts abundantly on your people,
  making some apostles, some prophets,
    some evangelists, some pastors and teachers,
  to equip the saints for the work of ministry,
  to build up Christ's body, the Church,
  and to fulfill your gracious purpose in the world.

*Family members and friends may be invited to stand where they are for silent prayer during the laying on of hands.*

*One by one the candidates go to the bishop and kneel. Calling each candidate by name, the bishop lays both hands on the head of each one. Other participating elders*

*also lay on hands. Bishops and others with ordaining responsibilities from other
communions may be invited to lay on hands also. Laity designated by the bishop to
represent the Church community may be included in the laying on of hands. While
hands are imposed, the prayer continues:*

Lord, pour upon *Name* the Holy Spirit
for the office and work of an elder,
in the name of the Father, and of the Son, and of the Holy Spirit.

*After laying on of hands on all candidates, the bishop, facing the candidates, with
both hands extended over them, concludes the prayer:*

Gracious God,
    give to these your servants the grace and power they need
    to serve you in this ministry,
    so that your people may be strengthened
    and your name glorified in all the world.
Make them faithful pastors, patient teachers, and wise counselors.
Enable them to serve without reproach,
    to proclaim the gospel of salvation,
    to administer the Sacraments of the new covenant,
    to order the life of the Church,
    and to offer with all your people
        spiritual sacrifices acceptable to you;
through Jesus Christ our Lord,
who lives and reigns with you,
in the unity of the Holy Spirit,
one God, now and for ever. **Amen.**

*The following sign act of delivering a Bible may be done immediately after the
laying on of hands and prayer for the Holy Spirit.*

*Then the bishop shall deliver to each candidate a Bible, saying:*

*Name*, take authority as an elder in the Church
    to preach the Word of God,
    and to administer the Holy Sacraments.

*An elder's stole, or chalice and paten together, may be given to each elder.*


## RECOGNITION OF ORDERS

*The bishop addresses all those whose Orders as elders are recognized. If the bishop
prefers, this may be done immediately prior to the laying on of hands.*

After due examination
    of your call and ministry in another part of Christ's holy Church,
    we now welcome you to this Communion.
You have given assurance of your faith and Christian experience.
You have renewed the vows of your ordination

and committed yourself to uphold faithfully
The United Methodist Church.
We rejoice that you have been called to serve among us,
and pray that the Spirit of God may guide your ministry.

*As each candidate comes forward, the bishop uses the following greeting:*

*Name*, we now recognize you as an elder in The United Methodist Church.

HYMN *

*Hymns are listed on 713.*

*If the Lord's Supper is celebrated, the new elders remain to assist the bishop and are joined by the new deacons and diaconal ministers. The service on 678-82 may be followed. If the Lord's Supper is not celebrated, the new elders return to their seats.*

*When the Lord's Supper is not celebrated, the service concludes as follows.*

## SENDING FORTH

PRAYER

*The bishop addresses the congregation:*

Let us pray.

We thank you, God,
    for raising up among us faithful servants
    for ministry in your Church.
Clothe them with your righteousness,
    and grant that we, with them,
    may glorify you by giving ourselves to others;
through Jesus Christ our Savior,
who lives and reigns with you,
in the unity of the Holy Spirit,
one God, now and for ever. **Amen.**

HYMN *

*If the closing hymn is a recessional, it should follow Dismissal with Blessing; otherwise it should precede Dismissal with Blessing.*

*Closing hymns are listed on 713.*

DISMISSAL WITH BLESSING *

*The bishop dismisses and blesses the people, saying:*

Go in peace
    to serve God and your neighbor in all that you do.
**We go in the name of Christ. Thanks be to God!**

GOING FORTH *

# INTRODUCTION TO THE CONSECRATION OF BISHOPS

"The task of superintending in The United Methodist Church resides in the office of bishop and extends to the district superintendent, with each possessing distinct responsibilities. From apostolic times, certain ordained persons have been entrusted with the particular tasks of superintending. Those who superintend carry primary responsibility for ordering the life of the Church. It is their task to enable the gathered Church to worship and to evangelize faithfully.

"It is also their task to facilitate the initiation of structures and strategies for the equipping of Christian people for service in the Church and in the world in the name of Jesus Christ and to help extend the service in mission" (*The Book of Discipline 1992*, ¶ 501).

"The office of bishop . . . exists in The United Methodist Church as a particular ministry. Bishops are elected . . . from the group of elders who are ordained to be ministers of Word, Sacrament, and Order and thereby participate in the ministry of Christ, in sharing a royal priesthood which has apostolic roots (1 Peter 2:9; John 21:15-17; Acts 20:28; 1 Peter 5:2-3; 1 Timothy 3:1-7).

"Bishops . . . share in the full ministry as ordained elders. The Body of Christ is one; yet many members with differing functions are all joined together in the one body (1 Corinthians 12:28)" (*The Book of Discipline 1992*, ¶ 503-504).

"Consecration of bishops may take place at the session of the conference at which election occurs or at a place and time designated by the conference. The consecration service may include bishops from other Jurisdictional and Central Conferences. It is strongly urged that the consecration service also include representatives from other Christian communions (see ¶ 512.1)" (*The Book of Discipline 1992*, ¶ 506.2.c).

The laying on of hands by other bishops is a custom that originated in the practice of the early church as a sign of episcopal unity and collegiality. The imposition of the hands of all the bishops present and prayer at the consecration of a new bishop now signify the bishop-elect's empowerment by the Holy Spirit and admission to the duties of episcopal ministry by those who share the same responsibility for oversight in the Church. The laying on of hands also signifies the bishop-elect's reception into the episcopal college to which the community has entrusted the representative *diakonia* of episcopacy in the Church. Only bishops should participate in the laying on of hands.

The senior bishop should be responsible for the service of consecration and should plan it in consultation with the Jurisdictional or Central Conference Episcopal Committee.

A bishop should preside at the consecration service. Other bishops, lay-persons, and clergy may also assist during the worship. Laity, diaconal ministers, and ordained clergy may participate in leadership during the Entrance, Presentation, and Proclamation.

The bishops-elect for consecration are presented to the presiding bishop using each bishop-elect's full name.

Red is the appropriate color for paraments and stoles.

Spouses and other family members of candidates for consecration should not participate in the laying on of hands. Family members and friends may be invited to stand where they are for silent prayer during the laying on of hands.

Care should be taken to enable members of the congregation to see the laying on of hands. Cameras, videocassette recorders, and other equipment should not be allowed to intrude upon the service.

Because consecrations are acts of the whole Church, the text and rubrics of The Order for the Consecration of Bishops are to be used as approved by the General Conference.

Updates to this service can be found at:
www.umcdiscipleship.org/services-for-the-ordering-of-ministry-in-the-united-methodist-church

# THE ORDER FOR
# THE CONSECRATION OF BISHOPS

## ENTRANCE

### GATHERING

*The service begins with the gathering of the people. Festive music may be offered while the people gather. The service may then continue with a procession including the worship leaders, bishop(s)-elect, and bishop(s).*

### PROCESSIONAL HYMN *

*If the hymn is to be a hymn of praise, it follows the Greeting. Processional hymns are listed on 713.*

### GREETING AND OPENING PRAYER *

*The presiding bishop begins; the people respond.*

The grace of our Lord Jesus Christ be with you all.

**And also with you.**

Our help is in the name of the Lord.

**The Creator of heaven and earth.**

Let us pray.

**Almighty God, by your Son Jesus Christ and the Holy Spirit
  you gave to your apostles many excellent gifts.
Give your grace to all servants of your Church,
  that we may with diligence and faithfulness
  fulfill our various ministries.
Grant that we your people may follow where you lead
  and live in joyful obedience to your will;
through Jesus Christ our Lord. Amen.**

*The people are seated.*

## PRESENTATION

*One layperson and one elder, chosen by the presiding bishop, present each bishop-elect to the presiding bishop, who stands before the Lord's table, facing the people, saying:*

Bishop *Name,*
we present to you *full name of bishop-elect,*
    an elder in the Church,
    to be consecrated a bishop in the Church of Jesus Christ.

*After each bishop-elect has been presented, the bishops-elect stand, and the presiding bishop addresses the congregation:*

People of God,
    *full name of (each) bishop-elect*
    *is (are),* by God's grace,
    to be consecrated bishop(s) in the Church.
*He (She, They) has (have)* been duly elected to this ministry.
We ask you to declare your assent.

Do you trust that *he (she, they) is (are)* worthy, by God's grace,
    to be consecrated bishop(s)?

**We do! Thanks be to God!**

Will you uphold *him (her, them)* in *his (her, their)* ministry
    as bishop(s) of the Church?

**With God's help, we will!**


## SALUTATION AND PRAYER

*The presiding bishop then says:*

The scriptures tell us
    that our Savior Jesus Christ spent the whole night in prayer
    before he chose and sent forth the twelve apostles.
The apostles also prayed before they appointed Matthias
    to be one of their number.
Let us offer our prayers to almighty God
    before *Name of (each) bishop-elect*
    *is (are)* consecrated for the work
    to which the Holy Spirit has called *him (her, them).*

The Lord be with you.
**And also with you.**
Let us pray.

*All pray in silence.*

*The presiding bishop continues:*

Almighty God, giver of all good things,
    by your Holy Spirit you have appointed
    a diversity of ministries in your Church.

Look in mercy upon *this* (*these*) your servant(s),
    now to be set apart for the ministry of a bishop,
    so replenish *him* (*her, them*) with holiness of life,
    and fill *him* (*her, them*) with the power of your Holy Spirit,
    that both by word and by deed,
    *he* (*she, they*) may serve you faithfully and joyously,
    to the glory of your name and the building up of your Church;
    through Jesus Christ our Lord,
    who lives and reigns with you and the Holy Spirit,
    one God, now and for ever. **Amen.**

*The bishop and bishop(s)-elect are seated.*


# PROCLAMATION

*Suggested scripture lessons are found on 711-12.*

## OLD TESTAMENT LESSON

## PSALM *

## NEW TESTAMENT LESSON

## HYMN OR ANTHEM *

*Hymns are listed on 713.*

## GOSPEL LESSON *

## SERMON

## THE APOSTLES' CREED * *See UMH 881, 882.*

## HYMN *

*Hymns are listed on 713.*

*During the hymn, the bishop(s)-elect come forward.*


# EXAMINATION

*The bishop(s)-elect stand facing the presiding bishop. The bishop examines the*
*bishop(s)-elect, saying:*

My *brothers and sisters,*
    you are to be consecrated bishop(s) in the Church of God.
All Christian ministry is Christ's ministry of reconciling love.

All baptized Christians are called
    to share this ministry of service in the world,
    to the glory of God and for the redemption of the human family.
From among the baptized
    some are called by God and set apart by the Church
        to serve God's people
    as diaconal ministers, deacons, elders, and bishops.

You have been ordained to the ministry of Word and Sacrament;
you are now called, as bishop(s) in the Church,
    to reaffirm the vows made at your ordination as elder(s),
    and to represent Christ's servanthood in a special ministry of oversight.

You are called to guard the faith, to seek the unity,
    and to exercise the discipline of the whole Church;
    and to supervise and support the Church's life, work,
    and mission throughout the world.

As servant(s) of the whole Church,
    you are called to preach and teach
        the truth of the gospel to all God's people;
    to lead the people in worship,
    in the celebration of the Sacraments,
    and in their mission of witness and service in the world,
    and so participate in the gospel command
        to make disciples of all nations.

As bishop(s) and pastor(s),
    you are to lead and guide
    all persons entrusted to your oversight;
    join in the consecration of bishops,
    ordain deacons and elders,
    consecrate diaconal ministers,
    and commission other ministers
        for service to the Church and to the world;
    and provide for the ministry of Word and Sacrament
    in the congregations committed to your care.

Your joy will be to follow Jesus the Christ
    who came not to be served but to serve.

Will you accept the call to this ministry as bishop(s)
    and fulfill this trust in obedience to Christ?

**I will, by the grace of God.**

Will you guard the faith, order, liturgy, doctrine, and discipline
    of the Church against all that is contrary to God's Word?

**I will, for the love of God.**

As bishop(s) and pastor(s), will you,
in cooperation with diaconal ministers, deacons, and elders,
encourage and support all baptized people
in their gifts and ministries,
pray for them without ceasing,
proclaim and interpret to them the gospel of Christ,
and celebrate with them the Sacraments of our redemption?

**I will, in the name of Christ,**
**the Shepherd and Bishop of our souls.**

Will you share with other bishops
in the supervision of the whole Church;
support the elders and take counsel with them;
guide and strengthen the diaconal ministers and deacons
and all others who minister in the Church;
and ordain, consecrate, and send others to minister in Christ's name?

**All this I will do, by the grace given me.**

May the God
who has given you the will to do these things
give you grace to perform them,
that the work begun in you may be brought to perfection. **Amen.**

## LAYING ON OF HANDS AND PRAYER

*The presiding bishop calls the people to prayer, saying:*

As *Name of (each) bishop-elect*
*is (are)* consecrated bishop(s) in the Church,
let us invoke the Holy Spirit on *his (her, their)* behalf
and pray for *him (her, them)*.

*The bishop(s)-elect kneel.*

*The people pray for them in silence.*

*The hymn* O Holy Spirit, By Whose Breath *( ♪ 223 or UMH 651) may be*
*sung.*

*The presiding bishop is joined by the other bishops participating. The presiding*
*bishop now extends hands over the kneeling bishop(s)-elect and begins the prayer of*
*consecration:*

God and Father of our Lord Jesus Christ,
giver of mercies and source of all comfort,
dwelling on high but having regard for the lowly,
knowing all things before they come to pass:
we give you thanks that from the beginning
you have gathered and prepared a people
to be heirs of the covenant of Abraham and Sarah,

and have raised up prophets, rulers, and priests,
never leaving your temple without a ministry.
We praise you also that from the creation
you have graciously accepted the service
of those whom you have chosen.

*Family members and friends may be invited to stand where they are for silent prayer during the laying on of hands.*

*The presiding bishop now lays both hands on the head of each bishop-elect, joined by the other bishops participating. Bishops and others with ordaining responsibilities from other communions may be invited to lay on hands also. The presiding bishop alone says over each person:*

Gracious God,
pour upon *Name* the Holy Spirit,
for the ministry of a bishop in your Church,
in the name of the Father, and of the Son, and of the Holy Spirit.

*When hands have been laid upon all persons, the presiding bishop, with both hands extended over them, continues to pray:*

Almighty God,
fill the heart(s) of *this* (*these*) your servant(s)
whom you have chosen to be bishop(s) in your Church
with such love of you and of all the people
that *he* (*she, they*) may feed and tend the flock of Christ,
serve in the ministry of reconciliation,
and supervise and support the life and work of the Church.
In all things may *he* (*she, they*) present before you
the acceptable offering of a pure, gentle, and holy life;
through Jesus Christ your servant,
to whom, with you and the Holy Spirit,
be honor and power and glory in the Church,
now and for ever. **Amen.**

*After hands have been laid on each person, a Bible is given to each new bishop with these words:*

*Name*, receive the Holy Scriptures.
Feed the flock of Christ,
defend them in Christ's truth,
and be a faithful steward of Christ's Word and Sacraments.

*After each new bishop has received a Bible, the presiding bishop says to them:*

Reflect upon the contents of this Book.
Give attention to reading, exhortation, and teaching.
Be to the people of God
a prophetic voice and a courageous leader
in the cause of justice for all people.

Be to the flock of Christ a shepherd;
support the weak, heal the sick,
    bind up the broken, restore the outcast,
    seek the lost, relieve the oppressed.
Faithfully administer discipline,
    but do not forget mercy,
    that when the Chief Shepherd shall appear
        you may receive the never-fading crown of glory. **Amen.**

## HYMN *

*Hymns are listed on 713.*

*If the Lord's Supper is celebrated, the new bishops remain to assist, and the service continues as follows. If the Lord's Supper is not celebrated, they return to their seats.*

*When the Lord's Supper is not celebrated, the service concludes with Sending Forth (709-10).*

## THANKSGIVING AND COMMUNION

### TAKING THE BREAD AND CUP

*The bread and wine are brought by representatives of the people to the Lord's table or uncovered if already in place. Deacons prepare the table for the Lord's Supper.*

*A hymn, doxology, or other response may be sung as the gifts are presented.*

### THE GREAT THANKSGIVING *

*This text is used by the bishop, while the congregation uses A Service of Word and Table III (UMH 15-16) or one of the musical settings (UMH 17-25).*

*The bishop may use the gestures suggested in the text.*

*The presiding bishop or the new bishops, standing behind the Lord's table, facing the people from this time through Breaking the Bread, begin the prayer:*

The Lord be with you.
**And also with you.**
Lift up your hearts. *The bishop may lift hands and keep them raised.*
**We lift them up to the Lord.**
Let us give thanks to the Lord our God.
**It is right to give our thanks and praise.**

It is right, and a good and joyful thing,
    always and everywhere to give thanks to you,
    Father Almighty, Creator of heaven and earth.

You built your Church
> on the foundation of the apostles and prophets,
> and instituted a holy ministry
> so that your prophetic and apostolic Word
> might be heard in the Church and in the world until the end of time.

And so,
> with your people on earth
> and all the company of heaven
> we praise your name and join their unending hymn:

*The bishop may lower hands.*

**Holy, holy, holy Lord, God of power and might,**
**heaven and earth are full of your glory.**
> **Hosanna in the highest.**
**Blessed is he who comes in the name of the Lord.**
> **Hosanna in the highest.**

*The bishop may raise hands.*

Holy are you, and blessed is your Son Jesus Christ.
Your Spirit anointed him
> to preach good news to the poor,
> to proclaim release to the captives
> and recovering of sight to the blind,
> to set at liberty those who are oppressed,
> and to announce that the time had come
> when you would save your people.
He healed the sick, fed the hungry, and ate with sinners.
By the baptism of his suffering, death, and resurrection
> you gave birth to your Church,
> delivered us from slavery to sin and death,
> and made with us a new covenant by water and the Spirit.
When the Lord Jesus,
> the great Shepherd of your flock, ascended,
> he sent forth the apostles
> to preach the gospel and make disciples of all nations.
He promised to be with them always,
> and sent the Holy Spirit to lead them.

*The bishop may hold hands, palms down, over the bread, or touch the bread, or lift
the bread.*

On the night in which he gave himself up for us,
> he took bread, gave thanks to you, broke the bread,
> gave it to his disciples, and said:
"Take, eat; this is my body which is given for you.
Do this in remembrance of me."

*The bishop may hold hands, palms down, over the cup, or touch the cup, or lift the cup.*

When the supper was over, he took the cup,
    gave thanks to you, gave it to his disciples, and said:
"Drink from this, all of you;
    this is my blood of the new covenant,
    poured out for you and for many
    for the forgiveness of sins.
Do this, as often as you drink it,
    in remembrance of me."

*The bishop may raise hands.*

And so,
in remembrance of these your mighty acts in Jesus Christ,
we offer ourselves in praise and thanksgiving
    as a holy and living sacrifice,
    in union with Christ's offering for us,
as we proclaim the mystery of faith.

**Christ has died; Christ is risen; Christ will come again.**

*The bishop may hold hands, palms down, over the bread and cup.*

Pour out your Holy Spirit on us gathered here,
    and on these gifts of bread and wine.
Make them be for us the body and blood of Christ,
that we may be for the world the body of Christ,
    redeemed by his blood.

*The bishop may raise hands.*

By your Spirit make us one with Christ,
    one with each other,
    and one in ministry to all the world,
until Christ comes in final victory
    and we feast at his heavenly banquet.

Through your Son Jesus Christ,
with the Holy Spirit in your holy Church,
all honor and glory is yours, almighty Father,
now and for ever. **Amen.**

## THE LORD'S PRAYER *

## BREAKING THE BREAD

*The bishop, still standing behind the Lord's table, facing the people, assisted by the new and participating bishops and elders as necessary, while deacons prepare the cups, breaks the bread in silence, or while saying:*

Because there is one loaf,
we, who are many, are one body, for we all partake of the one loaf.
The bread which we break is a sharing in the body of Christ.

*The bishop lifts the cup in silence, or while saying:*

The cup over which we give thanks is a sharing
in the blood of Christ.

## GIVING THE BREAD AND CUP

*The bread and wine are given to the people by the bishops, elders, deacons, diaconal ministers, and laity, with these or other words being exchanged:*

The body of Christ, given for you. **Amen.**

The blood of Christ, given for you. **Amen.**

*The congregation sings hymns while the bread and cup are given. In addition to hymns 612-41 and others listed in the index under Holy Communion (UMH 943), many other hymns in UMH are effective in expressing the people's loving communion with God and with one another. The people's knowledge and love of particular hymns are important considerations in the selection of appropriate hymns. It is particularly effective if the people can sing from memory during communion.*

*When all have received, the Lord's table is put in order by the deacons.*

## PRAYER AFTER RECEIVING

*A bishop says:*

Let us pray.

We thank you, gracious Lord, for giving yourself to us,
    and for uniting us in the fellowship of your Holy Spirit.
We bless you for raising up among us
    your faithful servant(s) *Name(s) of new bishop(s)*
    for the ministry of a bishop in your Church.
Clothe *him (her, them)* with your righteousness
    and grant that we, with *him (her, them)*,
    may glorify you by giving ourselves to others;
through Jesus Christ our Lord,
who lives and reigns with you,
in the unity of the Holy Spirit,
one God, now and for ever. **Amen.**

# SENDING FORTH

## PRAYER

*The following prayer is used only if the Lord's Supper has not been celebrated. The bishop says:*

Let us pray.

We thank you, gracious Lord,
   for raising up among us
   your faithful servant(s) *Name(s) of new bishop(s)*
   for the ministry of a bishop in your Church.
We pray that *he* (*she, they*) may be (an) example(s) of the new life in Christ
   in words and action, in love and patience,
   and in holiness of life.
Grant that we, with *him* (*her, them*), may glorify you
   by giving ourselves to others;
through Jesus Christ our Lord,
who lives and reigns with you and the Holy Spirit,
one God, now and for ever. **Amen.**

## HYMN *

*If the closing hymn is a recessional, it should follow Dismissal with Blessing, otherwise it should precede Dismissal with Blessing.*

*Closing hymns are listed on 713.*

## DISMISSAL WITH BLESSING *

*A new bishop dismisses and blesses the people.*

## GOING FORTH *

# SUGGESTED SCRIPTURE LESSONS

## OLD TESTAMENT

| | |
|---|---|
| Genesis 18:1-14a | Abraham and Sarah called |
| Exodus 3:1-18 | The call of Moses |
| Exodus 15:20-21 | Song of Miriam |
| Exodus 33:12-17 | My presence will go with you. |
| Numbers 11:16-17, 24-25a | Moses and the seventy elders |
| Judges 4:1-7 | Narrative of Deborah |
| 1 Kings 17:8-24 | Widow of Zarephath ministers |
| Esther 4:10-17 | Esther's plea for justice |
| Isaiah 6:1-8 | Here am I! Send me! |
| Isaiah 42:1-9 | A servant song |
| Isaiah 43:8-13 | You are my witnesses. |
| Isaiah 52:7-10 | Your God reigns. |
| Isaiah 55:6-11 | My word shall not return to me empty. |
| Isaiah 61:1-6a | The Spirit of the Lord |
| Jeremiah 1:4-10 | Before you were born I consecrated you. |
| Jeremiah 31:31-34 | A new covenant |
| Ezekiel 33:1-9 | The watcher's duty |
| Ezekiel 34:11-16 | God, the good shepherd |

## PSALM

| | |
|---|---|
| Psalm 23 (*UMH* 137, 754, 873) | The Lord is my shepherd. |
| Psalm 40:1-11 (*UMH* 774) | I delight to do your will, O my God. |
| Psalm 43 (*UMH* 778) | I will go to your altar. |
| Psalm 84 (*UMH* 804) | How lovely is your dwelling place. |
| Psalm 96 (*UMH* 815) | Worship the Lord in holy splendor. |
| Psalm 99 (*UMH* 819) | God the supreme ruler |
| Psalm 100 (*UMH* 821) | We are the people of God. |
| Psalm 119:33-40 (*UMH* 842) | Prayer for understanding |
| Psalm 122 (*UMH* 845) | I was glad when they said to me |
| Psalm 132 (*UMH* 849) | In praise of the temple |

## NEW TESTAMENT

| | |
|---|---|
| Acts 6:2-7 | Choosing deacons |
| Acts 9:36-42 | Paul and Dorcas |
| Acts 20:17-35 | Paul's farewell to the elders |
| Romans 10:9-17 | Those who preach good news |
| Romans 12:1-18 | The consecrated life |
| 1 Corinthians 1:18-31 | We preach Christ crucified. |
| 1 Corinthians 3:10-17 | No other foundation but Christ |
| 1 Corinthians 12:4-13 | Varieties of gifts |
| 2 Corinthians 3:4-9 | Ministers of a new covenant |
| 2 Corinthians 4:1-11 | Not ourselves but Christ |
| 2 Corinthians 5:14-20 | Ambassadors for Christ |
| Ephesians 3:14-21 | Strengthened with might |
| Ephesians 4:1-15 | Lead a worthy life. |

| Ephesians 5:15-21 | Be filled with the Spirit. |
| Ephesians 6:10-18 | Take the whole armor of God. |
| Philippians 4:4-9 | Rejoice in the Lord always. |
| 1 Timothy 3:1-13 | Qualifications of leaders |
| 1 Timothy 4:12b-16 | Do not neglect your gift. |
| 2 Timothy 1:6-14 | Rekindle the gift God gave you. |
| 2 Timothy 3:1-7 | In season and out of season |
| Hebrews 5:1-10 | Appointed for obedient service |
| Hebrews 12:1-6, 12-14 | Jesus, the perfecter of our faith |
| 1 Peter 4:7-11 | Good stewards of God's grace |
| 1 Peter 5:1-11 | An elder's qualities |

## GOSPEL

| Matthew 9:35-38 | The Lord of the harvest |
| Matthew 10:1-7 | The call of the twelve |
| Matthew 10:24-33 | Everyone who acknowledges me |
| Matthew 18:15-20 | Where two or three are gathered in my name |
| Matthew 20:25-28 | Not to be served but to serve |
| Matthew 28:16-20 | Make disciples of all nations. |
| Mark 10:35-45 | Whoever would be great among you |
| Luke 1:47-55 | Song of Mary |
| Luke 2:36-38 | Song of Anna |
| Luke 8:1-3 | Women who followed Jesus |
| Luke 10:1-12 | The Lord of the harvest |
| Luke 10:38-42 | Ministry of Mary and Martha |
| Luke 12:32-40 | Vigilant servants |
| Luke 22:14-30 | One who serves |
| Luke 24:44-49 | Witnesses with a message and a promise |
| John 4:7-42 | Woman of Samaria carries a message. |
| John 6:35-40 | I am the bread of life. |
| John 10:1-18 | The Good Shepherd |
| John 12:20-26 | Sir, we wish to see Jesus. |
| John 13:1-18 | Jesus washes the disciples' feet. |
| John 14:25-31 | The Holy Spirit will teach you all things. |
| John 15:9-17 | I have called you friends. |
| John 17:1-9 | Jesus prays for his disciples. |
| John 20:1-18 | Witnesses to the living Christ |
| John 20:19-23 | Receive the Holy Spirit. |
| John 21:15-19 | Feed my sheep. |

# SUGGESTED HYMNS IN *UMH*

## PROCESSIONAL HYMNS

*If the hymn is to be a hymn of praise, it follows the Greeting.*

554 All Praise to Our Redeeming Lord
555 Forward Through the Ages
552 Here, O Lord, Your Servants Gather
89 Joyful, Joyful, We Adore Thee
159 Lift High the Cross

547 O Church of God, United
66 Praise, My Soul, the King of Heaven
139 Praise to the Lord, the Almighty
545-6 The Church's One Foundation

## HYMNS DURING THE SERVICE

*Hymns may be used as responses to the scripture lessons or as acts of worship throughout the service.*

593 Here I Am, Lord
649 How Shall They Hear the Word of God
650 Give Me the Faith Which Can Remove
578 God of Love and God of Power
648 God the Spirit, Guide and Guardian
432 Jesu, Jesu (especially for diaconal
     consecration services)
398 Jesus Calls Us
580 Lead On, O King Eternal

584 Lord, You Give the Great Commission
396 O Jesus, I Have Promised
430 O Master, Let Me Walk with Thee
501 O Thou Who Camest from Above
583 Sois la Semilla (You Are the Seed)
408 The Gift of Love
436 The Voice of God Is Calling
344 Tu Has Venido a la Orilla
     (Lord, You Have Come to the Lakeshore);
     especially for diaconal consecration services

*See also this contemporary translation of the ancient ordination hymn,* Veni Creator Spiritus: O Holy Spirit, By Whose Breath ( ♪ 223)

## CLOSING HYMNS

*If the closing hymn is a recessional, it should follow Dismissal with Blessing; otherwise it should precede Dismissal with Blessing.*

413 A Charge to Keep I Have
566 Blest Be the Dear Uniting Love
438 Forth in Thy Name, O Lord
571 Go, Make of All Disciples
586 Let My People Seek Their Freedom

584 Lord, You Give the Great Commission
583 Sois la Semilla (You Are the Seed)
399 Take My Life, and Let It Be
585 This Little Light of Mine
582 Whom Shall I Send?

# XI. OTHER ANNUAL CONFERENCE AND DISTRICT SERVICES

## AN ORDER OF COMMITMENT
## FOR LAY SPEAKERS

*This order may be used at a district conference or another service of public worship, the district superintendent or a representative of the district Committee on Lay Speaking presiding. See* The Book of Discipline 1992 *(¶ 277-79) concerning the distinction between local church lay speakers and certified lay speakers and other provisions concerning lay speaking.*

*Leader to congregation:*

Brothers and sisters,
we gather here today to recognize those persons
   who have responded to a call to serve
   by becoming local church lay speakers and certified lay speakers.
A lay speaker is a member of a local church
   who is ready and desirous to serve the Church;
who is well informed on the Scriptures
   and on the doctrine, heritage, organization, and life
      of The United Methodist Church;
and who has received specific training to develop skills
   in witnessing to the Christian faith through spoken communication,
      church and community leadership, and caregiving ministries.
Those persons wishing to make this commitment
   will please present themselves.

*The candidates come forward and are introduced by name.*

*Leader to all candidates:*

Brothers and sisters,
   do you now, in the presence of these persons,
   renew your membership vow
      to be loyal to The United Methodist Church

nd faithfully participate in its ministries
by your prayers, your presence, your gifts, your service, and your witness?

**do.**

Do you believe you have been called by the Holy Spirit to use your skills
to lead in your church and community,
to expand your caring ministries,
and to witness to the Christian faith in worship and other settings?

**do.**

Do you intend to live a life
in keeping with the teachings and example of Jesus Christ?

**do.**

Do you believe the scriptures of the Old and New Testaments?

**do.**

Are you willing to serve your congregation
in any way called upon by your pastor or Charge Conference?

**am.**

Are you willing to take the initiative in program support
and give leadership to the total work of the local congregation?

**am.**

Are you willing to lead meetings for prayer, study, and discussion;
to assist in the conduct of worship;
and to care for others?

**am.**

Are you willing to continue your study,
improve your skills, and grow in wisdom and ability?

**am.**

*Leader to candidates for certified lay speaker:*

Have those of you seeking recognition as certified lay speaker
completed an advanced study program
as approved by the district Committee on Lay Speaking?

**have.**

Are you willing to communicate your faith,
offer leadership and resources, be involved in caring ministries,
lead worship,
and respond in any manner in which your services are requested
beyond your local congregation?

**I am.**

Have you met with the Committee on Lay Speaking
  to review your application
    and to consider the responsibilities of a certified lay speaker?

**I have.**

Have you faithfully ascribed to the requirements for lay speaking
  set forth in *The Book of Discipline?*

**I have.**

*Leader to pastors of the candidates:*

Pastors of these candidates, please stand.

*The pastors stand.*

You have heard the responses of these candidates.
Do you as their pastors recommend them
  as local church lay speakers and certified lay speakers?

**I do.**

*Leader to congregation:*

People of the district,
  as brothers and sisters of these candidates
    do you recommend them as servants of Jesus Christ?

**We do.**

Do you promise to support and help nurture them in this new ministry?

**We do.**

*Leader to all candidates:*

You have been recommended and endorsed,
  and have affirmed your commitment.
Therefore, by the authority granted to me
  by the Committee on Lay Speaking,
    I recognize you as local church or certified lay speakers
      with all the powers and responsibilities inherent with each.
Go forth to fulfill the ministry that you have received in the Lord.

*Leader to congregation:*

Let us pray.

**Almighty God, whose Word is truth,**
  **in the keeping of which is eternal life:**
**We thank you for these persons whom this day we set aside in your name**
  **as local church or certified lay speakers and as your servants.**

'repare them in body, mind, and spirit for their task
  and continue them in your grace,
  that they may increase and bless your Church through their labors;
hrough Jesus Christ our Lord. Amen.

*he leader presents the lay speakers with certificates and pins.*

# AN ORDER FOR PRESENTING LICENSES
# TO LOCAL PASTORS

*ocal pastors are licensed only by the bishop (The Book of Discipline 1992,
¶ 406.1). Their licenses may be presented in a public ceremony, which may take place:*
  *) Following the Proclamation of the Word in a service of worship of the congregation
    the local pastor is serving, with the district superintendent or a representative of
    the district superintendent presiding*
  *) At a district conference*
  *) At a session of Annual Conference*

*A representative of the district Committee on Ordained Ministry says:*

3rothers and sisters in Christ,
ve present to you *Name (these persons)* to be licensed as a local pastor(s).

*f more than one person is being licensed, their names are then read.*

*Leader to congregation:*

Dear friends,
*Name has (these persons have)* completed the requirements
  for the license as a local pastor
nd *is (are)* recommended by the District Committee on Ordained Ministry.
Ne have inquired diligently concerning *him (her, them)*
  and have found *him (her, them)* to be fit for this sacred vocation.

*Leader to candidate(s):*

Do you believe you are moved by the Holy Spirit to serve as a local pastor?
  do.
Vill you strive to live a life in keeping with what you preach?
  will.
You are hereby authorized to serve as a local pastor
  in the congregation to which you are appointed.
Take care that you perform these duties faithfully
  as much as you are able, the Lord being your helper.

Let us pray.

Almighty God, whose Word is truth,
  in the keeping of which is eternal life:

We thank you for *Name (these persons),*
  whom we set aside in your name as *a local pastor (local pastors).*
Prepare *him (her, them)* in body, mind, and spirit for *his (her, their)* task
  and continue *him (her, them)* in your grace,
that *he (she, they)* may increase and bless your Church
  through *his (her, their)* labors;
through Jesus Christ our Lord. Amen.

*A hymn may be sung and a Dismissal with Blessing given.*
*See hymns listed in UMH 940 under Discipleship and Service.*

# AN ORDER FOR
# ADMISSION OF CLERGY CANDIDATES
# TO MEMBERSHIP IN AN ANNUAL CONFERENCE

*This order may be used within an Annual Conference service of worship or as a separate service. It may be used when the classes are voted into Annual Conference o at any other time the bishop may designate.*

*The order may begin with a hymn of praise after which the bishop asks the registrar o another member of the Annual Conference to present persons to be admitted to probationary membership. Following their presentation, the candidates stand befor the conference, and the bishop addresses them:*

Brothers and sisters in Christ,
  this is a solemn hour in your life
  and a high moment in the proceedings of this conference.
You are following in the footsteps of those
  who have sought to spread scriptural holiness
    through the lands of the earth.
There is no calling more sacred than that which you now enter,
  and there is no privilege more meaningful
    than that which comes to you through this holy ministry.
In the presence of this Annual Conference I ask you:

Are you convinced that you should enter
  the ordained ministry of Christ's holy Church?

**I am.**

Are you willing to face any sacrifices that may be involved?

**I am.**

Are you in debt so as to interfere with your work,
or have you obligations to others that will make it difficult for you
  to live on the salary you are to receive?

No.

For the sake of a disciplined example,
   are you willing to respect the purity of life
      in body, in mind, and in spirit?

**I am.**

Are you willing to relate yourself in ministry to all persons
   without regard to race, color, or national origin,
      including receiving them into the membership of the Church?

**I am.**

Will you keep before you as the one objective of your life
   the advancement of the reign of God?

**I will.**

*Bishop to congregation:*

Let us pray.

**Almighty God,
accept our thanksgiving for these servants
   who have heeded Christ's call to the ordained ministry of the Church.
Fill them with the gifts needed in this sacred calling,
   prepare them to be true shepherds of the flock,
   and stir up in them prophetic insight and priestly holiness,
that they may become true and faithful pastors in Christ's holy Church.
We pray in the name of Jesus Christ our Lord. Amen.**

*The newly received probationary members are seated.*

*A hymn may be sung. Suggested from* UMH:

648-51 Ordination                     949 Hymns listed under Ordination
844 Hymns listed under Installation
      Services

*The bishop asks the chairperson of the Board of Ordained Ministry or another full
member of the Annual Conference to present persons to be admitted to full
membership and associate membership. Following their presentation, the candidates
stand before the conference, and the bishop addresses them:*

You have indicated that you are convinced
   you should enter the ministry of Christ's holy Church.
You have declared that you are willing to face any sacrifice
   that may be involved in the consecration of life.
You have indicated that you are so situated in life
   that you can accept the obligations of the itinerant ministry.
You have affirmed that you will respect the purity of life
   in body, mind, and spirit,

and that you will keep before you as the one objective of your life
   the advancement of the reign of God.
Remember the words of Christ, who said:
   "If any want to become my followers,
   let them deny themselves and take up their cross and follow me."

In accordance with the usage and *Discipline*
   of The United Methodist Church
   and the historic usages of our communion,
and in the presence of this conference, I ask you:

Have you faith in Christ?

**I have.**

Are you going on to perfection?

**I am, by the grace of God.**

Do you expect to be made perfect in love in this life?

**God willing, I do.**

Are you earnestly striving after it?

**With God's help, I am.**

Are you resolved to devote yourself wholly to God and God's work?

**I am so resolved.**

Do you know the General Rules of our Church?

**I do.**

Will you keep them?

**I will so endeavor.**

Have you studied the doctrines of The United Methodist Church?

**I have studied them.**

After full examination,
   do you believe that our doctrines are in harmony
      with the Holy Scriptures?

**I believe that they are.**

Will you preach and maintain them?

**To the best of my ability, I will.**

Have you studied our form of church discipline and polity?

**I have.**

Do you approve our church government and polity?

**do so approve.**

Will you support and maintain them?

**I will, with God's help.**

Will you diligently instruct the children in every place?

**I will.**

Will you visit from house to house?

**This is my commitment.**

Will you recommend fasting or abstinence, by both precept and example?

**I will so recommend.**

Are you determined to employ all your time in the work of God?

**That is my intention.**

Are you in debt so as to embarrass you in your work?

**I am not.**

Will you observe the following directions?
1) Be diligent. Never be unemployed. Never be triflingly employed.
   Never trifle away time;
       neither spend any more time at any one place
           than is strictly necessary.
2) Be punctual. Do everything exactly at the time.
   And do not mend our rules, but keep them;
       not for wrath, but for conscience sake.

**The Lord being my helper, I will.**

*Bishop to congregation:*

Let us pray.

**Most gracious God,**
   **you showed your love in sending Jesus Christ into the world**
       **that all might have life through him.**
**Pour out your Spirit upon your Church,**
   **that it may fulfill your command**
       **to preach the gospel to every creature.**
**Send laborers into your harvest,**
   **fill them with the Holy Spirit and with faith,**
   **defend them in all dangers and temptations,**
   **and hasten the time when your will shall be done,**
       **on earth as it is in heaven;**
**through the grace of Jesus Christ our Lord. Amen.**

*A hymn may be sung and a Dismissal with Blessing given.*

# A SERVICE CELEBRATING THE APPOINTMENT OF A DISTRICT SUPERINTENDENT

*The leader may be the resident bishop or the bishop's designated representative.*

GATHERING *See 16-17.*

PROCESSIONAL HYMN *

*See processional hymns suggested in 713 and in UMH 949-50.*

GREETING AND OPENING PRAYER * *See 17-21.*

The grace of the Lord Jesus Christ be with you.
**And also with you.**
Let us pray.

**Eternal God, by your grace you have set us together in your Church,**
**whose foundation is your Son Jesus Christ.**
**Grant your continuing grace, we pray,**
**to all who exercise leadership in your Church,**
**that they may with diligence and faithfulness**
**fulfill their various ministries;**
**and grant that we your people may follow them where you lead**
**and minister faithfully in the world;**
**through Jesus Christ our Lord. Amen.**

ANTHEM OR OTHER ACT OF PRAISE *See 21-22.*

PRAYER FOR ILLUMINATION * *See 22.*

SCRIPTURE *Suggested lessons:*

| | |
|---|---|
| Isaiah 42:1-9 | Here is my servant. |
| Isaiah 52:7-10 | God's messenger |
| Ezekiel 34:11-16 | God the True Shepherd |

PSALM 100 * *(UMH 821)*

SCRIPTURE *Suggested lessons:*

| | |
|---|---|
| Ephesians 4:1-7, 11-16 | Unity in Christ's body |
| Philippians 2:5-11 | The servanthood of Christ |
| Philippians 3:10-14 | Pressing toward the goal |
| 1 Peter 5:1-7 | Tend the flock of God in your charge. |

HYMN OR SONG * *Suggested from* UMH:

| | |
|---|---|
| 537-93 The Nature of the Church | 944 Hymns listed under Installation Services |
| 940 Hymns listed under Discipleship and Service | 949 Hymns listed under Ordination |

OSPEL * *Suggested lessons:*

John 10:11-16          The Good Shepherd
John 21:15-17          Feed my sheep.

# NTRODUCTION OF THE DISTRICT SUPERINTENDENT

*The resident bishop, if present, may make a statement regarding the appointment of the new district superintendent; or a letter from the resident bishop may be read by the leader; or the leader may make the introduction.*

# HE COVENANT SERVICE

*Leader to district superintendent:*

*Name,* you have been appointed to be among us
  for the ministry of Word and Sacrament;
  and called to a special ministry of supervision and leadership.
You are called to guard the faith, to seek the unity,
  and to exercise the discipline of the Church,
  and to supervise and support the Church's life, work, and mission.
Do you affirm your commitment to these ministries in our midst?

**I affirm my commitment to these ministries in your midst.**

*Leader to people:*

Brothers and sisters in Christ,
  as a people committed to participate in the ministries of the Church
  by your prayers, your presence, your gifts, your service, and your witness,
will you support and uphold *Name* in these ministries?

**We welcome you.**
**We celebrate your appointment to the *Name* District.**
**We affirm your leadership.**
**We pledge to you our support**
  **in our mutual ministry in the name of Jesus.**

# RESENTATION OF SIGNS OF DISTRICT SUPERINTENDENCY

*Representatives of the people of God come forward to make presentations. As each is received, the district superintendent responds,* **Amen,** *and places it on a table.*

*Name,* take this Bible, and be among us as one who proclaims the Word,
  for the edification of believers and the conversion of the world. **Amen.**

*Name,* take this water, be renewed in your baptism
  and renew us in ours. **Amen.**

*Name,* take this bread and cup,
  and keep us in communion with Christ and his Church. **Amen.**

*Name,* take this hymnal and book of worship,
  to guide us in our prayer and praise. **Amen.**

*Name,* take this towel and basin,
and be among us as one who serves. **Amen.**

*Name,* take this stole, and shepherd us as a pastor. **Amen.**

*Name,* take this *Book of Discipline,*
and strengthen our connections as United Methodists. **Amen.**

*Name,* take this globe,
and lead us in our mission to all the world. **Amen.**

SERMON *(or other response by the district superintendent)*

PRAYER

**Eternal God, bless the ministries of your Church.**
**We thank you for the variety of gifts you have bestowed upon us.**
**Draw us together in one spirit,**
    **that each of us may use our differing gifts as members of one body.**
**May your Word be proclaimed with faithfulness.**
**And may we be doers of your Word and not hearers only.**
**As we who have died and risen with Christ in baptism**
    **gather at his table and then scatter into the world,**
        **may we be one in service to others,**
**in the name of Jesus Christ our Lord. Amen.**

[OFFERING] *See 26-27.*

*An offering of money for some stated purpose may be received if desired.*

[HOLY COMMUNION]

*If Holy Communion is celebrated, the district superintendent presides, using the text on 678-82, beginning with Taking the Bread and Cup and continuing through Prayer after Receiving. The congregation uses A Service of Word and Table III (UMH 15) or one of the musical settings (UMH 17-25).*

DISMISSAL WITH BLESSING * *See 31-32.*

HYMN * *See 30-31.*

GOING FORTH * *See 32.*

# A SERVICE CELEBRATING THE ASSIGNMENT OF A BISHOP TO AN AREA

*A representative of the Jurisdictional or Conference Committee on the Episcopacy leads the service.*

GATHERING *See 16-17.*

PROCESSIONAL HYMN * *See processional hymns suggested in 713 and in* UMH *949-50.*

GREETING AND OPENING PRAYER * *See 17-21.*

The grace of the Lord Jesus Christ be with you.
**And also with you.**
Let us pray.

**Eternal God, by your grace you have set us together in your Church,**
    **whose foundation is your Son Jesus Christ.**
**Grant your continuing grace, we pray,**
    **to all who exercise leadership in your Church,**
**that they may with diligence and faithfulness**
    **fulfill their various ministries;**
**and grant that we your people may follow them where you lead**
    **and minister faithfully in the world;**
**through Jesus Christ our Lord. Amen.**

ANTHEM OR OTHER ACT OF PRAISE *See 21-22.*

PRAYER FOR ILLUMINATION * *See 22.*

SCRIPTURE LESSON Ezekiel 34:11-16    God the True Shepherd

PSALM 100 * *(UMH 821)*

SCRIPTURE LESSON Titus 1:7-9    The character of a bishop

HYMN * *Suggested from* UMH:

537-93 The Nature of the Church    944 Hymns listed under Installation Services
940 Hymns listed under    949 Hymns listed under Ordination
    Discipleship and Service

GOSPEL LESSON * John 21:15-17    Feed my sheep.

INTRODUCTION OF THE BISHOP

*Leader to bishop:*

Bishop *Name,*
    you have been consecrated to be a shepherd and servant,
and you have now been assigned
    as bishop of the *Name* Area of The United Methodist Church.

*Leader to the Chair of Committee(s) on the Episcopacy:*
Who will present Bishop *Name* for welcome to this area?

*Chair(s) of Committee(s) on the Episcopacy:*

I (We), the *Name* Area representatives
   of the *Name* Jurisdictional Committee on the Episcopacy,
do certify that Bishop *Name*
      [was duly elected a bishop of The United Methodist Church
         at the *year* Jurisdictional Conference, and] has been assigned
         by the *Name* Jurisdictional Committee on the Episcopacy
      to the *Name* Area.

I (We), therefore, present to this congregation Bishop *Name* to be
   welcomed to the area to which *he/she* has been assigned.

## THE COVENANT SERVICE

*Leader:*

The Church is the community of those called by God,
   justified by grace, and empowered by the Holy Spirit.
We who are baptized into Christ's death
   and raised with Christ in the resurrection
   are living members of the body of Christ
   who return thanksgiving to God
      in ministries of worship, nurture, witness, and service.

A bishop has been ordained to the ministry of Word and Sacrament;
   and to represent Christ's servanthood
      in a special ministry of oversight.

A bishop is called to guard the faith, to seek the unity,
   and to exercise the discipline of the whole Church;
and to supervise and support the Church's life, work,
   and mission throughout the world.

As a servant of the whole Church,
   the bishop is called to preach and teach
      the truth of the gospel to all God's people;
to lead the people in worship,
   in the celebration of the Sacraments,
   and in their mission of witness and service in the world,
   and so participate in the gospel command
      to make disciples of all nations.

The bishop is to lead and guide
   all persons entrusted to *his/her* supervision;
join in the consecration of bishops,
   ordain deacons and elders,
   consecrate diaconal ministers,
   and commission other ministers
      for service to the Church and to the world;

and provide for the ministry of Word and Sacrament
in the congregations committed to *his/her* care.

Let the shepherd who has been called
now affirm these ministries in our midst.

*Bishop:*

With God's help,
I promise faithfully to hear and to proclaim God's Word,
and rightly administer the Sacraments, as your pastor and servant.

*People:*

**With God's help,
we promise to join with you in the life of praise and thanksgiving,
and in the faithful use of the means of grace that God has given us.**

*Bishop:*

By the grace of Christ,
I promise to be among you as a teacher of the faith,
a pastor of souls, and a means to the unity of the body of Christ.

*People:*

**By the grace of Christ,
we promise to join with you in the life of learning,
in the nurturing of God's people,
and in the seeking of that oneness in Christ
which is Christ's gift to us.**

*Bishop:*

In the power of the Holy Spirit,
I promise to be for you a means of reconciliation and healing,
that all those who are burdened or oppressed may be made whole
and able to rejoice in the new life in Jesus Christ.

*People:*

**In the power of the Holy Spirit,
we promise to be, with you, faithful witnesses,
serving justice, showing mercy,
and in all things proclaiming the acceptable year of the Lord.**

*Leader:*

Let the people say, "Amen."

*People:*

**Amen and amen!**

## PRESENTATION OF SIGNS OF EPISCOPAL MINISTRY

*Representatives of the people of God present signs of the episcoal office to the bishop*
*As each is received, the bishop responds,* **Amen,** *and places it on a table.*

Bishop *Name,* take this pastoral staff,
    and be upheld and sustained by Christ the Good Shepherd
    as you exercise the ministry of a shepherd among us in Christ's name
**Amen.**

Bishop *Name,* take this Bible,
    and proclaim fearlessly the prophetic Word
      in the cause of justice and peace for all people. **Amen.**

Bishop *Name,* take this water,
    be renewed in your baptism and renew us in ours. **Amen.**

Bishop *Name,* take this bread and cup,
    and keep us in communion with Christ and his Church. **Amen.**

Bishop *Name,* take this towel and basin,
    and be among us as one who serves. **Amen.**

Bishop *Name,* take this stole,
    and be our pastor, preacher, and teacher;
encourage and support all baptized people in their gifts and ministries
    and pray for them without ceasing. **Amen.**

Bishop *Name,* take this *Book of Discipline,*
    guard the faith, seek the unity,
    exercise the discipline of the whole Church,
    and supervise the Church's life, work,
    and mission throughout the world. **Amen.**

Bishop *Name,* take this gavel,
    and preside in our Annual Conference(s);
appoint pastors and assign diaconal ministers to their ministries,
    and guide us in our common mission of love and justice,
    witness and service. **Amen.**

*Leader:*

Bishop *Name,* these are the signs of your ministry
    among the people of the *Name* Area of The United Methodist Church
Faithfully administer discipline, but do not forget mercy,
    that when the Chief Shepherd shall appear,
    you may receive the never-fading crown of glory.

*Bishop:*

In the name of Jesus Christ, the Head of the Church,
I gladly assume, with you and among you,

this ministry of Word, Sacrament, and Order,
of pastoral supervision, government, and service.
Strengthened by the love of God
and the remembrance of my consecration to the episcopacy,
I am resolved to serve faithfully and well
the congregations and people of the *Name* Area
as bishop, pastor, and friend.

*People:*

**On behalf of the congregations and people,
we receive you, Bishop *Name,*
with joy and thanksgiving, as our bishop and pastor.
We pledge to you our prayers, our loyalty, and our support
as you lead us in the ministry of reconciliation entrusted to us all.**

WELCOME AND ACCLAMATION

*Leader:* Welcome your bishop!

*The people acclaim their bishop with applause or other signs.*

SERMON OR OTHER RESPONSE BY THE BISHOP

PRAYER

**O God, Shepherd and Ruler of the faithful,
look with favor on your servant *Name,*
whom your Church has appointed bishop
and chief pastor of the *Name,* Area.
Grant that, by word and example,
*he/she* may assist those among whom *he/she* is placed,
so that *he/she* and the people entrusted to *his/her* care
may fulfill the promises that they have made this day;
grow together in unity, love, and service;
and at last attain everlasting life;
through Jesus Christ our Lord. Amen.**

[OFFERING] *See 26-27.*

*An offering of money for some stated purpose may be received if desired.*

[HOLY COMMUNION]

*If Holy Communion is celebrated, the bishop presides, using the text on 678-82,
beginning with Taking the Bread and Cup and continuing through Giving the
Bread and Cup. The congregation uses A Service of Word and Table III (UMH 15)
or one of the musical settings (UMH 17-25). After communion the following
prayer is offered by someone other than the bishop or by all:*

We thank you, gracious Lord, for giving yourself to us,
  and for uniting us in the communion of your Holy Spirit.
We bless you for raising up among us
  your faithful servant *bishop's first name*
    for the ministry of a bishop in your Church.
We pray that *he/she* may be to us an effective example
  in word and action, in love and patience, and in holiness of life.
Grant that we, with *him/her,*
  may glorify you by giving ourselves to others;
through Jesus Christ our Lord,
who lives and reigns with you,
in the unity of the Holy Spirit,
one God, now and for ever. Amen.

DISMISSAL WITH BLESSING * *See 31-32.*

HYMN * *See 30-31.*

GOING FORTH * *See 32.*


# A SERVICE OF FAREWELL
# TO A BISHOP OR DISTRICT SUPERINTENDENT

GATHERING *See 16-17.*

PROCESSIONAL HYMN *
  *See processional hymns suggested in 713 and in UMH 949-50.*

GREETING AND OPENING PRAYER *

The grace of the Lord Jesus Christ be with you.
**And also with you.**

Friends, we are gathered here this day
  to worship God and to witness to our common faith and ministry
    by celebrating the ministry of *Name.*

To God be all glory, honor, and praise.
**Thanks be to God! Amen.**

Let us pray.

**Almighty God,**
  **by your Holy Spirit your whole Church is governed and sanctified.**
**Direct us with your most gracious favor,**
  **that all our works begun, continued, and ended in you**
    **may glorify your holy name;**

**through our Lord and Savior Jesus Christ,**
**who lives and reigns with you and the Holy Spirit,**
**one God, for ever and ever. Amen.**

ANTHEM OR OTHER ACT OF PRAISE *See 21-22.*

PRAYER FOR ILLUMINATION * *See 22.*

SCRIPTURE *Suggested lessons:*

| | |
|---|---|
| Numbers 11:16-17, 24-25a | The elders receive the Spirit from Moses. |
| Joshua 1:7-9 | God's charge to Joshua |
| 2 Kings 2:1-12 | Elijah's spirit given to Elisha |
| Isaiah 42:1-9 | God's servant |
| Isaiah 61:1-8 | The Spirit of the Lord is upon me. |

PSALM OR CANTICLE * *Suggested from* UMH:

| | |
|---|---|
| Psalm 40:1-11 (*UMH* 774) | Blessed are those who trust in God. |
| Psalm 62:5-12 (*UMH* 787) | God alone is my rock and my salvation. |
| Psalm 99 (*UMH* 819) | The Lord reigns. |
| Psalm 138 (*UMH* 853) | All the rulers of earth shall praise God. |
| Canticle of Simeon (*UMH* 225-26) | Lord, now let your servant go in peace. |

SCRIPTURE

| | |
|---|---|
| Romans 12:1-18 | Love one another with mutual affection. |
| 1 Corinthians 4:9-17 | The apostles' ministry |
| 1 Corinthians 12:1-11 | Varieties of gifts but the same Spirit |
| 2 Corinthians 3:4-9 | Ministers of a new covenant |
| Ephesians 4:7, 11-16 | Unity in Christ's body |
| 1 Timothy 2:3-7; 3:1-7 | The qualifications of a bishop |
| Hebrews 5:1-10; 6:9-12 | God will not overlook your work. |

HYMN, ANTHEM, OR ALLELUIA * *See 23. Suggested from* UMH:

| | |
|---|---|
| 537-93 The Nature of the Church | 940 Hymns listed under |
| 949 Hymns listed under Ordina- |     Discipleship and Service |
|     tion | |

GOSPEL * *Suggested lessons:*

| | |
|---|---|
| Luke 10:1-9, 16-20 | Jesus sends out the seventy. |
| Luke 22:24-30 | The leader must be one who serves. |
| John 13:12-20 | You ought to wash one another's feet. |
| John 15:9-17 | I appointed you to bear fruit. |
| John 17:1-9, 18-21 | Jesus prays for believers. |

SERMON

*Someone other than the bishop or district superintendent preaches on a text such as one of the above with specific reference to the nature and meaning of spiritual leadership.*

## THE APOSTLES' CREED OR OTHER AFFIRMATION OF FAITH *

*See* UMH *880-89.*

## RECOGNITION OF THE BISHOP OR DISTRICT SUPERINTENDENT

*Leader to people:*

Brothers and sisters:
*Name* was ordained as an elder in Christ's holy Church
on the _____ day of _____, 19___, at *place.*
Through the grace of God, *he/she* has ministered in the name of Christ
at *places where the bishop or district superintendent has served.*
Now we celebrate this ministry and give thanks
to the One who has granted the harvest
and to *Name,* who has been a faithful and tireless laborer for the gospel.

*Family, friends, and clergy may briefly express their thanksgiving for the specific
spiritual gifts they have seen manifested in the ministry of the bishop or district
superintendent.*

*Leader to bishop or district superintendent:*

*Name,* you have been a faithful servant of Christ's holy Church.
In your life and ministry we have seen the work of God.

*People to bishop or district superintendent:*

**God's work in your life has renewed our faith
and inspired us to ministries in the name of Christ.**

*Leader to people:*

We pray that God will continue to work through *Name*
by strengthening the work already begun or accomplished among us.
Will you covenant to honor *Name's* ministry
through faithfulness toward God and God's people?

*People:*

**We will so honor *Name* and *his/her* ministry among us.**

*Leader to bishop or district superintendent:*

Will you honor the gratitude of these people
through your prayers for them and their ministry
and with other appropriate service as the Holy Spirit may direct?

*Bishop or district superintendent:*

I will so honor this people of God
and pray God's continued blessing upon their faith and work.

*Leader:*

Let us pray.

**Most bountiful God, the giver of every good gift,**
   **you have given each of us gifts**
      **for our season of labor in your service.**
**Bless and extend all your gifts,**
   **that they may glorify your name and heal and save your people;**
**through Jesus Christ our Lord. Amen.**

*A gift may be presented to, or on behalf of, the bishop or district superintendent in recognition of his/her ministry.*

*The bishop or district superintendent may make a statement of thanksgiving and may briefly state his/her plans for the future.*

## PRAYER OF INTERCESSION

Creating God,
   you are the Source of all that ever was, that is, and that is to come.
Direct us that we may do what is right, just, and merciful in your sight.
Lord, in your mercy, **hear our prayer.**

Redeeming God,
   you have created and redeemed us to be your people.
Continue to guide and sustain your Church, now and in the days ahead,
   that your will may be done on earth as it is in heaven.
Lord, in your mercy, **hear our prayer.**

Sustaining God,
   you have been present with your people from generation to generation.
Undergird your servant *Name* during this time of transition,
   and be with all who experience changes in life.
Lord, in your mercy, **hear our prayer.**

Almighty God,
   you have bound us together to work for your reign on earth.
Bless *Name* as *he/she* begins a new phase of ministry,
and grant that all of us, by drawing even nearer to you,
   may always be close to onr another in the communion of your saints;
through Jesus Christ our Lord. **Amen.**

## [OFFERING] *See 26-27.*

*An offering of money may be received for some stated purpose if desired.*

## [HOLY COMMUNION]

*If Holy Communion is celebrated, the bishop or district superintendent uses the text on 678-82, beginning with Taking the Bread and Cup and continuing through Giving the Bread and Cup. The congregation uses A Service of Word and Table III (UMH 15) or one of the musical settings (UMH 17-25). After communion the bishop or district superintendent may give thanks as follows:*

We thank you, gracious God, for giving yourself to us
  and for uniting us in the communion of your Holy Spirit.
We bless you for raising up among us your faithful servant *Name*
  for the ministry of *bishop (district superintendent)* in your Church.
We pray that *he/she* may continue to be to your people
  an effective example in word and action,
  in love and patience, and in holiness of life.
Grant that we, with *him/her*,
  may glorify you by giving ourselves to others;
through Jesus Christ our Lord,
  who lives and reigns with you, in the unity of the Holy Spirit,
  one God, now and for ever. **Amen.**

DISMISSAL WITH BLESSING * *See 31-32.*

HYMN * *See 30-31.*

GOING FORTH * *See 32.*

# A RETIREMENT RECOGNITION SERVICE

*The name of each person retiring should be printed in the bulletin. A summary of the life and ministry of each may also be printed.*

GATHERING *See 16-17.*

GREETING * *See 17-20.*

HYMN OF PRAISE * *See 17-20. Suggested from* UMH:

711 For All the Saints     60 I'll Praise My Maker While I've Breath
    (omit stanzas 4 and 6)     90 Ye Watchers and Ye Holy Ones
555 Forward Through the Ages

OPENING PRAYER * *See 20-21.*

PRAYER FOR ILLUMINATION * *See 22.*

SCRIPTURE LESSON(S) *Suggested lessons:*

2 Kings 2:1-15     The spirit of Elijah rests on Elisha.
Psalm 90 (*UMH* 809 or 117)     Our dwelling place in all generations
Philippians 3:7-16     Paul's testimony
2 Timothy 4:1-8     Paul's charge to Timothy
John 21:15-19     Feed my sheep.

SERMON

# RECOGNITION OF THE RETIREES

*The retirees and spouses come forward and are introduced by name.*

*Bishop:*

Brothers and sisters in Christ, you came to us from congregations
    where the Spirit of the Lord was upon you;
and you were charged to preach to the brokenhearted,
    to visit the captive, to anoint those who were bruised.
These things you have done.

*People:*

**We thank God for the community of the faithful
    in which the Word of God found response.
Countless persons have depended upon you for help.
In the providence of God, you know
    that both suffering and joy can be God's way of teaching and healing.**

*Bishop:*

At your ordination,
you received authority to read the Holy Scriptures
    in the Church of God,
    to preach the Word, to celebrate the Sacraments,
    and to Order the life of the Church.
At your consecration,
you received authority to equip the people of God,
    and to embody the unity of the congregation's worship
        with its life in the world.
By God's grace you did many things
    that seemed to be beyond your power.

*People:*

**We thank God that you were given the vision to be faithful.
Death and illness have not come on schedule.
The truth has not always been easy to preach.
We know something of the grace by which you have lived,
    and we thank God for your vision.**

*Bishop:*

Never think lightly of the great good
    that God has wrought through you.
Continue to be true to your calling.
May God's love and power be with you always.
Let us pray together.

**God of grace, you fill your servants with the vision.
You empower your servants with your Spirit.
We give thanks for the ministry of these women and men,**

**and for the ways in which you have ministered to us through them.**
**Give them a sense of your abiding presence,**
**that they may continue to love and serve you,**
**and ever grow in the grace and knowledge of Jesus Christ,**
**in whose name we pray. Amen.**

## RESPONSES FROM THE RETIRING CLASS

*Members of the retiring class may speak briefly to the conference.*

## ANTHEM

## PASSING OF THE MANTLE

*A representative of the retiring class and a representative of the new full member class kneel. The bishop takes the mantle (a cape or stole) and places it on the shoulders of the representative of the retiring class, saying:*

In the book of Kings we read of the prophet Elijah's ministry.
The mantle, symbolic of submission to God,
    fell upon the younger prophet, Elisha,
    and the spirit of Elijah rested upon Elisha.

*The representative of the retiring class rises and places the mantle on the shoulders of the representative of the new full member class, saying:*

I transfer this mantle from our generation to the young,
    indicating thereby
that the responsibilities and dedication of the older generation
    will be caught up and carried on by the young,
and the spirit of today's Elijahs will rest upon today's Elishas.

*The representative of the new class rises, turns to the retiring class, and says:*

We who come after you take up the mantle which falls upon us.
May we inherit a double share of your spirit.

*The bishop responds:*

I therefore, the prisoner in the Lord,
beg you to lead a life worthy of the calling to which you have been called,
    with all humility and gentleness, with patience,
    bearing with one another in love,
    making every effort to maintain the unity of the Spirit
        in the bond of peace.
There is one body and one Spirit,
    just as you were called to the one hope of your calling,
    one Lord, one faith, one baptism, one God and Father of us all,
    who is above all and through all and in all. (EPHESIANS 4:1-6)

HYMN * *Suggested from* UMH:

| | |
|---|---|
| 940 Hymns listed under Discipleship and Service | 583 Sois la Semilla (You Are the Seed) |
| 949 Hymns listed under Ordination | 399 Take My Life, and Let It Be |
| 396 O Jesus, I Have Promised | 344 Tu Has Venido a la Orilla |
| 338 Where He Leads Me | (Lord, You Have Come to the Lakeshore) |

DISMISSAL WITH BLESSING * *See 31-32.*

*Bishop:*

For everything there is a season,
　a time for every matter under heaven.
So, too, there is a time for movement, new adventure,
　fields of service not yet touched.
With love, we send you forth in the spirit of John Wesley:
May the world be your parish.

*People:*

**Go into the world and respond to the love of Christ in all you do.**
**Live out the vision God has given you.**
**May God's mercy, grace, and peace be with you.**
**May you be channels for God's mercy, grace, and peace**
**　to the world wherever you may be!**

*Bishop:* Amen!

*People:* **Amen!**

GOING FORTH * *See 32.*

# AN ANNUAL CONFERENCE MEMORIAL SERVICE

GATHERING *See 16-17.*

PROCESSIONAL HYMN OF PRAISE * *See 17-20. Suggested from* UMH:

| | |
|---|---|
| 949 Hymns listed under Processionals | 711 For All the Saints |
| 653 Christ the Victorious | 712 I Sing a Song of the Saints of God |
| 709 Come, Let Us Join Our Friends Above | 708 Rejoice in God's Saints |
| | 90 Ye Watchers and Ye Holy Ones |

*See also:*
Beloved, Now We Are the Saints of God ( ♪ *219*)

GREETING * *See 17-20.*

We have gathered here to celebrate the lives of those
　who have served faithfully through the years
　　and now share the triumph of Christ.

**We affirm with praise and thanksgiving the goodness of our Lord.**

Let us rejoice in God's presence with us, in death as in life,
among those who mourn
as with those who now see Christ face to face.

**In the midst of our grief we sing with joy,**
**for God's love is over all that has been made.**
**Blessed be God's glorious name for ever.**

OPENING PRAYER * *See 20-21.*

Tender and compassionate God,
we seek to know you through the hearing of your Word
and pray that we may go beyond hearing to obeying,
as shown by the faithful lives of your departed servants
whom we honor today.
We know that they are precious in your eyes,
worthy of your special attention and ours,
for they served well in the task that you gave them.
Grant that we may feel your presence
as did the followers who knew Jesus in the breaking of the bread,
and may we experience the fire within
that sent them out to share good news. **Amen.**

ANTHEM OR HYMN

*See UMH 652-56 and 700-12, other hymns listed under Funerals and Memorial*
*Services (UMH 941-42), and the suggestions on 160-61.*

PRAYER FOR ILLUMINATION * *See 22.*

SCRIPTURE LESSON(S) *Suggested lessons:*

| | |
|---|---|
| Isaiah 40:1-11, 28-31 | Comfort my people, says your God. |
| Isaiah 55:6-13 (*UMH* 125) | Canticle of Covenant Faithfulness |
| Psalm 23 (*UMH* 136, 137, 138, 754) | The Lord is my shepherd. |
| Psalm 46 (*UMH* 780) | God is our refuge and strength. |
| Psalm 90 (*UMH* 809) | God has been our dwelling place. |
| Psalm 91 (*UMH* 810) | Under God's wings we find refuge. |
| Psalm 121 (*UMH* 844) | My help comes from the Lord. |
| Romans 8:35, 37-39 (*UMH* 887) | Nothing can separate us from God's love. |
| 1 Corinthians 15:1-8, 12-20, 35-44, 53-58 | The resurrection of the dead |
| 2 Corinthians 4:5-18 | Glory in God |
| Ephesians 1:15-23; 2:1, 4-10 | Alive in Christ |
| Hebrews 11:1-2; 12:1-2 | So great a cloud of witnesses |
| 1 John 3:1-3 | We shall see God. |
| Revelation 7:9-17 | Multitude of the redeemed |
| Revelation 21:1-7, 22-27; 22:1-5 or Canticle of Hope (*UMH* 734) | A new heaven and a new earth |

| | |
|---|---|
| Matthew 5:1-12 | The Beatitudes |
| Luke 24:13-35 | Jesus at Emmaus |
| John 14:1-10a, 15-21, 25-27 | Let not your hearts be troubled. |

*Between lessons there may be a psalm, canticle, scriptural affirmation of faith, Gloria Patri, anthem, and/or hymn. See hymns suggested earlier in this service.*

## SERMON

*A hymn or an affirmation of faith may follow the sermon.*

## ACT OF REMEMBRANCE (NAMING OF THE HONORED DEAD) *

*The name of each of the honored dead is read aloud. After each name is read, the congregation may be asked to keep silence or to respond:* **Thank you, Lord, for this your servant.**

## PRAYER FOR THE SAINTS AND FAITHFUL DEPARTED *

**O God of both the living and the dead,**
    **we praise your holy name for all your servants**
      **who have faithfully lived and died.**
**We thank you for the sacred ties that bind us**
    **to those unseen who encompass us as a cloud of witnesses.**
**We pray that,**
    **encouraged by their example and strengthened by their fellowship,**
    **we may be diligent followers**
      **and that nothing will be able to separate us from your love**
    **in Christ Jesus our Lord. Amen.**

## [HOLY COMMUNION]

*See A Service of Word and Table II (UMH 12), III (UMH 15), or IV (UMH 26) and the musical settings in UMH 17-25. The bishop may use The Great Thanksgiving on 74-75.*

## HYMN AND DISMISSAL WITH BLESSING * *See 31-32.*

*If this hymn is a recessional, it follows Dismissal with Blessing. See hymns suggested earlier in this service.*

## GOING FORTH * *See 32.*

# XII. GENERAL CHURCH SERVICES

## THE ORDER FOR COMMISSIONING AS MISSIONARIES I

*This order is used by The General Board of Global Ministries for commissioning persons to the office of missionary.*

*Presiding bishop:*

Dear friends,
as we take part in this celebration of blessing and commissioning,
  we are reliving a practice of the early church.
We read in the book of Acts
  that the Holy Spirit set apart Saul and Barnabas for the work of mission,
  and the church at Antioch, after fasting and praying,
    laid hands on them and sent them out.
The early church eagerly sent its members to other peoples,
  to assist those who were already of the household of faith
    and those who did not yet believe in Christ.

Today we also send our sisters and brothers
  to serve the needs of the Church throughout the world.
This commissioning and sending will strengthen the bonds we maintain
  with the faith-filled communities to which they are going,
and the prayers we offer are an expression of the ties
  that bind us together in the larger body of Christ.

The Lord be with you.
**And also with you.**
Let us pray.

**Lord Jesus Christ,**
**you stretched out your arms of love on the hard wood of the cross**
  **that everyone might come within the reach of your saving embrace.**
**So clothe us in your Spirit that we, reaching forth our hands in love,**
  **may bring those who do not know you**
  **to the knowledge and love of you;**
**for the honor of your name. Amen.**

*Representative of The General Board of Global Ministries:*

These are the names
of those who are being sent by The United Methodist Church
as partners with Christ in mission, accompanied by our prayers:

*Candidates kneel as their names are read and their assignments are announced.*

*The bishop stretches hands over those being commissioned, saying this prayer of blessing:*

We bless you, O God, and we give you all the praise and glory.
We ask you to bless these your servants.
Fill the hearts of those we are commissioning
with the power of the Holy Spirit.
We send them forth as messengers of salvation and peace in your name,
marked with the sign of the cross and anchored in your grace.
Bless the crosses we now give
as a sign of Christ's love and a token of our faith. **Amen.**

*A cross is given to, and hands are laid upon the head of, each person commissioned. During the laying on of hands, the bishop says:*

*Name,* I commission you
to take the gospel of our Lord Jesus Christ into all the world,
in the name of the Father, and of the Son, and of the Holy Spirit.
**Amen.**

*Those who have been commissioned rise and turn to be greeted by the congregation.*

*A hymn may be sung. Suggested from UMH:*

| | |
|---|---|
| 563-90 Called to God's Mission | 648 God the Spirit, Guide |
| 433 All Who Love and Serve | and Guardian |
| Your City | 159 Lift High the Cross |
| 530 Are Ye Able | 424 Must Jesus Bear the Cross Alone |
| 451 Be Thou My Vision | 444 O Young and Fearless Prophet |
| 438 Forth in Thy Name, O Lord | 336 Of All the Spirit's Gifts to Me |
| 670 Go Forth for God | 436 The Voice of God Is Calling |
| | 338 Where He Leads Me |

# THE ORDER FOR COMMISSIONING
## TO THE OFFICE OF DEACONESS OR AS MISSIONARIES II

*This order is used by The General Board of Global Ministries for commissioning persons to the office of deaconess or as missionaries.*

*Presiding bishop to candidates:*

Dear *sisters and brothers,*
we rejoice that you have purposed

to devote your *lives* to Christian mission.
Your labors may take you to the mountains and the plains,
  to isolated villages or teeming cities.
You are to be among persons as those who serve
  in teaching, preaching, and healing.
In the varied activities of our common life,
  you will testify every day to the infinite love of God
  shed abroad in Christ Jesus.
Such a vocation confers a great privilege;
  it also lays upon you a solemn responsibility.
What you have done alone with God
  in consecrating your *lives* to this service,
  we now ask you to do publicly in the presence of this assembly.

Do you sincerely believe that you have been led by the Spirit of God
  to engage in this work and to assume its responsibilities?

**I do so believe.**

In humble reliance upon divine grace,
  do you make it the supreme purpose of your life
  to give yourself unreservedly to the work of Christ
    in your appointed field?

**I do, Christ being my helper.**

Will you be diligent in prayer, in the reading of the Holy Scriptures,
  and in such studies as increase your knowledge of God
    and God's plan for creation?

**I will endeavor so to do.**

Will you earnestly seek to carry forward your ministry
  in sincerity and love,
  cooperating humbly with your coworkers,
  under the direction of the Church?

**I will, Christ being my helper.**

*The people pray for the candidates in silence, after which the bishop says:*

Almighty God, Source of all mercies,
  graciously behold these your servants
  now to be commissioned as *deaconesses and missionaries*
    of your Church.
Endow *them* with your Holy Spirit,
  enrich *them* with your heavenly grace,
  and strengthen *them* for the tasks which lie ahead;
that in all *their* works,
  begun, continued, and ended in you,
  *they* may glorify your holy name,

and advance your blessed work;
through Jesus Christ our Lord. **Amen.**

*All those to be commissioned kneel. Designated representatives from the community assist the bishop in the laying on of hands. The bishop says:*

*Name,* I commission you
to take the gospel of our Lord Jesus Christ into all the world,
in the name of the Father, and of the Son, and of the Holy Spirit.
**Amen.**

*Those being commissioned pray the Covenant Prayer in unison:*

**I am no longer my own, but thine.**
**Put me to what thou wilt, rank me with whom thou wilt.**
**Put me to doing, put me to suffering.**
**Let me be employed for thee or laid aside for thee,**
**exalted for thee or brought low for thee.**
**Let me be full, let me be empty.**
**Let me have all things, let me have nothing.**
**I freely and heartily yield all things to thy pleasure and disposal.**
**And now, O glorious and blessed God,**
**Father, Son, and Holy Spirit,**
**thou art mine, and I am thine. So be it.**
**And the covenant which I have made on earth,**
**let it be ratified in heaven. Amen.**

*Presiding bishop to congregation:*

Christian friends, I commend to you *these persons*
whom we this day have recognized and commissioned
to carry into all the world
the sacred and imperishable message of eternal salvation.

**As members of this Christian assembly representing the whole Church,**
**we send you into service with your special gifts and graces.**
**We call you and support you.**
**You are our gift to the world.**
**We will receive you back again on behalf of all God's people.**

**Like you, we too have special gifts and graces,**
**particular endowments of mind and spirit,**
**through which God seeks to be made known in the world.**
**Together we are the people of God,**
**whose task is to participate in God's mission in the world.**
**We celebrate the gifts of life,**
**and we face the future with an unshakable hope.**

*Those who have been commissioned rise and turn to be greeted by the congregation.*

*Suggested hymns from UMH are listed on 741.*

# XIII. ACKNOWLEDGMENTS

United Methodist congregations may reproduce for worship and educational purposes any item from *The United Methodist Book of Worship* for one-time use, as in a bulletin, special program, or lesson resource, provided that the copyright notice and acknowledgment line for that item are included on the reproduction. This permission, however, does not extend to events (such as workshops and seminars) where admission is charged or registration fees are collected. Persons in charge of such events must write to copyright holders for permission.

Requests to reprint those items owned by The United Methodist Publishing House or Abingdon Press or Cokesbury, other than as outlined above, must be referred to Permission Office, Abingdon Press, 201 8th Avenue S., Nashville, Tennessee 37203. Requests to reprint items owned by other copyright owners, other than as outlined above, must be sent to the respective owner(s) listed below.

Permissions have been obtained for *The United Methodist Book of Worship*. Some items showing no copyright information may have copyright protection in other countries. Every effort has been made to trace the owner(s) and/or administrator(s) of each copyright. The Publisher regrets any omission and will, upon written notice, make the necessary correction(s) in subsequent printings.

Scripture, unless otherwise indicated, is adapted from the New Revised Standard Version of the Bible, © 1989 by Division of Christian Education of the National Council of Churches of Christ in the USA and is used by permission. Although copyright permission is not required for use of items from *The Book of Common Prayer*, as a courtesy, we recommend acknowledgment of this source.

## I. GENERAL SERVICES

Pages 13-171, containing the General Services of The United Methodist Church, are copyrighted and/or cited as follows:

15 The Basic Pattern of Worship © 1976, 1980 by Abingdon; © 1980, 1985, 1989, 1992 UMPH.

16-32 An Order of Sunday Worship Using the Basic Pattern © 1985, 1989, 1992 UMPH.

33-39 A Service of Word and Table I © 1972 The Methodist Publishing House; © 1980, 1985, 1989, 1992 UMPH.

41-50 A Service of Word and Table IV © 1957 Board of Publication, Evangelical United Brethren Church; © 1964, 1965, 1966 by Board of Publication of The Methodist Church, Inc.; © 1989, 1992 UMPH; renewal © 1992 UMPH.

51-53 A Service of Word and Table V with Persons Who Are Sick or Homebound © 1976, 1980 by Abingdon; © 1985, 1987, 1992 UMPH.

54-71 The Great Thanksgivings for Advent; Christmas Eve, Day, or Season; New Year, Epiphany, Baptism of the Lord, or Covenant Reaffirmation; Early in Lent; Later in Lent; Holy Thursday Evening; Easter Day or Season; the Day of Pentecost; and the Season After Pentecost © 1972 The Methodist Publishing House; © 1980, 1981, 1985 UMPH; © 1986 by Abingdon Press; © 1987, 1989, 1992 UMPH.

72-73 The Great Thanksgiving for World Communion Sunday © 1972 The Methodist Publishing House; © 1980, 1985, 1989, 1992 UMPH.

74-77 The Great Thanksgivings for All Saints and Memorial Occasions and Thanksgiving Day or for the Gift of Food © 1972 The Methodist Publishing House; © 1980, 1981, 1985 UMPH; © 1986 by Abingdon Press; © 1987, 1989, 1992 UMPH.

78-80 An Alternate Great Thanksgiving for General Use and A Brief Great Thanksgiving for General Use © 1972 The Methodist Publishing House; © 1980, 1985, 1987, 1989, 1992 UMPH.

86-102 The Baptismal Covenants I, II and II-A © 1976, 1980, 1985, 1989, 1992 UMPH.

103-10 The Baptismal Covenants II-B and III © 1964, 1965, 1966 by Board of Publication of the Methodist Church, Inc.; © 1989, 1992 UMPH; renewal © 1992 UMPH.

104 Congregational Pledge 1 © 1959 Board of Publication, Evangelical United Brethren Church; © 1992 UMPH.

111-14 The Baptismal Covenant IV © 1976, 1980, 1985, 1989, 1992 UMPH.

115-27 A Service of Christian Marriage I © 1979, 1980, 1985, 1989, 1992 UMPH. Intercessory Prayer and Blessing and Exchange of Rings © 1965 by Board of Publication of The Methodist Church, Inc.; © 1979, 1985, 1989, 1992 UMPH; renewal © 1992 UMPH. Thanksgiving and Communion © 1972 The Methodist Publishing House; © 1980, 1981, 1985, 1987, 1989, 1992 UMPH.

121 Alternative Texts for the Exchange of Vows © 1979 by Abingdon; © 1992 UMPH.

128-33 A Service of Christian Marriage II © 1964, 1965 by Board of Publication of The Methodist Church, Inc. © 1992 UMPH; renewal © 1992 UMPH. Declaration of Intention: Pastoral Charge #2 © 1959 Board of Publication, Evangelical United Brethren Church.

133-38 A Service for the Recognition or the Blessing of a Civil Marriage and An Order for the Reaffirmation of the Marriage Covenant © 1979 by Abingdon; © 1992 UMPH. Intercessory Prayer, Blessing of Rings © 1964, 1965 by Board of Publication of the Methodist Church, Inc.; © 1992 UMPH; renewal © 1992 UMPH.

139-57 A Service of Death and Resurrection © 1979, 1980, 1985, 1989, 1992 UMPH. An Order for Holy Communion © 1972 The Methodist Publishing House; © 1979, 1980, 1981, 1985, 1987, 1989, 1992 UMPH. A Service of Committal © 1979, 1985, 1992 UMPH.

158-66    Additional Resources for Services of Death and Resurrection © 1979 by Abingdon; © 1992 UMPH. Prayers For General Use and prayer #1 At the Service for a Person Who Did Not Profess the Christian Faith © 1964, 1965 by Board of Publication of The Methodist Church, Inc.; renewal © 1992 UMPH. Prayer #2 At the Service for a Child and prayer #3 At the Service for a Person Who Did Not Profess the Christian Faith renewal © 1971, 1972 by Abingdon Press. Prayer #2 At the Service for a Person Who Did Not Profess the Christian Faith © 1959 Board of Publication, Evangelical United Brethren Church.

167    Prayer #3 in Ministry with the Dying and prayers #2 and #3 in Ministry Immediately Following Death © 1992 UMPH.

168-69    A Family Hour or Wake © 1992 UMPH. Prayer © 1989 UMPH.

170-71    A Service of Death and Resurrection for a Stillborn Child © 1992 UMPH. Greeting and Prayer of Commendation, alt. © 1979, 1992 UMPH.

*The Book of Common Prayer*, 1928:

131    Blessing and Exchange of Rings, adapt.
132    Blessing of the Marriage, adapt.
129-30    Declaration by the Man and the Woman, adapt.
131-32    Declaration of Marriage, adapt.
133    Dismissal with Blessing, adapt.
130-31    Exchange of Vows, alt.
161    Prayer #1 At the Service for a Child, alt.
128-29    Wedding Greeting, adapt.

*The Book of Common Prayer*, 1979:

150    Commendation Prayer #3, alt.
134    Declaration by the Husband and Wife, adapt.
117    Declaration of Intention, alt.
120-23    Exchange of Vows; Exchange of Rings, alt.; Declaration of Marriage, alt.; Blessing of the Marriage, alt.
33    Opening Prayer, alt.
25-26    Prayer of Confession and Act of Pardon.
166-67    Prayers #1 and #4 in Ministry with the Dying, alt.
36    Preface, alt. (See also pp. 54, 56, 58, 60, 62, 64, 66, 68, 70, 72, 74, 76, 124, 152)
136    Reaffirmation of the Marriage Covenant, alt.
46-47    Seasonal Prefaces.

Permission for use of items controlled by other copyright owners must be obtained from the respective owners listed below.

Abingdon Press; 201 8th Avenue, S.; Nashville, TN 37203:
164    Prayer #3 For an Untimely or Tragic Death, adapt. from *Lift Up Your Hearts* by Walter Russell Bowie, 1939; renewal © 1984 Jean B. Evans, Elizabeth Chapman, and Walter Russell Bowie, Jr. Used by permission of Abingdon Press.

Collins Publishers; 8 Grafton St.; London W1X 3LA; England:
79    Prayer following the epiclesis, adapt. from *The Didache (The Teaching of the Twelve Apostles)*, "An Ancient Prayer" in *Prayers of the Eucharist: Early and Reformed* © 1975 compilation, editorial matter and translation of original texts, R.C.D. Jasper and G.J. Cumming.

The English Language Liturgical Consultation; 1275 K St., NW, #1202; Washington, DC 20005-4097:
34    Apostles' Creed, Ecumenical version, alt., from the English trans. of the Apostles' Creed originally prepared by the International Consultation on English Texts in 1975 and revised by ELLC in 1988. (See also pp. 89-90, 96-97, 107-08, 112)
36    Sursum Corda, alt., from the English trans. of "Lift up your hearts" prepared by ELLC 1988. (See also pp. 54, 56, 58, 60, 62, 64, 66, 68, 70, 72, 74, 76, 78, 124, 152)

Forward Movement Publications; 412 Sycamore St.; Cincinnati, OH 45202-4195:
138    Marriage Anniversary Prayer #2, adapt. from *Prayers for All Occasions*, © 1964 Forward Movement Publications. Used by permission.

International Commission on English in the Liturgy, Inc.; 1275 K St., NW, #1202; Washington, DC 20005-4097:
138    Marriage Anniversary Prayer #1, alt., text from *The Roman Missal* © 1973, ICEL. All rights reserved.
38    Memorial Acclamation text from *The Roman Missal* © 1973, ICEL. All rights reserved. (See also pp. 55, 57, 59, 61, 63, 65, 67, 69, 71, 73, 75, 77, 125, 153)
78    Prayer after Benedictus, adapt., text from *Eucharistic Prayer A* © 1986, ICEL. All rights reserved.
126-27    Wedding Post-communion Prayer, alt., text from *The Roman Missal* © 1973, ICEL. All rights reserved.

The International Consultation on English Texts; 1275 K St., NW, #1202; Washington, DC 20005-4097:
37    Sanctus and Benedictus from the English trans. of the Sanctus/Benedictus by ICET. (See also pp. 54, 56, 58, 60, 62, 64, 66, 68, 70, 72, 74, 76, 78, 124, 152)
38    The Lord's Prayer, Ecumenical Text from the English trans. of the Lord's Prayer by ICET.

Methodist Publishing House; 20, Ivattway; Peterborough PE3 7PG; England:
134    Declaration by the Husband and Wife, adapt. from *The Methodist Service Book* © The Methodist Conference 1975. Used by permission of Methodist Publishing House.

Morehouse Publishing; 871 Ethan Allen Highway; Ridgefield, CT 06877:
163    Prayer #1 For an Untimely or Tragic Death and
165-66    prayer #5 At the Service for a Person Who Did Not Profess the Christian Faith from *Burial Services* © 1980 Joseph Buchanan Bernardin. Used by permission of Morehouse Publishing.

The Uniting Church in Australia Assembly Commission on Liturgy; c/o Ian Culliman; 29 Menin Rd.; Corinda, Queensland, 4075; Australia:
168    Prayer #4 in Ministry Immediately Following Death, alt., from UNITING IN WORSHIP LEADER'S BOOK, © 1988, UCAACL. Used by permission of The Joint Board of Christian Education, Melbourne, Australia.

Westminster/John Knox Press; 100 Witherspoon St.; Louisville, KY 40202-1396:
135    Declaration of Marriage, adapt., reprinted from THE WORSHIP BOOK: Services and Hymns. © MCMLXX, MCMLXXII, The Westminster Press. Used by permission of Westminster/John Knox Press.
133    Greeting, adapt., reprinted from THE WORSHIP BOOK: Services and Hymns. © MCMLXX, MCMLXXII, The Westminster Press. Used by permission of Westminster/John Knox Press.
167    Prayer #1 in Ministry Immediately Following Death, alt., reprinted from THE FUNERAL: A Service of Witness to the Resurrection (Supplemental Liturgical Resource 4). © 1986 The Westminster Press. Used by permission of Westminster/John Knox Press.
166    Prayer #2 in Ministry with the Dying, reprinted from THE FUNERAL: A Service of Witness to the Resurrection (Supplemental Liturgical Resource 4). © 1986 The Westminster Press. Used by permission of Westminster/John Knox Press.

Wm. B. Eerdmans Publishing Co.; 255 Jefferson Ave. SE; Grand Rapids, MI 49503:
163-64    Prayer #2 for An Untimely or Tragic Death adapt. from "When Death Intrudes Untimely . . . an individual prayer" in *Dialogues with God* by O. Thomas Miles, Wm. B. Eerdmans Publishing Co.

## II. MUSIC AS ACTS OF WORSHIP

Items 173-223, containing the Music As Acts of Worship of The United Methodist Church, are copyrighted and/or cited as follows:

173    Words, Music: Hope Publishing Co.; 380 South Main Place; Carol Stream, IL 60188.

175    Words, Music: Stanley M. Farr; 518 Fairmont Rd.; Morgantown, WV 26505. B.N.: for Daniel Walker Irwin and his parents Jeff and Kathy on the occasion of his baptism.

176    Words, Music: English transliteration and musical transcription by Marilyn M. Hofstra; 820 Spring St.; Arcata, CA 95521. English paraphrase by Leona Sullivan; Rt. 3, Box 517; Broken Arrow, OK 74014.

177    Words, Music: Attributed to The Lumko Institute; Post Box 11; Lady Frere, Transkei; South Africa.

178    Words, Music: Ms. Leng Loh; 3515 Fourth Ave. #10; San Diego, CA 92103.

184    Words, Music: English transliteration and music transcription by Marilyn Hofstra; 820 Spring St.; Arcata, CA 95521. English paraphrase by Dorothy Gray; Route 2, Box 158; Carnegie, OK 73015.

187    Words, Music: Patrick Matsikenyiri; Shenandoah University; 1460 University Dr.; Box 683; Winchester, VA 22601. English trans. by G.I.A. Publications Inc.; Attn. Alex Harris, Dir. of Ops.; 7404 S. Mason Ave.; Chicago, IL 60638.

188    Words: English trans. by Gertrude C. Suppe; 3307 Michigan Ave.; South Gate, CA 90280. Music: Arrang. by Alvin Schutmaat, deceased May 1, 1987—all permissions given by his wife, Pauline Schutmaat; Cra. 55 #72-52; Barranquilla, Colombia.

189    Words: From *The Kingdom, The Power, and the Glory* (p. 5), Oxford University Press; Attn.: Miss Joyce Horn, Hymn Copyright; 7-8 Hatherly Street; London SW1P 2QT; England.

190    Music: William Farley Smith; 96 Reis Ave.; Englewood, NJ 07631.

197    Words: Fred A. Shaw/Neeake; 2757 West US 22 & 3; Maineville, OH 45039. Music: Traditional Shawnee as used by the Shawnee Nation United Remnant Band.

202    Music: Attributed to Alfred Bayiga; College protestante G. Schwab; B.P. 09; Edea; Cameroon.

203    Words, Music: Patrick Matsikenyiri with Church Music Service; Attn.: COM Director; The United Methodist Church Headquarters; Box 3408; Harare, Zimbabwe.

208    Words: United States Catholic Conference; 3211 Fourth Street, N.E.: Washington, DC 20017-1194. Music: © 1992 Gamut Music Productions; 704 Saddle Trail Court; Hermitage, TN 37076. All rights reserved.

210    Words, Music: James Ritchie; 1205 Huntingboro Court; Antioch, TN 37013.

211    Music: © 1992 Gamut Music Productions; 704 Saddle Trail Court; Hermitage, TN 37076. All rights reserved.

214    Words, Music: Steve Garnaas-Holmes; Bigforkcade Ave.; Bigfork, MT 59911.

216    Music: © 1992 Gamut Music Productions; 704 Saddle Trail Court; Hermitage, TN 37076.

220    Music: David Goodrich; 251 NE 38th St., A-101; Fort Lauderdale, FL 33334.

221    Music: David Goodrich; 251 NE 38th St., A-101; Fort Lauderdale, FL 33334.

223    Words: English trans. by John Webster Grant; c/o Emmanuel College; 75 Queens Park Crescent; Toronto, Canada M5S 1K7.

## III. THE CHRISTIAN YEAR

Items 224-421, containing the materials for The Christian Year of The United Methodist Church, are copyrighted and/or cited as follows:

227 Adapt. from Revised Common Lectionary © 1992, Consultation on Common Texts (CCT); Attn.: James M. Schellmann; 1275 K St., NW; Suite 1202; Washington, D.C. 20005.

245 From *The Book of Worship*, p. 67, © 1964, 1965 by Board of Publication of The Methodist Church, Inc.; renewal © 1992 UMPH.

249 From *The Book of Worship*, p. 35, 1944; renewal © 1971, 1972 by Abingdon Press.

250 From *The Book of Common Prayer*, p. 211, 1979.

251 From *The Book of Worship*, p. 68, © 1964, 1965 by Board of Publication of The Methodist Church, Inc.; renewal © 1992 UMPH.

252 Text from *The Roman Missal* © 1973, International Committee on English in the Liturgy. All rights reserved. ICEL; 1275 K Street, NW, Suite 1202; Washington, DC 20005.

253 From *Touch Holiness*, p. 13, © 1990. Used by permission of The Pilgrim Press; 700 Prospect Avenue East; Cleveland, OH 44115-1100.

254 From *Prayers for the Christian Year*, 2nd ed., p. 5, 1935. Text used by permission of Oxford University Press; Walton Street; Oxford OX2 6DP; England.

255 Altered from DAILY PRAYER (Supplemental Liturgical Resource 5, p. 295). © 1987 The Westminster Press. Altered and used by permission of Westminster/John Knox Press; 100 Witherspoon Street; Louisville, KY 40202-1396.

256 Text from *The Roman Missal* © 1973, International Commission on English in the Liturgy. All rights reserved. ICEL; 1275 K Street, NW, Suite 1202; Washington, DC 20005.

257 Text from *The Roman Missal* © 1973, International Commission on English in the Liturgy. All rights reserved. ICEL; 1275 K Street, NW, Suite 1202; Washington, DC 20005.

258 Adapt. from *The Hanging of the Greens*, by Sally Rhodes Ahner, © 1986 by Abingdon Press.

260 Additional blessings from the **Book of Blessings** for use in the United States of America © 1988, by the United States Catholic Conference, Washington, D.C. are used with permission. All rights reserved. USCC; 3211 Fourth Street, N.E.; Washington, DC 20017-1194.

261 Additional blessings from the **Book of Blessings** for use in the United States of America © 1988, by the United States Catholic Conference, Washington, D.C. are used with permission. All rights reserved. USCC; 3211 Fourth Street, N.E.; Washington, DC 20017-1194.

262 Adapt. from *From Hope to Joy*, p. 51, © 1984 by Abingdon Press.

266 Trans. and adapt. © 1992 UMPH.

274 Text from *The Liturgy of the Hours* © 1973, 1975 International Commission on English in the Liturgy. All rights reserved. ICEL; 1275 K Street, NW, Suite 1202; Washington, DC 20005-4097.

276 From *The Book of Worship*, p. 40, 1944; renewal © 1971, 1972 by Abingdon Press.

277 From *The Book of Worship*, p. 75, 1965.

278 "Send, O God, into the darkness. . ." from PRAYERS OF THE SPIRIT by John Wallace Suter. © 1971 by John Wallace Suter. Reprinted by permission of Harper Collins Publishers; 10 E. 53rd St.; New York, NY 10022.

279 Altered from DAILY PRAYER (Supplemental Liturgical Resource #5, p. 300). © 1987 The Westminster Press. Altered and used by permission of Westminster/John Knox Press; 100 Witherspoon Street; Louisville, KY 40202-1396.

280 Additional blessings from the **Book of Blessings** for use in the United States of America © 1988, by the United States Catholic Conference, Washington, D.C. are used with permission. All rights reserved. USCC; 3211 Fourth Street, N.E.; Washington, DC 20017-1194.

281 Trans. and adapt. © 1992 UMPH. Entrance from trans. and adapt. of "Las Posadas" by J. L. Gonzalez in *In Accord*, p. 56, 1981, by Friendship Press, Inc.; 475 Riverside Dr., Room 772; New York, NY 10115.

288 Covenant Renewal Service and Opening Prayer © 1992 UMPH. Wesley Covenant Service abridged by Ole E. Borgen.

294 Prayer from *Touch Holiness*, p. 24, © 1990. Used by permission of The Pilgrim Press; 700 Prospect Avenue East; Cleveland, OH 44115-1100.

301 From *The Book of Common Prayer*, p. 163, 1979.

308 From *The Book of Common Prayer*, p. 163, 1979.

311 © 1992 UMPH.

313 From *Book of Congregational Worship*, p. 100, 1920, © The United Reformed Church in the United Kingdom. URC; 86 Tavistock Place; London WC1H 9RT; England.

314 From *The Book of Worship*, p. 86, 1965.

315 From *The Book of Common Prayer*, p. 38, 1928.

316 Prayer from *New Handbook of the Christian Year*, p. 258, © 1986, 1992 by Abingdon Press.

318 From *From Hope to Joy*, p. 123, © 1984 by Abingdon Press.

319 From *Seasons of the Gospel*, p. 67, © 1979 by Abingdon.

321 A Service of Worship for Ash Wednesday © 1979, 1986 by Abingdon Press; © 1992 UMPH. Invitation to the Observance of Lenten Discipline, Thanksgiving over the Ashes, and Pardon from *The Book of Common Prayer*, pp. 264-69, 1979.

331 From *The Book of Worship*, p. 94, © 1964, 1965 by Board of Publication of The Methodist Church. Inc.; renewal © 1992 UMPH.

332 From *The Book of Worship*, p. 93, © 1964, 1965 by Board of Publication of The Methodist Church, Inc.; renewal © 1992 UMPH.

333 From *The Book of Common Prayer*, p. 166, 1979.

334 From *The Book of Common Prayer*, p. 166, 1979.

335 From *The Book of Common Prayer*, p. 168, 1979.

336 From *Altar Stairs*, 1928, The Macmillan Company. Rights administered by Casper L. Roberts, Esq., address unknown.

337 Altered from THE BOOK OF COMMON WORSHIP. © 1946 by The Board of Christian Education of the PCUSA; renewed 1974. Altered and used by permission of Westminster/John Knox Press; 100 Witherspoon Street; Louisville, KY 40202-1396.

338 A Service of Worship for Passion/Palm Sunday © 1979, 1986 by Abingdon Press; © 1992 UMPH. Opening Prayer from *The Book of Common Prayer*, p. 271, 1979.

346 From *From Ashes to Fire*, p. 97, © 1979 by Abingdon.

347 From *The Book of Common Prayer*, p. 168, 1979.

| | |
|---|---|
| 348 | From *The Book of Common Prayer*, p. 220, 1979. |
| 349 | From *The Order of Divine Service for Public Worship*, p. 148, 1921. Text used by permission of Oxford University Press; Walton Street; Oxford OX2 6DP; England. |
| 351 | A Service of Worship for Holy Thursday Evening (including Dismissal with Blessing by Don Saliers) © 1979, 1986 by Abingdon Press; © 1992 UMPH. |
| 354 | A Service of Tenebrae (including Dismissal by Don Saliers) © 1979, 1986 by Abingdon Press; © 1992 UMPH. English trans. of The Passion of Jesus Christ, by J. H. Charlesworth, based upon the 2nd Edition of the RSV with permission of the Division of Christian Education of the National Council of Churches of Christ in the United States of America. For permission write Dr. J. H. Charlesworth; CN 821; Princeton Theological Seminary; Princeton, NJ 08542. |
| 362 | A Service for Good Friday (including Dismissal by Don Saliers) © 1979, 1986 by Abingdon Press; © 1992 UMPH. |
| 367 | From *The Book of Common Prayer*, p. 283, 1979. |
| 371-72 | Easter Vigil, or The First Service of Easter © 1979, 1986 by Abingdon Press; © 1992 UMPH. Greeting, Opening Prayer, Introduction to the Service of the Word, collect for The Creation, collect for The Covenant Between God and the Earth, and collect for A New Heart and a New Spirit from *The Book of Common Prayer*, pp. 285-91, 1979. Easter Proclamation text from *The Rite of Holy Week* © 1972, International Commission on English in the Liturgy. All rights reserved. ICEL; 1275 K Street, NW, Suite 1202; Washington, DC 20005. |
| 390 | Text from *A Book of Prayers* © 1982, International Commission on English in the Liturgy. All rights reserved. ICEL; 1275 K Street, NW, Suite 1202; Washington, DC 20005. |
| 392 | From *A Cambridge Bede Book*, p. 15, by Eric Milner-White, 1936, Longmans, Green and Co. Ltd. Used by permission of Longman Group UK Ltd.; Longman House, Burnt Mill; Harlow, Essex CM20 2JE; England. |
| 394 | From *Seasons of the Gospel*, p. 79, © 1979 by Abingdon. |
| 395 | From DAILY PRAYER (Supplemental Liturgical Resource #5, p. 312). © 1987 The Westminster Press. Used by permission of Westminster/John Knox Press; 100 Witherspoon St.; Louisville, KY 40202-1396. |
| 396 | From *The Order of Divine Service for Public Worship*, p. 93, 1921. Text used by permission of Oxford University Press; Walton Street; Oxford OX2 6DP; England. |
| 397 | From *New Handbook of the Christian Year*, p. 218, © 1986, 1992 by Abingdon Press. |
| 399 | From *An Easter Sourcebook*, p. 163, 1988, Archdiocese of Chicago. Prayer by Gail Ramshaw. For permission write Gail Ramshaw; 7304 Boyer St.; Philadelphia, PA 19119. |
| 402 | Greeting from *From Ashes to Fire*, p. 232, © 1979 by Abingdon. |
| 403 | Reproduced from *The Scottish Book of Common Prayer* 1929, Scottish Episcopal Church; 21 Grosvenor Cres.; Edinburgh EH12 5EE; Scotland. |
| 404 | From *The Book of Common Prayer*, p. 226, 1979. |
| 406 | Greeting from *The Book of Worship*, p. 126, © 1964, 1965 by Board of Publication of The Methodist Church, Inc.; renewal © 1992 UMPH. |
| 407 | Altered from THE BOOK OF COMMON WORSHIP. © 1946 by The Board of Christian Education of the PCUSA; renewed 1974. Altered and used by permission of Westminster/John Knox Press; 100 Witherspoon Street; Louisville, KY 40202-1396. |
| 408 | From *From Ashes to Fire*, p. 248, © 1979 by Abingdon. |
| 412 | From *The Book of Common Worship* of the Church of South India, p. 41, 1963. Text used by permission of Oxford University Press; Walton Street; Oxford OX2 6DP; England. |
| 414 | Greeting from *From Hope to Joy*, p. 12, © 1984 by Abingdon Press. |
| 417 | From *From Hope to Joy*, p. 31, © 1984 by Abingdon Press. |
| 418 | From *Prayers and Services for Christian Festivals*, p. 103. Text used by permission of Oxford University Press; Walton Street; Oxford OX2 6DP; England. |
| 420 | From *From Hope to Joy*, p. 24, © 1984 by Abingdon Press. |

## IV. SPECIAL SUNDAYS AND OTHER SPECIAL DAYS

Items 422-444, containing the materials for Special Sundays and Other Special Days of The United Methodist Church, are copyrighted and/or cited as follows:

| | |
|---|---|
| 423 | Litany from *Flames of the Spirit*, p. 60, © 1985. Used by permission of The Pilgrim Press; 700 Prospect Avenue East; Cleveland, OH 44115-1100. |
| 425 | Based on "Oration of Chief Seattle" by Ted Perry, 1972; litany Copyright © 1992 by UMPH. |
| 426 | © 1992 UMPH. |
| 427 | From "Golden Cross Sunday: Resources for Worship," 1988, Mission Education and Cultivation Program Department, General Board of Global Ministries. Prayer © 1992 UMPH. |
| 428 | From *Peace with Justice in the Local Church*, p. 23, 1983, Peace with Justice Program, General Board of Church and Society. Prayer © 1992 UMPH. |
| 430 | From *The Rural Church Memo*, June 1990. Prayer © 1992 UMPH. |
| 431 | Prayer #1 © 1992 UMPH. Prayer #2 from *The Interpreter*, July/August, 1981, p. 4. United Methodist Communications; 810 Twelfth Ave. S.; P.O. Box 320; Nashville, TN 37202-0320. |
| 432 | From *The Book of Discipline of The United Methodist Church: 1992* (¶¶101-07) © 1992 UMPH. Litany © 1992 UMPH. |
| 433 | Litany from *The Interpreter*, October, 1988, p. 10. Reprinted by permission of Office of Loans and Scholarships BHEM; P. O. Box 871; Nashville, TN 37202-0871. |
| 435 | Letter from the Birmingham City Jail is used by permission of the JOAN DAVES AGENCY, New York NY. © in 1963 by Martin Luther King, Jr., renewed in 1991 by Coretta Scott King. For permission write Joan Daves Agency; 21 West 26th Street; New York, NY 10010. Prayer from *Share the Dream: The Martin Luther King Day Celebration Packet* © 1986 by Abingdon Press. |
| 436 | © 1992 UMPH. |
| 437 | Prayer from *Touch Holiness*, p. 222, © 1990. Used by permission of The Pilgrim Press; 700 Prospect Avenue East; Cleveland, OH 44115-1100. |

438 Additional blessings from the **Book of Blessings** for use in the United States of America © 1988, by the United States Catholic Conference, Washington, D.C. are used with permission. All rights reserved. USCC; 3211 Fourth Street, N.E.; Washington, D.C. 20017-1194.

439 Prayer from *The Book of Worship*, p. 392, © 1964, 1965 by Board of Publication of The Methodist Church, Inc.; renewal © 1992 UMPH.

440 Prayer by John Hunter from *Devotional Services*, p. 206, 1936, J. M. Dent & Sons Ltd.; 91 Clapham High Street; London SW4 7TA; England.

441 Additional blessings from the **Book of Blessings** for use in the United States of America © 1988, by the United States Catholic Conference, Washington, D.C. are used with permission. All rights reserved. USCC; 3211 Fourth Street, N.E.; Washington, D.C. 20017-1194.

442 © 1992 UMPH.

443 Prayer by Reinhold Niebuhr (1892-1971). For permission write Ursula M. Niebuhr; P. O. Box 91; Yale Hill; Stockbridge, MA 01262-0091.

## V. GENERAL ACTS OF WORSHIP

Items 445-567, containing the General Acts of Worship, are copyrighted and/or cited as follows:

449 From *The Book of Worship*, p. 151, © 1964, 1965 by Board of Publication of The Methodist Church, Inc.; renewal © 1992 UMPH.

450 From *The Book of Worship*, p. 134, © 1964, 1965 by Board of Publication of The Methodist Church, Inc.; renewal © 1992 UMPH.

451 From *The Book of Worship*, p. 134, © 1964, 1965 by Board of Publication of The Methodist Church, Inc.; renewal © 1992 UMPH.

452 From *The Book of Worship*, p. 136, © 1964, 1965 by Board of Publication of The Methodist Church, Inc.; renewal © 1992 UMPH.

453 From *Flames of the Spirit*, p. 67, © 1985. Used by permission of The Pilgrim Press; 700 Prospect Avenue, East; Cleveland, OH 44115-1100.

454 From *Bread for the Journey*, p. 54, © 1981. Used by permission of The Pilgrim Press; 700 Prospect Avenue, East; Cleveland, OH 44115-1100.

455 Attributed to *With All God's People: The New Ecumenical Prayer Cycle* p. 223, 1989, WCC Publications; 150 route de Ferney; 1211 Geneva 2, Switzerland.

456 From *Bread for the Journey*, p. 44, © 1981. Used by permission of The Pilgrim Press; 700 Prospect Avenue East; Cleveland, OH 44115-1100.

457 Prayer by Karl Ludvig Reichelt from "Aeropagus" Winter issue 1987. Altered by permission of the Tao Fong Shan Christian Centre; Tao Fong Shan Rd.; Shatin, N.T.; Hong Kong.

459 From *The Book of Worship*, p. 136, 1965.

460 From *The Book of Worship*, p. 94, 1965.

462 From *The Book of Worship*, p. 192, 1944; renewal © 1971, 1972 by Abingdon Press.

463 "O God, the Parent of our Lord. . ." from THE WORLD IN AT ONE IN PRAYER by Daniel J. Fleming (ed.). © 1942 by Harper & Row, Publishers, Inc. Reprinted by permission of HarperCollins Publishers; 10 East 53rd St.; New York, NY 10022.

464 From *Bread for the Journey*, p. 62, © 1981. Used by permission of The Pilgrim Press; 700 Prospect Avenue East; Cleveland, OH 44115-1100.

465 From the "Calendar of Prayer 1986-1987," p. 53, United Church Board for World Ministries; 700 Prospect Avenue; Cleveland, OH 44115.

466 From "Celebrating Together: Prayers, Liturgies and Songs From Corrymeela" © 1987 Corrymeela Press; Ballycastle; Co. Antrim BT54 6BP; Northern Ireland.

467 From *The Book of Common Prayer of the Church of England*, 1922.

468 From "The Gift is Rich," 1955, 1968, The Friendship Press; 475 Riverside Drive, Room 772; New York, NY 10115.

469 From *Touch Holiness*, p. 120, © 1990. Used by permission of The Pilgrim Press; 700 Prospect Avenue East; Cleveland, OH 44115-1100. Based on the poem "Bakerwoman God," © 1978 Alla Renee Bozarth, found in *Womanpriest: A Personal Odyssey*, rev. ed., Luramedia, 1988; and *Stars in Your Bones: Emerging Signposts on Our Spiritual Journeys*, Bozarth, Barkley, and Hawthorne, North Star Press of St. Cloud, 1990. For permission write Rev. Dr. Alla Renee Bozarth; 43222 SE Tapp Rd.; Sandy, OR 97055.

470 Used and adapt. with permission of Church Women United; 475 Riverside Dr.; New York, NY 10115. © 1980 from 1981 World Day of Prayer.

471 From *We Press On*, p. 24, 1979, The National Federation of Asian American United Methodists; 330 Ellis St., Room 508; San Francisco, CA 94102.

472 From WOMANPRAYER/WOMANSONG by Miriam Therese Winter © 1987 by Medical Mission Sisters; 92 Sherman St.; Hartford, CT 06105.

473 From *1987 United Methodist Clergywomen's Consultation Resource Book*, p. 61. Please use this credit line in lieu of seeking written permission.

475 Confession from *The Order of Divine Service for Public Worship*, p. 39, 1921. Text used by permission of Oxford University Press; Walton Street; Oxford OX2 6DP; England. Pardon from *The Book of Common Prayer*, p. 24, 1928.

476 Confession from *Divine Worship*, p. 35, 1935, Epworth Press; Room 195; 1 Central Buildings; London, SW1H 9NR; England. Pardon from *The Book of Worship*, p. 10, 1944; renewal © 1971, 1972 by Abingdon Press.

477 Confession from *Divine Worship*, p. 103, 1935, Epworth Press; Room 195; 1 Central Buildings; London, SW1H 9NR; England. Pardon from *The Book of Common Prayer*, p. 24, 1928.

478 Excerpt from *Gates of Prayer: The New Union Prayerbook* is © 1975, Central Conference of American Rabbis and Union of Liberal and Progressive Synagogues (London). Used by permission. CCAR; 192 Lexington Ave.; New York, NY 10016.

479 From *1987 United Methodist Clergywomen's Consultation Resource Book*, p. 57, written by Rev. Lydia S. Martinez. Please use this credit line in lieu of seeking written permission.

480 Two stanzas from a prayer from CONTEMPORARY PRAYERS FOR PUBLIC WORSHIP, edited by Caryl Micklem, SCM Press, 1967. For permission write SCM Press Ltd.; 26-30 Tottenham Road; London N1 4BZ; England.

481 © 1992 UMPH.

482 Prayer from Christian Renewal Centre, Northern Ireland. For permission write CRC; Shore Road, Rostrevor; Newry, Co. Down BT34 3ET; Northern Ireland.

483 From *Bread for the Journey*, p. 31, © 1981. Used by permission of The Pilgrim Press; 700 Prospect Avenue East; Cleveland, OH 44115-1100.

484 From Janet Weller, South West Manchester Group of Churches, UK, in *With All God's People: The New Ecumenical Prayer Cycle*, p. 80, 1989, WCC Publications; 150, route de Ferney; 1211 Geneva 2; Switzerland.

485 From *Bread for the Journey*, p. 60, © 1981. Used by permission of The Pilgrim Press; 700 Prospect Avenue East; Cleveland, OH 44115-1100.

487 Attributed to Church Women United, 1981 World Day of Prayer materials.

488 © 1987 Medical Mission Sisters; 92 Sherman St.; Hartford, CT 06105.

489 © 1992 UMPH.

490 From *Flames of the Spirit*, p. 76, © 1985. Used by permission of The Pilgrim Press; 700 Prospect Avenue East; Cleveland, OH 44115-1100.

491 © 1992 UMPH.

492 From *Bread for the Journey*, p. 46, © 1981. Used by permission of The Pilgrim Press; 700 Prospect Avenue East; Cleveland, OH 44115-1100.

493 © 1992 UMPH.

494 From *Jesus Christ—the Life of the World*, p. 6 (by WCC Worship Committee), © WCC Publications, Geneva, Switzerland. For permission write WCC Publications; 150, route de Ferney; 1211 Geneva 2; Switzerland.

495 From *The Book of Common Prayer*, p. 388, 1979.

496 From *The Book of Common Prayer*, p. 350, 1979.

500 Attributed to "Die Schoensten Gebete der Erde," 1964, Suedwest Verlag, GmbH & Co. KG; Goethestr. 43; 8000 Muenchen 2; Germany.

501 From *The Book of Common Prayer*, p. 37, 1928.

502 From *The Book of Common Prayer*, p. 547, 1928.

503 From *Praying for Unity through the Christian Year*, p. 27, 1956, Edinburgh House Press. Reprinted by permission of James Clarke & Co. Ltd., Cambridge. For permission write to JC & Co. Ltd.; P. O. Box 60, Cambridge CB1 2NT; England.

505 Prayer used in the Ecumenical Centre, Geneva, on the occasion of the visit of Pope John Paul II. From *With All God's People*, p. 311, 1989, WCC Publications; 150, route de Ferney; 1211 Geneva 2; Switzerland.

506 "O God, you have built your Church. . ." from A BOOK OF PUBLIC PRAYERS by Harry Emerson Fosdick. © 1959 by Harry Emerson Fosdick. Reprinted by permission of HarperCollins Publishers; 10 East 53rd St.; New York, NY 10022.

508 © 1991 Milton Vahey; 3165 Amber Rd., Marcellus, NY 13108.

509 © 1992 UMPH.

510 Attributed to *Prayers for Use in Public Worship*, p. 168, 1921, Alexander Brunton; Edinburgh; Scotland.

511 Source untraced.

512 From *Home Prayers*, p. 90, 1891.

513 From *The Book of Common Prayer*, p. 44, 1928.

514 Adapt. from *The Kingdom, The Power, and the Glory* © 1933 by Oxford University Press; renewed 1961 by Bradford Young. Used by permission of the publisher. Oxford University Press; 200 Madison Avenue; New York, NY 10016.

515 Adapt. from *The Kingdom, The Power, and the Glory* © 1933 Oxford University Press; renewed 1961 by Bradford Young. Used by permission of the publisher. Oxford University Press; 200 Madison Avenue; New York, NY 10016.

516 Attributed to "Morning and Evening Prayer," Church of Pakistan.

517 Altered from THE WORSHIPBOOK: Services and Hymns. © MCMLXX, MCMLXXII, The Westminster Press. Altered and used by permission of Westminster/John Knox Press; 100 Witherspoon Street; Louisville, KY 40202-1396.

518 Based on words from John Calvin, Switzerland, 16th cent. From *Contemporary Parish Prayers*, p. 106, Frank Colquhoun, ed., 1975, Hodder & Stoughton; 47 Bedford Square; London WC1B 3DP; England.

519 From *Acts of Devotion*, p. 11, F. W. Delly, comp., 1927, Society for Promoting Christian Knowledge; Holy Trinity Church; Marylebone Rd.; London NW1 4DU; England.

520 Adapt. from *The Kingdom, The Power, and the Glory* © 1933 by Oxford University Press; renewed 1961 by Bradford Young. Used by permission of the publisher. Oxford University Press; 200 Madison Avenue; New York, NY 10016.

521 Attributed to Wanda Lawrence.

522 Attributed to *UNICEF Book of Children's Prayers*, p. 67, William I. Kaufman, comp., published by Stackpole Books; Cameron and Kelker Streets; Harrisburg, PA 17105.

523 From *The Book of Common Prayer*, p. 217, 1928.

524 Attributed to an order of service from the Church of Pakistan.

525 From *The Book of Common Prayer*, p. 595, 1928.

526 From *Prayers for the Christian Year*, p. 103, 1935. Text used by permission of Oxford University Press; Walton Street; Oxford OX2 6DP; England.

527 From *1987 United Methodist Clergywomen's Consultation Resource Book*, p. 41, written by Rev. Elizabeth Lopez Spence. Please use this credit line in lieu of seeking written permission.

532 Text from *Book of Blessings* © 1988, International Commission on English in the Liturgy, Inc. All rights reserved. ICEL; 1275 K Street, NW; Suite 1202; Washington, DC 20005.

533 Additional blessings from the **Book of Blessings** for use in the United States of America © 1988, by the United States Catholic Conference, Washington, D.C. are used with permission. All rights reserved.

534 © 1992 UMPH.

535 Source untraced.

536 © 1992 UMPH.

537 Text from the *Book of Blessings* © 1987, International Commission on English in the Liturgy. All rights reserved. ICEL; 1275 K Street, NW; Suite 1202; Washington, DC 20005.

538 Source untraced.

539 From *Touch Holiness*, p. 209, © 1990. Used by permission of The Pilgrim Press; 700 Prospect Avenue East; Cleveland, OH 44115-1100.

540 © 1992 UMPH.

541 © 1992 UMPH.

542 From THE WORSHIPBOOK: Services and Hymns. © MCMLXX, MCMLXXII, The Westminster Press. Used by permission of Westminster/John Knox Press; 100 Witherspoon Street; Louisville, KY 40202-1396.

543 Source untraced.

544 Source untraced.

545 From *Service Book and the Ordinal of the Presbyterian Church of South Africa*, p. 27, 1921, Maclehose, Jackson & Co. Reprinted by kind permission of Macmillan Publishers UK; 4 Little Essex St.; London WC2R 3LF; England.

547 Additional blessings from the **Book of Blessings** for use in the United States of America © 1988, by the United States Catholic Conference, Washington, D.C. are used with permission. All rights reserved.

548 Excerpt from *Gates of Prayer: The New Union Prayer Book* is © 1975, Central Conference of American Rabbis and Union of Liberal and Progressive Synagogues (London). Used by permission. CCAR; 192 Lexington Ave.; New York, NY 10016.

550 From *The Book of Common Prayer*, p. 19, 1928.

551 From *The Book of Worship*, p. 183, 1965.

552 From *The Worship Resources of the United Methodist Hymnal*, p. 51, © 1989 UMPH.

553  From *The Book of Common Order*, p. 25, 1940. Text used by permission of Oxford University Press; Walton Street; Oxford OX2 6DP; England.

556  Attributed to "New Orders of the Mass in India."

557  From *I Sing Your Praise All the Day Long*, p. 40, 1967, The Friendship Press; 475 Riverside Drive, Room 772; New York, NY 10115.

558  Adapt. from Haudenosaunee Thanksgiving Address. For permission write Sue Ellen Herne; RR #1 Box 31; Roosevelt Rd.; Hogansburg, NY 13655.

559  From *Touch Holiness*, p. 241, © 1990. Used by permission of The Pilgrim Press; 700 Prospect Avenue East; Cleveland, OH 44115-1100.

563  From *1987 United Methodist Clergywomen's Consultation Resource Book*, p. 67. Please use this credit line in lieu of seeking written permission.

564  From *WOMANPRAYER/WOMANSONG* by Miriam Therese Winter © 1987 by Medical Mission Sisters; 92 Sherman St.; Hartford, CT 06105.

# VI. DAILY PRAISE AND PRAYER

Pages 568-80, containing the Orders of Daily Praise and Prayer of the United Methodist Church, are copyrighted and/or cited as follows:

569-71  An Order for Morning Praise and Prayer © 1989, 1992 UMPH.

572-73  An Order for Midday Praise and Prayer © 1992 UMPH.

574-76  An Order for Evening Praise and Prayer © 1989, 1992 UMPH.

577-80  An Order for Night Praise and Prayer and A Midweek Service of Prayer and Testimony © 1992 UMPH.

Permission for use of items controlled by other copyright owners must be obtained from the respective owners listed below.

Central Conference of American Rabbis; 192 Lexington Ave.; New York, NY 10016:

578  Prayer of Thanksgiving #2, "Jewish Prayer for Divine Providence" in *Gates of Prayer*, p. 35, 1975, CCAR.

Christian Conference of Asia Youth; G/F.; 2 Jordan Road; Kowloon; Hong Kong:

575  Prayer of Thanksgiving #2, from "Your Will Be Done," 1985, CCA Youth.

569-70  Prayer of Thanksgiving #2, alt. from "Your Will Be Done," 1985, CCA Youth.

International Commission on English in the Liturgy, Inc.; 1275 K St., NW, #1202; Washington, DC 20005-4097:

578  Prayer of Thanksgiving #1 text from *The Liturgy of the Hours* © 1973, 1975 ICEL. All rights reserved.

Order of Saint Luke Publications; 5246 Broadway; Cleveland, OH 44127-1500:

578-79  Commendation, alt., from The Book of Offices and Services After the Usage of The Order of Saint Luke, Timothy J. Crouch, O.S.L. ed. and comp. Cleveland (OSL Publications) © 1988. Used by permission.

Westminster/John Knox Press; 100 Witherspoon Street; Louisville, KY 40202:

569  Prayer of Thanksgiving #1 reprinted from THE WORSHIPBOOK: Services and Hymns, © MCMLXX, MCMLXXII, The Westminster Press. Used by permission of Westminster/John Knox Press.

572  Prayer of Thanksgiving, Joint Office of Worship, The Westminster Press/John Knox Press.

William G. Story; 1027 East Wayne Ave.; South Bend, IN 46617:

574-75  Prayer of Thanksgiving #1 trans. by Wm. G. Storey from the Greek.

# VII. OCCASIONAL SERVICES

Pages 581-612, containing the Occasional Services of The United Methodist Church, are copyrighted and/or cited as follows:

581-84  The Love Feast © 1992 UMPH.

585-88  An Order of Thanksgiving for the Birth or Adoption of a Child and An Order for the Presentation of Bibles to Children © 1992 UMPH.

590-91  An Order of Farewell to Church Members © 1992 UMPH. Prayer by E. Hawkins (England, 1789).

593  Creed from *The Book of Discipline of the United Methodist Church: 1992* (¶ 76) © 1992 UMPH.

593-95  An Order for the Recognition of a Candidate and An Order Recognizing One Who Has Been Ordained, Consecrated, or Certified © 1992 UMPH.

596  Prayer #2 in An Order for the Celebration of an Appointment: English trans. by Ole Borgen © 1992 UMPH.

598-99  An Order of Farewell to a Pastor © 1992 UMPH.

599-602  An Order for the Installation or Recognition of Leaders in the Church and An Order for the Installation or Recognition of Church School Workers © 1964, 1965 by Board of Publication of The Methodist Church, Inc.; © 1984 by Abingdon Press; © 1992 UMPH; renewal © 1992 UMPH.

602-04  An Order for the Commissioning of Class Leaders by David Lowes Watson © 1992 by UMPH.

604-05  An Order for the Installation or Recognition of Persons in Music Ministries © 1984 by Abingdon Press; © 1992 UMPH.

606-07  An Order for the Dedication of an Organ or Other Musical Instruments © 1964, 1965 by Board of Publication of the Methodist Church, Inc.; © 1984 by Abingdon Press; © 1992 UMPH; renewal © 1992 UMPH. Prayer, alt., renewal © 1971, 1972 by Abingdon Press.

607-08  An Order for the Dedication of Church Furnishings and Memorials, alt., renewal © 1971, 1972 by Abingdon Press.

608-10  A Service for the Blessing of Animals © 1992 UMPH.

610-12  A Service for the Blessing of a Home © 1984 by Abingdon Press; © 1992 UMPH. Greeting © 1964, 1965 by Board of Publication of The Methodist Church, Inc.; renewal © 1992 UMPH.

*The Book of Common Prayer*, 1979:

591-92  An Order for Commitment to Christian Service, alt.

595-98  An Order for the Celebration of an Appointment, alt.

586  Prayer of Thanksgiving for a Safe Delivery, alt.

585  Presentation and Call to Thanksgiving, adapt.

Consultation on Church Union; 151 Wall Street; Princeton, NJ 08540-1514:

586-87 Prayer of Thanksgiving for the Adoption of a Child; Prayer of Thanksgiving for the Birth of a Child; and Prayer of Thanksgiving for the Family from An Order of Thanksgiving for the Birth or Adoption of a Child, by the Commission on Worship of the Consultation on Church Union. © 1980 by Consultation on Church Union.

International Commission on English in the Liturgy; 1275 K St., NW, Suite 1202; Washington, DC 20005:

608-09 Gathering and Greeting, alt., text from the *Book of Blessings* © 1987, ICEL. All rights reserved.

609 Prayer with Responses, adapt., text from the *Book of Blessings* © 1987, ICEL. All rights reserved.

Karen Westerfield Tucker; The Divinity School; Duke University; Durham, NC 27706:

592-93 An Order for Commissioning to Short-Term Christian Service © 1991 Karen Westerfield Tucker.

Timothy J. Crouch, O.S.L.; 5246 Broadway; Cleveland, OH 44127-1500:

610 Opening Prayer © 1989 Timothy J. Crouch, O.S.L.

Foerlaget Sanctus; Box 5020; S-102 41 Stockholm; Sweden:

596 Prayer, alt., from *Kyrkohandbok foer Metodistkyrkan i Sverige*, p. 181, 1987, Foerlaget Sanctus.

United Church of Christ Office for Church Life and Leadership; 700 Prospect Ave. E.; Cleveland, OH 44115:

598-99 Words of release, adapt. by permission from "Order for Times of Passage: Farewell," **Book of Worship United Church of Christ** © 1986 UCC, OCLL, New York, NY.

The Uniting Church in Australia Assembly Commission on Liturgy; c/o Ian Culliman; 29 Menin Rd.; Corinda, Queensland, 4075; Australia:

588-90 Blessing, adapt.; Congregational Response, alt.; and Order of Service adapt. from A Celebration of New Beginnings in Faith, published in UNITING IN WORSHIP LEADER'S BOOK, © 1988, The UCAACL. Used by permission of The Joint Board of Christian Education, Melbourne, Australia.

584 Homecoming Service Prayer, alt., is adapted from A Litany for a Church Anniversary, published in UNITING IN WORSHIP PEOPLE'S BOOK, © 1988, The UCAACL. Used by permission of The Joint Board of Christian Education, Melbourne, Australia.

# VIII. HEALING SERVICES AND PRAYERS

Pages 613-29, containing the Healing Services and Prayers, are copyrighted and/or cited as follows:

615-23 A Service of Healing I and A Service of Healing II © 1992 UMPH. Thanksgiving and Communion © 1972 The Methodist Publishing House; © 1980, 1985, 1989, 1992 UMPH.

624-25 Prayers #1 and #3 in A Service of Hope after Loss of Pregnancy © 1992 UMPH.

626 Ministry with Persons Going through Divorce © 1992 UMPH.

627-29 Ministry with Persons with AIDS, Ministry with Persons with Life-threatening Illness and Ministry with Persons in Coma or Unable to Communicate © 1992 UMPH.

*The Book of Common Prayer*, 1979:

618 Preface, alt.

620 Thanksgiving over the Oil, alt.

The Christian Century Foundation; 407 S. Dearborn St.; Chicago, IL 60605-1111:

623-26 A Service of Hope after Loss of Pregnancy, portions adapt. from "Service of Hope" by Karen Westerfield Tucker. © 1989 CHRISTIAN CENTURY FOUNDATION. Reprinted by permission from the January-February 1989 issue of *The Christian Ministry*.

The English Language Liturgical Consultation; 1275 K St., NW, #1202; Washington, DC 20005:

618 Sursum Corda, alt., from the English trans. of "Lift up your hearts" prepared by ELLC 1988.

International Commission on English in the Liturgy; 1275 K St., NW, Suite 1202; Washington, DC 20005:

625-26 Closing Prayer #2, alt., text from *The Book of Blessings* © 1988, ICEL. All rights reserved.

619 Memorial Acclamation text from *The Roman Missal* © 1973, ICEL. All rights reserved.

The International Consultation on English Texts; 1275 K St., NW, #1202; Washington, DC 20005-4097:

618 Sanctus and Benedictus from the English trans. of the Sanctus/Benedictus by ICET.

Order of Saint Luke Publications; 5246 Broadway; Cleveland, OH 44127-1500:

621 Dismissal with Blessing, alt., from The Book of Offices and Services After the Usage of The Order of Saint Luke, Timothy J. Crouch, O.S.L. ed. and comp. Cleveland (OSL Publications) © 1988. Used by permission.

United Church of Christ Office for Church Life and Leadership; 700 Prospect Avenue East; Cleveland, OH 44115:

622 Confession and Pardon from *Book of Worship* ©, 1986.

United States Catholic Conference; 3211 Fourth Street, N.E.; Washington, D.C. 20017-1194:

627 Addiction Prayer, alt., additional blessings from the **Book of Blessings** for use in the United States of America © 1988, by USCC, Washington, D.C. are used with permission. All rights reserved.

Westminster/John Knox Press; 100 Witherspoon Street; Louisville, KY 40202-1396:

629 Prayer with Persons in Coma, alt., reprinted from SERVICES FOR OCCASIONS OF PASTORAL CARE (Supplemental Liturgical Resource, p. 69.). © 1990 Westminster/John Knox Press. Used by permission.

## IX. SERVICES RELATING TO CONGREGATIONS AND BUILDINGS

Pages 630-51, containing the Services Relating to Congregations and Buildings of The United Methodist Church, are copyrighted and/or cited as follows:

630-37  A Service for Organizing a New Congregation, A Service for the Breaking of Ground for a Church Building and A Service for the Laying of a Foundation Stone of a Church Building © 1964, 1965 by Board of Publication of The Methodist Church, Inc.; © 1984 by Abingdon Press; © 1992 UMPH; renewal © 1992 UMPH. Opening Prayer, alt., p. 633, Breaking of Ground, alt., pp. 634-35 from *Doctrines and Discipline of the Methodist Church 1956* (¶ 1931) © 1957 by The Board of Publication of The Methodist Church, Incorporated. Closing Prayer, alt., p. 637, from *The Book of Worship*, p. 472, 1944; renewal © 1971, 1972 by Abingdon Press.

637-42  A Service for the Consecration or Reconsecration of a Church Building © 1984 by Abingdon Press; © 1992 UMPH.

642-47  A Service for the Dedication of a Church Building Free of Debt and A Service for the Consecration of an Educational Building © 1964, 1965 by Board of Publication of the Methodist Church, Inc.; renewal © 1971, 1972 by Abingdon Press; © 1984 by Abingdon Press; © 1992 UMPH; renewal © 1992 UMPH.

648-51  An Order for the Leave-Taking of a Church Building and An Order for Disbanding a Congregation © 1992 UMPH.

*The Book of Common Prayer*, 1928:
639  Prayer of Consecration, adapt.

*The Book of Common Prayer*, 1979:
641  Consecration of the Baptismal Font, adapt.
640  Consecration of the Pulpit, adapt.

Permission for use of items controlled by other copyright owners must be obtained from the respective owners listed below:

The Inter-Lutheran Commission on Worship; The Division of Congregational Life; Evangelical Lutheran Church of America; 8765 West Higgins Road; Chicago, IL 60631:
648  Declaration of Purpose, adapt. in part from *An Order for Leave-Taking of a Church Building* (unpublished).

International Commission on English in the Liturgy; 1275 K St., NW, #1202; Washington, DC 20005-4097:
638  Declaration of Purpose, adapt., text from *Dedication of a Church and an Altar* © 1978, ICEL. All rights reserved.
643  Opening Prayer, adapt., text from *Dedication of a Church and an Altar* © 1978 ICEL. All rights reserved.

## X. CONSECRATIONS AND ORDINATIONS

Pages 652-713, containing the Consecrations and Ordinations of The United Methodist Church, are copyrighted and/or cited as follows:

654-60  The Order for the Consecration of Diaconal Ministers © 1992 UMPH.

663-69  The Order for the Ordination of Deacons © 1979 by Board of Discipleship, The United Methodist Church; © 1992 UMPH.

672-82  The Order for the Ordination of Elders © 1979 by Board of Discipleship, The United Methodist Church; © 1992 UMPH. Thanksgiving and Communion © 1972 The Methodist Publishing House; © 1979 by Board of Discipleship, The United Methodist Church; © 1980, 1985, 1989, 1992 UMPH.

685-97  The Order for Consecrations and Ordinations © 1979 by Board of Discipleship, The United Methodist Church; © 1992 UMPH.

700-10  The Order for the Consecration of Bishops © 1979 by Board of Discipleship, The United Methodist Church; © 1992 UMPH. Thanksgiving and Communion © 1972 The Methodist Publishing House; © 1979 by Board of Discipleship, The United Methodist Church, © 1980, 1985, 1989, 1992 UMPH.

*The Book of Common Prayer*, 1979:
679,  Preface, alt.
706

Permission for use of items controlled by other copyright owners must be obtained from the respective owners listed below:

The English Language Liturgical Consultation; 1275 K St., NW, #1202; Washington, DC 20005-4097:
679,  Sursum Corda, alt. from the English trans. of "Lift
706  up your hearts" prepared by ELLC 1988.

International Commission on English in the Liturgy, Inc.; 1275 K St., NW, #1202; Washington, DC 20005:
680,  Memorial Acclamation text from *The Roman Missal*
708  © 1973, ICEL. All rights reserved.

The International Consultation on English Texts; 1275 K St., NW, #1202; Washington, DC 20005-4097:
679,  Sanctus and Benedictus from the English trans. of
707  the Sanctus/Benedictus by ICET.

## XI. OTHER ANNUAL CONFERENCE AND DISTRICT SERVICES

Pages 714-39, containing the Other Annual Conference and District Services of The United Methodist Church, are copyrighted and/or cited as follows:

714-17  An Order of Commitment for Lay Speakers © 1992 UMPH.

717-18  An Order for Presenting Licenses to Local Pastors © 1964, 1965 by Board of Publication of The Methodist Church, Inc.; © 1992 UMPH; renewal © 1992 UMPH.

718-21  An Order for Admission of Candidates to Clergy Membership in an Annual Conference © 1964, 1965 by Board of Publication of The Methodist Church, Inc.; renewal © 1971, 1972 by Abingdon Press; © 1992 UMPH; renewal © 1992 UMPH.

722-30 A Service Celebrating the Appointment of a District Superintendent and A Service Celebrating the Assignment of a Bishop to an Area © 1992 UMPH.

734-39 A Retirement Recognition Service and An Annual Conference Memorial Service © 1992 UMPH.

*The Book of Common Prayer*, 1979:

723-24 Presentation of Signs of District Superintendency, adapt.

728 Presentation of Signs of Episcopal Ministry, adapt.

Permission for use of items controlled by other copyright owners must be obtained from the respective owners listed below.

Karen Westerfield Tucker; The Divinity School; Duke University; Durham, NC 27706:

730-34 A Service of Farewell to a Bishop or District Superintendent © 1991 Karen Westerfield Tucker.

## XII. GENERAL CHURCH SERVICES

Pages 740-43, containing the General Church Services of The United Methodist Church, are copyrighted and/or cited as follows:

740-41 The Order for Commissioning As Missionaries I © 1992 UMPH.

741-43 The Order for Commissioning to the Office of Deaconess or as Missionaries II © 1964, 1965 by

Board of Publication of The Methodist Church, Inc.; renewal © 1971, 1972 by Abingdon Press; © 1992 UMPH; renewal © 1992 UMPH.